HIDDEN HISTORY

HIDDEN HISTORY

THE SECRET ORIGINS OF THE FIRST WORLD WAR

GERRY DOCHERTY
AND JIM MACGREGOR

MAINSTREAM
PUBLISHING

EDINBURGH AND LONDON

First published in Great Britain in 2013 by
MAINSTREAM PUBLISHING COMPANY
(EDINBURGH) LTD
7 Albany Street
Edinburgh EH1 3UG

ISBN 9781780576305

A catalogue record for this book is available
from the British Library

Printed and bound in Great Britain by Clays Ltd, Elcograf S.p.A.

7 9 10 8

Dedicated to the victims of an unspeakable evil.

Acknowledgements

First and foremost we owe a debt to those writers and historians who, in the aftermath of the First World War, began to question what had happened and how it had come about. Their determination to challenge official accounts was largely dismissed by the Establishment, but they left a clear trail of credible evidence that has helped guide us through the morass of half-truths and lies that are still presented as historical fact. Without their cumulative effort, together with the profoundly important revelations of Professor Carroll Quigley, it would have been impossible for us to unpick the web of deceit woven around the origins of the war.

Special thanks are due to those who have encouraged our research over the years, made valuable suggestions and helped find sources to our enormous benefit. Will Podmore read our early chapters and offered sound advice. Guenter Jaschke has given us invaluable help in many ways, not least in providing and translating Austro-Hungarian and German political and military documents into English. Tom Cahill, American photojournalist and vibrant activist in the US Veterans against War movement, provided ongoing support, as did the American-Irish writer and political analyst Richard K. Moore. Other valued assistance came from Barbara Gunn in Ireland, Dr John O'Dowd in Glasgow and Brian Ovens, more locally.

We have to thank the ever-helpful librarians and researchers at the Scottish National Library in Edinburgh, both in the general reading rooms and the special documents section. We are grateful to the staff at the National Archives in Kew and the Bodleian Library, Oxford, especially in the special collections department, for their patience with us. Apologies are most certainly due to those we buttonholed and quizzed about missing documents, correspondence and papers at Oxford and Kew Gardens. As we were so correctly reminded, librarians and archivists can only provide access to the material that was passed into the library's safekeeping by the Foreign or Cabinet Offices. What was removed, withdrawn, culled or otherwise destroyed, was effected many years ago by those empowered to do so.

The good advice of our literary agent, David Fletcher, and the enthusiasm of our superb editor, Ailsa Bathgate, is genuinely appreciated, though we may not have said so at the time. Thanks too are due to the other members of the wonderful team at Mainstream, including Graeme Blaikie for guiding us through the photographic content with consummate patience. Above all we thank Bill Campbell, who displayed great enthusiasm for the project.

Finally, tremendous gratitude is due to Maureen, Joan and our families, who have patiently supported us through the long years of research and writing. While we have often not been there for them, they have always been there for us.

July 2013

Contents

Introduction

The history of the First World War is a deliberately concocted lie. Not the sacrifice, the heroism, the horrendous waste of life or the misery that followed. No, these were very real, but the truth of how it all began and how it was unnecessarily and deliberately prolonged beyond 1915 has been successfully covered up for a century. A carefully falsified history was created to conceal the fact that Britain, not Germany, was responsible for the war. Had the truth become widely known after 1918, the consequences for the British Establishment would have been cataclysmic.

At the end of the war Britain, France and the United States laid the blame squarely on Germany and took steps to remove, conceal or falsify documents and reports to justify such a verdict. In 1919, at Versailles near Paris, the victors decreed that Germany was solely responsible for the global catastrophe. She had, they claimed, deliberately planned the war and rejected all of their proposals for conciliation and mediation. Germany protested vehemently that she was not responsible and that it had been, for her, a defensive war against the aggression of Russia and France.

To the victors go the spoils, and their judgement was immediately reflected in the official accounts. What became the generally accepted history of the First World War revolved around German militarism, German expansionism, the kaiser's bombastic nature and ambitions, and Germany's invasion of innocent, neutral Belgium. The system of secret alliances, a 'naval race', economic imperialism, and the theory of an 'inevitable war' later softened the attack on Germany, though the spurious notion that she alone had wanted war remained understood in the background.

In the 1920s, a number of highly regarded American and Canadian professors of history, including Sidney B. Fay, Harry Elmer Barnes and John S. Ewart seriously questioned the Versailles verdict and the 'evidence' on which the assumption of German war guilt was based. Their work in revising the official Versailles findings was attacked by historians who insisted that Germany was indeed responsible. Today, eminent British war historians place the blame on Germany, though most are willing to concede that 'other factors' were also involved. Professor Niall Ferguson writes of the kaiser's strategy of global war.[1] Professor Hew Strachan maintains that the war was about liberal countries struggling to defend their freedoms (against German aggression),[2] while Professor Norman Stone states that the greatest mistake of the twentieth century was made when Germany built a navy to attack Britain.[3] Professor David Stevenson quite unequivocally writes that 'it is ultimately in Berlin that we must seek the keys to the destruction of peace'.[4] It was Germany's fault. End of story.

Several other recent accounts on the causes of the war offer alternative ideas. Christopher Clark's book, for example, looks on the events leading up to August 1914 as a tragedy into which an unsuspecting world 'sleepwalked'.[5] We reveal that far from sleepwalking into a global tragedy, the unsuspecting world was ambushed by a secret cabal of warmongers in London. In *Hidden History: The Secret Origins of the First World War*, we debunk the notion that Germany was to blame for this heinous crime against humanity, or that Belgium was an innocent, neutral nation caught unawares by German militarism. We clearly demonstrate that the German invasion of Belgium was not an act of thoughtless and indiscriminate aggression, but a reaction forced upon Germany when she faced imminent annihilation. From the day of its conception, the Schlieffen Plan[6] was a defence strategy and the last desperate act open to Germany to protect herself from being overrun simultaneously from east and west by the huge Russian and French armies massing on her borders.

What this book sets out to prove is that unscrupulous men, whose roots and origins were in Britain, sought a war to crush Germany and orchestrated events in order to bring this about. 1914 is generally considered as the starting point for the disaster that followed, but the crucial decisions that led to war had been taken many years before.

A secret society of rich and powerful men was established in London in 1891 with the long-term aim of taking control of the entire world. These individuals, whom we call the Secret Elite, deliberately fomented the Boer War of 1899–1902 in order to grab the Transvaal's gold mines, and this became a template for their future actions. Their ambition overrode humanity, and the consequences of their actions have been minimised, ignored or denied in official histories. The horror of the British concentration camps in South Africa, where 20,000 children died, is conveniently glossed over; the devastating loss of a generation in a world war for which these men were deliberately responsible has been glorified by the lie that they died for 'freedom and civilisation'. This book focuses on how a cabal of international bankers, industrialists and their political agents successfully used war to destroy the Boer Republics and then Germany, and were never called to account.

Carefully falsified history? A secret society taking control of the world? Britain responsible for the First World War? Twenty thousand children dying in British concentration camps? A cabal based in London whose prime objective was to destroy Germany? Lest any readers jump immediately to the conclusion that this book is some madcap conspiracy theory, they should, amongst other evidence, consider the work of Carroll Quigley, one of the twentieth century's most highly respected historians.

Professor Quigley's greatest contribution to our understanding of modern history was presented in his books, *The Anglo-American Establishment* and *Tragedy and Hope*. The former was written in 1949 but only released after his death in 1981. His disclosures placed him in such potential danger from an Establishment backlash that it was never published in his lifetime. In a 1974 radio broadcast, Quigley warned the interviewer, Rudy Maxa of the *Washington Post*, that 'You better be discreet. You have to protect my future, as well as your own.'[7]

The Anglo-American Establishment contained explosive details of how a secret society of international bankers and other powerful, unelected men controlled the levers of power and finance in Great Britain and the United States of America, and had done so throughout the twentieth century. Quigley's evidence is considered highly credible. He moved in exalted circles, lectured at the top universities in the United States, including Harvard, Princeton and Georgetown, and was a trusted advisor to the Establishment as a consultant to the US Department of Defense. He gained access to evidence from people directly involved with the secret cabal that no outsider had ever seen. Though some of the facts came to him from sources which he was not permitted to name, he presented only those where he was 'able to produce documentary evidence available to everyone'.[8]

Quigley noted a strong link between the highest echelons of power and influence in British government circles and Oxford University, particularly All Souls and Balliol colleges. He received a certain amount of assistance of a 'personal nature' from individuals close to what he called the 'Group', though 'for obvious reasons' he could not reveal the names of such persons.[9] Though sworn to secrecy, Quigley revealed in the radio interview that Professor Alfred Zimmern, the British historian and political scientist, had confirmed the names of the main protagonists within the 'Group'. Without a shadow of doubt, Zimmern himself was a close associate of those at the centre of real power in Britain. He knew most of the key figures personally and was a member of the secret society for ten years before resigning in disgust in 1923.

Quigley noted that the 'Group' appeared oblivious to the consequences of their actions and acted in ignorance of the point of view of others. He described their tendency to give power and influence to individuals chosen through friendship rather than merit, and maintained that they had brought many of the things he held dear 'close to disaster'. The great enigma of Professor Quigley lies in his statement that while he abhorred the cabal's methods, he agreed with its goals and aims.[10] Were these merely words of self-preservation? Be mindful of his warning to Rudy Maxa as late as 1974. Quigley clearly felt that these revelations placed him in danger.

Through his investigations we know that Cecil Rhodes, the South African diamond millionaire, formed the secret society in London during the last decade of the nineteenth century. Its aims included renewal of the bond between Great Britain and the United States, and the spread of all they considered to be good in English ruling-class values and traditions. Their ultimate goal was to bring all habitable portions of the world under their influence and control. The individuals involved harboured a common fear, a deep and bitter fear, that unless something radical was done their wealth, power and influence would be eroded and overtaken by foreigners, foreign interests, foreign business, foreign customs and foreign laws. They believed that white men of Anglo-Saxon descent rightly sat at the top of a racial hierarchy, a hierarchy built on predominance in trade, industry and the exploitation of other races. To their minds, the choice was stark. Either take drastic steps to protect and further develop the British Empire or accept that countries like Germany would reduce them to bit-players on the world's stage.

The members of this Secret Elite were only too well aware that Germany was rapidly beginning to overtake Britain in all areas of technology, science, industry and commerce. They also considered Germany to be a cuckoo in the Empire's African nest and were concerned about its growing influence in Turkey, the Balkans and the Middle East. They set out to ditch the cuckoo.

The Secret Elite were influenced by the philosophy of the nineteenth-century Oxford professor John Ruskin, whose concept was built on his belief in the superiority and the authority of the English ruling classes acting in the best interests of their inferiors. And they professed that what they intended was for the good of mankind – for civilisation. A civilisation they would control, approve, manage and make profitable. For that, they were prepared to do what was necessary. They would make war for civilisation, slaughter millions in the name of civilisation. Wrapped in the great banner of civilisation, this became a secret society like no other before it. Not only did it have the backing of privilege and wealth but it was also protected from criticism and hidden beneath a shroud of altruism. They would take over the world for its own good. Save the world from itself.

The secret society specifically infiltrated the two great organs of imperial government: the Foreign Office and the Colonial Office, and established their control over senior civil servants who dominated these domains. In addition, they took control of the departments and committees that would enable their ambitions: the War Office, the Committee of Imperial Defence and the highest echelons of the armed services. Party-political allegiance was not a given prerequisite; loyalty to the cause most certainly was.

Their tentacles spread out to Russia and France, the Balkans and South Africa, and their targets were agents in the highest offices of foreign governments who were bought and nurtured for future use. America offered a different challenge. Initially, the possibility of bringing the United States back into an expanded empire was discussed but, realistically, American economic growth and future potential soon rendered such an idea redundant. Instead, they expanded their powerbase to bring Anglophile Americans into the secret brotherhood, men who would go on to dominate the world through financial institutions and dependent governments.

What's more, they had the power to control history, to turn history from enlightenment to deception. The Secret Elite dictated the writing and teaching of history, from the ivory towers of academia down to the smallest of schools. They carefully controlled the publication of official government papers, the selection of documents for inclusion in the official version of the history of the First World War, and refused access to any evidence that might betray their covert existence. Incriminating documents were burned, removed from official records, shredded, falsified or deliberately rewritten, so that what remained for genuine researchers and historians was carefully selected material. Carroll Quigley's histories have themselves been subject to suppression. Unknown persons removed *Tragedy and Hope* from the bookstore shelves in America, and it was withdrawn from sale without any justification soon after its release. The book's original plates were unaccountably destroyed by Quigley's publisher, the Macmillan Company, who, for the next six years 'lied, lied, lied' to him and deliberately misled him into believing that it would be reprinted.[11] Why? What pressures obliged a major publishing house to take such extreme action? Quigley claimed that powerful people had suppressed the book because it exposed matters that they did not want known.

To this day, researchers are denied access to certain First World War documents because the Secret Elite had much to fear from the truth, as do those who have succeeded them. They ensure that we learn only those 'facts' that support their version of history. It is worse than deception. They were determined to wipe out all traces that led back to them. They have taken every possible step to ensure that it would remain exceedingly difficult to unmask their crimes. We aim to do exactly that.

Our analysis of the secret origins of the First World War uses Professor Quigley's academic research as one of many foundation stones, but goes far deeper than his initial revelations. He stated that evidence about the cabal is not hard to find 'if you know where to look'.[12] We have done that. Starting with the principal characters whom he identified (and the insider, Alfred Zimmern, confirmed), this book traces their actions, interlinked careers, rise to power and influence, and finally exposes their complicity in ambushing the world into war. Quigley admitted that it was difficult to know who was active inside the group at any given time, and from our own research we have added to his lists those whose involvement and actions mark them out as linked members or associates. Secret societies work hard at maintaining their anonymity, but the evidence we have uncovered brings us to the considered conclusion that in the era that led into the First World War, the Secret Elite comprised a wider membership than Quigley originally identified.

This book is not a fictional story conjured on a whim. Despite the desperate attempt to remove every trace of Secret Elite complicity, the detailed evidence we present, chapter by chapter, reveals a tragic trail of misinformation, deceit, secret double-dealings and lies that left the world devastated and bankrupt. This is conspiracy fact, not theory.

A great many characters appear in the narrative of this history and we have appended a list of key players for ready referral if required. The reader faces a tantalisingly difficult challenge. These immensely rich and powerful men acted behind the scenes, shielded by the innermost core of the Establishment, by a controlled media and by a carefully vetted history. The following chapters prove that the official versions of history, as taught for more than a century, are fatally flawed: soaked in lies and half-truths. Those lies have penetrated so deeply into the psyche that the reader's first reaction might be to discount evidence because it is not what they learned in school or university, or challenges their every assumption. The Secret Elite and their agents still seek to control our understanding of what really happened, and why. We ask only that you accept this challenge and examine the evidence we lay before you. Let your open-mindedness be the judge.

CHAPTER 1

The Secret Society

One wintry afternoon in February 1891, three men were engaged in earnest conversation in London. From that conversation were to flow consequences of the greatest importance to the British Empire and to the world as a whole.

THE OPENING PASSAGE OF PROFESSOR Carroll Quigley's book *The Anglo-American Establishment* may read like a John le Carré thriller, but this is no spy fiction. The three staunch British imperialists who met that day, Cecil Rhodes, William Stead and Lord Esher, drew up a plan for the organisation of a secret society that would take over the control of foreign policy both in Britain and, later by extension, the United States of America: a secret society that aimed to renew the Anglo-Saxon bond between Great Britain and the United States,[1] spread all that they considered good in the English ruling-class traditions, and expand the British Empire's influence in a world they believed they were destined to control.

It was the heyday of both Jack the Ripper and Queen Victoria. The latter, having confronted her anti-Semitic prejudices, began a personal friendship with a member of the Rothschild banking dynasty, which played such an important role in what was to follow;[2] the former allegedly murdered Mary Kelly, his fifth and possibly final victim, in London's fog-bound Whitechapel slums.[3] These two unrelated events captured the extremities of life in that era of privilege and poverty: sumptuous excess for the few, and penniless vulnerability for the many. Despite appalling social conditions, Victorian England sat confidently at the pinnacle of international power, steeped as it was in the 'magnificence' of the British Empire, but could it stay there for ever? This was the driving question exercising much serious debate in the cigar-smoke-filled parlours of influence, and the plan agreed between these three men was essentially an affirmation that steps had to be taken to ensure that Britain maintained its dominant position in world affairs.

The conspirators were well-known public figures, but it should be noted from the outset that each was linked to infinitely greater wealth and influence. The plan laid on the table was relatively simple. A secret society would be formed and run by a small, close-knit clique. The leader was to be Cecil Rhodes. He and his accomplices constructed the secret organisation around concentric circles, with an inner core of trusted associates – 'The Society of the Elect' – who unquestionably knew that they were members of an exclusive cabal devoted to taking and holding power on a worldwide scale.[4] A second outer circle, larger and quite fluid in its membership, was to be called 'The Association of Helpers'. At this level of involvement, members may or may not have been aware that they were either an integral part of or inadvertently being used by a secret society. Many on the outer edges of the group, idealists and honest politicians, may never have known that the real decisions were made by a ruthless clique about whom they had no knowledge.[5] Professor Quigley revealed that the organisation was able to 'conceal its existence quite successfully, and many of its influential members, satisfied to possess the reality of power rather than the appearance of power, are unknown even to close students of British history'.[6] Secrecy was the cornerstone. No one outside the favoured few knew of the society's existence. Members understood that the reality of power was much more important and effective than the appearance of power, because they belonged to a privileged class that knew how decisions were made, how governments were controlled and policy financed. They have been referred to obliquely in speeches and books as 'the money power', the 'hidden power' or 'the men behind the curtain'. All of these labels are pertinent, but we have called them, collectively, the Secret Elite.

The meeting in February 1891 was not some chance encounter. Rhodes had been planning such a move for years, while Stead and Esher had been party to his ideas for some time. A year earlier, on 15 February 1890, Rhodes journeyed from South Africa to Lord Rothschild's country estate to present his plan. Nathaniel Rothschild, together with Lord Esher and some other very senior members of the British Establishment, was present. Esher noted at the time: 'Rhodes is a splendid enthusiast, but he looks upon men as machines . . . he has vast ideas . . . and [is], I suspect, quite unscrupulous as to the means he employs.'[7] In truth, these were exactly the qualities needed to be an empire builder: unscrupulous and uncaring with vast ambition.

Cecil Rhodes had long talked about setting up a Jesuit-like secret society, pledged to take any action necessary to protect and promote the extension of the power of the British Empire. He sought to 'bring the whole uncivilised world under British Rule, for the recovery of the United States, for the making of the Anglo-Saxon race but one empire'.[8] In essence, the plan was as simple as that. Just as the Jesuit Order had been formed to protect the pope and expand the Catholic Church, answerable only to its own superior general and nominally the pope, so the Secret Society was to protect and expand the British Empire, and remain answerable to its leader. The holy grail was control not of God's kingdom on earth in the name of the Almighty but of the known world in the name of the mighty British Empire. Both of these societies sought a different kind of world domination but shared a similar sense of ruthless purpose.

By February 1891, the time had come to move from ideal to action, and the formation of the secret society was agreed. It held secret meetings but had no need for secret robes, secret handshakes or secret passwords, since its members knew each other intimately.[9] Each of these initial three architects brought different qualities and connections to the society. Rhodes was prime minister of Cape Colony and master and commander of a vast area of southern Africa that some were already beginning to call Rhodesia. He was held to be a statesman, answerable to the British Colonial Office in terms of his governance, but in reality was a land-grabbing opportunist whose fortune was based on the Kimberly diamond mines. His wealth had been underwritten by brutal native suppression[10] and the global mining interests of the House of Rothschild,[11] to whom he was also answerable.

Rhodes had spent time at Oxford University in the 1870s and was inspired by the philosophy of John Ruskin, the recently installed professor of fine arts. Ruskin appeared to champion all that was finest in the public-service ethic, in the traditions of education, decency, duty and self-discipline, which he believed should be spread to the masses across the English-speaking world. But behind such well-serving words lay a philosophy that strongly opposed the emancipation of women, had no time for democracy and supported the 'just' war.[12] He advocated that the control of the state should be restricted to a small ruling class. Social order was to be built upon the authority of superiors, imposing upon inferiors an absolute, unquestioning obedience. He was repelled by what he regarded as the logical conclusion of Liberalism: the levelling of distinctions between class and class, man and man, and the disintegration of the 'rightful' authority of the ruling class.[13] As they sat listening to him, those future members of the secret society, Esher and Rhodes, must have thought they were being gifted a philosophical licence to take over the world. Cecil Rhodes drank from this fountain of dutiful influence and translated it into his dream to bring the whole uncivilised world under British rule.[14]

Rhodes entered South African politics to further his own personal ambitions, allied, of course, to the interests of the highly profitable mining industry. Although he paid reverent service to Ruskin's philosophy, his actions betrayed a more practical, ruthless spirit. His approach to native affairs was brutal. In 1890, he instructed the House of Assembly in Cape

Town that 'the native is to be treated as a child and denied the franchise. We must adapt a system of despotism, such as works so well in India, in our relations with the barbarians of South Africa.'[15] The sense of superiority that he absorbed in his time at Oxford was expressed in plundering native reserves, clearing vast acres of ancestral tribal lands to suit gold and diamond exploration, and manipulating politics and business to the benefit of himself and his backers. Though he associated all his life with men whose sole motive was avarice, his expressed purpose was to use his ill-gotten wealth to advance his great ideal that the British Empire should control the whole world.[16]

Before he died of heart failure at the age of 48, and well aware that his lifespan would be limited, Rhodes wrote several wills and added a number of codicils. By 1902, the named trustees of his will included Lord Nathaniel Rothschild, Lord Rosebery, Earl Grey, Alfred Beit, Leander Starr Jameson and Alfred Milner, all of whom, as we shall see, operated at the heart of the secret society. Rhodes believed that 'insular England was quite insufficient to maintain or even to protect itself without the assistance of the Anglo-Saxon peoples beyond the seas of Europe'.[17] In the years to come, problems of insularity required to be solved and links with America strengthened. Implicit in his grand plan was a determination to make Oxford University the educational centre of the English-speaking world and provide top scholars, in particular from every state in America, with the finance to 'rub shoulders with every kind of individual and class on absolutely equal terms'. Those fortunate men who were awarded a Rhodes Scholarship were selected by the trustees in the expectation that their time at Oxford would instil 'the advantage to the colonies and to the United Kingdom of the retention of the unity of the Empire'.[18] Bob Hawke, prime minister of Australia, and Bill Clinton, president of the United States, can be counted amongst later Rhodes Scholars.

But this Empire-maker was much more than just a university benefactor. His friend William (W.T.) Stead commented immediately after Rhodes' death that he was 'the first of the new dynasty of money-kings which has been evolved in these later days as the real rulers of the modern world'.[19] Great financiers had often used their fortunes to control questions of peace and war, and of course influence politics for profit. Rhodes was fundamentally different. He turned the objective on its head and sought to amass great wealth into his secret society in order to achieve political ends: to buy governments and politicians, buy public opinion and the means to influence it. He intended that his wealth be used by the Secret Elite to expand their control of the world. Secretly.

William Stead, Rhodes' close associate in the secret society, represented a new force in political influence: the power of affordable newspapers that spread their views to ever-increasing numbers of working men and women. Stead was the most prominent journalist of his day. He had dared to confront Victorian society with the scandal of child prostitution in an outspoken article in the *Pall Mall Gazette* in 1885.

The details from his graphic exposé of child abuse in London brothels shocked Victorian society. The underworld of criminal abduction, entrapment and 'sale' of young girls from under-privileged backgrounds was detailed in a series of 'infernal narratives', as Stead himself described them. These painted a horrendous picture of padded cells where upper-class paedophiles safely conducted their evil practices on children.[20] London society was thrown into a state of moral panic, and, as a consequence, the government was forced to pass the Criminal Law Amendment Act. Stead and several of his enlightened associates, including Bramwell Booth of the Salvation Army, were later charged with abduction as a result of the methods used in the investigation. Although Booth was acquitted, Stead spent three months in prison.[21]

This is what earned Stead his place in Rhodes' elite company. He could influence the general public. Having embarrassed the government into making an immediate change in the law, Stead proceeded to campaign for causes in which he passionately believed, including education and land reforms, and in later years his was one of the most powerful voices demanding greater spending on the navy. Stead hoped to foster better relations with English-speaking nations and improve and reform British imperial policy.[22] He was one of the first journalistic crusaders and built an impressive network of young journalists around his newspapers, who in turn promoted the Secret Elite's ambitions throughout the Empire.[23]

The third man present at the inaugural meeting of the secret society was Reginald Balliol Brett, better known as Lord Esher, a close advisor to three monarchs. Esher had even greater influence in the upper echelons of society. He represented the interests of the monarchy from Queen Victoria's final years, through the exuberant excesses of King Edward VII, to the more sedate but pliable King George V. He was described as 'the *éminence grise* who ran England with one hand while pursuing adolescent boys with the other'.[24] Esher wrote letters of advice to King Edward VII almost daily during his eight-year reign,[25] and through him the king was kept fully appraised of Secret Elite business. His precise role in British politics was difficult to grasp even for his contemporaries. He chaired important secret committees, was responsible for appointments to the Cabinet, the senior ranks of the diplomatic and civil services, voiced strong personal opinion on top army posts and exerted a power behind the throne far in excess of his constitutional position. His role of powerbroker on behalf of the Secret Elite was without equal.

Two others quickly drawn into the inner elect of the secret society were Lord Nathaniel Rothschild, the international merchant banker, and Alfred Milner, a relatively little known colonial administrator who brought order and sense to the financial chaos in Egypt. Both of these men represented different aspects of control and influence. The Rothschild dynasty epitomised 'the money power' to a degree with which no other could compete. Alfred Milner was a self-made man, a gifted academic who began his working life as an aspiring lawyer, turned to journalism and eventually emerged as an immensely powerful and successful powerbroker. In time, he led the 'men behind the curtain'.

The Rothschild dynasty was all-powerful in British and world banking and they considered themselves the equals of royalty,[26] even to the extent of calling their London base 'New Court'. Like the British royal family, their roots lay in Germany, and the Rothschilds were possibly the most authentic dynasty of them all. They practised endogamy as a means of preventing dispersal of their great wealth, marrying not just within their own faith but also within their own immediate family. Of 21 marriages of the descendants of Mayer Amschel Rothschild, the original family patriarch, no fewer than 15 were between cousins.

Wealth begets wealth, never more so when it can provide or deny funds to governments and dominate the financial market on a global scale. The Rothschilds were pre-eminent in this field. They manipulated politicians, befriended kings, emperors and influential aristocrats, and developed their own particular brand of operation. Even the Metropolitan Police ensured that the Rothschild carriages had right of way as they drove through the streets of London.[27] Biographers of the House of Rothschild record that men of influence and statesmen in almost every country of the world were in their pay.[28] Before long, most of the princes and kings of Europe fell within their influence.[29] This international dynasty was all but untouchable:

> The House of Rothschild was immensely more powerful than any financial empire that had ever preceded it. It commanded vast wealth. It was international. It was independent. Royal governments were nervous of it because they could not control it. Popular movements hated it because it was not answerable to the people. Constitutionalists resented it because its influence was exercised behind the scenes – secretly.[30]

Its financial and commercial links stretched into Asia, the near and Far East, and the northern and southern states of America. They were the masters of investment, with major holdings in both primary and secondary industrial development. The Rothschilds understood how to use their wealth to anticipate and facilitate the next market opportunity, wherever it was. Their unrivalled resources were secured by the close family partnership that could call on agents placed throughout the world. They understood the worth of foreknowledge a generation ahead of every other competitor. The Rothschilds communicated regularly with each other, often several times a day, with secret codes and trusted, well-paid agents, so that their collective fingers were on the pulse of what was about to happen, especially in Europe. Governments and crowned heads so valued the Rothschilds' fast communications, their network of couriers, agents and family associates, that they used them as an express postal service, which in itself gave the family access to even greater knowledge of secret dealings.[31] It is no exaggeration to say that in the nineteenth century, the House of Rothschild knew of events and proposals long before any government, business rival or newspaper.

Throughout the nineteenth century, the Rothschild family banking, investment and commercial dealings read like a list of international coups. Entire railway networks across Europe and America were financed through Rothschild bonds; investments in ores, raw materials, gold and diamonds, rubies, the new discoveries of oil in Mexico, Burma, Baku and Romania were financed through their banking empire, as were several important armaments firms including Maxim-Nordenfeldt and Vickers.[32] All of the main branches of the Rothschild family, in London, Paris, Frankfurt, Naples and Vienna, were joined together in a unique partnership. Working in unison, the branches were able to pool costs, share risks and guarantee each other major profits.

The Rothschilds valued their anonymity and, with rare exceptions, operated their businesses behind the scenes. Thus their affairs have been cleverly veiled in secrecy through the years.[33] They used agents and affiliated banks not only in Europe but all over the world, including New York and St Petersburg.[34] Their traditional system of semi-autonomous agents remained unsurpassed.[35] They would rescue ailing banks or industrial conglomerates with large injections of cash, take control and use them as fronts. For example, when they saved the small, ailing M.M. Warburg Bank in Hamburg, their enormous financial clout enabled it to grow into one of the major banks in Germany that went on to play a significant part in funding the German war effort in the First World War. This capacity to appear to support one side while actively encouraging another became the trademark of their effectiveness.

Though they were outsiders in terms of social position at the start of the nineteenth century, by the end of that same epoch the Rothschilds' wealth proved to be the key to open doors previously barred by the sectarian bigotry that regularly beset them because of their Jewish roots. The English branch, N.M. Rothschild & Co., headed by Lionel Rothschild, became the major force within the dynasty. He promoted the family interests by befriending Queen Victoria's husband, Prince Albert, whose chronic shortage of money provided easy access to his patronage. The Rothschilds bought shares for Albert through an intermediary, and in 1850 Lionel 'loaned' Queen Victoria and her consort sufficient funds to purchase the lease on Balmoral Castle and its 10,000 acres.[36] Lionel was succeeded by his son Nathaniel, or Natty, who as head of the London House became by far the richest man in the world.

Governments also fell under the spell of their munificent money power. It was Baron Lionel who advanced Disraeli's Liberal government £4,000,000 to buy the Suez Canal shares from the bankrupt Khedive of Egypt in 1875, an equivalent of £1,176,000,000 at today's prices.[37] Disraeli wrote jubilantly to Queen Victoria: 'You have it, Madam . . . there was only one firm that could do it – Rothschilds. They behaved admirably; advanced the money at a low rate, and the entire interest of the Khedive is now yours.'[38] The British government repaid the loan in full within three months to great mutual advantage.

The inevitable progress of the London Rothschilds toward the pinnacle of British society was reflected in Natty's elevation to the peerage in 1885, by which time both he and the family had become an integral part of the Prince of Wales' social entourage. Encouraged by their 'generosity', the prince lived well beyond his allowance from the Civil List, and Natty and his brothers, Alfred and Leo, maintained the family tradition of gifting loans to royalty. Indeed, from the mid 1870s onwards they covered the heir to the throne's massive gambling debts and ensured that he was accustomed to a standard of luxury well beyond his means. Their 'gift' of the £160,000 mortgage (approximately £11.8 million today) for Sandringham 'was discreetly hushed up'.[39] Thus both the great estates of Balmoral and Sandringham, so intimately associated with the British royal family, were facilitated, if not entirely paid for, through the largess of the House of Rothschild.

The Rothschilds frequently bankrolled pliant politicians. When he was secretary of state for India, Randolph Churchill (Winston's father) approved the annexation of Burma on 1 January 1886, thus allowing the Rothschilds to issue their immensely successful shareholding in the Burma ruby mines. Churchill demanded that the viceroy, Lord Dufferin, annex Burma as a New Year's present for Queen Victoria, but the financial gains rolled into the House of Rothschild. Esher noted sarcastically that Churchill and Rothschild seemed to conduct the business of the Empire together, and Churchill's 'excessive intimacy'[40] with the Rothschilds caused bitter comment, but no one took them to task. On his death from syphilis, it transpired that Randolph owed an astonishing £66,902 to Rothschild, a vast debt that equates to a current value of around £5.5 million.

Although he was by nature and breeding a Conservative in terms of party politics, Natty Rothschild believed that on matters of finance and diplomacy all sides should heed the Rothschilds. He drew into his circle of friends and acquaintances many important men who, on the face of it, were political enemies. In the close world of politics, the Rothschilds exercised immense influence within the leadership of both Liberal and Conservative parties. They lunched with them at New Court, dined at exclusive clubs and invited all of the key policy makers to the family mansions, where politicians and royalty alike were wined and dined with fabulous excess. Collectively they owned great houses in Piccadilly in London, mansions in Gunnersby Park and Acton, Aylesbury, Tring, Waddeston Manor and Mentmore Towers (which became Lord Rosebery's property when he married Hannah de Rothschild). Edward VII was always welcome at the sumptuous chateaux at Ferrières or Alfred de Rothschild's enormous town house when enjoying a weekend at the Parisian brothels. It was in such exclusive, absolutely private environments that the Secret Elite discussed their plans and ambitions for the future of the world, and, according to Niall Ferguson, the Rothschild biographer: 'it was in this milieu that many of the most important political decisions of the period were taken'.[41]

The Rothschilds had amassed such wealth that nothing or no one remained outwith the purchasing power of their coin. Through it, they offered a facility for men to pursue great political ambition and profit. Controlling politics from behind the curtain, they avoided being held publicly responsible if or when things went wrong. They influenced appointments to high office and had almost daily communication with the great decision makers.[42] Dorothy Pinto, who married into the Rothschild dynasty, presented a tantalising glimpse of their familiarity with the centres of political power. Pinto recalled: 'As a child I thought Lord Rothschild lived at the Foreign Office, because from my classroom window I used to watch his carriage standing outside every afternoon – while of course he was closeted with Arthur Balfour.'[43] Foreign Secretary Balfour was a member of the inner circle of the secret society and destined to become prime minister.

Before he died in 1915, Natty ordered his private correspondence to be destroyed posthumously, denuding the Rothschilds' archives of rich material and leaving the historian 'to wonder how much of the House of Rothschild's political role remains irrevocably hidden from posterity'.[44] Just what would have been revealed in these letters to and from prime ministers, foreign secretaries, viceroys, Liberal leaders like Rosebery, Asquith and Haldane, to say nothing of the all-powerful Alfred Milner or top Conservatives like Salisbury, Balfour, and Esher, the king's voice and ears in the secret society? Ample evidence still exists to prove that all of these key players frequented the Rothschild mansions,[45] so what did these volumes of correspondence contain? There was no limit to the valuable information that Rothschild agents provided for their masters in New Court, which was then fed to the Foreign Office and Downing Street. Given that members of the Secret Elite removed all possible traces linking them to Rothschild, what Natty Rothschild ordered was precisely what was required to keep their actions hidden from future generations.

And what of the fifth name, the dark horse, the man behind the curtain? Alfred Milner was a key figure within the Secret Elite. He was returning home on holiday from his post in Egypt when the inaugural meeting was held but was already fully cognisant of Rhodes' proposal. On his arrival back in London he was immediately inducted into the Society of the Elect. Like Rhodes, he had attended Ruskin's lectures at Oxford and was a devoted disciple.[46] Milner was a man who commanded as much loyalty and respect as any Jesuit superior general.

Born in Germany in 1854, Alfred Milner was a gifted academic, fluent in French and German. Having no source of independent wealth, he relied on scholarships to pay for his education at Oxford. There he met and befriended the future prime minister Herbert Asquith, with whom he stayed in regular contact for the rest of his life. Clever and calculating, but without the gift of oratory, as a fledgling lawyer Milner augmented his salary by writing journalistic articles for the *Fortnightly Review* and the *Pall Mall Gazette*. There he worked alongside William Stead, whose crusading journalism appealed to him and whose campaigns in support of greater unity amongst English-speaking nations fostered a deep interest in South Africa.

Milner's fervour for the Empire and the direction it might take brought him into a very exclusive circle of Liberal politicians gathered around Lord Rosebery. In 1885, he was invited for the first time to Rosebery's mansion at Mentmore. Within a year, Rosebery was foreign secretary and, under his patronage, Milner advanced his career in the Civil Service. As Chancellor George Goschen's personal secretary at the Treasury, Milner was largely responsible for the 1887 budget. His abilities were admired and respected. He was offered the post of director general of accounts in Cairo and took it up at a time when the British government began to fully appreciate the strategic importance of Egypt and the Suez Canal. The Rothschilds handled Egyptian financial affairs in London and on that first home visit in April 1891, Milner dined with Lord Rothschild[47] and other highly influential figures within the Secret Elite. This was precisely the period when the secret society was taking its first steps towards global influence, yet even at that stage Professor Quigley could identify Milner as the man who would drive forward the Secret Elite:

> Rhodes wanted to create a worldwide secret group devoted to English ideals and to the Empire as the embodiment of these ideals, and such a group was created in the period after 1890 by Rhodes, Stead, and, above all, by Milner.[48]

It was always Milner.

Alfred Milner's dynamic personality drew like-minded, ambitious men to his side. His impressive organisational skills blossomed when, from 1892 to 1896, he headed the largest department of government, the Board of Inland Revenue. Milner was regularly a weekend guest at the stately homes of Lords Rothschild, Salisbury and Rosebery, and was knighted for his services in 1895. The following year he was recommended to the king by Lord Esher as high commissioner in South Africa, a post he made his own.

Perhaps the most remarkable fact about Alfred (later Viscount) Milner is that few people have heard his name outside the parameters of the Boer War, yet he became the leading figure in the Secret Elite from around 1902 until 1925. Why do we know so little about this man? Why is his place in history virtually erased from the selected pages of so many official histories? Carroll Quigley noted in 1949 that all of the biographies on Milner's career had been written by members of the Secret Elite and concealed more than they revealed.[49] In his view, this neglect of one of the most important figures of the twentieth century was part of a deliberate policy of secrecy.[50]

Alfred Milner, a self-made man and remarkably successful civil servant whose Oxford University connections were unrivalled, became absolutely powerful within the ranks of these otherwise privileged individuals. Rhodes and Milner were inextricably connected through events in South Africa. Cecil Rhodes chided William Stead for saying that he 'would support Milner in any measure he may take, short of war'. Rhodes had no such reservations. He recognised in Alfred Milner the kind of steel that was required to pursue the dream of world domination: 'I support Milner absolutely without reserve. If he says peace, I say peace; if he says war, I say war. Whatever happens, I say ditto to Milner.'[51] Milner grew in time to be the most able of them all, to enjoy the privilege of patronage and power, a man to whom others turned for leadership and direction. If any individual emerges as the central force inside our narrative, it is Alfred Milner.

Taken together, the five principal players – Rhodes, Stead, Esher, Rothschild and Milner – represented a new force that was emerging inside British politics, but powerful old traditional aristocratic families that had long dominated Westminster, often in cahoots with the reigning monarch, were also deeply involved, and none more so than the Cecil family.

Robert Arthur Talbot Gascoyne-Cecil, the patriarchal 3rd Marquis of Salisbury, ruled the Conservative Party at the latter end of the nineteenth century. He served as prime minister three times for a total of fourteen years, between 1885 and 1902 (longer than anyone else in recent history). He handed over the reins of government to his sister's son, Arthur Balfour, when he retired as prime minister in July 1902, confident that his nephew would continue to pursue his policies. Lord Salisbury had four siblings, five sons and three daughters who were all linked and interlinked by marriage to individuals in the upper echelons of the English ruling class. Important government positions were given to relations, friends and wealthy supporters who proved their gratitude by ensuring that his views became policy in government, civil service and diplomatic circles. This extended 'Cecil-Bloc' was intricately linked to the Society of the Elect and Secret Elite ambitions throughout the first half of the twentieth century.[52]

The Liberal Party was similarly dominated by the Rosebery dynasty. Archibald Primrose, 5th Earl Rosebery, was twice secretary of state for foreign affairs and prime minister between 1894 and 1895. Salisbury and Rosebery, like so many of the English ruling class, were educated at Eton and Oxford University. Adversarial political viewpoints did not interfere with their involvement behind the scenes inside the Secret Elite.

Rosebery had an additional connection that placed his influence on an even higher plane. He had married the most eligible heiress of that time, Hannah de Rothschild, and was accepted into the most close-knit banking family in the world, and certainly the richest. According to Professor Quigley, Rosebery was probably not very active in the Society of the Elect but cooperated fully with its members. He had close personal relationships with them, including Esher, who was one of his most intimate friends. Rosebery also liked and admired Cecil Rhodes, who was often his guest. He made Rhodes a privy counsellor, and in return Rhodes made Rosebery a trustee of his will.[53] Patronage, aristocratic advantage, exclusive education, wealth: these were the qualifications necessary for acceptance in a society of the elite, particularly in its infancy. They met for secret meetings at private town houses and magnificent stately homes. These might be lavish weekend affairs or dinner in a private club. The Rothschilds' residences at Tring Park and Piccadilly, the Rosebery mansion at Mentmore, and Marlborough

House when it was the private residence of the Prince of Wales (until he became King Edward VII in 1901), were popular venues, while exclusive eating places like Grillion's and the even more ancient The Club provided suitable London bases for their discussions and intrigues.

These then were the architects who provided the necessary prerequisites for the secret society to take root, expand and grow into the collective Secret Elite. Rhodes brought them together and regularly refined his will to ensure that they would have financial backing. Stead was there to influence public opinion, and Esher acted as the voice of the king. Salisbury and Rosebery provided the political networks, while Rothschild represented the international money power. Milner was the master manipulator, the iron-willed, assertive intellectual who offered that one essential factor: strong leadership. The heady mix of international finance, political manipulation and the control of government policy was at the heart of this small clique of determined men who set out to dominate the world.

What this privileged clique intended might well have remained hidden from public scrutiny had Professor Carroll Quigley not unmasked it as the greatest influence in British political history in the twentieth century. The ultimate goal was to bring all habitable portions of the world under their control. Everything they touched was about control: of people and how their thoughts could be influenced; of political parties, no matter who was nominally in office. The world's most important and powerful leaders in finance and business were part and parcel of this secret world, as would be the control of history: how it was written and how information would be made available. All of this had to be accomplished in secret – unofficially, with an absolute minimum of written evidence, which is, as you will see, why so many official records have been destroyed, removed or remain closed to public examination, even in an era of 'freedom of information'.

Summary: Chapter 1 – The Secret Society

- In 1891, a secret society comprising members of the English ruling class was formed in London with the long-term goal of taking control of the world.
- This organisation would have remained unknown had it not been for the research of the eminent American scholar Professor Carroll Quigley. He was given access to information that revealed the conspiracy and its impact on major events in the twentieth century.
- Funded and founded by Cecil Rhodes, a select group of men were chosen for the inner circle or 'elect' that would secretly control British colonial and foreign policy. Other associates were drawn in from time to time, and may or may not have known what they were involved in.

- Two essential components of their shared approach were secrecy and an understanding that the reality of power was much more important than the appearance of power.
- They built on the longstanding power and patronage that the Salisbury and Rosebery families exercised in British politics, but also included the Rothschild dynasty of international financiers who were very close to the British Establishment.
- In the early years, the leading activists were Cecil Rhodes, William Stead, Lord Esher, Alfred Milner and Lord Nathaniel Rothschild.
- Renewal and strengthening of the bond between Britain and the United States of America was a central plank of Secret Elite policy.
- By the mid nineteenth century, the House of Rothschild, based in London, Paris, Frankfurt and Vienna, dominated European finance.
- Their holdings branched out across the world into new investments in steel, railways and oil; Cecil Rhodes' diamond and gold companies were bankrolled by the Rothschilds.
- The Rothschilds preferred to operate behind other companies so that few realised exactly what and how much they controlled.
- They targeted and financed relatively indebted royalty, including members of the British royal family. They purchased the Suez Canal shares for Disraeli and gave generously to politicians whom they supported. In Britain, their generosity and patronage broke down many of the anti-Semitic barriers they had to endure.
- Nathaniel Rothschild was intimately associated with Cecil Rhodes and his secret society from the outset. The powerful alliance of the 'money men', the 'men behind the curtain' and the emergence of Alfred Milner as leader gave the Secret Elite a cutting edge to make Rhodes' dream a reality.

CHAPTER 2

South Africa – Disregard the Screamers

Cecil Rhodes, the son of an English vicar, left home as a 17 year old in 1870 to join his brother Herbert growing cotton on a farm in South Africa. The crop failed, but the brothers found work at the recently opened diamond fields of Kimberley.[1] Rhodes attracted the attention of the Rothschild agent Albert Gansi, who was assessing the local prospects for investment in diamonds. Backed by Rothschild funding, Cecil Rhodes bought out many small mining concerns, rapidly gained monopoly control and became intrinsically linked to the powerful House of Rothschild.[2] Although Rhodes was credited with transforming the De Beers Consolidated Mines into the world's biggest diamond supplier, his success was largely due to the financial backing of Lord Natty Rothschild, who held more shares in the company than Rhodes himself.[3] Rothschild backed Rhodes not only in his mining ventures but on the issues of British race supremacy and expansion of the Empire. Neither had any qualms about the use of force against African tribes in their relentless drive to increase British dominance in Africa. It was a course of action destined to bring war with the Boer farmers of the Transvaal.

In 1877, by the age of 24, Cecil Rhodes had become a very rich young man whose life expectancy was threatened by ill health. In the first of his seven wills he stated that his legacy was to be used for:

> The establishment, promotion and development of a Secret Society, the true aim and object whereof shall be for the extension of British rule throughout the world, the perfecting of a system of emigration from the United Kingdom, and of colonization by British subjects of all lands wherein the means of livelihood are attainable by energy, labour, and enterprise, and especially the occupation by British settlers of the entire continent of Africa . . . the whole of South America . . . the whole United States of America, as an integral part of the British Empire and, finally, the foundation of so great a Power as to render wars impossible, and promote the best interests of humanity.[4]

Rhodes' will was a sham in terms of altruistic intent. Throughout his life, he consorted with businessmen driven by greed,[5] and did not hesitate to use bribery or force to attain his ends if he judged they would be effective.[6] Promotion of the 'best interests of humanity' was never evident in his lifestyle or business practices. Advised and backed by the powerful Rothschilds and his other inner-core Secret Elite friends, the Rand millionaires Alfred Beit and Sir Abe Bailey,[7] whose fortunes were also tied to gold and diamonds, Rhodes promoted their interests by gaining chartered company status for their investments in South Africa.

The British South Africa Company, created by Royal Charter in 1889, was empowered to form banks, to own, manage and grant or distribute land, and to raise a police force (the British South Africa Police). This was a private police force, owned and paid for by the company and its management. In return, the company promised to develop the territory it controlled, to respect existing African laws, to allow free trade within its territory and to respect all religions. Honeyed words, indeed. In practice, Rhodes set his sights on ever more mineral rights and territorial acquisitions from the African peoples by introducing laws with little concern or respect for tribal practices. The British had used identical tactics to dominate India through the East India Company a century earlier. Private armies, private police forces, the authority of the Crown and the blessing of investors was the route map to vast profits and the extension of the Empire. The impression that Rhodes and successors always sought to give, however, was that they did what had to be done, not for themselves but for the future of 'humanity'. Imperialism has long been a flag of convenience.

The chartered company recruited its own army, as it was permitted to do, and, led by one of Cecil Rhodes' closest friends, Dr Leander Starr Jameson, waged war on the Matabele tribes and drove them from their land. The stolen tribal kingdom, carved in blood for the profit of financiers, would later be named Rhodesia. It was the first time the British had used the Maxim gun in combat, slaughtering 3,000 tribesmen.[8]

Leander Starr Jameson was born in Stranraer, Scotland. He trained as a doctor in London before emigrating to South Africa, where he became Rhodes' physician and closest friend. Jameson was more responsible for the opening up of Rhodesia to British settlers than any other individual. His place in history's hall of infamy was reserved not by the thousands of Matabele he slaughtered but by his abortive attempt to seize Boer territory in the Transvaal.

To further his grand plans, Rhodes had himself elected to the legislature of Cape Colony and began extending British influence northward. His most ambitious design on the continent of Africa was a railway that would run from

Cape Town to Cairo, which could effectively bring the entire landmass under British control. It would link Britain's vast colonial possessions from the gold and diamond mines of South Africa to the Suez Canal, then on through the Middle East into India. It would similarly provide fast links from southern Africa through the Mediterranean to the Balkans and Russia, and through the Straits of Gibraltar to Britain. Every link in that chain would hold the Empire secure. Whoever was able to control this vast reach would control the world's most valuable strategic raw materials, from gold to petroleum.[9]

THE RHODES COLOSSUS
STRIDING FROM CAPE TOWN TO CAIRO.

1892–Rhodes as Colossus, with telegraph line from Cape to Cairo.

(Reproduced with permission of Punch Ltd., www.punch.co.uk)

In 1890, when Rhodes became prime minister of Cape Colony, his aggressive policies reignited old conflicts with the independent Boer Republics of Transvaal and the Orange River Colony. The Boers (farmers) were descendants of the Afrikaner colonists from northern mainland Europe, including Holland and Germany. Many Afrikaners remained under the British flag in Cape Colony, but in the 1830s and '40s others had made the famous 'long trek' (*Die Groot Trek*) with their cattle, covered wagons and Bibles into the African interior in search of farmland and escape from British rule. A number settled in lands to the north across the Orange River that would become the Boer republic of the Orange Free State. Others trekked on beyond the Vaal River into what became the Transvaal. Further north, across the Limpopo and Zambezi Rivers, lay the African kingdoms of the Matabele tribes.

Like the British settlers, many of the Calvinist Boers were racist, but, whatever their shortcomings, they were excellent colonisers with a moral code that was far better than that of the 'money-grabbing, gold-seeking imperialist filibusters who were the friends of Cecil Rhodes'.[10] The British government had promised not to interfere in the self-governing Boer Republics, but that was prior to the discovery of massive gold deposits in the Transvaal in 1886. Prospects of untold wealth raised the stakes and created a new gold rush with a large influx of fortune-seeking prospectors from Britain.[11]

By the 1890s, the Boer Republics had become increasingly problematic for Rhodes. They did not fit easily into Secret Elite plans for a unified South Africa, nor his dream of the trans-African railway. The explosion of wealth in the Transvaal immediately transformed its importance. Political control lay in the hands of the rural, backward, Bible-bashing Boers, while economic control was increasingly in the hands of British immigrants sucked into the interior by the gold rush. These outsiders, or Uitlanders as the Boers termed them, had money but no political power. Despite the fact that Uitlander numbers in the Transvaal rapidly rose to twice that of the original Boer settlers, President Paul Kruger disbarred them from full citizenship until they had settled for a minimum of 14 years.

Kruger had left Cape Colony aged ten to trek northward with his family, and never outgrew his hatred and suspicion of the British.[12] His government placed heavy taxes on mining companies and made it almost impossible for the Uitlanders to acquire citizenship: two convenient reasons for the British to find fault.

British–Boer conflict was all about the Transvaal's gold. The Secret Elite wanted it and decided to take it by force. In December 1895, they planned to provoke an Uitlander uprising in Johannesburg as an excuse to seize the republic. Cecil Rhodes' close friend Dr Jameson, the British South Africa Company's military commander, simultaneously launched an armed raid from across the border to support the uprising. It was a hare-brained scheme cooked up by Rhodes and British-born Johannesburg business leaders, with the support of the British government.[13]

Alfred Beit and other members of the Secret Elite were deeply involved in planning, financing and arming the assault on the Transvaal. Months before it was due to take place, Rhodes disclosed his intentions to a close friend and member of the Secret Elite, Flora Shaw, the South African correspondent of *The Times*.[14] Shaw was a pioneering journalist in her own right and had worked closely with Stead at the *Pall Mall Gazette*. She was a personal friend of John Ruskin, who had encouraged her in her writings.[15] Thereafter, she wrote pro-Uitlander, anti-Boer articles in the London paper to prepare public opinion in England and grease the path to war.[16] Lord Albert Grey, yet another member of the inner core and a director of the British South Africa Company, sought official support for the uprising from Joseph Chamberlain, the colonial secretary in London.[17] Chamberlain was also given advance notice of the raid by the Liberal leader, Lord Rosebery.[18]

The uprising never materialised, for the Uitlanders were neither as unhappy nor as oppressed as Flora Shaw portrayed in *The Times*. Word of the intended raid had been leaked in Johannesburg, and President Kruger had his forces ready. Jameson and his men were surrounded and captured. The entire venture was a fiasco.

Rhodes was forced to resign as Cape Colony prime minister and ordered to London to appear before a parliamentary select committee. He became the focus of an international scandal that could have fatally damaged the Secret Elite. Something akin to panic sent urgent messages flying between the conspirators. Immediately Rhodes disembarked in Southampton he was met by Natty Rothschild carrying a confidential message from Joseph Chamberlain, who had secretly approved the raid. In political terms, Chamberlain could have been obliged to resign, but that would have left the Secret Elite even more vulnerable to relentless recriminations. Rhodes carried official telegrams he had received from Chamberlain that exposed the colonial secretary's complicity. A deal was there to be done. Consequently, this damning proof was withheld from the select committee, and the government made no attempt to limit the powers of the Rothschild/Rhodes British South Africa Company.[19] It was an exercise in damage limitation.

In London, Rothschild, Esher, Stead and Milner met urgently to determine the Secret Elite strategy of denial.[20] Barefaced lies were presented as truth. Chamberlain secretly visited Jameson in prison, and the good doctor agreed to keep his counsel.[21] Whatever happened in law, Jameson knew that the Secret Elite would ultimately protect him. In a further defensive move, Sir Graham Bower from the Colonial Office was persuaded to offer himself as a scapegoat. Bower, who had personally handled negotiations between London and South Africa, agreed to lie before the committee by insisting that Chamberlain knew nothing about Jameson's raid. Edward Fairfield, another Colonial Office civil servant who had handled the London end of the negotiations, refused to follow Bower's lead and give false testimony. What incredibly good fortune for Chamberlain, Rhodes and the Secret Elite that Fairfield died suddenly from a 'stroke'.[22]

In a manner that would become a regular occurrence down the years, every major witness who appeared before the select committee lied under oath. Prime Minister Salisbury, a member of the inner circle, insisted that Chamberlain himself should sit on the committee. When witnesses refused to produce documents or respond to questions, they were not pressed for answers. Whole fields of inquiry were excluded.[23] The Secret Elite were thus able to whitewash all of the participants save Leander Starr Jameson, whose position was impossible. He had after all been caught in flagrante. He accepted sole responsibility and spent just a few weeks in prison.

The raid proved a setback for Rhodes in terms of personal position, for he had lost the respect and support he had previously enjoyed from many Boers. He and his moneyed friends regrouped while the storm blew over, but the Transvaal's gold was always unfinished business. Soon after, pliant journalists began once more to flood Britain with propaganda about the alleged plight of the Uitlanders.[24]

The Jameson Raid elevated President Paul Kruger to legendary status in the Transvaal. He set about transforming his small army into an effective force of some 25,000 commandos armed with the most advanced guns and rifles. Combined with forces from the Orange Free State, the Boers could muster 40,000 men for action. Kruger was re-elected president of the Transvaal for a fourth term, and his standing amongst the Afrikaners there and in the Cape had never been higher.[25]

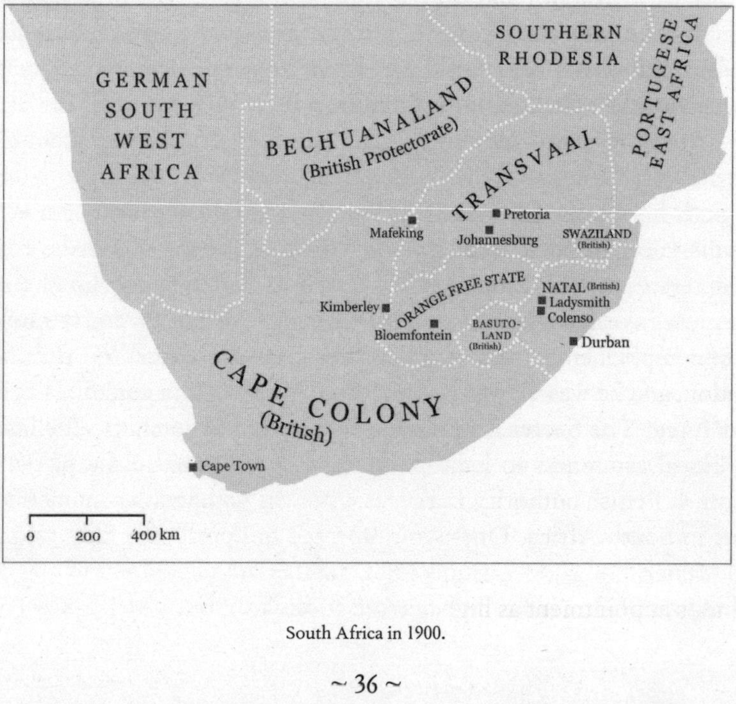

South Africa in 1900.

Cape Colony contained a majority of Afrikaners, though it was governed by Britain. Naturally, British rule was adversely affected both by the raid and Kruger's growing popularity. Rhodes had put at risk the very survival of that part of the British Empire to which he had dedicated his life. How ironic that the lure of gold drove him to reckless stupidity.

Of greater irony was the fact that he and Jameson were saved from eternal ridicule by the man who would pay the ultimate penalty for appearing to challenge the British Empire. The German Kaiser sent a telegram on 3 January 1896 to Paul Kruger congratulating him on preserving the independence of his country 'without the need to call for aid from his friends'.[26] Kaiser Wilhelm's telegram was portrayed in Britain as a veiled threat of Germany's willingness to support the Boers in any struggle against the Empire. The jingoistic British press raised a lasting storm of anti-German sentiment. *The Times* misconstrued the kaiser's note as an example of brazen German interference and proclaimed: 'England will concede nothing to menaces and will not lie down under insult.' The windows of shops owned by Germans in London were smashed, and German sailors attacked in the streets. In sharp contrast, the German diplomatic response was conciliatory. Taken aback by such unexpected reaction, Wilhelm replied to a letter from his grandmother, Queen Victoria: 'Never was the telegram intended as a step against England or your Government . . .'[27]

But the tide of public opinion had been turned and it was in no mood to turn back. 'A tawdry jingoism filled the air' and a new respect was found for Cecil Rhodes and Dr Jameson.[28] The Secret Elite propaganda machine turned Jameson's violence into an act of heroism and converted a shambolic, potentially very damaging incident to their advantage. Jameson, the butcher of the Matabele, was rewarded with a directorship of the British South Africa Company and would later be made prime minister of Cape Colony.[29]

Though his Secret Elite colleagues had saved him from derision and public disgrace, Rhodes' leadership was damaged. He remained a totally ruthless servant of the Empire, but his reckless attempt to oust the Boer government revealed a lack of political cunning. Worse, he had left behind a trail of complicit embarrassment that stretched back to the Colonial Office in London, and he was viewed by even his colleagues as a potential liability: a spent force. The Secret Elite required someone of intellect, intelligence and political astuteness to lead the secret society, pick up the pieces and re-establish British authority in the wake of the embarrassment caused by Rhodes in South Africa. One man fitted the bill perfectly: their man, Sir Alfred Milner.

Milner's appointment as high commissioner for South Africa was a coup for the Secret Elite. It was a post *he* had decided to take long before it was offered to him. The dangerous political tensions required a clear solution and could not be trusted to a less determined man. Milner was prepared to give the Empire the leadership it required by taking control of the South African government and confronting the Boers. His friend and colleague in the Society of the Elect, William Waldergrave Palmer, 2nd Earl Selborne, recommended him strongly to the colonial secretary at the same time as his other Secret Elite colleague Lord Esher was making a similar approach to the queen: a fair measure of the influence that the Secret Elite could exert inside the British government. The message put about by his friends was that Milner would have to be free to start *de novo*, pick his own team and be allowed to make his own decisions.[30] Chamberlain's first meeting with the new appointee remains a closed book, but though they differed in terms of the immediacy of a war, it later became apparent that both knew that it would be the only answer. Chamberlain insisted on patience because he had been personally damaged by the fallout from the Jameson Raid. He had to be sure that the public were behind him. Milner advocated an entirely different case for 'working up to a crisis'.[31] The difference between the two was temporal, and Milner used every contact he had to press the case urgently, even though it meant going behind his own boss's back.

Milner had been knighted for his services to the nation in 1895, but his promotion to high office in South Africa was spectacular. At the farewell dinner held by the Secret Elite in his honour, Milner was praised to the heights. Stead stated that he 'was an imperialist of the purest water, who could be relied upon to do all that can be done to make South Africa, from Table Mountain to Tanganyika, as loyally British as Kent or Middlesex'.[32] The dinner was organised by Lord Curzon and chaired by the future prime minister, Herbert Asquith. The guest list included Lord Rosebery, Sir William Harcourt, Lord Goschen, Arthur Balfour and Richard Haldane. These major British political figures had gathered to salute Sir Alfred Milner, one of their own, who ended his speech with a personal declaration that he was a 'civilian soldier of the Empire'.[33] How appropriate. Here was the man who would take up arms for the British race to which he was forever sworn.

On 14 April 1897, Milner set out for South Africa on a personal crusade to make it as loyally British as the garden of England. He would remain there for eight years, cement his role as leader and build a team of brilliant young acolytes to drive the Secret Elite agenda forward over the next 30 years. His mission was absolutely clear: govern South Africa, all of it, remove Boer obstacles to complete British domination and take the Transvaal's gold. Milner knew it would mean all-out war. He also knew that the only way to make such a war acceptable to the Cabinet and British public was to portray Kruger's Boers as the aggressors.

Sir Alfred Milner rarely met with Rhodes in South Africa but kept in constant touch using Edmund Garrett, member of the Society of the Elect[34] and newspaperman, as an intermediary. Milner felt that it was politically necessary to conceal their relationship, for Rhodes' reputation had been badly damaged and he was absolutely detested by many Boer communities.

In his first year in the Cape, Milner travelled around assessing the situation and weighing up alternatives. His appointment shortly after the raid disturbed the Boers, for he was known to be a determined Empire loyalist. And they had every reason to fear his unspoken intentions. In private letters to the colonial secretary, he stated very plainly that there was 'no way out of the political troubles in South Africa except reform in Transvaal, or war. And at present the chances of reform in the Transvaal are worse than ever.'[35] Although Chamberlain reminded him that their agreed strategy was to play the 'waiting game', that was precisely what Milner had no intention of doing. He was supported at every turn by Chamberlain's under-secretary, Selborne, who wrote secret and confidential letters to Milner in South Africa appraising him of Chamberlain's views and insisting that he must have a 'free hand and be backed up through thick and thin from here'.[36]

Sir Alfred Milner returned to England in 1898 to build support for 'an active and resolute policy of action'.[37] He travelled between London and the great watering holes of the Secret Elite, where he briefed members including Lords Curzon, Rosebery and Rothschild. He visited Arthur Balfour, Conservative leader in the Commons, and his former Balliol College classmate St John Brodrick, the man who within months would become secretary of state for war.[38]

Here, for the first time, the reader can see exactly how the Secret Elite worked. The colonial secretary persisted in his stance that Milner should delay until both public opinion and parliamentary objection had been turned in favour of war. Milner was straining at the leash because he knew that delay would only make the Empire look weak. He ensured that his own network prevailed. Joseph Chamberlain was effectively circumvented by his official representative in South Africa and, even had he known, there was nowhere he could turn to complain.

The high commissioner was invited to Windsor Castle by Queen Victoria, advised of course by Lord Esher, before going on to Sandringham, where a very affable future King Edward VII was anxious to have his advice. Milner instructed all the key members of the Secret Elite that there would have to be a war, whether his titular boss, Joseph Chamberlain, wished it or not.

Every one of these powerful individuals understood Milner's message. There was going to be a war in South Africa and they had to be ready to stand by him through what were certain to be difficult times.

Milner moved effortlessly from one front in which he was already the acknowledged master to a second where his contact base was equally impressive: the press. The British Army would be going to war, and the British public had to be softened up by a jingoism that would sweep all before it. The reaction to the kaiser's telegram had provided ample evidence of the public's aptitude for xenophobia, but Milner needed support too in the South African press. He recruited W.F. Monypenny from *The Times* to edit the *Rand Star*. Edmund Garrett, editor of the *Fortnightly Review*, was a loyal and trusted friend, and E.T. Cook at the *Daily News*, whose career Milner had advanced, was now trumpeting his virtues and supporting his solutions. In Britain, Harmsworth's *Daily News*, with a circulation in excess of 500,000 copies per day, was unstinting in its support for Milner and war.

The crisis, as far as the British public were made aware, had nothing to do with the Transvaal's gold. It stemmed from a disagreement about the limited rights of the Uitlanders and their ill-treatment by the Boers. The reader will immediately understand how much vested interest members of the Secret Elite had in Britain's imperial designs in South Africa. Rhodes, Alfred Beit, Abe Bailey (all Rand millionaires) and Lord Grey were directly involved with the British South Africa Company and, like the House of Rothschild, had serious financial and business investments that required to be protected. In truth, the coming war was all about the gold mines but was dressed as a clash of British immigrant workers' rights against Boer oppression.[39]

One journalist no longer applauded all that Milner did. One important voice who had initially been a committed supporter, as well as one of the original three conspirators, turned against them. William Stead had attended the 1898 Peace Conference at The Hague, undergone conversion to a different faith and returned as an apostle of international arbitration.[40] He publicly criticised Milner, who he could clearly see was steering Britain into a completely unnecessary war, and their long friendship (and his role in the secret society) ended acrimoniously.

Absolutely convinced of the brutal logic of his own analysis, Milner never wavered. British control of the Transvaal was essential, even though it meant war.[41] The only question that remained unanswered was how to bounce Paul Kruger into making the first move.

Consider the reality of Kruger's Transvaal. Boers were increasingly a distinct minority. Certainly, there were many British workers among the Uitlanders, but a large minority were Afrikaners from the Cape, Germans,

Frenchmen and even Americans – all white and earning good money.[42] The fact that they were effectively disenfranchised was a genuine concern to permanent settlers, but what did that matter to the itinerant workers? What possible incentive did they have to overthrow the Kruger government? None. Life under the Union flag promised no great advantage to the mass of gold-diggers and mine workers whose dream was to make a fortune and return home as wealthy men. In truth, the Jameson Raid had largely failed because Rhodes had hopelessly overestimated the strength of feeling amongst the Uitlanders. Milner did not leave such a basic prerequisite to mere chance.

He needed a genuine uprising from an angry and frustrated community that could appeal to the British government for help. Dissent had to be fermented throughout the Uitlander population. To this end, Alfred Beit wanted to unleash his Johannesburg agent and rabble-rouser Percy Fitzpatrick, but one major obstacle stood in the way. Fitzpatrick, arrested and jailed during the Jameson Raid, had been paroled on conditions that banned him from any political activity or criticism of the Kruger government. Quite incredibly, he was released from this bail condition by the Transvaal's state attorney and freed to stir Uitlander outrage at the shooting of one of their number in his own home by a trigger-happy Boer policeman. Five thousand protestors took to the streets, and salt was rubbed into the wound when several Uitlanders were arrested and set bail conditions five times higher than the police gunman at the centre of the storm. According to Fitzpatrick, those arrested were in the Market Square in Johannesburg simply to present a petition to the British vice-consul but were taken into custody under the Public Meetings Act. Bitter recriminations spewed forth, with Fitzpatrick pointing out that 'for taking the life of a British subject, £200 bail was sufficient, but for the crime of objecting to it, bail was set at £1,000'.[43] The cause became one of trampled civil rights.

Fitzpatrick encouraged further protest meetings in Johannesburg, and a petition was signed seeking redress through the British government. It was exactly what Milner needed: a popular cause. Late in March 1899, Milner met secretly with Percy Fitzpatrick in Cape Town and gave him instructions to continue stirring unrest and to feed damaging stories about Kruger to the British press.[44] Fitzpatrick was dispatched to London to present the Uitlander case to the British public. His book, *The Transvaal from Within*, became an instant bestseller,[45] promoted by the Secret Elite.[46]

Jan Smuts, the Transvaal state attorney who freed Fitzpatrick from the shackles of his parole, warrants considered attention. Prior to the Jameson Raid, Smuts had been Cecil Rhodes' close friend, trusted confidant and personal agent in Kimberley.[47] The 27-year-old Cambridge-trained lawyer believed passionately in South African unity under British rule, where both British and Dutch would settle their differences and coalesce into a single white nation.[48] His admiration was such that he saw Rhodes as the very man to carry forward this great ideal, and he became a vigorous supporter of a united South Africa within the British Empire. Then he completely changed tack. Apparently disaffected by the unlawful attempt to occupy the Transvaal by force, he abandoned his political philosophy, denounced his good friend Rhodes and reinvented himself. His conversion from Anglophile to Anglophobe was conveniently explained as a 'road to Damascus' moment. Born again as Rhodes's most vociferous critic, his violent anti-British agitation and uncompromising support for Kruger quickly yielded results. Despite his age and lack of experience, Kruger made him state attorney in Transvaal and his chief political advisor.[49]

Smuts' anti-English rhetoric and other draconian measures soon enraged the Uitlanders. In addition to their lack of voting rights, they complained bitterly about the levels of taxation, the state control of mining supplies and what they considered as a system of blatant extortion that took their wealth from Johannesburg and transferred it to the Boers in Pretoria.[50] Smuts' constant provocation of the Uitlanders was strangely at odds with President Kruger's attempts to calm the rising unrest, including a major concession on voting rights after just five years' residence instead of the previous fourteen. He was even prepared to grant preferential mining rights and reduce taxation levels.[51] This was Kruger's 'Great Deal', an astonishing turn of events that could have placated the dissenters and restored confidence in his government.

While the president was granting concessions and attempting to dampen down agitation from the anti-Boer press, Smuts seriously undermined him by arresting newspaper editors sympathetic to the Uitlander cause. Smuts was hell-bent on stirring Uitlander outrage. Strange indeed that in so short a time Rhodes' former close friend and ally was doing everything in his power to ensure that Milner got the one thing he and Rhodes most desperately wanted: war.

Smuts sensed a wavering in the political ranks and sent a memorandum to the Transvaal executive in September 1899 urging them to take the necessary steps to become 'one of the great empires of the world . . . an Afrikaner republic in South Africa stretching from Table Bay to the Zambezi'.[52] This was virtual Secret Elite-speak, reminiscent of Rhodes. Though it was voiced to upset the Uitlanders, Cape Afrikaners begged him to avoid war, accommodate the Uitlanders and placate the British government. Smuts would have none of their wise counsel. He retorted vehemently that if it was to be war, then 'the sooner the better. Our volk throughout South Africa must be baptised with the baptism of blood and fire.'[53] Two voices argued war – Milner and Smuts – apparently implacable enemies. As each week passed, tensions heightened. British troop movements unnerved Kruger, who could see that the Transvaal was threatened with invasion.

By October 1899, large numbers of British troops were sent to the Transvaal border in what was a calculated provocation. Kruger demanded their withdrawal, but Milner's response was to deliberately escalate the tension by sending yet more troops.

Milner got his war. Both the British and Boer representatives rejected the terms they demanded of each other, and to Milner's delight Kruger approved an ultimatum written by Smuts that accused Britain of breaking the 1884 London Convention, drawn up after the first Boer War of 1880–81. The text of the ultimatum was received in London with derision, delight and disdain. The *Daily Telegraph* didn't know whether to laugh or cry. The editorials rejoiced in the fact that 'Mr Kruger has asked for war, and war he must have'.[54] It was all to be over by teatime.

Boer soldiers advanced into Cape Colony on 12 October 1899 to attack an armoured train carrying supplies to Mafeking, and so began the Boer War exactly as Milner had planned. Kruger, in exasperation, made the first move before the British could bring even more troops into South Africa and was forever held to be the aggressor. In truth, he had been out-manoeuvred. Milner had the grace to confess in a letter to Lord Roberts, commander in chief in South Africa, that:

> I precipitated the crisis, which was inevitable, before it was too late. It is not very agreeable, and in many eyes, not a very creditable piece of business to have been largely instrumental in bringing about a big war.[55]

This was no immodest boast or rampant exaggeration. Milner's matter-of-fact explanation displayed the cold objectivity that drove the Secret Elite cause. War was unfortunate but necessary. It had to be. One year before, in a private letter to his friend Lord Selborne, Milner explained very clearly that the backward, almost medieval Boers could not be allowed to control the future of South Africa. 'The race-oligarchy [the Boers] has got to go, and I see no sign of it removing itself.'[56] The solution was simple. If they would not go, they had to be removed, and his placemen, Percy Fitzpatrick and Jan Smuts, had played their allotted roles in helping him precipitate that 'inevitable' crisis.

With a force that peaked at almost half a million men, more than double the entire Boer population of the Transvaal, against an estimated 40,000 Boers in the field, the British expected an easy victory. Easy? The first principle of Boer tactics was mobility, and though they vastly outnumbered the Boers, the British Army found it difficult to pin them down. The Boers' guerrilla warfare proved frustratingly effective against a military mindset anchored in Wellington's traditions. The war lasted almost three years and became the bloodiest, costliest and longest that the British Army had fought in almost a hundred years.

The Boer War provided little or no cheering news for the British public, but one report grabbed the national headlines and fired the imagination. It brought a young man with huge ambition to the public eye in a blaze of glory, though the account of his Indiana Jones adventure lacked the rigour of any independent corroboration.

Winston Churchill had been sent to South Africa as a war correspondent for the conservative *Morning Post* in 1899 and ended up in a Boer prisoner-of-war camp. The story, and it was largely his, derives from Churchill's autobiography.[57] According to his own account, he joined a reconnaissance mission aboard an armoured train on 15 November 1899 and was captured along with around 60 British officers and men when the Boers attacked it. Taken to Pretoria, they were held in an old school surrounded by a ten-foot-high corrugated-iron wall. Churchill gave an account of the derailment and his subsequent action in making a 'daring escape' to other journalists. The *Daily Telegraph* printed a dispatch from Reuters headlined 'Mr Churchill's bravery and coolness is described as magnificent'. The hero created himself.

What went unreported was that following his internment Churchill wanted himself classified as a non-combatant on the grounds that he was a journalist. He used his connections to send a begging letter to Alfred Milner on 24 November asking that he be included in a list of prisoners to be released and said that he had asked his mother to write to him through Milner.[58] He also submitted requests for his release on 26 November and 8 December,[59] and promised that 'if I am released I will give any parole that I may be required not to serve against the Republican forces'.[60] On 12 December, the Boer commander-in-chief agreed to release him, and some time thereafter Churchill was never seen again in the camp.

On his subsequent arrival in the Portuguese port of Lourenço Marques Churchill relayed an amazing adventure. He claimed to have cut through the fencing under the noses of the Boer guards and made a tortuous journey to freedom. His 'daring escape' became the stuff of legend. On his own and unable to speak either Afrikaans or Kaffir, but bolstered by the surprisingly large sum of £75 (worth over £6,000 in today's currency), he made the 250-mile journey to the safe haven of Lourenço Marques. His odyssey was worthy of any Greek hero of ancient myth. Crossing dangerous terrain and dodging the heavily armed Boer commandos who were out hunting for him, he eventually came to a railway track and leapt onto a train as it thundered past. This must have been accomplished with considerable difficulty, 'partly because of his dislocated shoulder'.[61]

In another fawning account, Churchill is said to have 'hurled himself upon a truck, and after an agonising struggle managed to remain crouching on the couplings between two wagons'.[62] Within a very short time, however, thirst forced him to leap off in search of water. Crawling on his belly, he dragged himself through swamps before coming across the Boer township of Witbank. He was unbelievably fortunate to knock on the door of 'the only family for twenty miles where he would not have been handed over'.[63] After three days in hiding, allegedly in the company of rats down a mineshaft, he got aboard another railway truck and concealed himself under bales of wool. It was the train to Delagoa Bay, freedom and 'a blaze of triumph'.[64] That is how Churchill told his story.

Controversy hung around his account like the rats in his mineshaft. There were accusations that he had behaved selfishly and badly by leaving on his own and creating such self-seeking publicity. Fortune and determined legal proceedings, however, seem to have removed such reservations. British officers in the camp, Captain Haldane, Sergeant Brockie, and Lieutenants le Mesurier and Frankland felt he had ruined their chances of freedom. Haldane's claims were strengthened by his refusal to appear in court on Churchill's behalf in a libel case against *Blackwood's Magazine* in 1912. Despite these contrary voices, his 'daring escape' turned Churchill into a public hero and gifted him a Conservative seat for Oldham in the parliamentary elections just a few months later.

Quite apart from the hero that was Churchill, British confidence ran well ahead of reality, and the Boer War proved beyond any shadow of doubt that the British Army was not fit for purpose. The war altered Milner's direct control of South African affairs, for the conduct of military operations was not within his remit. Perhaps he should have been very grateful, since fault for the many military embarrassments that followed could not be laid at his door. For Alfred Milner, war was a beginning, not an end in itself. What mattered was winning, controlling the gold fields, and then weaving the reconstructed South Africa into the fabric of the Empire.

Though it was a dirty war, dominated eventually by General Kitchener's tactics and the obscenity of British concentration camps, Milner learned a great deal that would be useful to the Secret Elite in the war of 1914–18. The military incompetence prior to Kitchener's arrival as chief of staff to Lord Roberts was alarming. Kitchener, however, proved to be difficult; he was not a team player. He was appointed by the War Office as a trouble-shooter, cutting through red tape, an organiser who rarely played second fiddle and not a man to give way to politicians.[65] In Kitchener's eyes, war was the responsibility of the armed forces, not civilians. He tended to be consumed by his own authority and did not listen to other points of view. When he altered the army-transport system in the middle of the war, despite the warnings of those who knew the South African terrain, the professional transport officers prophesied disaster, and it duly followed. Kitchener of Khartoum became known locally as 'Kitchener of Chaos'.[66]

The one fear that Alfred Milner carried in his heart, the one prospect that filled him with greater horror than a protracted war and the misery it brought, was the prospect of Kitchener offering the Boers a negotiated peace. Kitchener believed that by 1901 peace was both practical and desirable. Milner thought otherwise. He had not gone through the painstaking trouble of engineering this war simply to engage in a compromise through peace talks. Writing to Violet Cecil, the woman he would later marry, Milner admitted: 'My only fear is that he [Kitchener] may make promises to people to get them to surrender, which will be embarrassing afterwards to fulfil.'[67] His vision for a future South Africa was predicated upon outright victory and the total subjugation of the Boers to the British Empire. He dreaded a botched-up settlement, a 'Kaffir bargain' as he called it.[68] Quite apart from the gold, an early peace would not only save the face of the Boer leaders but also preserve their identity as a political force.

This was Milner's nightmare scenario. He wrote in January 1901 to Richard Haldane, the Liberal Member of Parliament whom he trusted most, that there was no room for compromise in South Africa; they must be out and out victors. The big difference between them was that Milner knew the grand plan. Kitchener did not. Winning the war was a necessity, but winning the peace in Milner's eyes was a complete necessity. He ensured that peace talks failed by directly lobbying the Conservative Cabinet through the Secret Elite in London. He was adamant there should be no talk of amnesty.[69] Kitchener's lack of political nous was revealed when he complained bitterly to the secretary of state for war, St John Brodrick, that Milner's policy was absurd and wrong: 'Milner's views may be strictly just but they are to my mind vindictive, and I do not know of a case in history when, under similar circumstances, an amnesty has not been granted'.[70] Given that Brodrick was Milner's close personal friend from Balliol College, and party to all that he went to South Africa to achieve, Kitchener simply undermined himself.

Sir Alfred Milner returned to London in May 1901 to assert his position and stiffen the resolve of any doubters. A reception committee that included government members of the Secret Elite met him at Waterloo Station. All the major politicians were waiting on the platform as the train drew in.

Prime Minister Lord Salisbury and his nephew, Arthur Balfour, leader of the House of Commons, led a delegation that included Lord Lansdowne, the foreign secretary, and the colonial secretary, Joseph Chamberlain. Sir Alfred Milner was whisked off through cheering crowds to Marlborough House, where his friend, the newly crowned King Edward VII, rewarded him with the Order of the Bath, made him a privy councillor and raised him to the peerage as Baron Milner. It was a public display of undiluted homage to the leader of the Secret Elite.

Within weeks, the Cabinet adopted Milner's policy in South Africa as their policy. Kitchener had been outmanoeuvred, and Lord Milner immersed himself in preparing the ground for success: continuing the war, re-opening the mines, ensuring the flow of wealth to his backers and getting the best of British talent into his own administration.

With his power confirmed absolutely, Milner returned to South Africa, where the brutal war continued for another full year. The Boer War started badly for Britain in military terms, and no matter how the supportive press exaggerated small successes, its popularity ebbed thanks to two infamous causes that the Liberal opposition made their own. The first was the public outcry that grew from one of Milner's rare mistakes.

The British welfare campaigner Emily Hobhouse, armed with credentials from Liberal MPs whom Milner trusted, solicited permission from him to visit the so-called refugee camps. What she saw there fired her sense of moral indignation, and rightly so. Set up as part of Kitchener's attempt to win the war, the concentration camps were by any standard abominable. From November 1900, the British Army had introduced new tactics in an attempt to break the Boers' guerrilla campaign. Kitchener initiated plans to flush out guerrillas in a series of systematic drives, organised like a sporting shoot, with success defined in a weekly 'bag' of killed, captured and wounded. The country was swept bare of everything that could give sustenance to the guerrillas, including women and children. Some 30,000 Boer farms were burned to the ground and their animals slaughtered. It was the clearance of civilians, virtually ethnic cleansing, uprooting a whole nation, that would come to dominate the public's perception of the last phase of the war.[71]

A total of 45 camps were built for Boer internees and 64 for native Africans. Of 28,000 Boer men captured as prisoners of war, almost all were sent overseas. The vast majority in the camps were women and children. Inadequate shelter, poor diet, total lack of hygiene and overcrowding led to malnutrition and endemic contagious diseases such as measles, typhoid and dysentery. Coupled with a shortage of medical facilities, over 26,000 women and children were to perish in the British concentration camps.

Emily Hobhouse's dispassionate *The Brunt of the War, and Where it Fell*, published in 1902, was more than just a political bombshell.[72] It exposed the disgusting truth about how Britain was conducting war against women and children. She detailed cases where every child in families of ten had perished in the camps, where Dutch charities were forbidden to provide much-needed condensed milk when it was freely available in Pretoria, and how as a consequence 'children were dying like flies'. The wives and children of men fighting for the Boer army were punished by being put on half the already meagre rations and given no meat whatsoever.[73] W.T. Stead was overcome by the evidence presented to him and wrote:

> Every one of these children who died as a result of the halving of their rations, thereby exerting pressure onto their family still on the battle-field, was purposefully murdered. The system of half rations stands exposed, stark and unashamedly as a cold-blooded deed of state policy employed with the purpose of ensuring the surrender of men whom we were not able to defeat on the field.[74]

All of this was conducted expressly on the orders of the British authorities. Concerted attempts were made to dismiss Hobhouse's revelations by claims that she was slandering British troops, but her exposé fired the Liberal leader Campbell-Bannerman's outrage over the 'methods of barbarism'[75] being used against the Boers. It was a phrase he hammered home time and again against the Conservative government. It was followed by another attack on the government by the virulently anti-war Lloyd George on 17 June 1901. He railed bitterly at his opponents: 'Why pursue war against women and children?' and pointed out with scathing derision that 'the rate of mortality among children is higher than that amongst the soldiers who have braved all the risks of the field'.[76] The following month, when statistical returns from the camps arrived at the War Office, it was clear that Hobhouse's worst fears had been confirmed. There were 93,940 whites and 24,457 blacks in 'camps of refuge', and the crisis was becoming a catastrophe as the death rates grew higher and higher.[77] To Milner, the life or death of 118,000 Boer and African civilians therein rated as an abysmally low priority. Friends like Richard Haldane dismissed the utter tragedy of the concentration camps as 'a great mess caused by the military authorities',[78] but no one should forget that Milner was morally responsible for the camps. He was the high commissioner.

Ten months after the subject had first been raised in Parliament, Lloyd George's taunts and Campbell-Bannerman's harsh words had been fully vindicated. In the interval, at least 20,000 Boer civilians and 12,000 Africans had died.[79] Lesser men would have been hounded from office, but Lord Alfred Milner was no lesser man.

The war was costing the British government around two and a half million pounds per month, and as the secretary of state for war, St John Brodrick, pointed out to Kitchener, they could not profit from any victories until 'the wheels of the gold mines began to turn'.[80] Milner too was anxious to restart production. His Secret Elite millionaire colleagues were dependent on him to pressurise Kitchener into reopening the Rand mines, and this duly happened.

There is no doubt that the Boer War was about mining rights and ownership of the Transvaal's gold. One immediate consequence of war, however, was that the gold stream dried up. The great mines like Robinson Deep and the Ferreira emptied their boilers, laid down their huge steel-crushing stamps and stopped all production. The Uitlander workers turned into panic-stricken refugees who only added to the chaos and fear in Johannesburg. Several operating mines were allowed to flood, lest the gold fell into Boer hands, but in November 1901 a small amount of dewatering began again, such was the urgency given to restarting the profit stream.[81]

Milner believed that the military commander's role was to win the war and accept the enemy's unconditional surrender, not discuss terms of surrender or a negotiated peace. His hackles were raised in March 1902, when the Boers agreed to meet with Kitchener, not him, to discuss peace. An urgent secret telegram was sent to London advising the colonial secretary that Kitchener's involvement could profoundly upset plans for the future administration of South Africa. Milner knew that Kitchener was very anxious to end the war and get away to India, and had no appreciation of the impact that 'dangerous concessions' could make.[82] Both Chamberlain and Milner agreed that the Boers needed to taste outright defeat.

Just days before peace negotiations finally began, Cecil Rhodes died at his home near Cape Town. It was the end of an era. Milner's place in the secret society was consolidated by his apostolic succession as leader, just as Rhodes had wished; though, in truth, Milner had assumed office after the Jameson Raid.

When the British delegation presented the Boers with terms of unconditional surrender, it was Jan Smuts who drew up their immediate acceptance. Smuts who drew up the ultimatum and Smuts who penned the proposal to accept Britain's terms without delay: so quick to go to war, so ready to grasp surrender. Had he undergone a second 'road to Damascus' conversion? Or was he always a Secret Elite placeman? The Treaty of Vereeniging was signed on 31 May 1902, and in consequence the Boer Republics were annexed to the British Empire. The winner took all. It has always been so. The Transvaal's gold was finally in the hands of the Secret Elite at the cost of 32,000 deaths in the concentration camps, including more than 20,000 children; 22,000 British Empire troops were killed and 23,000 wounded. Boer casualties numbered 34,000. Africans killed amounted to 14,000.[83] More British soldiers were killed by enemy fire in the Boer War alone than in all Great Britain's colonial wars in Asia and Black Africa from 1750 to 1913. The British mobilised nearly half a million soldiers, of whom 450,000 were sent directly from the mother country.[84] Milner's war proved costly in human terms, but he regained the gold mines.

Lord Milner was elevated to Viscount Milner by the appreciative Edward VII on 1 July 1902 and weeks later sworn in as governor of the Transvaal and the Orange River Colony. Discriminatory laws that had been enforced against non-whites remained untouched, and the policy of white supremacy continued. Milner was vexed to find that many of the troops whom he hoped would stay to populate South Africa were leaving because economic prospects looked bleak. He desperately wanted to root the Empire's future in the potential wealth of South Africa and urged Chamberlain in London to help him boost immigration by aiding the reconstruction of the country. He dreamed of developing a wider sense of British patriotism in South Africa, far in excess of that present in Canada or Australia, and was prepared to stay and fight for it.

In September 1902, after being handed the keys to 10 Downing Street by his uncle, Arthur Balfour asked his friend Milner to return home to take up the post of colonial secretary. It was unquestionably an acknowledgement of his high standing. Milner refused. Even when the king made it known that he was the royal choice, Milner stayed on to complete his task. He made it clear that Alfred Lyttelton, another member of the inner circle of the secret society,[85] should be appointed, and so he was.

This microscopic example demonstrates how the real power inside the Secret Elite worked. Milner held sway as their leader, and neither the prime minister nor the king denied him. Who else in the Empire would have dared override such authority? Theoretically, they had the power to insist Milner did as he was instructed, but both the head of government and the head of state bowed to his wishes and respected Milner's deep-seated view that completing the task in South Africa took priority.

Viscount Milner turned his attention to the practical business of transforming the country into a model British dominion. He administered the Transvaal and Orange River Colony as occupied territory, recruiting into the upper layers of his civil service a band of young men whom he had mainly recruited from his beloved Oxford University. This group, which became known as 'Milner's Kindergarten', replaced the government and administration of the two former republics and worked prodigiously to rebuild the broken country.[86]

'Milner's Kindergarten' comprised new blood from the best universities: young, educated men with a deep sense of duty and loyalty to the Empire and capable of populating the next generation of the secret society.[87] Milner's connection with All Souls and Balliol was particularly important in providing suitable recruits for his personal administration. The challenge was formidable. He estimated that there would be a short but important period after the war during which the British population could be increased through immigration. Prosperity would return when the gold-mining industry was restored and the hundreds of thousands of prisoners of war, civilians in concentration camps and native labourers, were resettled. Thirty thousand burned-out farms, smashed railway lines and a communications system in tatters would have to be restored. Thereafter, a united, self-governing, white community supported by black labour would see the benefits of being in the British Empire and want to become a vital and permanent part of it.[88] Milner needed men of quality to serve in the reconstruction of South Africa, and he was determined to enlist the very best brains with the greatest possible energy for the task ahead.[89] Oxford friendships, contacts with the Colonial Office and personal association with Milner were a good starting point, but above all they had to share his commitment to the Empire.

What marked out these young men, a collection of mere minor colonial administrators in 1902, is how their careers blossomed under the patronage of Alfred Milner and the Secret Elite. Of the eighteen men appointed by Milner to his administration in the 'Kindergarten', nine of them attended New College, Oxford, four went to Balliol, five were also Fellows of All Souls[90] and every one proved to be a Milner 'loyalist'. They were endowed with good fortune, education and family connections, and were skilled in personal relations.[91] Through Milner's patronage, and membership of the Secret Elite, they would all go on to high office in the British government and international finance, and become the dominant influence in British imperial and foreign affairs for the next 40 years.[92]

The unrelenting litany of political, academic and journalistic achievement of the men from Milner's Kindergarten is unparalleled. Ponder for a second on the likelihood of such success from any random group of university graduates in any period of history. They became viceroys, secretaries of state, permanent secretaries, governors general, ambassadors, knights of the realm, managing directors, bankers, industrialists, Members of Parliament, Members of the House of Lords, editors of major newspapers, professors of history, members of war cabinets, writers and guardians of the great imperial dream. These men were recruited by Alfred Milner, moulded, trusted and proven able. They went on to become the Secret Elite's imperial guard, the physical proof of its triple penetration of politics, the media and education. They were fired by his total dedication to the cause, and South Africa was their testing ground. Whatever else, Milner recruited and built formidable teams, and, as a result, had at his beck and call an unrivalled network of talent on which to draw for the rest of his life.

The post-war reconstruction of South Africa coordinated by the Kindergarten generated a general boom in work throughout the country and further huge profits for the Secret Elite. There was no incentive for the African workforce to return to the old jobs down the mines because higher paid work was plentiful elsewhere. Furthermore, mining was very dangerous work, with scant regard paid to workers' safety. Deaths in the mines averaged seventy-one per thousand workers in 1903, with the figures in July that year exceeding one man killed for every ten miners. 'Human life was being sacrificed, after a purgatory of toil and torture, for a wage of fifty cents a day.'[93] But investor profits were good. Milner and the mine owners were so desperate to augment the declining workforce that drastic measures were agreed. They looked to China, where there was a large source of surplus cheap labour.

The Chinese were lured to the South African mines with false promises and outrageous lies. They were led to understand that they would be living in pleasant garden cities where, once settled, families might join them. Fit and healthy applicants were selected and kept in sheds until embarkation. Then, under armed guard, they were loaded into the holds of ships for the journey.[94] The first ship to sail, the 3,400-ton iron-hulled SS *Ikbal*, left China on 30 June 1904 with over 2,000 men crammed in the hold like a classic eighteenth-century slave ship. It was mid-summer, with the temperature over 100 degrees Fahrenheit in the shade, as the *Ikbal* headed out for its 26-day voyage through the tropics. By the time it arrived in Durban, 51 men had died and their bodies dispatched overboard. The deaths proved no great loss to the organisers, however, for they had insured each man for $125 and netted a tidy profit from the insurance company.[95]

On arrival, the men were tagged like pieces of meat and sealed in railroad cars for the 30-hour journey to the Transvaal. The garden cities were a myth. In reality, the Chinese workers lived in huge hutted compounds beside the mines with 20 men in each small shack. They were unable to leave the compounds without a special permit and were fined for the slightest breach of the rules. The men worked ten hours a day for a wage of twenty-five cents. In addition, they had to work at lower rates for at least six months to pay back the costs of their passage from China. If any man failed to carry out his allocated work, he could be flogged and given a heavy fine. Although it was illegal, Milner approved the flogging of the Chinese workers as a necessary sanction, and the Conservative government backed him.[96] It was an act of classic, old-fashioned imperialism. Many who could not keep up with the backbreaking toil were in perpetual debt to the mines. If still alive after three years, they were to be shipped back to China like spoiled returned goods. 'These Chinese were brought over in the prime of life to be broken on the wheel within three years for the purpose of grinding out ever greater profits for the monsters of greed who owned them.'[97]

The problem for Milner was that he underestimated the impact that allegations of slavery and reports of vicious floggings would have on even his trusted Liberal friends like Asquith. Indeed, Milner was at times such a driven man that he failed to take account of the weight of opposition ranged against him. He warned his friend, Richard Haldane: 'If we are to build up anything in South Africa, we must disregard, and absolutely disregard, the screamers.'[98] It takes a very strong man to disregard the screamers: to ignore moral indignation, to put the cause before humanitarian concerns. Some frontline politicians find it all but impossible to stand against a torrent of public outrage, but those behind the curtain in the secret corridors of power can easily ignore 'sentimentality'. Remember those words. They will reverberate through the pages of this book: 'absolutely disregard the screamers'.

By 1905, public opinion in Britain had clearly turned against Milner, and with a general election due he decided that the best way forward was for him to withdraw from South Africa. Officially, the word was that his health was suffering under the strain of the momentous task of reconstruction; he was allegedly burnt-out.[99] Always in charge, Milner chose his moment carefully. It was vital to the Secret Elite that a change of government did not result in a change of imperial policy. Secret negotiations that would have long-term implications for British foreign policy were already taking place behind closed doors in London. Milner was needed there. His African quest could be left safely to his trusted Kindergarten, and Milner went so far as to nominate his Secret Elite friend, the Earl of Selborne, as his successor. In fact, Selborne was not too happy at being sent to South Africa, but he obeyed Milner, who wrote directly to Prime Minister Balfour saying that Selborne's appointment left him feeling the 'greatest possible relief'.[100] Yet again it was the leader of the Secret Elite who chose his own trusted man to continue the fight in South Africa, even though he did not particularly want the post.

Viscount Milner was well rewarded by his banking and industrialist friends for the tireless work he did to reinstate and increase their profits.

Within a year of his return to England in 1905 he was made a member of the board of the London Joint Stock Bank (later the Midland Bank), a director, later chairman, of Rothschild's Rio Tinto Co., a director of the Mortgage Company of Egypt and of the Bank of British West Africa. So many lucrative posts were offered to him that he was forced to refuse, amongst others, a directorship of both *The Times* and the armaments giant Armstrongs.[101]

Milner had a political vision for a Union of South Africa based on a great influx of British immigrants who would magically transform the language and the culture, but a severe drought wasted much of the agricultural land in 1903 and 1904, and his dream never materialised. While the veneer of British supremacy covered the reality of Afrikaner consolidation in the longer term, the mines were back in full production once the Chinese labourers were in place, and profits flowed back to the grateful international bankers who underwrote the investments. Political pressure from London and other parts of the Empire appeared to restore much of the autonomy of the former Boer Republics, and it was considered that a Liberal government would continue such a process, but Milner's war had not been in vain.

He left behind an impressive structure of able administrators dedicated to rebuilding the colonies. Furthermore, the Secret Elite's agents were in place throughout South Africa. The most compelling evidence that Jan Smuts was one of them is to be found in his activities after the Boer War. Professor Quigley revealed that Smuts was in the secret society's inner core and 'gained international fame chiefly because of this membership'.[102] Just as he had done before his supposed defection to the Boer cause, Smuts worked diligently for a union of South Africa under the British flag. Although the prime minister of the Transvaal was General Louis Botha, Jan Smuts was the dominant political figure. When the first cabinet of the new Union of South Africa was formed in 1910, it was largely Boer, with Louis Botha as prime minister. The real power, however, was retained by Jan Smuts, who held three out of nine important portfolios and completely dominated Botha.[103] Years later, the Secret Elite held a banquet in Smuts' honour in the Houses of Parliament, with Milner sitting at his right-hand side.[104] Smuts was always one of them.

And what of Jameson, butcher of the Matabele and leader of the shambolic raid? Without even a blush of embarrassment, Milner made him prime minister of Cape Colony, a suitable reward for his loyal service and silence.

An attempt was made in 1906 by Liberal Members of Parliament to put down a parliamentary motion that would name Viscount Milner and publicly shame him for permitting Chinese labourers to be flogged in the

Transvaal. It was intended as a severe censure from the House of Commons but was subtly amended by Winston Churchill, who had by this time re-invented himself as a Liberal Member of Parliament. He deliberately gave the impression that Milner had been sufficiently punished, was without income and no longer had influence over anything or anyone. Churchill told Parliament:

> Lord Milner has gone from South Africa, probably for ever. The public service knows him no more. Having exercised great authority, he now exerts no authority. Having held high employment, he now has no employment. Having disposed of events which have shaped the course of history, he is now unable to deflect in the smallest degree the policy of the day. Having been for many years, or at all events for many months, the arbiter of the fortunes of men who are 'rich beyond the dreams of avarice,' he is to-day poor, and I will add, honourably poor. After twenty years of exhausting service under the Crown he is to-day a retired Civil servant, without pension or gratuity of any kind whatever.[105]

Churchill's assurance that Milner had been retired permanently to some mythical poorhouse was a monumental deception. Milner would know public service again when *he* decided. He was not poor and never would be poor. The men whom Churchill deemed 'rich beyond the dreams of avarice' made sure of that. But of all the spurious parliamentary claims that Churchill made in defence of Alfred Milner, the most outrageous was that he was no longer able to 'deflect' the policies of the day. It was the very image behind which the master-manipulator could continue the work he had set himself to guide the Empire to a 'necessary war'. It mattered not a jot what Parliament thought of him.

Perhaps the most difficult fact with which the reader has to contend is that the Secret Elite had an absolute belief that elected, democratic government was no alternative to the kind of 'rule of the superiors' which Milner's Oxford mentor, Ruskin, had advocated. Just as Ruskin held a deep-rooted disbelief in democracy and saw the true instrument of social progress in the goodwill and intelligence of the upper classes,[106] so Milner held an absolute contempt for the British parliamentary system. He spelled it out in a letter he wrote in May 1902:

> Our political organisation is thoroughly rotten, almost non-existent. Never was there such an absurd waste of power, such ridiculous inconsequence of policy, not for want of men, but for want of any effective central authority, or dominant idea to make them work together.[107]

This self-styled British race patriot learned many lessons during the Boer War that shaped the Secret Elite's future action. The lack of backbone inside the British Cabinet to stand up to the voices clamouring against the continuation of the war in South Africa deeply annoyed him. The power given to Kitchener and the manner in which the military commander made rash promises to placate the Boers frustrated his long-term ambitions for the country. Forthcoming elections, public opinion, newspaper campaigns and political opportunism from Liberals like Campbell-Bannerman and Lloyd George turned his stomach. The ultimate success of the British race could not be left to the whim of political parties or changing government policy. Someone had to have the conviction to make hard decisions: to stand up to the 'screamers' and disregard them. Milner was that man, and members of the secret society endorsed him without reservation. He continued to generate Secret Elite strategy and control political decision making in Britain from behind the drawn curtain. He would go on to shape the course of history with a determination that was unbending, fuelled by the conviction of the 'race patriot'.[108]

Summary: Chapter 2 – South Africa – Disregard The Screamers

- Cecil Rhodes accrued a great fortune in gold and diamonds in South Africa thanks to the massive investment made by the Rothschild family.
- He was granted a Royal Charter for the British South Africa Company which permitted a private police force and army that was used brutally to grab more and more native territory.
- The Boer Republics were basically farming communities until the discovery of gold in the Transvaal transformed their absolute worth.
- Determined to take control of the Transvaal's gold, Rhodes and his associates hatched a hare-brained scheme to invade the colony. Its embarrassing failure threatened to expose the involvement of the Secret Elite in South Africa and London.
- Though the subsequent parliamentary select committee of inquiry whitewashed the conspirators, Rhodes' leadership was fatally damaged. Alfred Milner took the reins and had himself appointed high commissioner in Cape Colony.
- His objective was to provoke war, even though the colonial secretary Joseph Chamberlain advocated a no-war policy. Milner's Secret Elite network neutralised Chamberlain, and Milner advised his associates that war was absolutely necessary.
- With the experience of the Jameson fiasco in mind, Milner used political agents to stir up unrest in the Transvaal.
- Jan Smuts, once Rhodes' close friend and confidant, allegedly defected

to the Boers and was quickly promoted to the position of advisor to Kruger. Strangely, both he and Alfred Milner wanted exactly the same outcome: war.

- Despite tales of a Boy's Own nature garnishing Winston Churchill's self-penned story of a glorious escape from a Boer prison camp, the war went badly from the start, with the British Army proving beyond doubt that it was not fit for war in the Veldt.
- Kitchener was drafted in to South Africa to win the war and settle the Boers, but he was not a team player and his objectives did not match Milner's. Kitchener wanted surrender and conciliation; Milner wanted to crush the Boers and begin reconstruction under the British flag.
- Milner appointed administrators of the highest quality, trawled mostly from Oxford, and they shared his vision of an all-imposing Empire controlling the world.
- Two major 'problems' emerged that damaged Milner's reputation. The first was his acceptance of the concentration-camp system that caused the deaths of 32,000 women and children. The second was the system of immigrant Chinese labour employed to get the gold mines back into full production. The use of flogging as a form of punishment caused public outrage in Britain.
- Milner returned to Britain in 1905, having left South Africa in the hands of his trusted placemen. The changing nature of European alliances became an issue that required his presence in London. But many valuable lessons were learned by Milner and the Secret Elite during the war in South Africa.

CHAPTER 3

The Edward Conspiracy – First Steps and New Beginnings

THOUGH THE BOER WAR HAD finally ended in victory, with South Africa's gold and diamonds in the hands of the Secret Elite, it came at a cost greater than the number of lives lost. Britain had fewer friends than ever before. Living in 'splendid isolation', devoid of binding treaties with any other nation, had not been viewed as a handicap for as long as no other power on earth could challenge the primacy of British rule. However, by the beginning of the twentieth century, one European nation alone was rapidly gaining a position which threatened that dominance. Britain retained its immense global financial power and still ruled the waves in terms of the size of its navy and merchant marine, but industrial leadership and pre-eminence was passing to Germany with a rapidity that caused undeniable concern.

Following the Franco-Prussian War of 1870, the Kingdom of Prussia and surrounding principalities had merged to form Germany. When the bold Prussians defeated France, many in Britain, including the half-German Queen Victoria and her very German husband, Albert, were delighted that the upstart French, the traditional enemy of England, had been put in their place.[1] But the 'honest Teutons' did not stop there. The rapid scientific and industrial expansion of their newly unified nation was the most important single development in the half-century before the First World War.[2] Unification had given Germany a new standing in continental Europe, and from 1890 there was no question that she was outstripping both Britain and France.[3]

First one British industry then another fell behind German output, capacity or invention. Modern machinery, highly trained technical skills, application of scientific discoveries to production techniques and a will to adapt to the purchaser's wishes were just some of the reasons why Germany forged ahead. Her extraction of coal quadrupled between 1871 and 1906, production in pig iron quintupled and steel output rose from half a million tons in 1871 to twelve million in 1907.[4]

Germany, itself a former market for British products, had been transformed into a self-sufficient industrial nation. Then, having taken charge of the home market, its industries began to assert themselves abroad. Worried reports to the British Foreign Office confirmed that German iron and steel were being exported to areas of the world that Britain had long held as her own preserve, including Australia, South America, China and even Britain itself. In 1871, the German fleet consisted of a few sailing vessels plying the Baltic, but by 1900 the situation had changed dramatically, with over 4,000 ships carrying her merchandise across every ocean. In fact, the Hamburg-American shipping line became the largest in the world.

The Foreign Office viewed this competition in shipping much more seriously than rivalry in trade because it was a point of honour that Britannia ruled the waves. In addition, the mercantile navy had always served as a nursery for men of the fighting navy, and the rapid expansion in German naval activity alarmed the Secret Elite. The German chancellor, Theobald von Bethmann-Hollweg (referred to as Chancellor Bethmann from this point on in the text), stated that the British 'looked upon a Germany that kept on growing as an unwanted and troublesome intruder on the sanctity of British supremacy over the commerce and oceans of the world'.[5] The troublesome intruder had to be confronted.

British industrialists knew but rarely acknowledged that there was also a marked superiority in new German manufactures like organic chemicals and electrical goods. The British press carried bitter stories of the 'unfair' tactics of German salesmen spying on British trade practices, pandering to foreign countries and seducing them to the extent of, heaven forbid, translating brochures into their own language. By the turn of the century, German success was being denounced in exaggerated and over-excited terms, but the truth was ever more evident: German industrial expansion had left important sections of the British economy behind.

Having started its industrial revolution much earlier, British manufacturing suffered from comparative technological backwardness and the lack of new investment. A considerable portion of the profit from British industry was being invested in high-interest yielding portfolios and securities abroad, rather than re-invested in industrial modernisation at home. The German chancellor was correct in stating that the sanctity of British industrial supremacy was being challenged, but it was due as much to British complacency that leads were lost, opportunities missed and markets overtaken as it was to German growth. Better quality, cheaper goods were now coming from America and Japan, but mostly from Germany.[6]

The Secret Elite did not accept that German economic and industrial success was a just reward for their investment in better education and new technology. Together with its burgeoning industry, and a brand-new merchant fleet that promised future colonial expansion, Germany was also beginning to invest in oil production in Romania and Galicia.[7] This was even more alarming because the Secret Elite knew just how strategically important oil was for future industrial development and warfare. The German threat had to be removed, and war was the only means by which that could be achieved.

As far as the Secret Elite were concerned, there was no need to be squeamish or reticent about war. Britain had never experienced a single year of peace since the start of Queen Victoria's reign in 1837, with British forces having fought in over a hundred wars of imperial conquest across the globe.[8] The atrocities inflicted upon native Africans, Boer women and children, and Chinese slaves in South Africa exemplified the gross inhumanity of British imperialism. While many across the world railed and ranted at Sir Alfred Milner and General Kitchener, the principal perpetrators of these atrocities, King Edward ennobled them. Civilised nations were appalled. In India, Burma, Afghanistan, Sudan, Egypt, Nigeria, Rhodesia, on small islands and great continents, hundreds of thousands had been slaughtered or left to die of starvation in the wake of British imperial victories. What had Alfred Milner advised? 'Disregard the screamers.' Ironically, those classroom maps of the world that proudly showed the extent of the British Empire in all of its glory used blood red to depict the conquest.

If the Secret Elite were to achieve their great dream of world domination, the first step now had to be the removal of the Teutonic menace, the destruction of its economic prowess and restoration of the primacy of the British Empire. The plan presented great strategic difficulty. Friendless in her splendid isolation, Britain could never destroy Germany on her own. For a start, there was no continental foothold, and Britain's strength was her all-powerful navy, not a large army. Diplomatic channels had to be opened and overtures made to old enemies Russia and France. Friendship and alliances were required. This was no mean task since Anglo-French bitterness had been the main feature of the diplomatic scene over the previous decade, and war between France and Britain over Egypt had seemed a real possibility in 1895.[9]

Russia was also an imperial rival with designs of her own. In 1896, both Britain and Russia had considered using their fleets to take control of the Black Sea Straits and Constantinople. Here too there was an unrealised war, this time between Britain and Russia.[10] Historic antagonisms are not easily forgotten, but the Secret Elite were not interested in building genuine friendships. The huge armies of France and Russia were integral to the mammoth task of stopping Germany in its tracks. Put simply, the Secret

Elite needed others to undertake much of their bloody business, for war against Germany would certainly be bloody.

Over the previous 30 years, Britain had stood aloof from the quagmire of alliances, secret understandings and quasi partnerships between the nations of Europe. In breaking with tradition, and drawing venom from many Members of Parliament who saw in alliances the immediate danger of being trapped into war, the Secret Elite encouraged the foreign secretary into a surprising move. In 1902, the Conservative government announced the first ever alliance between any European power and an oriental country, Japan. It was a masterstroke. Britain and Japan entered into a formal alliance that they claimed stemmed from their joint interest in maintaining the status quo in China. Prime Minister Arthur Balfour berated the Liberal leader Campbell-Bannerman for implying that there was 'some occult reason lying behind the transaction'.[11] Of course there was. Both Germany and Russia had designs on Chinese trade, and Russia had expanded its railway system into Asia in order to advance its influence there. The Foreign Office was, as ever, a day's march ahead of the enemy.

Japan was the only country for whom the British shipyards had built an enormous tonnage of ships at the beginning of the century, including 'splendid battleships'.[12] At a stroke, the Secret Elite produced an ally who could block both Russian and German ambitions in the Far East. The Anglo-Japanese treaty sat on the back burner of international relations, apparently inoffensive and unthreatening, but it put down a marker and broke the spell of isolation to which so many in Britain clung instinctively. It may appear a strange tactic to deliberately antagonise a country that Britain needed in the longer term as an ally, but Russia had to be broken in the east before she could be remoulded in a manner that suited the Secret Elite.

Unlike Britain, Germany was no newcomer to international alliances. In 1879, Chancellor Bismarck had opened negotiations that led to Germany's alliance with Austria-Hungary. In 1887, he was also responsible for a secret agreement, the 'Reinsurance Treaty', between Germany and Russia. Bismarck was strategically astute. Potential enemies surrounded Germany, and his system of alliances offered the newly unified country time and space to grow strong.

Very full of himself, the young Kaiser Wilhelm II succeeded to the throne and dismissed Bismarck. He also chose to abandon the crucial alliance with Russia by deliberately allowing it to lapse without renewal. France, so completely beaten into submission by the Prussian/German State in 1870, lost no time at all in recognising an opportunity to align herself with Russia in a pact signed in December 1893. It was, on the face of it, a strange marriage of convenience, for the two countries were in many ways exact opposites. The French Republic could justifiably claim to be one of Europe's most democratic franchises, while Russia, at the other end of that political spectrum, was one of the last of the absolute monarchies. A Franco-Russian alliance, however, made understandable strategic and economic sense, since at that time they had common foes in Germany and Britain.[13]

Thus France and Russia combined in the 'Dual Alliance', while Germany, Austria-Hungary and Italy had come together in the 'Triple Alliance'. Before the Boer War, Britain had maintained friendly relations with Germany, but a sea change was taking place that demanded a complete rethink from the Secret Elite policy makers. Germany had to be knocked from its pedestal, its assumed ambitions curbed and the kaiser humbled. After centuries of mutual animosity, France, previously the most persistent and important British rival,[14] no longer posed a threat to the Empire. This change in attitude was reflected in the political storm that was deliberately generated after Kaiser Wilhelm's telegram of support to Kruger in 1896, while little regard was paid to the fact that French opinion had also been outspokenly hostile to Britain during the Boer War. During his visit to Europe, the French government welcomed President Kruger with ostentatious cordiality.[15] Although Kruger had specifically asked to meet the kaiser on that same visit, his request was turned down because Wilhelm did not want to upset British sensitivities. His consideration cut little ice with the British press.[16] Much was made of the kaiser's telegram, but in truth it was the German economic success story that stuck in John Bull's craw.[17] The telegram was used as a weapon in the growing armoury of British propaganda against Germany. France, on the other hand, was needed for the task ahead. Her criticisms of Britain, and cordial welcome for Britain's enemy, were conveniently overlooked.

In addition to the new relationship that needed to be crafted with France and Russia, four prerequisites had to be met before Britain went to war with Germany. Each required dedicated and long-term planning. Matters could not be left to chance. Irrespective of any change of government at general elections, the Secret Elite had to pursue a consistent foreign policy focused on preparing for a war that would see Germany crushed and the problem removed. To this end, both major political parties in Britain had to be under their control, whatever differences they might profess in domestic affairs. Second, the army, so thoroughly embarrassed by the heavily outnumbered Boers, had to be reorganised into an effective and powerful fighting force. The third requirement was more straightforward. The navy had to retain its supremacy on the high seas. That was a given fact of life anyway, but retaining supremacy meant modernisation and further investment. Finally, minds had to be changed. Men did not march to war on a whim. A massive and consistent propaganda drive was needed to create a German 'menace' and whip the British people into a froth of hatred towards Germany and Kaiser Wilhelm.

Initially, Germany's leaders were not overly concerned about the bitter anti-German rhetoric that followed the Boer War. Nor were they impressed by Britain's overtures to France. They believed that a Westminster government would never sanction such an alliance. Germany's basic mistake lay in a deep-rooted conviction that 'Britain could never draw close to her traditional French enemy, and certainly not to her bitter Russian rival'.[18] Like everyone else, they held to the naive belief that parliamentary government was thriving in Britain, unaware of the growing power and influence being exerted behind the scenes. While the Germans were slow to understand what was happening, others were not. Count De Lalaing, the Belgian ambassador in London, clearly realised the dangers. On 7 February 1905, he wrote to the minister of foreign affairs in Brussels:

> The hostility of the English public towards the German nation is founded apparently in jealousy and fear: jealousy in view of Germany's economic and commercial schemes; fear from the perception that the German fleet may perhaps one day become a competitor for naval supremacy . . . This state of mind is fomented by the English press, heedless of international complications . . . the spirit of jingoism runs its course unchecked among the people in England; and the newspapers are, bit by bit, poisoning public opinion.[19]

How right he was, but what he did not appreciate was the extent to which 'this state of mind' was being orchestrated. It was in meetings at select private clubs and weekend gatherings at stately homes like Tring and Mentmore that the anti-German propaganda was agreed and policy determined. The Secret Elite deemed Germany to be the greatest single barrier to their global takeover, so they created a German bogeyman and invested in him all of their own vices. Newspapers, magazines and novels spewed out their propaganda, week after week, month after month, and sadly the 'people in England' swallowed it with relish.

In a rapidly changing world where socialism, women's rights, trade unionism, parliamentary reform, land reform and a flurry of challenging demands were being presented to the government, the Secret Elite would require very strong political leadership and sustained support to see this through. Sustained support was the one thing that the Secret Elite could guarantee by ensuring that their trusted lieutenants and agents held key positions in government, the Civil Service, the army and navy and the diplomatic service, no matter which political party was in power. Alfred Milner was a consummate organiser, and his Secret Elite network stayed focused on their prime target despite all the political distractions at home.

Several weeks after the South African War ended in a victory soured by bitter acrimony, important changes took place in Britain. The Conservative prime minister, Lord Salisbury, resigned. In a blatant act of unashamed nepotism, he anointed his nephew, Arthur Balfour, as his successor, and thereby promoted another member of the Secret Elite to the highest political position in the Empire.[20] Balfour had been a member of the inner circle from the secret society's inception in February 1891, and his family background and political instinct gave him every advantage in British politics and society. His mother was a member of the immensely rich and powerful Cecil family that had dominated British politics for centuries. His godfather was the Duke of Wellington. Balfour's early career followed the pattern of many of his peers who entered the political arena with no specific ambition but with the ease and sense of entitlement that marked their upbringing. Balfour was ruling class through and through, but more, he belonged to that most powerful and determined group of wealthy and influential imperial loyalists whose secret agenda he could translate into policy in his new Conservative government. The change of prime minister was no change at all.

A much more significant change heralded the Secret Elite's most special weapon: Edward, prince of diplomats, king/emperor and inner-core co-conspirator. At 6.30 p.m. on 22 January 1901, 81-year-old Queen Victoria died at Osborne House on the Isle of Wight. Her death came as no surprise, since her health had been deteriorating for some time. Nevertheless, it was a shock to the nation because Victoria had been queen for 63 years and the vast majority had known no other monarch. Poignantly, it was her favoured grandson, Kaiser Wilhelm, who cradled her in his arms as she died.[21] Victoria may have been mourned by grieving subjects, but the ascent of Edward VII was crucially important to the Secret Elite.

The British royal family of Saxe-Coburg-Gotha was rich in German blood, and while the grand old lady sat on the throne, war with Germany had been unthinkable. King Edward VII, however, detested Germany as much as his late mother had been fond of it. He and Kaiser Wilhelm met at regular intervals when racing their grand yachts at Cowes, but Uncle Edward had little time for his nephew. This was in part due to the influence of King Edward's wife, Princess Alexandra of Denmark. She developed an almost paranoid hatred of Germany after Denmark lost the disputed territories of Schleswig-Holstein to it in 1864. Although Edward, when

Prince of Wales, frequently acted as host to the kaiser, he received very little assistance from his wife, 'who loathed all Germans in general and William in particular'.[22] She repeatedly wrote to her sister, the czarina of Russia, how untrustworthy he was, and frequently aired such opinions to her children. Edward's subsequent actions clearly indicated that he shared his wife's obsessive and venomous hatred of Germany.

It would have been impossible to pursue war with Germany without the undivided support of the royal family. That they themselves were of German blood was no impediment. The monarchy was viewed as the font of Englishness. They sat at the epicentre of the greatest known empire. Edward was the monarch with whom the Secret Elite and their entourage fraternised or slept.

Whether or not Edward VII hated his mother is a moot point, but he had cause to dislike her enormously. She disapproved of his lifestyle, his friends and his lack of royal reserve. And she told him so. Victoria was not afraid of speaking her mind. He disappointed her, never lived up to her expectations, and she was convinced that he would not amount to much. She blamed him for Prince Albert's death and wrote to her eldest (and favourite) daughter, Victoria, who was, briefly, the German empress: 'I never can or shall look at him without a shudder.'[23]

Victoria tried to keep Edward at arm's length from government business, and he was frustrated that he was less trusted with official papers than secretaries and ministers.[24] When Prime Minister Gladstone asked to include the Prince of Wales in the circulation of Cabinet papers, Victoria would not have it. She commented disparagingly that secrets should not be shared with one who talks too much.[25] But as *The Times* later observed with stunning clarity: 'The invitations to Malbrough House and Sandringham were by no means confined to the butterfly society.'[26] The future King Edward VII was no butterfly.

Edward's friends were not limited to the lush and the libidinous. Nor was he the hapless inconsequent that his mother believed. He had considerable gifts, amongst which were fluency in French and German. He was an attentive listener and a first-class speaker who could deliver an impromptu speech that captured his audience and concisely caught the moment. Edward rarely if ever used notes, and he had the capacity to include others in conversation as he moved round a room. He was charm personified, sharp and incisive, and completely belied the lampoon characterisations that belittled him.

From 1886, Lord Rosebery forwarded Foreign Office dispatches to him without the queen's approval. From that point on, 'every important foreign dispatch was placed at his disposal', and by 1892 Cabinet reports and proceedings were submitted to him.[27] He moved, unseen by the public eye, amongst politicians and nobility, government ministers and up-and-coming aspirants, diplomats, admirals and field-marshals, absorbing, considering and discussing future policy. His closest friends included Lord Esher and Lord Nathanial Rothschild. He took advice from Alfred Milner, was grateful to Lord Rosebery for the trust he showed in him as Prince of Wales, and he shared the Secret Elite philosophy for world dominance by the Anglo-Saxon race. After all, it was his Empire they intended to promote across the globe. Albert Edward, Prince of Wales, who ascended the throne on 22 January 1901, took the regal title of King Edward VII. As king, he operated at the heart of the inner core of the Secret Elite.

His greatest contribution lay in engineering the much-needed realignments in international relations that unpicked potential rivalries, smoothed over past difficulties and addressed the Secret Elite's prerequisite need to isolate Germany. Ultimate responsibility for British foreign policy lay, by precedent, with the elected government and not the sovereign, but it was King Edward VII who enticed both France and Russia into secret alliances with Britain within six short years. He was in effect the de facto foreign secretary. Many historians have denied his ambassadorial role, claiming that his foreign travels 'were visits of ceremony or of pleasure'.[28] What nonsense. Prime Minister Balfour's foreign policy proceeded exactly in line with the Secret Elite's grand design. Foreign Secretary Lansdowne facilitated the process, but it was King Edward who emerged as the driving force. His work was crucial, and the royal stamp of approval assured positive public opinion both at home and abroad. France and Russia were needed in a new capacity: as Britain's friends and allies. This was agreed in secret by the Secret Elite without the knowledge or consent of the Cabinet. The alliances would have been unacceptable to most Members of Parliament and the general public but were enacted for one single purpose: to throttle Germany. There was no real opposition to be voiced, because the real opposition did not know it was happening.

Befriending France was relatively straightforward. Though Napoleon III had admitted France was responsible for starting the Franco-Prussian war of 1870, many in France held a deep and bitter resentment towards Germany. The humiliation of the French forces in that war and the German army's siege of Paris still hurt badly 30 years on. In stark contrast, Bismarck's unification of Germany was hailed in Britain at the time as a desirable, even glorious, accomplishment. It was, however, accompanied by the thorny issue of the annexation of Alsace-Lorraine from France, which the French had always regarded as a crime: 'the brutal dismemberment of a nation'.[29] How the people of Alsace-Lorraine viewed it depended on their own historic background. By the turn of the century, most of them spoke German as their first language. In Bismarck's defence, it has been said that he had only been 'liberating' territory that had earlier been wrested from Germany by Louis X1V when Germany was weak and divided against herself.[30] Whatever the rights or wrongs of Germany's annexation of the provinces, a small, staunchly republican military cadre in France wanted revenge. These Revanchards[31] were determined never to rest until the 'Lost Provinces' were restored. It was this sense of loss, this strong nationalistic sentiment, which the Secret Elite in London encouraged and used to harness France for their ultimate war with Germany. For the Revanchards, an 'understanding' with Britain, a formal accord, was most welcome. They too needed allies.

Political relationships between France and Britain had been low-key in the aftermath of French criticism of the Boer War, but King Edward played a major role in smoothing things over and preparing the ground for an alliance. His accession to the throne had fundamentally changed the rules of engagement. Here was a man who loved all things French.[32] As prince regent, Edward had been one of the world's most well-travelled men, but his favoured destination was always France. During the Franco-Prussian War, his sympathies rested with the French cause, and in the months immediately after it he toured the battlefields round Sedan and Metz. The fascination that France held for him from boyhood had fully developed into that of the rampant Francophile, and he became extremely popular in Paris.

On private visits, and he was a frequent visitor, the Prince of Wales was welcomed in theatrical and artistic society. It was suggested that by 'freeing himself of all official etiquette' he was able to explore Parisian life so thoroughly 'that he became as familiar to the public of Paris as to that of London'.[33] Queen Victoria was not amused. She wrote of her 'very weak and terribly frivolous' eldest son to his sister Victoria in Germany:

> Oh! What will become of the poor country when I die! I foresee, if B[ertie] succeeds, nothing but misery – for he never reflects or listens for a moment and he [would] . . . spend his life in one whirl of amusements as he does now. It makes me very sad and angry.'[34]

Victoria always referred to her wilful son as 'Bertie', as he had been christened Albert Edward. In an effort to curtail his wayward lifestyle, the queen kept Bertie on the minimal royal stipend, but the Rothschilds and other members of his fawning entourage, like Sir Edward Cassel, quietly funded his dubious habits. He certainly became familiar with some very interesting characters, but behind the image of the 'playboy prince' that so worried his mother, Edward engaged with political and social circles that the Secret Elite sought to influence.

Edward frequented France as some might frequent a brothel: incognito, for personal pleasure and satisfaction. In point of fact, he visited the most luxurious brothel in Paris, Le Chabanais, so often that his personal coat of arms hung above the bed in one of the exclusive rooms. Heavily overweight, Bertie had a special 'love seat' built so that he could enjoy sex with several of the 'girls' at once.[35] He loved Paris; the Belle Époque naughtiness thrilled him. He was involved with many of the famous prostitutes of the period, and cartoons of the day struck a mighty likeness between him and a Toulouse Lautrec poster.[36]

France was always close to his heart, but not as close as his Empire. Not as close as the mighty aims of the Secret Elite. He was shielded from public awareness of his political machinations by the very playboy image he so readily embodied. It was hardly surprising that when the Secret Elite's charm offensive with France was at its height, King Edward was the spokesman. His appeal was personal and to the point. He, not the foreign secretary, Lord Lansdowne, brought the French on board. While Lansdowne dealt with the formal process of diplomatic exchange, Edward pressed the flesh. He was the Secret Elite's principal ambassador, bringing to fruition plans devised in the great country houses and clubs of England.

Edward the prince embraced the Secret Elite for their greater purpose. His meagre purse could never have addressed his gambling and whoring debts, his extravagant travels, parties and balls, or his horses and mistresses. He was accustomed to a lifestyle financed by other interested parties who were either inside or close to the Secret Elite.

Edward the king took his role at the centre of the Secret Elite very seriously, and he was the instrument through whom honours were used to bind friendships with the royalty of Spain, Portugal, Russia, Italy, Sweden, Persia and Japan, not excluding his relatives in Germany. In 1902 alone, Edward invested King Alfonso of Spain, Grand-Duke Michael of Russia, Prince Emmanuel Filiberto, a cousin of King Victor Emmanuel III of Italy, the Crown Prince of Portugal, and the ill-fated Archduke Franz Ferdinand as Garter Knights. Those who believe that Edward was not involved in diplomatic intrigue and dismiss his travelling court as a circus showpiece entirely miss the point. Or perhaps they choose to miss the point. King Edward's visits to foreign parts were designed to cement relationships, present British foreign policy as an act of benign friendship and unpick the alliances and commitments to Germany.

The Germans were clearly concerned about Edward's activities, but had no inkling of a secret society spinning a web of intrigue across Europe.

One by one the nations courted by King Edward VII were brought into a shared sphere of interest. What made his input so effective was the public manner in which he assiduously courted friendships. Contemporaries assumed that Edward's royal visits couldn't have any political importance because as often as not he travelled without a member of the Cabinet or the diplomatic corps. But consider his input to the new era of British 'openness' and the very necessary end of isolationism. He paid particular interest to the young King Alfonso of Spain, who in 1902 at the age of 16 reached his majority and assumed his right to rule. On the eve of his birthday, Alfonso was invested with the Order of the Garter. King Edward's relationship with the young monarch was positively avuncular to the extent that he acted as matchmaker by introducing Alfonso to his niece, Princess Victoria Eugenie. Lest the reader think that this is an example of Edward's consideration, think how valuable an alliance of royal families was with a country that had both Atlantic and Mediterranean coastlines. Within a few turbulent years, Britain was able to use that relationship to challenge Germany over control of Morocco.

Edward VII's links with Italian royalty were similarly important. How better to undermine Germany's alliance with Italy than frequent personal visits and the plying of gifts of honours and status on significant personages? A royal visit to Rome and Naples was arranged in 1903 during which King Edward the conspirator had discussions both with King Victor Emmanuel and the ageing Pope Leo XIII. His impromptu speeches proved to be disarmingly popular.[37] Edward took the opportunity to shower high honours on members of the Italian royal family, with knighthoods aplenty for the diplomatic corps and admirals and captains in the Italian navy.[38] In 1903 alone, Edward visited Rome, Lisbon, Paris and Vienna. German journalists at the time, and German historians afterwards, connected these to the '*Einkreisungspolitik*' or 'encirclement' policy. The Germans saw Edward as a Machiavelli among kings, but English historians Grant and Temperley later dismissed his visits as 'ceremonial'.[39] How can they reconcile his obvious interference in international politics with the claim that his visits were merely for social or ceremonial reasons? Incredibly, some historians even go so far as to omit King Edward entirely from the history of the origins of the First World War.

It was in France, though, that he first made his mark in 1903, displaying his gift of tact and a capacity to reach out over political reserve and speak to a wider audience. Edward's public statements were aimed to appeal to the French sense of self-worth, to herald a new beginning in international cooperation. He announced to the French media:

> The days of hostility between the two countries are, I am certain, happily at an end. I know of no two countries whose prosperity is more interdependent. There may have been misunderstandings and causes of dissension in the past, but that is all happily over and forgotten. The friendship of the two countries is my constant preoccupation.[40]

The king was then treated to a banquet at the Elysée Palace followed by horseracing at Longchamps. This pot-bellied, top-hatted, cigar-smoking, brandy-bloated, flamboyant lover of life, of friends, of their wives, was far more important in diplomatic and government circles than was ever acknowledged. So what if women of easy virtue were a constant distraction? Edward coped.

In the summer of 1903, two months after the king's trip to Paris, the president of France, Emile Loubet, paid him a return visit accompanied by the Revanchist Théophile Delcassé, whom Edward had met and befriended on an earlier trip. An immensely important warmonger, Delcassé set to work with Foreign Secretary Lansdowne on the terms of a joint agreement between the two countries. Old 'difficulties' were put aside, concessions agreed and a mutually acceptable solution found to Britain's control of Egypt and France's influence in Morocco. Eight months later, on 8 April 1904, the Entente Cordiale was signed. It marked the end of an era of conflict between England and France that had lasted nearly a thousand years. Isolation from the continent of Europe was formally abandoned. On the surface, the entente brought the two countries closer without any commitment to a formal military alliance. The talk was of peace and prosperity, but secret clauses signed that same day were to have very different consequences.

Some saw this as Edward's great autocratic design, as though he, and only he, wanted to formalise friendship with France, as if it was the king's personal gift to both nations. In his well-vetted memoirs, Sir Edward Grey, a long-serving agent of the Secret Elite, reflected on this moment with lyrical approval: 'The real cause for satisfaction was that the exasperating friction with France was to end, and that the menace of war with France had disappeared. The gloomy clouds were gone, the sky was clear, and the sun shone warmly.'[41] Put aside Grey's two-faced and self-serving image. The Entente Cordiale was indeed a diplomatic triumph, and there is absolutely no doubt that King Edward was the man responsible for delivering it on behalf of the Secret Elite, but the sunshine was to be short-lived. The real purpose behind the entente was war with Germany. Why else were the secret clauses signed on 8 April 1904 hidden from Parliament, from public knowledge and from other governments?

The Belgian ambassador to Berlin, Baron Greindl, was driven to the logical conclusion that 'British foreign policy is directed by the king in person'.[42] His conclusion was perfectly reasonable given the evidence he had before him, but Baron Greindl and many like him knew nothing of the powers behind the throne with whom the king was a partner in conspiracy. The Belgian chargé d'affaires in London, Monsieur E. Cartier, commented that 'the English are getting more and more into the habit of regarding international problems as being almost exclusively within the province of King Edward'.[43] What Monsieur Cartier failed to appreciate was that the king was not an agent of the elected government. He was not answerable to Prime Minister Balfour or Foreign Secretary Lansdowne, but they had no concerns over the king's influence in foreign affairs. They too belonged, as did His Majesty, to an inner circle of the utmost secrecy from which all effective foreign policy stemmed: the Secret Elite.

King Edward's association with the inner circle of the Secret Elite, and his role in their plan for the destruction of Germany, was strengthened by his first lieutenant, Reginald Balliol Brett, Lord Esher. He had been closely involved with Cecil Rhodes and Lord Rothschild in setting up the secret society in 1891 and was a member of the Society of the Elect with Lord Milner. Esher played a remarkable role for an unelected subject, an apparently independent mind, responsible to no politician. He turned down many top posts in government at home and in the Empire because he wanted to 'work behind the scenes rather than in public view'. His secret work was 'so important and influential that any public post would have meant a reduction in his power'.[44] He thus played a more important role than any Cabinet minister, viceroy of India or governor general of Canada. Esher's presence was welcomed in every aristocratic mansion, noble household and stately home in Britain. His influence was a guarantor of royal approval. He vetted newspaper editors, sat on official bodies, committees and investigations, and was rarely subject to public criticism, though his sexual preferences left him vulnerable to scandalous exposure.[45] Lord Esher's presence at the innermost court of the secret society, at the War Office, the Foreign Office or the Colonial Office, at meetings so secret that Cabinet ministers were excluded, was as unquestioned as his presence in any of the royal households.

When the South African War Commission was set up in 1902 to analyse the army's near disastrous performance in the Boer War, Esher was appointed as one of only three commissioners. Why? He was not a soldier, had no relevant military background, and his experience as permanent secretary to His Majesty's Office of Works hardly qualified him to do more than oversee Windsor Castle.

The king could not sit on a commission that the Secret Elite intended to use as a starting point for the complete reorganisation of the armed forces, but his right-hand man could. Esher wrote daily to King Edward with details of the evidence from every expert witness to the commission. He told the king that the defence of the realm was in such a perilous condition 'that it made it almost a crime to embark on any course of policy which might have involved the nation in a war'.[46] By any standards this was a shocking admission and one which touched on the Secret Elite's innermost fears. It was clear that reorganisation and modernisation of the British armed forces was essential. It was a momentous task that required careful preparation and political commitment. So much had to be achieved before they could tackle Germany.

Lord Esher's contribution proved invaluable. As a member of the War Commission, Esher interviewed all of the major politicians in both Conservative and Liberal ranks, and, as part of his role, assessed their views and commitment. These he discussed in private meetings with the king and his Secret Elite colleagues, so that when a change of government took place they could influence key appointments and ensure that their chosen men took charge.

The reshaping of the armed forces, for example, had to be led by a trusted man. It fell to Esher to ensure that the chosen incumbent in the War Office was such a trusted agent. He proceeded to influence the future development and organisation of Britain's military policy and appointments for the remaining years of King Edward's reign. His position was entirely unconstitutional, but his role continued unchallenged, protected by his membership of the Secret Elite and by the king's patronage.

One of the most important features of the Secret Elite plan for war was to keep an iron grip on foreign policy. The long-term drive to war had to be imprinted on the departmental mindset at the War Office, the Admiralty and, in particular, the Foreign Office. Governments might rise and fall, but the ultimate objective had to be sustained, no matter the politics of the day. To that end, a permanent Committee of Imperial Defence (CID) was established by Arthur Balfour. This secretive and very exclusive group first met in 1902 as an advisory committee to the prime minister on matters of national defence but was re-formed permanently in 1904. In addition to Balfour, the only original permanent member of this exclusive committee was Lord Roberts, commander-in-chief of the armed forces and longstanding friend of Alfred Milner. Esher recognised the strategic importance of the CID and the absolute necessity that its work remained hidden and at all times under the control of the Secret Elite. Afraid that a change of government would result in a radical element within the Liberal Party gaining control of the

CID, Esher pressed the prime minister to appoint trusted agents like Milner, Field Marshal Lord Roberts, and Roberts' up-and-coming protégé, Sir John French, as well as himself, as permanent members. Balfour partly acceded.[47] He sanctioned the appointment of both Esher and Sir John French to limitless tenure in the CID, and at a stroke the Cabinet was literally eclipsed from discussion on questions of defence. Esher's appointment was again of the utmost significance. He ensured that King Edward VII and his successor, George V, received regular secret reports on all CID business. More importantly, he ensured that Secret Elite designs were followed. All hidden from view and, in terms of cabinet government, strictly unconstitutional.

With dramatic simplicity, the Secret Elite turned Edwardian Britain from the rigid isolation of Victoria's reign to a country that embraced new 'friendships' and 'alliances' that suited their intentions in the twentieth century. They clearly identified Germany as the enemy at the Empire's gate and understood immediately that, on its own, Britain could not destroy her as a continental power. King Edward VII proved his worth as the pre-eminent ambassador by moving around the continent in apparent innocence, establishing personal connections with royal families, distributing honours with gay abandon and canvassing on Britain's behalf to ensure that Germany was surrounded by nations that enjoyed his patronage. Simultaneously, initial steps were made to reorganise and restructure the armed forces to radically improve their readiness for war. In this task, the Secret Elite were represented by Lord Esher, whose influence on the army and its future appointments was disproportionate to his constitutional right. But what hold did an unwritten constitution have on a subversive cabal that operated in conjunction with the king, well hidden from public knowledge? Even at that early stage, they understood the need to control foreign policy and the preparations for war, and to that purpose ensured the permanent membership of their unelected representative, Lord Esher, to the Committee of Imperial Defence. Reconstruction was under way.

Summary: Chapter 3 – The Edward Conspiracy – First Steps And New Beginnings

- The Secret Elite viewed German economic, industrial and commercial success as a direct threat to their global ambitions and believed that war was the only means by which they could be stopped.
- Britain could not engage in a war against Germany on her own and needed allies to provide the military manpower.
- Four lessons had been learned from the Boer War. Foreign policy had to be sustained no matter which political party was in office; the British Army needed a complete overhaul to make it fit for purpose; the Royal

Navy had to maintain all its historic advantages; the general public had to be turned against Germany.

- Britain's era of splendid isolation was brought to an end through an Anglo-Japanese treaty in 1902.
- The Secret Elite looked to Britain's old adversaries, France and Russia, as long-term potential allies, and King Edward VII emerged as their diplomatic champion.
- Edward was a natural Francophile whose playboy image served to screen his unconstitutional involvement in foreign affairs.
- Edward travelled all over Europe promoting the Secret Elite's plan, and he was the architect of the Entente Cordiale of 1904.
- Belgian diplomats accurately reported that the king's actions as de facto foreign secretary undermined Germany, but they did not know that he was acting on behalf of the Secret Elite.
- Lord Esher was appointed to the South African War Commission to analyse the reasons why the army had performed so poorly, and on the back of that and his close relationship with King Edward VII he became integral to army reconstruction.
- Esher was also a member of the secretive Committee of Imperial Defence set up to advise the prime minister on matters of defence, including foreign policy.
- Eager to keep control of this exclusive committee, Esher had himself appointed as a permanent member. Thus the Secret Elite dominated the reconstruction and realignment of the army and foreign policy from the start of the twentieth century.

CHAPTER 4

Testing Warmer Waters

THE ENTENTE CORDIALE WAS HAILED as proof positive of a new era of Anglo-French mutual understanding and friendship that would finally bury age-old antagonisms between the two. It did, but that was never its prime purpose. Pursuit of global dominance was at the core of every action taken by the Secret Elite, and the creation of alliances with France, followed some years later by Russia, were first and foremost arrangements of strategic necessity. Their large armies were required for the eventual destruction of Germany. Additionally, the secret terms hidden in the unpublished parts of the alliance were mutually approved to increase the power and influence of Germany's enemies, and push the Berlin government towards a possible war.

The entente heralded the end of disputes between Britain and France over North Africa and both declared that they had 'no intention of altering the political status' of Egypt or Morocco,[1] a sure sign that they meant exactly the opposite. *The Times*, the first organ of Secret Elite propaganda,[2] hailed the signing as 'the surest pledge of universal peace' and praised the part played by King Edward in bringing Anglo-French cordiality to a new level.[3] Old claims and counterclaims were to be put aside and French President Loubet and Foreign Minister Delcassé were presented as distinguished statesmen who deserved the gratitude of their fellow countrymen.[4]

The Entente Cordiale was not as it seemed. Top-secret codicils, hidden within its published articles, signed on that very same day, 8 April 1904, concealed the double-dealing upon which the entente had been settled. The secret clauses effectively guaranteed British control of Egypt in return for French control over Morocco. Britain had earlier promised to leave Egypt as soon as its financial affairs were in order, but such an open-ended promise meant nothing. The great financial houses in London – Rothschilds and Barings – had secured vast concessions by restructuring Egyptian finances.[5] They held large commercial interests there, and unfettered control of Egypt was a cash cow for these British bankers. Thanks to the Rothschilds, not only did the British government own most of the shares in the Suez Canal but it also acted as the strategic and commercial gatekeeper to the Gulf, the Middle East and India through the canal. Britain essentially controlled the entrance to the Mediterranean at Gibraltar and its exit at Suez. Do not imagine that strengthening the capacity to shut down the Mediterranean was a chance happening.

Hidden from parliaments and people alike, Britain agreed that France could take control of Morocco once they had effectively overthrown the sultan. In plain English, it was a carve-up. This paved the way for the annexation of Morocco by France with assured diplomatic support from Britain.[6] Other nations, countries on whom King Edward had recently showered honours, were sucked into the Mediterranean vortex by casual gifts of territories they did not own.

Italy's goodwill was secured by the promise of Tripoli. Spurred on by Britain, Italy agreed to the eventual French possession of Morocco in exchange for their acceptance of Italy's claims to the Tripoli-Cyrenaica area of northern Libya. In addition, Italy secretly promised to remain neutral if France was attacked by either Germany or Austria-Hungary.[7] The French reciprocated with a similar commitment should Italy be attacked. It was a pact of strict and mutual neutrality that in effect made a nonsense of Italy's commitment to any aggressive stance that the Triple Alliance might take.[8]

Relations between Britain and Italy had historically been amicable, and even within the context of the Triple Alliance, Italy had insisted that a clause be included recognising the fact that on no account would she go to war against Britain. With Kitchener and his army encamped literally next door in Egypt, Italy could never have moved into Tripoli without Britain's approval. Inside the Foreign Office, Secret Elite agents considered Italian royalty and government ministers who had been courted assiduously by King Edward as sympathetic allies. Edward's determination to prise them away from the Triple Alliance had begun in earnest.

King Alfonso's Spain was also held to be more than sympathetic to Britain and France. Edward VII's investment in the Spanish monarchy continued to bear fruit, and in colluding with France and Britain, Spain was assured a considerable part of Morocco's Mediterranean coast. Having surrendered any British interests in Morocco by deed of the entente, the Secret Elite chose Spain as the perfect surrogate replacement. Their most experienced diplomat, Sir Arthur Nicolson, was moved from Tangier to Madrid in 1904, and his presence guaranteed their involvement in all that followed.

Hidden behind the public announcements, the secret articles became the opening gambit in the Secret Elite's move to systematically provoke Germany. While they were prepared to concede minor points over

Newfoundland, Siam and West Africa, secret articles accompanying the treaty centred on Britain's control and assumed rights in Egypt, and France's own imperial plans for Morocco. It was designed to insult and antagonise Germany, whose rights and responsibilities in Morocco were every bit as strong as those of Britain or France. The major powers had jointly signed a mutually advantageous agreement in 1880 at Madrid, stating that Moroccan independence should be 'protected'. Britain, France and Germany, acting in unison, had promised that free trade with the country would be honoured. It was not some altruistic decision. They were simply a group of foreign exploiters happy to share the spoils of a weaker nation. But Germany was bound to react when the secret agreements of the entente came into play. She had a treaty with Morocco, kept a diplomatic representative in Tangier, had considerable growing commercial interests in the country and had cooperated fully with Britain in resisting any previous French attempts to claim a privileged position there.[9] Furthermore, she had no intention of allowing France and Britain to exclude her from the Mediterranean by a diplomatic agreement to which she had not been made party.

How did the perpetrators expect Germany to react? The Secret Elite network controlled the world's finest diplomatic and commercial spy rings and were well aware of the effect that their decisions would have. The diplomatic service was the best-informed and most proactive arm of British foreign policy, and they knew that Germany would learn the details of the secret arrangements. Germany was being deliberately put to the test.

News of the entente was first greeted by the German government with temperate approval. On 12 April, the German chancellor, Bernhard von Bülow, was questioned about it in the Reichstag. At that point in time he had no knowledge of the secret clauses and talked in terms of its benefit to world peace:

> Our interests there are commercial and we are especially interested that calm and order should prevail in Morocco. We must protect our commercial interests there but have no reason to fear that they will be set aside or infringed by any Power.[10]

Both the press and politicians in Germany accepted that a peaceful understanding between Britain and France was of benefit to everyone in Europe. Relations between Britain and Germany appeared to be harmonious. On the face of it, they had no reason to be concerned.

The French government took advantage of Britain's approval by acting as if it had some special governance over Morocco. Behind a mask of apparent good intent, a Franco-Spanish declaration of October 1904 stated publicly that they remained 'firmly attached to the integrity of the Moorish Empire under the sovereignty of the sultan'. It was a lie, an act of studied hypocrisy, because in yet another secret codicil they callously agreed to partition Morocco between them.[11] France and Spain intended to share the spoils of the country with Britain's full approval. On 6 October, the French ambassador in London, Paul Cambon, advised the British foreign secretary: 'Delcassé requests you to be good enough to keep the Convention entirely secret.' Lansdowne made it perfectly clear that the 'confidential nature' of the conspiracy would be 'duly respected'.[12] Delcassé was a man close to the heart of the Secret Elite, and his agreement with Spain to carve up Morocco was conducted with their consent. Secret Elite fingerprints touched every corner of this deal, but the question to be asked was: from whom were these actions being kept secret?

The answer is the British and French public, whose natural aversion to secret treaties was well understood. For sure, Germany would learn of them. There were too many indiscreet diplomats in Madrid and St Petersburg for Germany not to learn the truth within a relatively short period.[13] Diplomatic secrets rarely lasted long, and the Secret Elite knew, indeed hoped, that it would provoke a very angry German reaction, which would then be rejected as German propaganda against the entente.

Fortified by the entente and British collusion, the French could not stop themselves taking advantage of the fact that they already occupied Algeria and sought to expand their colonial stranglehold in northern Africa.[14] On 11 January 1905, the French ambassador at Tangier was ordered to submit a programme of unacceptable 'reforms' to the sultan. The Moroccan leader refused to bow to their demands and had no option other than to turn to Germany for support and advice.[15] Understandably, Germany had no intention of allowing Morocco's independence to be undermined by anyone. At the behest of the German chancellor, Kaiser Wilhelm, who had been enjoying a scheduled Mediterranean cruise for reasons of his health, reluctantly visited Tangier on 31 March 1905 to declare his support for the sultan.[16] According to the *New York Times*, Tangier was 'garlanded with flowers' and so much was spent on flags and bunting that 'no one could doubt that it meant more than merely a courteous welcome'.[17]

Though he spent only two hours there, the political significance of his message reverberated far longer. Kaiser Wilhelm made two fairly straightforward statements. The first asserted German commercial rights in Morocco and the second insisted that the sovereignty of the sultan and the integrity of Morocco must remain intact. Morocco's independence had never been questioned any more than the independence of Persia or Russia or of the United States.[18] An agreement, secret or otherwise, between Britain and France carried no authority to change that.

When the kaiser visited Tangier, he already knew about the secret articles attached to the entente and of the 'secret' Franco-Spanish Convention. He knew that deals had purposefully been concealed, and he was also aware that a series of 'reforms' had been prepared for the sultan's acceptance that were absolutely incompatible with Morocco's independence.[19] The German government declared that no one country should attempt to take control of Morocco, and, with dignified diplomatic propriety, the kaiser called for an international conference to resolve the matter. Von Bülow warned the international community that France might assume a protectorate over Morocco and expel other commercial competitors just as it had previously done in Tunis.[20] The sultan agreed with the kaiser's reasoned approach and invited interested parties to a conference in Tangier.

All hell was let loose in the British and French newspapers. Germany and the kaiser were ridiculed and vilified. The Secret Elite unleashed their outraged press to denounce the kaiser with unrestrained violence.[21] He was accused of deliberately attempting to destroy the entente as a prelude to making war on France. Wild claims of evil German intent poured out in a torrent of sheer vitriol, and any voice of reason was 'assailed as that of a traitor or a coward'.[22]

By creating the Moroccan Crisis, the Secret Elite successfully generated a fear and manufactured a menace where none existed. A British general election was in the offing, and a change of government seemed certain. Europe at peace with itself was the very last circumstance under which the Secret Elite wanted the incoming Liberal government to take office. That could have been a disaster. The public wanted the radical Liberals to cut spending on the navy and army immediately and redistribute the money to further social reform. Secret Elite ambition might have been thwarted by an incoming Liberal government, but serious steps that will be explained in detail later were already in place to protect their plans. The timing of the Moroccan Crisis was perfect. Just as the elections of January 1906 got under way, the international crisis generated alarm and created a climate of fear. Nothing more assuredly protects spending on armaments than a climate of fear.

And what had actually happened? Britain, France and Spain had acted without any international sanction.[23] There was no precedent in international law to justify their unwarranted intervention in Morocco. In France, Foreign Minister Delcassé was determined to stand his ground. He refused point-blank to accept a conference and depicted the kaiser's reasonable request as a challenge to the entente itself. His allies in the British and French press took up Delcassé's claim and grossly misrepresented the German position.

There was talk of war. Serious talk. Foreign Secretary Lansdowne secretly approved initial conversations between British and French military staff about preparations for war with Germany. The Belgian military staff was also included in direct talks with their British counterparts at this juncture. Hold on to this thought: Belgium was involved in secret military plans for a possible war of aggression against an unsuspecting Germany but almost a decade later would be presented as the innocent victim of German aggression.

King Edward was reported to have told French ministers 'that in case of need' Britain would intervene on the side of France.[24] Should you find it fanciful that Britain could have gone to war, consider the view of the president of the United States. After a private meeting with the British ambassador in May 1905, Roosevelt was left with the impression that the British government was 'anxious to see Germany humiliated' and 'quite willing to face the possibility of a war'.[25] One month later, in a letter to the German ambassador in Washington, Roosevelt wrote:

> I felt that if a war were to break out, whatever might happen to France, England would profit immensely, while Germany would lose her colonies and perhaps her fleet. Such being the case, I did not feel that anything I might say would carry any weight with England.[26]

Undoubtedly, Delcassé believed that he would have British support if it came to war with Germany,[27] but the French foreign minister pressed too hard. Prime Minister Rouvier greatly appreciated the private counsels he had with King Edward but shrank from the prospect of a war predicated on his refusal to take part in a conference. When it became apparent that all that the kaiser wanted was an international conference, and that the majority of the French parliament was in favour of such an accommodation, the clamour and outrage from the Secret Elite's press redoubled and moved swiftly to support Delcassé. As the Liberal MP E.D. Morel observed: 'the powerful occult influences which move behind the scenes and mould public opinion did their utmost to counteract the more moderate sections of French public life'.[28]

In this instance, the 'occult influences' failed. The secret Anglo-Franco-Spanish diplomatic arrangements were essentially a serious breach of trust towards the people and parliaments they were supposed to represent. That was the bottom line. Germany on the other hand sought transparency, not secret codicils. Germany was in the right.

Théophile Delcassé let his personal hatred of Germany sway both common sense and reason. He knew that powerful forces in Britain were entirely behind him and he thought he was unstoppable. Indeed, one observer felt that he was much closer to the king than he was to his own French colleagues, adding that Delcassé behaved 'as though he was one of King Edward's ministers'.[29]

Delcassé would not bend to any German request for a conference to settle the Moroccan question. More than that, he thought it 'intolerable' to yield to German pressure.[30] In June 1905, sensible heads within the French government realised the grave danger to European peace and sought a reasonable understanding with Germany. Delcassé vehemently defended his position of 'no surrender' but found himself overruled by the entire French cabinet and resigned.[31] Delcassé's fall from grace was a blow to the Secret Elite. Controversially, King Edward publicly invited him to a breakfast meeting, which surprised and alarmed many Parisians and the Belgian ambassador in Paris:

> Such a mark of courtesy to M. Delcassé at this moment has aroused much comment . . . Frenchmen feel that they are being dragged against their will into the orbit of English policy, a policy whose consequences they dread, and which they generally condemned by overthrowing M. Delcassé . . . People fear that this is a sign that England wants so to envenom the situation that war will become inevitable.[32]

Consider the implications. Delcassé had been forced out of the French cabinet, but King Edward responded with a very public display of support for the Revanchist cause. He could have held a private meeting with an 'old friend' but chose instead to draw attention to his unwavering support for Delcassé. He abused his undoubted popularity in France to publicly endorse a known warmonger. It was yet another example of the king's involvement in politics. He repeatedly broke the constitutional convention that a monarch should not interfere in politics, not just in Britain but in staunchly republican France. There could only have been one reason. The Secret Elite knew that the recovery of the 'Lost Provinces' was the emotional pull that would eventually stir Frenchmen to war with Germany, and King Edward was the means through whom they continued to express their support for Delcassé and the Revanchists.

The Germans considered Delcassé's resignation as a diplomatic triumph: recognition that the French architect of the devious secret articles had been abandoned by the voices of reason. Oblivious to the psychological effect that Delcassé's diplomatic humiliation was bound to have in the longer term, the kaiser genuinely believed that, with him gone, the thorny question of Alsace-Lorraine was now closed.[33] In fact, Delcassé's demise was an immediate point of contention in the British press, which began to treat the Moroccan Crisis as an Anglo-German affair rather than a Franco-German dispute. The Secret Elite presented matters as serious proof of Germany's aggressive power and France's defensive weakness.[34] King Edward signalled his strong support for France by studiously avoiding the kaiser in the autumn of 1905, and relations between the two plummeted to a new low. Wilhelm was suspicious of his 'mischief-making' uncle and expressed the view that some very influential people in England wished for war.[35] Unaware that he was talking directly to one of the 'very influential people' at the heart of the Secret Elite, the kaiser gave an interview to Alfred Beit during which he repeated allegations that Edward and Lord Lansdowne had threatened an invasion of Schleswig-Holstein[36] and complained bitterly about the cruel personal insults that the British press always levelled against him.[37] His thoughts were naturally passed from Beit to Lord Esher and King Edward.

After a year of deliberately manipulated international friction, with blustering, false allegations levelled against Germany, reason prevailed, thanks in no small way to the intervention of President Roosevelt, who agreed that America would take part in the mediation. A conference was held from 15 January to 7 April 1906 at Algeciras, the Spanish port on the Bay of Gibraltar. Thirteen nations including Morocco, Holland, Belgium, Austria-Hungary, Portugal and Sweden 'engaged in the delicate task of reconciling the French claims for predominance with the demand of equality for all'.[38] It took three months to agree a satisfactory resolution. The conference re-established political integrity for Morocco and agreed equal economic and commercial rights for all the powers, as Germany had long insisted was both right and proper.

While the end product was an inevitable compromise, the process provided evidence of how closely the British political and diplomatic elite supported France. The entente was not weakened. Far from it. Before the conference had opened, King Edward promised the French ambassador: 'Tell us what you want on each point and we will support you without restriction or reserves.'[39] The German envoy complained that the 'British were more French than the French'[40] and hinted that if the conference failed it could be blamed fairly and squarely on the British envoy, Sir Arthur Nicolson. This was a particularly astute observation, since Sir Arthur was earmarked for greater Secret Elite work within the Foreign Office and enabled their policies to hold fast inside Whitehall.

If the French were worried lest the new Liberal government that had taken office in Britain in 1905 would prove less supportive, Algeciras dispelled their doubts. Other commitments were also agreed at this precise point, to which we shall come shortly. Irrespective of the party in power at Westminster, the Secret Elite had an iron grip on British foreign policy. Was it feasible, as President Roosevelt suggested, that Britain really would have gone to war over Morocco in 1905 or were they simply testing the waters, determining how far they could push Germany? The lessons learned were salutary and saved gross embarrassment at a later date. First and foremost, they were not nearly ready to challenge the German army in Europe. Second, they had overestimated the strength of French Revanchism. There was no critical mass of popular feeling against Germany in France. Delcassé was more like the voice of the prophet crying in the wilderness than the focal point of a powerful political movement.

The French government, unnerved by their own insecurity about the strength of the entente, required reassurances that were to have long-term implications. Secret Anglo-French political and military conversations were stepped up and committees formed to ensure that the impetus for war with Germany was not lost in the desert sandstorm of Morocco or the political upheavals that seemed to threaten continuity in Britain and France. These were years of change through which the Secret Elite guided their forces with consummate skill, for their fingerprints are to be found on each and every major incident.

Summary: Chapter 4 – Testing Warmer Waters

- The Anglo-French Entente Cordiale of 1904 agreed British control of Egypt and recognised France's interests in Morocco.
- The German government accepted this at face value until January 1905 when it learned of both a Franco-Spanish agreement and secret clauses in the Entente Cordiale that gave France a colonial stranglehold in Morocco.
- The Secret Elite always knew that Germany would learn of these clauses and was bound to protect its legitimate interests in Morocco. The new French ally was encouraged to break an international treaty over Morocco in a deliberate attempt to antagonise Germany to the point of war.
- Germany declared the moves to undermine Morocco's independence 'unacceptable', but rather than risk war through a belligerent response, the kaiser proposed an international conference to resolve the issue.
- The British and French deliberately misrepresented this, and the kaiser's visit to Tangier, as a German plot to break the entente.
- In the summer of 1905, the Secret Elite in London and the Revanchist clique in Paris openly considered war.
- The French foreign minister, Delcassé, had the full backing of

King Edward VII and the Secret Elite, but the French parliament overwhelmingly rejected his warmongering and forced him to resign.

- The Secret Elite learned from this that they would have to thoroughly corrupt the French government before conditions were ripe for a move against Germany.

CHAPTER 5

Taming the Bear

The Entente Cordiale unquestionably signalled a dramatic shift in British foreign policy, but it was neither a formal alliance nor the first move to end Britain's 'splendid isolation'. It was a convenient act of friendship that drew both nations closer at a point where their other commitments might have driven them forcibly apart. France was allied to Russia, and Britain to Japan, and a war between Russia and Japan would have proved a serious blow for the Secret Elite had the entente not been in place. While in the long term Russia played a vital role in the web of European alliances, there remained in 1904 unfinished business in the Far East that had to be concluded before the Secret Elite could mould its relationship with Russia to its own advantage.

Britain and Russia had been at loggerheads for 20 years over claims and counterclaims on Persia, Afghanistan and China. The British feared that Russia ultimately intended to add India to her overstretched empire. Politicians talked repeatedly of the 'Russian menace' to India.[1] India was sacrosanct. Time and again the logistics and cost of defending what Disraeli had described as 'the brightest jewel in the crown' were raised in Parliament. Grave concerns were expressed about the numbers of troops needed to defend the borders of India. In 1902, it was estimated that 140,000 soldiers would be needed for that purpose. The question asked in Parliament was: 'Where are we going to get the other 70,000 British troops to add to the 70,000 already there, without denuding the United Kingdom of the forces necessary to uphold our interests in other parts of the British Empire?'[2] Astonishingly, the Secret Elite's solution lay in Japan. Informed through their diplomatic, industrial, commercial and banking ties, they knew that Japan was equally alarmed by Russia's intrusion into the Far East.

Japan had proved herself a major player in Far Eastern affairs by invading China in the Sino-Japanese War of 1894–95 and, to the astonishment of all, utterly defeating her gigantic neighbour. Japan promptly annexed Korea, Formosa and the Liaotung Peninsula of Manchuria with its strategic port of Port Arthur. Such impertinence from a 'lesser' nation offended Russia, France and Germany, who sent a joint ultimatum demanding the immediate withdrawal of Japanese troops from the peninsula and her warships from Port Arthur. The German demand was particularly rude and diplomatically inept. By expressing her intention to remove 'all menaces to peace in the Far East',[3] Germany made an unnecessary enemy of a nation that valued courtesy and despised the loss of face. Japan reluctantly complied, but insult was added to injury when Russia moved troops into the peninsula and berthed her warships in Port Arthur. At last she had access to a port that would not be icebound throughout the long Russian winters.

For the better part of a hundred years, the czar's empire had been 'groping southwards for a warm-water port',[4] and British opposition had been absolute to any advance towards the Black Sea Straits or the Persian Gulf. That resolve remained intact, but it was transparently obvious that Russia intended to enlarge her empire in the Far East and Port Arthur provided the perfect harbour. This the Secret Elite could not allow. Russia was in a position to threaten Britain's Far East trade and was one step closer to India.

The Russian empire held no secrets from the international financiers from whom they had to repeatedly borrow vast amounts of money, or the investors who developed the oil fields around Baku. Russian commercial and financial practices fitted poorly with their ambitious foreign policy, and the czar's treasury was drained of any reserves.[5] The Paris Rothschilds in particular raised huge sums in bonds to develop Russia's railways and small but growing industries. In 1894, a Rothschild-led syndicate raised a 400-million-franc loan for which Alphonse de Rothschild was decorated with the Grand Cross by the czar.[6] The Secret Elite knew that the Trans-Siberian Railway would enable Russia to transport its armies by rail from one side of the country to the other. The 6,365 miles of single track also provided great opportunities for the expansion of trade between Moscow and the Far East, in direct competition with British and Japanese interests.[7] Fully aware that the line was to be completed by 1905, the Secret Elite appreciated that there was a strict timeframe within which action would have to be taken before the might of the czar's armed forces marched into new conquests in China, Korea and Manchuria.

There were, however, no means by which the British Army or Royal Navy could effectively intervene. It was a conundrum solved by a stroke of pure genius. Impressed by the Japanese success against China and confident of their antipathy towards Russia, the Secret Elite promoted Japan as the England of the Far East.[8] The Japanese spent almost their last yen in the creation of a large army and a strong fleet,[9] much of it underwritten by international bankers in London. From the mid 1890s, British shipyards built warships for the Imperial Japanese Navy. The first pre-dreadnought battleship, the *Fuji*, was launched in 1897 from the Thames Ironworks in Blackwall, London, while her sister ship, the *Yashima*, was built by Armstrong Whitworth in Newcastle. When the *Asahi* was launched at John Brown's in Clydebank in 1899, she was the heaviest-ever Clyde-built warship to that date.[10] A ten-year Japanese naval programme, with the construction of six battleships and six armoured cruisers at its core, meant that in Britain the armaments industry thrived and the work was most welcome on the Clyde, Tyne and Thames. The last of these battleships, the *Mikasa*, was ordered from Vickers shipyard in Barrow-in-Furness at the end of 1898, for delivery to Japan in 1902. She took three years to complete, at the enormous cost of £880,000 (£74.5 million in current value).[11] As a rule, the Japanese ships were slightly smaller than their British counterparts but were consequently faster. Quietly and unobtrusively, Britain built the most modern battle fleet possible for the Imperial Japanese Navy, created jobs for its own shipyard workers, made substantial profits for the owners and shareholders, and effectively provided Japan with the means to police the seas in the Far East.

Events in China and Manchuria in 1900–01 further alarmed both countries. The Boxer Rebellion against the hated foreigners who had more or less stripped China of her natural resources was put down savagely by an international alliance. German, Russian, French, British, American, Japanese, Austro-Hungarian and Italian troops were sent to lift the siege of their legations in Peking. Russia, however, used the rebellion as a pretext to invade Manchuria and signalled her intention to stay. She was determined to partition China and end the open-door commercial policy that brought rich pickings to international traders. Japan brooded over the czar's intentions and appeared to waver between making an alliance with Russia and accepting their domination of China or allying with Britain and squaring up to them.[12]

Balfour's government in London had decided to break 500 years of insular tradition by wooing Japan.[13] The advantages of splendid isolation paled into insignificance in those Boer War years, with the looming threat of Russian expansion and the international scorn in foreign newspapers that had followed British military failures against the Boer farmers.[14] The Secret Elite could never dominate the world by sticking to hidebound tradition.

Negotiations were conducted in secret between Lord Lansdowne and the Japanese ambassador in London. An Anglo-Japanese treaty was signed on 30 January 1902. Some historians portrayed the treaty as a victory for Japan, claiming it had 'terrified' the British government into a 'rushed' agreement.[15] Terrified? Not in the knowledge that their common bond was a determination to stop Russian expansion in China and Manchuria. Rushed? It had been at least eight long years in the planning.

Britain's clear intention was to contain Russian expansion in the Far East and protect the British Empire, especially India, from a known predator. The official reason as stated in Parliament was the government's 'anxiety to maintain the status quo in China' and recognise Japan's rights in Korea.[16] The treaty stated that if either Britain or Japan became involved in war over China or Korea against a single enemy, the other would remain neutral. If, however, either became involved in war with more than one power, if, say, France joined Russia in a war against Japan, Britain would be bound to intervene on behalf of Japan.

Undoubtedly it was the subtext that angered Russia, and it might have caused the French considerable consternation had they not been more interested in King Edward's overtures for an Anglo-French entente. Essentially, Britain was giving Japan permission to go to war against Russia with a promise to cover its back if any other 'power' intervened. The implications for both France and Germany were clear. They should stay out of this. There were also a number of secret clauses wherein the British and Japanese governments agreed to permit each other's navies to use coaling stations and docking facilities, and maintain in the 'Extreme East' a naval force greater than any third 'power'.[17] What particularly appealed to the Secret Elite was the additional bonus it brought. With the war in South Africa bleeding resources, the treaty with Japan offered a cost-effective way to protect British interests in the Far East.[18] British naval power could be concentrated in and around the Atlantic and North Sea waters. The Imperial Japanese Navy would operate on Britain's behalf by proxy.

Parliamentarians were less than happy about the bombshell announcement on 12 February 1902. The treaty was 'a complete surprise', a 'bolt from the blue', a momentous departure from the 'time-honoured policy of this country'.[19] It was the first time Britain had concluded an offensive and defensive alliance with a foreign power, and the first that any European power had concluded with an Oriental race. Complaints were lodged about its secrecy, its sudden announcement as a fait accompli, the dangerous nature of an alliance that tied Britain 'hard and fast to the wheels of Japanese policy' and the fact that no one seemed to have previously thought it necessary.[20] To the taunt that Britain had sought the treaty, the under-secretary of state at the Foreign Office, Viscount Cranborne, elder son and heir of Lord Salisbury and cousin to the prime minister, retorted with the arrogance of a true aristocrat: 'It is not for us to seek treaties; we grant them.'[21]

Arrogant duplicity was at the core of the Secret Elite. Behind the illusion of munificent generosity, they sharpened their focus on every element that would serve their cause. The Secret Elite did not operate with transparency, nor seek the consent of Parliament. They took action as and when required to promote their agenda. Incidental matters drawn to the attention of Parliament, such as the practice of a British colony, namely Australia, of preventing the immigration of Japanese citizens was not their concern. As ever, their approach was to 'disregard the screamers'.

Two years later, on 8 February 1904, Japan put the treaty to the test with a pre-emptive torpedo-boat attack on Russian warships in Port Arthur. There was no declaration of war. It was reminiscent of the crippling strike by the British navy on the Danish fleet berthed at Copenhagen in 1807. A series of indecisive naval engagements followed that provided cover for a Japanese landing in Korea. From Incheon, the Japanese occupied Seoul and then the rest of Korea. The czar was ill-advised to order the Russian Baltic Fleet halfway and more around the world to liberate Port Arthur and settle the devious Japanese. It was a mission that began inauspiciously and ended disastrously.

On the night of 21 October 1904, the Gamecock fishing fleet sailed out of Hull to trawl their North Sea beat at the Dogger Bank, only to find ships of the czar's Baltic Fleet passing before them through the clearing fog. Waving and cheering, they gathered to watch what they thought were British naval manoeuvres. When the warships turned their searchlights towards them, the fishermen 'ceased their work, and laughed and revelled in the glare'.[22] Seconds later, the Russians opened fire. The trawler *Crane* was sunk, its captain and first mate killed, and six other fishermen wounded, one of whom died a few months later.

In the general chaos, Russian ships shot at each other. Fear and false information combined to make fools of the Russian navy. The outrage inflamed the British public. The Russians claimed that they had mistaken the fishing vessels for Japanese torpedo boats, which might sound ridiculous but the general nervousness of the Russian sailors and false reports about the presence of Japanese torpedo boats, submarines and minefields in the North Sea lent credence to their fears.[23]

The Dogger Bank incident assumed international status, with newspaper reports of headless fishermen, mutilated corpses and innocent victims.[24] Reparations were demanded. The Foreign Office sent an immediate note of protest to St Petersburg, and the Mayor of Hull wrote to the prime minister demanding 'the speediest and strongest measures to insure full redress'.[25] Matters were in danger of spiralling out of hand. Count Benckendorff, the Russian ambassador, was attacked as he got into his cab at Victoria Station and had to be rescued by police.

Foreign Secretary Lansdowne met urgently with Prime Minister Balfour and the king. The government had to exercise concerted damage-limitation to dampen down the violent anti-Russian outbursts. National newspapers regretted the targeting of Benckendorff and *The Standard* rebuked the mob for such a 'foolish demonstration'.[26] On 24 October, the *Daily News* carried an exclusive apology from the Russian ambassador: 'I authorise you to say from me to the people of England that I am absolutely certain that what occurred was a deplorable incident.' While acknowledging that the outrage was probably due to 'wicked negligence', the colonial secretary, Alfred Lyttelton, urged everyone to 'hold themselves entirely courteous to Russia, giving her every credit for her ready disavowal . . . and disassociating the many good people in Russia from any sympathy with such an outrage'.[27] *The Times* joined in with an editorial stressing that 'there is no wish to humiliate Russia or hurt her legitimate susceptibilities more than is absolutely demanded in the interests of justice'.[28]

What was going on? Russia was at war with Britain's one and only ally, Japan. The attack on the fishing fleet could have been construed as a reason for British intervention in the Russo-Japanese war, yet the Secret Elite moved instantly to maintain good relations with Russia. Why? Despite their fears over the security of India and distrust of Russia's intentions in China, they focused on their own long-term agenda. Never for one instant did they take their eyes off Germany. Paradoxically, while they intended Russia to fail in the Far East, there was no merit in further estranging her in Europe. Russia was earmarked for future use: against Germany.

In the French Foreign Office at the Quai d'Orsay, diplomats feared that the recently signed entente might be jeopardised. Just at the moment when Britain and France were colluding over Morocco and positioning themselves against the kaiser, this diplomatic crisis threatened the new spirit of harmony between London and Paris. Given that the French were formally allied to the Russians, the possibility of France being drawn into the Russo–Japanese war provoked real heart-search. No one could possibly have anticipated the Dogger Bank complications and the diplomatic impasse that ensued, but the Secret Elite had to find a solution.

Delcassé, always King Edward's favourite Frenchman, managed to get both Russia and Britain to agree to take the dispute to The Hague for an international arbitration.[29] Russian ministers had no notion of how deeply Delcassé was personally associated with the Secret Elite. He had a vested interest in France remaining on good terms with both Britain and Russia, and knew that delay would only allow the dispute to fester.[30]

As Russia's Baltic Fleet sailed ponderously in a seven-month sojourn from its northern habitat,[31] it was closely monitored by the Royal Navy, each coaling station noted, each vessel counted and watched. In the preceding years, the Secret Elite had given the Japanese navy access to large quantities of the best quality, practically smokeless, Welsh coal, while refusing to sell Russia even a pound of it, much to the annoyance of the czar.[32] Others were more helpful to the Russian fleet. Germany provided 60 coaling barges and France allowed them to use Cam Ranh Bay in French Indochina as a naval base.

For the Russians to be given this vital assistance, virtually on Japan's doorstep, was viewed as an affront, and the Japanese press demanded that Britain join in the war.[33] *The Times* called on Delcassé to deal with the breaches of neutrality with 'promptitude and firmness'. In a stern warning, the French were reminded that 'any action England may take is inspired by the strongest wish to avert the possibility of an incident that might dissolve the entente and compel them to take opposite sides in a great international controversy'.[34] This was a breathtaking example of double standards, as Britain had been supplying Japan with warships and coal for a decade in preparation for this moment.

Just days before the two warring fleets faced up to each other, a decision was taken in London to renew the terms of the Anglo-Japanese Treaty. The Secret Elite moved yet another piece on the chessboard of diplomatic intrigue. Lansdowne proposed a stronger alliance in which both Japan and Britain would go to war in support of each other if any country attacked either of them. This was a significant change. So too was the acknowledgement by the Japanese that Britain had the right to 'safeguard her possessions in India'.[35] Problems associated with the defence and security of India had greatly concerned the British Parliament for many years. The complexities of raising and transporting an army to protect her borders had been discussed in detail.[36] This was solved by the terms of the new treaty. Japan would act as a guarantor of the British Raj.

On 26 May, with the two opposing navies steaming towards their apocalyptic destiny, the Japanese ambassador presented a draft treaty to Lord Lansdowne that specifically included Britain's rights in India. The crown jewel had another guardian, a trusted ally who had the ability to react quickly to any threat from Russia or Germany in the future.

Bad though Dogger Bank had been, nothing prepared the czar for the disaster that awaited his Baltic Fleet in the Tsushima Strait between Korea and southern Japan. On 27–28 May 1905, the Japanese navy destroyed two-thirds of the Russian fleet. It had endured a voyage of over 18,000 nautical miles to perish in the Far East. The outcome was so significant that the battle of Tsushima was hailed, even in England, as 'by far the greatest and the most important naval event since Trafalgar'.[37] Two days of relentless fighting saw the British-built Imperial Japanese Fleet destroy all eight Russian battleships and all three of their smaller coastal battleships. Only one cruiser and two destroyers limped into Vladivostok.

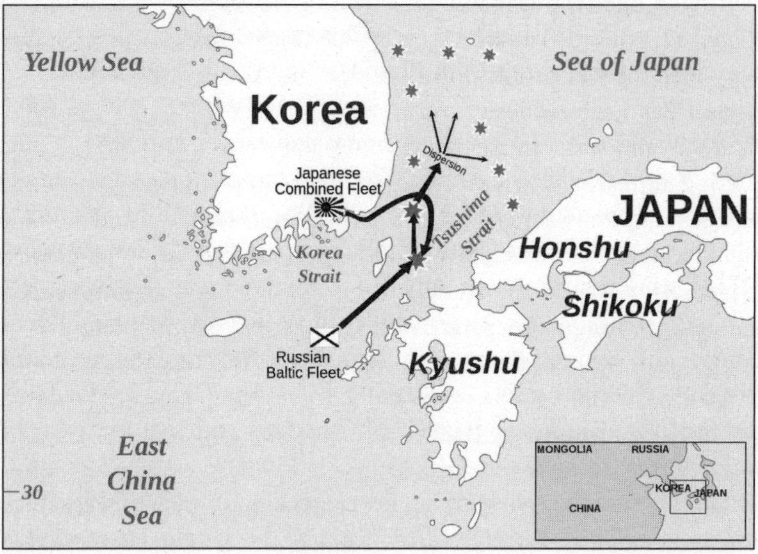

Battle of Tsushima, 27–28 May 1905.

Triumphant in the Far East, the Japanese were rewarded with enhanced international status and a peace settlement brokered by President Roosevelt in September 1905. They gained exclusive rights in Korea and control of the Liaotung Peninsula, including Port Arthur. Russia was forced to pay a huge war indemnity and grant Japan additional fishing rights in their territorial waters.

If this was a momentous victory for Japan, it held even greater significance for the Secret Elite; the real victors were in London. At a stroke, the problem of defending India had been transformed at little cost to the British exchequer. Indeed, the British-built battleships and cruisers had generated immense profits for the City.

During the war, an international consortium including British-owned banking houses like Barings, Samuels and the Hong Kong and Shanghai Bank raised over £5 billion at today's value to assist Japan. Almost half of Japan's war debt was financed through bonds sold mostly in London and New York.[38] Money was not a problem. Manipulators at the heart of the Secret Elite, like Esher, facilitated meetings held on Rothschild premises to help the Japanese financial envoy, Takahashi Korekiyo, raise their war chest. While banks with strong links to the Rothschilds were prepared to raise funds for Japan quite openly, the Rothschilds had to tread carefully because of their immense Russian investments, not least in the Baku oilfields. They were also very aware of the political repercussions that might ensue for Russian Jews who bore the harsh brunt of czarist anti-Semitism. That changed once the war was over. The London and Paris Rothschilds negotiated a further £48 million issue to help Japanese economic recovery.[39] At every turn the war profits flowed back to the Secret Elite.

Russia's Far Eastern designs lay in tatters. She had been trounced by land and sea, and was damaged and vulnerable. The warm-water port was gone. Civil unrest was widespread and revolution hung in the air. The 'Bloody Sunday' massacre of more than 500 protestors outside the Winter Palace in January 1905 was followed in February by the assassination of the czar's uncle. By March, the Russian army had suffered an unprecedented defeat in Manchuria. In April, ethnic grievances manifested themselves and in May the unions were demanding universal suffrage and parliamentary government. By June 1905, much of the navy had been destroyed and mutiny broke out on the *Potemkin*, Russia's most powerful battleship, in the Black Sea. July riots in Odessa saw over 6,000 civilians killed before a half-hearted step towards constitutional monarchy was proposed in August. In September, famine threatened and in October open revolt shut down factories, transport and manufacturing with 1,500,000 men on strike. November mutinies in Kronstadt were followed in December by a horrific pogrom of Jewish villagers in Odessa. Maltreatment of Jewish communities disgusted fair-minded people in Britain, and Russian influence stood at an all-time low. Time and circumstance favoured a radical move by the Secret Elite. Broken and almost friendless, the czar was ready to grasp the proffered hand from the very people who had reduced his empire to its withered state. Then, unexpectedly, the Kaiser almost stole the prize.

Kaiser Wilhelm had, since June 1904, been courting his cousin the czar to create an alliance between Russia and Germany that would change the face of European alliances. Emboldened by Delcassé's political demise but still concerned by his claims that the British were ready to go to war,[40] the kaiser made a bold move in July 1905. Germany had been very supportive of Russia during the war with Japan by providing the coal for the Baltic Fleet as it headed towards the Far East. In a series of telegrams and letters (released by the Bolsheviks in 1917), Wilhelm sought a new relationship with Russia. He suggested an alliance. Not only would it have undermined the entente but Germany's historic enemy, France, would have been left to choose either to throw her lot in with Russia, her ally, or abandon Russia and confirm an alliance with Britain. Wilhelm promised Nicholas that once the French realised that the British fleet could not save Paris, they would accept reality and fall in line behind them: 'In this way a combination of three of the strongest continental powers would be formed, to attack whom the Anglo-Japanese group would think twice before acting.'[41] He reasoned that it would guarantee peace in Europe by safeguarding both Russia and Germany.

Reeling from the defeat by Japan, Czar Nicholas secretly signed an alliance on 24 July 1905 on board his yacht moored off the Björkö Sound. No officials from the Russian court were present, no minister knew what had been proposed and agreed. It was to be their treaty. Nicholas was willing to grasp the hand of friendship from his cousin, who argued passionately that Russia had been badly let down by France. The kaiser understood exactly what Edward VII intended, and to reassure the czar he wrote again to him on 22 August 1905 that 'Britain only wants to make France her "cat's-paw" [tool] against us, as she used Japan against you.' It was an impressive assessment. He advised Nicholas that Edward, 'the Arch-intriguer – and mischief-maker in Europe', as the czar himself had called him,[42] had been hard at work trying to discover precisely what had transpired at Björkö.

Indeed he had. Rumours suggested that some private deal had been struck between the two royal cousins, but no one appeared to know precisely what it amounted to. King Edward asked Benckendorff, the Russian ambassador at London, to go to Denmark to find out what had been agreed.[43] He met there with the Dowager Empress of Russia and one of the key figures in the Secret Elite's network, the Russian ambassador to Copenhagen, Alexander Isvolsky. All were staunch Anglophiles. When Kaiser Wilhelm heard of this, he sent an angry telegram to the czar complaining that Edward had the audacity to use the Russian diplomatic service to his own ends. No one knew what had been agreed until the czar confided to his foreign minister, Count Lamsdorff, that he had signed a secret treaty with Germany on board his private yacht. As King Edward had said of him: 'Lamsdorff is such a nice man and lets me know all I want to hear.'[44] The cat was out of the bag. Suddenly, the Secret Elite were confronted by a potential alliance that threatened to blow their grand plan apart.

How they managed to kill the Björkö Treaty is further testament to the power the Secret Elite extended across Europe. Had it been formally ratified, Björkö would have signalled a realignment that transformed the balance of international alliances.[45] This dangerous treaty had to be quashed. Russian newspapers began immediately to attack the kaiser, who complained: 'The whole of your influential press, *Nowosti Nowie Wremja Ruskj*, etc., have since a fortnight become violently anti-German and pro-British. Partly they are bought by heavy sums of British money no doubt.'[46] His suspicions were not without foundation.

Russia was already in desperate financial straits after Tsushima and in need of fresh loans. The Paris Bourse had deeper, more reliable pockets than the Berlin banks[47] and had traditionally been the main source of financial backing for Russia. The Secret Elite threatened to pull the financial plug unless the czar came to his senses. Much to the disappointment of Kaiser Wilhelm, the opportunity to realign Europe towards a greater peace fell before it reached the first hurdle. Czar Nicholas backtracked and the treaty never was, though as Wilhelm bitterly reminded him: 'We joined hands and signed before God who heard our vows.'[48] His desperate appeal fell on deaf ears.

The kaiser was absolutely correct. The Secret Elite was prepared to use any nation as a cat's-paw, and Russia became the victim of British trickery, manipulated into a different treaty that was designed not to protect her or the peace of Europe but to enable the Secret Elite to destroy Germany.

In their eyes, a vulnerable czar had almost grasped the wrong hand of friendship, and the near-disaster at Björkö focused minds. Despite the alarming evidence of riots in the streets of St Petersburg and the slaughter of protestors at the Winter Palace on Bloody Sunday, King Edward began to court Czar Nicholas with the ultimate aim of a three-way alliance between Britain, France and Russia against Germany. The Russian navy was invited to visit Portsmouth at the king's request, and Russian officers and crew were brought to London and treated lavishly with banquets and nights out at the theatre. Much was made in the pliant press of the public warmth of the London crowds who cheered the Russians. *The Times* talked of a rapprochement with Russia as a natural and inevitable follow-on to the entente with France.[49] While the British public was softened up in anticipation of an alliance with Russia, the Bear was being enticed into a honeytrap.

The Secret Elite drew Russia in with a commitment that they never intended to deliver. Russia was secretly promised control of Constantinople and the Black Sea Straits, following a successful war against Germany.[50] This was Russia's holy grail, her 'historic mission'. She had long coveted free passage for her warships through the Straits, to the exclusion of all others.[51] From the reign of Catherine the Great, Russian leaders had entertained an ambition to control Constantinople in order to have a warm-water port and an unrestricted naval outlet to the Mediterranean. It promised access to trade, wealth and conquest.

For obvious reasons, not least the deafening public outcry that would have followed, the Anglo-Russian Convention signed on 31 August 1907 made no mention of Constantinople or the Straits but was crafted with reference only to Persia, Afghanistan and Tibet. Just as the French Revanchists had been offered the carrot of regaining Alsace and Lorraine, so the secret promise dangled in front of Russia was post-war control of the Black Sea Straits. It was yet another secret deal hidden from Parliament and the people, yet another spurious promise that Britain never intended to keep.

Basking in the success of his sterling work with King Edward in preparing the grounds for an alliance, the Russian diplomat Alexander Isvolsky was promoted in 1906 from a relatively unimportant post at Copenhagen to minister of foreign affairs in St Petersburg. This was a spectacular promotion and one that could not have taken place without support and influence. He was clearly a man who had proved his worth to the Secret Elite in the days and months after Björkö, and their financial rewards guaranteed his compliance. He was a bought man. Prior to this point, he had been bankrupt and had no personal wealth with which to promote his own career. Once linked directly by the king to Sir Arthur Nicolson,[52] who had been moved from Spain to be the British ambassador to St Petersburg, Isvolsky enjoyed a patronage whose source he would never fully comprehend.[53] He was, thereafter, a man of means with access to Secret Elite funds that promoted their ambitions as well as his own. In addition to the benefits of old-fashioned bribery, the new alliance gelled naturally because Isvolsky's aims harmonised with the London policy of encircling Germany.[54]

As this history unfolds, others will emerge whose services were bought and loyalty secured.

As was often the case in foreign affairs, the signing of the Anglo-Russian Convention was kept secret until Parliament had risen for the summer break, so denying the 'screamers' an opportunity to express their objections. The official terms of the convention were not made known until 25 September, leaving sufficient time for those journalists in the know to determine that such a diplomatic agreement with Russia was clearly to the benefit of the British Empire. And it was.

The central feature was a partition of Persia by which Britain gained a clear sphere of interest around Basra and the Gulf. These desert lands were to prove far from barren when the oil-rich fields were opened some six years later. British interests in the Gulf were deeply enmeshed with commerce, oil, the Suez Canal, the route to India, and the exclusion of Russia from a warm-water port. Foreign Office negotiators gained every advantage possible and in exchange gave promises that would never be kept. No mention was made of closing the net on Germany. Had she not been ruined by war with Japan, in desperate need of inward investment and incapable of pursuing the dream of a warm-water port by any other means, Russia might well have walked away from the convention. But she was exactly in the position that the Secret Elite had intended: on her knees. They raised her to her feet in the guise of the Good Samaritan.

An alliance with Russia, no matter how vague, was deeply unpopular with many sections of society, but Lord Curzon, from the inner circle of the Elite, defended the Liberal government in the House of Lords[55] and boldly announced that, in his view, it was all very natural. His claims were ridiculous and self-serving: 'I think there is no agreement that would generally be more acceptable to this House, or to the country, than one with Russia'.[56] Only a member of the aristocracy or the Secret Elite could have made such an outrageously untruthful statement. The czar and his brutal regime were totally anathema to fair-minded people everywhere.

Summary: Chapter 5 – Taming the Bear

- The major powers were astonished in 1902 when Britain formed an alliance with Japan.
- Britain supported her new ally by building a modern fleet for the Imperial Japanese Navy and providing huge loans for Japan's industrial development.
- In order to protect both British and Japanese interests in the Far East, the Secret Elite encouraged Japan to attack Russia.
- In a brutal war from 1904 to 1905, Japan decimated Russian forces in the East.
- An unfortunate incident with a British fishing fleet at Dogger Bank caused such public outrage against Russia that the Secret Elite had to calm the press.
- Although the British wanted Russia out of the Far East and away from India, their long-term aim was to draw her into an alliance against Germany.
- Kaiser Wilhelm virtually pre-empted this in July 1905 by signing a secret agreement with the czar at Björkö that would have blown apart the Secret Elite's grand plan.
- The Secret Elite in turn used all of their diplomatic, economic and political clout to negate the proposed Russo-German alliance before it could be made public and ratified.
- A second Anglo-Japanese Alliance in 1905 offered direct Japanese protection of India.
- As Kaiser Wilhelm correctly stated, Britain had used Japan to remove the Russian threat in the East and her intention was to similarly use France against Germany in Europe.
- The Secret Elite understood Russia's historic mission to gain an ice-free port and dangled the carrot of Constantinople and the Straits to entice

her. The Anglo-Russian Convention was allegedly about Persia, but in reality it paved the way towards an Anglo-French-Russian alliance against Germany.

- Having assisted King Edward and the Secret Elite to destroy the kaiser's Björkö agreement, Alexander Isvolsky was subsequently promoted to minister of foreign affairs at St Petersburg.
- Previously bankrupt, Isvolsky was bankrolled by the Secret Elite through the British diplomatic service.

CHAPTER 6

The Changing of the Guard

WHILE KING EDWARD AND THE Secret Elite were busy abroad building strategic alliances, it had been Arthur Balfour's misfortune to take over as prime minister in the wake of the unpopular South African War. His administration remained true to Secret Elite foreign policy but was split on tariff reform and various domestic issues. The Conservatives suffered regular by-election defeats to a very vocal and confident Liberal opposition waiting impatiently for office.

British democracy, with regular elections and changes of government, was portrayed as a reliable safety net against despotic rule. It has never been this. Although the 1884 Reform Act increased male voting rights to include adult householders and men who rented unfurnished lodgings to the value of £10 a year, an estimated 40 per cent still did not have the right to vote as a result of their status within society.[1] Women did not have the right to vote at all, while some men could vote twice, both at their place of business or university and at their home address. The ruling class held every advantage, and their contempt for the poor was undisguised. As Liberal MP Francis Neilson observed:

> At the end of 1905, it would have been difficult for Diogenes to find a country under the sun where there was so deep a contempt for the poor and the meek held by the ruling class . . . Labourers in agriculture at any wage from twelve to sixteen shillings a week; miners living in hovels.[2]

Apart from a small number of socialists funded by the trade unions, Members of Parliament were restricted to the well-to-do by the expense of office and by the fact that they were unpaid, a state of affairs that remained in place until 1911. A prohibitive deposit of £150 was required for any parliamentary candidate, a sum greater than the total annual income of most British families. Indeed, it equated to twice the annual wage of a policeman.[3]

Both the Conservative and Liberal parties had been controlled since 1866 by the same small clique that consisted of no more than half a dozen chief families, their relatives and allies, reinforced by an occasional incomer with the 'proper' credentials.[4] These incomers were generally recruited from society's select educational system, most prominently from Balliol or New College, Oxford, or Trinity College, Cambridge. If he proved valuable to the inner clique, the talented newcomer generally ended up married into one of the dominant families.[5] The Secret Elite made an art form out of identifying potential talent, putting promising young men into positions that would serve their future ambitions and slowly wrapping them in the warmth of Establishment approval and ultimate personal success.

Faced with the demise of the Conservative government in 1905, the Secret Elite had already selected their natural successors in the Liberal Party: reliable and trusted men immersed in their imperial values. Herbert Henry Asquith, Richard Burdon Haldane and Sir Edward Grey were Milner's chosen men and 'objects of his special attention'.[6] He wrote regularly from South Africa, met with them in secret when on leave in 1901 and actively instructed them on his policies.[7] Though they were groomed as a team, Haldane was his most frequent correspondent and, like many others, very much under his spell. He wrote to Milner during the Boer War: 'Just tell me how you wish us to act . . . and I will set about seeing what can be done. I have every confidence in your judgement.'[8] There was never any doubt about who was in charge.

Their remit was to ensure that the Liberals maintained a seamless foreign policy that served the grand plan: war with Germany. These three had more in common and mixed more readily with their Conservative opponents than with most of their own parliamentary colleagues.[9] Their Secret Elite connections were impeccable. Together with their good friend Arthur Balfour they shared similar university backgrounds and were intimately involved with the inner circles of the Secret Elite. They were also members of the exclusive dining clubs at Grillion's and The Club, which played a very significant role in developing the network that promoted British supremacy.

Herbert Asquith went to Balliol College, Oxford, and was a protégé of Lord Rosebery, under whose influence and patronage he blossomed. Elected to Parliament in 1886, he served as home secretary under Gladstone and later Rosebery from 1892 until the Liberals lost power in 1895.

Asquith's personal life provides a perfect example of how the Secret Elite inter-married, associated with one another and maintained their dominance over British foreign policy. If the first generation with whom Rhodes was directly associated belonged to the nineteenth century, dominated by Lords

Salisbury and Rosebery, the next generation that assumed power in the early twentieth century included many names already identified in this book as agents or members of the Secret Elite. Asquith attended Balliol with Alfred Milner, and they were in constant contact for many years. They ate their meals together at the scholarship table virtually every day for four years and as young lawyers had Sunday dinner together throughout the 1880s.[10]

Asquith's first wife died of typhoid fever in 1891, leaving him with five young children. In 1894, he married Margot Tennant, the free-spirited daughter of Sir Charles Tennant, director of the Nobel-Dynamite Trust Company, which by 1909 boasted the largest explosives manufacturing site in the world at Ardeer on the west coast of Scotland. Arthur Balfour was one of his closest friends and the best man at his marriage to Margot. Even when they were leaders of supposedly diametrically opposed parties, Balfour regularly dined with the Asquiths. He frequently joked that he had champagne dinners at Asquith's before going on to the House of Commons to verbally attack his host.[11] Ludicrous as this was, it served to highlight the hypocrisy of their public altercations in Parliament, where in matters relating to Secret Elite policy they supped from the same bowl.

Margot Tennant claimed in her autobiography to have written to Balfour from Egypt, where she had a brief affair with Alfred Milner before marrying Asquith, requesting that Milner be posted back to Britain and promoted to the Board of the Inland Revenue. She belonged to the country-house set known sarcastically as 'the Souls', essentially upper-class socialites, many of whom were directly associated with the Secret Elite, including George Curzon, St John Brodrick, Alfred Lyttelton and Asquith, and consequently she shared a number of friends with Milner. They were notorious for 'flitting about from one great country house to another or one spectacular social event to another at the town house of one of their elders'.[12]

Asquith, Haldane and Grey were close to Milner politically, intellectually and socially,[13] and even when the Conservatives were out of government from 1905 to (effectively) 1915, Milner continued to orchestrate Foreign Office decisions. It mattered not who was in power. The Secret Elite interacted 'just as if they were in office'.[14]

Edward Grey, also a Balliol man, had served as under-secretary in 1892 when Rosebery was at the Foreign Office. Grey's late father had been a royal equerry and regularly travelled abroad with Edward when he was Prince of Wales. This meant that Grey, who was King Edward's godson, had, through his father, strong ties to the royal family.

Asquith and Grey were trusted men and close to the king. They had colluded with Lord Rosebery as far back as 1890 in a long-term proposal to take over the Liberal Party leadership on behalf of what was termed the

Liberal Imperialist Group.[15] Their induction into the orbit of the Secret Elite came through the classic route of patronage and proven association. They were loyal men, loyal to Rosebery and the monarchy, loyal to the Empire.

Richard Haldane's rise to political office followed a different route and provides a fascinating insight into how the Secret Elite groomed able politicians for future use. R.B. Haldane came from the minor Scottish landed gentry of Cloan near Gleneagles. He gained a first-class honours degree at Edinburgh University, having spent a period in Göttingen studying German philosophy and learning to speak fluent German. This language skill was to prove an essential asset in a career that began unobtrusively when he was called to the Bar in London in 1879. There he met and was befriended by another talented lawyer, Herbert Asquith, and doors opened in front of him that might have otherwise remained closed. Haldane stood for Parliament as a Liberal in East Lothian and was duly elected. Talented, intellectual and affable, he became close friends with two rising young stars in Rosebery's government: Asquith and the more reserved Edward Grey. This was to become the triumvirate that ultimately enabled the Secret Elite drive to war with Germany.

As a backbencher, Haldane proved a poor orator. He was not included in Gladstone's government, though both Grey and Asquith were. Around this time, his circle of political friends and acquaintances expanded to include the purveyors of Secret Elite power in the Conservative Party: Arthur Balfour, Lord Curzon, George Wyndham and Alfred Lyttelton.[16] The Secret Elite drew him closer and closer into their confidence, and he was eventually introduced to the Prince of Wales in 1894. The two men developed a bond of trust and loyalty that strengthened in the first decade of the twentieth century when they regularly dined together. He was ever the king's loyal servant.

Haldane's long-term friendship with the Rothschild families was a mark, too, of their trust and confidence in him as 'one of them'. He considered himself 'very intimate' with both Lord and Lady Rothschild, and had a room at Tring reserved permanently for his weekend sojourns.[17] The close bond between Haldane and the extended House of Rothschild was marked by his frequent visits to the Paris branch of the family to spend time with Lady Rothschild's sisters and enjoy their sumptuous hospitality.

In the last years of the nineteenth century, the Liberal Party had almost rent itself asunder in a civil war between the aggressive 'Imperialists' led by Asquith, Grey and Haldane and the anti-war Liberals who always remained in the majority at grass-roots levels. The leadership was undermined and resigned in protest, claiming that the party 'was being infected by dangerous doctrines in foreign policy'.[18] It was, but no one realised how deep or how dangerous the infection would prove. Despite Haldane's repeated efforts to encourage Lord Rosebery to return to front-line politics, the Liberal Party elected Henry Campbell-Bannerman as their anti-war leader. Haldane's opposition to him never wavered. When Campbell-Bannerman placed the blame for the Boer War squarely on the shoulders of Joseph Chamberlain and Alfred Milner, he could not fathom the support that Milner was always guaranteed from Asquith, Grey and Haldane. He put it down to a 'perverse Balliol solidarity'. His bitter observation was that any criticism or doubt of Milner's policies was 'the unpardonable sin' and that the 'arch offender' in the Boer War scenario was Milner, 'but we can't get at him'.[19] The Secret Elite always threw a protective arm around its own, no matter the party in power. Campbell-Bannerman was right: Milner was an untouchable.

Why then did Richard Haldane, disillusioned as he was by Campbell-Bannerman and the Liberal Party, and a man whose political sympathies appeared to lie with the Conservatives, not cross the floor of the House of Commons and join them? The answer lay in the fact that the Secret Elite's greater purpose was served by his remaining a Liberal. Haldane's roots had taken inside the Secret Elite councils and he was judged to be a highly valuable asset. Alfred Milner considered him for the high commissioner's post in South Africa, but he was placed instead on a government committee on armaments.

Public concern about the state of the British Army was widely voiced in the press, and by 1902 it was accepted that defects in military organisation had to be tackled. Observers were surprised that the most serious contributions were coming from Haldane, a member of the anti-war Liberal party.[20] Placing Haldane in the War Office before the Liberals came to power was a very shrewd move by the Secret Elite. He was able to familiarise himself with the workings of the ministry and build positive relationships with senior British military personnel, who regarded him highly.

The king made Haldane a privy counsellor in August 1902,[21] an exceptional move because he was a backbench MP who had never held office.[22] But he, like Lord Esher, was the king's man. In January 1905, almost one calendar year before the Liberal Party entered government, King Edward invited Haldane to stay at Windsor Castle to discuss future plans for foreign policy and army reconstruction. The king and the opposition backbencher! How strange.

Haldane's relationship with Alfred Milner, Lord Esher and King Edward was exceptionally close.[23] The Secret Elite's other key political agents, Balfour, Lansdowne, Asquith and Grey, shared the innermost secrets of their respective parties with one another and with the king. There was always collusion on matters of foreign policy and the grand plan. This was where their allegiance lay, not to their specific party. Their duty was to the king, the Empire, to Milner's dream, to Rhodes' legacy. They confronted the same problems, analysed the same alternatives and agreed the same solution: Germany had to go.

Long before he announced it to his own party, Balfour gave Grey, Asquith and Haldane advance warning that he intended to resign as prime minister, giving them additional time to organise their political strategy. The immediate problem with this handover of power was Sir Henry Campbell-Bannerman. The man who would become the next prime minister had no knowledge of the Secret Elite. He was a radical. He was anti-war. He was a genial draper's son from Glasgow.[24] He was not one of them. But Campbell-Bannerman, who was committed to political change, had the overwhelming support of his party.

Though he was certain to lead the Liberals into government, the Secret Elite conspired with their trusted men to undermine Campbell-Bannerman's influence and power from within. The three conspirators, Asquith, Grey and Haldane, engaged in a plot worthy of Ancient Rome. They met in September 1905 at Grey's private fishing lodge at Relugas, a remote village in the north of Scotland, determined to be rid of Campbell-Bannerman. His acerbic opposition to Lord Milner had been very offensive to them, and indeed to Milner, who was by then the acknowledged leader of the Secret Elite. They resolved to demand that unless he agreed to go to the House of Lords and leave the leadership of the Commons to Asquith, none of them would serve in his Cabinet.[25] Haldane, who was always the driving force within this tight-knit group,[26] wrote immediately to the king's private secretary, warning that unless he, Grey and Asquith were in a position to shape policy inside the Liberal Cabinet, continuity of the grand plan would be impossible. Three weeks later, he was summoned to a meeting of the inner core of the Secret Elite at Balmoral. Present with the king were A.J. Balfour, prime minister and leader of the Conservatives, Lord Lansdowne, the foreign secretary, and the ubiquitous Esher. Thereafter, Haldane wrote triumphantly to Asquith that their Relugas plot was 'thoroughly approved in all its details' and that 'we have secured very cordial and powerful assistance'.[27]

An awesome conspiracy to thwart the Liberal Party's plan for peace and retrenchment was endorsed by the Secret Elite. They rubber-stamped a coup to undermine the democratic process, neuter the first man of the Liberal Party, and take control of the new government's foreign policy. Incredible though it might appear, the two most senior Conservative leaders were actively conspiring with the king and an unelected lord to decide the composition of a Liberal Cabinet. What would Liberal Party members have thought had they known that three of their most senior representatives were plotting in secret against their stated interests? How would they have felt had they known that the leader of the Conservative Party, their political adversary, was intimately involved? The prime minister in waiting, Campbell-Bannerman, had no notion that his 'loyal' colleagues had loyalties that lay elsewhere.

The 'Relugas Three' had sworn that they would not serve under Campbell-Bannerman's leadership, but the king stressed how important it was that they, the Secret Elite's chosen men, should be inside the Liberal Cabinet. Guided by Lord Esher, he personally asked Haldane to take the War Office.[28] King Edward then tried to persuade Campbell-Bannerman to go to the House of Lords, leaving control of the Commons to Asquith, Grey and Haldane. Campbell-Bannerman almost gave way to the pressure but was dissuaded by his wife, whose determination propped her wavering husband and temporarily thwarted the ambitious triumvirate. In an eventual compromise, they agreed to support Campbell-Bannerman provided Asquith was made chancellor of the Exchequer, Grey got the Foreign Office and Haldane the War Office. Continuity would be guaranteed. Control of foreign policy would remain in trusted hands, and a complete root-and-branch reorganisation of the War Office could begin under the watchful eye of the Secret Elite. Furthermore, by placing Grey and Haldane in these key posts, the Secret Elite kept firm control of the political leadership of the Committee of Imperial Defence and so ensured that only their men in the Cabinet fully appreciated the depth of preparation for eventual war with Germany.

And the beauty of it was that they were shielded from view by a radical Liberal Party intent on major social reform, content to let Edward Grey get on with his job in the Foreign Office, whatever that might be. How the Secret Elite must have laughed in their champagne at the notion of parliamentary democracy. The entire manoeuvre was agreed months before Arthur Balfour had even announced to his other colleagues that he was resigning. He did so in December 1905, and the king immediately invited Campbell-Bannerman to introduce his Liberal Government. Hey presto! Grey, Asquith and Haldane were appointed to the three senior Cabinet posts exactly as planned. The Secret Elite had all the king's men in place.

The Liberal Party had been invited to form a government in December 1905 without facing the electorate, but a general election was called in the New Year. Members went back to their constituencies to campaign, but the Relugas Three did not sit on their hands waiting for the result. Invigorated by the threats that stemmed from the confrontation with Germany over Morocco, they hit the ground running.

In the throes of the general election, and before the matter had been discussed with the prime minister, let alone the Cabinet, Grey and Haldane gave permission for joint Anglo-French naval and military planning for war against Germany to continue. During the previous government, the Committee of Imperial Defence, itself an organ of the Secret Elite, had established a permanent sub-committee to prepare schemes for combined naval and military operations.[29] Under the auspices of this top-secret committee, Lord Lansdowne had approved 'military conversations' with France for a possible immediate war against Germany. The French ambassador, Cambon, was deeply concerned that the Liberal government, which stood on an anti-war platform, might not maintain Lansdowne's commitment because Sir Edward Grey had not acknowledged it. There was a sense of panic in the Quai d'Orsay. Would Britain continue her support and stay true to all that had been promised to Delcassé? Advised of this by the *Times* war correspondent Charles Repington, Grey asked him to reassure the French that: 'I have not receded from anything Lord Lansdowne has said, and have no hesitation in confirming it'.[30] Armed with this reassurance, Repington dined with General Grierson, director of military operations and member of the Committee of Imperial Defence, who stated that Britain could put two divisions into Namur in Belgium within 13 days.[31]

Who was this journalist, Repington? Why was a war correspondent for *The Times* actively involved in the deepest secrets of British foreign policy? Eton old boy and ex-army officer, Repington had been dismissed for dishonourable conduct with a brother officer's wife. He was later employed at *The Times* by George E. Buckle, a close associate of Milner and the Secret Elite.[32] Professor Quigley demonstrated that *The Times* was their published voice and had been controlled by them since the 1890s.[33] What now became evident was that *The Times*, through its war correspondent, was directly involved in the secret machinations of the Foreign Office. How could a journalist know more about top-secret British commitments to France than the incoming prime minister?

With the final results of the general election still unannounced, General Grierson wrote to Brussels advising the Belgian chief of staff that the British government was prepared to put '4 cavalry brigades, 2 army corps and a division of mounted infantry' into Belgium, with the explicit intention of stopping a German advance.[34]

Plans to move British troops into Belgium? What exactly was going on? From 1905 onwards, Britain's military link with Belgium was one of the most tightly guarded secrets, even within privileged circles. General Grierson, who was director of military operations and a member of the

Committee of Imperial Defence, was present with Lord Roberts, Admiral Fisher, Prime Minister Arthur Balfour and the director of Naval Intelligence, Captain Charles Ottley, at the CID meeting on 26 July 1905. They agreed to treat the special sub-committee that would take forward joint planning with French and Belgian military personnel as so secret that minutes would not be printed or circulated without special permission from the prime minister.[35] They discussed the legal status of Belgian neutrality. A secret memorandum of 1 August 1905 included Gladstone's opinion that the 1839 Treaty of London (which recognised the neutrality and independence of Belgium), was not binding but added that British interests were 'now more than ever' opposed to the violation of Belgian neutrality.[36] The crucial point that the Treaty of London was not binding would be conveniently dropped in August 1914.

Grierson was tasked to drive forward the links with France and Belgium. On 16 January 1906, he opened official military 'conversations' with Major Victor Huguet in France, and on the same day wrote to Lieutenant Colonel Barnardiston, the British Military Attaché in Brussels, advising him that a British Force of 105,000 would be sent to Belgium if a war broke out between France and Germany.[37]

Documents found in Belgian secret archives by the Germans after they had occupied Brussels disclosed that the chief of the Belgian general staff, Major-General Ducarne, held a series of meetings with the British military attaché over the action to be taken by the British, French and Belgian armies against Germany in the event of war. A fully elaborated plan detailed the landings and transportation of the British forces, which were actually called 'allied armies', and in a series of meetings they discussed the allocation of Belgian officers and interpreters to the British Army and crucial details on the care and 'accommodation of the wounded of the allied armies'.[38] Grierson was kept fully informed and approved the joint agreements, but the documents show that confidentiality was stressed repeatedly, and above all the necessity of keeping the conversations secret from the press was explicitly spelled out.[39] Some observers have claimed that the Belgian government went no further than these preliminary talks because they were afraid that they might offend Germany and France,[40] but this flies in the face of other secret diplomatic revelations.

Historically, Anglo-Belgian ties ran deep. Queen Victoria was a favourite cousin of Leopold II, King of the Belgians, and Edward VII understood best how to close the deal between Britain and Belgium through him. The British government later cemented the relationship by allowing Belgium to annex that area of Africa called the Congo Free State. The quid pro quo was a secret agreement that was in everything but name an alliance. King

Where did European royalty come from? They are all cousins,

Leopold II sold Belgian neutrality for African rubber and minerals, and Britain acknowledged the annexation of the Congo in return for military cooperation that continued in absolute secrecy from that point forward. Thus Belgium bargained away her status as a perpetually neutral country by entering into a military compact with Britain.[41] The huge significance of this may not be immediately apparent but will become so when Sir Edward Grey's fateful speech of 3 August 1914 is thoroughly analysed.

In those dark January days, with the Moroccan crisis still unresolved, the Secret Elite intrigue drew Sir Edward Grey from his election meetings in Norfolk back to London for an urgent briefing from Lord Esher and Sir George Clarke,[42] a former Governor of Victoria who had become the first secretary of the Committee of Imperial Defence. Grey was 'well pleased' to learn that the armed forces had begun to coordinate planning for joint operations against Germany.[43] He wrote to Haldane on 8 January to advise him that war could be imminent and that he had been reassured by Admiral Fisher that the navy was so ready that it could 'drive the German fleet off the sea and into shelter at any time'.[44] The inference was that Haldane, as minister of war, should be equally prepared.

They met at Berwick on 12 January, where a momentous decision was taken. Haldane told Grey to inform the French that military communications should proceed directly and officially between General Grierson and the French Military Attaché.[45] They thus gave permission for a senior military director to coordinate planning with his French counterpart for war, without the knowledge or approval of the prime minister, the Cabinet, Parliament or the British people. From whom did their authority stem? No two men would dare commit Britain to such action unless they had the assured backing of an immensely powerful force. And they did. Haldane knew that Esher and the Committee of Imperial Defence approved of these moves. The king would certainly have been informed by Lord Esher. This was clearly driven by the Secret Elite.

At the same time as these ongoing machinations, the Liberal Party was vigorously campaigning across the country on a promise of 'Peace, Retrenchment and Reform'. Campbell-Bannerman began the campaign with a rousing rally in the Albert Hall, where he denounced war and promised that the Liberal foreign policy would be 'opposed to aggression and to adventure, animated by a desire to be on the best terms with all nationalities and to cooperate with them in the common work of civilisation'.[46] He added: 'We are fighting against those powers, privileges, injustices and monopolies which are unalterably opposed to the triumph of democratic principles.' These prescient words were further expanded into a vision for his government:

> It is vain to seek peace if you do not also ensure it. The growth of armaments is a great danger to the peace of the world. What nobler role could this great country assume than at this fitting moment to place itself at the head of the League of Peace?[47]

On such a promise, Campbell-Bannerman led his party to a landslide victory in 1906.

These were two irreconcilable positions. Campbell-Bannerman and his government were committed to peace, while Grey and Haldane had set the country on a course for war. Precedent dictated that agreement should be sought from the prime minister and the Cabinet, but this never happened. How did they manage to pull off one of the most devious deceptions in Parliamentary history? No official records survive to confirm what precisely happened, and the conspirators themselves sowed the seeds of confusion. Haldane claimed in his 'notoriously unreliable'[48] autobiography that he dramatically abandoned his election campaign over the weekend of 13–14 January to travel to London to advise Campbell-Bannerman of what had been agreed with the French and seek his approval.[49]

According to Haldane: 'He at once saw the point, and he gave me authority for directing the staff at the War Office to take the necessary steps.'[50] Charles Repington confirmed that Haldane told him that Campbell-Bannerman 'was very firm and clear on the point that we should be prepared for all emergencies and that conversations between the two staffs were permissible . . .'[51] This cannot be true. Campbell-Bannerman was not in London that weekend. He remained in Scotland throughout the elections and did not travel south to London until the night of the 26th. Drafts of various notes were allegedly copied to Campbell-Bannerman, but there is no evidence to support assertions that they were ever cleared with him.[52] Furthermore, Haldane later claimed: 'I saw Colonel Huguet [the French Attaché] and authorised him, Sir Neville Lyttelton and General Grierson to study together' plans for joint action against Germany.[53] If Haldane's recollection of these events, written privately in 1916, is accurate, the British secretary of state for war personally met with the French attaché and authorised plans that would have seen British troops rushed to Belgium in 1906. But at the time, and in the years that preceded the First World War, questions raised in Parliament about the British government's commitment to France were repeatedly answered with a reassurance that there were no such commitments.

Grey agreed with Esher that the prime minister should 'for the time being' be kept in the dark about military contacts.[54] On 9 January, he wrote to both Campbell-Bannerman at his home in Scotland and Lord Ripon,

Liberal leader of the House of Lords, to inform them that he had promised the French diplomatic support but no more.[55] Several days later, the prime minister received a note from his trusted Liberal colleague Lord Ripon, stating: 'Our engagements with France are, I understand, confined to a promise of full diplomatic support, and I have no doubt that the French government understand that we are bound to nothing beyond that.'[56] It is clear that Grey contacted both Campbell-Bannerman and Lord Ripon but was lying to them. The evidence proves that he and Haldane agreed to joint military preparations with France but told the prime minister that these were merely diplomatic conversations. It was a deliberate deception by Secret Elite placemen.

Arthur Ponsonby, Campbell-Bannerman's principal private secretary, knew nothing about the military talks. He was astounded by later claims made by Grey and Haldane that they had kept the prime minister fully informed. Ponsonby was adamant that 'C-B never apprehended the significance of conversations with France, nor did he see how we were being gradually committed.'[57] Had Campbell-Bannerman known what Grey and Haldane were up to, he would have confronted them. Given his staunch anti-war credentials, he would never have allowed Grey and Haldane to proceed.

In Grey's autobiography, he deliberately dissembled on the question of why the 'conversations' were never brought to the attention of the Cabinet, making out that the prime minister was ambivalent about when it might be discussed. He admitted that he 'ought to have asked for a Cabinet' meeting but could not remember why he failed to do so, claiming memory loss.[58] This is unbelievable. Just a few days later, the first Cabinet meeting of the new government passed without Haldane or Grey making mention of their cataclysmic decision. What seems even more incredible is that Campbell-Bannerman never raised the issue himself. Why? It is patently obvious that the wool had been pulled over his eyes. Numerous documented instances will be presented in our narrative which prove that the Relugas Three repeatedly lied to the Cabinet and Parliament about the existence of military agreements with France. It is a perfectly reasonable assumption that they were lying in their memoirs in suggesting that Campbell-Bannerman was kept fully informed. The problem remains that there is no evidence other than that given by the conspirators themselves in cynically sterilised accounts written long after Campbell-Bannerman was dead. No one was then in a position to refute their claims.

And what of Asquith? Although he appeared to have played little part in this particular aspect of the conspiracy, he had been kept fully informed, according to Haldane.[59] Asquith had never openly undermined Campbell-

Bannerman, who trusted him both as a political ally and a friend, but there can be no doubt about his treachery towards the ageing prime minister. The Relugas Three were constantly in cahoots, and Asquith operated as a buffer between them and Campbell-Bannerman, keeping his focus on domestic matters. Asquith's only contribution to the debate was denial.

Summary: Chapter 6 – The Changing of the Guard

- British politics was dominated by half a dozen families from the ruling elite. They tended to inter-marry, but fresh blood was recruited predominantly from Balliol and New College, Oxford.
- Faced with an imminent change of government, Asquith, Haldane and Grey were selected in order to ensure a seamless foreign policy. Each was closely associated with members of the Secret Elite and all were close to and admirers of Alfred Milner, with whom they were in regular contact.
- The three met at Relugas in September 1905, where they conspired to usurp the Liberal Party leader Campbell-Bannerman.
- Haldane confirmed their conspiracy with King Edward at Balmoral, in the company of Arthur Balfour and Lord Lansdowne, their political opponents.
- The king stressed the importance of their taking office in the new government even if Campbell-Bannerman refused to go to the Lords.
- Towards the end of the Conservative government, Balfour and Lansdowne created a secret sub-committee of the Committee of Imperial Defence, which began secret military 'conversations' with France and Belgium over the actions to be jointly taken in a war with Germany.
- The commitments made by Belgium and secretly continued thereafter nullified her status of neutrality.
- On taking office, Haldane and Grey approved the continuation of these secret agreements without first getting approval from the prime minister. They later claimed that he was informed, but there is no reliable evidence to confirm exactly what was said.
- They deliberately kept all knowledge of this from the Liberal Cabinet, because it was a step to war with Germany.

CHAPTER 7

1906 – Landslide to Continuity

The Liberal Party won the 1906 general election with a resounding victory. Having taken only 183 seats in 1900, they emerged with 397 Members of Parliament. The public had spoken. It was an overwhelming endorsement of 'Peace and Retrenchment'. The country was poised for reform. Former prime minister Arthur Balfour lost his Manchester seat but was quickly found another in the City of London. As leader of the opposition, he protected Asquith, Grey and Haldane from attacks by the Conservatives in matters of foreign policy.

Campbell-Bannerman's first Cabinet brought a very vocal and popular Liberal into Government, David Lloyd George. This young Welsh firebrand clearly stood out as a parliamentarian of considerable potential. So too did Winston Churchill, who had crossed from the Conservative Party two years before and been re-elected as a Liberal. Here was a Parliament bristling with new faces, keen to bring much-needed reform to Britain, yet even before the oath of office had been taken, the internal arrangements devised through King Edward, Lord Esher, Balfour, Haldane, Grey and Asquith ensured that foreign policy remained the preserve of the Secret Elite. Lloyd George reflected later that during the eight years that preceded the war, the Cabinet devoted a 'ridiculously small' percentage of its time to foreign affairs.[1]

Anti-imperialists in the eighteen-strong Liberal Cabinet comprised Campbell-Bannerman himself, Lloyd George and at least five other radicals. It may legitimately be asked how the Relugas clique could proceed with such a complex war conspiracy when faced with an anti-war prime minister and Cabinet. The straightforward answer is that they kept everyone else completely in the dark about their activities. Although Cabinet members and backbenchers frequently questioned foreign policy, Grey and Haldane repeatedly lied to them. It would be many years before the other Cabinet members learned of the dangerous military compact that had been secretly rubber-stamped.

Campbell-Bannerman left the all-important foreign policy to Sir Edward Grey, concentrating instead on issues such as Irish Home Rule and the alleviation of poverty. He was highly popular in the country at large but endured the double-whammy of having his authority undermined by the Relugas Three and suffering a personal tragedy. Shortly after Campbell-Bannerman became prime minister, his wife and inseparable companion, Lady Charlotte, took ill and died. It was an inestimable blow. Campbell-Bannerman's mental anguish unnerved him. The love and affection that had bound the couple together tortured him in his loss. Drained by the demands of office and his personal agonies, he cut a sad and lonely figure. The Irish MP T.P. O'Connor wrote of him:

> The Prime Minister, in 10 Downing Street, was less happy than the cottager that tramps home to his cabin . . . He was visibly perishing, looked terribly old, and some days almost seemed to be dying himself; and there was little doubt in the mind of anybody who watched him that if the double strain were prolonged, he would either die or resign.[2]

Campbell-Bannerman was a broken man, and the Relugas Three in the top Cabinet posts of Foreign Office, Exchequer and War Office pursued their cause without interference. One measure of how successfully they functioned was Lloyd George's revelation that every aspect of Britain's relations with France, Russia and Germany was met with an air of 'hush-hush'. He possibly did not realise how accurately he summed up Grey's dictatorial control of foreign policy in Cabinet when he confessed that he was made to feel that he had no right to ask questions 'since this was the reserve of the elect'.[3] How right he was. The information given to Cabinet was carefully filtered, and facts that would have enabled sound judgement were deliberately withheld.

Sir Edward Grey retained a tight personal grip on foreign policy within the Cabinet, but he never wielded real power inside the Foreign Office. Grey was the figurehead behind which the real power operated. The Secret Elite placed him in the Foreign Office not for his capabilities or knowledge of foreign affairs but because he was loyal and did as they advised. Grey was never Campbell-Bannerman's choice for foreign secretary. At least four other major politicians had better credentials, but Campbell-Bannerman had effectively been given little choice in the appointment. The Relugas Three came as a package.

Grey was a staunch imperialist on the extreme right wing of the Liberal Party and possessed no conspicuous intellectual talents.[4] He had idled his way through Balliol College, from where he was sent down for his indolence before being awarded an inglorious third-class degree. His outlook was utterly parochial. Northumberland was the centre of Edward Grey's world, and he knew more about its rivers and streams than the business of running an empire. His lack of interest in politics at university was clear to all, yet he became an MP at the age of 23. Although his family connections secured him a ministerial post as under-secretary at the Foreign Office from 1892 to 1895, his inept performance almost led to conflict with France. On leaving, he wrote in his diary: 'I shall never be in office again and the days of my stay in the House of Commons are probably numbered.'[5] A legion of observers would now add, if only . . .

Paradoxically, in the years when Britain was increasingly committed to a continental policy, her affairs were directed by 'one who seldom travelled outside the British Isles, and who had little first-hand knowledge of Europe and spoke no French'.[6] His very appointment was a paradox. Grey was unpardonably rude to Campbell-Bannerman, telling him point-blank that 'unless he took a peerage and transferred his leadership from the Commons to the Lords . . . he [Grey] would not take any part in the Government'.[7] Grey did not want to serve under a man whose contempt for Alfred Milner he resented and with whose espoused pacifism he was completely at odds, but the Secret Elite insisted. Grey's points of reference came not from Cabinet debate or House of Commons motions, nor from his own independent judgement, but from Grillion's and The Club, and from weekend collusion with the Milner Group in select stately homes. Is it conceivable that one man, one modestly educated man who, despite all of his advantages, never crossed the sea until 1914, nor spoke any foreign language, had the capacity to single-handedly control the foreign policy of the Empire? And control it so well that his judgement was held in great esteem?

No. Grey was surrounded in the Foreign Office by seasoned permanent secretaries like Sir Charles Hardinge and Sir Arthur Nicolson, who were proven Establishment men and associated with the Secret Elite. Hardinge was one of the most significant figures in the formation of British foreign policy in the early twentieth century. As a close confidant of King Edward, he travelled widely with him and played an important role in both the entente and the understanding with Russia.[8] Sir Arthur Nicolson, later Lord Carnock, who played a similar role in guiding Grey in the Foreign Office, was always at the centre at critical moments in Morocco, St Petersburg and eventually as permanent secretary in London. They controlled Britain's diplomatic reach across the world, while Grey fronted and deflected questions in Parliament.

Grey's presumed gravitas, his 'magisterial airs', as Lloyd George bitterly described them, his advantage in society, his 'correctitude of phrase and demeanour which passes for diplomacy'[9] invested in him a sense of the untouchable. He seemed to be above reproach. He appeared to know what other mortals did not know. It was rarely his place to have to explain himself to Parliament. He did not consider himself answerable to the large radical wing of the Liberal Party. In truth, as Niall Ferguson observed: 'There was more agreement between Grey and the opposition front bench than within the Cabinet itself, to say nothing of the Liberal Party as a whole.'[10] His contemporaries found him daunting, aloof and all too prepared to keep his own counsel. Grey did not argue his case but gave a judgement to which even Cabinet ministers felt there was no appeal, and few ever made one.[11] On the odd occasion that his policy was questioned, he would 'twist and turn' at each set of objections, voicing dire consequences for the nation's security or threatening resignation if crossed. With no strong centre of opposition to him within the Liberal Party, Grey had little problem operating above Cabinet scrutiny.

He had none of Haldane's brilliance, Asquith's capabilities or Lloyd George's eloquence, but he had credibility built on a myth. Promoted by a supportive right-wing press, Sir Edward Grey was above reproach. The industrial magnate Sir Hugh Bell, who worked for a time with Grey on the running of the North Eastern Railway, said: 'Grey is a good colleague because he never takes any risks; and he is a thoroughly bad colleague for the same reason.'[12]

Such a description hardly resonates with that of a key decision maker in charge of the most prestigious department of government in the British Empire. The Foreign Office was the hub of the imperial spider's web, linked through diplomatic and commercial channels to every part of the globe. Its incumbents plotted and planned ceaselessly for the 'good' of the Empire and the benefit of the Secret Elite. Grey was the perfect figurehead, but it was Hardinge and Nicolson who turned Secret Elite policy into practice.

In the War Office, Richard Haldane required no minders. He had the vigour, determination and intellect to tackle the mammoth task of reorganising a military set-up that was soaked in historic tradition and riddled with vested interest. The British Army still offered commissions to the sons of the noble and wealthy. Rank and its privilege were available at a price. Haldane approached his new job in the confident knowledge that he had the complete backing of King Edward, Lord Esher[13] and Alfred Milner. He told the House of Commons on 12 July 1906 that he intended to remould the army 'in such a fashion that it shall be an army shaped for the only purpose for which an army is needed . . . for the purpose of war'.[14] His main problem came not from the Army Council but from within his own party, burning with a zeal for social reform. Haldane knew he had to cut army expenditure to win the support of his own MPs and at the same time find the resources to invest in a different kind of fighting force.

He did this by dismantling coastal defence batteries with obsolete guns, closing a number of forts around London, reducing artillery and systematically reviewing all the constituent parts of the army with one question in mind: 'What is your function in war?'[15] Where Haldane did run into objections from traditionalists over the changing role of the militia and volunteers, he was able to call on support from King Edward, who summoned a conference of lords lieutenant from every shire and county of the British Isles to make clear his expectation that Haldane's reforms would have their active endorsement. The Secret Elite could not have made their aim clearer. They would have a modern army fit for the coming war.

Reforms included the creation of a general staff and, most crucially, the concept of an expeditionary force. Haldane had faith in the premise that the fleet would defend Britain's coast while the first purpose of the army was for overseas war. He built a dedicated expeditionary force of one cavalry and six regular divisions, which comprised 5,546 officers and 154,074 men. Haldane introduced an imperial general staff, including the military leaders from Britain's overseas dominions, and promoted officer-training corps in universities and public schools, which marginally extended opportunities to lead from the aristocracy to the wealthy upper-middle classes.

Few would have expected such an achievement in barely two years, but Haldane's extraordinary success was backed by the most powerful of Secret Elite allies, including the monarchy, senior military officers and *The Times*. He also gained the parliamentary support of a Liberal Party that had no understanding of his real purpose. Their minds were focused on the millions he cut from unnecessary spending.

One of the lessons Haldane learned was that a great deal of future coordination would be required to get the expeditionary force mobilised and transported to France in good time. When he took office, Sir Edward Grey informed the British ambassador to Paris, Sir Francis Bertie, that it would take two months to mobilise 80,000 men.[16] The French were mightily under-impressed. Prime Minister Clemenceau visited Britain in April 1907 and tried to persuade Haldane and Asquith to introduce conscription and create a great army that would 'take the field' along with France against Germany.[17] This French agitation was met with polite refusal. However, two points are worth noting. First, at the highest level of parliamentary government both countries discussed war against Germany. Second, Clemenceau must have been very badly briefed if he imagined that the

Liberal Party would for a moment contemplate compulsory military service. But the conversations continued apace.

Haldane's biggest problem lay with the Senior Service, as the Royal Navy styled itself. Preparation for an expeditionary force required joint naval and military planning, but the navy did not take kindly to the idea of providing a ferry service for the army or playing a subordinate role to it. It had, after all, been for centuries the most formidable naval fighting force in the world and at the forefront of British empire-building. Haldane quickly realised that there was no semblance of cooperation, or even understanding, between the Admiralty and the War Office. The past experience of wartime cooperation between the army and the navy was one long record of virtually unbroken misunderstandings and failure, mistrust and blame. In an attempt to bridge the gulf, Haldane used the Committee of Imperial Defence to promote the concept of a naval war staff. Sir Charles Ottley, then secretary of the Committee of Imperial Defence, wrote to him in some exasperation: 'Not one naval officer out of fifty has any knowledge of what the British Fleet will have to do in a war, or how it will do it.'[18]

The navy had a great and historic tradition, but the Secret Elite needed to ensure control from the inside, in the same way as they had with the army. Haldane did all he could to instigate change from the War Office, but knew in his heart that the navy could only be properly reformed from within the Admiralty. The man to whom they looked for help was Admiral Sir John (Jacky) Fisher, but the first sea lord was a man who had been allowed to plough his own passage and dictate his own policy. Fisher was ill disposed to tolerate any military, or worse, French interference. He was perfectly agreeable to the Secret Elite's coming war but did not believe in an expeditionary force being sent to Belgium. His preference was a joint naval and military attack on Schleswig-Holstein at the northernmost tip of Germany. It was a venture dismissed by both the British and French general staffs as impractical.[19]

The son of an army officer serving in India, Fisher had joined the navy as a 13 year old in 1854 and quickly rose through the officer ranks. In the early 1880s, when his duties as captain of HMS *Inflexible* brought him into close contact with the royal family, Prince Albert Edward befriended him.[20] Fisher contracted malaria in 1883 and during his recuperation Queen Victoria invited the dashing captain to stay with her at Osborne House for a fortnight.[21] Five years later, on his promotion to Rear Admiral, the queen appointed him her aide-de-camp. Thereafter, she knighted him in her birthday honours of 1894. Like Richard Haldane, Jacky Fisher did not belong to the Establishment. He boasted: 'I entered the navy penniless, friendless and forlorn. I had to fight like hell, and fighting like hell has made me what I am.'[22] He had progressed through the ranks and by the fates of fortune had been drawn into the elite circles surrounding the monarchy. Like Haldane, he was an able man. Both were tasked with bringing the country's armed services into the twentieth century. In October 1904, Fisher had breakfast with his good friend King Edward at Buckingham Palace and thereafter was sworn in as first sea lord. Both the army and the Royal Navy were, at that point, in the hands of loyal servants of the Secret Elite.

While friends in high places were undoubtedly a factor in elevating Fisher to the navy's top job, he was a man of vision who didn't hesitate to instigate revolutionary reforms that made the Royal Navy more effective for the job in hand. He valued ships for their fighting worth, and in 1904, with the German navy still in its infancy, he began a 'Ruthless, Relentless, and Remorseless' reorganisation of the British fleet. The navy was purged of 160 ships that, in his own words, could 'neither fight nor run away' and Fisher replaced them with fast, modern vessels ready 'for instant war'.[23]

The twentieth century heralded many advances in technology, and where this meant improvement and a better and more effective navy, Fisher never hesitated. He improved the range, accuracy and firing rate of naval gunnery, introduced torpedo boats and submarines to the fleet and, as first sea lord, was responsible for the building of the first huge dreadnought battleships. Of all Fisher's innovations, however, the most crucial was the introduction of oil to replace coal-fired boilers. Despite old-school admirals labelling him an eccentric dreamer, he insisted that fuelling the navy with oil would give Britain huge strategic advantages. There would be no telltale smoke to alert enemy vessels, and while nine hours might be required for a coal-fired ship to reach peak power, it would take only minutes with oil. Twelve men working a twelve-hour shift could fuel a vessel with oil, while the equivalent energy for a coal-fired ship required the work of five hundred stokers for five days. Crucially, the radius of action of an oil-powered vessel was up to four times as great as coal.[24]

Fisher got his way, but not without a tense and often bitter struggle with the Liberals and socialists in Parliament, who deemed the vast expenditure on new developments in naval warfare costly and wasteful.

Fisher's task of changing the framework of command within the navy was particularly challenging. By 1900, a naval officer would have found little difference in his career structure from the time of Nelson. Despite early reforms in 1902, and Fisher's long crusade to widen and democratise recruitment, the naval high command, like that of the army, remained the narrow preserve of the upper classes. Promotion was bound rigidly by the rules of seniority and class. As the *Naval and Military Review* later stated:

> The British Navy has long obtained an ample supply of capable officers . . . without recruiting from the Democracy to any visible extent . . . We should view with grave apprehension any attempt to officer the fleet at all largely with men of humble births.[25]

Such ingrained prejudice hampered Fisher in his reforms, and he would not have survived without the support on which he was able to call.

Although he did a sterling job in improving the navy, Fisher presented Haldane and the Committee of Imperial Defence with problems. He was a stubborn autocrat with a huge ego. He knew it all. No committee would be telling him what to do with his navy. If Germany was to be taken out, it was a job for him and his beloved ships.

On 12 April 1905, with the Moroccan crisis threatening to boil over into war, the first sea lord and Lord Lansdowne attended a meeting of the Committee of Imperial Defence, after which Fisher intimated to the foreign secretary that the dispute was a 'golden opportunity'[26] to bring forward war with Germany. Ever the war-hawk, Fisher confidently predicted that 'we could have the German fleet, the Kiel canal, and Schleswig-Holstein within a fortnight'.[27] Little wonder that Delcassé was able to claim in July 1905 that, if it came to war, the British fleet would be mobilised, seize the Kiel canal and land 100,000 men in Schleswig-Holstein. Fisher's ambitious plan to use the navy in a pre-emptive strike against Germany had clearly been shared with Delcassé, who told the French press. No matter how often it was denied by the British government, this caused great alarm in Germany.

Fisher strongly believed that Britain depended upon naval supremacy above all else, and that the army should be a subsidiary force. He called into question the huge budget allocated to the land forces and never tired of reiterating Sir Edward Grey's 'splendid words' that the British Army was simply a projectile to be fired by the navy. Fisher worked hard to influence the Committee of Imperial Defence and demanded that every plan for offensive hostilities against Germany should be subsidiary to the actions of the fleet. He was reluctant to discuss naval cooperation with the French, whom he distrusted, and kept even his most senior fellow officers in the dark. He did not believe in the plan for a military expeditionary force going to France. His preference was the Schleswig-Holstein option in conjunction with a close naval blockade to starve Germany into submission. His ideas were dismissed by an ever-growing number of the Committee of Imperial Defence, and some senior figures in the navy, but Fisher's option for a close naval blockade warranted much more consideration than it was given.

Despite the electoral promise of 'Peace and Retrenchment', Campbell-Bannerman's ideals were successfully thwarted. The first two years of the

Liberal government saw steady progress in building the foundations for war, though no one outside the Secret Elite's circles understood their true purpose. In January 1908, Campbell-Bannerman, who had suffered three heart attacks, fell terminally ill. The king 'really did wish to say goodbye to his Prime Minister',[28] but such an inconvenience would have interrupted his holiday in Biarritz, and he had no wish to return to fog-bound London. Sir Henry Campbell-Bannerman died in 10 Downing Street on Wednesday, 22 April. In an act of symbolic irony, Asquith was obliged to take the train to the South of France to kiss the royal hand before his appointment. King Edward was reportedly 'far too ill' to travel back to London for such a mere formality.[29] More likely he had no intention of interrupting his holiday just to appoint Asquith.[30] It remains the only instance in which a British prime minister has formally taken office on foreign soil.

There was much for Asquith to consider as he put the finishing touches to his government. The Secret Elite kept in close contact. Days before Asquith's formal visit to Biarritz, Lord Esher was able to note in his diaries that Lloyd George would become chancellor and Winston Churchill, president of the Board of Trade.[31] Asquith wrote from Biarritz to offer them those precise positions, so it is safe to assume that this was all approved by the Secret Elite beforehand. Some in the Liberal Party considered both men a danger, but this Cabinet needed to be balanced. Lloyd George had a large following on the backbenches and was popular with the working classes. Churchill had no such following but was energetic and single-minded. Asquith commented that 'Lloyd George has no principles and Winston no convictions'.[32] They appeared an extremely unlikely pairing. Winston Churchill came from the aristocracy and fully accepted class distinction as part of the British way of life. Lloyd George came from the opposite end of the social spectrum and was consumed at times by class-consciousness. Yet in the years that led to the First World War, they worked together in a formidable partnership.

Winston Churchill was an enigma for many in the inner circle of the Secret Elite. They all knew him and he knew all of them. Winston's family connections allowed him access to Arthur Balfour, Herbert Asquith, Lord Rosebery and Lord Rothschild, to mention but a few. His association with Alfred Milner dated back to South Africa, where he declared himself a great admirer of Milner's 'genius'.[33] By birth and connection, by education and politics, by instinct and breeding he had all of the necessary prerequisites. Churchill had, however, one fatal flaw, one characteristic that kept him at arm's length from the highest level of influence. He had an unstoppable capacity to be maverick. He had a need to see himself, and be seen by others, as the central player. He was useful as an agent to energetically promote big ideals, but his enthusiasms could not be fully controlled. His urge to portray himself as the government's action-man was at times laughable, but Churchill was an important political actor whom the Secret Elite influenced throughout his career.

Churchill was the product of a marriage of convenience. His father, Lord Randolph Churchill, son of the seventh Duke of Marlborough, was a spoiled playboy who wandered into Conservative politics, gambled and frolicked in the entourage of the Prince of Wales and died aged 46 from syphilis. His debts to Lord Nathaniel Rothschild would be calculated in millions of pounds in today's money. Randolph's wife, Jennie Jerome, was the daughter of an ambitious wealthy American businessman who paid a substantial sum to secure the marriage.[34] She gave birth to Winston in 1874, some seven and a half months after their wedding in Paris. Jennie had little time for motherhood, and Winston was abandoned to his nanny. He was kept at some distance from his parents and lacked maternal love and paternal interest. But what did that matter when surrounded by all of the advantages of privilege?

David George had no such advantage. Born in Manchester in 1863, his father William, a schoolteacher, died when David was one year old. He was sent to live with his uncle, Richard Lloyd, who gave him a nonconformist education and a new name, Lloyd George. Self-motivated and ambitious, he wrote, ungallantly, to Margaret Owen, later his wife: 'my supreme idea is to get on . . . I am prepared to thrust even love itself under the wheels of my juggernaut, if it obstructs the way'.[35]

Lloyd George was a gifted orator, though the Establishment saw him as a 'rabble-rouser'. He was elected to Parliament as Liberal MP for Caernarfon Boroughs in 1890 and became an outspoken critic of the Boer War. He saw it as 'an outrage perpetrated in the name of human freedom'.[36] While the war in South Africa was staunchly supported by Asquith, Grey and Haldane, Lloyd George stayed true to his core belief that it was an expensive waste, conducted in a blundering and cruel fashion.

Parliamentary exchanges between Churchill and Lloyd George after 1900 revealed some common ground, and a friendship of sorts developed into evening dinners and serious discussions about policy and government. By 1904, Churchill had decided to switch allegiance and abandon the Conservatives. The reason he gave was ostensibly the issue of Joseph Chamberlain's conversion to a new scheme of tariffs and imperial preference. Detractors believed that Churchill abandoned the party because it was about to lose the next election and he had little or no hope of attaining office, and certainly not high office.

There is another possibility. Was Churchill asked by the Secret Elite to defect to the Liberals in order to bring Lloyd George into their sphere of direct influence? While this might seem an outrageous question, later developments lend it credence.

Lloyd George had qualities that the Secret Elite could use: leadership, sharp and acerbic wit and popularity with the masses. He addressed colossal audiences, had no fears in parliamentary debate, cared passionately about social reform and had credibility in the public arena that was unsurpassed in its time. He was ambitious, relatively poor, had no additional sources of income, no benefactors or any likelihood of finding any in the capitalist bear-pit he railed against. His enemies were the wealthy, the aristocracy, the privileged, the warmongers and, of course, the House of Lords. He was a man of the people, but, as Asquith had said, he was not necessarily a man of principle. From the day he took office in Asquith's 1908 government as chancellor of the Exchequer, no one expected anything other than the Liberal government's absolute opposition to war, opposition to massive spending on the machines of war, opposition to the naval race and opposition to exorbitant wealth . . . all the core values that made Lloyd George the champion of Liberal radicalism. No one, that is, except the Secret Elite, who were preparing the ground to make him *their* man.

Although Churchill and Lloyd George were friends, they were also rivals. Both intended to be prime minister. They had a tendency to rile other Cabinet ministers, even Richard Haldane, when they started to demand cuts in military expenditure.[37] In their early years in government, Lloyd George labelled Haldane 'Minister of Slaughter'. Their crusade against the vast spending on the navy in particular brought them into conflict with Grey and Haldane, which caused initial discomfort. They were, in 1908, the 'younger generation knocking at the door',[38] and the Secret Elite monitored their progress with interest.

Summary: Chapter 7 – 1906 – Landslide to Continuity

- The 1906 Liberal landslide victory promised radical reform but brought no change in foreign policy.
- Grey continued the grand design for war with Germany and was cocooned in the Foreign Office with seasoned permanent under-secretaries who were part of the Secret Elite.
- A close examination of the list of politicians, diplomats and newspapermen who knew about the secret military 'conversations' provides a snapshot of key members of the Secret Elite in 1906.
- Haldane's reforms of the War Office had the full backing of King Edward and the Committee of Imperial Defence.
- He transformed the organisation of the British Army, but the navy

remained stuck in centuries-old tradition.

- Admiral Sir John Fisher introduced oil-driven warships and radically modernised the fleet.
- Fisher, however, believed in naval supremacy and that the army should play a subsidiary role. He would not budge from his stubborn belief that the German fleet should be 'Copenhagened' and that the Royal Navy should attack Germany in a pre-emptive strike. The CID resolutely refused to accept his plans.
- Campbell-Bannerman's death in 1908 gave the Relugas Three unfettered control of the government.
- The Secret Elite knew and approved the Cabinet reshuffle before it was confirmed to the ministers themselves.
- Two very different politicians, Churchill and Lloyd George, were given Cabinet posts from where their worth to the Secret Elite could be evaluated.

CHAPTER 8

Alexander Isvolsky – Hero and Villain

ALTHOUGH PREPARATIONS FOR THE LONDON Olympic Games and introduction of a bill to introduce an old-age pension proved a welcome distraction in 1908, try as he might the new prime minister could not avoid the prickly issue of Russia. Following the signing of the Anglo-Russian Convention the previous year, plans were set for what was billed as a family visit between King Edward VII and Czar Nicholas at Reval (now Talinn in Estonia) but was in fact the next step in the Secret Elite plan. The visit upset many sections of British society, who objected strenuously to any association with czarist Russia and its repressive regime. Asquith had barely taken office before he was being asked questions in Parliament that should have seriously embarrassed a Liberal prime minister. How could the king go to Russia when 100 members of the first Duma (Parliament) and 50 members of the second had been sent to Siberia or were held in prisons like common criminals, pending trials that might never take place? And what of the official and unofficial murders that still continued while the perpetrators went unchecked?[1] In the first two years of so-called 'constitutional reforms', 1,780 people had been executed and 15,557 imprisoned.[2] British trade unions, the Labour Party, churchmen and Asquith's own Liberal Party were united in their disgust at the vicious suppression of Russia's early attempts at democracy, but to no avail. What had Milner urged? 'Disregard the screamers.'

The new prime minister curtly reminded members of Parliament that it was not their business to make allegations about the internal conditions and policy of a foreign nation. Grey lied in the Commons on 28 May when assuring MPs that 'no new convention or Treaty is under discussion, nor is it intended to initiate any negotiations for one during the [king's] visit'.[3] Although Grey claimed that the visit was 'purely dictated by family affection' and without 'any suspicion of politics attached to it',[4] his own permanent under-secretary at the Foreign Office accompanied the king. The royal visit to Reval would lead to the realisation of a scheme that the

Secret Elite had devised years before: the encirclement of Germany.[5]

Protests in Parliament continued, but the Relugas Three did not buckle under pressure. When Asquith was asked if he was aware that the czar was to be accompanied by Pyotr Stolypin, his prime minister, and Isvolsky, his foreign secretary, while King Edward had no minister of the Crown with him, he feigned not to know the arrangements made by the Russian government.[6] It was unconstitutional for the king to discuss foreign affairs with other nations without the presence of a minister responsible to Parliament.[7] Rules? Regulations? Precedent? What did these matter to the Secret Elite in the pursuit of their great cause? They lied before the visit took place and lied after the entente was agreed.

Despite the moral, political and constitutional objections, the king and his entourage sailed off to the beautiful Estonian town that had never experienced such a profusion of royalty since Peter the Great captured it from Sweden some 200 years before. Both royal families, the Saxe-Coburgs and the Romanovs, were in full array, and the two days of talks were interspersed with banquets on board the royal yachts.

In the real world, protest continued but was studiously ignored. To the embarrassment of the Liberal government, the king was made an admiral of the 'young and growing fleet' that the Secret Elite were encouraging Russia to rebuild after the Tsushima disaster.[8] Massive profits were accrued by British and French bankers, and King Edward greased the path for his close friend, and Secret Elite financier, Sir Ernest Cassel, to be granted an interview with the czar. It was an abuse of his friendship, but the king had to repay his debts somehow.

One positive action stemmed from the meeting at Reval. King Edward responded to an appeal from the Rothschild brothers to speak to the czar about protection for Russian Jews under threat from brutal pogroms. He did, but little changed inside that anti-Semitic court.[9]

King Edward was accompanied by Admiral Jacky Fisher, the first sea lord, General Sir John French, inspector general of the army, and Sir Charles Hardinge, the Secret Elite's leading diplomat and the man who pulled the strings in the Foreign Office. The rabidly anti-German Admiral Fisher and Sir John French had discussed military and naval actions at the Committee of Imperial Defence in the presence of Asquith, Grey, Haldane and Lord Esher,[10] and the king's entourage was nothing more than a select sub-committee of that cabal. Fisher urged King Edward to support him in his plans to crush the German fleet before it could close the Baltic to the Royal Navy.[11]

On the bay off Reval on 9 June 1908, bathed in brilliant sunshine, the imperial and royal yachts, 'surrounded by British and Russian warships', set an impressive scene. Both czar and king spoke in English and emphasised the good relations that had replaced the coolness between the two countries in past years. After lunch, King Edward retired to his cabin with Premier Stolypin for 'a long private consultation'. As the *New York Times* reported the following day: 'nothing has been published'. Edward held private talks with the Russian prime minister, not his cousin the czar, on matters that have been kept secret. There was no official communiqué. Admiral Fisher and General French held private talks with Prime Minister Stolypin and Foreign Minister Isvolsky.[12] These too went unreported. Significantly, the Russians were known to be concerned about Germany's potential dominance of the Baltic, and Stolypin desperately wanted British support to 'prevent the Baltic becoming a German lake'.[13]

This was the trip that Edward Grey had assured deeply concerned MPs was 'purely dictated by family affection' and had no 'suspicion of politics attached to it'.

Reval was the final piece in a complex diplomatic strategy that started in Copenhagen with King Edward's loyal agent, then Russian ambassador to Denmark, Alexander Isvolsky. It was there in 1904 and 1905 that Isvolsky had, by his own account, long interviews with the king in which *they* settled the basis of the Anglo-Russian entente.[14] Shortly before the visit to Reval, the king and his entourage met secretly with Isvolsky in the Bohemian spa resort of Marienbad,[15] ostensibly to take the waters like tourists. Days later, Isvolsky moved on to Reval and was present there to greet the king on his arrival. He engaged in the public charade of being introduced to King Edward and his team as if for the first time.[16] When Stolypin met, first with the king and then with Fisher, French and Hardinge, he seems to have been unaware that Isvolsky had been at Marienbad or that their discussions had previously been rehearsed. Isvolsky, like his French counterpart, Delcassé, was truly King Edward's man.

Germany viewed this 'family gathering' with justified suspicion. What did the Anglo-Russian discussions really mean? Were they a cover for a secret alliance that would snare Germany between antagonistic nations? What were the unspoken subtexts? German newspapers declared that a mighty coalition had been formed against the Triple Alliance. It was a view shared by Belgian diplomats who recognised that King Edward had isolated the kaiser and that this new Triple Entente was 'united by a common hatred of Germany'.[17] All of which was repeatedly denied. Edward Grey claimed that Britain had simply removed any danger of a breach of peace 'either between us and France or us and Russia'. It was about 'friendship' and was not intended to 'isolate' Germany. Furthermore, Grey denied that Germany was isolated, as she had two great friends in the Triple Alliance: Austria and

Italy.[18] His shameless protestations polished a veneer of innocence over the Secret Elite triumph. Germany was now surrounded.

The czar made a reciprocal visit to Britain in 1909 in the company of Alexander Isvolsky. Public reaction was so heated that he dared not leave the safety of his yacht, *Standart*,[19] guarded as he was by two dreadnoughts and two hundred detectives.[20] He was mightily impressed when he reviewed the Northern Squadron of the British fleet off Spithead from the safety of his imperial yacht. One hundred and fifty-three combat ships were arranged in three parallel lines in a stunning show of naval power. The subtext was clear. Russia didn't yet have a fleet capable of defeating Germany, but her new friend, Britain, did.

What does it tell us about the extent to which the Secret Elite were prepared to go to isolate Germany? Public opinion mattered not. Liberal values were expendable. Human decency and democracy ignored. Their agents agreed the secret alliance and closed the net. The deed was done. All that now remained before war broke out was careful preparation and a suitable excuse.

Cue Alexander Isvolsky. The Russian was, first and foremost, the king's chosen man. He had been elevated from the relative obscurity of the Danish court in Copenhagen to the royal palaces of St Petersburg on Edward's personal recommendation. The Secret Elite controlled him, and their large bribes underwrote his lavish lifestyle. Isvolsky was central to the successful convention between Britain and Russia by which their major differences in Afghanistan, Tibet and Persia had been settled. He even managed to conclude a Russian agreement with Japan to define the spheres of influence between them in China.[21] For a foreign minister of a country that had recently been crushed by Japan, these were great achievements. They happened so readily because every action he took harmonised with the Secret Elite's policy.[22] It ensured that Russia and Japan would act together as a bulwark against German expansion in the Far East. Isvolsky's achievement was entirely predicated upon meeting the needs of his British masters. He formally closed the chapter on Russian imperial designs in the east and turned St Petersburg towards a new era of harmony with Britain, precisely as the Secret Elite had dictated.

Isvolsky's next move came in the Balkans, and it stirred more than just controversy. That backward corner of south-east Europe had long been troubled ground, and in the early years of the twentieth century the physical clash of cultures, language, religions and long-standing animosities was deliberately pressed into intrigue and war. The Ottoman Empire had ruled the Balkans for at least 400 years, but the deterioration of its control was underlined by a bankrupt government in Constantinople. A strong Ottoman

Empire had acted as a barrier to ambitious European expansion, but the fast-evaporating remnant of the great heyday of Ottoman rule signalled an outburst of calls for annexation, independence and political realignments by the numerous small nations comprising the Balkans.

The first element in what was to provide the slow-burning fuse for the First World War began in 1908 thanks directly to Alexander Isvolsky. Austria-Hungary had held administrative control of the Balkan provinces of Bosnia-Herzegovina since the Treaty of Berlin in 1878, and in the intervening 30 years had built roads, schools and hospitals.[23] Serbs, who comprised 42 per cent of the population, resented Austrian rule, but it was popular with a significant number of Muslims and Croats. In October 1908, Austria's decision to formally annex Bosnia-Herzegovina and bring it under direct rule from Vienna caused indignation both inside the province and, most vocally, in neighbouring Serbia. Russia had long made claim to be the protector of the Slavic peoples in the Balkans, and such a bold and provocative move could not have taken place without her agreement. So what happened?

Just days after his diplomatic intrigues with the Secret Elite at Marienbad and Reval, Isvolsky sent the Austrian foreign minister, Count Alois Aehrenthal, a memorandum. He proposed a meeting to discuss changes to the 1878 Treaty of Berlin without the knowledge or approval of the czar or the Russian government. He agreed to the Austro-Hungarian annexation of Bosnia-Herzegovina in return for a promise that Russian interest in the Straits and Constantinople would be supported by the Austrians.

From the start of the discussions, it was evident that Count Aehrenthal was acting in concert with his own government; Isvolsky was not. On 16 September 1908, they met in secret at Buchlau in Moravia. The Austrian minister was accompanied by diplomats and Foreign Office officials from Vienna.[24] Isvolsky had no one by his side to witness the talks, and no minutes were made during a meeting that lasted six hours. It was a very bold and dangerous move for any Russian politician to make on his own, but Isvolsky was not entirely on his own.

The British Foreign Office certainly knew what was being proposed before the 'top-secret' talks were concluded. Indeed, it was claimed that the Austrians had been encouraged by the British Foreign Office to proceed with the annexation.[25] Sir Edward Grey colluded with Isvolsky. He knew that the proposed action would deeply offend Serbia,[26] and both had agreed that she would be due compensation. This being so, the Secret Elite knew exactly what was being proposed and precisely what Isvolsky was doing.

On 6 October, Emperor Franz Joseph announced that Bosnia-Herzegovina had been annexed. With its accustomed two-faced approach to transparency, the British government proclaimed that it was unacceptable for any country to alter a treaty unilaterally.[27] A flurry of diplomatic protests followed. Inside the provinces themselves, the diverse population of Greek Orthodox Christians, Muslims and other Christian sects promised a dangerous mix of ethnic protest.

Isvolsky fanned the flame of Balkan nationalism. Serbia mobilised its army on 7 October and demanded that the annexation be reversed or, failing that, she should receive compensation.[28] When Serbia called for Russian military support, Aehrenthal publicly revealed Isvolsky's involvement in the secret deal. Alexander Isvolsky was undone. If he had hoped that diplomatic protocol would protect his anonymity, he was very disappointed. He blamed Aehrenthal, defaming him in a racist outburst worthy of any anti-Semitic Russian: 'The dirty Jew has deceived me. He lied to me, he bamboozled me, that frightful Jew.'[29] Isvolsky had put his career on the line by giving Russia's consent to the annexation without the knowledge or approval of the czar or his government and tried to blame it on an Austrian Jew. Did he?

Russia had not recovered from her devastating defeat by Japan and, embarrassed by Isvolsky's agreement and her military weakness, declined to intervene.[30] Some historians believe that a European war would have broken out in 1908 had the Russian military been at full strength.[31] Instead, the Serbians were deflated. Without the anticipated Russian support, they had no option but to pull back from the brink, but a bitter rage burned in their bellies against their powerful Austro-Hungarian neighbours. Isvolsky counselled Serbia to accept what had happened, with the chilling advice that they should prepare for future action.[32] Revenge has always been a dish best served cold. Thanks to Isvolsky's activities on behalf of his Secret Elite masters, their mission was accomplished. The Balkans had been successfully stirred, and Austria-Hungary emerged as public enemy number one.

Isvolsky was not working to his own agenda. He could not have seriously believed that the eternal conundrum of a warm-water port for Russia would be solved by his subterfuge. Given the 1878 Treaty of Berlin, there was no possibility that Germany, France, Britain, Italy, Austria-Hungary and the Ottoman Empire would grant joint approval for such a radical move. Wars had been fought for far less, and that was a point that Isvolsky must have understood. It did, however, point the way forward. The Secret Elite, the Foreign Office and Sir Edward Grey all knew how important Constantinople was to the Russians. Its gift was not in their hands, but the promise of it was a tantalising carrot they had every intention of dangling before the Russians at the right moment.

Isvolsky had been sold short at every turn. Mocked in St Petersburg as the Prince of the Bosphorus,[33] he faced dismissal and political oblivion, but his patron, King Edward, whose direct influence had raised him to foreign minister, stepped in once more on his behalf. The king wrote personally to his nephew the czar, reiterating his confidence in Isvolsky and his hope that he would remain in office.[34] He did, for the moment.

Undeterred, Isvolsky continued to stir the Balkan pot on behalf of his real masters. In a speech to the Russian Parliament, he advised the Balkan States to federate and encouraged the Greater Serbian policy aimed at the expulsion of Austria from the Balkan Peninsula. In December 1909, a secret military convention was concluded between Russia and the recently independent Bulgaria. Its fifth clause stated: 'The realisation of the high ideals of the Slav peoples in the Balkan Peninsula, which are so closely at Russia's heart, is only possible after a fortunate issue in the struggle of Russia with Germany and Austria-Hungary.'[35] In other words, war. Victory over Germany and Austro-Hungary was now the key to the realisation of all of their ambitions. The Secret Elite had reached into the very heart of czarist Russia and a touchpaper was set that would later find a murderous spark.

Isvolsky condemned the Balkans to six tortured years of miserable in-fighting, but he should not be seen as the real perpetrator. He was simply another foreign representative of the Secret Elite, who financed his lifestyle through their London and Paris banks. In many ways, the first part of his mission had been completed when he successfully demonstrated that war with Germany was the only route that Russia could take to the Straits of Constantinople. The military intent of all three members of the Triple Entente was thus harmonised through Russia's ambition to gain the Straits, France's drive to regain Alsace-Lorraine and Britain's masterplan to throttle Germany. A three-pronged spear was thrust towards the heart of continental Europe.[36]

What the Secret Elite had so successfully achieved was startlingly clever. The Balkan countries now had cause to fear that they might be the next target for Austrian annexation, while Russia had yet more proof that she could not act alone in any European intervention. An indebted Isvolsky was even more dependent on the support and financial largess of his London masters. Thanks to King Edward, he rode the storm at home. As far as the Secret Elite were concerned, Isvolsky had performed well. A gaping chasm had developed between Russia and the Austro-Hungarian Empire. Prior to 1908, relationships between St Petersburg and Vienna had been good, especially in regard to the Balkans.[37] Isvolsky's action single-handedly turned friendship into complete estrangement.

SUMMARY: CHAPTER 8 – ALEXANDER ISVOLSKY – HERO AND VILLAIN

- Despite widespread objections from MPs and the public, the Secret Elite pursued their objective to bring Russia into an entente by sending the king to Reval to meet the czar in June 1908 even although it broke with accepted protocol in diplomatic circles.
- King Edward took his Secret Elite advisors, members of the Committee of Imperial Defence, to liaise with Prime Minister Stolypin and Foreign Minister Alexander Isvolsky.
- The result was an agreement, sometimes called the Anglo-Russian convention, that dealt on the surface with issues about Persia, Afghanistan and Tibet but effectively isolated Germany and extended plans to go to war with Germany.
- Isvolsky, who was in the pay of the Secret Elite, plotted with them behind the czar's back before the meeting and was later credited with concluding in a matter of weeks both the entente and an alliance with Japan.
- Isvolsky's clandestine meeting with his Austrian counterpart Aehrenthal, which made Russia complicit in the annexation of Bosnia, was managed by the Secret Elite.
- Serbia called on Russian help to go to war against Austria, but the Austrians unmasked Isvolsky's role in the affair and the Russians had to step back.
- Isvolsky was ridiculed in the Russian press, but his position as foreign secretary was saved through the personal intervention of King Edward.
- Isvolsky continued to stir the Balkan states against Germany and Austria-Hungary. He encouraged a 'Greater Serbia' movement based on revenge and advised them to prepare for future action.
- The Secret Elite gained ground on several levels. The Triple Entente was cemented. The Balkans was stirred into a hornet's nest of nationalist and sectarian suspicion and bitterness. Russia realised that the only route to the Straits was through a successful war against Germany and no longer trusted Austria-Hungary.

CHAPTER 9

Scams and Scandals

THE SECRET ELITE ACHIEVEMENTS IN the first decade of the twentieth century were truly remarkable. They took complete control of South Africa's immense mineral wealth, British foreign policy and the Committee of Imperial Defence. The crowning glories of British diplomacy, Edward VII's diplomacy, were the ententes, which brought old enemies France and Russia to Britain's side. The balance of power between opposing alliances was allegedly meant to guarantee peace. It did no such thing. What the Triple Entente or 'understanding' actually entailed was never truthfully explained. Ramsay MacDonald, leader of the Labour Party, later reflected: 'As a matter of practical experience, the very worst form of alliance is the entente. An alliance is definite. Everyone knows his responsibilities under it. The entente deceives the people.'[1] It was for the very purpose of deception that arrangements with both France and Russia were created in the loose fashion of an 'understanding'.

Observant Liberals in the Cabinet sensed that the Triple Entente was effectively dragging Britain into the maelstrom of European politics, but no one could mount a serious challenge because Edward Grey reassured them that no *formal* obligations existed. He repeatedly promised that any decisions on possible military moves would always be left to the full Cabinet. In the strict sense of the term 'formal obligations', he was telling the truth. The Secret Elite shrewdly kept pen from paper and persuaded the French and Russians to agree to joint naval and military commitments on the basis of the old adage that an Englishman's word 'was his bond'. Edward Grey was thus able to deny they had created an *alliance* and declare that the Triple Entente had been agreed to secure the peace of Europe. The dirty work of preparing for the destruction of Germany was buried from sight but continued unabated.

The secret sub-group of the Committee of Imperial Defence had been set up with one purpose in mind: war with Germany. To ensure that Secret Elite aims were realised, it continually developed and refined plans for joint naval and military action with France and Russia. 'Secretly the Committee of Imperial Defence carried forward with great earnestness the plans for war, predicted by several "in the know" to begin in 1914.'[2] Plans included a naval blockade to deny Germany access to overseas trade and block her import of raw materials vital to war industries.[3] By 1907, accredited naval circles believed that Germany would quickly be brought to her knees by restricting her food supplies.[4] Sir Charles Ottley, secretary to the CID and director of Naval Intelligence, prophesied that British sea power would slowly grind the German people 'exceedingly small' and that 'grass would sooner grow in the streets of Hamburg'. He confidently prophesised that 'wide-spread dearth and ruin would be inflicted' on Germany.[5] Ottley was connected to different influences within the circles of the Secret Elite and stood to gain handsomely from a future war. Some might say disgracefully.

When he first took possession of the War Office, Richard Haldane learned that direct conversations between the English and French naval staffs, conducted on behalf of Britain by Admiral Jacky Fisher, were progressing on a satisfactory basis. What this meant was that progress was satisfactory to Fisher because he was conducting them on behalf of the navy, and he remained in charge. The plans for military cooperation were much less satisfactory because they did not rest in the hands of the War Office. As has already been noted with astonishment, the *Times* journalist Charles Repington had assumed the role of chief mediator between the British and French military staff in 1905.[6] The shocking fact is that the *Times* correspondent remained in a very privileged position within the War Office in the years leading up to 1914. Questions about Repington's role were asked in Parliament:

> When a man who has been an officer becomes the military correspondent of *The Times* . . . and given a room and access to papers in the War Office, it leads one to think that that gentleman does not always write what he really thinks to be true . . .[7]

No one denied this. As a journalist, Repington could have penned a sensational scoop. He didn't. Why? Was he a consultant, a reporter or a placeman for the Secret Elite in the guise of both? Did he continue as the unofficial mediator between the French and British military staff? What did he do to deserve the Legion of Honour from France and be made a Commander of the Order of Leopold by Belgium? Why has his real role been airbrushed from history? Clearly he was much more than just a humble journalist.

Haldane quickly introduced his plans for the formation of a highly trained, professional army to fight alongside France. Joint military planning was so intense and detailed that by 1906 senior officers believed that war with Germany was inevitable.[8] Top-secret Anglo-French military preparations entailed British and French staff officers reconnoitring the ground in France and Belgium upon which the forthcoming battles would be fought. Britain's director of military operations, Sir Henry Wilson, spent the summer months of 1906 reconnoitring the Belgian countryside on his bicycle, taking careful notes on the lie of the land, canals, railway crossings and church towers that would one day serve as observation posts. A gigantic map of Belgium, indicating the routes armies might follow, covered the entire wall of his London Office.[9] Sir Henry Wilson and the French general staff shared their deepest secrets. He was sure that war would come sooner or later and for years laboured to ensure that Britain was ready to act immediately.[10]

In addition to the British Expeditionary Force (BEF), Haldane set up the Territorial Army, the Officer Training Corps, the Special Reserve and the Advisory Committee for Aeronautics, which provided the fledgling aircraft industry in the United Kingdom. By 1910, he had achieved a complete revolution in the organisation of the British Army.

Haldane, Grey, Asquith and Esher retained an iron grip on the Committee of Imperial Defence and created within it an able secretariat. Sir Charles Ottley of the Naval Intelligence Department, one of Fisher's placemen on the CID, had been named secretary in 1907, and he in turn appointed as his assistants Maurice Hankey and Sir Ernest Swinton.[11] Hankey was Esher's chief protégé,[12] and the two were in constant communication. He later became a member of the Secret Elite and close to the inner circle. Swinton likewise became a member but belonged to one of the less central rings.[13] It is beyond any question of doubt that these Secret Elite agents ran the CID.

In 1906, the British electorate had voiced an overwhelming desire for peace and substantial reductions in spending on armaments, but the Secret Elite turned pacifism on its head through an age-old weapon: fear. Fear was required to stir the complacency of Edwardian England and counter the anger of workers on poverty wages evidenced in strikes and walkouts in mines, factories and shipyards across the land. Fear generates doubt and suspicion. Fear is the spur that has the masses demanding more and more weapons to defend homes and families, towns and cities. It has always been so. Generation after generation has been gulled into paying for the tools of destruction that are, in turn, superseded by yet more powerful weapons.

From the beginning of the twentieth century, the Secret Elite indulged in a frenzy of rumour and half-truths, of raw propaganda and lies, to create the myth of a great naval race. The story widely accepted, even by many anti-war Liberals, was that Germany was preparing a massive fleet of warships to attack and destroy the British navy before unleashing a military invasion on the east coast of England or the Firth of Forth in Scotland.[14] It was the stuff of conspiracy novels. But it worked. The British people swallowed the lie that militarism had run amok in Germany and the 'fact' that it was seeking world domination through naval and military superiority. Militarism in the United Kingdom was of God, but in Germany of the Devil, and had to be crushed before it crushed them. When the war ended and all of the plans and events that had taken place were analysed and dissected, were there any naval records found of secret German plans to invade England or for the secret building of more dreadnoughts? No. Not one.

Rarely have statistics been so thoroughly abused. The Secret Elite, through an almighty alliance of armaments manufacturers, political rhetoric and newspaper propaganda, conjured up the illusion of an enormous and threatening German battle fleet. The illusion became accepted, and historians have written that as 'fact' into contemporary history. These were the weapons of mass destruction of their time, but they could not be hidden from view. In the decade prior to the war, British naval expenditure was £351,916,576 compared to Germany's £185,205,164.[15] Had politicians such as Grey and Haldane been truly determined to 'crush militarism', there was plenty of work for them at home. The Triple Entente spent £657,884,476 on warships in that same decade, while Germany and Austria-Hungary spent £235,897,978.[16] The peacetime strength of the German army was 761,000, while France stood at 794,000 and Russia 1,845,000,[17] yet the claim that militarism had 'run amok' in Germany was presented as the given truth.

Fuelled by newspaper reports of massive increases in German warship building, of articles on the danger to 'our' sea routes, of exaggerated reports in Parliament that the German fleet would soon overtake British naval supremacy, the construction of more and more warships was demanded with patriotic zeal. A strong navy was never a party issue, for food supplies and the coherence of the Empire depended on the British fleet's ability to control sea routes against an enemy.[18] Whatever the cost, Britain had to outbuild Germany. In reality, the subsequent vast increases in naval spending were a response not to a perceived threat but to the 'vicious chauvinism' of those bent on the destruction of Germany.[19] What made it all so incredible was the fact that Grey, Asquith and Haldane drove the Liberal government into massive naval overspending at the very point where its express purpose was to alleviate poverty and introduce social reform. It was a breathtaking achievement.

Great ships were built and launched in Germany but not in the numbers bandied about in the British press. Quite apart from the Triple Entente, Britain alone held such an enormous lead over Germany that any question of a meaningful race was ludicrous. The notion that Britain had somehow fallen behind its capacity to protect her Empire was a convenience set to frighten politicians and the people. Like every other modern country with a blossoming mercantile fleet trading across the globe, Germany was perfectly entitled to protect itself. Chancellor von Bülow had stated in the Reichstag that Germany did not wish to interfere with any other country:

> but we do not wish that any other Power should interfere with us, should violate our rights, or push us aside either in political or commercial questions . . . Germany cannot stand aside while other nations divide the world among them.[20]

Von Bülow correctly noted that Italy, France, Russia, Japan and America had all strengthened their navies and that Britain 'endeavours without ceasing to make her gigantic fleet still greater'.[21] Without a navy, it would have been impossible for Germany to maintain a viable commercial position in the world. Britain, however, 'ruled the waves' and viewed Germany's growing fleet as an impudent challenge.

In June 1900, Admiral von Tirpitz had steered the second of two naval bills through the Reichstag to permit an expansion of their navy. He proposed the construction of 38 battleships over a 20-year period to protect Germany's colonies and sea routes. That's less than two per year. Keep this in mind.

What set alarm bells ringing within the Secret Elite was not German warship construction but their engineering innovations in merchant shipping that emerged from the dockyards of Hamburg, Bremen and Wilhelmshaven. German superiority in the commercial sea lanes could not be tolerated. The rapid growth of the lucrative commercial fleets of the North German Lloyd and Hamburg-America lines was outshining liners built in Britain. For a brief period, the SS *Kaiser Wilhelm der Grosse* was the largest and fastest liner on the Atlantic Ocean. This was followed by SS *Deutschland III*, which crossed from Cherbourg to New York in five and a half days, with a new speed record of 23.61 knots. International prestige was slipping from British-built liners. In 1907, the *Lusitania* regained the Blue Riband for the fastest crossing, outstripping the *Deutschland III* by 11 hours and 46 minutes. 'Bigger, Better and Faster' became watchwords for national one-upmanship.

The rough guide to Admiralty practice had long been based on the notion of a 'two-power standard': a navy capable of effectively outgunning the combined strength of the two next-strongest naval powers. Admiral Jacky Fisher played this navy card to great effect. A conveniently timed Admiralty Report 'disclosed' that no matter what number of ships Britain built, they could not guarantee the safety of the United Kingdom from aggressors 'on the opposite side of the North Sea' without a change in the quality of design and firepower. In 1905, this spawned the first of the dreadnoughts and an order to scrap old vessels. Entire classes of warship were condemned as useless. Around 115 vessels that had cost between £35 million and £40 million were scrapped. Astoundingly, thirty-four of these were only five years old.[22]

Fisher wrote confidentially to King Edward in 1907 that the British fleet was four times stronger than the German navy, 'but we don't want to parade all this to the world at large'.[23] The Secret Elite clearly knew that British naval superiority far exceeded the two-power ratio, but by encouraging Fisher in his manic obsession, the shipbuilding and armaments industry conspired with them to reap a rich dividend.

This was a falsely portrayed race Britain had to win to survive, and the only way of winning it was to stay further and further ahead of Germany. It was a media coup wrapped in a shipbuilder's dream. No one but a traitor could doubt the need to be fully armed against the kaiser's ambitions. Individuals who questioned the validity of the naval scare were dismissed as grumbling pacifists 'who neither knew what love of country meant, nor ever felt the thrill of joy that all the pomp and circumstance of Empire brings to men who think imperially'.[24] Bully-boy tactics turned honest concern into disloyalty in a blatant attempt to crush opposition to the crippling waste of increased naval expenditure.

In the midst of this paranoia, a scare story was concocted about a secret German naval building programme. On 3 March 1909, Mr Herbert Mulliner, managing director of the Coventry Ordnance Co., was brought to Downing Street to dupe the Cabinet. He told them that in the course of his job he had visited shipyards and armaments factories in Germany, and it was 'an accomplished fact' that an enormous and rapid increase in armaments production and naval construction had been taking place there over the past three years. Ten days later the revised 1909–10 Naval Estimates were published. The allocation was increased by £2,823,200 to £35,142,700.[25]

Despite this concession, the Conservatives under Arthur Balfour moved a vote of censure against the Liberal government's naval spending. The proposed increases were insufficient. The armaments lobby wanted even greater spending. Balfour warned the House of Commons that the margins between the British and German navies would be so reduced that it would result in a great blow to 'security which, after all, is the basis of all enterprise in this country'.[26] Balfour carried the banner for the Secret Elite and wrapped increased spending in words like 'security' and 'enterprise'. He insisted that Germany would have twenty-five dreadnoughts by 1912, whereas in reality she had nine. Time and again Balfour pounded home the Secret Elite message: more had to be spent on dreadnoughts.[27] Naval spending from 1901 to 1912 in Britain was £456 million compared to £179 million in Germany.[28]

A crowded meeting at the Guildhall on 31 March 1909 heard Arthur Balfour address several hundred shareholders of the armaments rings, the bankers and city investors.[29] They drank in his every word with dizzy approval. His rhetoric was filled with urgency, alarm and the dire consequences of indecision:

> You must build without delay, without hesitation, without waiting for contingencies, for obscure circumstances, for future necessities. You must build now to meet the present necessity. For believe me the necessity is upon you. It is not coming in July or November or April next . . . it is now that you must begin to meet it.[30]

Balfour's exhortation had a truly apocalyptic ring to it. It was an end-of-the-world prophecy designed to excite panic. The Secret Elite press, especially *The Times* and the *Daily Mail*, had fired the opening salvos in creating the 'German naval scare', and their propaganda swept the country off its feet. The summer of 1909 echoed to the cry of 'We want eight and we won't wait'. The propaganda machine turned a catchphrase into an axiom of national insistence. The public demand for more dreadnoughts became so vehement that the First Lord of the Admiralty, Reginald McKenna, who, like most of Asquith's Cabinet, was unaware of the Secret Elite, gave way. He accepted that by concealing its activities Germany might reach equality in naval power with Britain. McKenna stated that work on four extra British dreadnoughts would begin almost immediately. As a result, the Admiralty was prepared to lay down eight dreadnoughts in 1909. Few stopped to ask how this would affect social reforms and the eradication of poverty. From 1909 onwards, ever-greater sums poured into armaments production, and preparations for war speeded up.

The entire scare was a sham. Mulliner had been lying. It was 'one of the most disgraceful, cooked-up conspiracies' ever known in Britain.[31] What made it so utterly disgraceful was the fact that Asquith, Grey and Haldane *knew* he was lying yet invited Mulliner to Downing Street to convince the Cabinet that huge increases in naval spending were necessary. The statistics and so-called 'margins' between the British and German navies were grossly misrepresented. Winston Churchill later admitted that 'there were no secret

German dreadnoughts, nor had Admiral von Tirpitz made any untrue statement in respect of major construction'.[32] When Mulliner threatened to go to the press and reveal his role in the scare, he was bought off and retired to obscurity. Sir Edward Grey was eventually obliged to admit that every line Mulliner and the government had peddled was wrong, but the job had already been done. It was a shameful scandal that was quoted in Parliament many times over the next three decades as an example of just how far the armaments lobby would go to promote their own interests.[33] And Mulliner? He was easily replaced[34] and airbrushed from history, but the naval race is still peddled as a historic event. There was no race. Germany wasn't competing.

The massive rise in naval and military spending resulted in an equally massive increase in profits for the shareholders in armaments companies. Only the occasional lone voice braved the ridicule of a raging press. Lord Welby, former permanent secretary to the Treasury, saw what was happening, though he had no knowledge of exactly what or whom he was up against. He protested:

> We are in the hands of an organisation of crooks. They are politicians, generals, manufacturers of armaments, and journalists. All of them are anxious for unlimited expenditure, and go on inventing scares to terrify the public and to terrify ministers of the Crown.[35]

Lord Welby all but named the Secret Elite. These were indeed the men who planned and colluded to wage war on Germany . . . and made a profit on the way.

The average citizen in Britain considered the chief armaments firms to be independent businesses, competing in a patriotic spirit for government contracts, but this was far wide of the mark. They were neither independent nor competitive. These firms created monopoly-like conditions that ensured their profit margins remained high. In Britain, this armaments ring, or 'Trust' as it was known, consisted primarily of five great companies: Vickers Ltd; Armstrong, Whitworth and Co. Ltd; John Brown and Co. Ltd; Cammell, Laird and Co.; and the Nobel Dynamite Trust, in the last of which the family of Prime Minister Asquith's wife, Margo, held a controlling interest. The ring equated to a vast financial network in which apparently independent firms were strengthened by absorption and linked together by an intricate system of joint shareholding and common directorships.[36] It was an industry that challenged the Treasury, influenced the Admiralty, maintained high prices and manipulated public opinion.

Competition amongst British armaments firms had been virtually eliminated by 1901. Across Europe and the United States, armaments makers colluded in an international combine called the Harvey United Steel Co. to minimise competition and maximise profits. The five British armaments giants joined forces with Krupp and Dillingen of Germany, Bethlehem Steel Company of the United States, Schneider & Co. of Creusot in France, and Vickers-Terni and Armstrong-Pozzuoli of Italy.[37] Harvey United Steel provided a common meeting ground for the world's armament firms and accumulated royalties from those nations sufficiently civilised to 'construct armour-plated slaughter machines'.[38] It was highly successful in maintaining the demand for armaments that were bought by rival governments on the basis that they could not afford to be less well armed than their neighbours.[39]

These trade practices were shameless. Charles Hobhouse, Asquith's Treasury minister, wrote in his diaries that an armour-plating 'ring' of munitions manufacturers was robbing the Admiralty of millions of pounds of public money by collusion and malpractice. The group charged the Admiralty from £100 to £120 per ton for steel that cost them £40 to £60 to produce.[40] He knew but, like many other shareholders in the armaments industry, did nothing to stop it.

The Armaments Trust in Britain had its champions in both political parties, its friends at Court and its directors in the House of Lords and Commons. Its voice was heard in the press, and its 'apostles were in the pulpits of cathedrals and tabernacles'.[41] The churches were represented on its boards or shareholder lists by bishops of the Anglican Church. The vested interest carried its own 'vestry' interest.

Just as the profits of war never went to the ordinary people, so the profits of preparing for war were channelled into the pockets of the private investors. State-owned arsenals, dockyards and factories like Woolwich were deliberately run down, and five-sixths of the new naval construction contracts were awarded to private firms. Despite the protests from local Labour MPs, orders placed by the Admiralty or the War Office went mainly to the great armaments companies on whose boards senior military figures regularly sat.[42]

With the huge increase in naval building, the shareholders in Armstrong, Whitworth were receiving 12 per cent dividends with a bonus of one share for every four held. From the turn of the twentieth century, the dividend never fell below 10 per cent and on occasions rose to 15 per cent. Investments in armament shares provided windfalls for the well-to-do and the influential. In 1909, the shares list of Armstrong, Whitworth boasted the names of 60 noblemen, their wives, sons or daughters, 15 baronets, 20 knights, 8 MPs, 20 military and naval officers, and 8 journalists. Shareholder lists showed a marked connection between armaments share-holding and active membership of bodies like the Navy League, which promoted ever-greater warship construction.[43]

Armstrong, Whitworth and Co. shamelessly paid Rear Admiral Sir Charles Ottley as a defence director.[44] That the former director of Naval Intelligence and secretary to the Committee of Imperial Defence was ever in the employment of an armaments giant tells its own story. Vickers, one of the largest armaments firms in the world, had a similar list of notable shareholders.[45] Vickers and Armstrong were firmly entrenched in the governing class of Great Britain. With senior employees comprising retired military, naval and civil servants of the highest rank, the armaments firms possessed secret information supposedly restricted to the heads of the government. Shareholders included the nobility, senior politicians, admirals, generals and other members of the British Establishment who had direct access to the inner circles of power and were well equipped to apply political pressure.

Vickers grew through acquisitions of other companies into a vast concern with ordnance works in Glasgow, factories at Sheffield and Erith, and naval works at Walney Island. The London House of Rothschild was heavily involved in the Vickers takeover of the Naval Construction and Armaments Company, and issued £1.9 million of shares to finance the merger of the Maxim Gun Company with the Nordenfelt Guns and Ammunition Company. Nathaniel Rothschild retained a substantial shareholding in the new Maxim-Nordenfelt Company and 'exerted a direct influence over its management'.[46] Vickers was launched on the international road to prosperity backed by funding from Rothschild and Cassel.[47] The Secret Elite held sway at the very heart of the armaments industry.

The Rothschilds had always understood the enormous profits generated by these industries. Financing wars had been their preserve for nearly a century. Bankers, industrialists and other members of the Secret Elite, the same men who were planning the destruction of Germany, stood to make massive profits from it. War, any war, was a means of garnering wealth. Secret Elite bankers had provided Japan with high-interest-yielding loans to build a modern navy with which to attack Russia. The greater part of that victorious Japanese navy was constructed by the British yards from which the Secret Elite made even more profits. Of course, the Japanese people were left to foot the bill. After the Russian fleet had been destroyed at Tsushima, Russia was provided with high-interest-bearing loans of £190,000,000 to rebuild her navy. Much of the construction work went to factories and shipyards owned by the Secret Elite, and the cycle repeated itself, with the Russian people left to pay the price.[48] It was no different in

Britain. The great 'naval race' produced millions of pounds of profits, and the cost was met by the ordinary citizen.

One of the most enduring deceptions perpetrated by the agents of the Secret Elite was in regard to Italy. It was assumed that, as a signatory to the Triple Alliance with Germany and Austria-Hungary, Italy would have a dangerous naval presence in the Mediterranean should war break out. Any comparative naval statistics on the total size of opposing fleets given in Parliament or the press included Italian warships[49] and torpedo-boats but studiously ignored the irony that British armaments firms owned the very yards that were building those warships for Italy.[50] The British Armstrong-Pozzuoli Company, on the Bay of Naples, employed 4,000 men and was the chief naval supplier to Italy. The Ansaldo-Armstrong Company of Genoa, which belonged to the same British firm, built dreadnoughts and cruisers for Italy even although it was Germany's supposed ally.[51] Rear Admiral Ottley was a director of the Armstrong works at Pozzuoli in addition to being defence director of the parent company.[52] Ottley again. How much did he gain from his insider dealings?[53]

Vickers was also an important supplier to the Italian navy through combination with three Italian firms that constituted the Vickers Terni Co. Both Vickers and Armstrong also held a large proportion of the shares of Whitehead & Co., the torpedo manufacturer with works at Fiume in Hungary. During the war, Labour MP Philip Snowden angrily stated in the House of Commons:

> Submarines and all the torpedoes used in the Austrian navy, besides several of the new seaplanes, are made by the Whitehead Torpedo works in Hungary . . . They are making torpedoes with British capital in Hungary in order to destroy British ships.[54]

Throughout the war, those Whitehead torpedoes were also loaded into the tubes of German U-Boats and used against British shipping. Numerous individuals sitting in the warm comfort of Westminster or their exclusive London clubs or grand gothic cathedrals profited from the torpedoes that sent thousands of brave British seamen to cold graves in the Atlantic. These men made untold fortunes on the products of death and misery.

Some, at the inner core of the Secret Elite, conspired to make war to their own advantage. Some were simply in the business of providing the instruments of war. Some were mindless investors with no moral inhibitions.[55] Those in the high pulpits who profited from the war while extolling it as God's work included the bishops of Adelaide, Chester, Hexham, Newcastle and Newport, as well as Dean Inge of St Paul's

Cathedral.[56] They formed the legions of God who profited from the legions of hell.

In 1921, a sub-committee of the Commission of the League of Nations concluded that armaments firms had been active in the decades before in fomenting war scares and in persuading their own countries to adopt warlike policies that increased their spending on armaments. They were found guilty of bribing government officials both at home and abroad, and of disseminating false reports about the military and naval programmes of various countries in order to stimulate armament expenditure. The litany of accusations further indicted them for influencing public opinion through the control of newspapers in their own and foreign countries. The ring was directly criticised for all these activities and not least for ensuring the outrageous price of armaments, but nothing of any consequence was done about it.[57] The Secret Elite was not identified.

Summary: Chapter 9 – Scams and Scandals

- The Committee of Imperial Defence continued to host a secret sub-committee that continued to pursue military and naval 'conversations' with France.
- Richard Haldane at the War Office had to reorganise the military connections that had been left loosely in the hands of the *Times* correspondent Colonel Repington, a journalist with his own office at the War Office.
- The Secret Elite sanctioned a raft of fear stories and scares to generate the belief that Britain was being threatened by German naval construction in a race for survival.
- This propaganda was bolstered by an armaments scam that the Cabinet endorsed, the opposition of A.J. Balfour's Conservatives abused, and the naval lobby turned into a clamour for more dreadnoughts.
- The major British armaments firms formed close associations and partnerships. They made vast fortunes and engaged in national and international 'trusts' or 'armaments rings' that bled governments dry.
- Many key figures inside the Secret Elite gained handsomely from the trade of death, as did many members of the House of Lords, the Cabinet and the House of Commons. Even high-ranking churchmen were shareholders in this infamous scandal.
- British armaments were later to be used in the slaughter of British soldiers and sailors.

CHAPTER 10

Creating the Fear

THE SECRET ELITE HAS ALWAYS had a handle on the press. Newspapers have immense power to influence how people think and act. Important events in public life, including appointments and elections, are swayed by them. They like to portray themselves as standard-bearers for morality, for loyalty, for what is for the public good. When they get it right, they promote themselves with unconscionable arrogance. When they get it wrong, they simply move on to the next opinion. Few have absolute loyalty to a political party. They smell the wind and change their allegiance accordingly, but their concerted attacks can bring down politicians or blacken the character of public figures. Newspapers serve their owners and always have. When their owners are part of the greater conspiracy, democracy itself becomes a fraud.

Viscount Alfred Milner understood the role and the power of the press. From his earliest years in the *Pall Mall Gazette* in the 1880s, Milner's personal network of journalist friends included William T. Stead, editor of the *Review of Reviews*, George Buckle and later Geoffrey Dawson at *The Times*, Edmund Garrett at the *Westminster Gazette* and E.T. Cook at the *Daily News* and *Daily Chronicle*. All were members of the Secret Elite.[1] The combined impact of these newspapers and magazines gave the Secret Elite great influence over public opinion by directing editorial policies from behind the scenes, but it was the intimacy between *The Times* and the Foreign Office, the Colonial Office and the War Office that demonstrated just how deeply this symbiotic relationship ran.

Milner's good friend the *Times* correspondent Flora Shaw had been a welcome guest at the Colonial Office and 'was in the confidence of all concerned with Imperial Policy'.[2] Her task in justifying war in South Africa had been to insist day after day in *The Times* that President Kruger was refusing to address legitimate grievances in the Transvaal. Flora Shaw was also given the opportunity to rewrite history. *The Times* sponsored an updated *Encyclopaedia Britannica* and she was invited to revise the imperial sections, a task that involved 'rewriting a great many articles'.[3]

The connections between *The Times* and the Foreign Office continued through another known member of the Secret Elite, Valentine Chirol.[4] Formerly a Foreign Office clerk, Chirol moved to Berlin as the *Times* correspondent before returning to London to take control of their foreign department. From this powerful position, Chirol promoted Secret Elite policies for 15 years up to 1912. What he supported through his editorials became the policies that the government followed. With unerring certainty he promoted the Boer War, the Anglo-Japanese Alliance, the Entente Cordiale, the 1907 agreement with czarist Russia and increasing antagonism towards Germany.

Charles Repington, as we have seen, was yet another *Times* correspondent whose involvement in secret inter-government agreements belied his journalistic role. His access to Foreign Office and War Office civil servants, diplomats and secret papers went far beyond propriety.[5]

The Times was taken over and controlled by Milner's men in much the same way as they took control of All Souls College in Oxford: 'quietly, and without a struggle'.[6] Others might own the newspaper, but he ensured that its editorial leadership came from within the Secret Elite's trusted ranks. Members of the innermost circle swarmed all over *The Times*, writing editorials and articles, submitting news and views in line with their agenda. Professor Quigley stated that up to 1912 the old order inside the Elite, those initially associated with Lord Salisbury, were in charge, but after that point control passed seamlessly to Milner's close and trusted friend Geoffrey Dawson. Like all his favourites, Dawson had been personally recruited by Alfred Milner, originally for work in South Africa.[7] He poached him from the Colonial Office in 1901 and had him appointed editor of the *Johannesburg Star* before he left Africa in 1905.[8] When George Buckle was approaching the end of his tenure as editor of *The Times*, Dawson was sent for, spent a year hanging about the offices and was duly appointed editor-in-chief in 1912. That was how the Secret Elite worked: always one step ahead of the rest, sometimes two.

The Times could not boast a mass circulation. It never pretended to be a vehicle for mass propaganda. What Milner and his Secret Elite associates understood clearly was that *The Times* influenced that small number of important people who had the capacity to influence others. It represented the governing class, that elite of political, diplomatic, financial, wealth-bearing favoured few who made and approved choices for themselves and for others. It was part of the whole process through which the Secret Elite directed policy, by endorsing those elements that met their approval and deriding contrary opinion. When, for example, a member of the Secret Elite announced a policy on national defence, it would be backed up in an 'independent' study by an eminent Oxford don or former military 'expert', analysed and approved in a *Times* leader and legitimised by some publication favourably reviewed in the *Times Literary Supplement*.[9] Everyone involved in the process would in some way be associated with or approved of by the Secret Elite, including the writer of the anonymous review.

The revolution in newspaper circulation, with its popular daily papers, magazines and pamphlets, bypassed *The Times* in the first years of the twentieth century but did not alter its focus. The paper was, however, ailing and in danger of running at an unsustainable loss. Its saviour, Alfred Harmsworth, was, on first consideration, an unlikely guardian of the Secret Elite's public voice. As leader of the 'Yellow Press', a term of utter contempt derived from the sensationalist journalism developed in New York at the turn of the century, Harmsworth did not naturally belong inside the Elite, but, as his extensive stable proved, sensationalism sold newspapers and they wielded immense influence. He bought up a very large section of the London-based press, including the *Daily Mail*, the *Daily Mirror*, the *Daily Graphic*, *Evening News* and *Weekly Dispatch*. If he was not from the natural constituencies that bred Britain's elite, he was close to them.

Harmsworth had been very supportive of Alfred Milner during the Boer War, and his *Daily Mail* gave great prominence to Percy Fitzpatrick's *The Transvaal from Within*, which helped promote the need for war.[10] It brought him great profit. He spent large sums of money on stories that helped the circulation of the *Daily Mail* rise to over a million. Kipling's poem 'The Absent-Minded Beggar' was bought by his *Daily Mail*, set to music and sold to raise tens of thousands of pounds for ambulances and provisions for the troops.

Harmsworth was an innovator. He convinced Cecil Rhodes to give him an exclusive and entirely favourable interview which he published 'throughout the civilised world'.[11] Having been forewarned by his Secret Elite contacts that Arthur Balfour was about to resign in 1905, he scooped the story in an in-depth interview with the prime minister that included his plans for a general election.[12] Harmsworth was ennobled by King Edward that same year, took the title of Lord Northcliffe and was increasingly drawn into Secret Elite circles.

Gaining control of *The Times* was not straightforward. Northcliffe had a serious rival in Sir Arthur Pearson, proprietor of the *Daily Express*, and both bought up stock from the 68 major shareholders. Northcliffe was the Secret Elite's chosen man. His loyalty to the Empire, Milner and the king shone through. Lord Esher was sent to vet him on their behalf, since it was vital 'that the policy of *The Times* remained unchanged'.[13] Aided by the general manager, Moberly Bell, to whom he also had to make promises that '*The Times* of the future would be conducted on the same lines as *The Times* of the past',[14] Northcliffe gathered 51 per cent of the company stock and announced his ownership on 27 June 1908. Any fears that the editors, journalists, correspondents and readers might have expressed before his acquisition were quickly dispelled, for the only noticeable change he introduced was to the price. It fell from three pence to one penny.[15]

Northcliffe was a valuable contributor to the Secret Elite in their drive to vilify the kaiser, and his papers constantly repeated the warning that Germany was *the* enemy. In story after story, the message of the German danger to the British Empire, to British products, to British national security was constantly repeated. Not every newspaper followed suit, but the right-wing press was particularly virulent. In addition, Northcliffe had by 1908 bought up *The Observer* and the *Sunday Times*. According to Professor Quigley, the definitive assurances given by Northcliffe to the Secret Elite that their policies would be willingly supported brought him into the confidence of the Society of the Elect.[16]

What made Northcliffe and his associated newspapers so valuable was that the long-term plan to alienate public opinion against Germany could progress on two levels. *The Times* manipulated the 'elite' opinion in Britain, moulding policy and poisoning the climate, while the *Daily Mail* and its sister newspapers created sensational stories against Germany that excited the gullible of all classes. The *Morning Post*, whose unquestioning support for the myth of Winston Churchill's 'great escape' in the Boer War propelled him into politics, always promoted traditionally conservative views. It was even more committed to the Secret Elite cause after 1905 when one of its own, Fabian Ware,[17] became editor. A friend and trusted colleague of Milner himself, Ware ensured the *Morning Post*'s unstinting support against Germany.

A large and influential section of the British press was working to the rabid agenda of the Secret Elite in poisoning the minds of a whole nation. It was part of a propaganda drive that was sustained right up to, and throughout, the First World War. If *The Times* was their intellectual base, the popular dailies spread the gospel of anti-German hatred to the working classes. From 1905 to 1914, spy stories and anti-German articles bordered on lunacy.

In the years prior to the Entente Cordiale, the villain in scare stories and invasion claims had been France. In 1893, Lord Northcliffe (or Harmsworth, as he was then) commissioned a magazine serial called *The Poison Bullet* in which Britain was attacked one evening by the combined forces of Russia and France.[18] His aim was to stir public concern and underline the need for a larger fleet. The complete about-face in foreign policy at the start of the twentieth century was mirrored by an about-turn in popular storylines. It was Germany who was now spying on Britain, not France. It was Germany who was now plotting the downfall of the British Empire. It was Germany who was now the villain. The author of *The Poison Bullet* was the Walter Mitty of spy scare stories, William Le Queux. This was a man who found an extremely popular niche in cheap novels and scare stories, and made a fortune from them. His patron was none other than Lord Northcliffe. While *The Times* took a more high-brow approach to diplomacy and foreign policy, Northcliffe indulged his baser anti-German vitriol through the *Daily Mail*, where the editor, Kennedy Jones, operated on the basis of 'writing for the meanest intelligence'.[19] Northcliffe knew exactly what that entailed and was convinced that the British public liked a good hate. It was the perfect combination. By targeting Germany as the font of evil, the hate and the irrational spy and invasion stories gave the Northcliffe stables rich material to boost circulation and promote the war to which the Secret Elite were committed.

The literary war began in earnest in 1903 with the publication of Erskine Childers'[20] bestselling novel *The Riddle of the Sands*, which sounded the warning of a forthcoming German seaborne invasion of England. Written from a 'patriot's sense of duty', *The Riddle of the Sands* was an epic of its time, with secret plans that had 'seven ordered fleets from seven shallow outlets' carrying an invasion army across the North Sea, protected by the Imperial German Navy. He claimed it was written to stir public opinion so that slumbering statesmen would take action against the German 'menace'.[21] His novel galvanised the Admiralty to station a fleet permanently in the North Sea and brought Richard Haldane's plans to create a general staff for the army more popular support. As his biographer later claimed, Childers' book remained the most powerful contribution to the debate on Britain's alleged unpreparedness for war for a decade.[22] His was the single literary contribution that had merit and was the forerunner to John Buchan, John le Carré and Ian Fleming.[23]

In March 1906, Northcliffe commissioned William Le Queux to write *The Invasion of 1910*,[24] another scare serial, published in the *Daily Mail*.[25] It was utter drivel, badly written but meticulously researched. Le Queux spent several months touring an imaginary invasion route in the south-east of England assisted by the ageing former military legend and favoured son of the Secret Elite Lord Roberts of Kandahar, and the *Daily Mail*'s naval correspondent H.W. Wilson.[26] The chosen route included too many rural communities where circulation could never amount to much, so, in the interest of maximum profit and maximum upset, Northcliffe altered the route to allow 'the invaders' to terrorise every major town from Sheffield to Chelmsford.[27] The *Daily Mail* even printed special maps to accompany each edition to show where the invading Huns would strike the next day.[28]

It was an outrageous attempt to generate fear and resentment toward Germany. The personal involvement of Lord Northcliffe, Lord Roberts, who had been commander-in-chief of the army and a member of the Committee of Imperial Defence, and the naval historian Herbert Wrigley Wilson gave the impression that this was a work based on reality not fiction. In an act of mutual self-admiration, Lord Roberts publicly commended the novel to all who had the British Empire at heart, and Le Queux endorsed Lord Roberts' call for conscription to the armed forces. *The Invasion of 1910* was translated into 27 languages and sold over a million copies, though, to Le Queux's great embarrassment and considerable anger, in the pirated and abridged German version it was the Germans who won.[29]

Northcliffe was offensive and meant to be so. He explained his 'philosophy' in an interview with the French newspaper *Le Matin*:

> We detest the Germans cordially. They make themselves odious to the whole of Europe. I will not allow my paper [*The Times*] to publish anything which might in any way hurt the feelings of the French, but I would not like to print anything which might be agreeable to the Germans.[30]

He was, as the Belgian ambassador in London noted to his superiors in 1907: 'poisoning at pleasure the mind of an entire nation'.[31] He was indeed, but it was with the approval of the Secret Elite, whose ultimate success required fear and loathing to stir a hatred of Germany.

These ridiculous, poorly written and utterly outrageous stories raised the fear factor. People really believed that a German invasion was possible – likely, even. And the subtext, the very worrying additional threat that grew in the wake of this manipulation of public opinion, was the spy menace. Suddenly, the nation had been secretly infiltrated by thousands, no, hundreds of thousands, of spies. Success breeds imitation, and Le Queux soon found his spy plots and storylines about the German menace being pirated by other authors. E. Philips Oppenheim began his own crusade against German militarism, writing 116 barely readable and justifiably forgotten novels that made him a fortune. These included the 'revelation' that the kaiser intended to rule the German empire from London. Oppenheim claimed that 290,000 young men, all trained soldiers, were in place, posing as clerks, waiters and hairdressers, with orders to strike at the heart of Britain when the moment came.[32]

The spy mania sparked a forest fire whose heat generated genuine political concern. Even level-headed editors had trouble keeping the issue of spies and spying in perspective. By 1909, the net effect of Le Queux, and fellow charlatans who had jumped on this bandwagon to arouse a sleeping nation to a non-existent peril, was national paranoia.[33] The combination of the so-called naval race and the spectre of spies around every corner bred a rampant fear of Germany. The fiction was peddled as truth in the *Nation*, the *National Review*, the *Quarterly Review* and a whole host of editorials in the national press. These fantasies were swallowed whole by a readership far beyond what Winston Churchill called 'the inmates of Bedlam and the writers in the *National Review*'.[34] Secret Elite approval was reflected in Lord Esher's warning:

> A nation that believes itself secure, all history teaches is doomed. Anxiety, not a sense of security, lies at the readiness for war. An invasion scare is the will of God which grinds you a navy of dreadnoughts and keeps the British people in War-like spirit.[35]

The will of God, indeed. It was the will of the Secret Elite allied to its soulmates in the armaments industry.

By the autumn of 1907, Balfour and the Conservative opposition, bolstered by the press campaign, persuaded the government to appoint a further sub-committee of the Committee of Imperial Defence to consider the invasion threat.[36] The inmates were in danger of taking over the asylum. The sub-committee met 16 times between November 1907 and July 1908, and their report, published in October, rejected all of the invasion theories and surprise-attack scenarios. Such a message did not suit the Secret Elite, nor those promoting increased spending on the navy. Balfour, Lansdowne and the Conservatives portrayed it as a whitewash.

A further sub-committee of the CID was set up in March 1909 by Richard Haldane to examine the nature and extent of foreign espionage in Britain.[37] It recommended the creation of the British Secret Intelligence Bureau, a national intelligence service to operate both at home and abroad.[38] Haldane, who had been elevated to the House of Lords, moved the second reading of the Official Secrets Act in July 1911, stressing that his bill emanated from the deliberations of the Committee of Imperial Defence.[39] The first noble lord who rose to approve Haldane's Bill was both his and Lord Milner's friend Viscount Midleton, previously known as St John Brodrick, former secretary of state for war.

Such was the pressure to meet public expectation that the bill was rushed through its second and third readings in the House of Commons in a single afternoon with no detailed scrutiny and minimal debate.[40] Thus Asquith's Liberal government approved the setting up of what was to become the

British Secret Service through an Act of Parliament that was little more than a crisis reaction to public hysteria.[41] How ironic that the imaginary spies and outrageous scare stories from Le Queux and his ilk were responsible for the Secret Service Bureau. From these green shoots, planted in a flowerbed of fear and suspicion, both MI5 and MI6 were to grow into huge departments of national insecurity.

The deliberate undermining of public confidence by the press, and the excessive claims of imminent danger to the nation's survival voiced in Parliament and newspapers alike, slowly but surely eroded tolerance and trust. Liberal England was made to feel vulnerable. The influx of Polish and Russian refugees from the Jewish pogroms in the early years of the twentieth century had placed great social pressure on the East End of London, and a Royal Commission recommended the introduction of controls on their entry. These were not spies. They were desperately needy refugees, but fear of the foreigner now lurked deep in the national psyche.[42] They became the victims of Britain's first Aliens Act. A long-held tradition of succour for distressed peoples was the first casualty of the paranoia. The mounting fiction of bogus spy stories broke the resolve of Britain's traditional freedoms. The foreigner might not be what he seemed. The immigrant became a cause for concern where previously the proud tradition of liberalism made Britain a safe haven for the oppressed. The Official Secrets Act went much further than any before by empowering the authorities to arrest without warrant.[43] Freedoms eroded are rarely freedoms restored.

What the Official Secrets Act and the Secret Service Bureau achieved was greater protection for the Secret Elite. The ordinary man or woman on the streets of London, Birmingham or Glasgow had no need to be safeguarded against imaginary bogeymen. Nor had they anything to hide. The Secret Elite had much they needed to keep from the public eye: illicit agreements, illegal commercial deals, secret international treaties, preparations for war. This was what the Official Secrets Act was really about. The Secret Elite had made a vital move to further protect its own interests, not those of the British people.

SUMMARY: CHAPTER 10 – CREATING THE FEAR

- With his personal knowledge of the power of newspapers, Alfred Milner ensured that the Secret Elite gained control of a large section of the British press.
- The most important British newspaper, *The Times*, was given unprecedented access to the Foreign, Colonial and War offices.
- The Secret Elite vetted and approved Alfred Harmsworth as the new owner of *The Times* in 1908 because of his unstinting support for Milner

and the Boer War, and his anti-German sympathies.

- Harmsworth also controlled a large stable of popular newspapers with mass readership. Such was his value to the Secret Elite that he was elevated to the peerage as Lord Northcliffe. Henceforth he operated close to the inner circle.
- Northcliffe promoted deliberately concocted scare stories in his papers, including German invasions of England and the country being infiltrated by vast numbers of German spies.
- The ultimate aim was to undermine public confidence, create a menace where none existed and introduce legislation that eroded freedoms and protected the Secret Elite.

CHAPTER 11

Preparing the Empire – Alfred Milner and the Round Table

ALFRED MILNER REMAINED CONSUMED BY his ambition to ensure that the British Empire would dominate the world. He was a man on a mission. A large number of senior Conservatives, including Leo Amery, a fellow member of the inner core of the Secret Elite,[1] urged him repeatedly to enter Parliament. They saw him as their natural leader, but nothing could move Milner's resolve to remain in the shadows. In stepping back from the front line he avoided unwanted attention and was able to pursue his all-consuming agenda without the responsibility that attends representation. Contrary to the widely held belief that he withdrew altogether from politics following his return from South Africa in 1905, Milner set himself the mammoth task of preparing the Empire for war and bringing 'the most effective pressure to bear at once' if the necessity arose.[2] He gave serious consideration to how the different countries within the Empire would react to war with Germany. Haldane's reforms in Britain had prepared a small but highly trained British Expeditionary Force, but the Empire remained a vast untapped source of fighting men, the cannon fodder to ensure victory. In the early years of the twentieth century, Britain's Empire covered a very large portion of the earth's surface with a population of some 434,000,000, including over 6,000,000 men of military age.[3] This could neither be ignored nor taken for granted.

One of Milner's first tasks was to arrange a colonial conference in London in 1907. His stated agenda was to change the nature of the British Empire by creating an all-powerful imperial parliament that would reach across the world. At the same time, he had to ensure that the dominions were willing to stand by Britain in the coming war. He urged participants to be 'a single Power, speaking with one voice, acting and ranking as one great unity in the society of states'.[4] He pushed the heads of the dominions to develop a twofold patriotism: to their own homeland and to the 'wider fatherland'. If properly coordinated, the joint members of the Empire would become 'one of the great political forces of the world'.[5] His vision embraced an Empire of independent but loyal nations tied naturally to an imperial government constitutionally responsible to all the electors, with power to act directly on individual citizens. He brought together the leading lights to devise a plan for future cooperation that would lead to greater still ambition.[6] Quietly and unobtrusively, Alfred Milner sowed the first seeds for a world government. More immediately, he and his Secret Elite conspirators knew that when war came they had to be sure Australia, South Africa and the other great dominions of the Empire were ready and willing to stand shoulder to shoulder with Britain.

Australia's Premier Alfred Deakin was one of Milner's prime targets during and after the colonial conference. They shared a platform at the Queen's Hall on which Milner praised Australia's commitment to the Empire and stressed the links of race and loyalty that bound the two nations. On his journey home, Deakin wrote a letter urging Milner to take up the leadership of the 'Imperial Party'. As with many before him, he saw in Milner an inspirational character who could 'rally the younger men . . . attract a large section of British opinion which is waiting for a lead, and for an Empire Policy'. Such was Deakin's belief in Milner that he wrote: 'I can see no other man who will be so much trusted . . . You can turn the tide.'[7]

That was precisely the task that Milner set himself. He was no Canute, and he did not sit back and let events happen without asserting his convictions. One by one, he and his Secret Elite associates found ways to bind the dominions ever more closely to Britain. At the conference, a plan was adopted to organise dominion military forces in the same pattern as the British Army, so that they could be integrated in 'an emergency'. Milner's proposals led to a complete reorganisation of the armies of New Zealand, Australia and South Africa, with highly beneficial results.[8] Canada was the most challenging prospect. Its French-speaking Premier Wilfrid Laurier was a comparative outsider who was unmoved by appeals to Anglo-Saxon race unity.[9] Milner made Canada his priority.

At this time, Canada was recognised as the 'greatest dominion under the crown'.[10] British imperialists particularly treasured its wealth and future potential but feared that it might abandon its imperial connection in favour of closer economic and political cooperation with the United States. The well-proven Secret Elite tactic of manipulating colonial statesmen held little sway with the Canadian Premier. In Laurier's own words, the chief force they used to influence him was the pressure of a very select society. 'It is hard to stand up to the flattery of a gracious duchess . . . we were dined and wined by royalty and aristocracy and plutocracy and always the talk was Empire, Empire, Empire.'[11]

Milner decided that a coast-to-coast trip across Canada was necessary and prepared for the gruelling journey by meeting as many Canadians in Britain as he could. Amongst them was a young man whom the Secret Elite recognised as a future leader for Canada, W.L. Mackenzie-King. He met Milner at a Compatriots Club dinner in April 1908, recording in his diary: 'What was borne in upon me particularly in listening to Lord Milner was that . . . [it was] the furtherance of the power and strength of the British race that constituted the main purpose in their [imperialist] programme.'[12]

With the support of the Canadian Governor-General, Earl Grey, a member of the Secret Elite's inner core,[13] Milner toured Canada, crossing the country by rail to Vancouver. His message was one of praise for Canadian spirit and Canadian patriotism. He repeatedly stressed that Canada would be 'far greater as a member, perhaps in time the leading member, of that group of powerful though pacific nations, than she could ever be in isolation'.[14] His itinerary took him to Toronto and Montreal, where he reiterated his belief that he was a 'citizen of the Empire' whose final duty was to all the dominions of the Crown. 'That is my country,' was his bold pronouncement.[15]

The Secret Elite ensured that his trip was favourably reported in the British press. Northcliffe's *Daily Mail* hailed him as the 'brain-carrier of Imperial Policy' and forecast his rise to high office after a Conservative victory at the next election.[16] The subtext of Milner's message was much more subtle: power, duty, empire, loyalty. These were not chance remarks. His aim was to stir the Empire and its sense of collective responsibility. 'We should all cooperate for common purposes on the basis of absolute unqualified equality of status.'[17] The common purpose lay ahead.

On his return in June 1909, Lord Milner threw his energies into an Imperial Press Conference arranged and dominated by the Secret Elite. It was a grand affair that brought together over 60 newspaper owners, journalists and writers from across the Empire, both the governed (India) and the self-governing (Canada, Australia, South Africa and New Zealand). Six hundred of their counterparts from the British press, and politicians both in and out of government, mixed with military and naval staff at Shepherd's Bush Exhibition Hall. Lord Rosebery welcomed the delegates with warmth and dignity. The conference was, very tellingly, designed to rally the support of the Empire for the mother country in time of war and foster imperial cooperation in both defence and communications.

Rosebery's keynote address stressed that imperial defence was the most vital topic on the agenda. He warned that never before in the history of the world was there 'so threatening and overpowering a preparation for war'.[18] Though Germany was not mentioned by name, the clear inference was that the kaiser was responsible for the preparations for war. No evidence was presented for the simple reason that none existed. None, that is, beyond the vivid imaginations of the fiction writers encouraged by Northcliffe and his stable of alarmists. The appeal was directed to the delegates' sense of duty, their loyalty and, of course, their collective responsibility. Rosebery asked them to consider their heritage, their liberties and their race, the source of their language, and the institutions that made every single delegate present an essential part of the Empire. He called on them 'to take back to your young dominions across the seas' the message that 'the personal duty for national defence rests on every man and citizen of the Empire'.[19]

Asquith, Haldane, Churchill and Milner all addressed the delegates. Lord Roberts trumpeted his crusade for conscription from the platform. Milner argued that 'big armies . . . were a means of preserving peace'.[20] No expense was spared to accommodate and influence the journalists. The Australian delegate from *The Argus* of Melbourne wrote handsomely in admiration of Haldane and the British Army. He witnessed the presentation of colours to the new territorial regiments at Windsor and assured his readers that Germany would never dare invade Great Britain.[21] Armaments factories were visited in Manchester. Fairfields shipyard in Glasgow hosted the delegates and proudly displayed the destroyers being built for Australia. Honorary degrees were conferred on several leading newspapermen from Canada, Australia, India and South Africa. Every effort was made to impress – indeed, overawe – the visitors. The *pièce de résistance*, the grand propaganda coup that could never be trumped, was their visit to the naval review at Spithead, organised by Jacky Fisher himself. Geoffrey Dawson, representing then the *Fortnightly Review*, recorded his unqualified admiration. Moved by the overwhelming impact of 18 miles of battle-ready warships, he wrote that it was 'a wonderful sight and made me realise what British seapower is'. One of the journalists present noted that the fleet included seven dreadnoughts, 'so far the only ones afloat'.[22] Consider this last statement: 'so far the only ones afloat'. How can that square with Rosebery's assertion that others were engaged in 'threatening preparations for war'? The message the delegates were given was the same as that being delivered by the Northcliffe press: Britain and the Empire had to be prepared.

The final session of the Imperial Press Conference on 26 June was chaired by King Edward's personal advisor, Lord Esher, who examined the role of the colonies in 'imperial defence'. Delegates were wined and dined at the Waldorf before returning to inspire their readers across the Empire. The Imperial Press Conference was a major public-relations triumph. Northcliffe responded to congratulations on its success by claiming that it was 'one of the most important gatherings that has ever taken place in England'.[23] Replete with Secret Elite members and associates, what was the intended impact of this conference? They met Haldane, saw his new territorial army, Milner, Esher, Roberts, Rosebery, naval shipbuilders, Australian destroyers, the Spithead Review, with the reiterated message that big armies preserve peace. Crucially, these delegates were in position to encourage the young men of the colonies and dominions to sign their lives away in 1914. The success of these preparations should be judged by the level of willing volunteers from the Empire when war was declared.

Another important message learned from the conference was that bad news undermined efforts to promote the ideal of an empire gathered around a strong motherland that had to be defended at all costs. Delegates were deliberately shielded from reality during their carefully staged visit. The Secret Elite, and Milner in particular, were convinced that some concrete action had to be taken in order to stop the negative news stories of strikes, moral decay, social unrest, parliamentary discord and the general decline in standards that rolled off the British press and undermined confidence overseas. For those few weeks in June, a temporary truce had been called over dreadnoughts and budgets[24] because the Secret Elite fully understood that the old image of 'Merrie England', the 'Land of Hope and Glory', had to be sustained. Geoffrey Dawson advocated an 'Imperial Press Service' that pooled the news and was specifically designed to positively influence public opinion in every part of the Empire.[25]

While it was vital that the Empire was wholly organised for war, it was equally important that steps be taken to draw the dominions and colonies towards the Secret Elite vision of an all-powerful imperial parliament. The enthusiasm with which the press delegates departed for home was matched by the eagerness of a special breed of imperial zealots whom Milner had schooled in South Africa. The young men from his kindergarten returned to Britain fired with zeal. Guided by their mentor, they conspired to revolutionise the Empire by setting up small influential groups to promote the grand plan of imperial unification.[26] They dubbed themselves 'The Round Table', a grand Arthurian title which suggested equality of rank and importance, nobility of purpose and fairness in debate. In fact it was an unholy association of Rhodes' secret society. Milner was the authority to whom all gave recognition and service. His men from South Africa mixed with new adherents including Sir Alfred Zimmern, Sir Reginald Coupland and the American millionaires Waldorf and Nancy Astor, each of whom is named by Carroll Quigley as a member of the Secret Elite.[27]

Most members of the Round Table were lifelong friends. It was an intimate fellowship that held a high opinion of itself. They looked on one another with admiration and resolved to do great things together in the 'national interest'.[28]

Alfred Milner acted as both elder statesman and father figure, and his role in the Round Table was described as that of 'President of an Intellectual Republic'.[29] Their objective was to win power and authority in national and imperial affairs. Round Table groups were essentially 'propaganda vehicles' comprising a handful of influential people that Quigley believed were created 'to ensure that the dominions would join with the United Kingdom in a future war with Germany'.[30] Closer ties with the United States were also considered of crucial importance, and a Round Table group was established in New York to encourage links between Westminster and Washington, and high finance in the City of London and Wall Street. It was managed in secret, hidden from the electorate and the politicians, and went unreported in the press. Round Table members aimed to gain political influence and set the political agenda, but they were not willing to stand up in public. All was to be carried out in secret. How dangerous are those who believe that they have the capacity to think and plan for the nation's good, impervious to the will of the people and disdainful of democracy itself?

Funded originally by the South African gold 'bug', Sir Abe Bailey, Round Table groups were established in London, South Africa, Canada, Australia, New Zealand and the United States. They were also supported financially by the Rhodes Trust and wealthy Secret Elite members such as the Beit brothers in South Africa. Other contributors included the Astor family and wealthy individuals, trusts or firms associated with the international banking fraternity, including J.P. Morgan and the Rockefeller dynasty.[31]

Round Table members held private meetings, or 'moots', and worked out solutions to the national problems that fitted their philosophy.[32] Their plan involved the formation of powerful semi-secret groups in the major countries of the Empire to influence colonial governments and newspaper proprietors. It was a logical extension of the aims of the Imperial Press Conference. It advanced the fundamental idea of imperial unity. Once they had a blueprint and a body of supporters in all parts of the Empire, 'the quiet conspiracy could give way to a great crusade'.[33] Their techniques had been refined over the previous century, and Milner above all knew how to manipulate newspapers and influence editorials.

These individuals considered themselves the intellectual standard-bearers for Secret Elite policies. They promoted their aims anonymously in their periodical, *The Round Table: A Quarterly Review of the Politics of the British Empire*. The first article in the first issue of November 1910, 'Anglo-German Rivalry', was deliberately provocative. It set the tone for all the anti-German rhetoric that was to come. Carroll Quigley confirmed that this was the overriding purpose of the Round Table:

> There can be no doubt that the original inspiration for the Round Table movement was to be found in anti-German feeling. In fact, there are some indications that this was the primary motive and that the stated purpose of working for imperial federation was, to some extent at least, a mask.[34]

Unfortunately, he took that analysis no further. Nor can we find evidence, for secrecy surrounds almost everything that the Round Table organised. Indeed, as he put it: 'the whole group was so secretive that, even today, many close students of the subject are not aware of its significance'.[35]

The *Round Table* editor was Milner's protégé, Philip Kerr, but no name appeared in the magazine, neither editor nor contributors. Anonymity extended to an un-named secretary at 175 Piccadilly, to whom letters could be sent. The promoters claimed that they did not expect a large circulation but sought to directly influence a select public opinion.[36] Why they printed the journal without naming contributors was never explained, though at that level of conceit they probably didn't feel the need to justify themselves.

Practical politicians treated the *Round Table Quarterly Review* with deserved suspicion because it sought to influence power without responsibility. Nevertheless, the publications became an important forum for Secret Elite propaganda, and many of the ideas in later editions were translated into British foreign policy. Between 1910 and 1914, the *Round Table* exerted a tremendous influence on political thinking in every part of the Empire.[37] Essentially, it was an anti-German propaganda vehicle and an advocate of imperial unity.

Milner sent his most trusted acolytes to organise Round Table groups throughout the Empire. Between 1910 and 1912, Lionel Curtis travelled the world organising in India and Canada. Milner himself, accompanied by Philip Kerr, went back to Canada to inspire Round Table associates.[38] Their message, reinforced through articles in the Round Table's *Quarterly Review* and bolstered by their friends in the press, so carefully nurtured during the Imperial Press Conference, repeated the mantra of loyalty, duty, unity and the benefits of Empire . . . Empire . . . Empire. Members of Round Table groups across the world held influential positions in government, trade, commerce and banking. Theirs was a quasi-Masonic-Jesuit approach that allowed them to prepare the dominions for the coming war, hidden from the public view. It proved a resounding success. The Empire would be ready.

In the final analysis, Canada sent 641,000 men.[39] By 1917, it was delivering more than a quarter of the artillery munitions used by Britain on the Western Front. Over 250,000 Canadians worked in the armaments factories under the British Imperial Munitions Board.[40] South Africa provided 136,000 fighting troops as well as enlisting 75,000 non-whites.[41] Australia placed its navy under British command, and a total of 332,000 Australians went to war for the Empire. New Zealand provided 112,000 men, while India alone raised 1,477,000, including 138,000 men stationed on the Western Front in 1915.[42] In general, the governments that sent colonial troops paid for them.

Summary: Chapter 11 – Preparing the Empire – Alfred Milner and the Round Table

- Contrary to the belief that Alfred Milner retired from politics in 1905, he was heavily involved behind the scenes promoting imperial unity and preparing the Empire for war.
- He was instrumental in setting up a colonial conference in 1907 at which it became clear that considerable work was required to safeguard Canada's position within the Empire.
- The Imperial Press Conference in 1909, which was organised and dominated by the Secret Elite, proved an outstanding success. Its major theme concerned the duty and loyalty each dominion and colony owed to the 'Fatherland'.
- An imperial press service was specifically designed to disseminate good-news stories about Britain and influence public opinion throughout the Empire.
- At the same time, a secretive organisation, the Round Table, was created in London by Milner and his followers to influence governments about imperial unity and the defence of the Empire.
- These imperial 'think-tank-groups' were established across the British Empire and were funded by Secret Elite members and sympathisers.
- Their policies were published anonymously in the *Round Table* magazine.
- The entire organisation, which was hidden from public view, was highly antagonistic to Germany and would prove its worth in the years ahead.

CHAPTER 12

Catch a Rising Star and Put it in Your Pocket

THE SECRET ELITE WERE CONSTANTLY on the lookout for rising stars in politics and the diplomatic corps who might serve them well as agents. They would nurture, groom and fete them, and, if considered sufficiently malleable, draw them into the orbit of the group. None would join the select inner core, and most were not even conscious they were being controlled. Some may have guessed that they were indebted to an invisible force, but they asked no questions.[1] As we have seen, determined Revanchists in France, such as Delcassé, were considered particularly useful, as was Isvolsky, who dreamed of Russia's 'historic mission' to control the Straits. The key to compliance was the mutual desire to achieve their aims through the destruction of Germany. Public office, lavish lifestyles and personal gain were attractive by-products; ruthlessness, self-interest and avarice, essential prerequisites.

David Lloyd George was a politician identified, nurtured and drawn into the Secret Elite fold for several very important reasons. They considered him a potential asset unmatched by anyone else in the Liberal or Conservative parties. With his talent for skilful negotiation, the brilliant orator and audacious radical held sway with the working classes. He talked their language such that even militant trade union leaders accepted him. He had shown courage in taking a stance against jaundiced jingoism during the war in South Africa.[2] Lloyd George was so immediately associated with his anti Boer War stance, and his attacks on privilege and wealth, that his was the voice to which the people would listen and in which they could believe. Young, utterly ambitious and popular, he wasn't simply an orator at a time when the masses came to listen to great speeches, he was *the* inspirational orator of the age. His gift with words was dramatic, full of sound and fury. Ridicule and righteousness were the hallmarks of his vitriol, burning ambition the driving force behind his absolute determination to make it to the top. While he was determined to promote the social improvement of the lower classes, it was with even greater determination that he promoted David Lloyd George. It is worth repeating that as early as 1886 he had written to Margaret Owen, later his long-suffering wife, that 'my supreme idea is to get on . . . I am prepared to thrust even love itself under the wheels of my juggernaut if it obstructs the way.'[3]

Anything to get on. In that single phrase Lloyd George revealed his ruthless determination and greatest weakness, ambition. Detractors have called him 'a man without conviction',[4] claiming that he was shallow and opportunistic in most of his actions and at all times 'a man who did deals'.[5] And so it proved.

Campbell-Bannerman included Lloyd George in his 1906 cabinet, a radical balance to the Liberal imperialists like Grey and Haldane. The Secret Elite understood both the advantages and disadvantages of his presence there. He was a figurehead around whom men would rally, and his opinion carried great weight amongst many Liberal Members of Parliament. But how would he react to the vital question of war against Germany? Logically, Lloyd George was the man least likely to support their ambitions. If anyone could rally the Liberal Party and the country against war, it was him. Whoever he sided with would have a great advantage, and the Secret Elite set out to ensure that the advantage lay with them. Most crucially, no backbench MP or member of the public would ever suspect that a Cabinet in which Lloyd George sat would secretly be planning war. The Secret Elite's option was straightforward: he either had to be turned or turned out.

Lloyd George's performance as president of the Board of Trade in Campbell-Bannerman's government of 1905 caught their eye. He successfully steered a Merchant Shipping Act through that first parliamentary session, much to the benefit of the shipowners. His agreement to raise the Plimsoll line allowed ships to carry heavier cargoes but made them less stable. Losses of ships and men increased, but owners saved £8 million on building new ships and were appreciative of Lloyd George's willingness to act on their behalf.[6] It was a strange concession from the radical Liberal that gave rise to accusations that he had been responsible for the deaths of British seamen in the interests of the shipowners. The Social Democratic Forum, led by an old Etonian, described the raising of the Plimsoll line as:

> One of the most shameful things done to the working class of this country . . . Lloyd George has been officially murdering the seamen of British vessels in the interests of the shipowning class. This man George is an unscrupulous and murdering rascal.[7]

Lloyd George was clearly a man with whom the Secret Elite could do business. By averting a national railway strike in 1907, he again attracted their approval. *The Times* called him 'the greatest asset of the government with the commercial classes',[8] and he was subsequently invited to the state banquet for the visiting kaiser at Windsor Castle: a sure sign that his star was in the ascendancy.[9]

In April 1908, Lloyd George was made chancellor of the Exchequer in Asquith's first Cabinet, a remarkable promotion and one that raised his salary from £2,000 per year to £5,000.[10] But was the rising star already in the Secret Elite's ample pocket? Had they intended to destroy him, they could have done so several times over. By pandering to his many weaknesses and drawing him into a dependency, they did the very opposite.

Lloyd George harboured two serious cravings: a wealthy lifestyle and sex. Wealth and patronage the Secret Elite could provide in abundance, and he himself oozed the charm and dynamism, sometimes to the point of predatory insistence, to 'conquer' the opposite sex.

From his earliest days in Parliament, Lloyd George developed a taste for the 'good life'. His source of wealth necessarily came from others. Early attempts at speculative moneymaking were generally a disaster. He had been involved in a Patagonian gold syndicate that failed to realise the expected fortune and is alleged to have tried to sell his shares to an unwitting investor after he discovered there was no gold.[11] He progressed to the Liberal Party's front ranks and dined with King Edward. With typical immodesty he wrote to his brother that he had made a favourable impression on the king.[12] D.R. Daniel, a friend and companion in his early years, acknowledged that Lloyd George accepted funds from rich patrons without compunction. He stayed at the best hotels and dined at the best restaurants, had the most comfortable and most expensive seats reserved for him and expected to be treated as a . . . well, as a lord! It never seemed to embarrass him when he accepted favours. He exploited his wealthy supporters and they in turn fed his habit, knowing full well that there would be a payback.[13]

Lloyd George was constantly in trouble over his extra-marital relationships. Women were a damaging distraction, and fidelity was completely beyond him. His daughter claimed bluntly that he started having affairs soon after he was married.[14] He blamed his wife Margaret for his serial adultery because she was reluctant to move from Wales to London.[15] Lloyd George entered into relationships with scant regard for the women he left behind. His appendage was rumoured to be as large as his ego, but neither serve as adequate explanation for his sexual misbehaviour.[16] And of course it landed him in serious trouble. As early as 1897 he was forced to deny the allegation that he had fathered an illegitimate child with a Mrs Catherine Edwards.[17] Though that in itself would have meant his resignation from Parliament, he escaped being cited by her husband in court 'in rather mysterious circumstances'.[18] What these precisely were, we may never know, but 'mysterious circumstances' frequently surrounded him.

In 1908, scandalous rumours linked Lloyd George and Lady Julia Henry, wife of Sir Charles Henry MP, a Liberal colleague and millionaire merchant. The *Sunday People* inferred that Lloyd George managed to avoid being named as a co-respondent in the subsequent Henry divorce case because the injured husband had been bought off for £20,000.[19] Lloyd George looked into the political abyss and saw the darkness of final rejection. He was obliged to sue the *People* to save his name. Matters were so critical that the errant husband had to beg his wife Margaret to accompany him to court. According to his son, the desperate Lloyd George promised her: 'If I get over this, I give my oath that you shall never have to suffer this ordeal again.'[20]

He was represented in court by a team of legal colossi: Rufus Isaacs, the future Lord Reading and Lord Chief Justice; F.E. Smith, the future Lord Birkenhead; and Raymond Asquith, the prime minister's son. Ranged against this venerable trio was one of the most formidable advocates of the time, the Right Honourable Sir Edward Carson, KC MP. Here was the man who had personally nailed Oscar Wilde to the public pillory, stripped him of any vestige of dignity, frozen the caustic tongue with which Wilde had taunted the aristocracy, and destroyed for ever that self-styled genius.[21]

On 12 March 1909, the hyenas packed the press benches in anticipation of a legal free-for-all that might end the career of the most high-profile politician of that period. How many former lovers would Carson cite to demolish the chancellor's claims of innocence and fidelity?

What happened next gave rise to one of the greatest mysteries that ever surrounded the unscrupulous Welshman. Once Lloyd George had categorically denied the *People*'s allegations, Sir Edward Carson, representing the newspaper, did nothing more than ask a few meaningless questions. There was no cross-examination. No witnesses were called. The trial was over. Lloyd George had been raised from the edge of the abyss and retained his parliamentary office. Miraculously, he was deemed blameless. He had been grossly over-represented by the top legal brains in England, but to whom was Lloyd George forever indebted? The *People* had retained Edward Carson, the most expensive King's Counsel in the land, yet he failed to present their case. Why? What powerful strings had been pulled inside the hidden chambers of the legal profession?

It is impossible to determine precisely the point at which the Secret Elite drew Lloyd George into their web, but by rescuing his career they protected their chosen man. The rising star was not allowed to fall. In return, they gained an asset of peerless value. His indiscretions had been so numerous and his dependence on their largess become so strong that had he wished to turn back, he faced political oblivion. There was no escape from the web they had woven around him.

Six weeks after his court appearance, on 29 April 1909 Lloyd George presented his self-styled 'People's Budget' to the House of Commons.[22] A means-tested old-age pension had been introduced 12 weeks earlier and additional revenue was required to pay for it. The pension, which ranged from one shilling to five shillings per week, was for citizens aged over seventy who were living in poverty. Some 30 years earlier, Germany had introduced a significantly more generous old-age pension. While the banner-headline of the 'People's Budget' focused on social legislation, the £16 million shortfall in revenues was mainly caused by the additional spending on dreadnoughts. Much of the deficit that Lloyd George was trying to fill at the Exchequer was due to increased spending on defence.[23] By deliberately including a land tax that infuriated the gentry, Lloyd George designed his budget to provoke the House of Lords. On 30 July 1910, he addressed a massed gathering at Limehouse and waded into the Conservative opposition.[24] He directly attacked peers like the Duke of Northumberland for valuing land at 30 shillings an acre until the local authority wanted to build a school on it, whereupon the valuation rose instantly to £900 per acre.[25] In October, he roused the massive crowds at Newcastle by lambasting the House of Lords as '500 men, ordinary men chosen accidentally from among the unemployed' and claimed that they were forcing a revolution which would be eventually directed by the people.[26] Churchill also joined in the provocation, and Asquith did very little to control them.[27]

The bill's passage through the Commons took over 70 parliamentary days but was finally passed on 4 November. The next hurdle was the House of Lords, bedrock of Conservative peers and hereditary noblemen. It should have been a formality because in over 200 years a finance bill had never been formally rejected in the upper house.

The great debate in the House of Lords lasted six nights.[28] Their Lordships refused to accept the budget unless the country approved it through a general election. Uproar followed, but self-interest won the day. In his warped antediluvian approach to social justice, the gambling spendthrift Henry Chaplin MP, who owned some 4,000 acres of Lincolnshire, claimed that the old-age pension was 'the greatest possible discouragement to thrift'.[29] Alfred Milner deeply resented the 'People's Budget', railing against the 'utterly rotten and bad way of financing old-age pensions' because the shortfall would come from 'taxes raised exclusively from the rich'.[30] He told an audience of Conservatives in Glasgow that its consequences were 'evil'.

Consider Milner's words carefully. It was not the building of warships, the preparations for war, the commitment to Armageddon he deemed 'evil' but provision for the most vulnerable elderly people in Britain. His philosophy was straightforward and absolute: 'If we believe a thing to be bad, and if we have a right to prevent it, it is our duty to try to prevent it and damn the consequences.'[31] This was Milner at his most revealing: 'damn the consequences', so reminiscent of 'disregard the screamers'.

Lord Rothschild, who had vigorously campaigned for more dreadnoughts, also took up arms against the budget, denouncing it as 'the end of all, the negation of faith, of family, of property, of Monarchy, of Empire' – in short 'revolution'.[32] Such were the values the Secret Elite wanted to impose on the whole world in the name of the extended British Empire. When news of the defeat in the Lords came through, the great 'champion of the poor', Lloyd George, was dining at Frascati's, a top London restaurant in the Strand.

Having been subjected to bullying arrogance from their Lordships, Asquith threatened to reform the House of Lords and greatly reduce its constitutional powers. He dissolved Parliament and called a general election early in 1910. Recent by-election triumphs appeared to promise victory to the Conservatives, and their chosen government would have been led by Arthur Balfour and might have included Lord Curzon, Lord Lansdowne and, of course, though he professed no interest, Alfred Milner. At a stroke, all of the proposed legislation would have been abandoned and the business of governing returned to the safe hands of the natural elite.

Democracy dealt them a very different hand. In the ensuing election, the Liberals suffered serious reverses but held on to a majority, albeit of only two over the Conservatives, in a hung parliament.[33] The Liberals survived in power thanks to support from both the emerging Labour Party with 40 seats and the Irish Home Rulers with 82. Asquith's government now depended on the support of the Irish Members of Parliament, putting Irish Home Rule firmly back on the political agenda. There was frequent talk of Cabinet resignations, but none took place.[34] Asquith had not formally asked the king to create new peers, and the Cabinet was unsure on how it wanted to limit the powers of the House of Lords. Should it be elected? Did they require a referendum? No one had a clear view, and there was little hope that King Edward would rescue them. He did worse than that.

On 6 May 1910, King Edward VII died of a bronchial complication that was in no little way caused by his gluttony, his overindulgences and his constant smoking. He was sixty-eight years old and had been on the throne for nine. His intimate association with the Secret Elite through Lord

Esher, Lord Milner, Lord Lansdowne and others had guided British foreign policy into a very different twentieth century and done much to prepare the way for war. King Edward thoroughly disliked the constitutional change through which the Liberals claimed they were going to reform the House of Lords, and many Conservatives genuinely believed that Asquith had caused his death.

On 7 May, Alfred Milner and about 50 other peers took the oath and kissed the hand of King George V. A quarter of a million people filed past King Edward's catafalque at Westminster Hall. It was widely rumoured in the Conservative press that when Asquith came to pay his formal respects, Queen Alexandra told him bitterly, 'Look at your handiwork.'

Alfred Milner waited at Windsor to receive the body and attend the service at St George's Chapel. He predicted that in the new reign of King George V the British Empire would either be 'consolidated' or 'disrupted'.[35] Milner knew that with Edward dead and the Liberals still in power, the Secret Elite were themselves in uncharted waters. Although they used corrupt politicians to their own end, men who would sell their souls to stay in power were abhorrent to Milner. Even so, he was a pragmatist, prepared to work with anyone who would advance the great cause of British-race supremacy. The spirit of the dead king was invoked in a carefully worded editorial in Northcliffe's *Observer*. The editor, James Garvin, concocted a message from the grave calling for 'A Truce of God', as if the recently deceased king's last message to his grieving people was a plea for national unity exclusively revealed in the columns of *The Observer*[36] and blessed by the Almighty. His text ran:

> If King Edward upon his deathbed could have sent a last message to his people he would have asked us to lay party politics aside, to sign a truce of God over his grave, to seek . . . some fair means of making a common effort for our common country . . . let conference take place before conflict is irrevocably joined.[37]

Voice of the king? No, this was the voice of the Secret Elite.

A former columnist for the *Daily Telegraph*, Garvin had been handpicked by Northcliffe as the *Observer*'s editor. A true-blue Conservative and close friend of Admiral Fisher, Garvin was probably the last person to whom you might expect the Liberals to listen, but they did. With the approval of his Cabinet, Asquith called a 'constitutional conference' to see how far the two major parties might agree on a common approach and possibly even a coalition. A newspaper stunt was turned into a strategy, and it took 21 meetings of the 'constitutional conference' before the futility of such meaningless time-wasting was recognised.[38]

Lloyd George suddenly found he had a new message. A strident critic of the Conservatives in public, he became an advocate of compromise in private. According to Donald McCormick in *The Mask of Merlin*: 'In honeyed whispers he was heard at the dinner tables of Mayfair to give the words "Coalition Government" a melodious and seductive air.'[39] He held private meetings with Arthur Balfour that had to be kept secret even from his own Cabinet colleagues. Lloyd George was apparently prepared to concede a stronger navy, accept compulsory military service and agree a compromise on Irish Home Rule. It was a betrayal of virtually everything he had originally stood for, a betrayal of the wishes of the majority of the British people and a betrayal of his party. It did, however, safeguard his own position.

On 17 August 1910, he produced 29 pages of typescript that set out the case for a coalition government to 'unite the resources of the two parties'.[40] He proposed a formal alliance between Liberals and Conservatives that would have unquestionably sunk the constitutional reform. Britain, he argued, faced imminent impoverishment if not insolvency. Well, he was chancellor and would have had access to the Treasury figures. Despite the country's empty coffers, he proposed expensive compulsory military training. What? The great Liberal radical proposing conscription by any other name? The Conservatives would never have dared to go to the polls advocating this policy no matter how much they wanted to. It would have been electoral suicide. But Lloyd George? If anyone could convince the country, it was him. His memorandum did insist on the passage of bills already proposed for land, unemployment and insurance, but his view on constitutional reform and the Irish Question, especially the Irish Question, were stumbling blocks. Finally, he turned his attention to 'imperial problems', and his suggestions could have been written by Alfred Milner himself. Perhaps they were, for they read like a Round Table script. He advocated 'schemes for uniting together the Empire and utilizing and concentrating its resources for defence as for commerce'.[41] The rising star was now very firmly in the pocket of the Secret Elite.

Lloyd George's new 'philosophy', if indeed it was ever his, was a hybrid collection of ideas that would never have been acceptable to true Liberals. Obliged by the command of King George V to cut short a holiday in Austria, he shared his memorandum with the king at Balmoral before he had given his own prime minister sight of the document.[42] When he returned to his Welsh home, Winston Churchill and his wife Clementine immediately joined him. Churchill, of course, was more interested in what post Lloyd George had proposed for him than any other consideration.

Contemporary observers were concerned and perplexed. Charles

Hobhouse noted on 4 November 1910 that 'curious movements were taking place. Balfour has been daily at 11 Downing Street [the chancellor of the Exchequer's abode] for the last fortnight' and the details he wrote in his diary stated that a plan was afoot to defeat the government over the finance bill so that 'Balfour would become Prime Minister with Lloyd George as second-in-command'.[43]

Asquith should have quashed such disloyal behaviour, and it is absolutely untrue that he would have accepted proposals that effectively removed him from the office of prime minister. Yet here we have a new phenomenon: Lloyd George in furtive discussions with Arthur Balfour, the leading Conservative member of the Secret Elite.[44]

Like many of Lloyd George's political intrigues, this came to nothing. His proposals reeked of desperation, and neither the Liberal rank and file nor the Conservative Party itself was ever likely to accept such cut-and-dried machinations. His less than subtle moves to oust Asquith were abandoned. On 28 November 1910, with deadlock and stalemate in Parliament, the prime minister dissolved it and called a second general election. The result was almost exactly identical to the election held earlier in the year.[45] Yet again, the Liberal government could only survive with the help of the Labour Party and the Irish Nationalists.

This time they took decisive action. A Parliament Bill removed the right of the House of Lords to amend or vote down finance bills and reduced their powers to reject legislation from the House of Commons. Asquith had been given a secret undertaking by King George V that he would create the required number of Liberal peers to force through the constitutional changes.[46] With typical public-school bravado, their lordships opposed change from within by dividing themselves into two factions: the 'Hedgers' and the 'Ditchers'. Surprisingly, the 'Hedgers' were led by Lord Curzon, while Milner, who championed the 'Ditchers', was actively working throughout 'to incite as many as possible of the peers to vote against surrender'.[47] The final vote in favour of change was passed by 131 to 114. The Secret Elite had to protect the king from the embarrassment of creating hundreds of new peers, and they did not want to see nearly 250 'glorified grocers' inside their private chambers.[48]

The Parliament Act of 1911 was hailed as a great victory for the Liberals and a humiliating defeat for the Conservatives and the House of Lords. Balfour was the scapegoat. Denounced by the *National Review* in an article headed 'Balfour Must Go', he took the fall, and leadership of the Conservative Party was passed to Andrew Bonar Law.[49]

And what was this great victory? Had the House of Lords been crushed? Did hereditary peerage come to an end? Was there a marked reduction in the powers of the aristocracy? No, not at all. The House of Lords continued as a bastion of Conservative peers, introducing its self-promoting legislation and challenging social reform. Yet the Secret Elite had established another important bulkhead in Asquith's Cabinet in David Lloyd George. More, much more, lay ahead for the Welsh former firebrand who had shown willing to go along with their plans. He knew very well who paid the piper, and as long as he benefited personally and was maintained in the style and comfort to which he had become addicted, he was willing to dance to their tune. His star remained in the ascendancy, but its orbit had been dramatically changed.

SUMMARY: CHAPTER 12 – CATCH A RISING STAR AND PUT IT IN YOUR POCKET

- The Secret Elite identified and nurtured malleable politicians and diplomats across Europe and continued to seek emerging talent in Britain and the Empire.
- On the face of it, Lloyd George appeared to be the least likely politician in Britain to be brought under their influence. His anti-war rhetoric and aggressive stance against the aristocracy and landed gentry marked him out as a man of the people.
- His performance as president of the Board of Trade from 1906 caught their attention because of his willingness to concede to the interests of big business.
- Lloyd George's love of the good life and his insatiable sexual appetite rendered him vulnerable. His career could have been ended several times over had the Secret Elite chosen to destroy him. Instead, they protected his reputation, defended him against damaging allegations and saved his career.
- Although his 1909 budget was hailed as a great step forward in social reform, this masks the fact that half of the money raised was spent on preparation for eventual war with Germany.
- The House of Lords chose to reject the budget and the consequent constitutional crisis led to a general election in January 1910.
- Following King Edward VII's death, the Secret Elite promoted the idea of a coalition government comprising all their main political agents from both major parties.
- Contrary to his supposed 'principles', Lloyd George produced a memorandum that revealed an astonishing willingness to promote the Secret Elite agenda. It included most of the Round Table policies on defence, Empire, trade and military service as a basis for the coalition.
- It came to nothing and a second indecisive general election was held in

December 1910 with no change of government.

- What had changed was the fact that David Lloyd George was now firmly in the pocket of the Secret Elite.

CHAPTER 13

Moroccan Myths – Fez and Agadir

In the blazing hot summer of 1911, at the height of the tension between Asquith's government and the House of Lords, the Secret Elite deliberately took Europe to the brink of war by engineering a second crisis in Morocco. The reintroduction of Théophile Delcassé to the French cabinet marked a new era in their influence on French politics, as did the strategic switch of Alexander Isvolsky from St Petersburg to Paris. Within weeks, France displayed renewed aggression in Morocco by finding a pretext to send in a large military force. When it became an army of occupation, Germany objected. It was virtually 1905 revisited. The Secret Elite conjured the myth that Germany intended to build a naval base on the North African coast to threaten shipping lanes and so created an international storm. War was once more on the agenda.

The 1906 Algeciras Act solemnly proclaimed Morocco's integrity and independence, but secret deals had subsequently enabled bankers, concession hunters, land grabbers and speculators to slowly strangle the country. With British collusion and encouragement, the French systematically reduced the power of the sultan's government and steadily siphoned off its wealth. Moroccan resources were placed in hock to international bankers, with the entire customs revenues mortgaged to guarantee the interest paid to European bondholders on two major loans. The interest on a 1904 loan stood at 60 (sixty!) per cent. A 1910 loan attracted interest at 40 per cent.[1] Morocco, like most African countries, was bled dry by international exploitation.

The act had placed the Moroccan tribes under the joint jurisdiction of French and Spanish police forces, who proved very willing to crush any resistance. French brutality was relentless. In July 1907, local tribesmen in Casablanca reacted violently when European workmen removed gravestones from their native cemeteries to build a new harbour. French battleships retaliated by bombarding the town. Nearly every inhabitant was killed or wounded and the death toll numbered thousands.[2] It was an episode of spiteful revenge and a gross overreaction to the killing of nine European workers, including three Frenchmen. France took the opportunity to assert its 'imperial' control by sending in 15,000 troops with an order to enforce prompt and vigorous repression. An indemnity of two and a half million francs was imposed on the Chaouyas tribes because they had 'made war' against France by killing three French workmen.[3] It was a fearsome reprisal. French troops occupied Casablanca and a wide area round it. Typically, after the bombardment of the city, the French extracted $12,000,000 from the Moroccan government to cover the cost of their retribution.[4]

Lies about the incident were spread across the globe. The killing of nine foreign workers who had desecrated a Muslim burial ground was reported as a 'Massacre in Morocco'.[5] The *Daily Mail* raised the spectre of a Holy War and claimed that the 'massacre' had been 'premeditated and organised'.[6]

Within three weeks, the French claim was that the Moorish ports 'must stay in the hands of civilisation'.[7] Little mention was ever made of the excessive brutality of the French response. The *New York Times* reported that impartial observers believed that the French had gone to Casablanca to stay. 'They are repeating the history of the Americans in Cuba and the Philippines, of the French in Indo-China, and of the English in Egypt. They all started by fighting the natives and ended by keeping the country.'[8] The 'impartial observers' were absolutely correct.

The French Chamber of Deputies had on nine occasions between 1906 and 1911 passed resolutions by large majorities expressing its determination to uphold the Algeciras Act and disclaiming intervention in the internal affairs of Morocco. Like the British parliamentarians, the French were completely misled and had no knowledge of secret agreements. They believed that they were in charge of foreign policy, but, as the British MP and journalist E.D. Morel revealed, policy was being pursued by 'wire-pullers behind the scenes'.[9]

The Secret Elite's chief 'wire-puller' in France, the irrepressible Théophile Delcassé, was brought back into the French cabinet as minister of Marine in early March 1911. It was a greater tragedy than anyone could have imagined. The man forced to resign for taking France to the brink of war with Germany during the first Moroccan crisis was back in government and placed in charge of the French navy. The Frenchman had been described as 'an instrument' of the late King Edward VII, and though Delcassé was not officially involved in foreign policy, the Belgian ambassador Baron Greindl considered him 'far too ambitious and restless a man not to try and impress his ideas upon his colleagues. He would almost seem to have been invited to do so . . .'[10] By whom? Whose influence was used to revive the Revanchist?

Delcassé's impact was felt immediately. Ambassador Greindl noted that the president of the French Senate began to speak more openly of 'Revanche' than he had for years and that French newspapers found some cause or other for daily complaint against Germany. As soon as Delcassé returned to public office, France employed a policy of aggression in Morocco. It was not a coincidence.

Neither was Alexander Isvolsky's appearance in Paris as the newly appointed Russian ambassador to France. Isvolsky, who had stirred the Balkans in 1908 and craved Russian control of Constantinople, joined Delcassé, whose life's ambition was the return of Alsace-Lorraine. Both were inextricably linked to the Secret Elite. Isvolsky believed that he could more effectively orchestrate war against Germany from his base in Paris rather than the Foreign Office in St Petersburg.[11] The day after his return to the French Cabinet, Delcassé met Isvolsky, who described him as 'the most prominent member of the Cabinet'. He added that Delcassé saw his first task as 'the provision of a strong fleet and would ensure that the Cabinet would redouble its efforts in regard to the army'.[12] Although his given post was minister of Marine, Delcassé's forceful and dominating personality swamped the French foreign minister, Jean Cruppi, who was 'entirely without diplomatic experience'.[13] Delcassé was back and he meant business.

In Morocco, native discontent came to a head in the spring of 1911, when the French publicly executed Moroccan deserters. Allegedly, a revolt took place in the city of Fez. Alarming reports were generated by the French that the lives of Europeans in the almost inaccessible Moroccan capital were in danger.[14] French and British newspapers flooded the public with exaggerated stories of an entire European colony living in great fear and anguish. The ultimate fate of the women and children was described in most moving terms. Rebels had allegedly encircled Fez with a ring of 'iron and flame'.[15] There was talk of an international crisis, possibly war. It read like a French Mafeking.

Under the pretext of impending atrocities, a large French military contingent was sent to Fez. On 5 April, Jules Cambon, the French ambassador in Berlin, notified the Germans that a punitive expedition to rescue the Europeans would make it necessary for them to occupy the port of Rabat before moving into the interior of Morocco. Cambon promised that France would respect the Treaty of Algeciras and withdraw her troops as soon as order had been restored.[16] General Moinier reached the Moroccan capital at the head of a French expeditionary force in early May. He found the city perfectly quiet and the Europeans unmolested.[17] The rebels and their ring of 'iron and flame' had apparently disappeared like the morning dew. The phantom so dextrously conjured had disappeared in the night. The whole story had been concocted for devious purposes.[18]

On 2 May, John Dillon, the leading Irish Home-Ruler, asked the foreign secretary in the House of Commons if the government had received any reports from British agents in Morocco

> that Europeans in Fez were in danger or were unable to escape from Fez if they desired to do so, and had the British government any information to the effect that the Emperor of Morocco had sanctioned the advance of European troops on Fez?[19]

Sir Edward Grey avoided a straight answer. He retreated into a response that placed all responsibility for information about Fez on a verbal report from the French government. Keir Hardie weighed into the attack by asking about an international syndicate that was trying to gain control of Morocco's mineral wealth.[20] Sir Edward Grey ignored the question. He simply didn't give an answer. He knew that there were only ten British citizens in Fez, including six women and two children.[21] He knew there was no significant European colony. Equally, he knew that there had been no Moroccan attacks on Europeans.

The Secret Elite encouraged the French military invasion of Morocco purely to elicit a German response and bring about the desired international crisis. And what better excuse than to challenge the mining rights that the sultan had given to a German company which conflicted with the interests of the French Union des Mines Marocaines[22] in the guise of rescuing Europeans from a non-existent crisis?

Even after the reality of the situation became commonly known, Grey persisted in lying. His memoirs recorded that Fez was in danger and France was forced to send troops there to 'relieve the situation and prevent catastrophe'.[23] Baron Greindl telegraphed Brussels on 10 May:

> Since the Act of Algeciras . . . little by little the French have got possession of everything, taking advantage of incidents which have arisen automatically, and creating other openings when they were needed . . . Can the expedition now be regarded as anything else other than an act of the same farce? Sultan Mulai Hafid has already lost his precarious hold over his subjects, because he had to submit to become a mere tool in the hands of France.[24]

The perceptive Belgian diplomat was absolutely correct. France treated the Algeciras agreement like waste paper. It continued to conquer Morocco by direct military action and piecemeal occupation. It fomented internal discord and strangled the revenues of the Moorish government. The Secret Elite encouraged every step the French took while Europe was dragged nearer and nearer to the abyss. Baron Greindl observed that:

> The most interesting feature is the forbearance with which the German government pretends to ignore . . . the conquest of Morocco . . . She can choose between pretending not to see, and war, which the Emperor will not have, and which would be condemned by German public opinion.[25]

There was no appetite for war in Germany. The clamour for action, the undisguised overreaction, was entirely one-sided. Indeed, Kaiser Wilhelm, who believed that life was at risk in Fez, initially welcomed the French intervention to stabilise the sultanate.[26]

By the close of June, the entire country between the capital and the coast had been overrun by French troops.[27] When it became clear that the French army had no intention of leaving Fez, Germany reached the end of her patience. She complained that, despite assurances to the contrary, France was ignoring the Algeciras Act and ignoring German interests in Morocco with contemptuous disrespect. A symbolic protest was required. On 1 July, a German warship on its voyage home from southern Africa was rerouted to Agadir, a hitherto unknown town on the Atlantic coast of Morocco. The *Panther* was a gunboat of a thousand tons carrying two 10.5-calibre guns, six machine guns and one hundred and twenty-five men. In stark contrast to the wanton destruction meted out by the French navy on Casablanca, the small German gunboat anchored off the coast fired no shots and landed none of its crew.[28] Yet it was the *Panther* that drew all the venom.

At the same time, Germany presented a Note to the French government stating that their occupation of Fez was incompatible with the Algeciras agreement, respect for the sovereignty of the sultan and the integrity of Morocco. The German government was prepared to discuss a solution to the Moroccan question and willing to listen to any sensible proposal. Germany made it clear that she would not ask anything exorbitant of France and had neither landed men at Agadir nor had any intention of doing so.[29] She was seeking clarity and compensation, not war.

Although Britain had no territorial interest in Morocco, a wave of outraged anti-German bile filled the British press. Winston Churchill's view was that the *Panther* at Agadir was part of an untimely German attempt to set up a naval base from which it could attack allied shipping en route to the Canary Islands and South Africa.[30] It was an absurd suggestion, not least because the coast at Agadir had no deep-water harbour.[31] Sir Edward Grey would later resurrect the old chestnut that the *Panther* incident was yet another German attempt to break the Entente Cordiale, intended to provoke war with France.[32]

SOLID.

GERMANY. "DONNERWETTER! IT'S ROCK. I THOUGHT IT WAS GOING TO BE PAPER."

How the British and French press twisted the Agadir crisis to make the kaiser an object of derision.

(Reproduced with permission of Punch Ltd., www.punch.co.uk)

The warmongers breathed 'fire and brimstone' against Germany.[33] Edward Grey urged the French prime minister to adopt a belligerent attitude that would probably have led to war had he yielded to the advice.[34] In a moment of supreme irony, Sir Arthur Nicolson, permanent under-secretary at the Foreign Office since 1910, complained to the German ambassador in London that in anchoring the *Panther* off Agadir, Germany was violating the Act of Algeciras. He made no mention of the fact that France and Spain already had 100,000 troops occupying the country.

The Times of 20 July warned menacingly that Germany was claiming 'absolute European predominance',[35] and Grey personally blamed Germany for creating 'a new situation'.[36] According to his memoirs, Germany sent the gunboat to Agadir 'suddenly' after the French force entered Fez,[37] but in truth Germany had waited for almost two months while trying her best to resolve the situation through diplomacy.

Despite that, Sir Hew Strachan, emeritus professor of the history of war at Oxford University, and a fellow of All Souls, wrote in 2003:

> What had been a Franco-German dispute about colonial ambitions, designed to be resolved by diplomacy, now became an issue of vital national interest

> to Britain. Germany had deployed sea power beyond the purlieus of its immediate geographical waters; this was a direct threat to the premier navy in the world.[38]

Consider, please, the outrageous nature of this statement. A small German gunboat with a crew of 125 was painted as a 'direct threat to the premier navy in the world' and its presence as an 'issue of vital national interest to Britain'. Six days before the *Panther* dropped anchor in the Atlantic off Agadir, the entire British navy had paraded in a Coronation Review of the fleet at Spithead: 167 warships with an aggregate tonnage of over 1,000,000 tons, manned by 60,000 officers and men – the largest fleet ever assembled at that time, covering 18 square miles and arranged in 5 long main lines, with smaller lines filled with destroyers, submarines and torpedo craft, had been ceremonially inspected by the king on board HMY *Victoria and Albert III*.[39] The *Panther* was barely 1,000 tons. The royal yacht was almost five times heavier itself. Seen in the light of historical reality, Strachan's statement is absurd.

Like many of his contemporaries, Professor Strachan makes no mention of the secret treaties that carved up Morocco. The American writer Frederick Bausman suggested that: 'It is a good test of writers who discuss the cause of the war how they refer to the secret treaty of 1904. If they omit or do not reasonably discuss the secret part of the treaty, they must be viewed with caution.'[40] Good advice.

In the midst of diplomatic discussions between Germany and France, *The Times* kept up a barrage of protest. Its editorials and Paris dispatches were characterised by verbal violence. On 20 July, the newspaper stated that Germany was making outrageous 'demands' upon France and that no British government would tolerate them 'even if the French government were found feeble enough to do so!' The new French Premier, Joseph Caillaux,[41] was placed under great pressure to concede nothing to the Germans. *The Times* pressed for the despatch of British warships to Agadir. Every possible avenue was explored by the Secret Elite to promote their war with Germany. The following day, Sir Edward Grey summoned the German ambassador, adopted the same tone as *The Times* and reiterated the 'facts'. Grey hinted that it might be necessary to take steps to protect British interests.[42]

That same evening, the chancellor of the Exchequer was due to speak to the Bankers' Association in London. Before leaving for the Mansion House, Lloyd George went to seek the prime minister's approval for the content of his speech. According to Lloyd George, the prime minister immediately called Sir Edward Grey to the Cabinet Room 'to obtain his views and procure his sanction'.[43] While it was unusual for ministers of the Crown to make important speeches outwith their normal sphere of responsibility, Lloyd George was not known to seek permission from anyone before speaking his mind. Bluntly put, this was not his normal way. Yet here he was, inside the Cabinet Office with Asquith and Grey, rehearsing a hymn that came from their Liberal imperialist hymnal, not his nonconformist origins. In the plethora of interventions, protests and counterclaims, this one stood out above all. It was a moment of great significance. David Lloyd George abandoned the fundamental conviction on which his golden reputation had been forged. The man of the people, the man who above all stood for peace and retrenchment, the man who buried the Conservative Party in the mire of the Boer War, shook off the robes of pacifism and joined the horsemen of the apocalypse. With carefully chosen words he warned:

> I would make great sacrifices to preserve peace . . . but were a situation to be forced upon us by which peace could only be preserved by the surrender of the great and beneficent position Britain has won by centuries of heroism and achievement, by allowing Britain to be treated, where her interests were vitally affected, as if she were of no account in the Cabinet of Nations, then I say emphatically, that peace at that price would be a humiliation intolerable for a great country like ours to endure. National honour is no party question. The security of our great international trade is no party question; the peace of the world is more likely to be secured if all nations realise what the conditions of peace must be . . .[44]

What he said reverberated across Europe. Saint Paul's companions could hardly have been more surprised on the road to Damascus. The words may read mildly, but Lloyd George had drawn a line in the sand and crossed over to the dark side. 'The security of our international trade is no party question . . .'

What did he mean? How could a gunboat anchored off the Moroccan coast threaten the security of Britain's international trade? It was nonsense. A complete non-event, yet he was deliberately whipping up a storm of protest. What situation was being forced upon us (Britain) that involved the surrender of the great position Britain had won by centuries of heroism? What was he talking about? This was the rhetoric of pure imperialism . . . from Lloyd George. Tellingly, in his personal memoirs, Sir Edward Grey 'considered that there was nothing in the words that Germany could fairly resent . . .'[45] Germany. It was of course aimed at Germany, a dark warning from the former champion of peace.

The gunboat *Panther* sitting off Agadir justified nothing that Lloyd

George had said. A senior member of the British Cabinet made a serious, if veiled, threat to Germany in the knowledge and expectation that she would resent it. Riling Germany into a dangerous reaction was, of course, the whole point of the exercise. Paul Cambon, French ambassador to London, later admitted frankly to Lloyd George: 'It was your speech of July 1911 that gave us the certainty that we could count upon England.'[46]

The Secret Elite wanted war and were preparing for it. If it could be arranged for July or August 1911, it would have cut across the hated Parliament Bill and brought legislation to a halt. The crisis of the constitution would instantly be replaced by the unifying crisis of war in Europe. British naval and military preparations were stepped up. Army officers were recalled from leave, additional horses purchased for the cavalry, and the North Sea Squadron placed on a war footing.[47]

On the morning after Lloyd George's speech, *The Times* printed his inflammatory words in two articles in the same issue with accentuated notes and headlines.[48] It hailed his 'decisive and statesmanlike' references to Germany and portrayed him as national saviour. Europe had nothing to lose by his revelations on the 'true pretensions of Germany'.

The importance of the *Times* editorial lay in the fact that on the continent of Europe it was correctly held to represent the views of those in control of the British Foreign Office. A furious campaign followed in British newspapers and magazines, and raged for three months. Germany protested strongly about the insinuations and the 'hallucination' that she had considered establishing a naval base at Agadir. The German Note of complaint to Sir Edward Grey concluded: 'If the English government intended complicating and upsetting the political situation, and leading to an explosion, they certainly could not have chosen a better means than the Chancellor of the Exchequer's speech.'[49]

The entire Moroccan crisis had been set up to provoke Germany into war. That was not so startling, but that Lloyd George allowed himself to be used as the mouthpiece of the Secret Elite to fuel the flames of hatred against Germany most certainly was to most observers. Was this the moment for which his 'conversion' had been carefully prepared, an initial down payment to the Secret Elite who had rescued his career in 1909? If Britain had successfully engineered war in 1911, Lloyd George would have presented himself as the man of the people who had tried to warn Germany off. With every passing day, he grew closer to the Relugas Three. Inside Asquith's Cabinet, Charles Hobhouse certainly noted a much closer relationship between Lloyd George and Sir Edward Grey.[50]

Lloyd George was not the only new face in the inner circles of real power. He and Winston Churchill were brought quietly into the secret sub-committee of the CID that was responsible for the joint Anglo-French preparations for war: a sure sign of their standing with the Secret Elite. Asquith waited until Parliament had risen for the summer recess and ministers and backbenchers had left the sultry and oppressive city before summoning both men to a secret war meeting. This was an unprecedented act. It was a war briefing. To be there, in the company of the director of military operations, General Wilson, and Fisher's successor as first sea lord, Admiral Arthur Wilson, with the prime minister, the foreign secretary, the first lord of the Admiralty and the secretary of state for war, would have shaken lesser spirits. Not Churchill, nor Lloyd George, both of whom had previously given these colleagues a hard time in Cabinet, questioning military and naval spending plans and the cost of reorganisation. They had no idea what had been happening behind the closed doors of the War Office and the Foreign Office, but on 23 August 1911,[51] it was deemed that they had a need to know and could be trusted to pursue the imperial cause. That meeting was their initiation into a select fellowship who knew and understood that Britain was preparing for war with Germany. The only question that remained to be answered was: was now the time?

The meeting lasted all day. Great maps were produced and the details of the German Schlieffen Plan were demonstrated with amazing accuracy. General Wilson (later Field Marshal Sir Henry Wilson) was a dedicated and far-sighted soldier. He had been working since 1906 on one project: to support the French army in a war against Germany. He knew the French general staff and their army dispositions. Secret information was regularly relayed to him from the continent, and his own office was plastered with a gigantic map of Belgium on which every road, milepost, railway junction, river and canal had been identified following his reconnaissance trips through the Belgian countryside.

So it would start in Belgium, then. Three full years before the event, the Committee of Imperial Defence was taken through a meticulously accurate explanation of how war was to begin in 1914. Churchill was deeply excited by the prospect of war and with his customary conceit sent a memorandum to the CID forecasting how he imagined the first forty days of a continental war would proceed. In the event, his prognosis proved uncannily accurate.[52] The presentation by the first sea lord, Sir Arthur Wilson, was, in complete contrast, vague and singularly unimpressive. The Admiralty remained absolutely fixed on Fisher's view that a close blockade of enemy ports would be much more effective than the landing of an expeditionary force. He advocated keeping the army prepared for counter strikes on the German coast that would draw troops from the front line.

It soon became obvious that there was no agreed naval war plan at all.

Basically there was a fundamental impasse between the naval and military staffs. To be fair, a close blockade of the Channel and North Sea ports would have had a deadly impact on Germany's capacity to wage a longer war, but other influences ruled out such a strategy. Haldane was furious. Despite all of his sterling reorganisation at the War Office it was absolutely clear to everyone in that room that if war was declared in 1911, Britain would be found wanting. They did not have a plan of action agreed between the joint services.

The experience of attending the Committee of Imperial Defence stirred in Churchill a zeal that fired his imagination. There was going to be a war, and it could be very soon. He recorded that every preparation was made for war. The railway timetables for the movement of every battalion, 'even where they were to drink their coffee', were meticulously prepared.[53] An ongoing railway strike ended abruptly after a confidential statement was sent from Lloyd George to owners and workers' representatives. Thousands of maps of northern France and Belgium were printed for the Expeditionary Force. The press maintained a studied silence. Everything had to be organised in secret.

Churchill wrote a detailed letter to Grey and Asquith on 30 August advising them on what to do 'if and when the Morocco negotiations fail'. He actually believed that war was about to break out over Morocco. His advice to Sir Edward Grey was to

> Tell Belgium that, if her neutrality is violated, we are prepared to come to her aid, and to make an alliance with France and Russia to guarantee her independence. Tell her that we will take whatever military steps that will be most effective for that purpose.[54]

Yet again, the war planners brought Belgium into the equation. It had always been destined to provide the excuse for taking up arms against Germany. Winston Churchill was consumed by war fever, and for a few days in late summer war seemed probable.

In France, the radical Joseph Caillaux remained calm. He had formed his government in late June and withstood the pressure from the Secret Elite's men: Grey in London and Delcassé in Paris. Caillaux favoured conciliation rather than war. His socialist policies included the introduction of income tax, improved housing and the nationalisation of the railways.[55] Franco-German negotiations began in July and finally found a solution in the Treaty of Fez in November 1911, by which France was given a free hand in Morocco in return for a 'guarantee' that Germany's economic interests in that country would be safeguarded. Germany was, in addition, granted territorial compensation in the French Congo. As usual, it was an imperialist carve-up that denied the indigenous peoples of Morocco and the Congo any say in the matter.

In November 1911, two Paris newspapers, *Le Temps* and *Le Matin*, revealed the details of the secret articles in the 1904 entente, behind which Britain claimed to uphold the independence and integrity of Morocco while allowing France and Spain to abuse that country. The issue of Fez was a lie. The treaties and acts at Algeciras had been signed in bad faith. The indignation raised against Germany was founded on falsehood. In the December issue of the *Review of Reviews*, William T. Stead wrote a warning that was ignored at great cost:

> We all but went to war with Germany. We have escaped war, but we have not escaped the natural and abiding enmity of the German people. Is it possible to frame a heavier indictment of the foreign policy of any British Ministry? The secret, the open secret of this almost incredible crime against treaty faith, British interests, and the peace of the world, is the unfortunate fact that Sir Edward Grey has been dominated by men at the Foreign Office who believe all considerations must be subordinated to the one supreme duty of thwarting Germany at every turn, even if in so doing British interests, treaty faith and the peace of the world are trampled underfoot. I speak that of which I know.[56]

He did. As an initiate of the Rhodes secret society, Stead certainly spoke with unequalled authority. He had been part of them, worked for them, but ultimately rejected their warmongering philosophy. This was one of the very few occasions that someone who had been connected with the Secret Elite gave us a glimpse behind the curtain. Stead confirmed the point that we have made before. The men who dominated Sir Edward Grey and British foreign policy, Milner and his Round Table, were at the core of the Secret Elite. They believed that it was their supreme duty, and as acolytes of Ruskin they would have focused on the word 'duty', to defeat Germany, even if the peace of the world itself was trampled underfoot. Stead knew precisely what he was exposing: the British race zealots who sought world domination.

Thanks to both Kaiser Wilhelm and Premier Joseph Caillaux, the second Moroccan Crisis passed, as had the first, without recourse to war. It was the Secret Elite who were thwarted, but they had learned further. French politics had not been profitably corrupted. Delcassé had been rehabilitated and was impressively influential, but more was needed. They had to control the prime minister or the president of France. A staunch Revanchist was required in the Elysée Palace. Caillaux and his socialist-radicals would have to go.

Alexander Isvolsky had been successfully transferred to Paris and had made immediate contact with Delcassé. It was a partnership that promised much but would require greater resources to bribe politicians as well as the press. Nearer to home, Haldane had created his military staff and an army ready for instant action, but the navy, despite relentless investment, was disjointed. The Admiralty wanted to act alone. It knew better than everyone else. Both of these problems required firm solutions.

Summary: Chapter 13 –Moroccan Myths – Fez and Agadir

- Despite the guarantees given in the Algeciras Act, Moroccan independence and integrity were continually eroded by the French.
- Retribution against the local inhabitants at Casablanca in 1907 was grossly disproportionate and unnecessarily brutal.
- The French Chamber was completely misled about Morocco and had no knowledge of the secret agreements.
- Two major Secret Elite agents, Delcassé and Isvolsky, were the 'wire-pullers' influencing French foreign policy from 1911.
- A mythical rebellion at Fez was concocted and a large French military force sent to the city. Germany accepted the French promise that this was a temporary measure and that the troops would be removed as soon as peace had been restored.
- Despite these promises, it became an army of occupation, and Germany objected by sending a small gunboat to Agadir.
- The Secret Elite blew this out of all proportion with wild claims that Germany aimed to threaten sea lanes by establishing a naval base at Agadir. Their ludicrous propaganda claimed that Germany intended to push Europe into war.
- Lloyd George, once considered the arch radical and pacifist, joined the warmongers by making a deliberately antagonistic speech that aimed to rile Germany.
- Lloyd George and Winston Churchill were drawn into the Secret Elite's fold when the long-standing plans for war against Germany were shared with them. British preparations for war had been ongoing since 1906, down to the smallest detail. War was imminent.
- In France, the recently elected Premier Joseph Caillaux rejected the warmongering and entered negotiations with Germany.
- The kaiser and his ministers, while shocked by the malicious nature of the stories in the British press, refused to take the bait and agreed a diplomatic resolution.
- Thwarted, the Secret Elite realised that they would need to take complete control of the French government.

CHAPTER 14

Churchill and Haldane – Buying Time and Telling Lies

THAT SPECIAL MEETING OF THE Committee of Imperial Defence on 23 August 1911 was a pivotal moment on the road to the Secret Elite's war. Realisation dawned that the navy had to be given a similar shake-up to the army and be fully aligned with the secret war plans. The minister for war was alarmed by the 'highly dangerous' position caused by the 'grave divergence of policy', which, had Britain gone to war, 'might have involved us in a disaster'.[1] He despaired of the fact that 'Admirals live in a world of their own'.

It was a task that Haldane wanted to take up himself, believing that he was the only person equipped to cope with their intransigence.[2] Asquith agreed to a shake-up. He had been particularly annoyed, when trying to get immediate information, to discover that all the Admiralty staff took their summer holidays at the same time. It was effectively shut. Haldane was shocked that inside the Admiralty they had no strategic maps of Europe at all, since 'it was not their business'.[3]

Even although he had been elevated to the House of Lords as Viscount earlier in 1911 and was a favoured son of the Secret Elite, Haldane was not chosen to lead the navy. The task went to a jubilant Winston Churchill, who had pestered both Asquith and Sir Edward Grey to be given the post. The story goes that Asquith shut Haldane and Churchill together in a room at his holiday home near North Berwick and let them argue out who should be in charge.[4] Churchill claimed that he had been offered the key job while walking off the golf links at North Berwick.[5] Whatever the case, Churchill brought a fresh burst of energy to the Admiralty and shook it hard. His mission was clear-cut: 'to put the fleet in a state of instant and constant readiness for war'.[6]

Churchill was a culture shock for those who had grown accustomed to naval tradition. Officers and resident clerks were required to remain on duty night and day lest a surprise attack from Germany caught them unawares.[7]

One of the Sea Lords had henceforth to be on duty at all times in or near the Admiralty building,[8] and Churchill ordered a huge chart of the North Sea to be placed on the wall behind his chair, on which the daily disposition of the German fleet was marked with flags. He injected the Admiralty with a sense of clear and present danger, and put the department on a war footing. He ordered all naval magazines to be put under constant guard.[9] It was a measure of the paranoia generated by the spy stories that Churchill made such immediate moves.

Always a self-publicist, Churchill took credit for all that worked well. The Admiralty had commissioned oil-powered warships before he became First Lord. By February 1914 the navy had built, or was in the process of building, a grand total of 252 vessels that were either fitted for burning oil fuel only or fitted to burn oil and coal in combination, so the decision clearly predated Churchill, but he is credited with this radical change.[10] It all added up to a navy that was permanently prepared for war, which was exactly what the Secret Elite expected from a First Lord of the Admiralty.

Even with pliant and trusted men in the Cabinet, the Secret Elite had to keep their plan for war under tight wraps. Had the public known of their intention to manipulate a war with Germany, the government would have been swept from office. The regular meetings between military strategists from France and Britain that had been taking place in secret since 1905, sanctioned by Asquith, Grey and Haldane, were still only known to a privileged few, but secrecy was not easily maintained. Those in the know were bound to grow in number as the work of the Committee of Imperial Defence expanded. Foreign ministers and diplomats heard unconfirmed whispers or were included in confidential briefings. Newspaper editors and owners had sight of information that was kept from the public domain, but it could not last. By November 1911, sources from different parts of Europe made confident claims that secret deals had been done: deals that bound Britain to France and Russia through military and naval agreements that were repeatedly and officially denied in Parliament and in public.

There was a furious row in Asquith's Cabinet on 15 November, when details of the secret meeting of the Committee of Imperial Defence to which Asquith had summoned both Churchill and Lloyd George came to the attention of a number of ministers who had not been invited.[11] Lord Morley, himself a very senior minister, demanded an explanation about the joint planning between the French and British general staffs. How had this come about? Who sanctioned it? How could this have happened without the knowledge and approval of Cabinet? What precisely did it mean in terms of international commitments? No matter how much the Relugas Three squirmed, they could not find an answer to one telling question: if the 'conversations' really did not commit the country to war, why should information be withheld? Sir Edward Grey's lame and utterly insincere analysis of the conspiracy to keep the Cabinet in ignorance, as recorded in his official memoirs, meekly claimed 'there was no reluctance to have the whole matter discussed at the Cabinet. The only difficulty arose from the thing having gone on so long without the Cabinet generally being informed.'[12] Apparently, Grey, Haldane and Asquith had simply forgotten to inform Cabinet members in 1905 and never got round to bringing the issue up thereafter. What a pathetic excuse.

It was an awkward experience for the Relugas Three. Grey admitted that he regarded the agreements as a commitment to cooperate in military action with France, if that action was 'non-provocative and reasonable'.[13] Asquith took a different tack. He said that he still felt himself free under any circumstances to refuse Britain's cooperation. The general reaction round the Cabinet table was one of anger and anxiety. At best only five ministers were in the know – Asquith, Haldane, Grey, Churchill and Lloyd George. The other 13 could clearly see that military 'reciprocities' meant that, like it or not, Britain was at least partially committed to France in the event of war. Two Cabinet resolutions were formally tabled and passed unanimously. The first stated that 'no communication should take place between the general staff here and the staff of other countries which can, directly or indirectly, commit this country to military or naval intervention'. The second resolution ordained that 'such communications if they related to concerted action by land or sea, should not be entered into without the previous approval of the Cabinet'.[14] The Liberal Cabinet tried to assert some semblance of damage limitation. They genuinely believed that they had drawn a line in the sand before matters spiralled out of control. They were wrong.

Challenged in Parliament, Asquith was forced into denial. He resolutely assured the House of Commons: 'There is no secret arrangement of any sort or kind which has not been disclosed, and fully disclosed, to the public.'[15] In a parliamentary debate on foreign policy, Grey reiterated the lie:

> First of all let me try to put an end to some of the suspicions with regard to secrecy – suspicions with which it seems to me some people are torturing themselves, and certainly worrying others ... There are no other secret engagements.[16]

Asquith repeated his assurances a month later, strenuously insisting that 'There are no secret engagements with any foreign government that entail upon us any obligation to render military or naval assistance to any other

Power.'[17] These repeated, blatant lies were blanket denials of everything that they had sanctioned over the previous five years. The subtext was of serious concern to the Secret Elite. The British Cabinet and Parliament were clearly ill disposed to war with Germany and had been alerted to commitments that they rejected absolutely. Such potentially serious objections had to be circumvented.

The secrets and lies continued unabated. The Secret Elite sent an emissary to Berlin on 29 January 1912 in the guise of King Edward VII's personal banker, Sir Ernest Cassel. He and his German shipping-magnate friend Albert Ballin[18] requested a private audience with the kaiser in which a document was passed to him, allegedly prepared with the 'approval and knowledge of the English government'.[19] It appeared to be a formal offer of neutrality, conditional on a reappraisal of the proposed German naval programme. Cassel had been sent in secret, directly to the kaiser, without the apparent foreknowledge of the ambassadors of either country.[20] The British Cabinet was consequently told that a message had been sent from the kaiser through Ballin, asking Sir Edward Grey to come to Berlin to discuss armaments 'free from all entanglements'.[21] The British foreign secretary later claimed dubiety over the origins of the invitation. 'I never knew whether the suggestion had really emanated from a British or a German source.'[22] Of course he knew. Web upon web of outright lies covered his personal memoirs. The Secret Elite colluded with Grey, Churchill and Asquith in using Sir Ernest Cassel as a secret emissary. Churchill liaised directly with Cassel, who reported back to the Admiralty.[23] Grey did not go to Berlin on the flimsy excuse that he was required to deal with a miners' strike that was not even within his remit.[24]

Once the inner cabal had decided that Richard Haldane, the minister of war, would be sent to Berlin as the British representative, Grey, Churchill, Haldane and Sir Ernest Cassel drafted a reply predicated upon the belief that, in both countries, 'naval expenditure is open to discussion and there is a fair prospect of settling it favourably'.[25] Here once more we find that small shaft of light that catches the Secret Elite in action. They used a high-powered international financier and his German contact to secretly approach Berlin. Cassel was much more than a mere message boy. He negotiated directly with the kaiser to set up the meeting, took the reply secretly to Churchill and helped draft the telegram that was sent back to Berlin.[26] What power and influence did that demonstrate?

In contrast, Haldane had no power to negotiate a treaty.[27] Indeed, his instructions were explicitly not to bind or commit Britain to any pact.[28] His visit raised hope inside Germany that they could establish a new era of cooperation and friendliness with Britain. Chancellor Bethmann confided to Haldane that 'for two and a half years he had been striving to bring about an agreement between Germany and England'.[29] Haldane had no such mandate, nor any such intention.

Mainstream historians regularly described what followed as the 'Haldane Mission'. Its object was to 'reconcile', if possible, the differences between the two governments.[30] Their view is that the mission failed because of Germany's 'unwillingness to cease building a strong navy'.[31]

This is completely untrue. Before Haldane's departure, Grey assured the French ambassador that there was no question of opening negotiations with Berlin. His only desire was 'to learn the wishes of the German government and obtain information about the German fleet programme'.[32] In other words, Grey accepted the German hand of friendship but sent Haldane to Berlin primarily to glean confidential information about their naval programme. Haldane had been instructed to block any commitment to peace or negotiations, yet his 'Mission' has been portrayed as having been thwarted by German intransigence in rejecting British offers for naval reductions. Haldane's mission was to get hold of as many details as he could about German naval plans and promise nothing.

Despite an inflammatory speech by Winston Churchill delivered in Glasgow on the same day that Haldane arrived in Berlin, the minister for war was cordially received.[33] Churchill had claimed that Britain's fleet was a 'necessity' while the German fleet was a 'luxury', a provocation calculated to offend many in Britain and Germany who sincerely hoped for a better understanding between the two nations. Perhaps he was just sabre-rattling or, mindful that Haldane's visit was unpopular with Britain's allies, trying to give reassurance that the Admiralty had not gone soft on increased shipbuilding. He may even have considered that his stance would put pressure on the kaiser and his advisers and add weight to Haldane's position in Berlin. But in fact this was simply one more shameful pretence, a charade behind which Grey and the Foreign Office constantly confused their German counterparts.

On his arrival, Haldane promised that Britain was 'against any aggression by any nation' and repeated the great lie that 'we have no secret treaties'.[34] The Germans did not question his integrity and eagerly pursued a mutual agreement on 'benevolent neutrality' if either became entangled in a war where it was not the aggressor.[35] All of the enthusiasm for compromise stemmed from the Germans. The kaiser presented Haldane with a copy of their proposed naval building programme. To Haldane's surprise

> he had no objection to my communicating it privately to my colleagues. I simply put the documents in my pocket . . . I got some small modifications

agreed to in the tempo of battleship construction, and a little in reduction of expenditure on both sides.[36]

Without a single concession or quid pro quo, the Germans agreed to drop one dreadnought from their programme and postpone another two.[37] The chancellor and the kaiser were elated at the prospects for future understandings raised by these conversations with Haldane, and Bethmann promised that the success of the ongoing Anglo-German negotiations was 'the greatest object of my life now'.[38]

They were like two Dickensian gentlemen who had had their pockets picked by a master, been conned into surrendering part of the family jewels and believed naively that they had received something of worth in an empty promise. Convinced that considerable progress had been made, Bethmann sent a note to Grey on 3 March, summarising the three days of satisfactory conversations and suggesting a formula for political understanding. Armed with the details of the new German naval law, and empowered with the information Haldane had gleaned about German naval strength, the British Foreign Office replied that Haldane had not appreciated the magnitude of the new naval law nor made any unsanctioned promises.[39] Undaunted, the Germans promised to withdraw the proposed Fleet Law as it stood, in return for a pledge of British neutrality.[40] Grey made the usual spurious claim that Britain 'will neither make or join in any unprovoked attack upon Germany' but would not use the word 'neutrality'.[41] The Foreign Office prevaricated by asking more questions, demanding better explanations and seeking complicated data that would take time to compile. After months of inaction, it slowly dawned on the gullible kaiser that he had been the victim of an insincere 'political manoeuvre' to slow down his naval programme.[42] Such was Haldane's mission.

Undoubtedly, Britain's secret military and naval commitments to France had been the backbone of British foreign policy since 1906.[43] By the time Asquith and Grey were obliged to deny suggestions that secret agreements had been made with France, Haldane's plans to mobilise and concentrate the highly trained British Expeditionary Force on the Belgian border had been in place for a year. Churchill was not so fortunate. Vital naval coordination with France and Russia had yet to be agreed. Churchill was never one who felt a need to play by the rules. No Cabinet resolution was going to hold him back. Secret naval agreements went ahead, dressed in the garb of an Admiralty reorganisation. He used the occasion of his report to Parliament on 18 March 1912 to stoke the flames of German antagonism and make bold alterations to fleet displacement that presaged the preparations for war.

The first lord of the Admiralty loved these formal occasions in the House of Commons. The cut and thrust of the verbal duel fired his determination to have his way. He invited the Germans 'to take a holiday' that year. He proposed that if the German navy built no ships in 1912–13, neither would Britain. On the face of it, both countries would benefit, and the savings Germany would gain by cancelling three dreadnoughts would be accompanied by the savings that Britain would make by not building five new super-dreadnoughts. But Churchill couldn't stop revelling in his own acid wit. He pompously added that the five dreadnoughts 'wiped out' by such an arrangement were 'more than I expect they could hope to do in a brilliant naval action'.[44] There was no 'naval holiday'. Insulted by the British attitude, the German government proceeded to table new navy and army laws some four days later.

Churchill warned that his initial naval estimates would have to be increased from their original £44 million in the next year if Britain was to maintain its level of superiority. When the German plans were passed in the Reichstag, he promptly presented a million-pound supplement to his original estimate and accelerated the British building programme. While he appeared to be offering a solution to Germany in that they could accept a 'naval holiday', he was raising the stakes in a reckless game of overspend.

Churchill then surprised a packed House of Commons by announcing changes to the deployment of the British fleets. He moved the Atlantic Fleet from Gibraltar to the North Sea and the Mediterranean Fleet from Malta to Gibraltar, leaving only a small number of cruisers there. The North Sea Fleet was to be boosted to three battle squadrons. What message did that spell out to the German naval staff? What was the British navy planning to do? Members of Parliament were on their feet pointing out the very obvious dangers to Egypt and British grain supplies if these could not be defended by a sizeable British Mediterranean fleet. Churchill stood firm and answered his critics, but they wanted both a 'reasonable preponderance of naval strength in the North Sea, and a fleet in the Mediterranean'.[45]

What Churchill had proposed was in line with secret agreements already worked out between the British and French naval staffs, and on that very same day the French and Russian governments also agreed a secret joint naval pact. He could not tell Cabinet, because they had expressly forbidden such commitments. The Secret Elite had little interest in what the collective Cabinet thought, and their agents knew this well. Churchill, accompanied by Asquith, had met with Lord Kitchener at Malta in May 1912 and discussed how the British and the French fleets could be better stationed to maximise their advantage over Germany. While the issue of what comprised the Mediterranean Fleet took up heated parliamentary time, Churchill had already agreed the joint naval strategy for war.

Although the Cabinet instructed Sir Edward Grey on that very day (16 July 1912) to remind the French government that anything that was agreed between the naval and military experts must not be taken as a commitment to assist in a war,[46] he and Churchill took the Secret Elite strategy in the opposite direction.

On 22 July 1912, the Royal Navy reduced its Mediterranean fleet to a fragment of its former strength. The Atlantic Fleet joined with the Home Fleet to create battle squadrons ready to challenge the German High Seas Fleet. At the same time, France moved its entire battleship strength from Brest on the Atlantic coast to the Mediterranean, to challenge the notional power of the Austrians and Italians. (Italy was never likely to join in naval operations with Austria against Britain and the Admiralty knew this, but the pretence served its purpose.) Thus, without the permission or approval of the Cabinet or Parliament, Britain and France entered into active naval coordination in preparation for war at sea. They were committed to a focused mutual responsibility. When war was declared, the Royal Navy would protect France's Atlantic and Channel coasts, while the French navy would protect British interests in the Mediterranean.

Let there be no doubt about it, this agreement sanctioned British action if the German navy attacked the coasts of France. That alone made nonsense of all the claims of non-intervention in time of war. A country cannot stay neutral but agree to defend one side's interests.

The ordinary Member of Parliament had no inkling of these decisions. In the towns and cities of Great Britain, the populace got on with the business of the day, ignorant of the progress that was steadily being made towards war. Strikes in the docks, civil unrest in Ireland, suffragette disruption and the Olympic Games in Stockholm provided suitable distraction. The British press depicted the withdrawal of battleships from Malta and their new role in patrolling the North Sea as a response to the continuing German naval build-up. They painted a picture of Germany rebutting Britain's attempt to achieve a slow-down in the naval race, of Germany ignoring Winston Churchill's 'naval holiday'. It was always Germany's fault.

All of the suspicions aired in Parliament were fully justified. Commitments, albeit verbal, had been made, and were clearly understood. Under pressure from the French to have a written commitment, Grey broke his own rule and finally relented. It was an act he would have cause to regret. He did not permit a formal diplomatic exchange, but instead he wrote a private letter to the French ambassador in London, Paul Cambon, on 22 November 1912. It stated that 'the disposition of the French and British fleets respectively at the present moment is not based upon an engagement to cooperate in war'.[47] His weasel words were mere sophistry and hinged around the phrase 'at the present moment'. The only point that mattered was the future intention when a declaration of war would change everything.

The decision to relocate the fleets was taken by Churchill. The promise that the French coasts would be protected by the Royal Navy was inextricably linked to the overall strategy to maximise the concentration of British power against the German navy. Cambon's reply to Grey became the definitive example of Sir Edward's insincerity and cover-up, but that will be dealt with later.

The navy had been brought into line with the Committee of Imperial Defence and the preparations for war. The army had been reconstructed by Haldane and Esher, and its commitment was not questioned, but strangely its leadership remained under the spell of powerful old influences which need to be closely considered.

Summary: Chapter 14 – Churchill and Haldane – Buying Time and Telling Lies

- The Secret Elite realised that major changes were needed to modernise the administration of the Royal Navy, and Asquith chose Winston Churchill to put the fleet into a state of readiness for war.
- Churchill continued the Admiralty's high-spending regime with a programme that included a major switch from coal power to oil power.
- When details of the secret meeting of the Committee of Imperial Defence in August became known there was an unholy row in Cabinet. It was the first time that they learned about the 'conversations' with France that had been going on since 1905.
- Angry Cabinet members passed two unanimous resolutions that banned commitments to any foreign powers without their expressed approval.
- In Parliament, both Asquith and Grey repeatedly denied that Britain had made any secret commitments to any foreign power.
- An invitation from the kaiser led to Viscount Haldane's visit to Germany in February 1912. In fact, the initial approach had been made through Secret Elite agents. The net result of Haldane's so-called 'mission' was that Britain gained advance warning of the German naval plans, and Germany was deceived into thinking that some agreement on neutrality might be possible.
- Despite the clear instructions of Cabinet, Churchill reorganised the British fleet in secret negotiations with the French.
- The French repeatedly wanted written confirmation of Britain's commitment to them in a war with Germany. Uncharacteristically, Grey penned a vague letter to Ambassador Paul Cambon that was later to cause him embarrassment.

CHAPTER 15

The Roberts Academy

THE SECRETARY OF STATE FOR war may have thought that he held political control over the army, but a small coterie of very powerful senior officers were, first and foremost, loyal to Field Marshal, the Earl Roberts of Kandahar, friend and close associate of Alfred Milner and the Secret Elite. The son of a highly decorated British East India Company army general, Frederick Sleigh Roberts was born in India in 1832. Educated at Eton and Sandhurst, he served in many important British campaigns before going to South Africa to command the British forces in the Boer War. Although nominally retired as commander-in-chief of the British Army in 1905 with a £100,000 government gratuity (the equivalent of £8 million today), Roberts retained his imposing will over military affairs. The esteem in which he was held is reflected in the score of regimental honorary colonel posts he accepted, including such famous regiments as the Irish Guards, Sherwood Foresters and the Black Watch.[1] He was the first president of the Pilgrims Society of Great Britain,[2] a secretive organisation linking the very wealthy and privileged in America and Britain. Right up to 1914, Roberts played a highly significant role for the Secret Elite in selecting and shaping the military high command.

In addition to his leading role in the Pilgrims, Roberts was president of the National Service League, which advocated four years of compulsory military training for every man aged between 18 and 30. He ran a well-funded propaganda machine to generate fear of a German invasion of England and resolutely championed the need to prepare for the war against Germany. Fellow members of the National Service League included Alfred Milner, Rudyard Kipling, Leo Amery and Charles Repington. Donors included Lord Northcliffe and Abe Bailey.[3] At its peak, the National Service League had almost 100,000 members and over 200,000 subscribers.[4] In 1909, Lord Roberts addressed the House of Lords in doom-laden exaggeration:

> I want to ask you to take definite action in order to bring home to the

> public mind the gravity of the situation . . . our present system fails utterly to provide the necessary insurance against the dangers which may at any moment threaten us . . . an invasion of this country is not only possible, but . . . possible on a far larger scale than has usually been assumed . . . The question at issue is a vital one, and far too serious to be passed over lightly. Our very existence may depend upon it being wisely dealt with.[5]

Throughout the next five years, Roberts persisted in his scaremongering and made frequent demands for greater military spending. Backed by Arthur Balfour, he plagued the Committee of Imperial Defence like a spoiled child, with defiant insistence that an invasion of Britain by Germany was an eventuality that the government continued to ignore at its peril. Both Roberts and his naval compatriot, Admiral Jacky Fisher, always believed that they knew better than anyone else, though were staunchly agreed on the need to crush Germany. Roberts allied himself to Northcliffe newspapers to promote William Le Queux's fantasy, *The Invasion of 1910*.[6] Two years later, he wrote that: 'all patriotic men within this Empire should be made to see that . . . England, by neglecting her armaments, has drifted into a position which it is impossible to describe otherwise than a position of danger . . .'[7]

Lord Roberts had served with Alfred Milner in South Africa and knew Cecil Rhodes well. He was fully committed to Rhodes' and Milner's vision of an all-controlling Anglo-Saxon world power. How often do Secret Elite roots stem from South Africa and the Boer War?

As we have already seen, Milner organised and developed a talented coterie of Oxford graduates inside his South African administration, men who by 1914 held critical positions of power in the City, the Conservative Party, the Civil Service, major newspapers and academia. Carroll Quigley specifically dedicated a chapter in his seminal *Anglo-American Establishment* to this 'Kindergarten',[8] the men who rose to high office in government, industry and politics. He appointed, trained and developed his chosen men to drive forward the Secret Elite agenda with conviction. To the same end, Roberts used his South African experience to create an equivalent military kindergarten, his own coterie of trusted officers who were to dominate British military life for the next 20 years.[9] In order to avoid possible confusion between the Milner and Roberts kindergartens, we have chosen to name the latter Roberts' 'Academy'. Through Milner and Roberts, the Secret Elite's political and military strategy was as one.

Officered through the privileged route of Eton and Sandhurst, the army was known for its 'gallantry', its 'self-indulgent amateurism and well-bred bearing',[10] but had not been noted for its ability or its views on the importance of systematic thinking or planning. The Boer War provided embarrassing proof of that. The unquestioning loyalty of the army was taken for granted by the ruling class, but a 'new army', a slick modern fighting force, was required for the massive task that lay ahead. While Haldane was tasked with reorganising and modernising the armed forces, Roberts set out to provide its leadership. His drive to replace the 'old gang' was given momentum by Arthur Balfour in the House of Commons and Sir George Clarke and Lord Esher in the Committee of Imperial Defence.[11]

Lord Roberts acted as chief military advisor to Balfour and Bonar Law, but his key influence lay in placing the principal military personnel within the War Office. Roberts' Academy included men promoted to the very highest ranks of the armed forces, including John French, Henry Wilson, William Robertson, Henry Rawlinson and Douglas Haig.[12] Their careers were launched on the strength of the little field marshal's support and their acceptance of his self-determined 'advanced ideas'.[13] To a man, they owed Roberts everything, having been chosen in the first instance in South Africa for their unquestioning loyalty to him and his 'vision'. In turn, they brought with them their own coteries of loyal personal followers who would form a 'new army' fit for purpose: the Secret Elite's purpose.[14]

John Denton Pinkstone French, born in Kent in 1852, was the oldest member of the Roberts Academy. The son of a Royal Navy commander, French followed in his father's footsteps by joining the navy. After four unsatisfactory years at sea, he transferred to the army through the convenient back door of the militia.[15] French obtained a commission in the 19th Hussars and was promoted to major in 1883. He almost ended his career by being cited for adultery with a brother officer's wife while on leave but survived the scandal.[16] Reduced to half-pay, French borrowed a large amount of money, reputedly the grand sum of £2,000, from a junior officer, Douglas Haig, to pay off debts incurred through speculation and save his career.[17] French was posted to South Africa, where he commanded the Cavalry Division during the Boer War. His friendship with Lord Esher was 'no handicap'.[18] Well, no man's was. He was promoted to general in 1907 and, on Esher's recommendation, made inspector-general. From his base in the War Office, French was responsible for ensuring that army units attained the appropriate levels of training and efficiency. His royal credentials were impeccable. In 1908, French accompanied King Edward VII on his visit to the czar at Reval and was appointed aide-de-camp to King George V in 1911. Despite his lack of staff experience or study at Staff College, he was installed as chief of the imperial general staff (CIGS), the professional head of the British Army. Thereafter he was promoted to field marshal and became the second-ranking serving officer in the British Army after Lord Kitchener. When appointed chief in 1912, French stated that war with Germany was an 'eventual certainty' and that he intended to ensure that the army prepared for it.[19]

French was not academic and, with a mind closed to books, was more renowned for 'irritability than mental ability'. Indeed, King George V confided in his uncle: 'I don't think he [French] is particularly clever, and he has an awful temper.'[20] By reputation, French alternated between extremes of aggressiveness and depression, and was easily swayed by gossip. He was loyal, trusted and biddable. What more did the Secret Elite need? As ever, an exclusive background helped.

Henry Rawlinson attended Eton and Sandhurst before military service in Burma and India. Family connections had brought him into close contact at an early age with both Kitchener and Lord Roberts. Rawlinson first came under Roberts' influence in India, where he served as his aide-de-camp. He gained a reputation of being hard and cold, and of putting his own advancement first. This stubborn disregard for others would best be illustrated at the Battle of the Somme.[21] Rawlinson fought in the Boer War before being promoted to colonel and made commandant of the British Army's Staff Training College at Camberley in 1903. Three years later, he moved to Aldershot and was replaced at Camberley by Henry Wilson.

Sir Henry Wilson, the most industrious and committed member of Roberts' Academy, was an Ulster-Scot whose career positively thrived under Roberts' patronage. Having failed to pass the entrance exams to the royal military academies at Woolwich and Sandhurst on five occasions, despite intensive private tuition, Wilson also took a back-door route into the army.[22] He joined the Longford Militia before transferring to the Rifle Brigade. Wilson had a flair for impressing influential people, including Lord Roberts, who helped him to 'prosper' in the South Africa campaign.[23] The commander-in-chief had lost his only son in the war, and Wilson was considered by some to have become his surrogate.

Roberts considered the post of 'supreme importance to the future of the army', since through it the staff 'doctrine' could be thoroughly influenced. How ironic that the Secret Elite chose an officer who had repeatedly failed his entrance exams as commandant of staff training. But this was not chiefly about education; it was about indoctrination. Wilson had risen from captain to brigadier general in five years: an unheard of advancement by any standard.[24] He immediately wrote to Roberts: 'I know well how much I owe you, Sir . . . and it is no exaguration [sic] to say that the whole of my career and future prospects have been of your making.'[25] Sycophantic but true.

As soon as his appointment at the Staff College was confirmed, Wilson cycled to visit Roberts at his home at nearby Englemere, where they discussed future plans.[26] It was a journey he made several times every week over the next three years, keeping Roberts informed of all military developments and general army gossip. Wilson also repeated the much longer trips he had made to reconnoitre the Belgian borders in 1906. He traversed the frontiers from the Channel to the Swiss border by train and bicycle, making notes on the topography with detailed precision. His staple lecture at the Staff College was on 'Frontiers', and he was rightly recognised as the military authority on the Belgian, French and German borders.

In 1910, Wilson left Camberley to take up the post of director of military operations at the War Office and advisor to the government and the Committee of Imperial Defence. He immediately crossed to France for further talks with General Foch, then commandant of the French Staff College. In Paris, Wilson visited the British military attaché, Colonel Fairholme. He was not impressed with what he found, noting in his diary: 'there is much that I will change here, and, I suppose, in the other Military Attachés. They appear to me to be dealing with details and with peace, and not with war.'[27]

This was the same Sir Henry Wilson who had briefed Asquith, Grey, Lloyd George and Churchill during the Agadir incident, who was responsible for the British Expeditionary Force and knew the precise details of the plans for war. He also knew that Haldane had authorised the general staff to discuss possible eventualities with not only the French but also the Belgian general staff.[28] Shortly after joining the War Office, Wilson had dinner with Alfred Milner and Sir Arthur Nicolson, 'both of whom he was to be much associated with in the future'.[29] Several weeks later, General Foch came over from Paris, and Wilson took him to discuss plans with Nicolson at the Foreign Office. As a regular member of the Committee of Imperial Defence, Wilson sat at the heart of military decision making and ensured that the Secret Elite were fully acquainted with all that was going on.[30]

Joint war planning with France took on an immediate new impetus on Wilson's appointment as director of military operations. Over the next four years, he repeated his visits to the Franco-Belgian and Franco-German frontiers three and four times every year. On each visit he made bicycle or motor tours of the anticipated battlefields, taking careful notes and conferring with members of the French general staff. All the while, Haldane, Asquith and Grey were maintaining the disingenuous position that military 'conversations' were 'just the natural outcome of our close friendship with France'.[31] In her Pulitzer Prize-winning *The Guns of August*, Barbara Tuchman made it very clear that Britain was committed to war by 1911 at the latest. She highlighted the fact that the plans worked out by the joint general staffs 'committed us [Britain] to fight whether the Cabinet liked it or not'.

Of course they did. It was their prime objective. These military conversations were formal, undertaken in secret by the chosen few, such as Henry Wilson. Make no mistake about it, despite repeated denials in Cabinet, and to Parliament and the people, the Secret Elite had absolutely committed Britain to war with Germany.

By February 1912, General Joffre, commander-in-chief of the French army, was able to inform the French Supreme War Council that he could count on six British infantry divisions, one cavalry division and two mounted brigades totalling 145,000 men. In tribute to Henry Wilson, Joffre had named the British Expeditionary Force, L'Armee 'W'. He explained that the BEF would land at Boulogne, Havre and Rouen, concentrate in the Hirson-Maubeuge region and be ready for action on the 15th day of mobilisation. In the autumn of 1912, Henry Wilson returned to France to attend manoeuvres with Joffre and Grand Duke Nicholas of Russia. Thereafter they went to St Petersburg for talks with the Russian general staff. In 1913, Wilson visited Paris every other month to confer with the French staff and to join manoeuvres of the XXth Corps guarding the frontier.[32]

The fact that Henry Wilson kept in constant touch with the French and Russian military had to be concealed, and all the preparatory work on 'Plan W' was carried out in the utmost secrecy. It was of paramount importance that the Secret Elite plans for war were confined to half a dozen officers 'who did even the typing, filing and clerical work'.[33] A wider involvement risked the inclusion of someone with a sense of moral decency who might have blown the conspiracy apart. It is impossible to be certain if Barbara Tuchman was referring to the Roberts Academy when she noted that no more than six British officers were aware of the top-secret plans for war. The numbers certainly fit.

Another member of Roberts' Academy, William (Wully) Robertson, was unique in that he served for the first 12 years of his military career as a private. He passed the entrance exam to become an officer, was transferred to the Dragoon Guards and entered Camberley entirely on merit. During the Boer War, he served directly under Lord Roberts and was drafted into the Academy. Thereafter, his promotion was rapid. In 1905, he was appointed assistant director of military operations and decorated as a Companion of the Order of the Bath. In 1906, he went to France with General Grierson to study the lie of the land along the Franco-German border. In a later visit that same year, he joined Major Victor Huguet, the former French military attaché in London who had been the initial contact for the 'informal conversations' in 1905, and, in consultation with the French general staff, they selected landing bases and staging areas for the British Expeditionary Force.[34]

In 1910, Robertson took over from Wilson as commandant at Camberley. He commented: 'there was no position in the army where greater influence for good or evil can be exerted over the rising generation of officers'.[35] This was exactly why Roberts had placed his own appointees there. Roberts retained huge influence through his Academy even when he 'retired'. As long as his values were instilled in others, the Staff College continued to produce officers shaped in Roberts' image. And they did. In 1913, Robertson was moved to the War Office as director of military training, by which point the higher reaches of military command were dominated by the Academy.

The member of Roberts' Academy who achieved greatest notoriety was Douglas Haig. The youngest offspring of a wealthy Scottish whisky distilling family, Haig attended Brasenose College, Oxford, where he joined the exclusive Bullingdon Club but failed to achieve even a humble pass degree before moving to Sandhurst. He was unpopular with fellow student officers, who considered him a spoilt, dour and highly abrasive individual.[36] Seconded to the Egyptian army after Staff College, Haig served in the 7th Hussars, in Kitchener's campaign against the Dervishes. Thereafter, he was posted as a staff officer with the Cavalry in South Africa, ending the Boer War as commander of the 17th Lancers. Haig was heavy-handed and aggressive with the men under his command, especially junior officers, and made a point of keeping his distance from them at mealtimes.[37] Roberts considered these characteristics as eminently suitable for a member of his Academy and ensured Haig's rapid promotion. Appointed aide-de-camp to King Edward in 1902, he became the youngest major-general in the army two years later. In 1906, he was moved to the War Office as director of military training, an appointment that had 'been strongly urged by King Edward'.[38] Flattered with a knighthood, Haig worked closely with Richard Haldane to create a general staff, develop the Territorial Army and organise the British Expeditionary Force. In 1911, following a two-year spell in India as chief of the general staff and promotion to lieutenant-general, Haig was moved to Aldershot as general officer commanding.

Two of the Academy men who would lead the British Army into the Secret Elite's war, Haig and French, held military views forged in old-fashioned wars. They firmly believed in the paramount value of the cavalry and argued that so long as the cavalry charge was maintained, all would be well. Haig stated: 'Artillery seems only likely to be really effective against raw troops' and confidently declared: 'Cavalry will have a larger sphere of action in future wars . . . Besides being used before during and after a battle as hitherto, we must expect to see it employed strategically on a much larger scale than formerly.'[39] Despite the fact that they knew the devastating power of the machine gun, as witnessed in the Sudan and Rhodesia, the Academy leadership remained committed to the past.

The Royal Commission on the War in South Africa clearly demonstrated that officers had failed to recognise the root problem of the fusillade and the difficulty and danger for soldiers crossing open ground swept by machine guns. But the lesson had not been learned. The cavalry school dominated military high command in the years before the war, and the careers of those who deigned to argue otherwise withered. The British Army's selection process singularly failed to bring to the fore officers best fitted for leadership. Outstanding officers failed to gain promotion on the basis of merit.[40] Others, who were unquestioningly loyal to Roberts, rapidly climbed the career ladder despite their mediocrity. There was an idiosyncratic promotion structure based on personal favouritism and this had a negative impact on the army's later performance.[41] Top military positions were bestowed at the whim of a man who had absolutely no right to interfere in such decisions. As a consequence, the ordinary British soldier would pay a heavy price in the years to come. Such was the quality of the Roberts Academy. They listened to him, they followed him and they flourished.

Others who served under Roberts in the Boer War included General Louis Lipsett, who was sent to Canada in 1911 as general staff officer. His remit was to put into action the policy agreed at the Imperial Conferences of 1907 and 1909, when the heads of state from all the dominions and colonies had gathered in London. The Secret Elite were very conscious of the fact that military training among the British and dominion armies had to be standardised. General Sir Alexander Godley was likewise despatched to New Zealand to provide advice and training. Godley was detested by the New Zealand troops, but their military preparedness for 1914 was excellent.

While Milner's Kindergarten was drawn from an academic and social elite, men whose talent, intellect and ability was prized, Roberts' Academy maintained the old-boy networks that constrained army leadership. Milner recognised talent and shaped it into a formidable force for the advancement of the Empire, while Roberts favoured men who thought like him and followed him faithfully but had little discernible talent. Milner's men were loyal to him, to the Empire and to each other. Roberts' Academy were loyal to their leader but undermined each other if it meant personal advancement. Both knew that war with Germany was planned. Both served the Secret Elite cause at the expense of democracy and were willing to sacrifice others, but only Milner's men became part of the Secret Elite. Roberts was intrinsically associated with Milner, Esher, Balfour, the royal family and the inner core of the Secret Elite, but he was being used. Through him, they had control of the army leadership. His 'retirement' was little more than a front behind which he influenced military appointments, policy and preparations for war.

The Roberts Academy comprised a small group of egotistical, self-promoting officers who were intensely loyal to the old field marshal and the secret agenda to which he was committed. They should not be considered patriots, for they actively planned to take Britain to war against the expressed wishes of Parliament and the people. Their loyalty was to a small clique of conspirators, not the nation. Some believed that the sword and lance would outmatch the machine gun. They, of course, were not amongst those who would be sacrificed to the slaughter.

SUMMARY: CHAPTER 15 – THE ROBERTS ACADEMY

- A small coterie of very powerful army officers rooted in the South Africa campaign owed their allegiance to Lord Roberts, a close associate of Alfred Milner and the Secret Elite.
- Although retired, Roberts retained immense power in military and political circles and was an advisor to the Conservative Party.
- He was the first president of the Pilgrims Society of Great Britain, 1902–14, and president of the National Service League, which advocated conscription.
- Roberts was responsible for promoting scare stories about invasion through the Northcliffe press.
- He created an 'Academy' of high-ranking officers, including Generals French, Wilson, Rawlinson, Robertson and Haig.
- The Academy controlled the Staff College at Camberley, military operations at the War Office and army representation on the Committee of Imperial Defence.
- Men from the Roberts Academy were responsible for the military planning and operations of the First World War.

CHAPTER 16

Poincaré – The Man Who Would be Bought

MANIPULATING KEY PLACEMEN INTO POSITIONS of political power in any country is a complex challenge but one in which the Secret Elite were well practised. The radical French prime minister Joseph Caillaux, who had instigated diplomatic negotiations with Germany and resolved the crisis over Agadir, had to be replaced. His belief that 'our true policy is an alliance with Germany'[1] was incompatible with Secret Elite plans. Caillaux had many enemies but none more deadly than Alexander Isvolsky, the principal foreign agent of the Secret Elite. Though he had given up his post as Russian foreign secretary in 1910 and moved from St Petersburg to Paris as the Russian ambassador, Isvolsky had not been demoted or reduced in rank. His principal roles were to coordinate war preparation between Russia and France, and help corrupt French politics.

Isvolsky was provided with substantial funds to bribe the French press into turning public opinion against Caillaux and like-minded politicians. A right-wing Revanchist lawyer Raymond Poincaré was selected as the man to replace Caillaux and lead France to war. Born in Lorraine, Poincaré was consumed by hatred of Germany and harboured a fierce determination to regain the province for France. He later conceded: 'I could discover no other reason why my generation should go on living except for the hope of recovering our lost provinces . . .'[2]

Be clear about this: from the outset, Poincaré knew that he was funded and supported by outside agencies to turn France against Germany. He was fully aware that he owed his political success to hidden forces that sponsored his rise to power in France. He sold his soul to the Secret Elite in order to regain Alsace-Lorraine. Poincaré was personally involved in the bribing of the French press, advising Isvolsky 'on the most suitable plan of distribution of the subsidies'.[3] Subsidies indeed. This was outright corruption in its most blatant form. French newspaper editors were paid large sums of money to subject Caillaux to a torrent of abuse. Vilifying Caillaux, they alleged that he had negotiated with the kaiser behind the back of his ministerial colleagues and needlessly conceded French colonial territory in Africa to Germany. Revanchists in the Senate quite ludicrously portrayed the African bushlands Caillaux had given up in return for European peace as a second Alsace-Lorraine 'torn from the bleeding body of France'.[4] Under immense personal and political pressure, Caillaux resigned in January 1912. Poincaré was elected as prime minister and foreign minister, and, for the first time, France was committed to the Revanchist cause. It was a pivotal moment in European history.

The new prime minister of France owed everything to Isvolsky and his controllers. Within hours of his installation, Poincaré went to Isvolsky's office to assure him of France's absolute solidarity with Russia.[5] Note the sequence of events. The prime minister immediately went in person to see Isvolsky rather than the ambassador being called to the prime minister's office. This clearly proved who called the shots in the relationship. Poincaré was a bought man who fully understood his indebtedness and did everything but kiss the dapper little Russian's hands. From the start, he carefully fashioned French foreign policy to meet Sir Edward Grey's approval, and it was to the British Foreign Office that he looked for direction.[6]

After two frustrating years dealing with anti-war politicians in Paris, Alexander Isvolsky was overjoyed. He wrote elatedly to Sergei Sazonov, his own chosen replacement at the Russian Foreign Office, that the French War Ministry was now energetically preparing for 'military operations in the very near future' and that Poincaré intended to discuss these matters with him 'as frequently and thoroughly as possible'.[7] Some weeks later, Isvolsky informed Sazonov that Poincaré's first concern was 'to prevent a German movement for peace'.[8] Under his direction, the nature of the Franco-Russian agreement changed from a defensive alliance to open support for aggressive Russian intervention in the Balkans. Furthermore, Poincaré had assured Isvolsky that France would give Russia armed support if she became involved in a war with Austria and Germany.[9] With Poincaré in power, Isvolsky was renewed in his purpose, and the chronicle of the two years that followed is the story of their victory over all opposition in France and Russia.[10] They cooperated and assisted each other to attain their personal dreams: the return of Alsace-Lorraine to France and Russian control over Constantinople and the Straits.

Poincaré's legal skills and forceful personality saw him dominate the French cabinet, and from the first day of his premiership he pursued an anti-German foreign policy that had been given no explicit public approval.[11] He was faced with one particular problem. Georges Louis, the French ambassador in St Petersburg, one of France's most able diplomats, was staunchly against war. Ambassador Louis was aware of the change to the nature of the Franco-Russian Alliance and spoke out strongly against it.[12] Henceforth, his days were numbered.

Raymond Poincaré was not particularly subtle. In April 1912, he curtly rejected German overtures of friendship.[13] He was perplexed about Haldane's 'mission' to Germany, but the British Foreign Office quietly reassured him that nothing had changed and reminded him how the entente worked in practice. Nothing could be committed to writing. Secret agreements of such a magnitude between Britain and France, and Britain and Russia, had to remain unwritten. Thereafter, Poincaré appeared entirely comfortable with verbal assurances from London. Speaking with studied admiration of the late British monarch, he noted that 'King Edward regarded it as entirely superfluous to set down in writing the understanding between Powers'.[14]

Be certain that he did. Isvolsky was able to report back to Sazonov in June 1912 that: 'Neither France nor England has cause to desire modification of present relations . . . Signature of this or that other formal document . . . would not reinforce in any manner this guarantee.'[15] You can almost hear King Edward's calm reassurance through these very words. In reality, there was greater harmony and mutual confidence between France and Britain though they were only 'friends' than between France and Russia with their formally signed treaty. The commitment was absolute, yet Asquith and Grey continued to deny solemnly in Parliament that Britain had any secret agreements that bound her to participate in a continental war.[16]

When Russia was deliberately and steadily fomenting trouble in the Balkans in August 1912, Poincaré visited St Petersburg to assure Sazonov of French and British support, and to conclude further military agreements. The French prime minister was accompanied everywhere by Isvolsky, while Ambassador Georges Louis was pointedly kept well away from the discussions. They did not trust their own ambassador with policy changes to which they knew he would object.[17] Poincaré promised Sazonov that France would follow Russia into a war with Germany[18] and assured him that 'England' was ready to come to France's aid with her military and naval forces. The French war plan, Plan XVII, detailed the elaborate provisions already in place for the British Expeditionary Force's transportation and concentration on the Belgian frontier. Poincaré begged Sazonov to 'preserve the most absolute secrecy in regard to the information'.[19]

The other matter that required attention was finance. Russia remained desperately short of capital for war preparations. During his visit, Poincaré pointedly linked financial support from France to an increase in the efficiency of the crucial Russian railway lines leading to the frontiers with Germany. He was particularly insistent that the timescale required for mobilisation and advance of the Russian army towards the Polish–German border had to be reduced to a minimum.[20] French capital was also to be used for specific war enterprises in Russia such as naval construction, armaments production, railway carriages and the infrastructure to move everything effectively. A major Paris bank, L'Union Parisienne, was the principal vehicle for much of the funding. Linked as it was to the Rothschilds through Baron Anthony de Rothschild, this had all the hallmarks of Secret Elite funding for Russia's war machine. [21]

Given that Russia had serious problems maintaining its own internal investment, Isvolsky's capacity to find funds to promote Secret Elite objectives is worthy of examination. By the onset of the First World War, 80 per cent of direct Russian government debt was held in Paris.[22] When they tried to arrange a flotation of railway securities at half a billion francs annually, Poincaré's government gave approval based on certain promises: the Russian army had to be increased, and construction of designated strategic railroads up to the German border, which had been agreed in advance with the French general staff, was required to begin immediately.[23]

Despite its name, the centre point of French banking was not the Bank of France. It was an organisation controlled by a handful of private banks amongst which two were more powerful than all of the others combined: the 'Haute Banks' of Mirabaud and Rothschild. Indeed, the Rothschilds and their relatives were consistently on the Board of Regents of the Bank of France.[24] Investment banks, the first line source of funding, were dominated by the Rothschild Banque de Paris et de Pay Bas (Paribas) and the Banque de L'Union Parisienne, a nominal rival. Though separate, they frequently shared directors. The Rothschilds' Paribas Bank controlled the all-powerful news agency Havas, which in turn owned the most important advertising agency in France.[25] Like Lord Natty Rothschild in London, Baron Edouard de Rothschild in Paris controlled massive swathes of global investment banking. The London and Paris cousins worked in tandem so that the funds that flowed to Russia were strictly directed to the war aims of the Secret Elite.

The large amount of money Isvolsky used to corrupt French politics and the French press appeared to come from Russia. It did, but only via a circuitous route. The slush fund was siphoned off from the huge loans that were transferred there from Paris. This indirect funding structure meant that the money was borrowed in Paris, at a cost to the Russian taxpayer, and redirected back to France to provide Isvolsky's slush fund. It was a clever system whereby all of the loan debt and the interest accrued on it was ultimately repaid by the Russian people. Poincaré understood enough about the power of money to change the banking rules in 1912 so that any applications for international loans had to be approved through himself as foreign minister.[26] This allowed him to work closely with all of the bankers to whom he directly and indirectly owed his position, and channel the funds required by Russia and Serbia to prepare for war.

Poincaré had made an impressive start in international politics, and his commitment to a shared cause made him an invaluable asset to the Secret Elite. They were, however, conscious of the vagaries of French politics. Prime ministers tended to come and go with vulgar repetitiveness, and there had been six incumbents over the previous six years. The post of president, on the other hand, was guaranteed for a seven-year period. The presidency would thus offer Poincaré, and by default the Secret Elite, a greater permanence to pursue their war agenda. They enthusiastically backed his candidacy in the 1912 presidential election against an avowed anti-war, anti-Russian opponent, Emile Combes.

The choice was stark, and Isvolsky understood the absolute necessity of securing Poincaré's election. He urgently telegraphed Sazonov for further funds to bribe the press and members of the Senate and Chamber of Deputies,[27] telling him, 'Should Poincaré fail, which God forbid, it will be a disaster for us.'[28]

The sums involved were enormous. Isvolsky requested three million francs alone to buy off the *Radical*, a paper owned by one of Poincaré's most outspoken opponents in the Senate.[29] The money was passed directly by Isvolsky to an intermediary and on to the French minister of finance, Louis-Lucien Klotz, who shamelessly disbursed it to the politicians who would effectively vote for Poincaré.[30] The general public did not at that time vote for their president. Electors were limited to senators and deputies, which made bribery and corruption relatively straightforward. The Secret Elite went to great lengths to ensure that the money could not be traced back to Russia or, worse still, to Paris and London. Poincaré's opponents were bribed to vote for him and opposition was silenced.[31] Nothing was left to chance.

Congress duly elected Poincaré on 13 February 1913, and the fate of Europe was sealed. Traditionally the president had been seen as merely a figurehead, but Poincaré's first act was to award himself much greater powers. In his inaugural address, he declared that he would play a more active part in politics than his predecessors and radically altered the philosophy of the French government. 'The diminution of executive power is desired neither by the Chamber nor by the nation . . . it is not possible for a people to be really peaceful, except on the condition of always being ready for war.'[32] His dictatorial approach was underlined by the immediate removal of Georges Louis from his ambassadorial post in St Petersburg.

The late King Edward's chosen agent, Théophile Delcassé, the most rabidly anti-German politician in French public life, replaced him. Isvolsky telegraphed St Petersburg: 'Delcassé is entirely devoted to the idea of the very closest association between Russia and France . . . He is empowered to offer Russia all the financial assistance required, in the form of railway loans.'[33] The new president meant business.

Raymond Poincaré altered the regulations which determined the composition of France's Supreme War Council, giving himself the power to convene the council under his own chairmanship.[34] He announced a well-funded campaign to introduce a military service law that extended the period of national service from two to three years and dramatically increased the size of France's standing army.

The Northcliffe press enthusiastically backed the plan. In London, *The Times* ran a passionate campaign in support of Poincaré's three-year law and poured ridicule on its opponents like the socialist Jean Jaurès.[35] The *Times* correspondent in St Petersburg reported that, with simultaneous changes in the Russian army, their peacetime footing would be 1,400,000. He boldly claimed that 'by general consent the Russian army has never been in better condition'.[36] Though that itself had yet to be put to the test, these changes gave the Franco-Russian military forces an enormous numerical advantage over the united German and Austrian armies.

On 12 June 1913, Baron Guillaume, the Belgian ambassador in Paris, warned his foreign minister in Brussels that Poincaré's exorbitant expenditure on the French army posed an alarming dilemma. France would 'either renounce what she cannot bear to forgo [Alsace-Lorraine], or else [go to] war at short notice'. Clearly, Poincaré was not preparing for the former. Guillaume noted that infatuation with the military had created a kind of popular frenzy and that French people were not allowed to express doubt about the three-year law 'under pain of being marked as a traitor'. The propaganda, which had been carefully planned and executed, 'began by helping to get Poincaré elected president' and continued 'regardless of the dangers that it is creating. There is great anxiety throughout the country.'[37] The French people were right to be anxious.

Raymond Poincaré proved to be a worthy investment for the Secret Elite. He put reconciliation with Germany to the sword, prepared his nation for war and declared unswerving loyalty to Britain and Russia. Guided by Isvolsky, he stood ready to manipulate unrest in the Balkans and take advantage of the crisis to provoke a European war. The war he wanted so much. The war that would win back his beloved 'lost provinces'.

Poincaré's election had been secured through bribery, corruption and a huge investment in influencing public opinion through the press. This classic control of the levers of power, which Carroll Quigley so rightly described as the Secret Elite trademark, was not limited to Europe but was simultaneously being manipulated in the United States of America.

Summary: Chapter 16 – Poincaré – The Man Who Would be Bought

- The Secret Elite used their principal agent in Paris, Alexander Isvolsky, to undermine Prime Minister Joseph Caillaux and have him replaced by a rabid Revanchist, Raymond Poincaré.
- Poincaré knew that he was indebted to Isvolsky and foreign bankers, newspapers and politicians who funded his corrupt campaign.
- Under Poincaré, the nature of the Franco-Russian alliance was fundamentally comitted to war, not defence. Thus he visited Sazonov in St Petersburg to reassure him of French and British commitment to war with Germany.
- By 1914, over 80 per cent of Russian debt was owed to French banks. Poincaré and his backers insisted that these loans were conditional on increases in the Russian military and a modernised railway infrastructure that would speed up mobilisation against Germany.
- The French banks and the Bank of France were controlled by a very few major financiers, amongst whom the Rothschilds were a dominant power. The Houses of Rothschild in London and Paris worked in tandem to service the loans required for Russia through other banking fronts.
- Poincaré's position as prime minister was relatively insecure, so the Secret Elite promoted his election to president in 1913 through a massive programme of bribery and corruption.
- Once elected, Poincaré immediately increased the powers of the president, sacked his more pacifist ambassador in Russia, George Louis, and replaced him with the Revanchist champion Delcassé.
- Much to the approval of the Secret Elite, Poincaré introduced a three-year law to increase the strength of the French army.

CHAPTER 17

America – A Very Special Relationship

RHODES' SECRET SOCIETY GREW STEADILY and became ever more sophisticated in the first decade of the twentieth century. Its aim of bringing the entire world under British influence remained paramount, and Milner's Round Table associates travelled the globe to spread the gospel of the Empire.[1] The great financiers and merchant bankers centred in the City, the financial and banking district of London, shared the vision of a single world power based on English ruling-class values. In his 'Confession of Faith', Rhodes had written of bringing the whole uncivilised world under British rule, and the 'recovery' of the United States to make the 'Anglo-Saxon race but one Empire',[2] by which he meant a white, Anglo-Saxon, Protestant America working in tandem with like minds in England. Clearly the United States could not be 'recovered' by force of arms, so wealthy elites in America with a similar mindset would have to share in the control.

Rhodes Scholarships favoured American students, with one hundred allocated there, two for each of the fifty states and territories, whereas a total of sixty were made available for the entire British Empire. The 'best talents' from the 'best families' were to be nurtured at Oxford University and imbued with an appreciation of 'Englishness' and the importance of the 'retention of the unity of the Empire'.[3] Rhodes recognised the opportunities on offer to those who possessed great wealth to control politics and governments, and his ambition was driven by an understanding that the markets could be used to 'achieve political ends'.[4] The world was entering an era of financial capitalism where wealthy international investment bankers, the 'money power', were able to dominate both business and government if they had the concerted will to do so.[5] This new money power seeped into the British Establishment and joined the aristocratic landowning families who had ruled Britain for centuries. Together, they formed the heart of the Secret Elite.

From 1870 onwards, London was the centre of Britain's greatest export: money. Vast quantities of savings and earnings were gathered and invested at considerable profit through the international merchant banks of Rothschild, Baring, Lazard, and Morgan in the City. There, influence and investments crossed national boundaries[6] and raised funds for governments and companies across the entire world.[7] The great investment houses made billions, their political allies and agents grew wealthy, and the nascent British middle class was desperate to buy into a share of their success. Edward VII, both as king and earlier as Prince of Wales, swapped friendship and honours for the generous patronage of the Rothschilds, Cassel, and other Jewish banking families like the Montagus, Hirschs and Sassoons, and in so doing blew away much of the stigma of anti-Jewish bigotry inside British 'society'. The Bank of England was completely in the hands of these powerful financiers, and the relationship went unchallenged.

The Secret Elite appreciated America's vast potential and adjusted the concept of British race supremacy to Anglo-Saxon supremacy. Rhodes' dream had only to be slightly modified. The world was to be united through the English-speaking nations in a federal structure based around Britain.[8] Like Rhodes, Alfred Milner believed that this goal should be pursued by a secret political and economic elite influencing 'journalistic, educational and propaganda agencies' behind the scenes.[9]

The flow of money into the United States during the nineteenth century advanced industrial development to the immense benefit of the millionaires it created: Rockefeller, Carnegie, Morgan, Vanderbilt and their associates. The Rothschilds represented British interests, either directly through front companies or indirectly through agencies that they controlled. Railroads, steel, shipbuilding, construction, oil and finance blossomed in an often cut-throat environment, though that was more apparent than real. These small groups of massively rich individuals on both sides of the Atlantic knew one another well, and the Secret Elite in London initiated the very select and secretive dining club, the Pilgrims, that brought them together on a regular basis.

On 11 July 1902, an inaugural meeting was held at the Carlton Hotel attended by around 40 members of what became known as the London Chapter of the Pilgrims Society, with a select membership limited by individual scrutiny to 500.[10] Ostensibly, The Pilgrims was created to 'promote goodwill, good friendship and everlasting peace'[11] between Britain and the United States, but its highly secretive and exclusive membership leaves little doubt as to its real purpose. This was the pool of wealth and talent that the Secret Elite drew together to promote its agenda in the years preceding the First World War. Behind an image of the Pilgrim Fathers, the persecuted pioneers of Christian values, this elite cabal advocated the idea that 'Englishmen and Americans would promote international friendship through their pilgrimages to and fro across the Atlantic'.[12] It presented itself as a spontaneous movement to promote democracy across the world,[13] and most of the membership truly believed that. But the Pilgrims included a select collective of the wealthiest figures in both Britain and the United States who were deeply involved with the Secret Elite. They shared Rhodes' dream and wanted to be party to it.

The London Pilgrims soon established a tradition that they should be the first to entertain each new American ambassador to Britain and that his first official speech should be at a Pilgrims dinner. They also hosted a farewell dinner for each new British ambassador departing for Washington and welcomed him back after his tour of duty. The New York branch of the Pilgrims was launched at the Waldorf-Astoria on 13 January 1903[14] and comprised the most important financiers, politicians and lawyers on the eastern seaboard. They established a similar tradition of close interaction with British and American ambassadors.[15] These ambassadorial connections with the Pilgrims would prove crucial in linking the foreign secretary in London and the secretary of state in Washington to the Secret Elite and its agenda for war. A number of the American Pilgrims also had close links with the New York branch of the Secret Elite's Round Table.

In Britain, at least 18 members of the Secret Elite, including Lords Rothschild, Curzon, Northcliffe and Esher, and Sir Edward Grey and Arthur Balfour attended Pilgrims dinners, though the regularity of their attendance is difficult to establish. Such is the perennial problem with secret groups. We know something about the guests invited to dinner but not what was discussed between courses.[16] In New York, members included both the Rockefeller and Morgan dynasties, and many men in senior government posts. Initially, membership was likewise limited to 500, and it was agreed that any American resident in London who was proposed for membership should first be vetted by the New York committee.[17] The power elite in America was New York centred, carried great influence in domestic and international politics, and was heavily indulgent of Yale, Harvard and Princeton universities. Within a short period of time they created an American version of what Carroll Quigley termed the triple-front penetration of politics, the press and education.[18] The Pilgrims Society brought together American money and British aristocracy, royalty, presidents and diplomatic representatives. It was indeed a special relationship.

Of all the American banking establishments, none was more Anglocentric than the J.P. Morgan bank, itself deeply involved with the Pilgrims. In the complex world of investment banking, the Morgan empire owed everything to a Massachusetts-born American, George Peabody, who set up a banking firm in London in 1835 to deal in American railroad securities. He later recruited a fellow American, Junius Morgan, father of J.P. Morgan, as a partner in the venture, but they faced ruin when a run on the banks in 1857 almost bankrupted the company. Though rivals were keen to drive the firm out of business, a massive £800,000 loan from the Bank of England, which would have a current equivalence of half a billion pounds, saw them emerge with an enhanced reputation.[19] Nathaniel Rothschild had developed a close relationship with George Peabody, and he in turn proved to be a loyal and grateful friend.[20] The crisis claimed four banks, yet Peabody, Morgan and Company was saved. Why? Who initiated the rescue? The Rothschilds held immense sway in the Bank of England and the most likely answer is that they intervened to save the firm. Peabody retired in 1864, and Junius Morgan inherited a strong bank with powerful links to Rothschild.

The question to be asked is what the Rothschilds had to gain by such acts of generosity? Their rescue packages for failing banks or companies always came at a price. Once saved, the concern would be allowed to continue trading under its old name, and usually with its previous owners and directors, but henceforth it would act as a front company for the Rothschild dynasty. It would move securities, trade on stock markets, front deals and buy up other companies under the old retained name, and few would know that the Rothschilds were the real purchasing power behind them. When Barings Bank faced similar collapse in 1890, Nathaniel Rothschild headed the emergency committee of the Bank of England. He not only donated £500,000 directly but through his cousin, Baron de Rothschild, persuaded the Bank of France to contribute £3 million in gold to stave off the crisis.[21] There can be no doubt that by the early twentieth century numerous major banks, including J.P. Morgan and Barings, and armaments firms, were beholden to or fronts for the Rothschilds.

The Morgan family wore their affinity to England like a badge of honour. Despite stinging criticism from Thomas Jefferson that Junius's father-in-law, the Rev. John Pierpont, was 'under the influence of the whore of England',[22] his son, John Pierpont Morgan, was sent to the English High School in Boston and spent much of his younger years absorbing British traditions. He was an ardent Anglophile and admirer of the British Empire. In 1899, J.P. Morgan travelled to England to attend an international bankers' convention and returned to America as the representative of Rothschild interests in the United States.[23]

It was the perfect front. J.P. Morgan, who posed as an upright Protestant guardian of capitalism, who could trace his family roots to pre-Revolutionary times, acted in the interests of the London Rothschilds and shielded their American profits from the poison of anti-Semitism. In 1895, the Rothschilds secretly replenished the US gold reserves through J.P. Morgan and raised him to the premier league of international banking.[24] In turn, his gratitude was extended to another Rothschild favourite and one of the most powerful men in England, Alfred Milner. In 1901, Morgan offered Milner a then massive income of $100,000 per annum to become a partner in the London banch of J P Morgan,[25] but Milner was not to be distracted from the vital business of the Boer War. J.P. Morgan became the Empire loyalist at the heart of the American Establishment.

A second powerful bank on Wall Street, Kuhn, Loeb & Co., also served as a Rothschild front. The history of this bank dated from the Civil War, when two successful German immigrants, Abraham Kuhn and Solomon Loeb, amassed a fortune selling uniforms to the North. They ploughed the profits into a small banking house in New York and went back to their Frankfurt roots to find a partner who had banking experience in the European arena. Kuhn and Loeb offered the post to Jacob Schiff, who came from a family close to the Rothschilds.[26] He had been born in the house his parents shared with the Rothschilds in the Jewish quarter of Frankfurt.[27]

Schiff was an experienced European banker whose career straddled both continents, with contacts in New York, London, Hamburg and Frankfurt. Edward Cassel was his long-standing friend and was appointed Kuhn, Loeb's agent in London. Schiff even dined with King Edward on the strength of Cassel's close friendship with the king.[28] Jacob Schiff married Solomon Loeb's daughter and, backed by Rothschild gold, quickly gained overall control of the Kuhn, Loeb Bank.[29]

Schiff returned to Germany and recruited two of his nephews, Paul and Felix Warburg, from the M.M. Warburg bank in Hamburg. Both married into the Kuhn, Loeb firm and became important players in the lucrative securities market that underpinned the railroad bonanza. Like J.P. Morgan, Barings and Kuhn, Loeb, the M.M. Warburg Bank owed its survival and ultimate success to Rothschild money. It had faced bankruptcy but was rescued by a vast injection of funds from Credit-Anstalt, a Rothschild bank in Vienna.[30] These inter-related European banking families understood the nature and politics of the time. The balance of financial power rested in the City in London, but the real opportunities increasingly lay in the United States. That Jacob Schiff and Paul and Felix Warburg were German was of no relevance to their growing allegiance to America. International financiers do not limit themselves to any national boundary. Theirs is a global market.

Schiff and the Warburgs became naturalised Americans. Shedding their German citizenship was only part of a strategy that accommodated the position of these rich immigrants in New York society, though they did not entirely abandon Europe. Paul Warburg maintained his partnership in M.M. Warburg, which, following the Rothschild rescue, became a major bank in Germany's booming economy. The eldest Warburg brother, Max, another who had served part of his apprenticeship with Rothschild in London,[31] controlled their European base. He was the natural representative for Kuhn, Loeb in Germany, and kept in touch with his brother Paul on a daily basis.[32] Insider knowledge always played a key role in the pursuit of profit, and what this generation of bankers who were closely linked to the Rothschilds knew was that war in Europe was not far off.

The strategic alliances with the House of Rothschild and J.P. Morgan played an important part in determining Warburg's meteoric rise in American banking. Of even greater strategic importance was Jacob Schiff's relationship with J.D. Rockefeller. Schiff became the financial strategist for Rockefeller's Standard Oil, which was then refining about 90 per cent of all crude oil in the United States. Rockefeller, who helped to fund the Secret Elite's New York Round Table, was an unscrupulous thug, ruthless in his determination to trample opposition and throttle competition. He used monopolistic control in oil by creating a 'Trust' that squeezed rivals until they were shorn of sufficient profit to continue trading. He indulged in secret deals to undercut his competitors and expanded his control of the oil business across the entire American continent.[33]

Rockefeller's labour relations belonged to an age of brutality. Strikes were mercilessly crushed and workers denied basic rights. His worst excess came in 1913 during a miners' strike at Ludlow, where his private agents evicted families, brought in deputies in armoured cars and sprayed machine-gun fire on striking miners. Tents in which the evicted workers and their families were sheltering were deliberately set on fire, and two women and eleven children were roasted alive. Undeterred, Rockefeller extolled the 'energetic, fair and firm way' that his mining company had conducted itself.[34] Such desperate inhumanity in the pursuit of profit contrasted with the public image Rockefeller presented of Christian benevolence and cultural philanthropy.

On the surface, there were periods of blistering competition between the investment and banking houses, the steel companies, the railroad builders and the two international goliaths of oil, Rockefeller and Rothschilds, but by the turn of the century the surviving conglomerates adopted a more subtle relationship, which avoided real competition. A decade earlier, Baron Alphonse de Rothschild had accepted Rockefeller's invitation to meet in New York behind the closed doors of Standard Oil's headquarters on Broadway. John D. Archbold,[35] Standard Oil's chief negotiator, reported that they had quickly reached a tentative agreement and thought it desirable on both sides that the matter be kept confidential.[36] Clearly both understood the advantage of monopolistic collusion. It was a trend that they developed to their own advantage. Much of the assumed rivalry between major stakeholders in banking, industry and commerce was a convenient facade, though they would have the world believe otherwise.

Consider, please, this 'convenient facade'. Official Rothschild biographers would have us believe that Rothschild interest in America was limited and that the American Civil War led to 'a permanent decline in the Rothschilds' transatlantic influence'.[37] All our evidence points in the opposite direction. Their associates, agents and front companies permeated American finance and industry. Their influence was literally everywhere. J.P. Morgan, the acknowledged chieftain of the Anglo-American financial establishment, was the main conduit for British capital and a personal friend of the Rothschilds.[38] Jacob Schiff of Kuhn, Loeb, another close friend of the Rothschild family, worked hand-in-glove with Rockefeller in oil, railroad and banking enterprises. In December 1912, *Truth* magazine stated:

> Mr Schiff is head of the great private banking house of Kuhn, Loeb & Co, which represents the Rothschild interests on this side of the Atlantic. He has been described as a financial strategist and has been for years the financial minister of the great impersonal power known as Standard Oil.[39]

If the article was written to shock Wall Street, it failed abysmally. What it demonstrated was that Jacob Schiff, the Pilgrim, was both a Rothschild agent and a trusted associate of J.D. Rockefeller, the Pilgrim. Morgan, Schiff and Rockefeller, the three leading players on Wall Street, had settled into a cosy cartel, behind which the House of Rothschild remained hidden but retained immense influence and power. Control of capital and credit was increasingly concentrated in the hands of fewer and fewer men until the rival banking groups ceased to operate in genuine competition.[40]

US politicians readily succumbed to the money-power influence. The Rothschilds' first agent in the United States, August Belmont, served as the chairman of the Democratic Party National Committee from 1860 to 1872.[41] The Morgan bank had an enormous influence on President Grover Cleveland, who spent most of his life inside the Morgan empire. Virtually all of his senior appointments were Morgan men, with an occasional place at the table for other bankers. His first secretary of state, Thomas F. Bayard, was a close ally and disciple of August Belmont. The dominant secretary of state in the second Cleveland administration was a leading lawyer for banking interests and was on the board of a Morgan-run company.[42] Men close to Rothschild had the Democratic Party sewn up.

Rockefeller and his empire also treated the federal government with barely disguised contempt. His aforementioned chief executive John D. Archbold procured the services of elected representatives by including them on the company payroll. One senator from Ohio was paid $44,000 in a six-month period, while another from Pennsylvania received $42,500.[43] Archbold was called to testify before a committee investigating the dubious contributions that Standard Oil had given to Republican campaign funds. He claimed that President Theodore Roosevelt was aware of the $125,000 contribution made previously by the Standard Oil Company to the Republican Party. Roosevelt was adamant that he had ordered his campaign team to reject such donations. Whatever the truth, the government of the United States, irrespective of which party was in power, was in the grip of the big banks close to Rothschild, Rockefeller and the Secret Elite.

The Morgan–Rockefeller–Kuhn, Loeb axis on Wall Street planned to consolidate their grip on America by setting up a central bank that, like those in Europe, would be owned and controlled not by government but by banks. Their banks. The problem facing the money power was that banks and bankers were not popular with the ordinary citizen in the United States, and there was widespread public antipathy towards a central bank. The Secret Elite's solution was to deliberately create a banking crisis that would frighten the populace into accepting banking reforms. Shortly after a five-month spell in England in 1907, J.P. Morgan found the perfect opportunity. A rogue speculator, Augustus Heinze, owner of the Knickerbocker Bank, had been surreptitiously using depositors' money in an attempt to corner the stock of the United Copper Company. Its value had been pumped up to $62 per share but two days later closed at $15 per share. Heinze lost a fortune and the Knickerbocker Bank immediately faced problems over its solvency.[44] When the National Bank of Commerce, part of Morgan's financial empire,[45] publicly refused to accept Knickerbocker cheques, rumours spread rapidly. Morgan's decision scared other institutions from offering financial support[46] and next morning, 22 October, the Knickerbocker depositors were so desperate they withdrew $8 million during a three-hour run.[47] Depositors at other banks across America panicked, attempted to withdraw their savings, and the anticipated domino effect kicked in.

Having caused the crash, Morgan took personal charge of reversing it, though he was neither elected nor appointed to the task.[48] In so doing, he assumed the mantle of saviour of the American banking system. With the government's approval, Morgan browbeat bankers and Trust company presidents into contributing to the rescue package.[49] Rothschild hailed Morgan as 'a man of wonderful resources. His latest action fills one with admiration and respect for him.'[50] It was a vote of approval from the boss of bosses to one of his trusted lieutenants.

The panic of 1907 ran like a true Rothschild scam, orchestrated by Morgan to 'prove' the absolute necessity of a central bank. Something had to be done. The Senate was warned: 'we may not always have Pierpont Morgan with us to meet a banking crisis'.[51] Thereafter, the establishment of a central bank was presented as the solution to avert future financial crises.[52]

In 1915, a Committee of the House of Representatives, chaired by Congressman Arsène Pujo, presented a report on the banking business and demonstrated that Morgan placemen held multiple directorships in interrelated banks, insurance companies and giant business corporations. Pujo demonstrated that the banking system was run like an exclusive private club,[53] and that the New York Stock Exchange dealt in dishonest, unwholesome speculation.[54] In the recent panic, malpractice by the major banks had made the situation much worse and resulted in banking collapses which they used to their own advantage.[55] The abuse of ordinary stockholders,[56] the unhealthy increase in the control of money centred on New York,[57] and the multiple affiliations inside major banking houses like J.P. Morgan, the First National Bank of New York, National City Bank and Kuhn, Loeb & Company, made appalling reading. Big business in the US lay in the hands of just a few men who controlled the banks. Pujo's evidence proved that 5 banking firms held 341 directorships in 112 corporations valued at over $22 billion.

Pujo dissected the rampant abuses of financial power, and his final report revealed corporate banking abuse at a pandemic level.[58] The report was, however, not what it seemed. Like many other commissions before and after, it shied away from penetrating questions on the crucial matter of foreign investment houses and their massive influence over US banking and industry. The name Rothschild remained unspoken. Amongst the few politicians who railed against the corruption in American banking, Congressman Lindbergh and Senator La Follette stood tall. They never ceased to demand that the system be thoroughly cleansed and repeatedly called for an investigation with teeth. Tellingly, they were denied access to the Pujo Committee. The only witnesses allowed to testify were the bankers themselves.[59]

The entire object of the run on the banks was to frighten the public into believing that urgent reform of the banking system was necessary to protect their savings and that Wall Street should be brought under control.[60] The public, who had objected to a central bank for many years, had to be made to believe that banking reform was precisely what was needed. No one appeared to appreciate that the biggest advocates of banking reform were the bankers themselves. Their standing in the community assumed toxic proportions in terms of the popular reaction, but they used that to pursue their near impossible dream of a US central bank. The lie was repeated over and over again that only a central bank could bring banks and bankers to public account. The case they put forward argued that the government would regulate and control banking in the interests of the people, but nothing could have been further from the truth. This was a colossal fraud perpetrated by the money power. As Professor Quigley explained, these bankers sought 'nothing less than to create a world system of monetary control in private hands, able to dominate the political system of each country and thus the economy of the world as a whole'.[61] That could only happen if the United States had a central bank like those in England and France.

Contrary to widespread belief, the Bank of England was not a public institution but was operated and controlled by bankers such as the Rothschilds and brooked no semblance of political interference. In France, there was a more complex system of seniority and stability, where a number of traditional banking families were considered part of an elite Haute Banque that in turn controlled the Bank of France.[62] Two dominant private French banking firms, Rothschild and Mirabaud, were more powerful than all the others put together.[63] In Germany, the Reichsbank was a private institution with the power to print money but was much more directly under the control of the government than either the Bank of England or the Bank of France.[64] The money power in New York wanted the same control that the bankers in England and France enjoyed: namely, freedom from government interference, the right to print money, control of rates of interest and to stay safely anonymous behind an executive appointed by themselves.

This is why Paul Warburg was on hand. The German banker had been chosen by the money power to drive forward their ambitious plan for a US central bank. Though Jacob Schiff brought him to New York to help him run the Kuhn, Loeb bank, Warburg still committed six months of each year to his family bank in Hamburg. Following the 1907 panic, Paul was presented as the guru of central banking who 'just happened' to be in New York, and 'just happened' to decide to file for American citizenship. He was a 'reluctant warrior' who appeared just in time to sweep into battle for the noble cause of a central bank.[65] The fable would have us believe that the *New York Times* 'just happened' to ask Paul (who could hardly write in English) to pen an article about banking reform. He dusted off an essay he 'just happened' to have written when he arrived in America and it was duly published on 12 November 1907 under the headline 'Defects and Needs of our Banking System'.[66] He followed that up with a short piece in the *New*

York Times Annual Financial Review entitled 'Plan for a Modified Central Bank'. Warburg argued that nothing short of a central bank would solve the currency problem. He expanded upon these initial thoughts with the publication of 'A United Reserve Bank of the United States' and was duly dispatched across America on a promotional tour, lecturing on the values of a central bank. Congressmen and senators were bombarded with advice. Pamphlets and articles were penned in favour of a banking system that would mystically put control 'back in the hands of the people' and break the grip of the money trust.[67] And thus the lie was spread.

Senator Nelson Aldrich of Rhode Island was chosen by the Secret Elite to be the voice of 'sound economics' in the Senate. A wealthy businessman and father-in-law of John D. Rockefeller Jr, Aldrich was known as 'Morgan's floor broker in the Senate'.[68] Shameless in his excesses, he used public office to feather his own very large nest. Public service was to him little more than a cash cow. He built a 99-roomed chateau and sailed a 200-foot yacht.[69] Over a two-year period, Paul Warburg and J.P. Morgan worked steadily on their corrupt senator to turn him into an 'expert' on banking systems. Congress appointed a National Monetary Commission in 1908 with Aldrich as chairman, to review US banking. Its members toured Europe, supposedly collecting data on various banking systems. Aldrich's final report, however, was not the product of any European study tour but of a collective conspiracy.

In November 1910, five bankers representing Morgan, Rockefeller and Kuhn, Loeb interests met in total secrecy with Senator Aldrich and the assistant secretary to the US Treasury on Jekyll Island, an exclusive resort off the coast of Georgia. Of the seven conspirators, five – Senator Aldrich, Henry Davison, Benjamin Strong, Frank Vanderlip and Paul Warburg – were members of the Pilgrims.[70] Their objective was to formulate a central banking bill that would be presented to Congress as if it were the brainchild of Aldrich's Monetary Commission. In a scenario more reminiscent of a B-movie plot than the confused reality of the super-wealthy, the group travelled from New Jersey to Georgia in Senator Aldrich's private railway carriage with blinds drawn, using aliases and purporting to be on a duck-shooting trip.[71] Regular servants were sent away and temporary replacements hired lest anyone was recognised. Their paranoia stemmed from the justified fear that should any journalist see them all together, the whole conspiracy would be blown apart.[72] For nine days, they thrashed out the details of a central banking system that the Secret Elite wanted put in place. The title 'Central Bank' had to be avoided in order to deceive the American people, so they decided to misname it the 'Federal Reserve System', though it would be neither federal nor a reserve.

The proposed 'System' was to be owned entirely by private banks, though its name implied that it was a government institution. Individuals from the American banking dynasties, including Morgan, Warburg, Schiff and Rockefeller, would hold the shares. It was to be a central bank of issue that would have a monopoly of all the money and credit of the people of the United States. It would control the interest rate and the volume of money in circulation. The Federal Reserve System constructed on Jekyll Island had powers that King Midas could never have contemplated. The objective was to establish a franchise to create money out of nothing for the purpose of lending, get the taxpayer to pick up any losses and convince Congress that the aim was to protect the public.[73]

When the proposals took shape in Congress, there was one overarching flaw. Senator Aldrich insisted on appending his name to it, despite Paul Warburg's warning that it would automatically be associated with Wall Street and prove an unnecessary obstacle. The ego prevailed, and Warburg's concerns proved justified. The Aldrich proposals never went to a vote. President Taft refused to support his bill on the grounds that it would not impose sufficient government control over the banks. The money power decided that Taft had to go. Their support in the 1912 presidential election swung behind the little-known Democrat candidate, Woodrow Wilson. The speed with which Wilson was bounced from his post at Princeton University in 1910 to governor of New Jersey in 1911, then Democratic Party nominee for the presidency in 1912 made him the Solomon Grundy of US politics. Grass-roots Democrats in New Jersey were opposed to having Wilson imposed on them by 'the big interests' in New York,[74] but they quickly caved in.

Rarely has there ever been such a concerted and focused effort to remove a Republican president from office and replace him with a Democrat party-puppet. Sponsored by Cleveland H. Dodge, director of Rockefeller's National City Bank, and a friend of both Rockefeller and Morgan, Woodrow Wilson was thrust into the presidential race in 1912. The money power opened a campaign office for him at 42 Broadway, and over two-thirds of his campaign funds came directly from Wall Street.[75] Wilson lied about his politics during the campaign and betrayed the Democratic heritage of Presidents Jefferson and Jackson by courting the bankers and representing their interests. His public utterances were a masterclass in hypocrisy.[76] He campaigned in 1912 under the banner of 'New Freedoms' and opposition to monopoly powers, yet within a year had given the banks exactly that.

No matter the extent of financial backing, Wilson could never have defeated a popular president like Taft without devious tactics crafted by his political puppet-masters. Clear favourite for a second term in office, Taft's chance of success was seriously undermined when another Republican, former president Theodore Roosevelt, entered the race. Financed by Morgan's associates in Wall Street, Roosevelt created a third force, the 'Bull-Moose' Party, from thin air[77] and effectively split the Republican vote. While the Morgan team were destroying Taft's chance of victory, Paul Warburg and Jacob Schiff completed the pincer movement by backing Wilson[78] and ensuring his election. Wilson won with 42 per cent of votes cast, Roosevelt took 27 per cent while Taft could only muster 23 per cent. The remainder went to the socialist candidate Eugene Debs. The Republicans were also routed in the Senate elections, where the Democrats emerged with a clear majority.[79]

Not only did the money power put their man in the White House, they also gave him a minder, Edward Mandell House, a 'British-trained political operative'.[80] Woodrow Wilson was president of the United States but this shadowy figure stood by his side, controlling his every move.

Like Esher, and to some extent Milner, House preferred to influence politics from behind the scenes, rather than take public office.[81] He had been part-educated in England and was credited with swinging the Democratic Convention in Baltimore in 1912 behind Wilson.[82] He became Woodrow Wilson's constant companion from that point onwards, with his own suite of rooms in the White House. He was also in direct, sometimes daily, contact with J.P. Morgan Jr, Schiff, Warburg, and Democrat senators who sponsored the Federal Reserve bill.[83] House guided the president in every aspect of foreign and domestic policy, chose his cabinet and formulated the first policies of his new administration.[84] He was the prime intermediary between the president and his Wall Street backers.[85] This president was not to be left to his own devices. The governance of America fell, step by step, under the juggernaut of investment bankers closely linked to the Rothschilds.

The original Aldrich Bill was revised, renamed and steered through both Houses of Congress with great speed. On Tuesday, 23 December 1913, the technically named Glass-Owen Bill (it was barely distinguishable from the Aldrich Bill rejected by Taft two years previously) was finally presented to the Senate. It provided for 'the establishment of Federal Reserve banks, for furnishing an elastic currency, affording means of rediscounting commercial paper, and to establish a more effective banking system in the United States, and for other purposes'.[86] Despite loud and constant protestations from senior Republican senators, the sub-committee that had been set up to find solutions to contentious points was usurped by the Democrat majority. Every contentious issue was decided in favour of the elite bankers.

What had started off as a proposal for public ownership of the stock and government control of the banks ended up as a system whose stock was owned by the banks and controlled by the banks. In impotent frustration, Senator Bristow of Kansas pointed out that 'every provision in this bill that was in favour of the banks has been retained. The provisions that were struck out were provisions in the interests of the public.'[87] After four hours of political sniping, the bill was formally passed through the Senate by 43 votes to 25, with a further 27 senators not voting.[88] Later that day, in the House of Representatives, the lone voice of Representative Finlay H. Gray railed against the Wall Street bankers and their 'deliberate plan and conspiracy to discredit the national bank currency [so] that there might be reared upon its ruins a central autocratic bank under private control'.[89]

Too late: the horse had well and truly bolted. The bill was rushed through on the Tuesday night before Christmas 1913, signed quickly by the compliant President Wilson, and legally in place as an act of Congress before the morning newspapers hit the streets. Most importantly, by clever sleight-of-hand political manoeuvring, it was precisely the opposite of what the public had been promised.

What impact did this have on the well-coordinated Secret Elite plans for war? What did it matter if the richest economy in the world gifted control of its money supply to its major private bankers? Wars require to be financed and cost immense sums of money. In Britain, France, Russia and Germany the national coffers were almost bare. Outrageous spending on armaments and growing indebtedness had left virtually every treasury in Europe dangerously close to empty. A new source of funding was required, a supply of money that could expand in line with the demand of desperate nations willing to pay handsomely for massive loans. Now that was something that a US central bank, unfettered by government control, responding to unlimited demand, could do. The Federal Reserve Act was passed in December 1913, and the seven-man board took office on 10 August 1914, by which time the war . . . but we are running ahead of ourselves.

Rhodes' American dream took shape. Close links with the American Establishment had been cemented through the Round Table and the Pilgrims, and grew in strength behind the closed doors of private dinners in London and New York. The Anglo-centric money power had finally established its central bank in time for the Secret Elite's war.

Consider the last two chapters and ponder this significance. By February 1913, two major powers, the United States and France, had new presidents who were elected to office through the machinations of the Secret Elite. Woodrow Wilson had been elevated to the presidency of America by the money power in the United States. Raymond Poincaré's election was likewise paid for by bribery and corruption funded through bankers and financiers in London and Paris. The Secret Elite had positioned key players in the governments of Britain, France, Russia and the United States. Politics, money and power were the pillars on which the Anglo-Saxon elite would destroy Germany and take control of the world.

Summary: Chapter 17 – America – A Very Special Relationship

- Cecil Rhodes appreciated the importance of the United States in pursuit of a world dominated by the 'Anglo-Saxon race'. More Rhodes Scholarships were awarded to the United States than anywhere else.
- The real aristocracy in America was the money power that comprised the obscenely rich industrialists, financiers and oilmen who dominated politics and society.
- The Pilgrims was an exclusive society founded in 1902 ostensibly to 'promote goodwill and friendship' between Britain and the United States. It provided a pool of wealth and exclusivity through which the Secret Elite could spread its values and increase its power.
- Secret Elite politicians and businessmen attended Pilgrim functions, but no records exist of the private discussions fostered in these exclusive gatherings.
- Economic power was increasingly invested in a small number of New York-based family dynasties, including the houses of Morgan and Rockefeller. The Rothschilds were closely associated with Morgan and other emerging banks and bankers in New York, including Kuhn, Loeb & Co., Joseph Schiff and Paul Warburg, and did not withdraw from the American market.
- The money power sought to convince politicians that the United States, like European nations, required a central bank to control the system of money. The 1907 banking crisis happened because the bankers wanted to prove their point that a central agency was required to bring stability to banking.
- Corrupt politicians, in particular Senator Nelson Aldrich, fronted the drive to have congressional approval for a central bank.
- He colluded with other banking conspirators representing Morgan and Rockefeller, most of whom were Pilgrims, to promote a Federal Reserve Bank for the United States.
- It failed to pass into law and the money power turned against President Taft. They manipulated the presidential election of 1912 to have Taft replaced by a puppet president, Woodrow Wilson.
- A Federal Reserve System passed into law in December 1913. It gave ownership and control of the money supply in America to private banks.

CHAPTER 18

The Balkan Pressure Cooker – 1912–13

By 1912, the Secret Elite had spent over a decade in pursuit of their ultimate aim to create a new world order through the destruction of the old. The Northcliffe press was steadfastly preparing the public for war against the 'Evil Hun', but no amount of propaganda would have the required impact if Britain or her allies were seen to be the aggressor. It had to be Germany. The question was: how? Both attempts at goading Germany to strike the first blow over Morocco had failed miserably because the kaiser and his government agreed diplomatic solutions.

The problem was complex. Britain could not enter into war with Germany without good cause, and the cause had to be close to home. There were no circumstances in which war against Germany could be declared in support of Russia. The British people despised czarist Russia. Would they be prepared to go to war on behalf of France if the German army moved on Paris? They might, but the possibility of war was not sufficient. The Secret Elite needed certainty. Britain could only be brought in once the Germans had been forced into a defensive retaliation by Russia or France. Germany had to appear to be the aggressor. The British cause for war would be manufactured by German reaction provided their army advanced through Belgium. British and French war plans had since 1905 assumed that the Germans would do so, but first and foremost they had to wait for a German response to provocation.

The answer lay in a strategy that encouraged Russia to be aggressive and fulfil her historic ambitions in the Straits, and brought Britain into play once Germany reacted to it. The cause for Russia would lie in the Balkans; for France it would always be Alsace-Lorraine. Britain had no just cause unless the Secret Elite could manufacture it.

Though the Balkans was a little-known, backward region in the south-east corner of Europe, fragmented by mountain ranges running in every direction, the Secret Elite recognised the explosive potential of Balkan nationalism and harnessed it. Many historians have cited Russia as the instigator and financier of the Balkan troubles in its drive to push the Ottomans from Europe and Austria from Bosnia-Herzegovina,[1] but they have virtually ignored, or failed to recognise, the hidden British influence. The growth of national resentment across the Balkans against Turkey and Austria-Hungary was deliberately stirred by agents of the Secret Elite.

Left to their own devices, Balkan countries had neither the infrastructure nor investment capital to make the most of their natural resources. Romania and Serbia were particularly dependent on international bankers, and, as a consequence, real wealth flowed out of the Balkans into London, Paris and Vienna. European financiers sucked all they could from the Serbian national economy before taking serious steps to develop its industry. The banks used local agents, influential politicians, legislators and government ministers as intermediaries between the European stock exchange and Serbia. Leon Trotsky, at that juncture a correspondent in the Balkans for the Kiev newspaper *Kievskaya Mysil*,[2] wrote caustically: 'One and the same door here leads to a ministry and to a bank directorship.'[3]

Trotsky's assessment was perfectly judged. Corruption blossomed. Government officials were bribed with directorships of banks and oil companies. Spending on armaments and the weapons of war outpaced genuine investment in Serbia's future. Used and abused: that was the fate of the Balkans.

Serbia was groomed for a very special role. She was perfectly placed as the epicentre for a seismic explosion that would blow away the old order. With her many nationalist Pan-Slav and fiercely anti-Austrian secret societies, Serbia provided the perfect location from which the Secret Elite could activate the European war. Austria's annexation of Bosnia-Herzegovina in 1908 generated a deep, bitter and lasting resentment amongst the Serbs, not least because it defied their ambition to bring all Serb peoples into a unified state called Yugoslavia.[4] Serbia's long-standing hatred of Austrian rule grew exponentially from the first day of the annexation in 1908 until it culminated in war.[5] The Serbs could never have waged successful war against the might of Austria on their own but were assured of Russian support by Isvolsky, who actively encouraged Serbia to wrest Bosnia-Herzegovina from Austria as their rightful entitlement. Serbia's finance minister, Milorad Draskovic, confidently claimed: 'Our people have faith in Russia. It is said of us that we are merely Russia's armed camp. We do not take that as an insult.'[6]

It was not by accident that Alexander Isvolsky played a significant role in creating these perilous conditions in the Balkans. The Secret Elite used him and their diplomatic and commercial agents in Serbia and Bulgaria to identify prominent individuals and organisations that they could influence. Far from being passive observers, the Secret Elite in London made certain that their agents influenced events at every opportunity. Received wisdom acknowledged that by 1912 Serbia was 'completely an instrument of Russia',[7] and in one sense it was. The instructions, the finance and the promises of support all stemmed from St Petersburg to Russian diplomats in Belgrade, a state of affairs that seemed to underscore their commitment to Serbia. In reality, these Russian diplomats were taking their orders from men who we believe were controlled by the Secret Elite: Isvolsky and his puppet, Sazonov. Furthermore, the real sources for their slush funds could be traced to Paris and London. The complex chain of command that was established extended to include one of the most competent and influential of Russian diplomats, Nicholas Hartwig.

Hartwig was known and well respected in London. He had formerly been Russian ambassador at Tehran and was deeply involved in the successful rapprochement between Russia and Britain over their differences in Afghanistan. Hartwig was hailed as 'a diplomatist of the Isvolsky School'[8] and 'the pupil and alter-ego of Isvolsky'.[9] In 1906, he had been one of the favourites for the post of Russian minister of foreign affairs, but it was Isvolsky who triumphed, not least because King Edward influenced the czar on his behalf. Hartwig might have succeeded Isvolsky in 1909, but the weaker and more malleable Sazonov, whose father-in-law happened to be Prime Minister Stolypin, was favoured by the outgoing Isvolsky. Instead, Hartwig's talents were recognised in a crucial posting to the Serb capital, Belgrade.

Bear in mind that, hitherto, Serbia had been viewed as a backwater: a small primitive country of pig farmers with a disgraceful history of regicides and little in the way of valuable resources.[10] Strange, is it not, for such an important and highly considered diplomat to be relegated to a remote outpost in south-eastern Europe? Unless, of course, there was a significant task ahead that he was uniquely qualified to accomplish.

Within a short time, Nicholas Hartwig held immense power in Belgrade and was considered by some to be the real ruler of Serbia.[11] He stoked anti-Austrian ambition, raised nationalist expectations and indulged in warmongering by insisting that Serbia had to become the Slavic advance post in the Balkans and must annex Bosnia-Herzegovina and the South Slavic districts of Hungary.[12] The Russian diplomat Eugenii Shelking noted that 'shortly after his arrival in Belgrade, Hartwig had created an exceptional position for himself. The king, Prince Alexander, Prime Minister Paschitch [Pasic] – none of these made any decision without first consulting him.'[13]

Nicholas Hartwig controlled and directed the Serbian leaders, but that was insufficient to realise his ambition. He gathered round him a viper's nest of Serbian mafiosi and Russian collaborators, plotters and schemers who stoked the fires under a pressure cooker of disillusion that was kept simmering near the boil. The Russian military attaché, Viktor Artamanov, and the Serbian chief of military intelligence, Colonel Dimitrijevic, regularly exchanged secret information gleaned from trusted agents in Austria-Hungary. Russian money covered the necessary 'expenses'.[14] These were unscrupulous men in unscrupulous times, whose place in history had yet to reach its nadir. The inflated expectations which they raised for a Greater Serbia stretched beyond sanity. Bosnia-Herzegovina, Serbia and Bulgaria festered in bitter resentments. All could claim that they had suffered from broken promises, unrealised dreams and unachieved potential.

Colonel Dimitrijevic was known throughout Serbia by his nickname, Apis (the Bull), a reflection of his physical strength and presence. He had been wounded in the brutal assassination of King Alexander and Queen Draga in 1903.[15] In dishonourable circumstances, he and his fellow officers stormed the royal palace in Belgrade, shot the royal couple dead and hacked them beyond recognition with bayonets before throwing the mangled corpses from an upper window of the palace.[16] While this regicide shocked and revolted most of the crowned heads of Europe, Apis emerged as a national hero, an ardent nationalist and loyal supporter of King Petar, whose succession he had delivered. He possessed considerable personal charm and became the real power and influence inside Serbian military politics.[17]

Apis was intimately associated with the 'Black Hand', otherwise known as 'Unification or Death', the underground secret society dedicated to the destruction of Austria-Hungary. Despite the atrocities, and a past history which left the Serbian monarchy despised in the courts of Europe, Hartwig praised Black Hand as 'idealistic and patriotic'.[18] As the founder and dominating spirit, Apis 'was the most influential officer in Serbia'.[19] Encouraged, financed and protected by the Russian agents Sazonov had placed in Belgrade, Apis was instrumental in promoting 'a type of Serbian activity which was bound, sooner or later, to bring about an acute Austro-Serbian crisis'.[20] In Colonel Apis and his Black Hand, the Secret Elite recognised and cultured the dormant virus that would, in one moment in June 1914, infect the body-politic.

Hartwig proved himself a worthy disciple of Isvolsky by helping to create an alliance of Balkan states known as the Balkan League. Given that these countries detested one another, Hartwig achieved his aim in the face of overwhelming odds. The Balkans was a quagmire of ethnic bitterness, religious tension and nationalist squabbling that had festered over centuries of Turkish misrule. Whatever the apparent disinterest that the Great Powers feigned, or the protestations made on behalf of one state or another, there was the constant whiff of rampant self-interest in the air when they turned their attention towards that region. The nascent states and aspiring breakaway nations were even more unpredictable. Like jealous hyenas tearing into the carcass of a wounded beast, they all wanted either to grab more for themselves or stop the others feasting on the hapless Ottoman victim. Despite their protestations, no one was innocent. As individuals, they could quickly be at each other's throats, but if they ran as a pack, these hyenas would be especially dangerous to Austria. This was why the Secret Elite supported the formation of a Balkan League. Together they were virtually equivalent to a separate Great Power.[21]

By almost curious coincidence, there was one other figure, this time based in Bulgaria, who emerged as if from the ether to work with Hartwig in creating the Balkan League. Preliminary negotiations were 'conducted in profound secrecy' and the promoters of the alliance 'employed as intermediary Mr J.D. Bourchier, the *Times* correspondent in the Balkan Peninsula . . .'[22] Who?

James David Bourchier, of Anglo-Irish stock, educated at Trinity College, Dublin, and Cambridge University, assistant master at Eton with impeccable credentials, went on holiday to the Balkans in 1892 and within a short time became the *Times* correspondent. Bourchier settled in Sofia, where he found a role as an unattached diplomat, mixing with heads of state and royalty. At what stage does coincidence begin to smell? This is a story that has all the hallmarks of a Secret Elite placement.

A telegram to Isvolsky from the Russian ambassador in Bulgaria in November 1912 identified a representative of *The Times* who claimed that 'very many people in England are working towards accentuating the complications in Europe [the Balkans]' to bring about the war that would result in the 'destruction of the German Fleet and of German trade'.[23] Though not named, it had to be Bourchier. He had confided in the Russian ambassador and spelled out precisely the overall Secret Elite agenda, without realising that his conversation would be relayed back to Isvolsky in Paris. The telegram exposed the whole objective in a nutshell. 'People in England' were working towards making the Balkans ever more explosive, to bring about war and destroy Germany and German trade. It could not have been put more succinctly.

Edith Durham, the English writer and traveller who exposed many of the horrendous atrocities during the subsequent Balkan Wars, also confirmed that Bourchier was deeply involved with the Balkan League.[24] Like other contemporary commentators, she had no reason to suspect that the real source of power and influence lay behind Alexander Isvolsky in Paris, from which vantage point he began to stir the Balkan pot. As Professor Sidney Fay, the American historian, observed:

> To the Serbians, Isvolsky continued to give secret encouragement, urging them to prepare for a happier future in which they could count on Russian support to achieve their Jugo-Slav ambitions . . . He encouraged them to regard it [Bosnia-Herzegovina] as a Serbian Alsace-Lorraine.[25]

This was a particularly enlightening observation on Isvolsky's role in the Balkans. In Paris, he openly endorsed the right-wing government led by Poincaré, whose Revanchists held the return of Alsace-Lorraine as the holy grail of French foreign policy. He was the man who traded Bosnia-Herzegovina to the Austrians in 1908 on the empty promise of their support for Russia's gaining the Straits. He had been quite prepared to surrender the Bosnian province but somehow absolved himself from that responsibility. By 1912, he had changed his tune by advocating that Serbia seize Bosnia-Herzegovina, making it their cause célèbre.

Consider then the midwives in attendance at the birth of the Balkan League: Isvolsky, who promoted the idea when he was Russian foreign minister, and always the company man; Hartwig, approved by London, sent to Serbia to strengthen control in Belgrade; and Bourchier, a correspondent of *The Times*, itself an organ of the Secret Elite. The two unlikely bedfellows, Serbia and Bulgaria, were eased into an alliance that would not have been considered 'natural'. The men who guided them had ulterior motives. They were not fired by nationalist sympathies.

Summary: Chapter 18 – The Balkan Pressure Cooker – 1912–13

- By 1912, the Secret Elite had failed twice to goad Germany into war.
- The simmering nationalist tensions in the Balkans were stoked by Secret Elite agents to destabilise the region and create a flashpoint.
- They set up a line of command that appeared to lead to St Petersburg but was in fact based in London. It went from the Foreign Office to Isvolsky in Paris, Sazonov in Russia and Hartwig in Belgrade (Serbia).
- The Russian ambassador Hartwig was closely associated with Colonel Apis and his powerful terrorist organisation, the Black Hand.
- The Balkan League was created by Isvolsky, Hartwig and Bouchier, three individuals linked to the Secret Elite.
- The League brought the disparate Balkan nations together in an alliance that threatened both Turkey and Austria-Hungary.

CHAPTER 19

From Balmoral to the Balkans

In September 1912, with the Balkan League beginning to assert itself, King George V invited Sazonov to join him and Sir Edward Grey at Balmoral. Sazonov claimed in his memoirs that he spent six days in the Aberdeenshire countryside locked in private talks with the king and Sir Edward Grey, in the company of the Russian ambassador to Britain, Count Benckendorff, and Bonar Law, leader of the Conservative opposition.[1] The official memoirs of both Grey and Sazonov suggest that virtually no discussion took place on the Balkans crisis, even although it had reached boiling point and war was just about to break out. How strange. Their differing recollections of the private discussions are at serious odds on one key matter.[2] Sazonov, whose correspondence the Secret Elite could not edit in the aftermath of the Russian Revolution, telegraphed the czar afterwards to tell him triumphantly:

> An agreement exists between France and Great Britain, under which in the event of war with Germany, Great Britain has accepted the obligation of bringing assistance to France not only on sea but on land, by landing troops on the continent. The King touched on the same question, and expressed himself even more strongly than his Minister . . . He said, 'We shall sink every single German merchant ship we shall get hold of.'[3]

In fact, Poincaré had told Sazonov in confidence about Britain's secret commitment some weeks earlier, but now he had the confirmation he so desperately needed.

Balmoral 1912 offers the perfect example of how the Secret Elite managed international politics through their agents and how they controlled the official records of these events. The king was asked to invite Sazonov to his Scottish country estate and charmed him with the elegance of royalty. The foreign secretary, diplomats, the leader of the opposition and others were in attendance. We do not know who else visited or stayed over, who dined with the guests and walked or fished or hunted with them. The details that were made public acted as a smokescreen behind which the real politics took place. Nothing that could incriminate was traceable. It was agreed with nods and handshakes. Verbal consent was sufficient. Matters of real importance were concealed from Parliament and the people by sophistry and carefully prepared official records. Judgements were made. Opinions were shared. Strategy was considered and agreed. Sazonov emerged thrilled with the heady intoxication of regal flattery, clearly understanding that war was coming and that Britain would play its part. His excited telegram to the czar, quoted in part above, is a reliable account of what he believed he heard. The only questions that remained unanswered were: how soon and by what means war against Germany could be induced by way of the Balkans.

Grey's dismissive memoirs stated that the main focus at Balmoral was 'that wearisome subject' Persia.[4] The subsequent memorandum drawn up by the Foreign Office on 4 October 1912 is exactly as Grey claimed: boring, long-winded and focused on Persia, Afghanistan, consular representation, the Trans-Persian Railway and border disputes.[5] His silence on the Balkans is deafening. Sazonov spent four consecutive days with the British foreign secretary discussing world affairs[6] and two weeks later the First Balkan War broke out, yet he claimed that it didn't merit inclusion in their discussions. Elsewhere in his writings, Grey talked about the pent-up hatreds of generations that exploded into war in the Balkans, a war he described as 'just' on the grounds that it involved the emancipation of Christian subjects of Turkey.[7] But we are asked to believe that nothing was said about it at Balmoral. This was, of course, a deliberate deception.

Sazonov's account of Balmoral mentions 'the impetuous outburst' of the Balkan States, as if he had no prior knowledge of their intentions. He communicated regularly with Isvolsky about the war that he knew was about to break out. They had planned it. Serbia and Bulgaria were, after all, obliged to hold off until Russia gave the go-ahead.[8]

Sazonov was not a well man. His health had been an ongoing problem for him. He was in awe of Sir Edward Grey, a politician at the pinnacle of his powers. Sazonov and Isvolsky owed their very positions to the influence that Grey represented. The Secret Elite set the agenda. Sazonov and Grey most certainly discussed the Balkans. In a private letter to the British ambassador to Russia written on 21 October 1912, a matter of one month later, Grey confided: 'The fact is that he [Sazonov] was, at Balmoral, much concerned at the blaze he had kindled in the Balkans by fomenting an alliance of the Balkan States.'[9] So much for the integrity of his memoirs. Sir Edward Grey clearly wanted to keep secret any record of the Balkan discussions, but diplomatic exchanges have since exposed his deception.[10]

The Russian press was mightily unimpressed that Sazonov's visit to Britain had resulted in no visible support for their Balkan ambitions, and the Foreign Office was alerted to the disappointment this caused. British ambassador Sir George Buchanan sent Grey a dispatch quoting an article in *Novoe Vremya* that questioned the value to Russia of having an entente with England. Written by Stolypin, brother of the recently assassinated Russian prime minister, it captured the very truth that the Secret Elite sought to bury. Buchanan paraphrased Stolypin's argument: 'In a war with Germany, England would endeavour to drag Russia and France into the struggle which would be one of existence for her but which could not fail to be prejudicial to Russia's interests.'[11] Stolypin was one of a number of Russians who recognised that there was a fundamental divergence of interests between Britain and the czar's empire. At every turn, Britain was opposed to Russian designs in Persia, Afghanistan, the Straits and the Balkans, and Stolypin was absolutely correct in his warnings that Britain intended to drag Russia into a war with Germany.

Every overture to Russia since 1905 was occasioned by its value in an all-out war with Germany. Press rumblings and reported grievances in Russia over British interests in the Balkans and Persia might well have disturbed the Secret Elite's grand plan. So the royal card was played. The king was asked to write privately and personally to the czar to reassure him that Sazonov's visit had been entirely satisfactory, that the most friendly and intimate relations between the two countries should be maintained and to express the hope that their cordial and frank links would continue. Sir Arthur Nicolson, Grey's minder in the Foreign Office, more or less dictated the king's letter, stating that the czar was 'the all-important factor'.[12] In the autocratic Russian empire, keeping the czar 'on side' was absolutely vital to the Secret Elite no matter how the Balkan disturbances ended.

Isvolsky had known about the plans for war in the Balkans some 18 months before the outbreak.[13] He was, after all, the first to encourage the small nations to come together in a formal Balkan League. His fingerprints were all over a treaty that bound Serbia and Bulgaria to declare war against Turkey. Its secret clauses gave Russia the role of arbiter to decide when that war could begin and insisted that the Balkan League accept Russian decisions on any points of disagreement.[14] Isvolsky and Sazonov had ownership of this attack on Turkey, but their orders came from London. The final decision always lay in London.

Myths in history tend to become self-perpetuating. One such myth that grew into accepted popular culture in the early twentieth century was that Russia had a profound and binding right to protect Serbia, as if there was some deep Slavic bond between them. Serbia was not wholly a Slav nation; nor was Russia. There was no long-standing affection between the two. When one could use the other to advantage, they did so. At all other times, 'each intrigued for or against the other'.[15] Isvolsky had proved how little Serbia meant to Russia in 1908 when he agreed that Austria could annex Bosnia-Herzegovina. He never forgave the Austrian 'betrayal', as he saw it, and carried a personal grudge to his grave. But it suited Russian self-importance to perpetuate the pretence of being the protector of all Slavic people. There were large numbers of Slavs in Bosnia who considered themselves 'kin' to their Serbian 'cousins'. They constituted a deep reserve of disaffection from which disruption against Austria could be stirred.

Russia had funded the murder of one Serbian dynasty more inclined to Austria, that of King Alexander and Queen Draga, and replaced it with another that was undeviatingly sympathetic to Russia.[16] Russia abused her influence with Serbia to keep constant pressure on Austria-Hungary. The continual and wearing disruptions began to annoy Austria so much that the choice was either endless costly bickering or a sharp decisive war to punish Serbia. As Edith Durham observed:

> Austria, exasperated by the repeated outrage of the Serbs, and aware of the activity of Hartwig at Belgrade, realised that she was marked down as Russia's next victim on the proscribed list, and that the hour was arriving when she must kill or be killed.[17]

Wars do not just happen; small skirmishes do. Wars have to be financed in advance and repaid with interest. When the Paris banks showed a studied lack of interest in Bulgaria's approach to borrow heavily for the war against Turkey, it was Isvolsky who ensured that they got what they needed. Serious pressure was applied to French bankers in favour of Bulgaria. Their minister of finance, Todorov, met personally with Isvolsky in Paris in June 1912 to thank him and update him on Bulgarian plans.[18] But Isvolsky was the procurer, not the source. He had access to other 'backers', and they were not to be found in Russia.

Two distinct conflicts took place on the south-eastern flank of Europe in 1912 and 1913. The first was a concerted attack on Turkey by the combined nations of the Balkan League. In October 1912, Serbia, Bulgaria, Montenegro and Greece, 'secretly backed by England', declared war on Turkey and stripped her of most of her European possessions.[19]

Turkey was the first target, but the Balkan League was also directed against Austria. Without doubt, the League had a twofold agenda. They believed that the simplest and best solution would be the simultaneous break-up of Turkey and the downfall of Austria-Hungary. Deals were agreed. Serbia would take Bosnia-Herzegovina, Romania would have Transylvania, and Bulgaria would be free from Romanian interference.[20]

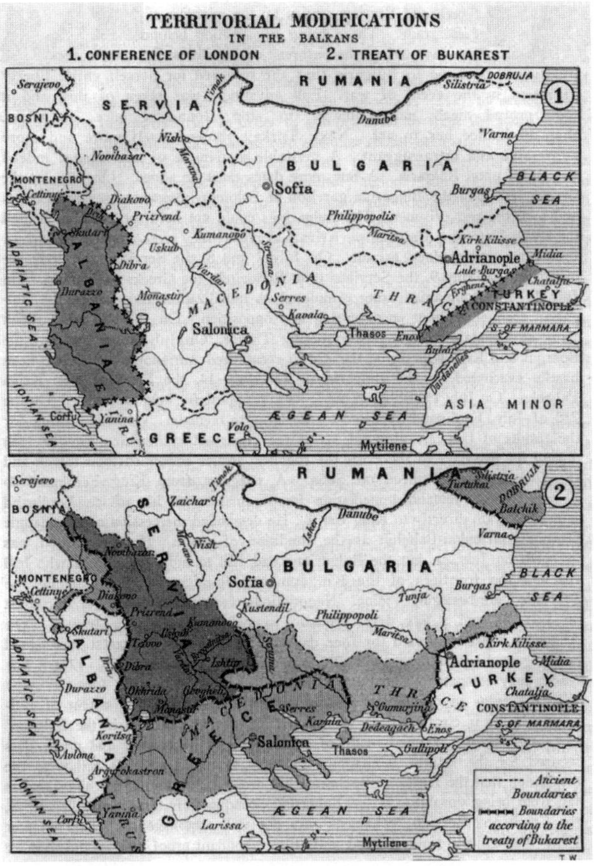

The Balkans 1912–13.

The First Balkan War was short, not particularly sweet, and humiliating for Turkey. An all-out conflict that might draw in the Great Powers never materialised. Austria did not intervene, and Kaiser Wilhelm made it clear that he would 'under no circumstances' be prepared to go to war with Russia or France on account of the Balkan nations.[21] This undoubtedly disappointed those who hoped, indeed planned, that it would lead on to a greater European war.

On 25 November 1912, the German government called for a joint settlement of the crisis, and an ambassadors' conference was held in London in December. Sir Edward Grey claimed to have taken no part in the discussions as 'they did not touch British interests and were not our affair'.[22] As we have already shown, the exact opposite was the case. Like Pontius Pilate, Grey had a propensity to wash his hands of responsibility for difficult decisions.

In fact, the London conference brokered only a temporary truce. Nothing was permanently resolved. The one thing that could be guaranteed was continual bickering and aggressive anti-Austrian antagonism emanating through Serbia. Georges Louis, while still the French ambassador at St Petersburg, had no doubt that Hartwig was stirring Serbia against Austria. He reported that Hartwig had incautiously remarked that 'the affair of Turkey is settled. Now it is the turn of Austria.'[23] That the plan was set is undeniable, but Ambassador Louis was not a player in the Secret Elite's grand scheme. He was removed for his troubles.

Despite the many pressing demands at home, the Secret Elite had stepped up their preparations all through the period of Balkan strife. On 5 December 1912, Isvolsky reported:

> Lately, in the most rigorous secrecy, the Chief of the English General Staff, General Wilson, arrived in France, and on this occasion various complementary details have been elaborated . . . Not only military but other representatives of the French Government have participated in this work.[24]

Two weeks later, Isvolsky telegraphed Sazonov, warning that the Austrian cabinet might make a critical move, causing a Russian response 'which in turn would inevitably and automatically drag first Germany and then France into the war'.[25] Poincaré viewed this possibility with perfect calm, aware of French obligations under the alliance, and firmly resolved to act. All the necessary steps had been taken. Mobilisation on the frontier had been examined, war materiel was in place and processes and procedures for going to war with Germany were understood and agreed with the military command.[26]

Raymond Poincaré was on the point of introducing his three-year army bill to increase the time enlisted men would stay in the forces from two years to three. It rapidly led to a huge increase in French military manpower. Edward Grey secretly assured Poincaré that Britain would support France and Russia as 'an obligation of honour' should the Balkans trouble lead to a European war.[27] Sazonov telegraphed Isvolsky asking him to reassure the French that Russia too was ready. He rebutted claims that Russia had done nothing to build up its forces. In fact, some 350,000 reservists had been retained within the colours. In addition, 80 million roubles had been allocated for extraordinary army requirements and for the Baltic Fleet, while some of the divisions in the Kiev command had been brought closer to the Austrian frontier.[28]

To all intents and purposes, Britain, Russia and France were in a state of alert, checking on one another's readiness. The question being asked in the dark corridors of power in London, Paris, St Petersburg and across other European capitals was: is a general war going to break out this time? French and Russian military preparations continued unabated. All that was needed was a 'satisfactory' incident in the Balkans to precipitate the war. The French people were subjected to a campaign of anti-German and anti-Austrian propaganda in the papers whose editors and writers were being bribed by funds obtained by Isvolsky.[29] Newspapers in the UK had spent the better part of a decade softening up the British public for war. Behind a mask of indifference to the Balkans, the warmongers in Britain were almost ready.

Perhaps the most telling evidence that Europe stood on the brink in 1912 comes from Belgium. In November 1912, the parliament in Brussels held a secret sitting at the insistence of King Albert to consider urgent precautionary measures. The king disclosed to a hushed chamber that he had evidence that Belgium was in dire and imminent danger. A drastic and far-reaching military programme that had been first advocated by his predecessor, Leopold II, some 30 years previously, was adopted immediately. The strength of the Belgian army was raised to 150,000 men in the field, with 60,000 in auxiliary services and 130,000 allocated to defensive garrisons: 340,000 men in total. It was an enormous expansion of armed forces in a supposedly neutral nation of 7,500,000 people.[30]

What was the nature of King Albert's evidence? Where did it come from and why was it given directly to him? These were not the normal channels through which secrets were passed. The accepted protocol was for kings and royalty to liaise with each other while government ministers shared and exchanged news and views. So who alerted the king? The only reason he would have taken such exceptional action was a warning that a European war was imminent. A second cousin to the late King Edward, Albert had an absolute trust in the British royal family.[31] Though no evidence could be produced to prove that this was his royal source, none would have had more impact.

There was another aspect to the Belgians' sense of impending crisis. According to evidence later published in New York, the Belgians were advised in November 1912 by the British military that as soon as a European war broke out, 160,000 men would be transported to Belgium and northern France, with or without the permission of the Belgian government.[32] Bear this in mind: 'with or without the permission of the Belgian government' – the British planned to be in Belgium when war broke out. This sense of ongoing crisis was fully justified because the Balkans were far from settled.

Following the first Balkan War, Bulgaria claimed rights to territory she had taken from Turkey. Her claim rested upon the pre-war treaty agreed with Serbia by which definite portions of the captured lands were to be allocated to each country. Serbia, disgruntled at having been ordered by the Great Powers to vacate areas allocated to her in Albania, demanded a portion of the land she had previously agreed should go to Bulgaria. Bloated by early success, Serbia strutted threateningly, like the young thug who knows he can flex his muscles against a bigger boy because he has the protection of an older bully. Serbia relied on the promised support of Russia to push for more than she had already gained. Russia was their provider, guarantor and arbiter. Bulgaria, having suffered by far the greatest number of war casualties, refused and insisted that the terms of the treaty be adhered to. She called on Russia to fulfil her agreed role as arbiter. Much to the anger and resentment of the Bulgarian government, the czar responded by paying an overtly friendly visit to Bulgaria's old adversary, Romania. To make matters worse, Russia backed the Serbian claims and in so doing forfeited Bulgaria's friendship.

The League was split irrevocably. Skirmishes between Bulgarian and Serbian troops on their communal border led to a Second Balkan War in June 1913. Serbian forces, aided by Romania and Greece, committed terrible atrocities as they penetrated deep into Bulgaria. Russia, France and Britain looked on passively as Bulgaria was soundly beaten. The Turks took the opportunity to invade Bulgaria and snatch back some of their territory ceded after the first Balkan War. The Treaty of Bucharest on 10 August 1913 brought a second temporary peace to the region but at considerable cost to Bulgaria, which had lost most of the territorial gains made from the First Balkan War. In stark contrast, Serbia doubled its territory and 'now posed an even greater threat to Austria-Hungary, both externally and by encouraging the sizeable Serbian minority within the dual monarchy (Bosnia-Herzegovina) to demand its independence'.[33]

There was a feral nature to Balkan warfare that accepted atrocities as the natural course of events. The Serbian practice of decapitating the dead or captured enemy and impaling their heads on poles was positively medieval. The extermination of entire villages or the merciless bayoneting of women and children was commonplace. The Russian press, and that of Western Europe, was excoriated by Trotsky, Durham and others 'for its conspiracy of silence about the atrocities being committed by the Slavs of the Balkans against the Turks'.[34]

Disgusted by the behaviour of the Serbian army, Edith Durham left the Balkans for London and rushed to the Foreign Office to plead the case for a Muslim population that was being systematically subjected to humiliation, torture and death. Muslims were being coerced into conversion to Christianity. She recorded that, each day, civilians were taken from their villages and summarily executed, writing: 'as the victims fell the earth was shovelled over them, whether living or dead . . . Men were plunged into ice-cold rivers and then half roasted till they cried for mercy. And conversion to Christianity was the price.'[35] Medieval barbarity was reintroduced with a vengeance. The Carnegie Commission that was later set up to investigate such crimes against humanity made clear that the accusations were true. These atrocities were planned and executed by the Serbian Black Hand.

Durham was fobbed off by the Foreign Office. The British Establishment did not want to know. Sir Edward Grey had deemed it a 'just' war on the grounds that Christians could now be protected from the Ottomans.[36] In truth, the Secret Elite needed the murderous Black Hand and their leader, Colonel Apis, for a hugely important task.

In the summer of 1913, Serbian troops re-occupied Albanian territory, even although it was supposed to be protected by the Great Powers. Yet more atrocities followed. Britain was approached directly by the Austrians to use its influence as a matter of urgency to effect a Serbian withdrawal. Sir Edward Grey happened to be 'out of town for the weekend' and his under-secretary, Sir Eyre Crowe, declined to take action on the grounds that he did not think that Grey would approve a demand for immediate withdrawal by the Serbs.[37]

Austria-Hungary was seething and prepared to send aid to Albania. A major European war became more likely by the hour. An emergency telegram was sent to the Russian army from the czar stating that an order for mobilisation in the western military command caused by any political complications on the western frontier was to be treated as an order for the start of hostilities against Austria and Germany.[38] In other words, the military command had to treat an order for general mobilisation emanating from St Petersburg as an indication that the talking had ended. Such a mobilisation meant war, and it meant war with Austria and Germany.

The temperature kept rising as the pent-up frustrations in the Balkan pressure cooker rose to bursting point. European war was only averted in 1913 because Russia ordered Serbia to move back from the brink after the Austrians served an ultimatum on Belgrade. The Serbians were furious but had no option but to comply.

Why did Russia take this decision in 1913 but respond to a similar situation in 1914 with a full mobilisation of its armies? Was it a function of their state of readiness for war? Possibly. But, as far as the Secret Elite was concerned, the *raison d'être* for the Balkan crisis was to get Austria to react to severe provocation in order to draw Germany in. This was not, at its core, about Austria. It was about Germany. It had always been about Germany.

Kaiser Wilhelm would not be drawn. He was not willing to support an Austrian onslaught against Serbia. Instead, he consistently focused on low-risk diplomatic solutions, to the extent that there was considerable frustration in Vienna at his apparent inability to understand the serious threat that Austria believed she faced from her enemies in Belgrade.[39] Contrary to the ubiquitous image of the warmongering Kaiser Bill, so beloved of British propaganda, Wilhelm urged Austria to make concessions to the Serbs and seek peaceful co-existence. When Germany pressurised Austria to accept a diplomatic resolution, a continental war in 1913 became impossible. Germany had to be at the forefront, had to be seen as the aggressor.

And what had the Secret Elite learned from it all? It was clear that the British public had little stomach for war over a Balkan nation. With so many local distractions – Ireland, the suffragette demands, strikes and social unrest – public interest in the Balkans was virtually non-existent, and sympathy for Russia was at a low ebb. Many Members of Parliament, especially the Liberal Radicals, spoke disparagingly about the czarist regime with its pogroms and repressions.[40] Serbia, Bosnia, Slavic nationalism: these were not the concerns of the British people in 1913. If a war did break out, 'hell mend them' was the attitude. It had nothing to do with Britain, had it? Not only had more work to be done to fully prepare the British people for war, but Germany wasn't taking the bait.

The Secret Elite understood the history of genocide and massacre in the Balkans, and had a grasp of undetermined disputes that could be put to great advantage. They could see that Austria was bristling with frustration. Its national pride, its international standing, its very patience was being undermined by Serbian aggression. Austria lay like a coiled spring that Serbia continued to prick and prod in the hope and expectation that one day it would explode. And when that happened, Germany would be pitched into action. Surely.

Summary: Chapter 19 – From Balmoral to the Balkans

- Sazonov met with Sir Edward Grey and King George V at Balmoral in 1912. Both he and Grey claimed not to have discussed the Balkans. The lies and disinformation that stemmed from those four days of meetings offer a perfect example of how the Secret Elite covered their real business.
- Sazonov reported to the czar that Britain was secretly committed to support France in a war with Germany both by land and sea.
- Secretly backed by England, the Balkan League attacked and humiliated Turkey.

ABOVE: Professor Carroll Quigley

RIGHT: Cecil Rhodes

Alfred Milner

Lord 'Natty' Rothschild

Milner (sitting) chose his personal staff with great care, preferring Balliol and Oxford graduates who would later blossom under his patronage.

Alfred Milner (sitting second left) and Lord Roberts (with arm in sling) at Cape Town, 1900, with key members of the Roberts Academy.

Jan Smuts, Boer hero and inner-core member of the Secret Elite. (Library of Congress)

Prime Minister Balfour (sitting at desk with pen in hand) with Foreign Secretary Lansdowne (centre) at a Committee of Imperial Defence meeting.

Arthur Balfour, friend and protector of the Liberal imperialists. (© Getty Images)

Edward VII in his regal glory. His major role in the origins of the First World War has been hidden. (Portrait by Samuel Luke Fildes)

The Relugas Three

Grey

Haldane

Asquith

Even in retirement, Lord Roberts was a national icon.

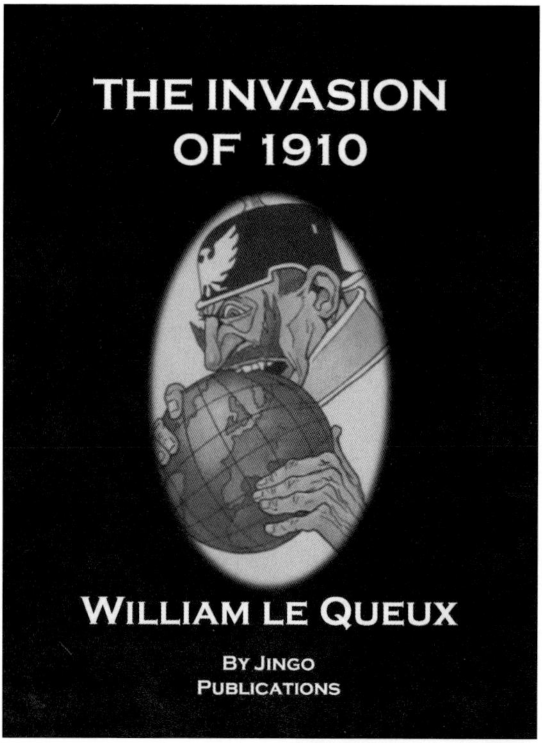

Le Queux's ridiculous spy 'novel' featuring the kaiser as the evil world-grabbing 'Hun'.

Often in cahoots, 'the terrible twins' – Churchill and Lloyd George – were by 1912 in the pocket of the Secret Elite.

Sir Edward Carson

Paul Warburg

Three crucial Secret Elite placemen

President Raymond Poincaré

Lord Crewe, Winston Churchill and Sir Edward Grey (right) dressed 'to kill'.

Wilson, Joffre and Huguet – the men who led the secret 'conversations' so often denied in Parliament.

- All-out war was avoided because the kaiser would not contemplate it and called for a peace conference in London.
- The Second Balkan war targeted Bulgaria and Austria's allies. The Secret Elite chose to ignore the evidence of brutal massacres by Serbian troops.
- Austria was consistently undermined and challenged by Serbia. The treatment of Albania was deplorable, but Germany refused to let her ally be suckered into war because of Serbia.
- Yet again the kaiser would not be drawn into the conflict. He favoured diplomatic solutions.
- The lesson learned was this: Austria was seething at the abuse she suffered from Serbia and was at her wit's end. Austria would be the Achilles heel.

CHAPTER 20

Sarajevo – The Web of Culpability

THE SECRET ELITE FAILED TO find their spark for the international conflagration in the Balkans because Germany, in the person of the kaiser, restrained Austria-Hungary from overreacting to Serbia's deliberate provocation. Indeed, the Dual Monarchy was concerned that the German ambassador in Belgrade in 1914 was decidedly pro-Serb and had influenced the kaiser to take a comparatively benign attitude towards the Serbian cause.[1] Yet it was clear that Austria could only absorb so much pressure before the integrity of the state was destroyed.[2] The war-makers required an incident so violent, threatening or dangerous, that Austria would be pushed over the brink.

Austria-Hungary was aware of the dangers that lay across the Serbian border. Their military intelligence had intercepted and deciphered a large number of diplomatic telegrams that detailed Russian involvement with several Serbian activist groups.[3] They knew that Isvolsky's placeman in Belgrade, Nicholas Hartwig, was manipulating the Serbian government to destabilise the region. They knew that Hartwig was in control of the internal politics of Serbia. They knew of his links back to Sazonov in St Petersburg, and to Isvolsky and Poincaré in Paris, but they were not aware of the real power centred in London. No one was.

The links in the chain of command from London went further, deeper and more sinister when extended from Hartwig into the Serbian military, their intelligence service and the quasi-independent nationalist society, the Black Hand. And deeper yet into the young Bosnian political activists who were willing to pull the trigger in Sarajevo – students whose ideas on socialism and reform were influenced by revolutionaries like Trotsky. As each level in the web of culpability extended away from the central Secret Elite chain of command, precise control became less immediate. Sazonov in St Petersburg considered that Hartwig in Belgrade was 'carried away occasionally by his Slavophile sympathies'[4] but did nothing to curtail him. Hartwig in turn supported and encouraged men whose prime cause he willingly shared and whose actions he could personally approve but not at every stage control.

Hartwig, the Russian ambassador, worked in close contact with his military attaché, Colonel Viktor Artamanov, who had been posted to Belgrade to advise and liaise with the Serbian army. These men were intrinsically linked to the assassins in Sarajevo by their chosen agent, the founder and dominating figure in the Serbian Black Hand and the most influential military officer in Serbia, Colonel Dragutin Dimitrijevic, or Apis.[5]

The English traveller and Balkan commentator Edith Durham described the Black Hand as a mafia-type society, Masonic in secret self-promotion, infiltrating the Serbian military, civil service, police and government. It produced its own newspaper, *Pijemont*, which preached intolerance to Austria-Hungary and 'violent chauvinism'. It became the most dangerous of political organisations, a government within the government, responsible to none. Crimes were committed for which no one took responsibility. The government denied any knowledge of it, yet King Petar was elevated to the throne by these men. Efforts by responsible politicians to tackle the subversion of good government by the Black Hand came to nought.[6] Hartwig's friendship and respect for Apis may be measured by his description of his group as 'idealistic and patriotic',[7] and there is no doubt that it suited Hartwig's purpose to approve Apis's promotion to chief of intelligence in the summer of 1913.

It is important that we clearly identify every link in the chain of responsibility that surrounded the fateful assassination in Sarajevo in June 1914. Apis was deliberately given responsibility for an intelligence organisation financed from Russia and informed by Bosnian Slavs. His life's purpose was the establishment of a Greater Serbia. He was first, foremost and always a Serb. He worked in collusion with Hartwig's military attaché, Artamanov, and secured a promise from him that Russia would protect Serbia should Austria attack them in the wake of his actions.[8] For Apis, what was required was a demonstration of Serbian self-determination that would bring about permanent change and force the issue once and for all.

The Austrian government presented the opportunity in March 1914 when they announced that Archduke Franz Ferdinand, heir to the Hapsburg dual monarchy, would visit Sarajevo in June. Political assassination as a means to an end was not a new concept. In the five years prior to 1914, lone assassins, mostly Serbian citizens of Austria-Hungary, made a series of unsuccessful attempts against Austro-Hungarian officials in Croatia and Bosnia-Herzegovina.[9] In 1912, two unsuccessful attempts were made on the viceroy of Croatia and royal commissioner for Austria-Hungary, and in 1914 a similar attempt on the life of a royal commissioner was foiled. The Austrian government had reliable information that Serbian agitators 'in conjunction with influential Russian circles' wished to strike a decisive blow against the Austrian monarchy,[10] but had no precise details.

Apis's organisation was prepared. It had infiltrated a revolutionary group, Mlada Bosna (the Young Bosnians), and equipped and trained them to carry out the Sarajevo assassination. The Young Bosnians held high ideals, far more intellectual than the narrow chauvinism of the Black Hand. They wanted to go beyond independence from Austria-Hungary to change the primitive nature of Bosnian society. They challenged the authority of existing institutions of state, church, school and family, and believed in socialist concepts: egalitarianism and the emancipation of women. The Young Bosnians stood for modernism, intellectualism and a brave new world.[11] They were spurred by revolution, not narrow nationalism.

Apis knew just the man to organise and lead an assassination team of Young Bosnians, Danilo Ilić. He had worked as a schoolteacher and as a bank worker, but in 1913 and 1914 he lived with his mother, helping her run a small boarding house in Sarajevo. Ilić was leader of the Serbian Black Hand terrorist cell in Sarajevo, and as such was known to Colonel Apis personally.[12] Ilić was also a close friend of Gavrilo Princip, the student destined to fire the fatal shot.

Apis used three trusted Serb associates in planning the assassination. His right-hand man, Major Vojislav Tankosić, was in charge of guerrilla training and brought the would-be assassins to a secret location in Serbia where his specific role was to ensure that the Young Bosnians knew how to handle guns and bombs effectively. He was tasked to teach them the art of the assassin and get them back over the border and into Sarajevo safely. The second, Rade Malobabić, was the chief undercover operative for Serbian military intelligence. His name appeared in Serbian documents captured by Austria-Hungary during the war that describe the running of arms, munitions and agents from Serbia into Austria-Hungary under his direction.[13] His assessment was that the Young Bosnians were capable of the task. The third Black Hand conspirator was Milan Ciganovic. He supplied the assassination team with four revolvers and six bombs from the Serbian army's arsenal. Crucially, each of the assassins was given a vial of cyanide to take after they had murdered the archduke. Their suicides would ensure that the trail could not be traced back to Apis and Hartwig.

Ciganovic played another equally important role. He was a trusted confidant of the Serbian prime minister, Nikola Pasic, and was ultimately protected by him from the volcanic fallout after Sarajevo. Critically, Ciganovic's involvement meant that members of the Serbian government knew in advance about the proposed assassination and had time to consider the consequences.[14]

Everything appeared to be running smoothly, but Serbian intrigues hit political turbulence at precisely the wrong moment. The unity of Serbia's political, military and royal leaders, nestling behind the muscle of their Russian minders, had been a feature of Serbian success in the Balkan Wars. Prime Minister Pasic, Colonel Apis and King Petar were all supported by Ambassador Hartwig towards the ambitions of a Greater Serbia. But suddenly, just days before the planned assassination, a power struggle erupted for control of the country. Apis attempted to organise a coup to dismiss Pasic, allegedly over a minor detail of precedence, but found that his power base in the Serbian military had shrunk. Many of his senior colleagues who had been involved with him since the first regicides in 1903 had died naturally or been killed in the Balkan Wars. The old order inexorably changes. Even his closest friends baulked at unleashing military force against the civilian authorities.[15] Many Serbs expected Apis to win outright victory in this power struggle, but his foray into civil politics diluted the aura that had been associated with his leadership of the Black Hand. The Serbian cabinet drafted stringent measures against Black Hand membership, retiring highly placed officials and transferring others to the anonymity of remote Serbian outposts.[16]

But the killer blow to Colonel Apis's aspirations came from two external powers. Russia, more accurately the Sazonov/Isvolsky axis, would not countenance the removal of Prime Minister Pasic and his cabinet. Hartwig slapped down any notion of resignations. At the same time, Poincaré let it be known that a Serbian opposition regime could not count on financial backing from Paris.[17] The king, caught between old loyalties and Russian pressure, withdrew from political life. He transferred his powers to Prince Alexander, who resented Apis's authority in Serbian military circles.

Look again at these events. With the assassination just days away, the last thing that Sazonov/Isvolsky, Poincaré and the Secret Elite would have entertained in June 1914 was a change of government in Serbia that did not owe its very existence to their power and money. Apis, the ultra nationalist, was not a man to take orders. He had desperately wanted to attack Bulgaria in 1913, but Pasic (no doubt under instruction from Hartwig) had refused to sanction the order.[18] Apis was neither deferential to Prince Alexander nor under Hartwig's thumb. He knew that Pasic was weak and subservient to Russia. It was as if metaphorical scales had suddenly dropped from his eyes and he understood for the first time that the Russians were exploiting him and his beloved Serbia for their own purposes.

Apis may also have had second thoughts about the assassination based on his own prospects for survival. He had clearly shaken the ruling cabal in Serbia. Prime Minister Pasic knew about the intended assassination, and in consequence the cabinet allegedly closed the borders to known or suspected assassins. If true, was this self-preservation on their part an attempt to make it look like the Serbian government had nothing to do with the shooting? Hartwig too knew details of the plans but never imagined they could be traced back to him. Crucially, he did not know that the Austrians were well aware of his intrigues because they had possession of decoded diplomatic correspondence between Russia and Serbia.[19]

Apis ordered a trusted agent to go to Sarajevo and instruct the Young Bosnians to abort the mission. It was all too late. They were safely ensconced in Sarajevo, ready for the appointed day and ill-disposed to accept any postponement. The Young Bosnians had slipped out of Belgrade on 28 May and been secretly routed across the border by sympathetic frontier guards. Ciganovic had ensured they had weapons and cash. The senior officer on the border guard at the time, a member of the Black Hand, had been placed there on special assignment by Apis's intelligence department.

Yet the archduke need not have been killed. Warnings about the perilous nature of his safety abounded. Despite this, the governor of Bosnia, General Potiorek, was determined that the visit would go ahead. Desperate pleas from the chief of police, who believed that the Archduke was in grave danger, were ignored. The very date of the visit, 28 June, was particularly provocative. It was St Vitus' Day, historically and emotionally significant to the Serbs, the anniversary of the Battle of Kosovo Poyle (1389), the victory that unified the Serbian nation against the Turkish invader.

That alone should have been a warning. The police chief's fears were dismissed by the governor and ridiculed by Sarajevo's military committee when he requested a cordon of soldiers to line the streets as a precaution. He pleaded with them not to publish the route of the archduke's cavalcade through the city, but was ignored. Newspapers carried detailed notice of the time and place to view the archduke's entourage.[20] A request that additional police officers be brought in from the country was rejected because it would cost too much. Security measures were left in the hands of providence.

The conspirators, and there were seven in the Young Bosnian team, stood at intervals along the avenue called Appel Quay – or the 'Avenue of Assassins' as the archbishop of Sarajevo would later dub it – and mingled freely with the crowds for an hour and a half before the archduke's arrival. Though Bosnia could boast a first-class political intelligence, no one – no police officer, no undercover police agent, no vigilant citizen – questioned them.[21]

The events of what might safely be deemed the world's most devastating assassination have been well documented. A botched bomb-throwing left the archduke shaken but physically unmarked. Officials in the following car were not so lucky. His cavalcade stopped briefly before continuing to the town hall. Strained speeches made pretence that all was well. Despite the shameful outrage, troops were not called in from the barracks, nor additional police summoned for protection. Franz Ferdinand demanded to go to the hospital to see for himself how one of the governor's assistants, wounded by the bomb blast, was faring.[22] Incredibly, the cavalcade returned along the same 'Avenue of Assassins' on which the first bomb had been thrown but turned into the wrong street. Potiorek ordered the driver to stop and reverse. In doing so, he placed the archduke directly in front of young Princip, who promptly shot both him and his unfortunate wife, Sophie. The police arrested Princip on the spot before he could attempt suicide.

And on a chance wrong turn we are expected to believe that the world went to war.

Governor Potiorek's behaviour was astonishing. The entourage was on its way to the hospital, but Potiorek ordered the driver to proceed to the governor's residence instead. Confused? We should be. A meticulously planned assassination succeeded, despite the amateurism of the conspirators, only because the victim was more or less served up on a plate. Had Potiorek acted in shock, or did he know it was already too late? It was suggested at the time that Austria had set up the assassination deliberately in order to provoke a war. In the bitter rage of accusation and counterclaim that followed after 1914, all sides made allegations against one another. In the 1920s, and over the decades since, much evidence has come to light from documents that had been 'lost' or removed 'unofficially'. There is now a huge body of diplomatic evidence that links Russia and Serbia to the assassination,[23] but none that supports the suggestion that the low-security visit of Archduke Ferdinand to Sarajevo was in some way organised with the intention of exposing him to the risk of assassination.

Had the great crime gone to plan, all the Young Bosnians would have committed suicide. They were expendable. Dead Bosnians tell no tales. The links in the chain of responsibility would have been broken. The headline they sought was of a noble death-pact assassination that would leave the authorities completely bewildered and the coffee houses of Europe abuzz with revolutionary admiration. Cabrinovic, who threw the first bomb, immediately swallowed his cyanide and leapt 15 feet into the shallow River Miljacka. Police officers hauled him out of the mudflat, vomiting uncontrollably. The cyanide failed to be effective for any of the Young Bosnians. There was to be no self-directed martyrdom.

With suspicious ease, the Austro-Hungarian authorities arrested all but one of the Sarajevo assassins, together with the agents and peasants who had assisted them on their way. How they managed to track all of the alleged conspirators so quickly begs the question of how much they knew in advance. The major charge against the Young Bosnians was conspiracy to commit high treason, which carried a maximum sentence of death. Within a few days of the assassination, the Austrians had set up a judicial investigation. They were convinced that the Young Bosnians had been equipped from Belgrade and that the plot had originated from there. What the Austrians desperately needed to know was the extent to which Pasic's government was directly involved.[24] The Austro-Hungarian Foreign Ministry sent its top legal counsellor, Dr Freidrich von Wiesner, as official investigator to Sarajevo.

On 13 July 1914, he forwarded an interim report to Vienna containing three major points:

1. The Greater Serbia movement aimed to sever the southern Slav region from Austria by revolutionary violence. He pointed an accusatory finger at Narodna Odbrana, yet another Serbian nationalist movement, possibly confusing it with the Black Hand, stating that the Belgrade government let it have an absolutely free hand.
2. He named Major Tankosić and 'the Serbian official Ciganovic' for training and supplying the assassins with weapons, and both the frontier authorities and the customs officers for smuggling them into Bosnia. These facts he deemed 'demonstrable and virtually unassailable'.[25]
3. He concluded by stating cautiously that there was no conclusive proof at that time of the Serbian government having any knowledge of the assassination or having cooperated in planning it.

Dr von Wiesner's oral report, delivered some two days later, was more comprehensive. By then he had unearthed more evidence of Serbian complicity, but his telegrammed report of 13 July was destined to be hijacked and later grossly misrepresented by the American delegation at the War Guilt Commission in 1919. Their two most senior delegates, Secretary of State Robert Lansing and Counsellor James Scott Brown, deliberately extracted a 31-word 'soundbite' from von Wiesner's brief report, which they claimed 'proved' that Austria had no evidence against Serbia that justified war.[26] It was a deliberate misrepresentation that gave the impression that Dr von Wiesner believed that Serbia was 'utterly innocent' in 1914.[27] Such a falsification suited their cause. It was used as part of the post-war onslaught against Germany and Austria to lay the blame for war entirely on their shoulders. The Americans, Lansing and Brown, now stand accused of deliberately falsifying history in a desperate attempt to malign Austria and Germany.

By October, when the Young Bosnians were brought to trial, the Austrian authorities had overwhelming evidence of Serbian complicity. Despite this, the conspirators insisted in deflecting blame from Serbia. Under cross-examination, Princip was defiant: 'I believe in unification of all South Slavs in whatever form of state and that it be free of Austria.' Asked how he intended to realise his goal, he responded: 'By means of terror.'[28]

Although they had been trained in Serbia, the Young Bosnians had no knowledge of the influences that had been exerted further up the chain of command. Indeed, few if any within that chain knew who was empowering the next link. Princip and his group genuinely believed that they were striking a blow for freedom and emancipation, and could not bring themselves to accept that they had been duped into firing someone else's bullets.

The Austrian court did not accept their attempts to hold Serbia blameless.[29] The verdict was decisive. The court ignored Princip's claims and stated bluntly that the military commanders in charge of the Serbian espionage service collaborated in the outrage. Four of the Young Bosnians were executed by hanging in February 1915, but the younger members, like Princip, were given prison sentences. He died in prison in 1918 from tuberculosis exacerbated by a botched amputation.[30] Crucially, the trail of culpability had not been covered over.

Above all else, the Secret Elite had to ensure that no links could be traced back to Russia. Evidence of her complicity in the archduke's death would have altered the balance of credibility for the entente cause. All links to Sazonov in particular had to be airbrushed. That in turn meant that the web of intrigue between Serbia and Russia had to be cleansed. The outbreak of war in August slowed down this process but only delayed the outcome.

The Russian ambassador died in very strange circumstances. On a routine visit to Baron von Gieslingen, Austrian ambassador at Belgrade, on 10 July 1914, Hartwig collapsed and died from a massive 'heart attack'. The Serbian press immediately published several inflammatory articles accusing the Austrians of poisoning Hartwig while he was a guest at their legation. The Austrians, of course, knew from decoded diplomatic telegrams that Hartwig was at the centre of intrigues against Austria-Hungary.[31] Was this the old-fashioned style of retribution, or were the Secret Elite simply very fortunate that the 57-year-old diplomat dropped dead in the Austrian legation?

Denials echoed around Europe, nowhere more vehemently than in Britain, where the Secret Elite had to vilify any suggestion that Russia was involved with internal Bosnian or Austro-Hungarian politics. *The Times* led the outcry:

> The latest suggestion made in one of the Serbian newspapers is that M de Hartwig's sudden death in the Austro-Hungarian Legation at Belgrade the other day was due to poison. Ravings of that kind move the contempt as well as the disgust of cultivated people, whatever their political sympathies may be.[32]

Ravings indeed. *The Times*, and those it represented, clearly wanted to quash such speculation. It was far too close to the truth. If the idea that Hartwig had been murdered because he was involved in the archduke's assassination gained credence, British public opinion would turn even further against Russia. At the request of the Serbian government, Hartwig was buried in Belgrade in what was virtually a state funeral. Every notable Serbian, including the prime minister, attended. Officially, Hartwig suffered death by natural causes. Unofficially, a very important link in the chain of culpability was buried along with his corpse.

Some three years later, with the tide of war turned violently against Serbia, the Austrians demanded the immediate arrest and trial of Colonel Apis and the officers loyal to him. They were indicted on various false charges unrelated to Sarajevo at a Serbian court martial held on the frontier at Salonika. On 23 May 1917, Apis and eight of his associates were sentenced to death; two others were sentenced to fifteen years in prison. One defendant died during the trial and the charges against him were dropped. The Serbian High Court reduced the number of death sentences to seven. Regent Alexander commuted four others, leaving three to face the firing squad.[33]

Colonel Apis effectively signed his own death warrant when he confessed to the Salonika court that 'in agreement with Artamonov [*sic*], the Russian military attaché, I hired Malobabić to organise Ferdinand's murder upon his arrival in Sarajevo'.[34] The explosive part of that statement was the opening phrase 'in agreement with Artamonov'. His revelation of Russian involvement had to be silenced. Much to his own despair, for Colonel Apis truly believed right up to the moment of death that his contacts in England, France and Russia would intervene on his behalf,[35] he was executed on 26 June 1917 by firing squad. In reality, Apis was silenced: put to death by order of a Serbian government that desperately needed to permanently bury its complicity with Russia in the Sarajevo assassination.[36] It was judicial murder.

By one means or another, the lower edges of the web of culpability were blown away. The Young Bosnians had in their naivety been willing sacrifices to a cause they never knew existed. Hartwig was dead. Murdered? Probably, but all that really mattered was that his voice would never be heard again. Our understanding of his role in managing the Russian intrigues has to remain, at best, incomplete. There was plenty to hide and no doubt at all about Russian complicity.[37] The Soviet collection of diplomatic papers from the year 1914 revealed an astonishing gap. During the first days of the October Revolution in 1917, Hartwig's dispatches from Belgrade for the crucial period between May and July 1914 had been removed by an unknown person from the archives of the Russian Foreign Ministry. Three years dead and his was a voice they still had to gag.[38] Finally, Apis and his Black Hand associates were removed from any future inquiry or the temptation of a lucrative memoir. Blown away, all of them, in the expectation that the truth about their contributions would disappear in the confusion of war.

Summary: Chapter 20 – Sarajevo – The Web of Culpability

- The assassination of Archduke Ferdinand was orchestrated through a chain of culpability that stretched from Sarajevo to Belgrade, Belgrade to St Petersburg and then on to Paris and London.
- The Russians Hartwig and Artamanov liaised with the Serbian nationalist Dimitrijevic (Apis) and the Black Hand organisation to underwrite and plan the assassination.
- The Young Bosnians, a much more idealistic and intellectual group, became the agents through whom Apis planned the assassination.
- The assassination was almost called off at the last moment by Apis when an internal political power struggle in Serbia broke out between him and Prime Minister Pasic, but the Russians, through Hartwig, quashed the attempted coup.
- Protection for the archduke on the day of the assassination was so negligible as to make it incomprehensible to today's reader.
- The assassins' attempts to commit suicide failed because the cyanide did not work. Serbian complicity was easily proven but steps were taken to remove any evidence that might link the organisation to Russia or even further back.
- The Austrians had broken the Serbian diplomatic codes and captured documents that detailed anti-Austrian activities. Following the assassination, they amassed a significant body of evidence implicating Serbia.
- Hartwig died, almost certainly murdered, at the Austrian embassy in Belgrade. Apis was shot by firing squad in 1917 on a trumped-up charge unrelated to Sarajevo. Hartwig's correspondence with Sazonov in Russia mysteriously disappeared in 1917. Princip died in prison from tuberculosis in 1918. These deaths 'coincidentally' protected the chain of command that led back to St Petersburg, Paris and London.

CHAPTER 21

July 1914 – Deception, Manipulation and Misrepresentation

The First Weeks

The smouldering distrust and racially inflamed tensions that continually raised the political temperature in the Balkans after the uneasy peace of 1913 were very deliberately reignited by the assassination of Franz Ferdinand. Civilised Europe was stunned by his murder. His uncle, the elderly Austrian emperor Franz Joseph, went into shock. Acrid demands for retribution filled the air. It took careful planning and considered judgement on the part of the Secret Elite to fan the understandable outrage and bring about the great European conflagration for which they had planned since before 1905. Furthermore, it required the highest level of diplomatic skill and political nous, allied to press connivance, unseen sleights of hand and downright lies to achieve the ultimate goal of war with Germany. War apparently started by Germany; war that would once and for all crush Germany and re-affirm the pre-eminence of the British race.

While the archduke's murder has generally been accepted as the spark that lit the fuse, it did not make the subsequent war inevitable. Far from it. The act in itself presented no cause for a world war. Assassinations and political murders were not uncommon in these troubled parts, with royalty, prime ministers, political opponents and religious leaders all victims in the recent past.[1] This was different. The Secret Elite deliberately and systematically whipped the consequences of Sarajevo into a raging wildfire that could not be extinguished.

From the hub of the Foreign Office in July 1914, Sir Edward Grey and his ambassadorial guard abused their position in order to trick both Austria-Hungary and Germany into a European war. A diplomatic network of highly experienced ambassadors committed to the Secret Elite vision of the pre-eminence of the British race was in place throughout the European capitals: Sir George Buchanan in St Petersburg, Sir Maurice de Bunsen in Vienna, Sir Edward Goschen in Berlin and Sir Francis Bertie in

Paris. Each was entrusted with the task of manipulating the Balkan crisis into a war that would see the Anglocentric influence dominate the world. Highly confidential information and instruction passed to and fro between them and London, where Sir Eyre Crowe and Sir Arthur Nicolson headed Grey's personal praetorian guard in the all-powerful Foreign Office. Even where the major players appeared to be Russian (Sazonov and Isvolsky) or French (Poincaré and Maurice Paléologue, the French Ambassador at St Petersburg in 1914), their actions were sanctioned from London.

The last days of June and the first week of July were, on the surface, comparatively calm. An outpouring of sympathy for Austria and its monarchy followed the initial shock of the assassination. In a parliamentary address on 30 June, Prime Minister Asquith stated that Emperor Franz Joseph 'and his people have always been our friends'. He spoke of the 'abhorrence of the crime and the profound sympathy of the British Parliament'.[2] In France, President Poincaré expressed his 'sincere condolences'.[3] Profound sincerity did not last long.

Franz Ferdinand had not been particularly popular in some Austrian circles because of his morganatic marriage[4] and the suspicion that he favoured Austria-Hungary's Slavic subjects. In many ways he was relatively enlightened about democratic rights and freedoms, a philosophy that was not shared by the Hapsburg traditionalists.

Despite the archduke's high office and his position and rank as heir-apparent, his funeral was decidedly low-key. The Austrian foreign minister, Count Leopold Berchtold, allegedly wanted it that way. Kaiser Wilhelm definitely intended to go. Franz Ferdinand had been a close personal friend, and it was his duty to show public respect to the ageing emperor.[5] The kaiser, however, developed diplomatic lumbago[6] when it was put about that a dozen Serbian assassins were making their way to Vienna to kill him.[7] Prince Arthur of Connaught was the designated representative for King George V, but quite suddenly, on 2 July, he and all other members of European royalty cancelled. Every one. Fears were expressed that other assassins were ready to do away with any passing royalty. No collection of funereal crowned heads gathered in Vienna.

Count Berchtold did not want a rabble of royalty descending on Vienna. He hoped to spare the ailing emperor the vexation of a long funeral ceremony.[8] Perhaps Berchtold feared that a gathering of emperors, kings and princes in Vienna would have distracted the Hapsburg government in its determination to seek retribution from Serbia. It most certainly suited the Secret Elite that Berchtold was left unfettered by interference from visiting dignitaries who might have cautioned care.

Isvolsky, the Secret Elite's Russian puppet-master, knew immediately what the success of the mission in Sarajevo meant. On the following day, he left Paris in utmost secrecy and slipped out of the public eye. His given role was to hold everything together in the Russian capital. The czar would need careful handling, and Foreign Minister Sazonov's resolve had caused concern from time to time. President Poincaré, Prime Minister Vivani and senior French diplomats were expected in St Petersburg on a mission that Isvolsky had helped organise some six months previously, though no fixed date had been agreed until after Sarajevo. On 20 July, they assembled for one purpose: to ensure that Russia triggered a war with Germany. If Isvolsky failed to put steel into the Russian backbone and there was no war, the dream of Constantinople and the Straits might forever be gone. Isvolsky disappeared for three crucial weeks before the St Petersburg meeting. There is no known record of his whereabouts.[9]

This vital gap in our knowledge of Isvolsky's whereabouts is not due to chance. No record remains of his diplomatic activities from the beginning of July 1914, and this from an agent who sent prolific notes and information to his French and Russian contacts on a daily basis. Who would have sought to blank out his contribution to the slide to perdition? Since the French leaders Poincaré and Vivani were scheduled to visit St Petersburg, and he had decamped there to be with Sazonov and the czar, Isvolsky would certainly have been in communication with them prior to the visit. He would likewise have kept in regular contact with Sir Edward Grey, either through Buchanan, the British ambassador in St Petersburg, or one of his Foreign Office acolytes. Sadly, we can but speculate. Isvolsky's biographer hints that his diplomatic telegrams from that time were deliberately destroyed.[10] Whatever and wherever, we can be sure that Isvolsky was actively influencing the Franco-Russian resolve to provoke a war with Germany, backed, as ever, by the Secret Elite.

One other burning question remained unanswered: what, precisely, would Austria do? Serbia could not go unpunished. A sense of justified indignation consumed the Austrian people. Sarajevo was the latest in a series of insults and challenges that threatened the very prestige of a nation that called itself a Great Power. Nor did the assassination stop the onslaught from Belgrade. Sir Maurice de Bunsen, the British ambassador in Vienna, telegraphed London to say that Serbian newspapers were 'behaving shamefully' and virtually elevating the assassins to martyrs.[11] When the Serbian press referred to Austria-Hungary as 'worm-eaten', Conrad von Hötzendorf, Austrian chief of staff and head of the militarist party in Vienna, bristled at the inaction of his government. He believed that by its constant yielding to Serbian provocation, Austria had given the impression that she was impotent and this in turn encouraged Serbia to be ever more aggressive. Von Hötzendorf was convinced that Austria had to choose between being slowly strangled by its noxious neighbour or making a final effort to prevent its own destruction. Severe military measures had to be taken against Serbia in an act of self-preservation.[12]

This was exactly the response the Secret Elite hoped they would get from the Austrians. Their challenge now was to encourage the key decision makers in Austria-Hungary to overreact without realising they were being led into a greater confrontation.

Within a few days, the telegraph wires were hot with diplomatic intrigue. Even prior to the archduke's inauspicious funeral, the Belgian ambassador to Berlin was able to tell Brussels that the Austrian government would demand that Serbia set up an inquiry into the assassination and permit Austro-Hungarian police officers to take part in it. The ambassador added:

> The Pachitch [Pasic] Government, having deliberately shut its eyes to the hotbed of anarchist propaganda in Belgrade, ought not to be surprised at being required to take energetic measures against the guilty persons, instead of continuing to treat them with blind tolerance.[13]

Before the archduke had been laid to rest, diplomats were clearly well informed about Austrian intentions. This information was also known to the respective Foreign Offices in London, Paris and St Petersburg. Despite their professed surprise and exaggerated pretence of shock, the key agents of the Secret Elite knew by the second day of July that the Austrians would demand a full investigation. Critically, at that early juncture, the Belgian ambassador clearly identified the nub of the question: 'Will Serbia consent to tolerate the assistance of Austro-Hungarian police agents? If she refuses on the grounds that it will be an infringement of her sovereign rights, will such a dispute break out into open hostilities?'[14] It certainly would. Crucial information was to hand, and positions were already being taken in those early days of July. The Secret Elite knew then that the instrument with which they could deliberately fan the flames was the question of Serbia's 'sovereign rights'.

Serbia continued to goad Austria and made little pretence of being contrite. Why? Why did the Serbs continue to aggravate the situation, unless of course they, and others, were determined to provoke a reaction? The *Times* correspondent reported on 1 July that newspapers in Belgrade were claiming that the assassination was a consequence of the bad old Austrian police system and a lack of real liberty in Austria. The Russian press was equally aggressive. They placed the responsibility for Serb agitation on those who, 'like Franz Ferdinand', sowed discord between Roman Catholic Croats and

Orthodox Serbs. The *Novoe Vremya*[15] published a long indictment of anti-Slav policy which alleged that the archduke was its leading protagonist. If the powers that controlled Serbia, both internally and from St Petersburg, had wanted to caution restraint, then this provocation would never have been tolerated. But the assassination had not been meticulously planned as some singular act of defiance. The flames could not be doused.

The *Westminster Gazette*, owned by Waldorf Astor from the Secret Elite's inner-circle,[16] stated that 'Austria cannot be expected to remain inactive'.[17] The *Manchester Guardian*, always influential in Liberal circles, declared that Serbia's record was unmatched as a tissue of cruelty, greed, hypocrisy and ill faith. 'If it were physically possible for Serbia to be towed out to sea and sunk there, the air of Europe would at once seem clearer.'[18] It could hardly have made its position more obvious. With one exception, *The Times*, all English newspapers recognised that Austria had suffered intense provocation and acknowledged her right to take the strongest measures to secure the punishment of those concerned. The weekly paper *John Bull*, which had a wide readership among the working classes, was equally adamant that Austria's position was 'just'.[19] Small wonder, then, that Berchtold believed that he had the backing of the British government. Editors with direct access to key members of the Cabinet offered him sympathetic support for direct action.

The British public were consumed by their own immediate crisis. Though it is not absolutely true to say that they had their heads turned exclusively elsewhere, the overwhelming newspaper interest centred on Ulster, parliamentary uproar over Irish Home Rule, gun running and the Ulster Volunteers. All of these threatened a civil war in a very real sense.[20] Day by day, week by week, the Loyalists in Ulster and the Home-Rulers in the southern counties captured the headlines and raised the horrendous spectre of a civil war that would spill over onto mainland Britain. How convenient, then, that for most of the month of July home affairs dominated learned debate, while Sir Edward Grey and the Foreign Office went about their business in almost monastic silence, unburdened by the need to keep the Cabinet informed of the developing crisis in Europe.

Austria was determined to deal with Serbia as an act of self-preservation,[21] but it would have been impractical to attempt this without the approval of her great ally, Germany. A letter from Emperor Franz Joseph was delivered to the kaiser at Potsdam on 5 July, underlining Austria's desire to take definitive action. After discussing the representations from Vienna with his advisors, Kaiser Wilhelm gave his unqualified approval, the so-called German 'blank cheque'. This was later misrepresented as a binding promise to give Austria military support against Serbia with the deliberate intention of bringing about a European-wide war. It was nothing of the sort. Certainly the kaiser encouraged Austria to take whatever action she believed necessary to put Serbia in its place,[22] but few in Germany believed that Russian military intervention in a localised dispute was a realistic possibility. Russia had no defence treaty with Serbia, and Austria had no intentions whatsoever of using force against Russia. It was inconceivable to the kaiser that the czar would actively support the 'regicides' in Serbia.[23]

One of the most deliberate historical misrepresentations of the twentieth century took root in that Potsdam meeting. A great lie was concocted by the Secret Elite that, before going on holiday, the kaiser convened a crown council meeting at Potsdam on 5 July and revealed his determination to make war on an unsuspecting Europe.[24] The myth holds that he was advised to wait a fortnight in order to give German bankers time to sell off their foreign securities.[25] Such blatant fabrication has since been unmasked as part of the orchestrated propaganda constructed to 'prove' that Germany intimidated Austria into attacking Serbia in order to draw Russia into the conflict.[26] In the years immediately after the war, the deliberate lie that the kaiser was the instigator of war passed into accepted history as 'truth'. Children learn in school, and students repeat in examinations, that war was the kaiser's doing. In fact, the only signal he transmitted back to Vienna was that, whatever Austria decided, Germany would stand by her as an ally and friend. His near-desperate efforts to claw Berchtold back from the precipice at the end of the month demonstrated the sincerity of his attempts to maintain the peace of Europe. If the kaiser is to be held at fault at all, it might be for not restraining Berchtold earlier. The difference between Sir Edward Grey and the kaiser was that only one of them was plotting war.

From Vienna, the British ambassador Sir Maurice de Bunsen advised the Foreign Office that the situation was dangerous and might rapidly deteriorate.[27] Other diplomats conveyed the same burning sense of urgency to their respective governments, but Grey, Poincaré and Sazonov did nothing to reduce the tension. The Secret Elite agenda required them to play a deadly game of charades that left Berchtold convinced that Europe understood his dilemma. Austria-Hungary had to stop the Serbian-inspired rot. Grey played his cards perfectly. He may never have read Sun Tzu's *Art of War*, but the first rule of all war is deception, and deception was an art at which Sir Edward Grey and his Foreign Office associates were absolute masters.

Reassured by support from across Europe, Berchtold came to the logical conclusion that he was expected to punish Serbia for the crime of Sarajevo. Other governments, even the entente governments, appeared to approve the need for retribution.[28] Indeed, the Austro-Hungarian ministerial council was concerned that if they did not take strong action, their own Slav and Romanian subjects would interpret it as weakness.[29] They agreed to make stringent demands on Serbia. Nothing else would stop their vicious intrigues. The die was cast, but few in Britain knew that the dice were even rolling.

A number of interlocking steps were being taken secretly in Britain so that war would not catch the nation unprepared. An apparently unrelated debate took place in the House of Commons on 7 July that was fundamentally engineered to strengthen both naval supplies and the British control of the route to India before anyone embarked on war. Winston Churchill, backed strongly by his ministerial colleague Sir Edward Grey, steered the government's Anglo-Persian Oil Company bill through Parliament, oblivious to the loud objections from Liberal Free Traders and Conservative and Unionist opposition. They objected vigorously to a £2,000,000 buyout of the recently created oil company, based in distant Persia,[30] but the oil-rich sands were economically important and strategically significant. Churchill's navy was rapidly being converted from coal to oil power and he, together with the Relugas gang, knew that it would very soon sail to war. Questions were raised about the wisdom and commercial efficacy of the Persian oil purchase. Other British oil suppliers were seriously upset, but the timing was perfect. It was a calculated move. Oil supplies were guaranteed for the navy; the Empire made more secure. All the while, Parliamentarians thought that they were debating issues of funding and the ethics of government ownership of private companies. The plot was far thicker than that. Churchill and Grey pulled off a magnificent strategic coup just weeks before the declaration of war.

A secure supply of oil was but one of a very specific number of conditions that had to be simultaneously contrived before the Secret Elite could start their war. Each in its own way was part of the grand deception. Relations with Germany in 1914 appeared to be on a surer, more positive footing than for each of the last three years. The crises of Morocco and the Balkans appeared to have receded. That was an integral part of the deceit. They ensured that the public and the press were kept at arm's length from informed discussion about Europe in the weeks prior to 4 August. Whatever else, in any public forum, and in Parliament in particular, the chance of Britain being involved in a European war was downplayed. The deception went deeper. Members of the Cabinet were denied crucial information that was circulating inside the deepest recesses of the Foreign Office. Only the Secret Elite's agents were trusted. Parliamentary debates had to be focused away from the Austro-Serbian dispute and, in particular, they had to avoid mention of British involvement with Russia. Had any person of note stood upon a public platform and announced that within weeks the British Expeditionary Force would be on its way to war in support of miserable Serbia and the despised czar, they would have been laughed from the stage, mocked and ridiculed. Such circumstances were not just beyond reason, they were beyond folly. That could never happen without the cleverest of deceptions, the most careful manipulation of headstrong men and the complete misrepresentation of Germany's intentions.

From the outset, Sir Edward Grey worked constantly to deceive the kaiser and his advisors. On 9 July, the German ambassador in London, Prince Lichnowsky, was repeatedly assured by Grey that Britain had entered into no secret obligations that would come into play in the event of a European war. Lichnowsky confidently assured his government that 'England wished to preserve an absolutely free hand to act according to her own judgement in the event of continental complications'.[31] He also reported that Grey said he would be willing to persuade the Russian government to adopt a more peaceful and conciliatory attitude towards Austria.

Pure deception. Grey had been intimately associated with the commitments made through the Committee of Imperial Defence since 1905. His commitment to the Secret Elite's cause overrode honesty. He did nothing to reconcile Russia and Austria. In fact, his ambassador in St Petersburg, Sir George Buchanan, was there to steady Sazonov's shaky hand in the desperate drive to war.

You might have expected the foreign affairs debate in the House of Commons on 10 July to have discussed the growing tensions in the Balkans or the Austrian response to Sarajevo. What about British concerns over Serbia or the rumours circulating in newspaper and diplomatic circles all over Europe that Austria was planning to punish Serbia severely? What would Russia do? Might relationships between the Great Powers turn dangerously sour? It was an opportunity for serious debate that would have warned the nation of ominous developments that could well lead to a continental war. If the Foreign Office had honourably tried to raise the level of public awareness, then this was the logical platform. But these questions were never raised. The very last outcome the Secret Elite wanted was to allow time and opportunity for a powerful anti-war lobby to be established. The debate was a masterclass in deception. Members of Parliament had their democratic say about commercial interests and allegations of other nations acting unfairly against British companies and investors. It set a tone of self-interest that was occasionally broken by a shard of enlightenment.[32] Honourable members discussed China, India, Persia and Russia, the Hong Kong and Shanghai Bank, improving relations with Germany, Portugal and Turkish Armenia but not the crisis in the Balkans. Sir Edward Grey said not a word to criticise or disagree with major points that were completely at odds with the true objectives of the Foreign Office, and then ignored them completely. Had it not been so serious, so calamitous, so despicable, the reader might find it amusing to appreciate how successfully he used the House of Commons to lull the country at large, and the Germans in particular, into believing that Britain had not the slightest concern that the events in Sarajevo might lead to a continental war.

The Liberal MP for Stirling, Arthur Ponsonby, stood in the House and praised the improved relations between Britain and Germany. He hailed the recent successful visit of the British fleet to Kiel as an example of 'how friendly relations are between Germany and Britain', and in consequence asked for a commitment to reduce military spending 'to prevent civilisation being submerged'.[33] This was exactly the kind of signal that inspired German confidence in the British government's good intentions. Ponsonby was perfectly serious, as was his Liberal colleague Joseph King, who drew appreciation from other members when he attacked czarist Russia's religious intolerance towards Jews. His contempt for their anti-Semitic practices was clearly expressed in the statement: 'I consider that a country which abuses the right of free entry, is outside the brotherhood of nations.' Travellers who professed the Jewish faith were systematically denied entry to Russia, even on a British passport, which meant that some of the most prominent and powerful men in the Houses of Parliament could not go there.[34]

What music to the ears of the German ambassador when Joseph King compared the scandal of Russia's behaviour to the goodwill and affection for 'countries like Germany, which stand with us in the forefront of civilisation'.[35] Again and again, honourable Members of Parliament, completely ignorant of the Secret Elite agenda, underlined the much-improved relationship between Britain and Germany.

Ultimately, not one word spoken in the debate mattered. British foreign policy was not to be sidetracked at the last moment by rising to the bait of Liberal ideology. Not a word was said about the festering sore that poisoned Austro-Serbian relationships. It was as if the ominous events in the Balkans had no relevance in London. It all played into the hands of Grey and the ultimate deception. The British people's contempt for Russia might be palpable, but that meant nothing to him. At that very moment, Grey's men were manipulating St Petersburg towards a war to destroy Germany. That would not be achieved without the Russian armies. While Parliament praised the new warmth in the Anglo-German relationship, the Foreign Office continued its preparations to blow it apart. The date was 10 July 1914.

Had the Austrians simply invaded Serbia immediately after the archduke's funeral, international opinion would have understood why, but Berchtold was old-school and believed that diplomatic niceties and due process required to be followed. He sought appropriate permissions, waited patiently for full reports of the investigations, presented the case to the Emperor Franz Joseph and discussed the issue over and again with his top diplomat Alexander, Count Hoyos, and with the Hungarian premier, Count Istvan Tisza. Every formal link in the procedural chain was observed. It was the Hapsburg way. Three whole weeks were wasted. Three weeks in which those plotting war were gifted time to collude and prepare. Berchtold would not be rushed.[36] He patiently waited Dr von Wiesner's final conclusions.[37]

Despite the volume of evidence implicating Serbia, Belgrade repeatedly protested its innocence and denied any complicity in the assassination. While these lies were repeated in the Russian press, the Austrian government had positive proof that Serbia was involved and that Hartwig had directed it.[38] Wiesner's report was merely the formal confirmation that due process demanded.

Though pressure for action mounted by the day, Berchtold stuck to protocol. On 14 July, he dutifully explained to the ageing emperor that demands would be made to Serbia in a very firm 'Note'. These included an immediate end to anti-Austrian propaganda and anti-Austrian teaching in schools; public apologies for the assassination from King Peter and the Serbian government; direct Austrian police involvement in the criminal investigations within Serbia and the immediate surrender of those complicit in the murder. Such details were much in line with what was already known in London. Secrets did not remain secrets for long in the sieve of international diplomacy. Too many ministers and civil servants had sight of the proposed text of the Austrian Note as it was discussed, finalised and presented to the emperor and his advisors.

On 16 July, the British ambassador at Vienna, Sir Maurice de Bunsen, telegraphed Sir Edward Grey with a detailed account of the Austrian indictment against Serbia.[39] He itemised the demands that would be made and the fact that Austria would insist on unconditional compliance. De Bunsen stated that there was a genuine belief in Austria that Russia would not seek to protect racial assassins. He added that Austria also believed she would lose her position as a Great Power if she did not act definitively.[40] It was exactly as the Foreign Office expected.

Unaware that their intentions were already widely known, the Austrians decided they should postpone delivering their demands to Serbia until after Poincaré's visit to St Petersburg. They believed this would reduce the danger of his spurring Sazonov to respond to the Note with a macho Russian overreaction. Berchtold was encouraged by Germany to keep the problem and the solution local. He was prepared to wait. One important element in his thinking had been clarified on 14 July. If Austria was obliged to mobilise for war and Serbia backed down at that point, he instructed that the Serbs would be required to pay the colossal cost of Austrian mobilisation. Brinkmanship in the Balkans had almost become a way of life, and Berchtold's advisors were alive to the possibility that Serbia might go to the edge before accepting all of their conditions. Berchtold added a codicil that accommodated such a last-minute Serbian stand-down. There was, therefore, an understanding that Austria might not need to go as far as war with Serbia if she agreed to the demands at the last moment.

From 16 July, the diplomatic buzz centred exclusively on the forthcoming Austrian Note to Serbia, and the vocabulary sharpened to a threatening barb. Amongst the entente diplomats, in the rat runs of conspiracy in London, St Petersburg and Paris, the forthcoming Note further mutated from 'ultimatum' into 'unacceptable ultimatum'. Berchtold's gravest mistake was in withholding the demands to Serbia for three weeks in the expectation that it mattered that Poincaré had departed from Russia. In fact, the delay was counterproductive. Poincaré might have been at sea, but Berchtold was the one marooned by his own procrastination. He gifted the Secret Elite precious time to prepare an orchestrated response.

Berchtold was also the victim of a cruel deception. Each of the three entente governments used their diplomatic corps to lead him down a blind ally by encouraging him to believe that 'there was little probability indeed' that their reaction to the Note would go beyond a diplomatic protest.[41] Newspaper editorials and political comment had been repeatedly favourable to Austria. British ambassador Sir Maurice de Bunsen convinced Berchtold that Britain would not intervene. Edward Grey's professed indifference to the Austro-Serbian quarrel was considered proof of this disinterest. He repeatedly said that he had no right to intervene.[42] Poor Berchtold. The reassurances spurred him on to disaster.[43]

Within three weeks of the Sarajevo assassination, the Secret Elite network had successfully manipulated the unfolding events in Austria and Serbia. They embarked on a mission to ensure that Russia's determination to support Serbia against Austria remained firm, in the full knowledge that Germany would be dragged into the conflict. Simultaneously, they repeatedly and disingenuously assured Berlin of their good faith and noble intention. Britain, France and Russia expressed an unreserved understanding for the Austrian case against Serbia, but by the third week in July these same politicians were poised to declare a complete rejection of Austria's response. Count Berchtold had been drawn into a well-constructed trap that the Secret Elite strategists hoped would net a greater prize. War with Germany.

Summary: Chapter 21 – July 1914 – Deception, Manipulation and Misrepresentation

- The Secret Elite ensured that the murders in Sarajevo were fanned into a full-scale international crisis by manipulating key individuals in Vienna and St Petersburg, using their ambassadorial agents who were already in place.
- There was widespread initial support for Austria-Hungary after the assassination of Archduke Franz Ferdinand.
- Through overtures of friendship and mutual understanding, the Secret Elite went to considerable lengths to deceive Germany, unwittingly assisted by the genuine goodwill of many parliamentarians.
- This encouraged Count Berchtold to a bold response that would stop the Serbian aggression once and for all.
- It is claimed that, in a deliberate attempt to force a war on Europe, the kaiser gave an unconditional assurance to Austria by a so-called blank cheque. In fact, Austria-Hungary's need to respond to Serbian aggression was endorsed by others including Britain and the British press.
- The kaiser and his advisors supported a local solution to a local problem and made absolutely no special preparation for war.
- Consumed by the troubles in Ireland, the British Parliament and Cabinet were kept entirely in the dark about the dangers of the Austrian–Serbian dispute.
- Churchill and Grey used this opportune moment to purchase the Anglo-Persian Oil Company, guaranteeing oil for the navy and stamping British authority on the Gulf.
- Berchtold's insistence on diplomatic protocol, and his three-week delay until after Poincaré's visit to Russia, gave the members of the entente time to redefine their stance and prepare their response to the Austrian Note.
- Berchtold was about to walk into a trap, and the Secret Elite expected Germany to follow dutifully.

CHAPTER 22

July 1914 – Leading Europe Towards the Brink

St Petersburg became the focal point of meaningful decision making in Europe from mid July 1914. That is not to infer that the czar or Sazonov suddenly asserted themselves and stood determined to see this through. Far from it. At each stage, the Secret Elite placemen were physically present to continually and positively reassure the czar and Sazonov that they were making the right decisions, reinforcing them in the certainty that their actions were being forced on them by Austria, and behind Austria, mendacious Germany. Grey knew that Sazonov would make the defence of Serbia an issue of national pride, and that the aggressive Russian response would draw Germany into the trap of a European war. Paléologue and Buchanan, the French and British ambassadors in St Petersburg, were there to constantly embolden him and keep him from wavering from this course as the pressures of such an onerous task increased. Poincaré's presidential visit had been scheduled to renew promises of a joint attack on Germany that would destroy their common enemy and open the Straits to Russian shipping and commerce. The golden carrot of Constantinople and the Straits was almost within the Russian reach.

Every player was aware that Austria had constructed a list of stern demands to punish Serbia. It was an open secret. Grey, of course, knew that Sazonov would make an issue of defending Serbia, and Buchanan's task was to keep the Russian foreign minister sufficiently confident to attack Austria, if and when she took retaliatory action against Serbia. Buchanan telegraphed that Sazonov had warned that 'anything in the shape of an Austrian ultimatum could not leave Russia indifferent'.[1] Little wonder Serbia felt secure. The Serbian prime minister, Pasic, in the midst of an election campaign that would define his political future, had time on 19 July to forward a telegram to all Serbian legations instructing them to impress on foreign governments Serbia's 'desire to maintain friendly relations with Austria-Hungary'. It is surely a matter of regret that he had not sent such instructions earlier to the Serbian press. He further warned that his government could never comply with demands that 'might be directed against the dignity of Serbia, and would be unacceptable to any country which respects and maintains its independence'.[2]

The dignity of Serbia? An oxymoron, surely. Pasic's message was clear. The Austrian Note, as the demands were termed, had to be depicted as the act of a bully against a small, independent country. This approach was far more astute than any Pasic had previously taken. It had all the hallmarks of a professional diplomatist. Others had surely conspired to guide him through the diplomatic minefield. By 19 July, the entente governments knew the basis of the Austrian Note and had their response in place. They were prepared to react in unison the moment it was delivered. Berchtold's delay had given them time to work out their retaliation in advance. This Machiavellian duplicity required careful planning, first-rate diplomatic cunning and the speedy preparation and distribution of a 'hymn sheet' from which Grey, Isvolsky, Poincaré, Sazonov and Pasic could sing in unison the moment the Austrian demands were delivered They all objected loudly to any implied threat to Serbia's 'sovereignty'.

Historians have described the visit of President Poincaré and Prime Minister Vivani to St Petersburg from 20 to 23 July 1914 as a ceremonial state occasion of no particular consequence.[3] If that was so, why did they not wait until after the international crisis had settled before embarking for Russia? The entire French diplomatic service was aware of the implications that a war between Austria and Serbia would have for France. They knew that an Austrian declaration against Serbia would draw an equal response from Russia; that if Russia took arms against Austria, Germany would be obliged by her alliance to become involved. More pertinently for the French, if Russia went to war, they were bound by treaty to join her. They knew that a crisis of unprecedented severity was at hand. Yet we are asked to believe that this goodwill exchange had no particular purpose. Poincaré and Vivani could have easily delayed in Paris until the crisis had passed. They did not. They chose to go to St Petersburg and boarded the warship *La France* at Dunkirk on 15 July. After five days at sea, Sazonov, Isvolsky and Paléologue (the French ambassador at St Petersburg) warmly welcomed them to Russia.[4] This was no innocent state visit. Nor was its timing a matter of chance.

Poincaré's very presence in St Petersburg was ominous. If he had sought a peaceful resolution to the Austro-Serbian crisis, a letter to the czar would have been sufficient. Had Poincaré warned the Russians that France would not go to war over Serbia, that would have been the end of the matter. Nicholas II would never have had the confidence to act alone. Poincaré stiffened his resolve.[5] Every action taken by Poincaré resonated with the Secret Elite agenda. On his arrival, he boarded the czar's yacht, *Alexandria*, and immediately went into deep and private conversation with him.[6]

There was an air of pronounced irony in Poincaré's toast to the czar at the state dinner in which he suggested that France would pursue 'in intimate and daily collaboration, the work for peace and civilisation for which both governments strove daily'.[7] Was he unaware of the Cossacks in the streets, the assaults on women and children, trams overturned and wrecked in riots that went on overnight? Civilisation had rarely been worse served. The *Times* correspondent in St Petersburg wrote: 'Thanks to the admirable arrangements, the unruly elements were successfully kept off the main thoroughfares during President Poincaré's visit, which passed off without a hitch.'[8] The unruly elements were removed from view, cruelly beaten and even killed, but to the privileged *Times* readership these victims of poverty and oppression were mere flotsam and jetsam: the incidentals of history.

Poincaré held court in St Petersburg. Reports of his private conversations with the czar were carried in the press, but no word was written about the substance of their discussions.[9] Indeed, French diplomatic telegrams were altered and suppressed after the war, to conceal the true nature of Poincaré's visit.[10] He met in the Winter Palace with many of the foreign ambassadors to Russia. His discussion with the Japanese ambassador prepared the way for Japan's intervention later on the side of the entente. He assured Sir George Buchanan that the czar was very conciliatory about Persia. Doubtless the oil purchase had rattled a few Russian samovars. When it came to his formal introduction to the Austrian ambassador, Poincaré talked about his French ancestors but spoke not a word about the tension over Serbia.[11] The president of France was on a mission, as he had been in 1912. How strange that in both years that a European war was seriously possible (1912 and 1914), Poincaré made a state visit to Russia. This was no coincidence. The purpose of Poincaré's visit was to reassure the czar and Sazonov that France would stand beside them, and to encourage them to begin military preparations immediately for war with Germany. Every Russian at court in St Petersburg knew that the enemy was Germany and that war would be the outcome. Paléologue wrote in his account of ostentatious banquets how the Grand Duchesses Anastasia and Melitza, the respective wives of Grand Duke Nicholas and Grand Duke Peter, were ecstatic at the prospect that 'War is going to break out. Nothing will be left of Austria. You will get Alsace-Lorraine back. Our armies will meet in Berlin. Germany will be annihilated.'[12] Clearly, it consumed their thoughts with joyous anticipation. In fact, as elsewhere in Europe, the ruling classes saw war as the solution to civil unrest, unemployment and loose talk of revolution. Poincaré had a willing audience. The Russian military hailed him enthusiastically. They too were convinced that war was 'inevitable'. Poincaré's endorsement was precisely what they wanted to hear.[13]

Buchanan sent a telegram to the Foreign Office in London on 24 July, summarising Poincaré's visit: 'The French ambassador gave me to understand that France would not only give Russia strong diplomatic support, but would, if necessary, fulfil all the obligations imposed on her by the alliance.'[14] Poincaré and Sazonov had agreed the deal. When Russia went to war against Germany and Austria, France would fulfil her commitment to Russia. This telegram explicitly proved that by 24 July Sir Edward Grey knew that his world war was ordained. The document was concealed from the world for ten years. As Isvolsky's biographer, Stieve, concluded: 'The blank cheque for world war, signed first by Poincaré in 1912, was now signed again.'[15] It was no more and no less than that. While historians have focused on the mythical notion of Germany's blank cheque to Austria given at Potsdam, the real cheque for war – which would be endorsed by Britain – was that which Poincaré signed in St Petersburg.

In the Foreign Office, Buchanan's telegram was subjected to minute scrutiny, and the private notes attached to it demonstrated the inner convolutions of Secret Elite thinking.[16] Sir Eyre Crowe's surgical analysis cut to the heart of the matter. Whatever the merits of the Austrian case against Serbia, he believed it would be 'impolitic' to interfere in St Petersburg or Paris, 'dangerous', even. Dangerous? As in, any intervention from Britain might stop them starting a war?

Put all of this into perspective. Austria had suffered assassination, humiliation and taunts from Serbia, but that didn't count. Russia and France had agreed that they would stand together and go to war, which seemed perfectly reasonable to Sir Eyre Crowe, so Britain should simply let that happen. He phrased his diplomatic comments in the following way: 'The point that matters is whether Germany is or is not absolutely determined to have this war now.'[17] His twisted logic flew in the face of what he already knew. It was not Germany that was determined to 'have this war now'; it was the Secret Elite. Years of careful and intricate planning would come to nought if, once again, Germany refused to be drawn in – just as she had done in 1912 and 1913. Crowe's reasoning contained an awesome revelation:

> Our interests are tied up with those of France and Russia in this struggle, which is not for the possession of Serbia, but one between Germany aiming at a political dictatorship in Europe, and the Powers who desire to retain individual freedom.[18]

Ask yourself this question: what were the coincident interests between Britain and Russia? Shared ambition that could only come to blows in Persia? No, it was war with Germany. Would Britain ever have seriously contemplated giving Russia possession of the Straits? No. Was Russia a land of individual freedoms? No. The very notion of the czarist empire being associated with freedoms was ludicrous. Not one single Jewish Member of the British Parliament was free to travel into Russia.[19] This twisted, illogical bias was nothing more than the bile of Secret Elite philosophy. Crowe ended his minute with a recommendation that the fleet be mobilised as soon as any of the Great Powers made their first step to war, but Edward Grey had previously checked that point with Winston Churchill. The fleet was ready and waiting for the coming storm.

Feelings in Britain were running high about Ireland, not about Russia, Austria or Serbia. Nor was there any sense of concern about Germany. Lloyd George had, during a finance bill debate on 23 July, praised the improving relations between Germany and Britain. He looked forward with confidence to a time when the lunacy of international arms spending might reduce the ridiculous tax burden on the British nation:

> Take a neighbour of ours. [He meant Germany.] Our relations are very much better than they were a few years ago. There is none of that snarling which we used to see, more especially in the Press, of those two great, I will not say rival nations, but two great Empires.[20]

On the very day that Austria's Note was presented to the Serbian government, the British chancellor of the Exchequer publicly praised Germany with a speech that hinted at better times ahead. Little wonder the Germans were confused. Little wonder Sazonov immediately required reassurance of Britain's real intentions.

In contrast to the deceptions and secret memorandums that hid the real aims of Lloyd George and his trusted accomplices, German politicians had been trying to keep the Austrian response in context. Secretary of State Gottlieb von Jagow suggested in the *North German Gazette* of 19 July that a 'localised war' was sufficient and appropriate.[21] It was straightforward: leave Austria and Serbia to fight it out between them.

There were historical precedents that justified such thinking, including Britain's own war with the Transvaal, and the United States in her fight against Spain in 1898.[22] Russia and France, however, had no intention of holding the proverbial jackets while Austria sorted 'poor' Serbia. A localised Austro-Serbian affair was never an option for the Secret Elite. The whole point was to draw Germany into war.

Bethmann, the German chancellor, remained quietly assured that all proper protocols were being followed, though he was concerned at the slow pace of Austrian decision making. He sent instructions to the German ambassadors in St Petersburg, London and Paris to stress that Austria had every just cause to punish Serbia.[23] He stated that unless Austria was willing to 'dispense for ever its standing as a Great Power', it had to enforce its demands. Bethmann was confident that in the aftermath of Archduke Ferdinand's assassination, the czar would understand the need for the monarchs of Europe to stand together against a political radicalism that sought to put an end to emperors and czars, kings and queens and all the trappings of monarchy.[24]

Austria presented the Note to Serbia once Poincaré and the French delegation had departed St Petersburg on 23 July. The delay was futile. The French and Russians had already made their fateful, but still secret, tryst and Sazonov's commitment to protect Serbia was absolute. All had been determined long before the Austrian demands became public.[25] Berchtold insisted that the Note was non-negotiable: 'We cannot enter into negotiations with Serbia with regard to our demands, and cannot be satisfied with anything less than their unconditional acceptance within the stated terms; otherwise we should be obliged to draw further consequences.'[26]

Baron von Gieslingen, the Austro-Hungarian minister at Belgrade, handed the Note to the Serbian government at 6 p.m. on Thursday, 23 July. It comprised ten demands that had been leaked over the preceding weeks and, as far as Berchtold was aware, had caused little obvious anxiety. Basically, the Serbs were instructed to stop anti-Austrian publications, dissolve the secret society Narodna Odbrana, put an end to the teaching of anti-Austrian propaganda in schools and sack all civil servants and military personnel who were openly anti-Austrian. The Note insisted that Austro-Hungarian police be permitted to cooperate with the Serbs and take part in a judicial inquiry into the conspiracy that had led to the assassination in Sarajevo. Known conspirators – and here the Note correctly named Tankosić and Ciganovic – had to be placed under arrest, as had those who flagrantly assisted the assassins by smuggling arms and explosives over the border into Bosnia. They wanted to know why high-ranking Serbian officials had continued to verbally assault Austro-Hungary even after the outrage. Finally, a 48-hour deadline was set for an unequivocal acceptance of every point. Virtually every demand was already known to the Secret Elite agents, including the timescale for a reply.

Berchtold and his advisors were totally unprepared for what happened next. Despite all of the international support and encouragement that they had been given over the preceding weeks, what followed was an orchestrated overreaction from Russia, France and Britain, whose well-coordinated pretence at outrage was completely at odds with previous sentiments. Those who had encouraged strong Austrian action now declared that, rather than aiming for justice from Serbia, Austria was abusing the situation as a pretext to provoke a war. The argument turned in a most bizarre way. Austria was accused of having presented 'no evidence' of the Serbian complicity, and they insisted that 'more time' ought to be given for the Serbian Reply.[27] It was a sham, a blatant attempt to gain additional time for the Russian and French military preparations.[28] Austria remained unmoved and insisted on a Reply within 48 hours.

On 24 July, Austro-Hungarian ambassadors were subject to verbal abuse when they presented their demands of Serbia to the entente governments. In St Petersburg, Sazonov exploded at the Austrian ambassador, constantly interrupting his attempt to explain the Note. 'I know what you want. You want to go to war with Serbia . . . you are setting fire to Europe.'[29] Point by point, Sazonov challenged and rejected every part of the Austrian Note. How dare the Austrian government demand the dissolution of Narodna Odbrana? Why were they insisting that Austrian police officers be involved in the investigations?[30] His lack of perspective made nonsense of this unprofessional tantrum, but since he already had detailed knowledge of the demands, it was a sham.

Sir Edward Grey met with Count Mensdorff, the Austrian ambassador to Britain, at Downing Street on the morning of 24 July. Given that he was not known to rush to judgement, Grey's immediate pronouncement that the Note was 'the most formidable document that has ever been addressed from one state to another'[31] was ridiculous. When Mensdorff tried to explain the merits of the case, Grey rejected the arguments as 'not our concern'. He could hardly have been more dismissive. This too was a sham. It was different in Paris. With all the senior ministers who might have dealt with the Austrian explanation literally at sea, the Note was handed to the minister of justice, whose moderate and unemotional reaction was in complete contrast to the paroxysms elsewhere. No one had thought to give him sight of the entente's official script. With near indecent haste, Paul Cambon, the French ambassador at London, was ordered back to France to hold the fort at Quai D'Orsay.

While the entente foreign ministers orchestrated as close to a perfect storm of indignation as they could muster, several British newspapers considered the Austrian demands to be perfectly justified. The *Manchester Guardian*, the *Daily News* and the *Daily Chronicle* all voiced a reasoned understanding of the Austrian position. Of the conservative newspapers, the *Daily Telegraph* was the most impartial. It supported the Austrians in 'demanding full and prompt repudiation of all those nefarious schemes which have politics as their excuse and murder as their handmaid'.[32] The *Manchester Guardian* deeply regretted that Russia was prepared to threaten 'extreme measures' if strong Austrian action was forced upon Serbia. As its editorial explained, Austria had a good reason to be overbearing towards Serbia, but 'Russia's threat of war is a piece of sheer brutality, not disguised by her sudden discovery of the sacredness of the balance of power in Europe'.[33] It was a sarcastic but justified rebuff to the Russian presumption of interest in Serbian affairs. Predictably, *The Times* was batting for the other side. An editorial, published two days before the Note was handed over, under the heading, 'A Danger to Europe', supported the Russians and cast doubt on Austrian intentions to localise the war.[34] As ever, the voice of the Secret Elite was a step ahead.

Asquith decried the Austrian Note as 'bullying and humiliating',[35] but in private he confided to his secret love, Venetia Stanley, that: 'the curious thing is that on many, if not most of the points, Austria has a good and Serbia a very bad case . . . but the Austrians are quite the stupidest people in Europe'.[36] He knew that Grey had greatly exaggerated his reaction to the Austrian demands but could never say so in public. Indeed not. Their public stance, their pretence of outrage, represented a prepared position that aligned the Foreign Office with the outbursts from Sazonov in Russia and Poincaré once back on French soil. By undermining Austria-Hungary they were simultaneously undermining the one nation that would stand with her: Germany.

Members of Asquith's Cabinet knew only what they read in the newspapers. With the singular exception of the notorious five,[37] they were ignorant of the entente connivance in the Austria–Serbia dispute. Cabinet met on the afternoon of 24 July and discussed shootings in Dublin and the shipping of German guns to the Irish Volunteers at great length, and then, almost as an aside, the rapidly deteriorating Serbian crisis was raised. According to Winston Churchill, the discussion on Ireland had reached its inconclusive end and the Cabinet was about to separate when Sir Edward Grey produced the Austrian Note, which he claimed had just been brought to him from the Foreign Office. The message they wanted Cabinet members to believe was that this was 'an ultimatum such as had never been penned in modern times'.[38]

Charles Hobhouse, the postmaster-general in Asquith's 1914 Cabinet, wrote in his diary:

> Grey broke in to say that the Ultimatum by Austria to Serbia had brought us nearer to a European Armageddon than we had been through all the Balkan troubles. He had suggested that Germany, France, Italy and the UK should jointly press Austria and Russia to abstain from action, but he was certain that if Russia attacked Austria, Germany was bound to come to the latter's help.[39]

If Churchill's recall was correct, Grey must have staged the delivery for dramatic effect. We know that the Note had not 'just been brought' to Grey that afternoon but was handed to him in Downing Street that morning, when he had ranted at Count Mensdorff.[40] That apart, look how the Foreign Office had twisted the Note into an 'Ultimatum'. Hobhouse even gave the word a capital letter. Notice too how in Hobhouse's version it was not Germany that was at fault. The key to war or peace was Russia: 'If Russia attacked Austria, Germany was bound to come in.' That would be the same Russia just given a blank cheque by Poincaré. The same Russia with which, Sir Eyre Crowe had advised, it would be 'impolitic' and 'dangerous' to interfere.

In all of the bluster, the claims and counterclaims that were lodged once war began, focus was placed on the Austrian Note as if it were the cause of war itself. Austria, however, had been on the receiving end of Serbia's troublemaking and broken promises for years. The Serbian government had participated in the criminal activities of various societies in Serbia and their outrageous anti-Austrian invective. In the days and weeks before the Note was delivered to Belgrade, Austria had amassed considerable evidence on the assassins and their controllers.[41] What they were demanding was the minimum required for a normalisation of relationships. No vague promises, no procrastination. The basis for a positive resolution to what had proved an intractable problem was laid on the table. It was non-negotiable but fair. How else could they have begun to build a lasting, constructive and meaningful future? The Note comprised the minimum conditions that would guarantee Austrian safety from the Serbian menace.[42]

At 3 p.m. on 25 July – that is, three hours before the end of Austria's forty-eight-hour deadline – Serbia formally mobilised its armed forces. Frantic military preparations got under way. State archives, the treasury and the civil service decamped from Belgrade to the interior city of Nish. Before they handed over their Reply, and in the knowledge that it failed to meet the Austrian demands, the Serbians declared their intent. Serbia was getting ready for war. Not that they were the only ones in a hurry. Pasic personally delivered the formal Reply a few minutes before 6 p.m. on 25

July, and the Austrian ambassador and his entire legation were on their way home on the 6.30 p.m. express from Belgrade.

The Serbian Reply was carefully crafted and moderate in character.[43] It not only won the approval and sympathy of the entente powers but also of neutrals everywhere. It even commanded the admiration of Berchtold, who described the Reply as 'the most brilliant example of diplomatic skill which I have ever known', but he added that though it appeared to be reasonable, it was 'wholly worthless in content'.[44] The diplomatic language certainly had all the hallmarks of a professional tactician. Pasic had previously relied on Hartwig, the Russian ambassador, whose untimely death ought to have left him bereft of ideas. Yet, out of nowhere, this comparative nonentity apparently produced a masterstroke of international diplomacy. Pasic was reputedly a lost, floundering soul without his Russian mentor, so who was behind the Serbian Reply?

Belgrade had immediately appealed to Sazonov, Paléologue and the czar for help.[45] Behind the scenes, the telegraph lines between London, Belgrade, St Petersburg and Paris nearly went into meltdown. Sir Edward Grey telegraphed Belgrade on Friday evening (24 July) at 9.30 p.m. to advise the Serbs on how they should respond. He specifically suggested that they 'give a favourable reply on as many points as possible within the limit of time, and not to meet Austria with a blank negative'. He wanted them to apologise, express regret for the conduct of their officials and reply in a manner that represented the best interests of Serbia. Grey refused to give any further advice without liaising directly with Russia and France.[46] His time-serving words sufficed to cover the fact that Britain, France and Russia had already agreed their joint position.

The greatest input to the Serbian Reply came from Paris in the person of Philippe Berthelot, assistant director for political affairs at the French Foreign Office. He was one of the most senior diplomats in Europe and highly regarded by Poincaré and the Secret Elite. Berthelot first admitted that he had outlined the extremely astute Reply for Serbia and later boasted that he actually drafted its very wording.[47] He reaffirmed Grey's advice that Serbia should offer immediate satisfaction on all points except the one that affected her sovereignty. In St Petersburg, Sazonov had likewise counselled the Serbs on extreme moderation.[48]

The Secret Elite primed the Serbians with a staged strategy. Step one had been Pasic's telegram of the 19th, a honey-dripped appeal for support based on a plea for dignity, respect and independence. Step two was to get Pasic out of Belgrade. They knew that the Austrians intended to present their demands on 23 July, so ensured that Pasic was out of the Serbian capital on an election campaign, an arrangement that was released in advance to the press of Europe.[49] (This was a ploy to force the Austrians to extend the time permitted for an official response. It didn't work.) Finally, they had ensured that there were no significant chargés d'affaires or ambassadorial representatives from any of the entente powers in Belgrade that weekend, so that, whatever transpired, no one from France, Russia or Britain could be associated with the official response.[50]

The input from London, Paris and St Petersburg represented a massive public-relations offensive on behalf of Serbia. The Reply was couched in very conciliatory language, with feigned humility and apparent openness and sincerity. European opinion still sided with Austria rather than Serbia, and that would have been reinforced had the Serbs presented an arrogant or insulting Reply. Serbia had to be reinvented as a brave and helpless little nation that had gone beyond the boundary of national dignity in surrendering to Austria's harsh demands. Of all the diplomatic ruses before the war began, there was no cleverer 'subterfuge than the planning of the Serbian response to Austria'.[51]

To the unwitting, it appeared as though all points bar two had been accepted and that 'poor little Serbia' had yielded to the immense and unfair pressure from her neighbour. Kaiser Wilhelm, for example, returned from his three-week cruise and hailed the Serbian Reply as 'a triumph of diplomacy' when he first read it.[52] Wilhelm jotted on it: 'a brilliant performance for a time-limit of only 48 hours. This is more than one could have expected!'[53] He was convinced that the Austrians would be satisfied and that the few reservations Serbia had made on particular points could be cleared up by negotiation. Kaiser Wilhelm's immediate and spontaneous response clearly indicated his belief, indeed his joy, that all risk of war had been removed. 'With it [the Serbian response] every reason for war falls to the ground.'[54]

Wilhelm's analysis was sadly naive. He accepted the Serbian concessions at face value, but the Austrians did not. The Reply included carefully constructed conditions and reservations that were not immediately apparent.[55] First impressions can often be misleading. While the Serbian response appeared to consent to virtually every Austrian demand, it was so hedged with qualifications that the Austrians were bound to take umbrage. Only two of Austria's demands (numbers 8 and 10) were accepted in their entirety, while the answers to the others were evasive.[56] Reservations and lies had been carefully disguised by skilful dissembling. For example, where the Note insisted on the arrest of Tankosić and Ciganovic, the Reply stated that Ciganovic had fled and it had not been possible to arrest him. The implication that the Serbians were actually trying to arrest him was a lie. Ciganovic was a personal friend of Pasic, and the prime minister knew that his friend had been secretly re-accommodated with the full knowledge and assistance of the Serbian chief of police.

The most important Austrian demand was rejected outright. Berchtold insisted that judicial proceedings be taken against everyone associated with the assassination plot and that Austro-Hungarian police officers be directly involved in the investigations. Serbia baulked at this, claiming that such an intrusion would be a violation of her constitution. That was not the case. The Austrians had demanded that their police be allowed to assist in the investigation of the crime, not that its officials be allowed to participate in internal Serbian court procedures. There were numerous precedents for such cross-border police involvement.[57] But the Serbs nailed their colours to this spurious assertion and claimed that the Austrian Note was an infringement of their sovereignty. How strange. The Belgian ambassador had warned three weeks earlier that Serbian sovereignty would become the central issue.

The Secret Elite knew that Austria would not accept the Reply. It was specifically designed to be rejected. No amount of cosmetic wordplay could cover the fact that it did not accede to the Austrian stipulations. The lie that Austria-Hungary deliberately made the Note so tough that Serbia would have no choice but to refuse it has, unfortunately, been set in concrete by some historians. The argument put forward generally claims that:

> War was to be provoked, and the murder of the Archduke provided a perfect occasion. The Austrians were told that they should use it to attack Serbia, Russia's client, and the means chosen was an ultimatum, containing demands that could not be accepted without the loss of Serbian independence.[58]

This was the myth that the Secret Elite wanted to promulgate, namely that Austria was 'told' by Germany to attack Serbia. The best lie is the big lie. If Austria was hell-bent on war with Serbia, why did she entertain the gruelling three-week diplomatic route? Freed from extraneous interference, the Austrian army was entirely capable of defeating Serbia. Hawks in the Austrian military had demanded an immediate attack, but the diplomats insisted on the long-delayed Note that unwittingly gave Britain, France and Russia time to lay their trap.[59] The Serbian Reply, and Austria's consequent reaction, sprang that trap.

On 25 July, Sir George Buchanan in St Petersburg penned a strictly confidential telegram to Sir Edward Grey. It arrived in the Foreign Office at 10.30 p.m. The message could not have been clearer: 'Russia cannot allow Austria to crush Serbia and become the predominant Power in the Balkans, and, secure of support of France, she will face all the risks of war.'[60]

THE POWER BEHIND.

AUSTRIA (*at the ultimatum stage*). "I DON'T QUITE LIKE HIS ATTITUDE. SOMEBODY MUST BE BACKING HIM."

The Russian Bear waits as the Austrian Eagle swoops down on the Serbian bait.

(Reproduced with permission of Punch Ltd., www.punch.co.uk)

From whose imagination did the notion of Serbia being crushed by Austria spring? No such aim had ever been put forward by Berchtold. The allegation that Austria wanted to crush Serbia was yet another piece of propaganda manufactured to justify the entente over-reaction. But worse still was the French connection: the blank cheque. 'Secure of support of France', Russia was prepared to 'face all the risks of war'. Buchanan spelled out the absolute reassurances that Poincaré had given to Sazonov. These were in fact more than reassurances; this was an incitement to war. Poincaré was inviting Sazonov to lead the line, promising that both countries would march behind the same banner. It was precisely what the Secret Elite had planned.

It was not the Austrian Note that made war inevitable, it was the Serbian Reply designed to provoke the reaction for which Russia, France and Britain were prepared.

Summary: Chapter 22 – July 1914 – Leading Europe Towards the Brink

- St Petersburg became the centre of critical decision making.
- The Secret Elite agents, Poincaré and Isvolsky, aided by Paléologue and Buchanan, were there to ensure that the czar and Sazonov took a firm stance against Austria.
- Poincaré went to St Petersburg, as he had done in 1912, to promise that France would go to war on the side of Russia if Germany took arms on the part of Austria. This was the real 'blank cheque' for war.
- Sir George Buchanan ensured that Grey was fully conversant with the progress towards war and was regularly at Sazonov's side to reassure him.
- Russia, and Russian policy towards her own people, was anathema to most cultured and knowledgeable Britons. They would never have accepted a military alliance with Russia.
- In Parliament and in the Cabinet, details were withheld about the deterioration in international relations until 24 July.
- Germany was deceived into thinking that her relations with Britain had substantially improved through parliamentary, press and diplomatic discussion, while Secret Elite agents in the Foreign Office were plotting her destruction.
- Austrian foreign minister, Berchtold, was repeatedly assured that other nations understood the need for a sharp Austrian retaliation, while, unknown to him, Britain, France and Russia prepared a collective and entirely negative response to the demands contained in the Austrian Note.
- The demands made by Austria were neither unexpected nor unfair. The responses from the entente group were disproportionately over-excited. Berchtold's delay gifted them a three-week window in which to manufacture their considered reaction.
- The Serbian Reply was a diplomatic triumph designed by the Secret Elite to appear conciliatory but trigger the Austrian military threat and all that would ensue.
- Germany had become concerned at the slow pace of the Austrian demands on Serbia, and the kaiser for one was delighted that the Serbian Reply seemed to remove any likelihood of war.
- The Serbian Reply sprang the trap that had been laid for Berchtold.
- The Secret Elite's race to war was gathering momentum. Sir Edward Grey knew by 25 July that Russia was prepared to face all risks of war.

A Jew has many reasons for each action.

CHAPTER 23

July 1914 – The First Mobilisations

WITHIN HOURS OF POINCARÉ'S DEPARTURE from St Petersburg on 23 July, the success of his mission became clear. Russia began mobilising her vast armies and took an irrevocable step towards war in Europe. The Secret Elite's agent had completed his prime objective.

In the first decades of the twentieth century, the general mobilisation of the armed forces of a major power signalled its intent on war. Plans for bringing together regular army units, conscripts and reserves, equipping these troops and transporting them to border assembly points had been worked out with great precision. Modern railway systems were the key. The entire process had to be conducted by rail and the general staffs had worked for years to perfect their timetables. From the moment the command to mobilise was given, everything had to move at fixed times, in precise order, down to the number of train axles that would pass over a given bridge within a given time.[1] Each action in the mobilisation process led logically to the next, in lockstep precision, combining in a practically irreversible escalation to war. In terms of strategic planning, the assumption was that the advantage lay always with the offence, and that speed was of the essence. European leaders believed that a one-to-three-day lead in mobilisation was militarily significant for the course of the war, leaving vulnerable anyone who delayed.[2]

The Franco-Russian military convention was very specific in declaring that the first to mobilise must be held the aggressor, and that general mobilisation 'is war'.[3] All responsible military and political authorities in France, Russia and Britain subsequently acted on that supposition. The chief of Russian general staff for mobilisation in 1892 clarified the convention that mobilisation by one of the major powers was a decisive act of war because beyond that point 'no further diplomatic hesitation is possible'. All effective diplomatic manoeuvring, deals and agreements had to be concluded before a mobilisation. Once begun, there was no turning back.[4]

The Franco-Russian Alliance was clearly based on the assertion that mobilisation equated to war.[5] Both Russian and French general staffs not only viewed mobilisation as an outright act of war but also insisted that all normal operational decisions be based on that assumption.[6] It is important to clarify that the Russian and French governments understood precisely what mobilisation meant when the decisions were taken in July 1914.[7] Once the order was given and the machinery for mobilisation set in motion, there was little possibility of stopping it.

The kaiser and his military advisors observed the same rule that general mobilisation was the first decisive step towards war. They knew they had no choice but to respond in kind if a general Russian mobilisation was ordered. In such a scenario, the moment Germany mobilised in self-defence, the Franco-Russian Alliance would be triggered. The French would mobilise to support Russia, and Germany would be faced with war on two fronts. This was no secret. Both alliances knew precisely how the other would react in the event of war.

Germany was to be compelled to fight war on two fronts and would be greatly outnumbered by the combined forces of Russia, France and Britain. The czar's army alone was much larger than that of the kaiser, though neither better trained nor equipped. With her more modern road and rail networks, Germany's advantage lay in the rapidity of her mobilisation. In comparison, Russia's military machine was slow, cumbersome and burdened by inefficiency. A mobilisation across the vast lands of the Russian empire, with inadequate infrastructure, less-developed railroad systems near the German frontiers and inefficient local military authorities was necessarily slow. Russia's strategic aim was to reduce this natural German advantage by keeping her mobilisation secret for as long as possible.

In 1912, in the midst of the Balkan troubles, Russia claimed to have annulled the order that the proclamation of general mobilisation was equivalent to the declaration of war, but their secret military protocols clearly contradicted this:

> It will be advantageous to complete concentration [mobilisation] without beginning hostilities, in order not to deprive the enemy irrevocably of the hope that war can still be avoided. Our measures for this must be masked by clever diplomatic negotiations, in order to lull to sleep as much as possible the enemy's fears ... If by such measures we can gain a few days they absolutely must be taken.[8]

Poincaré departed St Petersburg late on 23 July. Several hours later, on the morning of the 24th, General Nicolai Ianushkevich, chief of the Russian general staff, called General Dobrorolsky, the chief of mobilisation, to his office and asked if he had everything ready for the proclamation of mobilisation of the army. He had, but was aghast when Ianushkevich added 'against Austria-Hungary only'. Dobrorolsky knew that partial mobilisation against Austria was a dangerous, impossible folly. It had to be a general mobilisation aimed at Germany.[9]

At a meeting of the Council of Ministers held at three o'clock that same afternoon, 24 July, the Russians decided to mobilise 1,100,000 men in the four southern military districts of Odessa, Kiev, Moscow and Kazan, together with both the Baltic and Black Sea fleets.[10] The czar further agreed that preparation should be made for the mobilisation of 13 army corps at a date to be determined by Sazonov. The minister of war was authorised to 'proceed immediately to gather stores of war materiel' and the minister of finance directed to call in at once all Russian money in Germany and Austria. This, remember, was still 24 July, the day before the Serbian Reply was due for submission.[11]

The Russian Military Command comprised class-ridden elitists, self-infatuated aristocrats, time-servers and careerists, who did not doubt their capacity to defeat both Austria and Germany at the same time. Undeterred by the stupidity of changing their chiefs of the general staff six times in nine years, they firmly believed that Russia was ready for war and bound by her word of honour to France to move against Germany.[12]

After the hastily convened meeting of the Council of Ministers on 24 July, Foreign Minister Sazonov lunched with ambassadors Buchanan and Paléologue at the French Embassy. These were the Secret Elite's diplomatic enforcers, who ensured that London and Paris were kept fully updated. Sazonov confirmed that the czar had approved both the mobilisation of over 1 million men and the Russian navy. The imperial order (*ukase*) was not to be made public until he, Sazonov, considered that the moment had arrived to enforce it, but all the necessary preliminary preparations for the mobilisation had already begun.[13]

Sazonov confirmed that Russia was prepared to 'face all the risks', and Paléologue reiterated Poincaré's 'blank cheque', placing France unreservedly on Russia's side. Poincaré had explicitly instructed Paléologue to reassure Sazonov by prompt and persistent promises of French support.[14] The French ambassador informed Sazonov that he had also received a number of telegrams from the minister in charge of foreign affairs, and that not one of them displayed the slightest sign of hesitation. Russia was mobilising for war, and France placed herself unreservedly by her side.[15]

Sazonov was thus constantly reassured that France would stand shoulder to shoulder with Russia, but what about Britain? Grey and King George V had assured him of British support at Balmoral in 1912, but he was confused by the overtures of friendship voiced by Britain to Germany. Sazonov was not sufficiently astute to realise that such mind games were designed to mislead and were part and parcel of the deception. Germany had to be led to believe until the very last minute that Britain would remain neutral. An official treaty between Britain and Russia, which Sazonov so desperately desired, would have destroyed that cover. Grey was determined to hold to the official line that 'England' could be more effective if she posed as a mediator at all costs.[16] His charade had to be maintained. Germany had to be kept guessing.

The following morning, 25 July, the Russian Council of Ministers rubber-stamped the military plans and confirmed their readiness for war.[17] Telegrams were sent out in secret ciphers, halting military manoeuvres throughout the Russian empire. Military divisions were instructed to return immediately from their summer camps to their regular quarters. Troops were to be equipped and prepared for transportation to their designated areas on the frontiers.[18] Cadets undergoing training at the St Petersburg Military Academy were immediately promoted to the rank of officer, and new cadets enrolled. A 'state of war' was proclaimed in towns along the frontiers facing Germany and Austria, and a secret order given for the 'Period Preparatory to War'.[19] This enabled the Russia military command to take extensive measures for mobilisation against Germany without a formal declaration of war. Meanwhile, on the diplomatic front, ambassadors and chargés d'affaires, ministers and imperial officials continued the pretence that they sought a peaceful resolution to the Austro-Serbian crisis and bought precious time for the military. Russia had begun a secret mobilisation in incremental stages before the Pasic government in Serbia had even responded to the Austrian Note.

Sir George Buchanan urged Sazonov to be cautious lest Germany got wind of the mobilisation, reacted immediately and Russia was portrayed as the aggressor.[20] Buchanan did not suggest that Sazonov should stop the Russian mobilisation, far from it, but urged him to keep it well hidden from German view. It was important that the mobilisation be as far advanced as possible before the Germans became aware of the military build-up on their frontiers. Furthermore, the Secret Elite in London needed to be able to portray Germany as the aggressor, to entice Germany into firing the first shots and so avoid a situation where Russia could be blamed for starting the war. At all costs, blame had to be laid at Germany's door. The British public would never accept war unless Germany was seen as the aggressor. This absolute conviction became Britain's diplomatic mantra. Although Buchanan later denied it, the French ambassador, Paléologue, even went so far in his memoirs as to recall Buchanan telling him: 'Russia is determined to go to war. We must therefore saddle Germany with the whole responsibility and initiative of the attack, as this will be the only way of winning over English public opinion to the war.'[21] The Secret Elite and their agents knew exactly how the unfolding events would have to be manipulated to dupe the British public.

Sir Edward Grey stubbornly insisted throughout the whole crisis that the Austro-Serbian dispute did not concern him.[22] This lie went unchallenged. He chose to distance himself and the Foreign Office from what transpired in Vienna and Belgrade, and its impact on St Petersburg. By making no parliamentary reference to events in that part of the world, he hid the Secret Elite's diplomatic incitement to war behind a screen of apparent lack of interest in the Austro-Serbian conflict. He consulted daily with Sir Arthur Nicolson and had a powerful anti-German ally in Sir Eyre Crowe. These two almost outbid each other in their distaste for Germany and their indulgence of Russia.[23] Grey's minders never veered from the Secret Elite doctrine. Inside Grey's Foreign Office, the Empire loyalists behaved like a swarm of Jesuit zealots pledged to an anti-German inquisition. In sharp contrast, the foreign secretary's public stance was of mute disinterest in the events that they expected to lead to war. Theirs was an ignominious deception, for they knew that this was a dispute from which a general war would ensue, and, far from being disinterested, they were intimately complicit.

Sir Edward Grey's attitude was very matter-of-fact. In his telegraphed reply to Buchanan on 25 July, he accepted that the critical step of Russian mobilisation had raised international tension to the next level. He expressed no criticism or undue alarm. Instead he blamed the 'brusque, sudden and peremptory' nature of the Austrian demands, which in his eyes made it 'almost inevitable that in a very short time Austria and Russia will both have mobilised against each other'.[24] Later that day, he repeated this view in a diplomatic letter to Horace Rumbold, the British ambassador in Berlin. He predicted that Europe would soon be confronted by a moment when 'both Austria and Russia would have mobilised'.[25] Grey's message to Russia was not one of horror and dismay, or protestation that mobilisation would lead to war. He was waiting for it. Indeed, there is much substance to the view that 'Grey actually encouraged Russia to mobilise'.[26]

Meanwhile in Belgrade, at 3 p.m. on 25 July (three hours before responding to the Austrian Note), Pasic's government, confident of Russian military support, announced Serbia's mobilisation against Austria. At 9.30 that same night, the Austrians responded by declaring a partial mobilisation (some 22 divisions) of its army against Serbia.[27] Austria had made it patently clear that in the event of such a mobilisation, war would remain localised and no territorial claims would be made on Serbia. She intended to occupy Belgrade until such time as Serbia agreed to all of their demands.

This Austrian mobilisation was deliberately misrepresented as a direct challenge and threat to Russia, and the reason for Russian mobilisation. That is a ridiculous claim. The Russian mobilisation had been agreed in principle before Poincaré left St Petersburg and before Austria had even delivered the Note to Serbia. Another fiction put about was that the Russian mobilisation was meant to act as a deterrent to war. What nonsense. It was the first act of war, and all involved knew it. The notion that it could be seen as a deterrent is groundless. They clearly understood that to order mobilisation was to cross the Rubicon: there could be no turning back.[28]

Maurice Paléologue, the French ambassador, offered an interesting insight into what was happening on the streets of the capital:

> At seven in the evening [the 25th] I went to the Warsaw Station [in St Petersburg] to bid farewell to Isvolsky, who was leaving to rejoin his post. Great activity at the terminus, the trains crowded with officers and troops. All this points to mobilisation. We hurriedly exchanged our views of the situation and both arrived at the same conclusion: this time it is war.[29]

Hour by hour, Russia secretly edged closer to war.[30]

On 26 July, the czar officially approved 'partial' mobilisation against Austria. A telegram was despatched from Paléologue to Poincaré on board *La France*. It concluded: 'Russian opinion makes it clear that it is both politically and morally impossible for Russia to allow Serbia to be crushed.'[31]

Poincaré's visit had been successful, his mission accomplished. Apart from the outrageous exaggeration that Austria intended to crush Serbia, the telegram confirmed that nothing would stop the Russians moving to war against Austria. That, of course, meant war against Germany too. Russia's frontier districts adjoining Austria and Germany were put on a war footing as rapidly and discreetly as possible, though Sazonov assured the German ambassador, Count Pourtales, that no mobilisation orders of any kind had been issued.[32]

It was a complex package of lies, deception and misrepresentation that added up to false justification, deliberate manipulation and a downright determination to wage war on Germany.

Summary: Chapter 23 – July 1914 – The First Mobilisations

- By the accepted conventions of the time, general mobilisation by a major power was the first act of war.

- The French–Russian (entente) game plan was to ensure that Germany was attacked on two fronts: that is, from the east and west simultaneously.
- The Secret Elite's grand plan tightened further when Poincaré and the French agreed in principle with the Russians to joint mobilisation during his visit to St Petersburg. Poincaré repeatedly assured the czar and Sazonov of the absolute commitment of France.
- Any wavering on the part of the czar or Sazonov was bolstered by the reassurances from his diplomatic minders, Paléologue (French ambassador) and Buchanan (British ambassador). The Russian military were preparing for war and delighted with their French allies.
- Sir Edward Grey also encouraged mobilisation by declaring his calm acceptance of its 'inevitability', while Buchanan cautioned Sazonov to make sure that Germany did not get wind of what was happening.
- Buchanan and Grey knew that the British public would not go to war unless Germany was the proven aggressor.
- The Serbian government mobilised at 3 p.m. on 25 July, and the Austrians followed with a partial mobilisation against Serbia at 9.30 that evening.
- Russian mobilisation had been agreed while Poincaré was still in St Petersburg, and the evidence of troop movements was recorded by diplomats. The czar accepted partial mobilisation of the Russian armies on 26 July.

CHAPTER 24

July 1914 – Buying Time – The Charade of Mediation

Before the war, Sir Edward Grey's reputation rarely suffered from contemporary attack no matter what he did. The Secret Elite protected him at every turn. The foreign secretary fronted their ambitions with absolute loyalty, and his reward was to be treated with reverence by *The Times*, King George V, the British Establishment and sympathetic international leaders. He was an untouchable, the epitome of right-minded, educated Englishness, of impeccable family and the best of clubs. Sir Edward Grey was held in such high esteem that his clever manipulation of the July crisis and his consequent misrepresentation of events to Parliament and to his Cabinet colleagues was accepted at face value. The verdict of his time claimed that he 'acted splendidly in a great crisis, and did everything possible to avert war'.[1] He did not. Grey delivered the war.

His strategy from 25 July onwards was to make it appear that he sought answers to intractable problems by offering plausible solutions, and to urge the Germans in particular to cling to the hope that peace was still possible. Grey knew precisely what had been arranged by and through Poincaré's visit. Sazonov and the Russian military had begun mobilisation. His prime objective was to gain time for the Russians by delaying Germany's defensive response. He achieved this by presenting Britain as an 'honest broker' for peace. Sir George Buchanan in St Petersburg ensured that Grey was kept fully informed, thus allowing him to don the mantle of peacemaker to Russia's advantage. British neutrality sat at the epicentre of this charade like a prize exhibit at an auction. Sazonov desperately wanted Grey to openly commit to the entente, but to no avail.[2] The Germans repeatedly sought clarification about 'England's' intentions, but Grey held to the official line. Britain was not bound by any obligation to enter into war. He had told this lie so often he might even have started to believe it.

Over that weekend of 25–26 July, while the Russians secretly began their mobilisation, the British political leaders left town for their country pastures. The German ambassador, Prince Lichnowsky, arrived unannounced at the Foreign Office with an urgent message from Chancellor Bethmann, imploring Sir Edward Grey to use his influence at St Petersburg against any form of mobilisation. No one was available to see him, and Lichnowsky had to postpone his appeal until Monday.[3] It was an old trick and such a simple deception. By being allegedly out of touch for the weekend, formal diplomacy was put on hold and the Russians were gifted two more valuable days for mobilisation.

Grey's convenient absence stalled Lichnowsky but did not in any way hinder the Foreign Office from repeatedly making diplomatic moves aimed at buying more time for Russia's military preparations. An offer of British mediation was immediately accepted by Germany but rejected by Sazonov and Poincaré.[4] Grey then proposed that the ambassadors of Italy, Germany and France should meet with him in London to find a peaceful solution to the diplomatic conflict.[5] This offer was made in the full knowledge that Italy had long planned to betray her commitment to the Triple Alliance. Germany and Austria were themselves aware that it was very unlikely that the Italians would support them. Bethmann believed that 'the ill-will of Italy appeared almost a certainty'.[6] As matters stood, Germany knew she would find herself isolated at the conference and that the vote count was bound to be three to one in favour of Russia's view. A further stumbling block was the insistence that Austria accepted the Serbian Reply as a basis for negotiation.[7] No specific condition was placed on any other nation, and Russia remained free to continue her 'preparatory measures'.[8] In truth, the conference was proposed not as a means to find a settlement but to give the massive Russian military machine time to move its armies up to the German frontier.

Germany advocated the eminently more sensible proposition that direct negotiations between Vienna and St Petersburg offered the best chance of peace. Grey agreed, but Sazonov did not. Knowing full well that Austria had just declared the Serbian Reply unacceptable, Sazonov said he considered it satisfactory and the basis for talks on which Russia 'willingly held out her hand' to Austria.[9] This was yet another of the 'peace proposals' that Grey, Sazonov and Poincaré knew could never be acceptable. Forewarned that any peace proposal emanating from Grey was a ruse, Poincaré and Isvolsky knew how they were expected to respond. When Grey suggested a solution and Germany accepted, Poincaré or Sazonov would say no. Likewise, if Germany proposed a peace move, Grey would accept and be seen as the man of moderation, but either Poincaré or Sazonov would then reject it. War was the object, not peace.

During that same weekend of 25–26 July, with the British Cabinet absent from London, Sir Arthur Nicolson in the Foreign Office kept his finger on the beating pulse of the European crisis. Across at the Admiralty, another secret decision drew war ever closer. At four on the Sunday afternoon, the first sea lord, Prince Louis of Battenberg (who had been appointed to replace Jacky Fisher in 1912), sent, with Churchill's prior approval, an order to the fleet to remain concentrated at Spithead. Quietly and unassumingly, the fleet was mobilised. Note the coincidence: both the first lord of the Admiralty and the foreign secretary were absent from their posts, yet key departmental decisions were taken that deliberately brought war ever closer. As far as the public were concerned, nothing untoward was happening. It was just another summer weekend.

Churchill and Prince Louis of Battenberg acted without the authority of the Cabinet or the king, but it hardly mattered since the entire British Grand Fleet 'just happened' to be gathered at Spithead for the King's Review. The massed ranks of Britain's navy had been effectively mobilised since 15 July 1914. The official Royal Review took place on the 18th, but the fleet had not been disbanded back to its sectoral locations in the Atlantic, across the Empire or closer to home in the North Sea. It had been mobilised in full view of Germany. What a magnificent deception.

On Sunday, 26 July, Prince Henry of Prussia was at Cowes on the Isle of Wight, sailing his magnificent yacht *Germania*, when he received an invitation to dine with King George in London. Henry was the kaiser's younger brother and grand admiral of the German Fleet. This was no chance meeting but one primed by the Secret Elite to deceive the kaiser. Over a private dinner, the king promised that 'we shall try to keep out of this, and shall remain neutral'.[10] The reassuring news was telegraphed that same evening to Berlin. The king, like his late father, always played his part in the Secret Elite programme that cut across the bonds of the extended royal families of Europe. Though the kaiser and Prince Henry were his cousins, King George had no hesitation in maintaining the deception. Naturally, the kaiser laid great store in the promise. Here was something infinitely more worthy than the huckstering of politicians. He had the word of a king.[11]

Every sacred moment was put to good use by the Russian military command. Over that same weekend, Russian frontier districts adjoining Austria and Germany were put on a war footing as rapidly as possible. Because the minister of war had the authority to call out the reservists and militia for service in those districts, this was carried out without the sanction of the czar. And so, on 26 July, Russia's secret mobilisation measures began in earnest. That very day, Sazonov assured the German ambassador, Count Pourtales, that no mobilisation orders of any kind had been issued. He denied it to his face. The consequence of this deception would be clear later when Germany was taken by surprise by the rapidity with which the Russian troops poured into East Prussia.[12] The French maintained their constant pressure on St Petersburg. Prime Minister Vivani repeated over and over again that France was fully resolved to fulfil all her obligations to the alliance. Innocent though that might sound, the meaning was clear. 'We will stand together in war': unspoken but understood. He also reiterated the same urgent advice that Buchanan had passed on from London: the Russians had to proceed as secretly as possible in their military preparations to avoid giving the Germans any excuse to reciprocate. Isvolsky sent an almost identical message.[13] These men who posed as ambassadors of peace on the European stage were united in their shameless deceit. They sought war and, in its pursuit, to gain every advantage over Germany.

Diplomatic proposals and counter-proposals criss-crossed Europe over the next five days as a variety of options for mediation, negotiation or direct interventions emanated from London, Berlin, Vienna and St Petersburg. Some were genuine; some were intended to deceive. Grey's suggestions were consistent in that they always supported the Russian position and never at any time sought to question or constrain Sazonov. More ominously, the Foreign Office began to insist that German preparations for war were much more advanced than those of France or Russia.[14] No evidence from the British archives has ever been presented to justify this allegation.[15] Britain had thousands of representatives, businessmen, bankers, tradesmen and tourists in Germany during those crucial weeks. Military and naval attachés, consuls in all the larger cities and, of course, senior diplomats in Berlin all served to represent the interests of the British Crown. No one filed an official report warning of German preparations for war. The major newspapers had foreign correspondents in Germany. They observed nothing untoward. Not just that. No other diplomatic mission shared Grey's unwarranted view.[16] The anti-German cabal of Grey, Nicolson and Crowe created yet another myth.

The German government's views were published in the *North German Gazette* on Monday, 27th. They voiced support for the Austrian action and strongly advocated a localised solution. Disturbing intelligence was steadily filtering into the German Foreign Office that Russian military activity had been seen in locations close to the border. Twenty-eight different reports became a cause for concern. The Danish foreign minister even went so far as to state categorically that the Russians were preparing to mobilise in military districts facing the Austrian and German frontiers.[17] Prince Lichnowsky asked Sir Edward Grey directly if he knew what was happening in Russia. Despite what he had already learned from Buchanan, Grey flatly denied that Russia was in the process of calling up reservists.[18]

When Kaiser Wilhelm and his advisors returned to Berlin from their summer holidays on Monday, 27 July, there was a relatively calm atmosphere. General Helmuth von Moltke, chief of the German general staff, took the precaution of sending instructions to the German Foreign Office that would only be activated if peace negotiations failed. It was a draft of the ultimatum to be sent to Belgium in the event of war. Clearly he had to cover all eventualities, but neither he nor the kaiser was planning to start a war.[19] Moltke wrote reassuringly to his wife in the expectation that it would be a fortnight before anything definite was known.[20] Such optimism, though a considerable misjudgement, was based on the German belief that a European war could be avoided.

As far as Moltke and the kaiser were concerned, the most likely, and certainly the desired outcome, was a localised war between Austria and Serbia. Berlin officials felt vexed that Berchtold in Austria had failed to keep them fully informed and had delayed so long in taking action. The attitude of the Italian government, though not unexpected, remained disturbing. Count Szogyeny, the Hungarian ambassador in Berlin, noted that Italy, 'in the case of a general conflict, would not fulfil its duty as an ally of the Triple Alliance'.[21] He believed that Austrian demands on Serbia would be used as an excuse by Italy to renege on its commitment. Vexation turned to alarm when four further telegrams arrived in Berlin revealing Russian troop movements close to the German borders. The Russians had placed the town of Kovno in a state of war and mined the mouth of the Duna River.[22]

Despite the fact that her army would not be in a position to invade for at least another fortnight, Austria declared war on Serbia on Tuesday, 28 July.[23] In an instant, the diplomatic options changed. The kaiser knew that Berchtold had to have his pound of Serbian flesh, but he was very unhappy at this sudden turn of events. Wilhelm had been impressed with the Serbian Reply. In his judgement, the few reservations Serbia had made on particular points could be settled by negotiation, but he clearly understood the Austrian dilemma. In his eyes, as in theirs, the Serbs were Orientals, hence 'liars, tricksters and masters of evasion'.[24] Having been obliged to mobilise twice in the previous two years against Serbian aggression, Austria demanded both a cast-iron guarantee that Serbia meant what was said and recompense for having to mobilise the army for a third time. He proposed a temporary military occupation of a portion of Serbia – the 'Kaiser's

Pledge'. This tried and tested solution was similar to that which Germany had employed in France in 1871. Let the Austrians occupy Belgrade until Serbia accepted their demands, but stop at that. There should be no full-scale invasion but a qualified occupation that would satisfy honour all round. The kaiser went further. He took the initiative to put an end to this dangerous period in European history by stating that 'on this basis, I am ready to mediate for peace'.[25]

Matters accelerated beyond Wilhelm's control. Sir Arthur Nicolson received a telegram from Buchanan, stating that 'Russia had mobilised in the Southern districts'.[26] Behind the scenes, the Secret Elite were also mobilising for the final push.

They approached the endplay on the route to war with meticulous care. Lord Nathaniel Rothschild made an unscheduled visit to Prime Minister Asquith to advise him on the preparations that his bank had put in place to prepare for war. He had received a banker's order from his family branch in Paris to sell a vast quantity of consols for the French government. This would have resulted in a substantial outflow of money from London to Paris, which he refused to approve.[27] The stock markets across Europe were extremely nervous. Asquith confided this to Venetia, adding: 'it looks ominous'.[28] All agents of the Secret Elite were linked together through that most powerful advantage, knowledge, and they knew that the mobilisation taking place in Russia meant war. They were fully aware that Germany would eventually be forced into a defensive retaliation through the Schlieffen Plan.[29] They knew through their bankers that the money markets were braced for the impact of war. Every shard illuminated aspects of the Secret Elite's foreknowledge. They knew because they were responsible.

On the evening of 28 July, Chancellor Bethmann sent a telegraph to Vienna putting pressure on Berchtold to negotiate and immediately notified Britain and Russia that he had done so. Germany was cooperating to maintain the peace. Bethmann was doing all he could to persuade Berchtold to hold frank and friendly discussions with St Petersburg. He informed the British ambassador that 'a war between the Great Powers must be avoided'.[30] Bethmann was determined to make Austria reconsider the consequences of events that were unfolding, but by the following morning he had received no response from Berchtold. All that day he waited in vain for an answer. Berchtold's silence was unnerving. More and more reports were relayed to Berlin confirming Russian mobilisation. Moltke was able to report that France was also taking preparatory measures for mobilisation: 'it appears that Russia and France are moving hand in hand as regards their preparations'.[31] There was much cause for concern in Berlin. The German military authorities demanded precautionary defensive measures. That evening, Bethmann indignantly fired off another three telegrams to Berchtold, adamant that there was a basis for negotiations.[32] His subtext was that Germany's blank cheque could be cancelled.

The German ambassador in London telegraphed Berlin on the 29th to say that the British believed that a world war was inevitable unless the Austrians negotiated their position over Serbia. Lichnowsky begged Sir Edward Grey to do all he could to prevent a Russian mobilisation on Germany's borders. The consequences would be 'beyond conception'.[33] Grey promised to use his influence and keep Sazonov as 'cool-headed as possible'.[34] Far from trying to calm Sazonov, however, Grey made no attempt at intervention. Instead, he met again with Lichnowsky that evening and sowed the seeds of confusion that deliberately included conditions and suppositions that mixed hope with dire warnings.[35]

Grey wrote four dispatches on 29 July that were later published as official documents in the British Blue Book.[36] After the war, when some limited access was granted to national and parliamentary archives, it transpired that the telegrams had never been sent. It was part of a cosmetic charade to imply that Britain had made every effort to prevent war.

Bethmann and the kaiser, on the other hand, genuinely tried to apply the brakes and gain some control of the deteriorating situation. The German chancellor vigorously opposed any military measures that would ruin his diplomatic appeals. Unfortunately, he was almost the last man standing in that particular field. In Berlin, they held to the fading hope that British diplomats were men of honour, and great store was placed on the reassurances that King George V had recently given to Prince Henry of Prussia. The prince was convinced that the king's statement 'was made in all seriousness' and that England would remain neutral at the start, but he doubted whether she would do so permanently.[37] Germany pursued peace right up to the last minute. As Lloyd George later put it: 'The last thing that the vainglorious kaiser wanted was a European war.'[38] His and Bethmann's valiant efforts failed because the Secret Elite and their agents had already engineered their war.

Sazonov anguished over the final decision. He was given to illness and depression, with mood swings and bouts of genuine self-doubt. If it was his weakness that initially attracted the Secret Elite to endorse his elevation to minister, it was also a problem that required careful handling. Sir George Buchanan was rarely far from his side. Nor was Paléologue, the French ambassador. When the news of Austria's declaration of war on Serbia reached St Petersburg, Sazonov was gripped by a dangerous emotional cocktail of fear, suspicion, pressure from the military and the elation of possibly winning Constantinople. Concerned that Sazonov and the czar might lose their nerve at the eleventh hour, or that the czar could be talked out of war by his cousin the kaiser, the Secret Elite ensured that they received constant reassurance. The czar sent a desperate and revealing telegram to Wilhelm that gave a rare insight to his personal anguish:

> I appeal to you to help me . . . I foresee that very soon I shall be unable to resist the pressure exercised upon me and that I shall be forced to take extreme measures which will lead to war . . .[39]

Clearly, Nicholas II was overwhelmed by the pressure being put on him by the warmongers and was burdened by the realisation that his actions, not the kaiser's, would lead to war. His telegram was essentially a *cri de coeur*, a plea from his soul.

The kaiser was not impressed by what he saw as a confession of the czar's personal weakness, but Wilhelm's mind was also exercised by Socialist anti-war demonstrations on the streets of Berlin, which he refused to tolerate. He ordered martial law.[40] These were indeed troubled and distracting times in many European capitals.

The czar's telegram crossed one sent to him by the kaiser at 1.45 a.m. on 29 July. Wilhelm advised him that he, as kaiser, would do his utmost to induce Austria-Hungary to obtain a frank and satisfactory understanding with Russia. The telegram ended: 'I hope confidently that you will support me in my efforts to overcome all difficulties which may arise.'[41] His appeal was genuinely made and honestly intended. Germany continued to give time to find a peaceful solution – in contrast to Russia, which was already on the move.

During the afternoon of the 29th, Nicholas II caved in to pressure and signed the order for the general Russian mobilisation. As his telegram showed, he knew it meant war.[42] But he remained ill at ease. Several hours later, following a personal plea from the kaiser that Russian mobilisation meant it would be impossible for him to continue to act as mediator for peace, the czar reversed his decision.[43] At 9.30 p.m., urgent instructions were sent to the St Petersburg Telegraph Office to halt the general mobilisation. The Russian general staff were outraged at the stupidity of such a command. Allegations were later made that they continued the full programme for general mobilisation despite the czar's order. In fact, Russia had been in the process of mobilising since the 25th, and the military had no intention of losing the precious five-day advantage they had already gained.[44]

Europe in 1914. Germany and Austria-Hungary stand alone. Italy did not join in the Triple Alliance. (Map courtesy of the Arizona Geographic Alliance, School of Geographical Sciences and Urban Planning, Arizona State University; Becky Eden, cartographer)

Intelligence reports citing Russian troop movements along her frontiers were continually relayed to Berlin. Moltke could not afford to delay a military response for long. He was responsible for the defence of Germany, and it would have been completely incompetent to wait and see how events unfolded before reacting to the Russians. He was not fooled by their assurances that they had not yet mobilised or that no reserves had been called up. He warned the chancellor that 'she [Russia] has been getting herself so ready for war that, when she actually issues her mobilisation orders, she will be able to move her armies forward in a very few days'.[45] The kaiser, however, did not want to give Russia, France and particularly Britain any excuse to block negotiations for peace, and overruled Moltke.

In London that evening, 29 July, the Secret Elite's political placemen, Grey, Asquith, Haldane and Churchill, held a private meeting to discuss what Asquith called 'the coming war'.[46] Apart from Lloyd George, these were the only senior British politicians who knew what was about to happen. Parliament, in both Houses, was completely ignorant of the fact that Britain was going to war. Maurice Hankey, the Secret Elite's invaluable secretary to the Committee of Imperial Defence, advised them to declare a 'precautionary period' on the road to war. Hankey was indispensable and at the centre of all the major decision making. He was the keeper of minutes, the organiser of instructions: the man who linked the centre of the Cabinet to the Civil Service.

Churchill left the meeting, went straight to the Admiralty and ordered the British fleet to proceed immediately to war stations at Scapa Flow in the Orkney Islands. The Grand Fleet may have been mobilised in full view, but it passed through the Straits of Dover in total secrecy. There was no glory for the British navy as it sneaked away in the dark of night with lights extinguished. Ten days previously it had paraded with all flags flying before the king in a line that stretched for forty miles.[47]

On the 29th, while the kaiser was working to preserve the peace, the fleets and armies of his opponents were busily preparing for war.[48] Chancellor Bethmann could see that Germany was being progressively surrounded by the proverbial 'ring of steel', and his last ray of hope lay in the British government's announcement that it wanted nothing more than to cultivate friendship with Germany. How was he to know that it was simply part of Sir Edward Grey's deception? Bethmann was left with no alternative but to put Britain's 'friendly' overtures to the test. He discussed the critical European situation with Goschen, the British ambassador in Berlin, and detailed a number of promises that Germany would honour if Britain agreed to remain neutral. He was being honest and forthright: qualities that were alien to the Machiavellian instincts in the British Foreign Office. And in his openness, Bethmann gave a hostage to fortune. He was quoted as saying: 'provided that Belgium did not take sides against Germany, her integrity would be respected after the conclusion of the war'.[49] This was the moment for which the Secret Elite had been waiting. Goschen immediately telegraphed the German proposals to the Foreign Office.

Sir Eyre Crowe, one of Grey's minders at the Foreign Office, reacted with affected indignation when the telegram arrived. His instant verdict was that these were 'astounding proposals' that reflected very poorly on Bethmann. More pertinently, he portrayed the German chancellor's words as proof that 'Germany practically admits her intention to violate Belgium'.[50] His intemperate language was mimicked by Sir Edward Grey, who rushed to Asquith to report that Germany had 'despicably' tried to bargain Belgium's future against Britain's neutrality. In his memoirs, Grey recorded his 'despair' when he read Bethmann's 'dishonouring proposal'.[51] Despair? He felt nothing of the kind. Belgium had always been the answer; it was only a matter of time before the Belgian question would be raised. And witness too the vocabulary with which they rushed to damn Bethmann's serious and honest proposals on neutrality. When he addressed the House of Commons the following day, Grey made no mention of the proposals from Germany that he and his advisers had already rejected.[52] Bonar Law, the Conservative leader, asked if there was any information that the foreign secretary could give to the House regarding the critical events in Europe. Grey replied: 'There is very little that I can say.' He knew he could not possibly divulge the German offer, since a majority in the Cabinet and the House of Commons would agree to neutrality and vote to keep Britain out of a war. If Russia wanted to start a European war over Serbia and her assassins, and France blindly followed, the most popular parliamentary view would have been to let them get on with it. Grey concluded: 'We continue to work to preserve European peace.' It was a well-prepared soundbite, and Bonar Law asked no follow-up question.[53] Neither man wanted to open a debate on British neutrality.

Bonar Law knew far more than was made public. Several key Members of Parliament supportive of and supported by the Secret Elite were in the Conservative Party and sat on the opposition front bench. Balfour was paramount as the conduit between the party leaders, trusted on both sides and absolutely at the heart of the Secret Elite. On 30 July, Asquith attended a secret meeting at Bonar Law's Kensington villa together with the Ulster Unionist Leader Sir Edward Carson, ostensibly to discuss Ireland. The real purpose was to coordinate plans in the immediate run-up to war. The prime minister shared the latest intelligence from Berlin, which showed that the German government was counting on the Ulster crisis to affect British foreign policy. They were given sight of documents from the Belgian ambassador who had reported that 'Britain was paralysed by internal dissentions and her Irish quarrels'.[54] The most important was from the German chancellor, whose telegram was portrayed as attempting to buy Britain's neutrality.[55] Asquith believed that this was clear proof that Germany expected Britain to remain neutral in the coming war because of the debilitating effect of a possible civil war in Ireland.

It would be easy to forget that Asquith was sharing these secrets with his lover[56] and leaders of the opposing party, while men who should have been informed, members of his own Cabinet, were not. The secretary of state for Ireland knew nothing about this. For reasons that will be made clear in the following chapter, the Ulster representatives were given very special treatment and exclusively made party to the fact that war was imminent. Behind the backs of the mass of government supporters, and a large majority of the Cabinet, a cross-party cabal of Secret Elite placemen was briefed in advance. The apparent runaway train that was Irish Home Rule would have to be switched to a safer track, but that would be arranged in good time. With trusted men on board, the Secret Elite could confidently start the countdown to the events that would bounce the British people into their long-planned war. In the meantime, Ulster was an impressive smokescreen behind which more than a 100,000 Irishmen could be turned into a fighting force right in front of the kaiser's eyes.

Towards the end of July, Chancellor Bethmann was the only European leader who sought to prevent war and find an equitable solution. On the morning of 30 July, both he and the kaiser sent telegrams pleading with Austria to accept mediation. Berchtold paid no heed to the advice. A very angry Bethmann sent him yet another urgent message reiterating that Austria's intransigence was placing Germany in an 'untenable situation' and insisting that Austria accept mediation. Bethmann restated that he accepted Austria's right to seek retribution but refused to be drawn into a world conflagration through Austria-Hungary not respecting his advice.[57]

It was, quite literally, a command. Desist. Berchtold was 'most emphatically' being told to accept mediation.[58] He had to give way or the so-called blank cheque would bounce and explode in his face. Berchtold finally realised that his plans for retribution against Serbia had to be revised within the parameters set by Germany. He had spent beyond his limit.

With Berchtold at last prepared to negotiate, Bethmann clung to a glimmer of hope that all was not yet beyond repair. Austria gave assurance that she would not annex any part of Serbian territory or violate Serbian sovereignty, and the kaiser promised Russia that he would compel Austria to cease military operations and remain satisfied with the temporary occupation of Belgrade.[59] Since the Austrian army would not be in a position to occupy Belgrade for another two weeks, there was still ample time for negotiations. If the Austrians agreed to 'halt in Belgrade', if Britain's friendly overtures were genuine, if Grey put pressure on Sazonov to stop the Russian mobilisation, peace was still within the bounds of possibility. If the kaiser sent another heartfelt plea to the czar, would he agree to listen to his own cousin? Poor deluded, hapless men. They had been deceived, all of them. Grey had no intention of restraining Sazonov or accepting any German proposals or preventing war. He never had.

On 30 July, at 1.20 a.m., the kaiser sent a despairing telegram to Czar Nicholas unequivocally placing responsibility for war on his cousin's shoulders.

> My ambassador is instructed to draw the attention of your government to the dangers and serious consequences of a mobilisation . . . If, as appears from your communication and that of your Government, Russia is mobilising against Austria-Hungary . . . The whole burden of decision now rests upon your shoulders, the responsibility for peace or war.[60]

His cousin's appeal to reason struck a chord. Deep in those early morning hours, his mind uncluttered by the baying of warmongers, Nicholas made a bold decision to stop the madness. He telegraphed the kaiser that he would send his personal emissary, General Tatishchev, to Berlin with explanations and instructions that would broker a peace. Tatishchev was the czar's own representative at the emperor's court and as such was outside the control or influence of politicians or the military. Czar Nicholas's message held great promise, but Tatishchev never made it to Berlin.[61] Unbeknown to the czar, Sazonov had him arrested and detained that night just as he was about to enter his compartment on the St Petersburg–Berlin train.[62] It was an act of treason. Sazonov secretly defied the czar's express command and thwarted the highest level of personal diplomacy between the two heads of state. By hauling Tatishchev off the train, he removed what would have become an awkward complication: one that could have stopped the war. It was a high-risk strategy in a high-risk game.

Sazonov, urged on by senior members of the Russian military in St Petersburg, begged the czar to ignore the German pleas. The telegrams from Kaiser Wilhelm had clearly influenced him, but Sazonov insisted that they were a ruse, that the Germans were lying and trying to buy time to split the Russian and French alliance and so leave Russia vulnerable to a devastating attack. Czar Nicholas relented under the sustained pressure and on the afternoon of 30 July again ordered general mobilisation. This time, nothing would be permitted to stop it.[63]

Sazonov instructed General Janushkevich to issue the order then 'smash his telephone' and keep out of sight for the rest of the day in order to frustrate any further attempt by the czar to countermand the mobilisation.[64] It was a conspiracy inside the conspiracy. Every action that could possibly be taken to continue Russian mobilisation and bring peace talks to an end was approved by Sazonov and the military. A new era in world history had been sanctioned. In Dobrorolsky's own words, war was 'irrevocably begun':[65] deliberately, wilfully begun by Sazonov, Poincaré and Sir Edward Grey, all at the behest of the Secret Elite in London.

The Germans neither mobilised first nor rushed to mobilisation when the news of the Russian decision reached Berlin on Friday, 31 July. Bethmann had been desperately seeking confirmation from Vienna that they would listen to him and 'Halt in Belgrade', so giving the kaiser the opportunity to stop the needless war. The time for diplomacy had passed. Moltke was naturally anxious. Restraint gave advantage to Germany's enemies, and these lay both to the east and west of the country. It was too late to avoid war. The official announcement of Russia's mobilisation closed all doors to peace.

The czar's order had been decreed while the kaiser was putting severe pressure upon Austria-Hungary to negotiate[66] and the British were secretly making their own preparations. The fleet was at war stations, and on 31 July it was reported that:

> Thousands of feet tramped Channel-wards; regiment after regiment with full kit wound through London Streets as the bells from tower and steeple called the folk to prayer. In Whitehall crowds parted to let a regiment march through. They marched on past the War Office and the Admiralty, but no one knew their ultimate destination.[67]

Thus the British navy was mobilised and the army began mobilisation before Parliament or the Cabinet had even had the opportunity to discuss the possibility of Britain going to war.

The timing was choreographed to perfection. Within hours of Austria relenting to sustained German pressure, and with the real possibility that successful talks could be held, the door to peace was deliberately, firmly and finally slammed shut by the official Russian mobilisation. Kaiser Wilhelm sent another telegram to the czar on 31 July. He was hurt and disillusioned. His friendship and family ties apparently counted for nothing. While he had been mediating for peace at the behest of the czar, the Russians had taken full advantage and mobilised. The pfennig dropped. His good intentions had been skilfully abused by deceitful men. Wilhelm had received 'trustworthy news of serious preparations for war, even on my eastern frontier'.[68] Despite the fact that he had been deliberately misled and knew that his first responsibility was to his own people, the kaiser tried once more to convince the czar that disaster could be averted. He warned his cousin that:

> It will not be I who am responsible for the calamity which threatens the whole civilised world. Even at this moment it lies in your power to avert it. Nobody threatens the honour and power of Russia, which could well have waited for the result of my mediation.[69]

Every word was true. Russia was under no threat. Nicholas could have chosen to wait for a solution to the problem between Serbia and Austria.

At the same time, Kaiser Wilhelm, the man who still stands accused of starting the catastrophic war, had made every possible effort to avoid it. One important measure of his inner feelings is how he responded to the news that war was inevitable. Was he elated, filled with unbridled joy? No. Was this the moment for which he had yearned? No. Wilhelm's anguish was clearly reflected in a note he wrote that day:

> I have no doubt about it: England, Russia and France have agreed among themselves . . . to take the Austro-Serbian conflict for an excuse for waging a war of extermination against us . . . the stupidity and ineptitude of our ally is turned into a snare for us . . . The net has been suddenly thrown over our head, and England sneeringly reaps the most brilliant success of her persistently prosecuted purely anti-German world policy against which we have proved ourselves helpless . . . From the dilemma raised by our fidelity to the venerable old Emperor of Austria, we are brought into a situation which offers England the desired pretext for annihilating us under the hypocritical cloak of justice.[70]

And he was right on every count. He could hardly have expressed the Secret Elite strategy more succinctly. Like a wounded animal caught in a trap, he realised too late that it had all been a set-up. Around noon on Friday, 31 July, the kaiser went to Berlin for a final conference with Bethmann and Moltke. At 1 p.m., he proclaimed the 'Threatening Danger of War', not a mobilisation but a formal announcement that mobilisation would take place within 48 hours.[71] It was to be war. German military authorities needed to move fast. Their mobilisation was based on the understanding that Germany, under attack from two sides, would have to advance firstly on France and then turn on Russia.

Summary: Chapter 24 – July 1914 – Buying Time – The Charade of Mediation

- From 25 July onwards, Sir Edward Grey's diplomatic efforts were geared to buy precious time for the secret Russian mobilisation. Every suggestion he made over the next five days favoured that.
- Grey abused his friendship with Lichnowsky by implying that Britain was unlikely to play any part in a 'ruinous' war.
- The Secret Elite placemen made strenuous attempts to maintain an appearance of normality while secretly effecting every possible preparation for war.
- King George V was instrumental in deluding the kaiser and his brother that 'England' would remain neutral.
- The Foreign Office put about the lie that Germany was secretly mobilising and better prepared for war than Russia and France.
- Several of the telegrams that Sir Edward Grey allegedly circulated to diplomatic contacts were in fact never sent. It was yet another part of the great deception that he appeared to make every effort to avoid war.
- Based on an expectation of British neutrality, Germany remained optimistic that a war between Austria and Serbia would remain localised,

despite evidence of Russian movements on her border.

- Bethmann and the kaiser became vexed with Berchtold and the Austrians, who did not respond to their insistence that they should hold talks with the Russians.
- The czar wavered between a general and full mobilisation in response to the pleas from the kaiser to avoid war, but Sazonov and the military convinced him that delay was out of the question.
- While Bethmann in Germany was desperately trying to find ways of maintaining peace, and with Berchtold constrained and ready to take a step back from the precipice, the door was finally slammed shut on that option when Russia announced full mobilisation on 30 July.

CHAPTER 25

Ireland – Plan B

In that last week of July when Russia was mobilising her armies on the German border, war became certain. The Secret Elite had known for at least a decade that when Germany reacted to the Russian mobilisation, she would have little option but to simultaneously advance on France through Belgium. They were confident that this German breach of Belgian 'neutrality' would provide their *casus belli*, but what if Parliament overwhelmingly rejected entering the war on the pretext of defending Belgium? Or what if Germany did the unexpected and poured her armies directly over the French border further south through Alsace and Lorraine? The Secret Elite had a fall-back position, a Plan B. They always had.

Astonishing as it sounds, that fallback position was to be civil war in Ireland. You will find no evidence of this in history books. It isn't there. But look hard at the extraordinary evidence presented in the following pages and decide for yourself. We will demonstrate how the Secret Elite wilfully promoted strife between the mainly Protestant Unionist north and the largely Catholic Nationalist south, and had their agents arm both opposing camps with weapons purchased in Germany. If, for whatever reason, their justification for taking Britain to war could not be found in a German violation of Belgium, civil war in Ireland would immediately have been ignited. Banner headlines in the pro-war British press would have immediately blamed Germany. The kaiser would have stood accused of arming both sides in a devious attempt to neutralise Britain through internal conflict. Outrage on the streets would most certainly have followed, with public insistence that the country immediately join France and Russia against the evil 'Hun'.

A similar plan had been considered with Alfred Milner in the run-up to the Boer War. His Balliol College friend and member of the inner core of the Secret Elite, Philip Lyttelton Gell,[1] whom Milner made a director of the British South Africa Company, wrote to him in July 1899, insisting that more direct action be taken to stir war. Gell described the British public as the 'uninstructed mass of limp opinion' and added that 'Something more has got to happen before the government could prudently take the initiative in bloodshed . . . a fresh murder would start the people . . . people would like that if the murder was really brutal.'[2] Though he was talking about the Transvaal in 1899, the same remarks applied to Sarajevo in 1914. Of even greater interest was a fall-back position to which Gell made direct reference: the importation of guns and ammunition to South Africa. His view was that if the British public realised that the Boers had imported arms from Germany to be used against British subjects, the cause for war 'would be popular and obvious'.[3] And Kruger had taken such a step. In the aftermath of the Jameson Raid, the Boers imported 37,000 Mausers from Krupp's factory in Germany.[4] The ploy was identical. Both in 1899 and 1914, the Secret Elite had a considered fall-back plan involving guns and ammunition provided by Germany that would have turned public opinion in favour of war.

Civil war in Ireland was never the intention, but the appearance of one had to be real, and the Secret Elite wielded the power to take matters as far as they deemed necessary. Churchill was later to admit that 'German agents reported and German statesmen believed that England was paralysed by faction and drifting into civil war'.[5] The carefully engineered 'crisis' in Ireland presented coincidental bonuses. A large paramilitary force in the north, the Ulster Volunteer Force (UVF), marched, drilled and trained with rifles for months before the outbreak of war under the instruction of former senior British Army officers. After the outbreak of war, a considerable number of these men enlisted with the 36th (Ulster) Division of the British Army. Perhaps of greater importance was that with public attention focused on Ireland, the Secret Elite created a very convenient smokescreen behind which they prepared for action on the continent. When the 5th Battalion, the Black Watch, was ordered to muster on 31 July, the soldiers assumed they were headed for Ireland, only to be thoroughly disappointed that their allotted task was to protect the Tay Bridge from an imaginary invasion force. 'We thought we were going to Ulster when we got orders last night . . . there would have been some excitement there.'[6] Plenty of 'excitement' lay ahead, but not in Dundee or Belfast. While historians and commentators wrongly use the concept of inevitability in conjunction with the First World War in July 1914, the only war that seemed inevitable then to the people of Britain was war in Ireland.

The Secret Elite was not responsible for centuries-old religious animosities in Ireland, but they manipulated them to their own ends. Ireland was riven by religious antagonisms between the historic Protestant ascendancy in the industrial north, and an agricultural Catholic majority in the south. The country was divided between those who wished Ireland greater degrees of self-government, and the pro-Empire Loyalist Protestants who held themselves to be British first, foremost and for ever.

The 1914 crisis was generated in the first instance by the introduction of a Home Rule Bill for Ireland. Two previous Home Rule Bills had been thrown out at Westminster: the first in 1886 was outvoted in the Commons and the second in 1893 was rejected by the House of Lords. After the general election of 1910, the political arithmetic in Westminster radically changed, with a hung parliament and the Liberals dependent on the support of Irish Home Rule MPs to cling to power. The quid pro quo was yet another Home Rule Bill to establish a parliament in Dublin. Control of the treasury, taxation, the armed forces and, most importantly, foreign policy would, however, remain firmly at Westminster. Ulstermen feared above all a role reversal where Protestants would become second-class citizens inside a Catholic state.[7]

Had it not suited their purpose, the Secret Elite could have brought down Asquith's government and replaced it, but the formation of a Liberal/Conservative coalition was put to one side. Mistakenly believing they were an integral part of a great democracy, backbench MPs from opposing sides waved their order papers at one another and bayed across the House of Commons with jeers and insults,[8] while their leaders met cordially behind the scenes, briefed each other and ensured that what was happening in Ireland was under their control.[9] It mattered little to the Secret Elite which of their teams was running the government, just as long as the path to war was being followed diligently. In pursuing the Home Rule Bill with all their might, the Liberal team of Asquith, Grey, Churchill and Lloyd George was doing just that. The Secret Elite fanned the fear, tension, hatred and religious bigotry on both sides. Churchill and Lloyd George deliberately antagonised the Ulstermen, while Bonar Law and his team professed loyalty to them. The entire charade was carefully stage-managed.

Though he had no experience of leadership, Edward Carson, a lawyer and Unionist MP for Trinity College, neither an Ulsterman nor an Orangeman but a Dublin MP,[10] was chosen by the Secret Elite to stir Protestant Ulster. He championed their heritage, their genuine and deeply held commitment to the Protestant cause and raised a battle-frenzy against Home Rule. Carson was a creation of the Secret Elite. He owed his political fortune to Arthur Balfour of the inner circle. As secretary for Ireland in earlier years, Balfour had appointed him as his chief prosecuting attorney, arranged a safe parliamentary seat and elevated him to the post of solicitor general in his 1903 government. Balfour was proud to boast that he had 'made Carson'.[11]

Carson's second in command in Ulster, James Craig, was a millionaire

Belfast whisky distiller who served as an officer of the Imperial Yeomanry in South Africa, where his capture and release by the Boers was in stark contrast to the treatment meted out in the British concentration camps. Like most of the Secret Elite's placemen in Ulster, Craig's involvement in the Boer War under Lord Roberts gave him the stamp of an Empire loyalist whom they could trust. He rejoiced in Ulster's place in the Empire.[12] He was Unionist MP for East Down and grand master of the Orange Lodge of County Down. James Craig had an organisational and administrative flair that served Ulster well, and he formed a very effective partnership with Edward Carson.

Once the Home Rule Bill had been introduced to Parliament in April 1912, the Ulster Unionist Council was urged to stand firmly against it. The council appointed a commission 'to take immediate steps, in consultation with Sir Edward Carson, to frame and submit a constitution for a provisional government in Ulster'.[13] Carson in turn promised the Protestants that 'with the help of God, you and I joined together, will yet defeat the most nefarious conspiracy that has ever been hatched against a free people'.[14]

There was indeed a nefarious conspiracy, but it extended far beyond the four provinces of Ireland. Carson's commission was to keep a firm hand on Ulster, maintain its integrity and lead its Protestant lodges and Unionist clubs. He had to fan the flames while preserving that narrow margin between dissent and rebellion.

Powerful politicians made public their support for Ulster. Bonar Law, Balfour's successor as leader of the Conservative Party, was both a friend and admirer of Sir Edward Carson. He waded into the murky Irish waters on Easter Tuesday, 1912, at an enormous demonstration, well in excess of 100,000 strong, at the Balmoral showground near Belfast. Seventy special trains ferried Unionists and Orangemen from all parts of the province. Opening prayers from the primate of All Ireland and the moderator of the Presbyterian Church marked the solemnity of the occasion, where, symbolically, the Unionist Party of Great Britain met and grasped the hand of Ulster Loyalism.[15] Bonar Law brought 70 members of the British Parliament with him, including Lord Hugh Cecil, Walter Long, Ian Malcolm and Leo Amery, all intimately connected with the Secret Elite. Bonar Law, son of a Canadian Orangeman and himself an Ulster Scot, invoked the memory of the siege of Derry, rousing the crowd with a passionate speech that ended: 'You have saved yourself by your exertions and you will save the Empire by your example.'[16]

Rudyard Kipling, another member of the Secret Elite,[17] was equally unstinting in his loyalty. His poem 'Ulster 1912', first published in the *Morning Post* on 9 April 1912, expressed fear and loathing as seen through the eyes of an Ulster abandoned by England, where 'we know the hells prepared by those who serve not Rome'.[18] Every prejudice was dressed in the Union flag. The passion of ordinary working-class Irish Protestants was whipped into a lather by fear that they were about to be surrendered as hostage to 'Catholic Dublin'. But they did not start a civil war. No one broke rank. Carson and his allies in the lodges and clubs of Ulster maintained a remarkable and impressive discipline in the province.

Demonstrations of loyalty and solidarity continued with a public declaration of formal defiance. On 28 September 1912, Sir Edward Carson was first to sign Ulster's Solemn League and Covenant. Staged-managed to perfection, Carson demonstrated his wonderful sense of occasion by walking the hundred yards from the Ulster Hall to the City Hall, escorted by guards from the Orange lodges and Unionist clubs of Belfast, with the Boyne Standard[19] borne before him. Altogether, almost half a million people pledged their opposition to Home Rule by signing the covenant or, in the case of women, the 'declaration'. They promised to

> stand by one another in defending . . . our cherished position of equal citizenship in the United Kingdom and in using all means . . . to defeat the present conspiracy to set up a Home Rule parliament in Dublin.[20]

Thousands more who could prove their Ulster origins signed in Ireland, England and Scotland.[21] It was all carefully choreographed.

At Westminster in January 1913, Carson tried to use parliamentary procedure to exclude the whole province of Ulster from the Home Rule Bill, but his amendment was defeated. Consequently, preparations for a breakaway provisional government and all that it involved in Ulster were stepped up dramatically.[22] On 13 January 1913, an illegal private army, the Ulster Volunteer Force, was formally established. Recruitment was limited to 100,000 men aged from 17 to 65 who had signed the covenant, the pure-blood loyalists. On the advice of Lord Roberts, Carson appointed the retired lieutenant-general Sir George Richardson to lead the Ulster Volunteers.[23] Richardson was in residence in Belfast within the month, and a series of parades were organised to introduce him to the volunteers. Sir Edward Carson boldly stated that the UVF was no longer a collection of unrelated units but, under the general's leadership, an army. At Antrim on 21 September, he warned:

> we have pledges and promises from some of the greatest generals in the [British] army, who have given their word that, when the time comes . . . they will come over and help us to keep the old flag flying.[24]

It was no empty boast. Lord Roberts' Academy would see to that.

The Ulster Unionists had other powerful and determined friends inside the Secret Elite, including Milner, Curzon, Balfour, Walter Long and Leo Amery, in addition to the entire Conservative Party, leading newspapers and influential industrialists. Like Carson, each played clearly defined roles in stirring the Ulstermen to a frenzy of fear and resistance against Asquith's government: an 'enemy' that would not listen to their pleas. Few outside the inner sanctum of the Secret Elite appreciated exactly how much control was vested in Alfred Milner, who emerged from the backrooms of manipulative politics to play a pivotal role.

No one was more influential, more determined and more willing to take action than Milner.[25] He wrote a 'very confidential' private letter to Carson on 9 December 1913 in which he pledged his total commitment to Ulster and offered his services as one who disbelieved in 'mere talk'. Connected as he was to all the organs of power, Milner knew precisely what the government intended and reassured Carson that 'they are just passing the time'.[26] The entire construct was a charade. No one in London intended to subvert the people of Ulster, but the possibility of an impending civil war had to be given substance to prepare for Plan B. Milner assured Carson that he would 'paralyse the arm which might be raised to strike you'. In other words, there were huge risks involved in unleashing dark forces throughout Ireland, but Milner reassured Carson that the British Army would not be used against Ulstermen. Carson had to control the UVF, and Milner had to control the army response. Read between the lines of this illuminating letter and you will understand the nature of the audacious plan. Milner and the Secret Elite knew that the government would not subvert Ulster no matter how it might seem. Most importantly, Milner promised to 'paralyse' any move by the army against the UVF. This was the Secret Elite's covenant with Ulster: we will guarantee your safety and integrity, and nullify the government's military authority in Ireland.[27] But the charade had to continue. And it did.

Words brought encouragement, but it was deeds that mattered. Milner's promise to Carson was backed by a vast Secret Elite fund.[28] Waldorf Astor, the émigré American millionaire and a member of the Secret Elite's inner core,[29] donated £30,000. His astonishing benevolence equated to £2.25 million in current money. Rudyard Kipling gave a similar donation.[30] Lord Rothschild contributed £10,000, as did the wealthy Duke of Bedford and Lord Iveagh, the multi-millionaire head of the Guinness family. Intriguingly, one contributor, 'C', was not identified, even in a very secret document, leaving fair speculation as to whom that might have been. The Secret Elite amassed over £100,000 (approximately £8 million today) for

Carson's work in Ulster, and its spending provoked great alarm. Milner also wanted to use parliamentary process to blunt the British military in Ireland, but no politician would follow that ploy.[31]

General Sir Henry Wilson, senior member of the Roberts Academy, was at that point director of military operations at the War Office and advisor to the government and the Committee of Imperial Defence. This was the same Sir Henry who had repeatedly reconnoitred Belgium for the Secret Elite, briefed Asquith, Grey, Lloyd George and Churchill during the Agadir incident, who was responsible for the British Expeditionary Force and knew the precise details of the plans for war with Germany. Like Lord Roberts, Henry Wilson was full of admiration for his friends in the UVF. From January 1914, though the British Army saw very little of him, he regularly slipped over to Ulster to hold secret meetings with the Unionist leaders and observe at close hand the UVF forces as they exercised. Incredibly, the director of military operations at the War Office in London was in cahoots with the very people in Ulster with whom his own troops might be in imminent conflict, and he had access to their plans and organisation.

Colonel Hacket Pain, a Boer War veteran under Lord Roberts' command, currently UVF chief of staff,[32] issued a secret programme on 7 February 1914 for full mobilisation of the UVF. An undated, unsigned memorandum headed 'The Coup' recommended 'a sudden, complete and paralysing blow'.[33] All rail links, telegraph, telephone and cable lines were to be severed, all roads into Ulster closed, and all British Army depots of arms, ammunition and military equipment seized, along with supply depots for British troops and the police. Weapons were only to be used if fired upon, but any attempt to arrest UVF commanders was to be forcibly resisted. It was a plan; armies have to have plans, and it leaked.

In March 1914, Ulster almost exploded, or so it appeared. The Unionists claimed that Liberals, including Churchill and Lloyd George, had concocted a spurious accusation that a plot had been hatched in Ulster to grab control of arms and ammunition in army stores. Churchill was deliberately provocative in a speech on 14 March at Bradford, where he warned of bloodshed in Ulster and threatened to put these grave matters 'to the proof'.[34] He ordered a squadron of battleships, cruisers and destroyers from the coast of Spain to Lamlash on the Isle of Arran, menacingly close to Belfast. Both political factions of the Secret Elite in London were vigorously and successfully stirring the Irish cauldron. At the same time, John Seeley, the secretary for war, drafted an instruction to Sir Arthur Paget, the commander-in-chief of the British Army in Ireland, to take special and urgent precautions to ensure that the stores in Armagh, Carrickfergus, Omagh and Enniskillen were properly guarded. Paget was yet another officer who had served and been promoted under Lord Roberts' command in the Boer War.

Rumours were spread that the British government intended to arrest the leaders of the Ulster Unionist Council, and *The Times* warned sternly that 'any man or government that increases the danger by blundering or hasty action will accept a terrible responsibility'.[35] All that followed has generally been brushed aside by historians as confusion and misunderstanding, muddled by exasperated Cabinet ministers and political opportunists. Not so. What followed was proof of the absolute authority of the Secret Elite over the British military establishment and its key officers.

Milner had promised that he would paralyse the arm raised against Ulster, and he did.

He had invited General Wilson to the exclusive seclusion of Brooks's Club as early as November 1913 to ensure he knew that the Secret Elite would look after its own. They were effectively plotting treason. Milner assured him that if any army officers resigned rather than order their troops in against the UVF, the incoming Conservative administration would ensure that they were fully reinstated.[36] Wilson duly informed colleagues so that it reached the ears of serving officers everywhere, precisely as intended. There was a similar move from Sir Edward Carson, who asked Milner to guarantee a fund for officers who decided to resign rather than 'violate their consciences'.[37] The seeds of rebellion took root.

When Paget was ordered to reinforce strategic points in Ulster against 'evil-disposed persons' who allegedly intended to raid British Army stores,[38] he did not consider the action justified.[39] Consequently, Paget was summoned to London on 18 and 19 March, where he received direct instructions from a sub-committee at the War Office that included Sir John French, another senior member of the Roberts Academy.[40] Immediately after the meeting, French discussed its conclusions with General Wilson, who, on that same night, dined with Milner and Carson, the men dedicated to protect Ulster against any move by the British Army. Why? Was Wilson informing them of the War Office decisions that had been leaked to him by Sir John French, or taking instruction on how to interpret them? Most likely it was both of these. There were no circumstances under which Milner, Carson, Wilson or, indeed, French, who was chief of the imperial general staff, would permit a move against Ulster. The most senior officers in the British Army actively intrigued with the men who controlled the UVF to prevent any attempt to enforce Home Rule.[41] Was this not treason?

Strangely, though the special sub-committee and the War Office were involved with Paget over the two-day period, no records were kept. Such action was highly suspect and for that reason mystery has always surrounded the 'mutiny' incident at the Curragh that was 'a consequence' of the meeting at the War Office.[42] On the 20th, Paget presented his subordinates in Ireland with an unprecedented opportunity to decide matters for themselves. Officers 'domiciled' in Ulster were to be allowed to absent themselves from duty during any forthcoming operations. Paget's exact words were that these officers 'would be permitted to disappear' until the Ulster crisis was resolved, then return to their posts 'as if nothing had happened'.[43]

The effect was electrifying but hardly surprising. Within hours of his return to Ireland, Paget telegrammed the War Office to say that 'Officer commanding the 5th Lancers states all officers except two, and one doubtful, are resigning their commissions today. I much fear the same conditions in 16th Lancers. Fear men will refuse to move.'[44] Less than five hours later, Paget sent a second telegram: 'Regret to report Brigadier and fifty-seven officers, 3rd Cavalry Brigade, prefer dismissal if ordered north.'[45]

Defiance swelled precisely as Milner intended. The wires in Ireland and Britain were hot with news about a mutiny at the Curragh. General Haig, commander in chief at Aldershot and a member of Roberts' Academy,[46] went to Downing Street to tell the prime minister that his own men strongly supported their fellow officers in Ireland.[47] Wilson, French, Paget and Haig, some of the most senior military figures of the day, sided against the government, but not one army officer was accused of treasonous action.

Politicians lied about the circumstances. Denial swirled above Westminster like a breaking storm. It is a matter of record that Richard Haldane made a statement in the House of Lords that the government had no intention of giving orders to the troops to intervene. These words were seen as a pledge that under no circumstances would the government use troops in Ulster. Haldane later illegally changed the Hansard proof-copy by altering the sentence to read 'no immediate intention'.[48] Everyone involved bent the truth to the Secret Elite's advantage.

Though Bonar Law denied it, he kept open communication with officers at the Curragh.[49] An anonymous telegram was sent from there to the Conservative leader at the Commons at 5.40 p.m. on 20 March that simply told him: 'General and all cavalry officers Curragh division resigned today.'[50] Bonar Law knew it would happen, as did Balfour, Milner, Carson, Lord Roberts, General Wilson and Sir John French. They had, after all, facilitated it. Discussions relating to the episode were not recorded, but Seeley made the unforgivable mistake of exposing the fact that the government condoned the conspiracy by signing a memo stating that the army would not be ordered to take up arms against Ulster. Sir John French made a similar mistake by initialling the document, and thus exposed his collusion. When news of the 'mutiny' broke and all hell was let loose in

Parliament, Seeley and French paid for their indiscretion and resigned. This conveniently deflected blame from the main conspirators. The Secret Elite's golden rule was never to put anything incriminating on paper, and if an instruction had to be written, ensure that it was burned afterwards.

The Curragh 'incident' was carefully staged proof that 'the arm raised against Ulster' could be paralysed. As usual, Milner's will prevailed. There was 'unparalleled fury' in Parliament that, according to Winston Churchill, 'shook the state to its foundations'.[51] In an ugly Westminster puppet-show controlled by the Secret Elite, their agents railed against one another and kept Ulster in the headlines. Between mid March and the end of July 1914, more than 700 parliamentary questions were raised over this action, blocking serious debate and causing such a backlog that Asquith was eventually forced to refuse to accept any more. But all eyes stayed fixed on Ulster.

And what of Churchill and Lloyd George, who had stirred alarm in provocative speeches at the height of the 'crisis'? Churchill's declaration at Bradford that 'there are worse things than bloodshed' was widely reported, and Lloyd George deliberately raised the hackles of Protestant Ulster in a tirade at Huddersfield on 21 March: 'Orangemen professed to be shocked that force should be used for setting up a great free self-governing Parliament in Ireland, but when did Ulster acquire detestation of coercion?'[52] Together, Churchill and Lloyd George created an atmosphere in which it was widely believed that the Liberal government was on the point of bullying Ulster into accepting Home Rule.[53] One half of the Secret Elite's political team was inciting bitterness and anger in Ulster while the other half was declaring its complete support and loyalty. The Curragh incident was brushed aside, excused as a 'misunderstanding', but the tensions in Ireland continued to rise towards boiling point.

Throughout the weeks of outrage and posturing, a more dangerous conspiracy unfolded, a conspiracy that could never have been successful without the knowledge and permission of several governments across Europe. Events were so coincidental that it is possible to wonder if the one did not deliberately conceal the other. In a story more cliff-hanging than any John Buchan adventure, the legend was that Major Fred Crawford, director of ordnance of the UVF,[54] procured twenty-four thousand modern rifles and over three million rounds of ammunition[55] under the noses of the German, Norwegian, Danish and British authorities, and landed them in a 'brilliant' operation the like of which Ulster had never seen.

The narrative of the gun-running episode was truly amazing. Crawford, another officer who had served and gained promotion under Lord Roberts' command in South Africa, spoke no German but 'found' an armaments supplier in Hamburg willing to sell him a vast quantity of rifles, bayonets and bullets. He was commissioned to buy these on behalf of the UVF. Four days before the Curragh 'incident', the UVF secured the services of a Norwegian collier, the SS *Fanny*. That accomplished, Crawford met with two members of the Secret Elite, Walter Long and Bonar Law, in London on 27 March, and delivered a secret letter from Sir Edward Carson. Long had access to the funds raised by Milner and the Secret Elite, and arranged for him to take ownership 'of a very large cheque'.[56] They shook his hand and wished him 'God speed and a successful issue'.[57] Crawford's evidence tied Bonar Law and Walter Long to the gun-running plot. The leader of His Majesty's opposition was directly involved in providing guns and ammunition for use against His Majesty's army in Ulster. Was that not treason? Had not others been summarily executed in past times for raising arms against the Crown? Indeed, yet this was part of the grand conspiracy that they dared not call treason. This time it was called 'Loyalty'. Crawford needed cash to buy ships at short notice and deal with unforeseen contingencies, of which there were several. The Secret Elite provided.

Once he had purchased the rifles in Germany, Crawford steered them through the Kiel Canal in a barge to rendezvous with the SS *Fanny* in the Baltic. Does anyone imagine that such a cargo could have passed unnoticed through the Kiel Canal in March 1914? During the transfer of weapons from the barge, Danish customs officers came on board and confiscated their papers, believing that their destination was Iceland, where, coincidentally, home-rulers sought independence from Denmark. Yet they managed to slip away into the night, thanks, according to Crawford, to the intervention of Psalm 90.[58] Reports of their arrest were printed in the daily papers, with *The Times* correctly stating that the destination of the guns was Belfast, not Iceland.[59] The UVF assumed that the plot had been a disastrous failure. Not so. Miraculously, Psalm 90 prevailed and the *Fanny* negotiated the English Channel, avoided any intervention from the Royal Navy and sailed round the Welsh coast to Tenby. Crawford was authorised to buy a second collier, the *Clyde Valley*, in Glasgow, to which the arms were transferred. After a further name change, the collier headed for Belfast Lough as the *Mountjoy II*.

Throughout the night of 24–25 April 1914, the UVF unloaded 216 tons of weapons and ammunition at Larne, Bangor and Donaghadee. At Larne, telephone lines were cut, roads blocked and railway lines closed. The town was locked down and, just to make sure that the guns were landed safely, a decoy ship sailed into Belfast Lough so that the Customs and Excise men had an excuse for their inaction in Larne. The weapons were dispersed around Ulster under the command of UVF assistant quartermaster General

Wilfrid Spender.[60] Seen as a rising star in the British Army, Spender had been through the staff college at Camberley, assisted Sir Henry Wilson at the War Office, and served on the Committee of Imperial Defence. With no ties whatsoever to Ulster, he inexplicably gave up his glittering military career in 1913 to become a renegade with the UVF.

Were it not an act of treason in itself, the landing of the UVF guns would have warranted a special award for exemplary planning. The police were physically blocked from the docks and Customs officers boldly refused permission to examine the cargo. It was a tremendous coup for the Ulster Volunteers. Carson in London received a coded one-word telegram: 'Lion', which signalled that Ulster was now armed. Lord Roberts read about the success in special editions of the morning newspapers and rushed round to congratulate Carson in person.[61] More pertinently, the whole process was completed under the knowing eyes of the authorities in Germany, Denmark, Dublin and London. Reduced to a single headline, Germany had armed Ulster.

Every action causes a reaction, and the sight of an armed Ulster precipitated a military response from the south. A new, young generation of Irish nationalists regarded the Irish parliamentary party of John Redmond with ill-disguised contempt. Redmond was an Empire loyalist who seemed to have more in common with Sir Edward Carson than he did with the mass of Irishmen he presumed to represent. Sinn Fein, the Republican nationalist movement formed in 1905 to seek an end to British rule in Ireland, accused him and his party of being subservient to English political party considerations and actively detrimental to the best interests of Ireland.[62] He maintained great faith in the British Empire and steadfastly refused to recognise its capacity for brutality.[63] Happy to play the parliamentary game, constrain radicalism and acknowledge the king emperor, Redmond danced to a Secret Elite air.

In November 1913, totally disenchanted with Redmond, a disparate group of nationalists set up the Irish Volunteer movement of some 170,000 men.[64] But, significantly, they lacked weapons, military experience and united leadership. Two opposing forces are needed for a civil war, and in that aspect the Irish Volunteers were useful to the Secret Elite, but they had to move quickly to take control of the movement. In a late, desperate move, John Redmond forced its provisional committee to accept his nomination of 25 new members.[65] Civil War could hardly break out if only one side had weapons, so the Secret Elite moved to arm the nationalist volunteers.

Ponder, please, the main protagonist, the man who was chosen by them to provide guns for the south: Erskine Childers. Author of *The Riddle of the Sands* and arch advocate of Britain's so-called 'military unpreparedness' turned into a gun-runner? The man whose 1903 book concluded that Germany was 'pre-eminently fitted to undertake an invasion of Great Britain' and that Britain was ill prepared to prevent it[66] emerged in 1914 as an enemy of the state. How likely was that?

The unqualified success of his spy thriller brought the Cambridge-educated Childers into contact with the like-minded defender of the Empire Lord Roberts. The novel provided Roberts and his National Service League with a valuable tool to excite fear and anti-German sentiment. Childers insisted his story was true, the names of the characters having merely been altered, and advocated that every man in Britain should be trained for service in either the army or navy. The book ran to three print runs in 1903, two in 1904 and 1905, and was reprinted again in 1907, 1908, 1910 and 1911.[67] Winston Churchill praised *The Riddle of the Sands*, admitting that it influenced the Admiralty's decision to establish three completely new naval bases to deal with the so-called German naval threat. Erskine Childers was a champion of the British Establishment. In his earlier book, *In the Ranks of the C.I.V.*, about his active service in the Boer War with the City Imperial Volunteers, Childers sang the praises of Lord Roberts and extolled his bravery and his popularity among the rank-and-file soldiers.[68] Later, in writing the preface for Childers' book *War and the Arme Blanche*, Roberts reciprocated the compliment:

> . . . no one has dealt so exhaustively and so logically with this aspect of cavalry in war as Mr Childers. He has gone thoroughly into the achievements of our cavalry in South Africa . . . In conclusion I would ask you, my brother officers, in whatever part of the Empire you are serving, and whatever branch, to read this book.[69]

It was a ringing endorsement from Britain's 'greatest living soldier'.

Childers' background was elitist and refined. He went to a private boarding school with Lionel Curtis and Basil Williams of Milner's famed Kindergarten. Williams, a member of the Secret Elite,[70] was his lifelong friend, as was Churchill's personal assistant and close friend Eddie Marsh. Childers' cousin and mentor, Hugh Childers, had, in recent years, been home secretary and chancellor of the Exchequer in the Conservative government. Thomas Erskine, the lord chancellor, was his ancestor. Childers was held in such high esteem by the Secret Elite that he was invited to write volume three of the *Times History of the South African War* in conjunction with Basil Williams and Leo Amery. He visited America in 1903 and wrote 'there were no limits to the possibilities of an alliance of the English-speaking races'.[71] It was the vocabulary of the Pilgrims. Childers was steeped in the traditions of upper-middle-class England, loyalty to the king and defence of the Empire. Although not named by Carroll Quigley as a member of the Secret Elite, he was exceedingly close to many at its heart. For Childers, the growth, development and expansion of the British Empire represented the best possible solution for all the economic and social problems facing the nation. Childers abhorred egalitarianism,[72] and his philosophy was close to that of Milner and the Round Table. His friendships, background, philosophy and writings marked him out as a man who was highly regarded by the Secret Elite.

Childers believed that Ireland's peace and prosperity was intrinsically linked to, and best assured by, remaining part of the United Kingdom. Yet according to his biographer, Andrew Boyle, this staunch British patriot became involved in gun-running for Republican rebels because, 'suddenly, as if dazzled by a blinding vision, the views of Childers changed almost overnight'.[73] Astonishing.

He disappeared to Ireland in the spring of 1911 to hold discussions with leading industrialists, government officials, Unionists and Home-Rulers. Subsequently, Childers wrote a treatise in favour of a Home-Rule structure in Ireland, more Liberal, more understanding of the Catholic position and openly critical of Empire loyalists with whom he suddenly appeared to be completely at odds. Taken at face value, his Framework of Home Rule demonstrated his conversion from an anti-German, British Empire loyalist, to a rebel Empire-breaker, yet he retained his important associations with individuals close to the Secret Elite. It was as if he had rebranded his philosophy to appeal to a new audience. Crucially, it proved to be a passport into the trust of the Irish Volunteers.

Early in May 1914, Childers and a group of friends met at the plush Mayfair home of Alice Stopford Green, a house that had echoed with the conversation of many of the most distinguished political and literary figures of the age, including Winston Churchill, James Bryce and Lord Morley.[74] Alice, the widow of an Oxford University history professor, was in close contact with influential men within the British Establishment and Secret Elite. Others at the meeting included Sir Roger Casement, Captain George Fitzhardinge Berkeley, Lord Ashbourne, Sir Alexander Lawrence, Mary Spring Rice and Conor O'Brien. Like Stopford Green and Childers, they all belonged to a privileged class. They conspired to raise £1,523 (a not inconsiderable sum worth over £120,000 today) to buy weapons for the Irish Volunteers.[75] While generous, it paled in comparison to the £100,000 raised effortlessly by Milner for the UVF in the north.

Born into a prosperous Irish Protestant family, Alice Stopford Green was the daughter of the rector of Kells and granddaughter of the Church of Ireland Bishop of Meath. Professor Quigley identified her nephew, Robert J. Stopford, as a member of the Secret Elite.[76] She was a close friend of Viscount Bryce, former British ambassador at Washington and a president of the Pilgrims Society. Dublin-born Sir Roger Casement was at that time a distinguished British Foreign Office diplomat,[77] though his later involvement in Irish politics cost him his life. Lord Ashbourne came from a line of wealthy Protestant, Anglo-Irish landed gentry. Mary Spring Rice was the daughter of Lord Monteagle. Her great-grandfather had been chancellor of the Exchequer and secretary of state for war. She was the niece of Sir Cecil Spring-Rice, the British ambassador to the United States and a Pilgrim. Conor O'Brien, cousin of Mary Spring Rice, was the son of Sir Edward O'Brien, a wealthy Irish Protestant landowner. Sir Alexander Lawrence was the son of Brigadier General Sir Henry Montgomery Lawrence. His late uncle had been viceroy of India. Captain George Fitzhardinge Berkeley, the son of Major George Sackville Berkeley, attended the prestigious Wellington College then Oxford University, where he was awarded a Blue for cricket. This was not a typical terrorist cell.

Childers and an accomplice, Darrell Figgis, son of an Irish-born tea merchant in Ceylon, went to Hamburg, where, despite a German ban on the export of weapons to Ireland, they purchased a quantity of virtually obsolete rifles. It was no coincidence that the arms deal was conducted through the same agent who supplied the Ulster Volunteers months earlier. Several weeks later, in July 1914, Childers and his wife Molly sailed their yacht, *Asgard*, to pick up the armaments. Captain Gordon Shephard, a close friend, helped crew. Educated at Eton and Sandhurst, Captain Shephard was an experienced sailor and a member of the prestigious Royal Cruising Club. Immediately after the gun-running mission, he returned to his post with the Royal Flying Corps. By the time of his death in action in 1918, he was a much-decorated brigadier general in the British Army and the highest-ranking officer in the Flying Corps to die in action.[78] Such profiles did not match known terrorists.

A second yacht, the *Kelpie*, owned and crewed by Conor O'Brien, assisted *Asgard* with the gun-running. They rendezvoused with a German ship off the Belgian coast and transferred the weapons at sea. *Asgard* sailed back to Ireland through the assembled ranks of the British fleet at Portsmouth. A destroyer allegedly bore down on them at full speed, but they were not ordered to heave-to. No one appeared to consider it suspicious that the yacht was stacked at every point with rifles and lay extremely low in the water. They endured dense fog and were hit by the 'worst storm seen in the Irish Sea for 30 years'.[79] Childers had to lash himself to the wheel to hold course, so the story goes, but, like Churchill's adventures in South Africa, these gallant deeds lacked independent corroboration. To heroic acclaim from the nationalists, Childers landed his tranche of the consignment at Howth near Dublin on Sunday, 26 July 1914. At the same time, far to the east, the Russians began their secret mobilisations against Germany. Only the Foreign Office and their Secret Elite minders knew of both events.

Under the guise of an organised Sunday 'drill', the volunteers marched in broad daylight from Dublin to Howth to collect the weapons. Police and coastguards were warned off. It looked like a re-run of the UVF experience at Larne until soldiers of the King's Own Scottish Borderers, having failed to apprehend the gun runners or seize their weapons, clashed with a jeering, taunting crowd on Bachelor's Walk by the Liffey. Stones and insults were thrown, and the troops fired into the crowd, killing three and injuring thirty-eight.[80] Asquith was shocked by the news, not of the landing of the arms but of the civilian deaths, which he realised would be deeply resented in Dublin.[81] They were.

When the *Kelpie* returned to Irish waters with her tranche of weapons, Conor O'Brien was reluctant to land them directly at Kilcoole because 'he and his yacht were well known to the authorities there'. The weapons were transferred at sea to another yacht, *Chotah*, which was owned by Sir Thomas Myles, president of the Royal College of Surgeons in Ireland. Myles became honorary surgeon to King George V and was awarded the prestigious Order of the Bath. Assisting him in the gun-running was the Hon. James Creed Meredith, KC, the son of Sir James Creed Meredith, a wealthy Protestant Anglo-Irish landowner and deputy grand master and treasurer of the Grand Lodge of the Freemasons of Ireland. Trust us, please. It is beyond our capabilities to make this up. The roll call of honour for gun-runners against the Crown was completed when Colonel Fred Crawford of the UVF was awarded the CBE.

The disparity between the gun-running in Ulster, with 24,000 modern rifles landed at Larne, and the 1,500 aged weapons that made it to Howth, was very obvious. However, if carefully crafted, the subjective historian and the biased journalist, the corrupt politician and the prejudiced observer could say that both sides were armed for civil war. Reduced to a single headline, Germany had armed the Nationalist Volunteers.

By July, the words 'civil war' and 'inevitable' hung around Britain like the proverbial albatross. King George V was certain of it because 'the cry of civil war is on the lips of the most responsible and sober-minded of my people'.[82] He was asked to call an all-party conference on Home Rule, but his intervention was to no purpose. There was no spirit of compromise, no last-minute reprieve. The time had not yet come. Edward Carson added to the drama of the moment: 'I see no hopes of peace. I see nothing at present but darkness and shadows. We shall have once more to assert the manhood of our race.'[83] This was melodrama of the highest order, for there was no possibility of Ireland bursting into flames as long as Carson continued to keep Ulster in close check. The opposing Irish Volunteers had neither the weapons nor the will to wage a debilitating war on Ulster. The British Army would not have permitted it. Civil war was an illusion conjured by politicians and newspapers loyal to the Secret Elite. They and they alone were in control. The hopelessness and tension that filled the spring and early summer of 1914 were genuine. The despair of the Ulster Protestants and the well-versed concerns voiced in Parliament were mostly sincere. Scaremongering was a strategic ploy, for in the realm of 'higher politics' the few connected to the Secret Elite knew precisely what they had done. Do not lose sight of the fact that these individuals had been planning war with Germany for over a decade.

Looking back with the advantage of hindsight, something disturbing emerges from these episodes, something that jars. These folklore 'heroes' of both the north and the south of Ireland who defied the Crown, armed civilians and gave credence to a coming civil war enjoyed most unusual careers thereafter. Immediately war with Germany was declared, the Admiralty telegraphed the headquarters of the Irish Volunteers in Dublin directly and requested that Erskine Childers make urgent contact with them. The Admiralty Intelligence Department knew where to find Erskine Childers, and they knew about the *Asgard* and the gun-running. It was organised by and through them. How else could the yacht have passed through the midst of the greatest fleet ever assembled without being stopped and searched? Winston Churchill, prompted by his personal secretary Eddie Marsh, one of Childers' closest friends, had personally ordered his naval staff to contact Childers, the man who knew Germany's North Sea coastline in great detail.[84] One can only wonder what the Irish Volunteers would have thought had they seen Erskine Childers shaking hands with Winston Churchill and saluting Admiral Lord Jellicoe on 22 August 1914, before stepping into his own office in the Admiralty.[85]

What was it really about? We know that the Secret Elite and the Committee of Imperial Defence had long been prepared for war against Germany, and that it was of the utmost importance that Germany appeared to take the first steps. What would have happened had General Moltke decided to abandon the well-advertised Schlieffen Plan and attacked France on a different frontier? Had Belgium's neutrality been honoured, what could the Secret Elite have done? There had to be a Plan B, an alternative scenario that would create such an outrage that war with Germany would follow. Consider the following. Germany had supplied both sides of the

Irish divide with arms. The guns and ammunition had been sourced in Hamburg and were all traceable back there. Imagine the outcry if a cowardly explosion in a Belfast lodge or a Dublin pub had slain dozens of innocents in early August 1914, or rogue gunmen had slaughtered unarmed civilians in the name of either cause? Blame would have quickly focused on the fall guy who had allowed the illicit weapons deals to go through: the kaiser. Why was so little made of Germany's part in the gun-running? Remember the covenanter motto: 'put your trust in God and keep your powder dry'. The Secret Elite were able to keep their powder dry because they did not have to revert to Plan B.

Summary: Chapter 25 – Ireland – Plan B

- The Secret Elite had long known that the Schlieffen Plan meant large numbers of German troops would pass through Belgium. This breach of Belgian neutrality would become the *casus belli*, the justification for war. If the Germans avoided Belgium, the Secret Elite required a fall-back position. Ireland became Plan B.
- Age-old religious animosities were deliberately stirred in order to bring the Protestant majority in Ulster into a state of potential conflict with the predominantly Catholic south. Both sides were armed by the Secret Elite with weapons purchased in Germany. If required, 'civil war' would have been declared and Germany blamed. At every stage, the Secret Elite were in control.
- The introduction of a Home Rule Bill was used to generate unrest. Edward Carson was sent to Ulster to take charge. He created a large Protestant paramilitary wing, the Ulster Volunteer Force, comprising some 100,000 men who had signed the covenant. It was a large and illegal private army that the British Establishment actively supported.
- Alfred Milner assured Carson that he would not allow the British Army to take up arms against the UVF. Army officers at the Curragh were encouraged to refuse to move against the UVF. Senior figures in the army, the government and the opposition front bench colluded to make this possible.
- Secret Elite funds were used to procure weapons and ammunition in Germany. UVF officers brought them by sea to the north-west coast of Ireland and distributed them throughout Ulster. Officials in the police, coastguard and British Army were ordered to turn a blind eye.
- In the south, a large nationalist Catholic force formed spontaneously as a reaction to the arming of the UVF. Through John Redmond, the Secret Elite moved quickly to ensure their control over it. Erskine Childers, an agent of the Secret Elite who had earlier infiltrated the

nationalist movement and won their trust, proceeded to arm them. He and a group of upper-class Protestant friends with close links to the British Establishment and Secret Elite funded the purchase of weapons and ammunition from Germany, and delivered them to the south in their yachts.

- The scene was set for civil war should the Secret Elite need it to provide the *casus belli*. In addition, the entire venture provided a convenient distraction and smokescreen behind which preparations for war were rapidly progressed.

CHAPTER 26

August 1914 – Of Neutrality and Just Causes

In the last week of an epoch that was rushing towards oblivion, the warmongers in London, Paris and St Petersburg forced the pace with unrelenting determination. Localised Austrian retribution on Serbia had deliberately been transformed by the Secret Elite into an altogether greater cause for carnage. Diplomacy had been made to fail. Dishonest men could now throw up their hands in horror and cry 'inevitable' war. Democracy was contemptuously abused by hidden forces that had the political and financial power to manipulate public opinion. Propaganda misrepresented motive, moulding fear into hysteria and empowering the madness that swept reason aside. The great plan for war against Germany that would establish the primacy of the British Empire was almost complete. The last requirement was the 'just cause' to win over and inspire the British people.

On Saturday, 1 August, Isvolsky sent a telegram from Paris to St Petersburg:

> The French War Minister informed me, in hearty high spirits, that the Government have firmly decided on war, and begged me to endorse the hope of the French General Staff that all efforts will be directed against Germany . . .[1]

France had 'firmly decided on war' almost 24 hours before Germany had announced mobilisation or declared war on Russia. General Joffre was straining at the leash. He sent Poincaré a personal ultimatum that he would no longer accept responsibility for the command of the French army unless a general mobilisation was ordered.[2] Poincaré did not need much encouragement. At 4 p.m. that day, telegrams ordering the French general mobilisation were sent from the central telegraph office in Paris. By that point, Serbia, Austria, Russia, France and Great Britain had begun military measures of one sort or another. Germany alone among the powers concerned had not yet done so.[3]

That afternoon, the German leaders gathered at the kaiser's palace in Berlin. Bethmann and von Jagow arrived with sensational news from Lichnowsky in London: the British government had just given a promise that France would remain neutral under a British guarantee. Hugely relieved, the kaiser called for champagne. He sent a telegram to King George: 'If Britain guarantees the neutrality of France, I will abandon all action against her.'[4] The king summoned Grey to Buckingham Palace that Saturday evening to help frame a response. King George replied: 'I think there must be some misunderstanding of a suggestion that passed in friendly conversation between Prince Lichnowsky and Sir Edward Grey.'[5] There was no British guarantee of French neutrality. It had simply been another delaying tactic, a ruse to gain whatever advantage.

At 5 p.m., after waiting in vain for twenty-four hours for an answer to his telegram demanding that the Russians stop all military movements on his border, the kaiser ordered general mobilisation. Germany was the last of the continental powers to take that irrevocable step. How does that possibly fit with the claim that Germany started the First World War? An hour later in St Petersburg, Pourtales, the German ambassador, went to Sazonov and asked him three times if the Russian government would halt the mobilisation. In the full knowledge that it meant a European war, Sazonov replied that it would continue. Count Pourtales handed him Germany's declaration of war and burst into tears.[6] Time: 6 p.m., 1 August.

Germany's declaration was an understandable reaction but a tactical mistake. Russia had been mobilising with the definite intent of attacking Germany, but Sazonov had been instructed that he should not make an actual declaration of war. The vital message oft repeated by Grey to Poincaré and Sazonov was that France and Russia must, as far as possible, conceal their military preparations and intent on war until Germany had swallowed the bait. The British people would never support the aggressor in a European war, and it was imperative that Germany should be made to appear the aggressor. It was akin to bullies goading, threatening and ganging up on a single boy in the school playground, but the moment he had the audacity to defend himself, he was to blame.

What else could Germany have done? She was provoked into a struggle for life or death. It was a stark choice: await certain destruction or strike out to defend herself. Kaiser Wilhelm had exposed his country to grave danger and almost lost the one precious advantage Germany had by delaying countermeasures to the Russian mobilisation in the forlorn hope of peace. The German army depended entirely upon lightning success at the very start of a war on two fronts. Germany's only effective defence was through offence.

On 1 August, the London *Daily News* declared:

> The greatest calamity in history is upon us . . . At this moment our fate is being sealed by hands that we know not, by motives alien to our interests, by influences that if we knew we should certainly repudiate . . .[7]

The *Daily News* had summed up the situation perfectly. The British people knew nothing of the hands that were sealing their fate. They would never have gone to war in support of Russia. Indeed, in a war between Russia and Germany, there was every chance that the man in the street would support Germany. Public opinion was not clamouring for war; every liberal, radical and socialist paper in the kingdom stood against participation in a European conflict. Nor was there any obvious sign of rabid jingoism. Yet.

The Secret Elite knew precisely what would move public opinion: Belgium. If Britain's excuse for entering the war was focused well away from Russia, then Grey's final requirement would fall into place and the lock would be sprung. The people would clamour for war if the cause became the defence of 'gallant little Belgium' against a contemptible German invasion. It was Belgian neutrality that would furnish him with the best excuse for entering the war.

Grey turned Belgian neutrality into his cause célèbre. He told the German ambassador, Prince Lichnowsky, that it would be extremely difficult to restrain public feeling in Britain if Germany violated Belgian neutrality. Lichnowsky asked whether Grey could 'give me a definite declaration of the neutrality of Great Britain on the condition that we [Germany] respected Belgian neutrality'.[8] It was an astonishing suggestion, an enormous concession and one that could have spared Britain and Belgium the horrors of war. Lichnowsky was prepared to concede exactly what Grey claimed the British Cabinet wanted. Belgian sovereignty would be respected in exchange for a promise of Britain's neutrality. Duplicitous as ever, Grey blurred the issue and avoided an honest reply, reassuring Lichnowsky that 'for the present there was not the slightest intention of proceeding to hostilities against Germany'.[9]

When the kaiser read the diplomatic note from his ambassador, he wrote in the margin:

> My impression is that Mr Grey is a false dog who is afraid of his own meanness and false policy, but who will not come out into the open against us, preferring to let himself be forced by us to do it.[10]

Right again, Wilhelm, though Grey still had two objectives: to gain as much time as possible for Russia and to turn the public in favour of war.

Astonishingly, Lichnowsky's proposal on neutrality was never revealed to the Cabinet or House of Commons. Had it been, a significant majority would likely have agreed to it. Grey's deception might never have come to light had Chancellor Bethmann not exposed this offer in the Reichstag on 4 August:

> We have informed the British Government, that as long as Great Britain remains neutral, our fleet will not attack the northern coast of France, and that we will not violate the territorial integrity and independence of Belgium. These assurances I now repeat before the world . . .[11]

Grey ensured that every offer of peace and neutrality from Berlin was rejected or suppressed, while at the same time his Cabinet colleagues were informed that he was outraged by the way in which Germany had 'put aside all attempts at accommodation while marching steadily to war'.[12]

Inside Asquith's Cabinet, Charles Hobhouse saw a marked change in the foreign secretary at this time. Hobhouse wrote in his diary that from the moment it became clear that Germany would violate Belgian neutrality, Grey, who was 'sincerity itself, became violently pro-French and eventually the author of our rupture with Germany'.[13] Grey became violently pro-French? How little Hobhouse and most of his Cabinet colleagues knew of the real Grey, knew of his years of secret planning for war on Germany, knew of the agreements he had put in place with France. Their ignorance was, to an extent, understandable. On four separate occasions over the previous two years, Grey and Asquith stood at the despatch box in the House of Commons and solemnly assured Parliament that Britain was entirely free from any secret obligations to any other European country.[14] In a private letter to his ambassador in Paris, Grey noted: 'there would be a row in Parliament here if I had used words which implied the possibility of a secret engagement unknown to Parliament all these years committing us to a European war . . .'[15]

Hobhouse was not witnessing a sudden change in Grey's attitude but an unmasking, the revelation of his real commitment to a cause that could not be named: the Secret Elite's war to destroy Germany. Hobhouse saw Grey in a new light as the 'author of our rupture with Germany'.[16] Did he belatedly realise that Sir Edward Grey bore heavy responsibility for the First World War?

Clearly, Grey was poisoning the Cabinet atmosphere with pro-French, anti-German rhetoric. Crucially, he now placed Belgium at the centre of the heated discussions. The issue was suddenly about loyalty to Belgium and about Britain's standing as a Great Power, which would be damaged for ever if she stood aside while Belgium was 'crushed'. He diverted the arguments away from Russian mobilisation, misrepresented the kaiser's intentions and made no mention of Serbia. He cited the treaty dating from 1839, falsely claiming that it obliged Britain to take up arms in defence of Belgium. Asquith and Churchill agreed, but Grey met strong resistance from the majority of the Cabinet.[17]

He later claimed that the question of Belgian neutrality emerged for the first time at the end of July 1914. Long after the war ended, when the Secret Elite had to mask and carefully reinterpret their pre-war actions, he wrote that Chancellor Bethmann's very mention of Belgium on 29 July 'lit up an aspect that had not been looked at',[18] as if it had suddenly dawned on him and the Foreign Office that Belgium would play a strategic part in a continental war. It was an outrageous lie, and one that has been perpetuated ever since. Sir Hew Strachan, professor of the history of war and a fellow of All Souls at Oxford University, gave a different interpretation: 'But Belgium was not decided that the invader would be German. Right up until the war's outbreak it continued to espouse a policy of pure neutrality, treating all its neighbours as potential enemies.'[19] That is profoundly untrue. Belgium was in cahoots with the entente countries, most specifically Britain. Belgium was not some unknown and forgotten corner of Europe that history bypassed on a regular basis. It had long been a battlefield in continental wars, and sat in a natural basin between the Jura Mountains and the English Channel. Belgium was the northern gateway to Paris or, indeed, Berlin.

Confidential Belgian documents, to which we made detailed reference in Chapter 6, completely refuted Grey's nonsense and proved that top-secret military agreements between Britain and Belgium had been in place since 1906, when the Committee of Imperial Defence and the War Office began the process of modernising the British Army. This accord included comprehensive arrangements for military cooperation and elaborate plans for the landing of British troops[20] who were scheduled to disembark at Dunkirk and Calais in such numbers that half of the British Army could be transported to Belgium within eight days of mobilisation. The British supply base was to be moved from the French coast to Antwerp in Belgium as soon as the North Sea had been cleared of German warships. Lieutenant Colonel Barnardiston, the British military attaché to Brussels, had emphasised to the chief of the Belgian general staff, Major-General Ducarme, that these arrangements had to be kept 'absolutely confidential' and known only to his minister and the British general staff.[21]

In 1912, when the likelihood of a European war over the Balkans became a serious possibility, Anglo-Belgian military arrangements had been further refined. Secret guidebooks for the British military dated that year contained highly detailed maps of Belgian towns, villages and rural areas, including railway stations, church steeples suitable for observation posts, oil depots, roads, canals and bridges. British–Belgian military tactics had been worked out in fine detail, including the role of intermediary officers, interpreters, English translations of Belgian regulations, hospital accommodation for the British wounded and more. Barnardiston's successor as British military attaché to Brussels, Lieutenant-Colonel Bridges, confirmed to the Belgians that Britain had an army composed of six divisions of infantry and eight brigades of cavalry – 160,000 men in all – and that 'everything was ready' to go.[22] Remarkably, the minutes of the meeting between Colonel Bridges and the Belgian chief of staff in 1912, General Jungbluth, stated that the British 'would have landed her troops in Belgium in all circumstances',[23] with or without Belgian consent, if Germany attacked France. Where would that have placed the sanctity of Belgian neutrality? By February 1914, the rate of exchange for payment of British soldiers fighting in Belgium had been fixed; that was some six months ahead of the conflict.[24]

Britain and Belgium had been deeply involved in joint military preparations against Germany for at least eight years. Bethmann's honourable proposal on 29 July[25] regarding the integrity of Belgium brought no sudden and unexpected enlightenment as Sir Edward Grey would have us believe. It brought him a tangible excuse. He had, from that moment on, diplomatic 'proof' of Germany's 'ill-intentions'. On 1 August, Grey telegraphed Brussels urging the Belgian leaders to maintain their absolute neutrality.[26] It was essential that Belgium kept up the charade of neutrality until the very last, in order to provide Grey with his trump card.

Belgian 'neutrality' was a sham. Grey knew perfectly well that she would side with Britain, France and Russia against Germany. It had long been so arranged. Northcliffe's newspapers would ensure that the public outrage turned against Germany with a truly spiteful venom, and the Secret Elite could start their war. Sir Edward Grey was fully aware that Belgium had actually been mobilising her armed forces for almost a week, under the guise of self-protection against anyone who might try to cross the Belgian border. To this effect, a mobilisation order had been issued by the Belgian government on 24 July, and on 28 July three classes of army reserves were called up.[27] The Belgians were as ready as they could be to repulse the German invader. It was no coincidence that this 'neutral' little country began military preparations against Germany on the very same day that both Russia and France began theirs.[28]

The Secret Elite elevated the independence and sovereignty of Belgium to a higher level of moral obligation, just as they had with Serbia's 'dignity and sovereignty'. Such altruistic and chivalrous sentiments suited their public stance, while behind the scenes they manipulated, dictated to, interfered with and essentially controlled these little 'independent' countries. It was no different from the manipulation of Russia, which they exerted through their puppets Isvolsky and Sazonov, and France through Poincaré. The hypocrisy of Grey and the Secret Elite knew no bounds. They were fully aware that Germany would, by necessity, have to cross Belgium in its defence against France. Such temporary use of a right of way was very different from a permanent and wrongful invasion. There were precedents: during the Boer War, British troops were permitted passage across neutral Portuguese territory to fight in South Africa.[29] The scale of the British hypocrisy over Belgium was indeed breathtaking. The armed forces of British imperialism had been trampling uninvited over countries across the world for centuries. Such British action was, of course, always regarded as a self-evident right.

Grey's imperious stance was given backbone by his Foreign Office mentor, Sir Eyre Crowe, who provided him with answers to all of the objections voiced in Cabinet in a secret and detailed memo.[30] Sir Eyre Crowe's commitment to the Secret Elite cause was so absolute that he carried the conviction of the infallible zealot. He rejected the argument that Britain should not engage in a European war by pointing out that unless they were used, the maintenance of an all-powerful navy and dedicated expeditionary force was nothing less than an abuse of resources forced on the country at enormous and wasteful expense. Crowe dismissed the signs of commercial panic in the City and in stock markets across Europe as part of Germany's well-laid plans for war. He accused German financial houses of being 'notoriously' in daily contact with the German embassy and plotting the downfall of the British Empire. This was somewhat precious given the close links between the British government and the House of Rothschild, Baring and Lazards. Neutrality he dismissed as a dishonourable act; the entente was praised as a moral bond. Eyre Crowe repudiated the claim that 'England cannot in any circumstance go to war' by stating that any other action would be political suicide. His parting shot was a rally call to arms: 'I feel confident that our duty and our interest will be seen to lie in standing by France in her hour of need. France has not sought the quarrel. It has been forced upon her.'[31] These were the values that the British Cabinet was asked to accept: a litany of lies that were repeated so often they became accepted as fact.

Could the Secret Elite placemen convince the Cabinet that Britain had no option but war? Asquith confessed in a letter to his beloved Venetia that he had a problem. The Cabinet was not merely split on the question of going to war; it was massively against such an epoch-changing step. No one should underestimate the enormity of the challenge that Grey and Asquith faced, even though Northcliffe and *The Times* and all of the powerful agencies that operated behind the political screen backed them to the hilt. This was a Cabinet that had no intention of going to war, or of approving a war; a Cabinet that represented a political party that would never vote for war and a population that had no concept of the war that was planned for them. If ever a disparate group required careful man-management it was Asquith's Liberal Cabinet. How he, Grey, Haldane, Churchill and Lloyd George achieved the Secret Elite objective remains a testament to how good men can be worn down by expectation, pressure, false information and inflamed public reaction to turn their back on what they know to be right.

Asquith convened a special Cabinet meeting on Sunday, 2 August 1914. Had a vote on Britain's involvement in a European war been taken at the outset, only the known stalwarts would have been in favour. The other campaign-hardened political veterans were set against it. Lord Morley complained that they had known nothing of the extent of the military and naval agreements with the French. They began to appreciate that 'a web of obligations, which they had been assured were not obligations, had been spun round them while they slept'.[32] But realisation dawned slowly, and Asquith was sufficiently astute to avoid rushing to a decision by a show of hands.

Those anxious, heavy-hearted, loyal Liberals, whose consciences and years of commitment to peace made the meeting almost unbearable, struggled with the enormity that was suddenly presented to them. Sir Edward Grey kept secret the German proposal on neutrality. It was never voiced as an option. Had Cabinet ministers been given all relevant information and time to consider the options, discuss the implications with significant others in their constituencies and prepare themselves properly, matters would likely have taken a very different turn. Instead they had to listen to situation reports from Berlin, Paris, St Petersburg, Vienna and Belgium that caught them by surprise and were presented in a manner that vilified Germany.

Talk of resignations – three, perhaps four – darkened the mood and threatened to tear the Cabinet apart. Asquith faced the prospect of having to form a coalition government with the Conservative and Unionist opposition. It had no appeal, but if needs dictated Asquith knew he could count on them to go to war. He had in his pocket a letter from the Conservative leaders Bonar Law, Lord Lansdowne and Austen Chamberlain that promised unhesitating support for the government in any measures that were required to assist Russia and France in their war against Germany. Their view was that it would be 'fatal to the honour and security of the United Kingdom to hesitate in supporting France and Russia at the present juncture'.[33] It was a letter that had been written at the suggestion of Balfour in the inner circle of the Secret Elite. Just as Sazonov was provided with reassurance by the Secret Elite agents, so Asquith and Grey were assured that they were not alone.

Asquith begged Cabinet ministers John Burns,[34] Sir John Simon, Lord Beauchamp, Joseph Pease and others who were clearly swithering not to make a rash decision. He implored them to wait at least until Sir Edward Grey had addressed Parliament. The semblance of a united Cabinet, however illusory, would have a greater impact on the general public than a clear division of opinion, and would avoid the identification of figureheads around whom opponents of the war might rally. The Secret Elite would not entertain any unwelcome diversions as they took the final decisive step to push Britain into the war. The non-interventionists, those who did not want any involvement at all, were not themselves united. Some would accept war if Belgium was violated. The pros and cons of neutrality were thrashed around the Cabinet table. Eventually, a loose consensus agreed that Sir Edward Grey would tell the House of Commons that Britain could not stand aside if Belgium was invaded, that France would be given maritime support, and Germany would be advised of this.[35]

The opening Cabinet session lasted for three hours, from 11 a.m. to 2 p.m., at which point Asquith scribbled a note to Venetia: 'We are on the brink of a split.'[36] The prime minister was renowned for his excessive drinking, but he was no dupe. He above all knew the enormous hurdle faced in turning the Cabinet round to accept war, not least because he was certain that a good three-quarters of his own party stood for 'absolute non-interference at any price'.[37] He did everything possible to avoid putting a decision to the vote. And his tactic worked.

Churchill was by far the most eager for war. Asquith wrote: 'Winston very bellicose and demanding immediate mobilisation.'[38] The Cabinet had refused to give him permission to proceed with the mobilisation of the fleet, but Churchill sent the order anyway.

Sir Edward Grey was not to be outdone. At 3 p.m. on that Sunday afternoon, during an interval between the two Cabinet meetings, he called the French ambassador, Paul Cambon, and confirmed that if German warships came into the Channel to attack France, the British navy would sink them. This should have been subject to Parliamentary approval, though in the event Parliament was never asked. Cambon was careful to hide his elation. If Britain was prepared to take sides to protect the Channel coast, she was halfway to a full commitment to war. He would later comment: 'The game was won. A great country does not make war by halves.'[39] Cambon knew it and Sir Edward Grey knew it. Britain was going to war.

And what of David Lloyd George, the erstwhile pacifist and dazzling, devious darling of the radical masses in whom the hope and trust of the anti-war Liberals had been invested? Lloyd George appeared to be on the side of the 'non-interventionists'[40] and should have been their natural leader. They assumed that he was, but were very mistaken. Lloyd George had long since sold his soul to the Secret Elite. Had he been allowed to remain a free agent, an anti-war Liberal group headed by him would have represented the Secret Elite's gravest nightmare. The damage he could have caused was literally boundless. A splinter Cabinet led by a national figure, a rallying point for the Liberals and the Labour Party in Parliament, would have spelled disaster for the warmongers. But Lloyd George was not what he seemed. It was not for his own sake that he had been saved by the Secret Elite from public scandal, extra-marital excesses, from court cases and from the opprobrium of the Marconi Scandal, been favoured with a wealthy lifestyle and mistress and kept in a luxury he could never have personally afforded. Lloyd George simply continued his long-term payback.

The Cabinet met again that evening. Grey informed them that he had told Cambon of their agreement to protect France if the German navy attacked her Channel coastline. Nothing further was decided. No one appeared to realise what Cambon instantly surmised. Britain had taken sides. The Liberal Cabinet tottered on the brink of disintegration. Ten or eleven ministers were still against war.[41] Not undecided; still against the war. Surely the essential qualities of British fairness, decency and parliamentary democracy would safeguard the nation from a disaster that its elected representatives did not want? A number of the less prominent Cabinet ministers looked to Lloyd George for leadership at that moment but found none. Lord Morley felt with hindsight that the Cabinet would have collapsed that night if Lloyd George had given a lead to the waverers, and Harcourt appealed to the chancellor to 'speak for us'.[42] To no avail. Lloyd George led the opponents of war into a cul-de-sac and left them there.

In Brussels that August evening, the German ambassador handed over the sealed letter that Moltke had earlier forwarded into his safe-keeping.[43] It stated that Germany had reliable information that France intended to attack her through Belgium and she would therefore be forced to enter Belgium in response. If Belgium did nothing to halt this invasion, Germany promised that, once the war was over and peace resumed, she would evacuate the territory, make good any damage done and pay for food used by her troops. However, if the movement of German troops was opposed, Germany regretted that she would have to regard Belgium as an enemy. The Belgians were given 12 hours to reply: that is by 7 a.m. on 3 August.[44]

King Alfred of Belgium sent a message to Sir Edward Grey to confirm that Belgium would refuse the German request and appealed for British support. The telegram was timed to perfection for Grey's vital speech in the House of Commons later that day. It provided ammunition to sway the Cabinet and Parliament. How could anyone of moral standing reject gallant little Belgium's desperate plea for help?[45]

In London in the small hours of Monday, 3 August, with his Cabinet abed and blissfully ignorant of his intentions, Asquith quietly advanced all preparations for war. He wrote out the authorisation for mobilisation of the British Army. Lord Haldane personally delivered it to the War Office at eleven o'clock that morning and issued the very orders that he had prepared years before when he held the office of minister for war.[46] The first steps had already started five days earlier, but the instructions had to be made official. The Secret Elite had, through its agents, authorised the general mobilisation of both the British navy and army without the approval of the Cabinet or Parliament.

Later that warm bank holiday morning, ministers returned yet again to Downing Street. Just before Cabinet, Asquith met privately with the Conservative leaders Bonar Law and Lord Lansdowne. He advised them that if a critical number of Liberal ministers resigned, a coalition government would be the only way forward. He knew he could rely on their support for war since the Conservative leaders were fellow agents of the Secret Elite.

In Cabinet, Asquith announced the resignations of John Burns and Lord Morley, and the junior minister Charles Trevelyan. He asked if he should go to the king to offer his resignation or if coalition government might be the answer. It was essentially blackmail. He knew that the waverers were extremely reluctant to bring down the Liberal government at this critical juncture in Britain's history. No further offers of resignation were tendered. The Cabinet broke up in some disarray. No vote had been taken on the critical issue of Britain going to war. It was such a clever ploy. By continually seeking a consensus, Asquith wore down his Cabinet critics and created the illusion of debate. Later, much later, another prime minister would substitute the myth of weapons of mass destruction for the myth of Belgian neutrality.

Inside Parliament, Sir Edward Grey had far more support from the opposition benches than from his own party. Balfour, Bonar Law, F.E. Smith and Carson had been advised in advance of the likelihood of war[47] and promised unreserved support. In the House of Lords, many powerful men stood ready to ensure that every sinew was strained to approve war. Lords Derby, Lansdowne, Rothschild, Curzon and Milner, the beating heart of the Secret Elite, were joined by the press baron Lord Northcliffe and the financial, industrial and commercial interests that bore no single name. Grey would be the focus of attention in Parliament, but at no stage was he acting alone.

As Members of Parliament gathered in the House of Commons at 3 p.m. that day, bursting with expectation and apprehension, many would have read the *Times'* full-blooded call to arms against Germany. 'The blame must fall mainly on Germany' was its rant. How ridiculously ironic that the editorial, written by Geoffrey Dawson, complained of Germany 'mobilising behind a mask of conversations', when the very opposite was the case. The villains who had mobilised behind such a mask were Russia, France and Britain. Accusations of a German invasion of France, a German resolve to crush France, a forthcoming German invasion of Holland and Belgium were followed in that editorial by an appeal to duty, both in Britain and in the Empire. 'When Britain goes to war, the whole Empire is at war.'[48] It was one day ahead of itself.

The Times was the voice of the Secret Elite and well informed in all aspects of its business. It carried a detailed insider report on the arduous Sunday Cabinet meetings and talked disparagingly of the few Cabinet 'dissidents' who did not want intervention. Mr Asquith was cheerfully advised that it would be 'no disadvantage' to bring some new blood into his administration. To claim that *The Times* was one step ahead was not an empty boast. Germany, for example, did not declare war on France until 6.15 p.m. that very day. It was but a taste of the lies and propaganda that would necessarily follow.

Summary: Chapter 26 – August 1914 – Of Neutrality and Just Causes

- As the Great Powers in Europe hurled themselves towards a continental war, the Secret Elite required a just cause for British involvement.
- The German chancellor, Bethmann, handed the perfect excuse to Sir Edward Grey through promises about the future status of Belgium as a bargaining pawn for British neutrality.
- Grey's pretence in his memoirs that the issue of Belgium was an aspect that had not been previously considered was an outrageous lie. The Secret Elite had known that Belgium and northern France would be the prime location for the British forces since discussions first got under way with France in 1905.
- It was vital to Grey's plan that Belgium remained outwardly neutral even though the secret arrangements meant that Belgian neutrality was a deception.

- Primed and supported by Sir Eyre Crowe and Sir Arthur Nicolson in the Foreign Office, Grey planned his assault on an unsuspecting Cabinet to stop them voting against British involvement in the coming war. Gaining their support proved a daunting task.
- He and Asquith secretly liaised with and advised Secret Elite politicians in the Conservative and Unionist parties to bring them on board and guarantee a parliamentary majority in support of war.
- Cabinet members were subjected to immense moral pressure on the issue of Belgium's future, especially from Grey, Haldane and Churchill. Asquith posed as an impartial chair but let it be known that he too would resign with Grey if the Cabinet went against the foreign secretary.
- Lloyd George would have been a formidable leader of the non-interventionists had he decided to oppose the war, but in fact his actions misled his Cabinet colleagues.
- Cabinet opponents to the war were in a majority, but were either neutralised (Lloyd George) or browbeaten into accepting that the best option for the country was to wait until Grey had spoken in Parliament on 3 August before resignations took place.
- Unbeknown to the Cabinet, and without permission, Churchill mobilised the fleet and Asquith sent Haldane to the War Office to mobilise the army. Grey contacted Paul Cambon, the French ambassador, to confirm that Britain would defend the French coast from any attack by the German fleet, thus ending any semblance of British neutrality.

CHAPTER 27

The Speech That Cost a Million Dead

CONSIDER THIS UNQUESTIONABLE FACT. THE final act which transformed the continental war into a world war was ordained by the Secret Elite. The person who fronted that decision, who did indeed snuff out the lamps all over Europe, was the man who allegedly made that observation, the secretary of state for foreign affairs, Sir Edward Grey.[1] The tipping point was his statement to the House of Commons on Monday, 3 August 1914, and its subsequent impact on Parliament, the nation and the Empire.

To most Members of Parliament, the events of that Bank Holiday Monday came in a blur of excitement and disbelief. One Irish Member recalled how it was only at the point where parliamentary attendants began to set out additional seats in the chamber of the Commons that he realised 'something wholly unusual was expected'.[2] So many Members of Parliament crammed into the claustrophobic chamber that even the additional seating could not cope. There was an electricity of expectation, an uncertainty, an apprehension that few had ever experienced.

Yet even before they had time to gather, the Relugas Three took preparation for war to the brink. On Asquith's instructions, Haldane returned to his old stamping ground at the War Office and summoned the Army Council. By his own account, the generals had their breath 'somewhat taken away' when he announced that he carried the prime minister's authority to immediately mobilise the Expeditionary and Territorial forces, the Special Reserve and the Officers' Training Corps. To the astonishment of the public, trains to Newhaven and Southampton were requisitioned for the exclusive use of the military. He wrote that 'it was a matter of life and death'.[3] All of this took place before Grey rose to speak.

In all that follows, it is important that the reader fully understands that Sir Edward Grey made a statement to Parliament, and through Parliament and the press to the nation.[4] It was not a debate. Grey was not subjected to questions from MPs, nor asked to explain himself. Time and again he and his co-conspirators had promised that any British military commitments or naval agreements with France or Russia would require the official approval of the House of Commons. All understood this to mean an informed debate in Parliament followed by a vote. There was no debate. There was no vote. The Secret Elite and their agents did not seek democratic approval for anything they had previously organised or engineered, and they did not seek parliamentary approval for taking Britain to war. By clever turn of phrase and repetitive lie, Grey deceived the House of Commons into believing that it 'was free to make the most momentous decision in history'.[5]

The warmongers hailed Grey's position as statesman-like and noble, and talked of duty and loyalty, obligations and integrity. The many voices raised against this same speech were drowned out by Secret Elite agents in Parliament, dismissed by most of the daily newspapers, and have been more or less ignored altogether by historians. It was not a great speech – Leo Amery mocked it as narrow and uninspiring[6] – but, nevertheless, it was of monumental importance. The House of Commons has rarely hung on the words of a secretary of state for foreign affairs with such studied attention. Sir Edward Grey set the tone by announcing that peace in Europe 'cannot be preserved'[7] and distanced himself and the Foreign Office from any previous involvement or collusion. His moral stance stemmed from a claim that 'we have consistently worked with a single mind, with all the earnestness in our power, to preserve peace'.[8] Given his connivance with Isvolsky and Sazonov, Poincaré, the Committee of Imperial Defence, the secret agreements and understandings, and all of the scheming that had encouraged Berchtold and the Austrians to make the demands on Serbia, that was a breathtaking lie. He accepted that Russia and Germany had declared war on each other, almost as if to say, what could be done about that? The implication that Britain, and British diplomats, had had nothing to do with these events was entirely false.

Grey's appeal to British interests, British honour and British obligations was lifted from Sir Eyre Crowe's memorandum,[9] which is hardly surprising since he would have carefully rehearsed his speech with his Foreign Office accomplices before facing the Commons. He stressed that the House was 'free to decide what the British attitude should be' and promised to publish parliamentary evidence that would prove how 'genuine and whole-hearted his efforts for peace were'.[10] When these were made available to Parliament at a later date, the diplomatic notes had been carefully selected and included three telegrams that had never actually been sent.[11] Worse still were the carefully amended versions: absolute proof of Foreign Office double-dealings.

Grey admitted that 'conversations' had been going on for some time between British and French naval and military experts, but MPs did not realise that he had sanctioned these since 1906, without seeking permission of the Cabinet. He produced a letter from the French ambassador, Paul Cambon, which conveniently explained that whatever the disposition of the French and British fleets, they were not based on a commitment to cooperate in war. It was a downright lie, but MPs and the British people had to be misled. In response to an interruption from Lord Charles Beresford, Grey was obliged to confess that the letter had been written some two years previously, yet had never been revealed to Parliament. Much worse than that, he read out only part of a formal letter between his office and the French authorities, deliberately omitting the crucial final sentence: 'If these measures involved action, the plans of the General Staffs would at once be taken into consideration and the governments would then decide what effect should be given to them.'[12]

The plans of the general staffs? What plans? How did this come about? There would have been uproar amongst the Liberals, the Labour Party and Irish Home Rulers had Grey revealed that plans for joint military action had been agreed between the general staffs of both nations. All of the denials that had been made to Prince Lichnowsky and the kaiser would instantly have been unmasked. All of Prime Minister Asquith's previous statements in Parliament denying that secret agreements tied Britain to France in the event of a war with Germany would have been revealed as deliberate deceptions.[13] In his personal memoirs, published in 1925, Sir Edward Grey claimed that the charge of omitting the final sentence was not brought to his notice till 1923. He could only imagine that he had been interrupted when reading the letter or 'perhaps I thought the last sentence unimportant, as it did not affect the sense or main purport of what had already been read out'.[14] Ridiculous. Truly and utterly ridiculous. That final sentence would have destroyed Grey's speech and exposed years of secret preparation for war.

Grey repeatedly stressed that the government and the House of Commons was perfectly free to decide what to do and that no previous diplomatic arrangements stood in the way of democratic decision making. In fact, he had absolutely no intention of asking the House of Commons for its opinion. The Secret Elite's was the only opinion that mattered.

When he reminded the House that Britain had a long-standing friendship with France, a voice from the surrounding seats shouted 'and with Germany', but the remark was pointedly ignored. With amazing hypocrisy and deceptiveness he painted a fanciful picture of the northern and western coasts of France standing 'absolutely undefended'. He asked how the public would react if a foreign fleet (everyone knew it could only be German) bombarded the undefended coasts of France within sight of Britain's shores. He admitted that he had assured the French ambassador that in the event of hostile operations against the French coasts or shipping, the British fleet would step in to support and protect them, subject, as always, to the mythical approval of the House of Commons.

What a stunning confession. Two days previously, Grey's under-secretary, Sir Arthur Nicolson, had reminded him that it was at Britain's behest that France had moved her fleets to the Mediterranean in 1912 on the absolute understanding that the British navy would protect her northern and western coasts.[15] Grey was describing a strategy that the Admiralty and Foreign Office had initiated two years earlier but was falsely implying that it had only just been agreed because of the escalating European crisis. The entire construct was false. He admitted that the fleet had been mobilised and the army was in the process of full mobilisation, though he felt it necessary to add that, as yet, no troops had left the country.

The foreign secretary took some time warming up his audience before unveiling the focal point of his statement: Belgian neutrality. His trump card was his greatest lie, for Belgium was neutral only in name. The heavy veil of secrecy that had been drawn over Belgium's preparations to side with Britain and France against Germany proved its worth. In a moment of time that caught the purpose of Grey's dramatic delivery, this was his *coup de théâtre*. The stunning presentation of 'neutral' Belgium as the innocent victim of German aggression was biblical in its imagery and grotesque in its deceit. The Treaty of 1839,[16] which allegedly obliged Britain to defend Belgian neutrality, was dredged up as the reason for taking Britain to war. This despite repeated pronouncements by Asquith and others which denied that there were any treaties or alliances which compelled Britain to go to war.[17]

An emotional telegram from the King of the Belgians to his good friend King George pleading for assistance was read to the crowded Commons. The fact that it had been delivered from Buckingham Palace hot foot to Grey was intended as a signal to MPs from the king that the country had an obligation towards Belgium. Grey invoked emotional blackmail. If Belgian neutrality was abused by Germany, he asked, would Britain, endowed as it was with influence and power, 'stand by and witness the perpetration of the direst crime that ever stained the pages of history, and thus become participators in the sin'?[18]

The 'direst crime that ever stained the pages of history'? Had no one in the Foreign Office read Edith Durham's account of the slaughter of thousands of innocents in the Balkans? Were the massacres in Albania, Serbia and Bulgaria of no consequence? Had Grey forgotten the atrocities in the Congo, where the Belgian king's mercenaries slaughtered millions, outraging world opinion in 1908?[19] But then most of these people were black or Muslims or from other such ethnic groups, and therefore of little value in Secret Elite thinking. Sir Edward Grey's hyperbole and melodramatic statements were truly worthy of ridicule, but his words were greeted with loud cheers from the jingoistic Conservatives on the opposition benches.[20]

Grey had long known that his entire argument would be predicated on Belgian neutrality. It had been absolutely vital that Belgium remained apart from the entente and did not seek membership, so that its neutrality could be construed as a sacred issue, a point of principle that necessitated British support when the time came. Consider the whole charade of neutrality that the Secret Elite used to manipulate British foreign policy. No formula for British neutrality could ever square with the naval and military obligations that had been agreed directly with France, and more indirectly with Russia. There was no neutrality; it was another lie, a shameless posture to deceive Germany and bring about war.

He painted a picture of Europe in a state of collapse, stating that if Belgium fell, 'the independence of Holland will follow . . . and then Denmark'. Neither happened. He was strident in his determination to present the case for war as inevitable. His claims became ever more excitable. The impact of going to war was described as such that 'we shall suffer but little more than we shall suffer even if we stand aside'. Grey prophesied an end to foreign trade – a ridiculous assertion, given the power of the British navy and the spread of the British Empire. *The Guardian* later lambasted his lack of commercial knowledge and his ignorance of the workings of trade,[21] but he was pushing every alarm button, raising every fear, pandering to every prejudice.

Yet he found one bright spot in all of his well-rehearsed alarm: Ireland. In the midst of all the doom and gloom and talk of imminent civil war, he asserted that the Irish question was no longer an issue 'which we feel we have now to take into account'. Why? What had happened to justify such an unexpected claim? From what authority could he suddenly draw the conclusion that the 'general feeling throughout Ireland' was in favour of British foreign policy?

Edward Grey's double-speak lent him the appearance of a man of honour. In reality, he was deliberately guiding the nation to a world war. He could not contemplate Britain's 'unconditional neutrality'. Such action was bound to 'sacrifice our respect and good name and reputation before the world, and should not escape the most serious and grave economic consequences'. His doom-laden statement promised suffering and misery 'from which no country in Europe will escape and from which no abdication or neutrality will save us'.[22] He made great play of the notion that 'the most awful responsibility is resting upon the government in deciding what to advise the House of Commons to do'. The House of Commons was not being offered a choice; it was being advised that there was no choice.

He sat down to a storm of cheering and acclaim from the Conservatives, part orchestrated, part genuine. Leo Amery caustically found it 'so long and so dull that I more than once fell asleep'.[23] As an inner-circle member of the Secret Elite, Grey's speech would have come as no surprise to Amery, but he admitted that it was better received by the Liberals than the government had expected.[24] The majority of Liberal MPs were stunned by what they had heard. Suddenly, without debate, consensus or warning, the government, their Liberal government, was on the brink of declaring war. Irish Members were bemused to hear that the Irish question was about to suddenly evaporate and no longer pose a problem should Britain go to war. Had the Ulster Unionists promised unconditional support? Had the south?

What followed was truly remarkable. The leader of the Conservative and Unionist Party, Bonar Law, solemnly acknowledged that the government had done everything in its power to preserve peace, but 'if any other course is taken, it is because it is forced upon them, and that they have no alternative'. This same man had described Asquith, Churchill, Lloyd George and Grey as 'the most incompetent, policy-less people to be found on earth'[25] and warned they were drifting to disaster. Barely three weeks before, Bonar Law boldly told Edward Grey that if he could not use his influence to preserve peace in his own land (Ireland), he could do no good abroad.[26]

These members of the Secret Elite played the parliamentary game of charades to preserve the facade of democracy. Sir Edward Grey knew well in advance that fellow placemen in the Conservative Party would support war. Churchill had carefully vetted their attitude[27] and Asquith was sent a personal letter of unqualified Conservative support. Hours before Grey's speech, Asquith had yet again been reassured that the Conservatives would stand with him by Bonar Law and Lord Lansdowne.[28] Conservative support in the House of Commons was a prearranged pantomime, a pantomime that played well to the press gallery. The Secret Elite had never let party politics interfere with its spheres of influence. They controlled them all.

That John Redmond, leading member of the Irish Home Rule party, should have risen to promise the support of Catholic Ireland appeared much more astonishing. His bold suggestion that Ireland could defend itself, thus releasing the British Army for service elsewhere, was astounding but effective. Asquith noted gratefully that Redmond 'cut in effectively' to offer support to the government.[29] Even his very language had a sense of stage-management. No one on the Irish Home Rule benches expected Redmond to make any comment. There had been no prior consultation, as was both customary and obligatory on important issues. Redmond was, by understanding and agreement, more of a party chairman than a leader. John Dillon, the most important of the Irish Home-Rulers, was in Dublin on that fateful afternoon. Redmond acted in his own right[30] and officially there had been no consultation between him and the government. It appeared that he had simply been swept away by Grey's rhetoric, but an article in *The Times* on 1 August, stating that government troops could be withdrawn safely from Ireland,[31] exposed that as a lie. There was also evidence that Redmond met with Asquith immediately before Grey's speech.[32] *The Times*? Secret meetings? Deals? What was Redmond's association with the Secret Elite?

Of the party leaders, only Ramsay MacDonald stood firm against the swelling tide of orchestrated 'inevitability'. He rejected the idea that the country was in danger. He ridiculed the concept of statesmen appealing to their nation's honour and reminded the Commons that Britain had 'fought the Crimean War because of our honour. We rushed into South Africa because of our honour.'[33] MacDonald asked what was the use of talking about going to the aid of Belgium when what was really happening meant engaging in a pan-European war that was going to alter the boundaries of many nations? He wanted to know what this would mean for Russian domination when it was over.

Then, quite remarkably, this historic assembly, which has long considered itself the champion of free speech, was denied precisely that by the prime minister. Members wanted to discuss Grey's statement at length. Had he not just said that the House was free to decide what the British attitude should be? Asquith responded by promising an early opportunity for discussion. 'Today?' shouted a number of Members of Parliament. The reply was unequivocally negative. There would be no debate that day. The Commons had listened in good order to a singularly biased statement, laced with emotional blackmail, but was refused permission to discuss these affairs at that very point where delay made any response worthless. A very fragmented Cabinet had been ground into acquiescence. The decision to go to war had already been taken by the Secret Elite, by their Cabinet agents, through the mobilisations of fleet and army, by the Northcliffe press, and all with the full knowledge of the monarch. They were not interested in alternative views.

Asquith and his pro-war colleagues cynically abused democracy, but democracy has the capacity to express itself in unexpected ways. The prime minister had tried to close the matter to debate, but the speaker of the House of Commons was not privy to the secret machinations and made an unexpected offer. He suggested a procedural manoeuvre that would allow the House to adjourn at 4.35 p.m. and reassemble at 7 p.m. that same night. Asquith was not to have his way.

The secretary of state for foreign affairs left the House of Commons immediately. His work was far from finished. He had, by his own admission, decisions to make, but there was one thing he knew for certain. It did not matter whether that decision was to declare war on Germany or to impose impossible conditions on her. He knew that 'conditions meant war just as surely as a declaration of war. Respect for the neutrality of Belgium must be one of the conditions, and this Germany would not respect.'[34] Yet another lie, demolished entirely by the evidence in Chapter 26, but a lie that Grey had to repeat many times to make it feel like the truth.

Churchill caught up with him outside the Commons and asked what he intended to do next. He was eager to get started. Grey's reply was stunning in its complicity but a masterstroke: 'Now we will send them an ultimatum to stop the invasion of Belgium within 24 hours.'[35] It was the condition to which he knew Germany could not accede. Having set the nation to focus on Belgium, to make it the point of honour, Grey immediately proceeded to lure Germany into a position where it would appear that Britain had no alternative other than go to war. That was a certainty, for he knew the German army was already on its way through Belgium.

Meanwhile, that same afternoon Haldane summoned a War Council. Lord Kitchener, now consul general in Egypt, 'who happened to be in London', was present.[36] What was more astonishing was that Haldane invited Lord Roberts to attend his select council: a remarkable invitation given that Roberts had retired from his post of commander-in-chief of the British Army ten years earlier.

But Roberts had never retired. Roberts, who had shared so many platforms with his friend Alfred Milner, and was at the heart of the Secret Elite, was still the decision maker. His influence dominated military thinking through the promoted members of his Academy. It was they who liaised with the French and Belgian general staffs and prepared the detailed plans for the British Expeditionary Force. It was they who would lead the British Army to war. This was their purpose.

When the House of Commons reconvened at 7.20 p.m. on 3 August 1914, the prime minister and foreign secretary were cheered, mainly by the opposition. Sir Edward Grey opened by announcing that he had received information from the Belgian legation in London not available to him when he made his speech earlier in the afternoon.[37] It was the details of the German Note to Belgium sent the previous evening at 7 p.m., which offered friendly neutrality if the German troops were allowed safe passage. Yet again, Grey was lying to Parliament. A telegram from the French ambassador in London to French Prime Minister Vivani proved that Grey had been told about the German offer by Paul Cambon on the morning of 3 August, hours before his initial statement.[38] Grey had withheld this information from the Cabinet and thereafter from Parliament so that his centrepiece on Belgian neutrality could be portrayed as an absolute condition for declaring war on Germany. Had it become known that the Germans had offered the Belgians terms for neutrality, his whole argument would have been destroyed.

A number of prominent Liberals rose to challenge Grey's claims and express their horror at the prospect of war being visited on Britain. Philip Morrell stressed that Germany had never refused to negotiate and had guaranteed Belgian integrity.[39] He added: 'we are going to war now because of fear and jealousy fostered by large sections of the press . . . the fear and jealousy of German ambition, that is the real reason'. He summed up the calamitous situation by ending: 'I regret very much at the end of eight years of the policy which has been pursued of the Triple Entente, that it should have landed us into such a war as this.' This theme was continued by Edmund Harvey,[40] who claimed that war had been caused 'by men in high places, by diplomatists working in secret, by bureaucrats who are out of touch with the peoples of the world . . .'[41] Keir Hardie implored the government to consider the plight of the poor, the unemployed and 'starving children'. Both Houses of Parliament had unanimously passed a bill for the relief of the Stock Exchange, but Hardie was more interested in a bill to compel local authorities to feed local schoolchildren. He was barracked from the Conservative benches when he added: 'Most of the members of this House have more of a direct interest in the Stock Exchange than they have in the sufferings of the poor.'[42] Little changes.

Though this short adjournment debate ended at 8.15 p.m., a further debate on Grey's speech began again at the insistence of angry Liberal members.[43] It was a futile exercise. Most of those whose minds the anti-war Members of Parliament sought to change chose not to stay. They were off preparing for war. Lloyd George, though, was present at the start to answer a question on food supplies.

Percy Molteno, the Liberal MP for Dumfriesshire and an outspoken critic of the Boer War, was first on his feet to detail the many assurances given to Parliament over the previous years that there were no unpublished agreements which would hamper or restrict the freedom of the government or Parliament to decide whether or not Great Britain should participate in a war.[44] He felt desperately let down by the government he had long supported and asked bitterly of Asquith and Grey who had 'informed the people that they were a government of peace, and they would seek to maintain peace' whether they were not compelled to honour their obligations to their supporters? In a passage that would echo down the ages and still resonates a century later Mr Molteno declared:

> They have brought us to the brink of disaster without our knowing, and without our being warned. I say that at the last moment, they should give the people of this country a chance to decide. This is a continuation of that old and disastrous system where a few men in charge of the State, wielding the whole force of the State, make secret engagements and secret arrangements, carefully veiled from the knowledge of the people, who are as dumb driven cattle without a voice on the question. And nobody can tell the country what are the important considerations that ought to weigh with us in taking part in this tremendous struggle.[45]

What an apt metaphor. The dumb driven cattle were being herded towards the global abattoir for reasons they would never properly know. A few men wielding the whole force of the state, with secret arrangements and secret agreements, had unleashed the demon war and sanctioned the slaughter. Molteno pointed an accusatory finger at the politicians who had fronted the decision, but it was the Secret Elite who hid their all-powerful influence behind the carefully veiled parliamentary screen.

Another Liberal, W. Llewellyn Williams, accused Grey of disguising his motives and falsely arousing war fever:

> If you had asked any man in this country, whatever his politics might be, whether he would calmly contemplate the entrance of his country into this quarrel, he would have said, 'No' . . . Even today this country does not want war . . . Now is the only time to speak before the war fever has come to its height. I beg and implore this Government . . . to use every effort in their power to avert this terrible calamity, not only to our own prosperity, but to the civilisation of the world.[46]

Others questioned the impact in constituencies where factories were closing down and people could hardly afford to buy bread for their family. Russian opportunism was repeatedly criticised. In his absence, Grey was berated for 'the sinister injustice' of seeing Germany as the enemy while ignoring that fact that Russia had mobilised her forces first. It was a basic truth. Russia had mobilised first. Russia had caused the war. The objectors could see that Britain was being railroaded into war and asked what benefit it would be if Germany were crushed by an all-conquering Russia? One Liberal Member wanted to know why Belgian neutrality was suddenly of such vital consequence to Britain's national honour when no one suggested making war to protect the integrity of Finland, which was being suppressed by a 'semi-civilised barbaric and brutal' Russia?

The warmongers sought to close the quasi-debate by shouting down speakers, but such loutish behaviour only served to spur on the North Somerset Liberal MP Joseph King. He did not hold back. Why had only one Member of Parliament voiced support for the foreign secretary, even although he apparently had the wholehearted approval of both government and the official opposition? Was the Cabinet united? Who would resign? He continued to tear apart the pretence of parliamentary unity by asking why the Conservative Members from Ireland had not given immediate assurances of their support. By the time Mr King reminded them that 'a short time ago the Hon. Members [from Ulster] were declaring they would invite the kaiser over',[47] he was being drowned out. His views on Russia and the expediency of their mobilisation are worthy of note. King stated that because of all the internal uprisings, localised and national strikes and threats of civil war, Russia had mobilised her army and thrown the whole of Europe into war for its own sake. They had no great political or patriotic motive other than to preserve the privilege of the ruling classes. He concluded: 'if we are fighting for Russia at the present time, we are fighting for an amount of tyranny and injustice and cruelty which it is quite impossible to think of without the deepest indignation'.[48] His views were perfectly valid and completely justified, but what he could not grasp, what none of them could grasp, was the much more sinister fact that Russia, like France, was being used to a greater Secret Elite purpose.

Joseph King's final point was equally stunning. When Franz Ferdinand's assassination was first announced, the prime minister had proposed a resolution 'which was accepted in solemn silence'. Asquith had extended his tender respect to the great family of nations headed by the Austrian emperor, and he offered them 'affectionate sympathy'. Five weeks later, that same government was proposing to wage war against them. King called it 'tragic, bitter and cynical'. He asked if British foreign policy had become so shifting and changing that the people to whom every sympathy was offered one day were our declared foes the next. He was not given an answer. What he could not understand because of all of the confusions around him was that foreign policy had not changed one iota since the moment that the Secret Elite decided that Germany had to be crushed. The lies, the deviousness, the secrecy, the posturing and the pretence had ambushed the voices of reason raised against war.

As each and every contributor attacked government policy, challenged every step, asked more and more telling questions, it became ever more evident that there was a very strong body of articulate opinion ranged against Sir Edward Grey. At which point, Arthur Balfour, former Conservative prime minister and a member of the Secret Elite's inner circle, rose menacingly. He had heard enough. Balfour derided their objections as the 'very dregs and lees of the debate, in no way representing the various views of the Members of the House'. With consummate arrogance he patronised all that had been said before his interruption, stating that what they were engaged in was a 'relatively impotent and evil debate'.[49] How could this be a serious occasion, he asked, when none of the senior government ministers were present?

What spurious nonsense. Senior government ministers had actively chosen not to be present. If these discussions were denied the trappings of a 'serious occasion', it was entirely because those ministers refused to be there. Balfour betrayed his real purpose when he 'ventured to think' that the points which had been raised might be misunderstood in the country and would certainly be misunderstood abroad.[50]

Was Balfour sent in to bring it to a halt? He said as much when he alluded to the damage these opinions might do abroad. War had not been formally declared, but Parliament was being silenced, and it took a former Conservative prime minister to bring the discussions to a close. Arthur James Balfour, member of the Society of the Elect of the Secret Elite, personal and long-term friend of Milner, Lansdowne, Curzon, Asquith, Grey and Haldane, did the job for them. *The Guardian* described the evening debate as 'serious and patriotic, and its prevailing tone reflected that of sober opinion in the country'.[51] Amery called the voices raised against war 'the radical crank section',[52] and *The Times* dismissed the whole protest in a single sentence.[53]

When Grey forwarded that infamous ultimatum to Berlin, it required a positive reassurance that Belgian neutrality would not be violated by Germany. The deadline was set for midnight on 4 August 1914. At some stage during the day an unknown person realised that Greenwich Meantime was set one hour behind Germany, and a decision was taken to advance the deadline to match the time in Berlin. There has never been an official explanation why such a decision was made, or by whom, or at what stage in the day. This decision had to be sanctioned by Sir Edward Grey, so the question to be asked is: why? Is this the action of a man who had reputedly tried every possible diplomatic channel to protect the peace of Europe? No. The two actions do not sit together. Was Sir Edward Grey afraid of some last-minute change of heart by the German military or a timely intervention by the kaiser? Perhaps, as A.J.P. Taylor famously wrote, they just wanted to get it settled and go to bed.[54] Yes, that is precisely what happened. They wanted to get this war against Germany started, and no insignificant time difference would be allowed to halt it.

The German High Command was taken aback by Grey's ultimatum. Chancellor Bethmann fulminated at British duplicity in a speech delivered to the Reichstag on 4 August.[55] He lambasted Sir Edward Grey for secretly encouraging France and hence Russia. He argued that war would have been impossible if the British Cabinet had made it absolutely clear to all the parties that they were not prepared to allow a continental war to develop from the Austria–Serbia conflict. Britain, he claimed, sought to take advantage of the international crisis by seizing the opportunity to destroy her greatest European competitors in the markets of the world. He dismissed Belgian neutrality as a lame excuse, a mask to cover the main intent, which was to destroy German economic power, assisted by two great continental armies from Russia and France. Bethmann accused Britain of seeing herself as the '*arbitrium mundi*', the self-appointed ombudsman on the international stage. He was correct on every point, but official histories would mock his justified rage.

Thus the *casus belli*, the German invasion of Belgium, had been steamrollered through Parliament, the opposition flattened and the 'screamers' ignored. Once Asquith knew that war with Germany would be declared, he urgently contacted Edward Carson to cancel Plan B. It was no longer needed. Professor Quigley revealed that the Ulster Unionist leader had a prepared coded telegram ready to be dispatched to the UVF to seize control of Belfast at his given signal.[56] This ultra-secret strategy was revealed to the inner-core Round Table member Lionel Curtis by Carson himself once the war was under way.[57]

If an unbiased observer was invited to take a hard look at how the British Empire in all of its manifestations went to war, they would be amazed that such a process of undemocratic decision making permitted a tiny clique of elected officials, bolstered by a larger, less visible, but overwhelmingly influential cabal, to achieve their ultimate goal: war with Germany. The Cabinet played no part whatsoever in this process once it had sanctioned the primacy of Belgian neutrality. No one, with the possible but unrecorded exception of the prime minister, was given sight of the ultimatum sent by Sir Edward Grey. Before he had even sent it, Grey was fully aware that the condition he demanded had already been violated. German troops were heading into Belgium. The Cabinet did not authorise the declaration of war. It was never asked to. Parliament itself was informed of events, belatedly, but was given neither proper time to debate nor any opportunity to vote on war or neutrality. Opposition to the war was stifled as quickly as possible. The first time that any vote could have taken place was on 6 August, when the government sought approval for the finances they imagined would sustain a war that they had entered two days earlier. Nor were governments and parliaments across the Empire consulted. Millions of subjects of the king found themselves at war against an enemy about whom they had no knowledge.[58]

So, who declared war?

Technically, it was King George V who, as a matter of royal prerogative, had to sanction the proclamation of a state of war from 11 p.m. on that fateful night. A Privy Council meeting was held late on in Buckingham Palace. It began at 10.30 p.m. in the presence of His Majesty, one Lord of the Realm[59] and two court officials; it ended with the royal assent. It was a dark deed done by a lesser monarch in the presence of men whose names are long forgotten. The act was purely symbolic but ultimately catastrophic. It was as if some medieval right cursed the twentieth century. The will of the Secret Elite was sanctioned by a pliant monarch whose pen unleashed the hounds of hell.

Summary: Chapter 27 – The Speech That Cost a Million Dead

- Sir Edward Grey's statement on 3 August 1914 was not a debate, so he was not challenged on the issues he put before the House of Commons when he sat down.
- He began by stressing the utter lie that he and his Foreign Office colleagues had done everything possible to preserve peace in Europe.
- While he reiterated, yet again, that Parliament was free to decide what British attitudes should be, he never at any point sought its opinion.
- He deliberately gave the false impression that the 'conversations' with France that had been ongoing since 1905 made no commitment to go to war by omitting to tell Parliament that these included plans agreed by both general staffs.
- He introduced the imaginary scenario whereby the German fleet might bombard the undefended French Channel coast without explaining that the disposition of the French and British fleets had been arranged at Britain's behest in 1912 and on the understanding that the British fleet would protect the French coast.
- The whole issue of neutrality, of the 'violation' of Belgian neutrality and its consequences, was the central argument in Sir Edward Grey's cause for war. Appeals for help from the Belgian king to King George were introduced as a means of indicating support for action from the monarchy.
- Grey's language became increasingly excited. Talk of the 'direst crime

that ever stained the pages of history', and the claim that Britain would suffer equally badly whether she was involved directly or not, was pure nonsense.

- At the end of Grey's speech, Bonar Law, the Conservative leader, rose in pre-planned approval to voice total and unconditional support for the government's action.
- John Redmond spoke for the Irish Home-Rulers and most surprisingly promised their support too. What deals had been done?
- The only party leader to speak out immediately against the tone and the content of Grey's speech was the Labour leader, Ramsay MacDonald.
- Members of the House of Commons asked for an immediate debate but were rebuffed by Prime Minister Asquith. However, to the chagrin of the Secret Elite, the speaker of the House of Commons agreed to find time to discuss the issues later that night.
- Grey immediately left Parliament to send the fateful ultimatum to Germany, knowing full well that the invasion of Belgium, which was the central British condition, was already under way. It was a declaration of war.
- When the House of Commons reconvened, there was an outpouring of bitter objections to Sir Edward Grey's statement, especially from Liberal MPs who felt personally betrayed by what they had heard. Grey's statement was ripped apart. Pointed and unanswered questions were raised about Russia, the lies previously told in Parliament and the fearful consequences of war.
- The clamour against any proposed war was stopped in its tracks by one of the most senior Secret Elite agents in Parliament, A.J. Balfour. He rose to demand an end to the proceedings because the debate was unrepresentative and would give a poor impression to the public. (That could only have happened if the 'debate' had been reported in the newspapers.)
- Once the *casus belli* of Belgium was achieved, Plan B became redundant.
- War was formally proclaimed by King George V at Buckingham Palace on 4 August 1914.

CONCLUSION

Lies, Myths and Stolen History

In August 1914, the Secret Elite began the war they so coveted. In Britain, Liberal, Labour and Irish Nationalist Members of Parliament were in shock, stunned by the fait accompli Sir Edward Grey presented on 3 August 1914. They had been ambushed and betrayed. Cast adrift by the excited jingoism, democracy looked on in impotent disbelief. And it was all predicated on a myth: the myth of Belgian neutrality. From 1906 onwards, Britain's military link with Belgium was one of the most tightly guarded secrets, even within privileged circles.

Documents found in the Department of Foreign Affairs in Brussels shortly after the war began proved Anglo-Belgian collusion at the highest levels, including the direct involvement of the Belgian foreign secretary, had been going on for years.[1] Like the 'conversations' with French military commanders, the Belgian 'relationship' was never put in writing or adopted as official policy by Britain, since that would have risked exposure to Parliament and the press.[2] Indeed, because Belgium's behaviour violated the duties of a neutral state, the Secret Elite could not entertain any move to openly include them in the entente. That act alone would have put an end to neutrality and with it their best cause for war. Professor Albert Geouffre de Lapradelle, the renowned French specialist on international law, explained: 'The perpetually neutral state renounces the right to make war, and, in consequence, the right to contract alliances, even purely defensive ones, because they would drag it into a war . . .'[3]

The American journalist and writer, Albert J. Nock, completely destroyed the lie of Belgian 'neutrality'. In his words:

> To pretend any longer that the Belgian government was surprised by the action of Germany, or unprepared to meet it; to picture Germany and Belgium as cat and mouse, to understand the position of Belgium otherwise than that she was one of four solid allies under definite agreement worked out in complete detail, is sheer absurdity.[4]

And yet this absurd notion was used to take Britain into war and has been propagated ever since by British historians. Belgium posed as a neutral country in 1914 like a siren on the rocks, set there to lure Germany into a trap, whimpering a pretence of innocence.

Every ruse was used to vilify Germany and the kaiser. The carnage was barely under way before blame was heaped on them. German responsibility was allegedly based on the official 'books' of diplomatic documents published by each government. The British Blue Book, which contained the diplomatic exchanges from just before the start of the war, was presented to Parliament on 6 August. Arranged in chronological order, the 'evidence' appeared to be complete, candid and convincing: a studied confirmation of Sir Edward Grey's 'determined efforts to preserve peace'.[5] Later evidence released from Moscow in the wake of the Russian Revolution clearly showed that three of the telegrams Grey had presented to Parliament as proof of his attempts to prevent war had never even been sent. The claim by the British ambassador in St Petersburg, Sir George Buchanan, that, with one exception, all of the diplomatic exchanges between him and the Foreign Office were included in the Blue Book was a scandalous lie.[6] Professor Sydney Fay of Harvard found that 'more than a score' had not been included and that important passages from telegrams and letters had been judiciously cut.[7]

The Russian Orange Book contained 79 documents that emphasised her efforts for peace, but it concealed the truth about Russia's mobilisation and blamed the Central Powers.[8] The Orange Book omitted the conciliatory proposals that had been made by Germany during the July crisis and all evidence of the aggressive Franco-Russian policies.[9] The long-delayed French Yellow Book likewise suppressed some telegrams altogether and altered others to imply the French desire for peace and German guilt for the war.[10]

The Secret Elite were ruthless in their manipulation of official documents. The French Yellow, British Blue and Russian Orange Books were riddled with omissions and misinformation to conceal the truth and were faithfully portrayed by their propaganda machines as evidence of German guilt.

The German White Book[11] was presented to the Reichstag on 3 August, and its brevity (it contained only 27 telegrams and letters) gave rise to the myth that Germany had only printed selections that suited her cause. A great mass of telegrams had been exchanged between Germany and Austria in the days and hours before publication of the White Book, and, even had they been published, it would have been impossible to read and digest their contents in such a short time.[12] In 1919, Karl Kautsky, the German socialist leader (and no lover of the kaiser's regime), released volumes of evidence on the origins of the war. The Kautsky documents comprised 1,123 records which proved absolutely that Germany made every effort to avoid the war and that evidence to the contrary was a pure myth.[13]

The Secret Elite control over four years of mindless slaughter will be explained in detail in our next book in the *Hidden History* series. On 11 November 1918, the armistice with Germany was signed in General Foch's railway carriage in the forest of Compiègne, north of Paris. It was claimed that the kaiser waged war to expand the German empire and tyrannise Europe, while Britain, France and Russia had made every possible effort to prevent it. The jaundiced analysis was that 'Germany deliberately worked to defeat all of the many conciliatory proposals made by the Entente Powers and their repeated efforts to avoid war'.[14] Germany was 'guilty of the greatest crime against humanity and freedom that any nation calling itself civilized had ever committed'. The terrible responsibility for millions of war dead was placed firmly at Germany's door because 'she saw fit to gratify her lust for tyranny by resort to war'.[15] These lies were presented as 'truth'.

The Secret Elite mobilised all the resources at their command, including universities, the press, the pulpit and the whole machinery of government to preach this false gospel of guilt. The kaiser and Germany were vilified. The Allied Powers were glorified. Their men, after all, had fought and died for 'civilisation'.

Treaty negotiations in Paris were crammed with representatives from Britain, France and the US who were closely linked to the Secret Elite. The few German delegates permitted to attend Versailles asked for proof of Germany's alleged guilt but were denied it. In truth, none existed. They asked for an independent investigation into the responsibility for war but were denied it. They asked for a non-partisan commission to examine the archives of all the warring nations and to question the principal leaders but were denied. No defence was permissible. On 28 June 1919, the formal peace treaty was signed in the Palace of Versailles. It had taken the Secret Elite exactly five years from the murders in Sarajevo to achieve their aim. The German delegates were obliged to sign Article 231, accepting all blame:

> The Allied and Associated Governments affirm, and Germany accepts, the responsibility of herself and her allies, for causing the loss and damage to which the Allied and associated Governments and their nationals have been subjected as a consequence of the war imposed upon them by the aggression of Germany and her allies.[16]

By signing, Germany acquiesced and accepted sole responsibility for the

First World War. A starving, desperate nation had been confronted with the choice of admitting her 'guilt' at once or suffering an Allied occupation with every likelihood that an admission of guilt would ultimately be extorted in any case. Professor H.E. Barnes stated:

> Germany occupied the situation of a prisoner at the bar, where the prosecuting attorney was given full leeway as to time and presentation of evidence, while the defendant was denied counsel or the opportunity to produce either evidence or witnesses.[17]

The lies, vindictive reparation schemes and headline-grabbing assertions continued long after 1918 in order to protect the real culprits in this crime against humanity and conceal the truth from the world. In his groundbreaking book *The Anglo-American Establishment*, Professor Carroll Quigley dared to reveal how the Secret Elite continued their malicious influence and controlled and manipulated the truth through their triple-front penetration of politics, the press and education:

> No country that values its safety should allow what the Milner group accomplished – that is, that a small number of men would be able to wield such power in administration and politics, should be given almost complete control over the publication of documents relating to their actions, should be able to exercise such influence over the avenues of information that create public opinion, and should be able to monopolize so completely the writing and the teaching of the history of their own period.[18]

The Rhodes secret society, expanded as it was by Alfred Milner and his acolytes into the Secret Elite, had achieved stage two of their great plan: war with Germany. The combination of money power, intellectual conviction and ruling-class mentality, the All Souls, Oxford, power base and the aristocratic heritage harnessed to the Northcliffe stables had ambushed Germany into a war in 1914 and now ambushed the truth about their complicity in the war's origins.

From the conception of the secret society, members of the Secret Elite took exceptional care to remove all traces of their conspiracy. Letters to and from Alfred Milner were culled, removed, burned or otherwise destroyed.[19] Milner's remaining papers, held in the Bodleian Library, Oxford, bear witness to the zeal with which much evidence of wrongdoing has been obliterated. Secret dispatches that he sent to his friend Lord Selborne have disappeared. Milner burned private and personal telegrams[20] and what remains of the cull undertaken by Lady Violet Milner after his death represents only the bare rump of his voluminous correspondence. Incriminating letters sent by King Edward were subject to an order that on his death they must be destroyed immediately. Admiral Jacky Fisher noted in his *Memories* that he had been advised by Lord Knollys, the king's private secretary, to burn all letters sent to him by the king. Fisher consequently burned much of his royal correspondence but couldn't bear to part with it all.[21] Lord Nathaniel Rothschild likewise ordered that his papers and correspondence be burned posthumously lest his political influence and connections became known. As his recent biographer commented, one can but 'wonder how much of the Rothschilds' political role remains irrevocably hidden from posterity'.[22] That is exactly what they tried to do: hide their role in causing the First World War from posterity.

If anything, the systematic conspiracy of the British government to cover all traces of its own devious machinations was far worse and utterly inexcusable. Even if we assume that the surviving records of the Committee of Imperial Defence were accurate, what remains tells us more about what is missing. Cabinet records for July 1914, covering the 4th to the 21st, relate almost exclusively to Ireland.[23] Discussion about the Balkans? None. Belgium? None. No paper appeared that weighed concerns and consequences of a German invasion of Belgium. It had to appear that this conundrum had suddenly been sprung on Britain.

While the official notice in the Public Record Office List of Cabinet Papers warns that 'the papers listed . . . are certainly not the whole of those collectively considered by Cabinet Ministers', the gap is breathtaking, and no effort has been made to explain why crucial records are missing or what happened to them. Nothing is included from 14 July until 20 August, by which time the First World War had entered its third week. It beggars belief that so much has disappeared, been destroyed, burned or 'not been kept for whatever reason'.[24] In fairness to the librarians and custodians of the Public Record Office, they could only catalogue what was passed to them from the Cabinet Office, the Foreign Office, the War Office and the Colonial Office. The British public has a right to know the full extent of what has been secretly retained, hidden or gone 'missing'.

In the early 1970s, the Canadian historian Nicholas D'Ombrain began researching War Office records. He noted:

> The Registry Files were in a deplorable condition, having suffered the periodic ravages of the policy of 'weeding'. One such clearance was in progress during my foray into these files, and I found that my material was being systematically reduced by as much as five-sixths.[25]

Astonishingly, a large amount of 'sensitive' material was actually removed as the researcher went about his business. Where did it go? Who authorised its removal? In addition, D'Ombrain noted that minutes of the Committee of Imperial Defence and 'circulation and invitation lists' together with much 'routine' correspondence had been destroyed.[26] What still required to be hidden from historians and researchers in 1970? That D'Ombrain found five-sixths of the total files melting away in front of him demonstrated clearly that others still retained a vested interest in keeping the evidence of history hidden.

Official memoirs covering the origins of the First World War were carefully scrutinised and censored before being released. Sir Edward Grey's *Twenty-Five Years* is an appalling excuse for a record of fact, and the convenience of his failing memory rings hollow. Lloyd George's *War Memoirs* naturally centre on himself but contain pieces that suggest a censor's pen. Instead of detailing the help he received from Lord Rothschild at the very start of the war, Lloyd George restrained his comment to 'it was done',[27] leaving the reader to wonder precisely what 'it' was. Ambassador Sir George Buchanan's memoirs, *My Mission to Russia and other Diplomatic Memories*, contained information too revealing for publication. His daughter Meriel stated that he was obliged to omit passages from his book on pain of losing his pension.[28]

Utterly unacceptable as this is, in the light of the lies that have been purveyed as history, it is surely of even greater concern that Carroll Quigley pointed an accusing finger at those who monopolised 'so completely the writing and the teaching of the history of their own period'. There is no ambivalence in his accusation. The Secret Elite controlled the writing and teaching of history through numerous avenues, including the Northcliffe stables, but none more effectively than Oxford University. Almost every important member of the Milner Group was a fellow of one of three colleges – Balliol, New College or All Souls. The Milner Group largely dominated these colleges, and they, in turn, largely dominated the intellectual life of Oxford in the field of history.[29] The influence of the Milner Group at Oxford was so powerful that it controlled the *Dictionary of National Biography*, which meant that the Secret Elite wrote the biographies of its own members.[30] They created their own official history of key members for public consumption, striking out any incriminating evidence and portraying the best public-spirited image that could be safely manufactured.

The immediate advantage lay with the victors, and they ensured that their voluminous histories carried the message that the 'Great War' had been Germany's responsibility. Kaiser Wilhelm, viciously maligned by the Secret Elite, abdicated on 28 November 1918 and went into exile in Holland.

His memoirs, published in 1922, strongly defended Germany's innocence. For years, few believed Wilhelm's protestations, but the steady release of documents from Russia and Germany in the 1920s drew others to question the official 'evidence'. American historians began to pay closer attention to the war's origins, including Sidney Bradshaw Fay, professor of history at Harvard and Yale. He published articles in 1920 that led to demands for a 'revision' of the Versailles war-guilt conclusions. Fay's masterly twin volume, *The Origins of the World War*, first published in 1928, was matched by another powerful denunciation of the lies, *The Genesis of the World War* by Harry Elmer Barnes, professor of history at the prestigious Columbia University. It went deeper and further than Professor Fay's work in supporting Germany, but, like Carroll Quigley's history *Tragedy and Hope*, it was suppressed. Barnes explained:

> A major difficulty has been the unwillingness of booksellers to cooperate, even when it was to their pecuniary advantage to do so. Many of them have assumed to censor their customers' reading in the field of international relations as in the matter of morals. Not infrequently have booksellers even discouraged prospective customers who desired to have *The Genesis of the World War* ordered for them.[31]

Booksellers unwilling to sell books? That was surely an unusual situation, unless of course other influences – powerful, moneyed influences – wanted to restrict the circulation and squeeze the life from such work. Barnes expanded the historic debate by inviting German and Austrian politicians who played key roles in July 1914 to provide eyewitness evidence for a special edition of the *New York Times Current History Magazine* in July 1928. The result was a fierce rejection of German war guilt.[32] The Secret Elite grew concerned. If this revisionist historical research was allowed to continue unabated, they faced the possibility of being unmasked. The peasant revolt had to be put down.

A steady stream of anti-revisionist histories that once more blamed Germany for causing the war began to appear. In 1930, American historian Professor Bernadotte Schmitt, who had studied at Oxford, published *The Coming of the War: 1914*. His work was heavily biased against Germany and reaffirmed her war guilt. Schmitt was awarded the Pulitzer Prize and, fittingly, the George Louis Beer Prize from the American History Association. Beer was specifically named by Professor Quigley as a member of the American branch of Rhodes' secret society.[33] Was it simply a coincidence that Schmitt had been a Rhodes scholar and was consequently awarded a major honour in memory of a Rhodes devotee who was the

American correspondent for Milner's Round Table journal?

One year later, Professor M.H. Cochran of the University of Missouri demolished Schmitt's work. Among other things, he proved that it contained major errors and used false methodology to 'uphold the fantasies of 1914'. He demonstrated that Schmitt's book was 'an appalling attempt, clothed in the elaborate trappings of scholarship, to uphold with pro-British bias the Entente myth which mountains of objective historical evidence had discredited since 1920'.[34]

In 1961, Fritz Fischer, professor of history at Hamburg University, rocked the academic world with his book *Germany's Aims in the First World War*. He presented selected evidence from German archives to 'prove' Germany had indeed deliberately abused the archduke's assassination and the July crisis as an excuse to go to war. Here, surely, was the final proof: German fault proven by a German historian. *The Times* immediately sang the praises of Fischer's book in the *Literary Supplement*:

> A brilliant example of history written from the original records . . . It is by far the most comprehensive study of its subject yet produced and, startling as some of its conclusions must at first appear, it seems unlikely that they can be seriously challenged in view of the weight of the evidence . . .[35]

The book helped suppress the truth for decades, but in 2006 Marc Trachtenberg, professor of political science at the University of California, demolished Fischer's thesis. Amongst other elementary 'errors', Fischer had distorted and misrepresented documents, and paraphrased conversations that did not correspond to the actual wording.[36]

Although now widely accepted as highly suspect, Fischer's thesis continues to receive support in Britain. Among others who have recently held it up as sound history is Hartmut Pogge von Strandmann, professor of modern history at Oxford. Professor von Strandmann was a student of Fischer's before he moved to Oxford in the 1960s as research fellow and junior dean at Balliol College.

The Oxford link goes ever on. Norman Stone, one of von Strandmann's professorial predecessors between 1984 and 1997, wrote: 'Princip stated if I had not done it, the Germans would have another excuse. In this, he was right. Berlin was waiting for the inevitable accident.'[37] Sir Hew Strachan, Chichele professor of the history of war at Oxford and a fellow of All Souls, also absolved Britain and France of blame. His conclusion was that for those liberal countries struggling to defend their freedoms (against Germany), the war was far from futile. With reference to Poincaré, Professor Strachan wrote: 'he firmly believed that the solidarity of the alliance system in Europe helped create a balance which prevented war'.[38] The Oxford don added:

> the original purpose of the Anglo-French Entente of 1904 was not to create a united front against Germany, but to settle the two powers' long-standing imperial rivalries in North Africa . . . The Kaiser . . . had little interest in Morocco but he was anxious to disrupt the Anglo-French Entente.[39]

No mention here of the secret clauses and what they hid.[40] No mention either of Poincaré the Revanchist, or his blatant anti-German outbursts.

A.J.P. Taylor, a fellow of Magdalene College and lecturer in modern history at Oxford from 1938 to 1963, was a prolific and popular historian from the 1960s until his death in 1990. He was the classroom 'guru'. Virtually every school course in modern history in the land used A.J.P. Taylor's texts. When he decided that it was not true to claim that 'mobilisation means war',[41] then that was what was learned as fact, no matter the evidence from Russia, from France, or from the waves of diplomatic telegrams warning them to mobilise in secret. In like vein, Sir Michael Howard, formerly Chichele professor of the history of war at Oxford, fellow of All Souls and emeritus professor of modern history at Oxford, denied the automatic implication of mobilisation, claiming that 'Russian mobilisation gave her [Germany] the excuse'.[42]

So the mobilisation of between one and two million Russian soldiers on Germany's border was simply an excuse for her to go to war: a war on two fronts that she had desperately striven to avoid? Little evidence was offered by either of these learned authorities. They spoke *ex cathedra*, pronouncing the verdict of Oxford on the causes of the First World War like medieval popes, and God help the student that questioned their divine bull.

The message has been made clear: blame Germany. It is our opinion that modern histories of the First World War should be treated with critical caution, especially those that have emanated from Oxford University, the spiritual home of the Secret Elite. In Britain generally, diaries and memoirs have been censored and altered, evidence sifted, removed, burned, carefully 'selected' and falsified. Bad as this is, it is of relatively minor importance compared to the Secret Elite's outrageous theft of the historical record from across Europe. In the immediate post-war years, hundreds of thousands of important documents pertaining to the origins of the First World War were taken from their countries of origin to the west coast of America and hidden away in locked vaults at Stanford University. The documents, which would without doubt have exposed the real perpetrators, had to be removed to a secure location and hidden from prying eyes.

A 45-year-old 'mining engineer', Herbert Clark Hoover, was the Secret

Elite agent charged with the mammoth task of removing incriminating documents from Europe. During the war, Hoover played a major role for the Secret Elite in operating an emergency food-supply organisation that was allegedly created to save starving Belgian civilians. In reality, the Commission for Relief of Belgium (CRB) had a much more sinister motive that will be revealed in our next book.

An American by birth, Herbert Hoover worked in an Arizona mine owned by the Rothschilds. His geological surveys won high praise, and he came to the attention of Rothschild mining experts.[43] Sent in 1897 to manage Australian gold mines, Hoover proved himself ruthless. He became notorious as a hard, callous manager who cost lives by cutting back on safety props and was cordially hated by even the toughest of the Australian miners.[44]

In the early years of the twentieth century, Hoover moved to China and fraudulently gained control of the state-owned Kaiping coalmines. The Secret Elite in London backed Hoover's activities to the extent that Royal Navy ships were sent in to protect his interests. The Chinese government eventually took legal action against him in the London courts, and Hoover was forced to confess that he had used repeated threats and brute force to claim ownership of the mines.[45]

Through the Chinese Engineering and Mining Company, which became 'an octopus, racketeering in the stock market, racketeering in the mines and racketeering in human lives',[46] Hoover expanded his own empire. He supplied the British South Africa Company with the Chinese labourers whose abuse cost Alfred Milner dear,[47] and his Rothschild/Milner links were embedded in his racketeering excesses. His co-director in the mining company, and its highly profitable slave-driving sideline, was Emile Francqui, an ex officer in the forces of King Leopold of Belgium. Francqui had 'distinguished' himself in the brutal Belgian regime that massacred, tortured and mutilated millions of natives in the Congo to provide vast profits for Leopold's company.[48] This same Francqui later worked closely with his 'humanitarian' colleague, Herbert Hoover, to relieve the starving children in Europe – or so it was officially portrayed. Hoover's bloody reputation was revised during the war to project the false image of an enlightened Quaker philanthropist, a caring man who had repatriated Americans stranded in Europe in August 1914 and gone on to head the CRB. Hoover the ruthless, evil racketeer was reinvented as Hoover the saviour of starving children.

In early 1919, Herbert Hoover was given another important task by the Secret Elite as they set about removing documentary evidence about the origins of the First World War. They reinvented him again, this time as a scholarly individual who 'loved books' and wished to collect manuscripts and reports relating to the war because they would otherwise 'easily deteriorate and disappear'.[49] No government gave official sanction to his removal of historical artefacts. It was theft dressed as a philanthropic act of preservation for the use of future historians. Indeed, like the thief in the night, stealth was the rule of thumb.

On the basis that it was kept 'entirely confidential', Ephraim Adams, professor of history at Stanford University, a close friend of Hoover's from their student days, was called to Paris to coordinate the great heist and dress it in a cloak of academic respectability. Hoover 'donated' $50,000 to the project, recruited a management team of 'young scholars' from the American army and secured their release from military service. His team used letters of introduction and logistical support from Hoover to collect material and establish a network of representatives throughout Europe.[50] He persuaded General John Pershing to release 15 history professors and students serving in various ranks of the American Expeditionary Force in Europe and sent them, in uniform, to the countries his agency was feeding. With food in one hand and reassurance in the other, these agents faced little resistance in their quest. They made the right contacts, 'snooped' around for archives and found so many that Hoover 'was soon shipping them back to the US as ballast in the empty food boats'.[51]

Hoover recruited an additional 1,000 agents whose first haul amounted to 375,000 volumes of the 'Secret War Documents' of European governments.[52] Hoover's $50,000 'donation' would have paid for around 70 of these agents for a year, and it has not been possible to discover from which sources he funded the other 930. Most likely they were American or British military personnel released to Hoover under the direct orders of the Secret Elite, in which case the ultimate source of their funding was the British and US taxpayer.

Hoover's backers believed that there would only be ten years within which the most valuable material could be 'acquired', but it could take 'a thousand years' to catalogue it. The collection was accelerated to a 'frenzied pace'.[53] They were primarily interested in material relating to the war's origins and the workings of the Commission for Relief of Belgium. Other documents relating to the war itself were ignored. The secret removal and disposal of incriminatory British and French material posed little or no problem for the Secret Elite, and, surprisingly, once the Bolsheviks had taken control, access to Russian documents proved straightforward. Professor Miliukov, foreign minister in the old Kerensky regime, informed Hoover that some of the czarist archives pertaining to the origins of the war had been concealed in a barn in Finland. Hoover later boasted that 'Getting them was no trouble at all. We were feeding Finland at the time.'[54]

The Secret Elite thus took possession of a mass of evidence from the old czarist regime that undoubtedly contained hugely damaging information on Sarajevo and Russia's secret mobilisation. Likewise, damning correspondence between Sazonov and Isvolsky in Paris, and Sazonov and Hartwig in Belgrade, has been 'lost' to posterity. As shown in Chapter 19, the Russian diplomatic papers from 1914 revealed an astonishing gap. Ambassador Hartwig's dispatches from Belgrade for the crucial period between May and July 1914, when the decisions on Franz Ferdinand's assassination were being finalised, were removed from the archives of the Russian Foreign Ministry by an unknown person. These were documents of momentous importance that would have changed for ever the myth of Sarajevo.

It might at first appear strange that the Bolsheviks cooperated so willingly by allowing Hoover's agents to remove 25 carloads of material from Petrograd.[55] According to the *New York Times*, Hoover's team bought the Bolshevik documents from a 'doorkeeper' for $200 cash,[56] but there were darker forces at play that we will examine at a later date.

The removal of documents from Germany presented few problems. Fifteen carloads of material were taken, including 'the complete secret minutes of the German Supreme War Council' – a 'gift' from Friedrich Ebert, first president of the post-war German Republic. Hoover explained that Ebert was 'a radical with no interest in the work of his predecessors',[57] but the starving man will exchange even his birthright for food. Hoover's people also acquired 6,000 volumes of court documents covering the complete official and secret proceedings of the kaiser's war preparations and his wartime conduct of the German empire.[58]

Where then is the vital evidence to prove Germany's guilt? Had there been proof it would have been released immediately. There was none. Possession of the German archives was especially crucial since they would have proved conclusively to the world that Germany had not started the war.

By 1926, the 'Hoover War Library' was so packed with documentary material that it was legitimately described as the largest in the world dealing with the First World War.[59] In reality, this was no library. While the documents were physically housed within Stanford, the collection was kept separate and only individuals with the highest authorisation and a key to the padlock were allowed access. In 1941, 22 years after Hoover began the task of secreting away the real history of the First World War, selected documents were made available to the public. What was withheld from view or destroyed will never be known. Suffice to say that no First World War historian has ever reproduced or quoted any controversial material housed in what is now known as the Hoover Institution on War, Revolution and Peace. Indeed, it is a startling fact that few if any war historians have ever written about this illicit theft of European documents to America: documents that relate to arguably the most crucially important event in European and world history. Why?

Before his death in 1964, Hoover reflected that the institution had to constantly and dynamically point the road to 'peace', to 'personal freedom' and 'private enterprise'.[60] His words betray an Orwellian doublespeak, a contradiction conjured from the past by the rewriting of history. To him and his ilk, black was white, war was peace. 'Personal freedom' was restricted to rich, white Anglo-Saxons, not men of Chinese origin such as those he sold into slavery, or the black people his good friend Francqui mutilated and butchered in the Congo. 'Private enterprise' was the obscene profits they made from such atrocities. It was the language of the Secret Elite.

What this *Hidden History* has revealed is not reflected in British historical writing. Perhaps one day it will be. What is taught in classrooms and lecture halls bears no resemblance to the narrative in this book. Some historians have worn a straightjacket, limited by their willingness to go no further than the official evidence provided by departments of state, government reports, selected documentation, officially sanctioned histories and well-cleansed memoirs. Those who consider that the only true history is that which can be evidenced to the last letter necessarily constrain their own parameters. The individual who attempts to climb a mountain by taking only the given pathway may well discover that, far from reaching the summit, he/she has become a cross-country runner moving between markers deliberately set to confuse.

Ian Bell, the renowned Scottish journalist, wrote recently:

> What is known has to be said. What happened has to be faced. History, that baffling mess, has to be confronted. When you fail in the duty to truth, malevolence fills the vacuum. The evidence for that miserable proposition has been accumulating for generations.[61]

After a century of propaganda, lies and brainwashing about the First World War, cognitive dissonance renders us too uncomfortable to bear the truth that it was a small, socially advantaged group of self-styled English race patriots, backed by powerful industrialists and financiers in Britain and the United States, who caused the First World War. The determination of this London-based Secret Elite to destroy Germany and take control of the world was ultimately responsible for the deaths of millions of honourable young men who were betrayed and sacrificed in a mindless, bloody slaughter to further a dishonourable cause. Today, tens of thousands of war memorials in villages, towns and cities across the world bear witness to the great lie, the betrayal, that they died for 'the greater glory of God' and 'that we might be free'. It is a lie that binds them to a myth. They are remembered in empty roll calls erected to conceal the war's true purpose. What they deserve is the truth, and we must not fail them in that duty.

APPENDIX 1

The Secret Elite's Hidden Control and Connections, 1891–1914

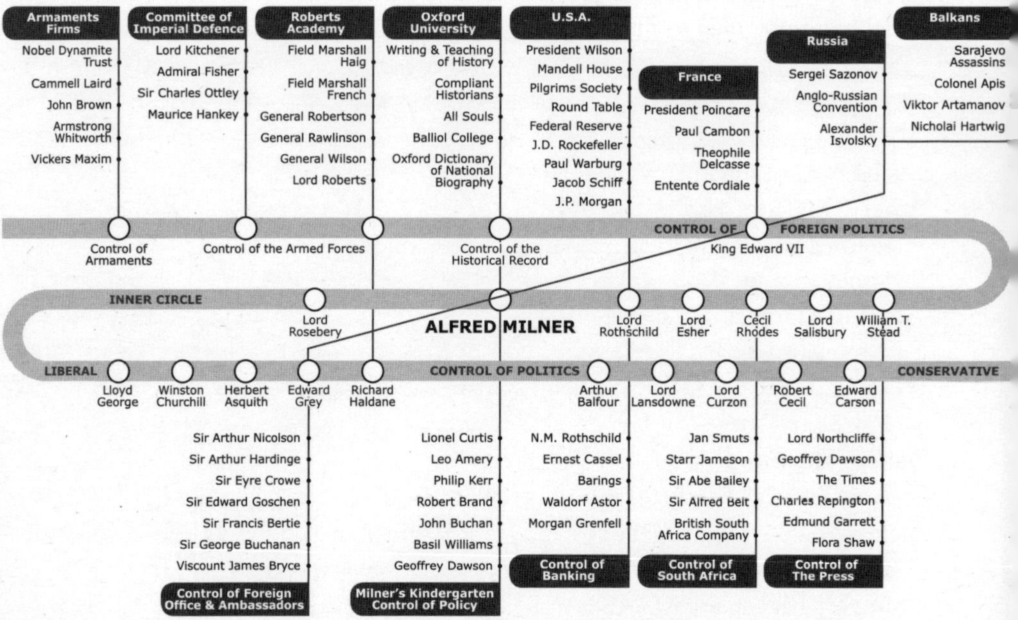

APPENDIX 2

Key Players

KEY LIST A

Members and associates of the Secret Elite up to 1914. Those given by Professor Quigley as members of the Rhodes secret society are marked *. Final honours given to them by the Crown are underlined.

Albert Edward Saxe-Coburg (Edward VII) – King/Emperor of United Kingdom and dominions 1901–10, responsible for entente with France and Russia, much-travelled diplomat and schemer for Empire

Amery, Rt Hon. Leo* – Balliol, All Souls, Kindergarten, Round Table, lifelong friend of Alfred Milner, Conservative MP, Companion of Honour

Asquith, Herbert – Liberal imperialist, Relugas Three member, British prime minister 1908–16, 1st Earl of Oxford and Asquith

Astor, Waldorf* – American-born, Eton and Oxford, newspaper owner, 2nd Viscount Astor

Balfour, Rt Hon. Arthur* – British prime minister 1902–05, leader of Conservative Party, foreign secretary 1916–19, 1st Earl of Balfour

Bailey, Abe* – Tied to Rhodes and South African goldbugs, heavily fined for Jameson Raid involvement, financially supported Round Table and imperialist causes, KCMG

Beit, Alfred* – Millionaire colleague of Cecil Rhodes, involved in supporting Jameson Raid, founder of De Beers and British South Africa Company, imperialist, Round Table financier, gifted chair of Commonwealth history to Oxford University, given baronetcy

Bertie, Francis – Ambassador at Paris 1905–18, played a major role in the Entente Cordiale, privy counsellor, several knighthoods, including Grand Cross Order of the Bath, Viscount Bertie of Thame

Buchanan, George – British ambassador at St Petersburg 1910–17, played major role from 1910 in reassuring Russian foreign minister Sazonov, Knighthood, privy counsellor

Carson, Edward – Barrister and Conservative MP, Ulster Unionist leader, Knighthood, 1st Baron Carson

Cassel, Ernest – German-born banker, financier and businessman, close to King Edward VII and Lord Esher, friend of Alfred Milner, sent to Berlin before Haldane's 'Mission', Knight Grand Cross of the Order of the Bath

Cecil, Lord Robert* – Conservative politician, son of Lord Salisbury, Viscount Cecil of Chelswood

Chamberlain, Joseph – Conservative, secretary of state for colonies during the Boer War

Childers, Erskine – Influential author, friend of Lord Roberts and Churchill, cousin to Chancellor Hugh Childers, apparent 'gun-runner' for Irish Nationalists but immediately recruited to Admiralty duties at start of war

Churchill, Winston – Aristocrat who moved naturally in Secret Elite circles, self-publicist, and opportunist, maverick Conservative who crossed to Liberals in 1904, home secretary 1910–11, First Lord of Admiralty 1911–15, Knight Companion Order of the Garter

Crawford, Fred – Director of ordnance for the UVF, responsible for the successful importation of German guns to Larne, Commander of the British Empire

Crowe, Eyre – German-born diplomat, Foreign Office mentor to Sir Edward Grey, wrote key memoranda about the need for war with Germany, Knight Grand Cross of the Order of the Bath

Curtis, Lionel* – Milner's Kindergarten, All Souls, Round Table, Beit lecturer in colonial history, Oxford 1912

Curzon, George – Eton and Balliol, All Souls, Grillion's, viceroy of India 1899–1905, chancellor of Oxford University, 1st Marquis Curzon of Kedleston

Dawson, Geoffrey* – Eton, Oxford, All Souls, Milner protégé, Kindergarten, Milner had him appointed editor of the *Johannesburg Star*, editor of *The Times* 1912–19, prominent imperialist

de Bunsen, Sir Maurice – British ambassador at Madrid 1906–13, Vienna 1913–14, Knighthood and 1st Baronet de Bunsen of Abbey Lodge

Esher, Reginald* – Co-founder of Rhodes' secret society, South African War Commission, permanent member of Committee of Imperial Defence, personal friend and representative of King Edward, Viscount Esher

Fisher, John (Jacky) – Admiral, first sea lord 1904–10, 1914–15, close to Milner and British royal family, advised 'Copenhagening' German fleet, 1st Baron Fisher

French, John – Roberts' Academy, Anglo-Irish Cavalry officer in Boer

War, chief of imperial general staff 1912, commander in chief of British Expeditionary Force 1914, Viscount Fisher, 1st Earl Ypres

Goschen, Edward – Ambassador at Berlin, 1908–14, Knight Grand Cross Royal Victorian Order, privy counsellor and 1st Baronet of Beacon Lodge

Grey, Albert* – Governor General of Canada 1904–11, Rhodes trustee, British South Africa Company, Grand Cross Order of the Bath

Grey, Sir Edward – Balliol, Grillion's and The Club, Liberal imperialist, member of Relugas Three, British foreign secretary 1905–16, Viscount Grey of Fallodon

Haldane, Richard B. – Liberal imperialist, member of Relugas Three, secretary of state for war 1905–12, lord chancellor 1912–15, favourite of King Edward, Viscount Haldane of Cloan

Hankey, Maurice* – Background in naval intelligence, assistant secretary to Committee of Imperial Defence in 1908, secretary from 1912, ensured that every government department, save the Treasury, had a war book prepared in advance of August 1914, 1st Baron Hankey

Hardinge, Sir Charles – Diplomat, ambassador at St Petersburg 1904–06, permanent under-secretary at Foreign Office 1906–10 and 1916–20, personal friend and advisor to King Edward VII, accompanied him on all foreign diplomatic tours, 1st Baron Hardinge of Penshurst

Jameson, Leander Starr* – Scottish doctor, close personal friend and colleague of Rhodes and Milner, took the blame for the botched Jameson Raid in the Transvaal, imprisoned in Holloway, rewarded by Secret Elite, prime minister of Cape Colony 1904–08, freedom of cities of Edinburgh, London and Manchester, Knighthood, KCMG and 1st Baron Jameson

Kipling, Rudyard – British author, poet and imperialist, personal friend of Cecil Rhodes and Alfred Milner, Kipling wrote jingoistic poems in praise of militarism, connected to Lord Roberts, Ulster and the Empire, awarded Nobel Prize for Literature in 1907

Kitchener, Herbert – British soldier and national hero, commander-in-chief 1914–16, secretary of state for war 1914–16, 1st Earl Kitchener

Lansdowne, Henry – Governor General of Canada 1883–88, viceroy of India 1888–94, secretary of state for war 1895–1900, foreign secretary 1900–05, senior and influential Conservative, close confidant of A.J. Balfour, Marquis of Lansdowne

Long, Walter – Conservative politician, backed by Lord Salisbury, chief secretary for Ireland 1905, member of the Ulster Defence League, 1st Viscount Long

Lloyd George, David – Liberal MP, anti-war, chancellor of Exchequer 1908–16, involved in many scandals, 1st Earl Lloyd George of Dwyfor

Milner, Alfred* – Balliol and fellow of New College, intimate of Rhodes, acknowledged leader of the Secret Elite from around 1900, created the Boer War, governor of Cape Colony and high commissioner for Southern Africa 1897–1901, mentor for the Round Table, Conservative politician, 1st Viscount Milner of St James

Nicolson, Arthur – Senior diplomat, ambassador at Madrid 1904–05 and St Petersburg 1906–10, permanent under-secretary at the Foreign Office 1910–16, controlled the Foreign Office and guided Edward Grey, attended Committee of Imperial Defence, close to Alfred Milner, member of Grillion's, Knight Grand Cross Order of the Bath, 1st Baron Carnock

Ottley, Charles – Director of Naval Intelligence 1905–07, secretary to Committee of Imperial Defence 1908–12, director of Armstrong Whitworth & Co., Knighthood, KCMG

Paget, Arthur – Commander-in-chief in Ireland 1912–14, deeply involved with the Curragh incident, two knighthoods, Knight Grand Cross Order of the Bath, Knight Grand Cross, Royal Victorian Order

Repington, Charles – Ex-army officer, war correspondent and journalist, had his own office in the War Office, wrote for *The Times*, linked to the joint discussions with French military

Rhodes, Cecil John* – Founder member of secret society, Oxford scholar, British race patriot, used his fortune to promote the British Empire to control civilised world, millionaire South African gold and diamond magnate, British South Africa Company, prime minister of Cape Colony 1890–96, Rhodesia named after him, owed much to Rothschild funding, donated his estate to Rhodes Scholarships and the trustees had great power in using his fortune, complete faith in Alfred Milner – his chosen successor and trustee, privy counsellor

Roberts, Frederick Sleigh – Most senior British Army officer of his time, last commander-in-chief before post abolished in 1904, founder of the Roberts 'Academy' – trusted officers schooled in his own image – advocated conscription and increased spending on army, close friend of Milner and Esher, 1st Earl Roberts, Viscount St Pierre

Rosebery, Lord* – (Also known as Archibald Primrose, Lord Dalmeny) Eton and Oxford, British prime minister 1894–95, leading Liberal, patron and friend of Milner and the Relugas Three, 5th Earl Rosebery

Rothschild, Nathaniel* – International banker and financier, head of British branch of Rothschild dynasty, close Cambridge friend of Prince Albert Edward, later Edward VII, whose gambling debts he covered generously, trustee of Rhodes' early wills, friend of Milner, used J.P. Morgan as front to cover family involvement in America/Wall Street, massive investor in gold, diamonds, oil, steel, railways and armaments, 1st Baron Rothschild

Selborne, Earl* (W.W. Palmer) – Lifelong Oxford friend of Milner, worked on his behalf as under-secretary at the Colonial Office, KCMG, privy counsellor

Shaw, Flora* – Pro-Boer War *Times* columnist, friend of Milner and corresponded with him to promote the war in South Africa, belittled the alarmists on concentration camps and rewrote the 'History of the South African War' for *Encyclopaedia Britannica*, Dame Flora Shaw, Lady Lugard

Stead, William T.* – Co-founder of Rhodes' secret society, campaigning journalist, imperialist, pro-naval spending, fell out with Secret Elite over the Boer War and removed as trustee of Rhodes' last will

Williams, Basil – Milner's Kindergarten, close friend of Erskine Childers, professor of history at Edinburgh University 1925–37, contributor to the *Oxford History of England*, OBE

Wilson, Henry – Protégé of Lord Roberts, brigadier general of Camberley Staff College, director of military operations at the War Office, pro Ulster Unionist and UVF admirer, prepared plans for BEF, member of Committee of Imperial Defence, secretly briefed Milner and Conservatives against his own government, 1st Baron Wilson of Currygrane

Key List B

British politicians and writers NOT associated with the Secret Elite

Campbell-Bannerman, Sir Henry – Liberal leader and prime minister 1905–08

Durham, Edith – British traveller and writer who wrote extensively about the Balkans and the ethnic massacres, highly critical of British Foreign Office, which ignored her work

Morel, Edmund – Journalist, author and socially aware MP, imprisoned for his pacifism, wrote extensively about the warmongers, outspoken critic of Grey and Asquith, one of the most important pre-war commentators

Morley, John – Prominent Liberal, secretary of state for India, resigned as lord president of the council in 1914 because Grey and Asquith declared war, Viscount Morley of Blackburn

Ponsonby, Arthur – Eton and Balliol, Liberal MP, outspoken critic of Sir Edward Grey, went to the House of Lords in 1930

Key List C

Foreign personnel. Those we consider agents of the Secret Elite are identified with an *.

Aehrenthal, Count Alois – Austrian minister of foreign affairs 1906–12

Artamanov, Viktor – Russian military attaché in Belgrade, key link between Hartwig and the Sarajevo assassins

Caillaux, Joseph – French prime minister 1911–12, socialist, anti-war, resolved the conflict with Germany over Morocco

Cambon, Jules – French ambassador at Berlin 1907–14, head of French Foreign Ministry 1914–18

Cambon, Paul* – French ambassador at London 1898–1920, played important role in entente and in diplomatic exchanges that helped cement Anglo-French relations

Ciganovic, Milan – Conspired with Serbian military and secret service to help the Young Bosnians, informant for Prime Minister Pasic, who shielded him after the assassination

Delcassé, Theophile* – French foreign minister 1898–1905, Revanchist, anti-German, friend of King Edward VII, played major role in entente, dismissed from government in 1905, reinstated in 1911 as minister of marine, ambassador at St Petersburg 1913–14, supported by Secret Elite

Dimitrijevic, Dragutin – (Apis) Serbian nationalist leader, head of Masonic-like secret order the Black Hand, commanded large military following, complicit in regicide of King Alexander in 1903, initially supported Prime Minister Pasic

Greindl, Baron Jules – Belgian ambassador at Berlin 1888–1912, very astute, his observations were highly accurate

Guillaume, Baron – Belgian minister at Berlin

Hartwig, Nicholas – Russian minister at Tehran 1906–08, minister at Belgrade 1909–14, controlled Pasic government in Serbia, Isvolsky's alter ego, died 1914 under suspicious circumstances

Isvolsky, Alexander* – Russian ambassador at Copenhagen 1903, friend of King Edward VII, Russian foreign minister 1906–10, ambassador to Paris 1910–16, bribed French press and deputies, close to Poincaré and Delcassé, stirred trouble in Balkans, died suddenly while writing memoirs

Jaurès, Jean – French Socialist leader, strongly anti-war, assassinated 31 July 1914, his assailant was acquitted

Lichnowsky, Prince – German ambassador at London 1912–14, said to be very pro-English and had been sucked into 'society' in London

Louis, George – French ambassador at St Petersburg, disliked and dismissed by Poincaré, distrusted the Revanchists, was kept away from the real business when French government visited Russia in 1912

Malobabić, Rade – Chief undercover operative for Serbian military intelligence, helped plan assassination in Sarajevo

Morgan, John Pierpont* – Pilgrim, New York banker and financier, closely associated with the Rothschild dynasty, anglophile, worked to achieve Federal Reserve

Nicholas II – Czar, weak-willed and vacillating hereditary leader of Russia, his government struggled against popular labour unrest and demands for democracy, responding with disgraceful attacks on strikers and vicious anti-Jewish pogroms

Pasic, Nikola – (Paschitsch) Prime minister of Serbia (five terms 1891–1918), directed by the Russian ambassador, Hartwig

Princip, Gavrilo – Student assassin, shot Archduke Ferdinand and his wife in Sarajevo, alleged to have started the First World War

Poincaré, Raymond* – Revanchist prime minister (five terms), president of France 1913–20, indebted to Isvolsky and Secret Elite funding for winning office, anti-German, pro-war politician and colleague of Delcassé

Sazonov, Sergei* – Russian foreign minister 1910–16, served in London embassy before being appointed successor to Alexander Isvolsky, who remained his trusted mentor and advisor

Schiff, Jacob* – Pilgrim, New York banker and financier, Kuhn, Loeb & Co., friend of Sir Ernest Cassel and Rothschilds, played a leading role in raising funds for Japan during war with Russia

Shelking, Eugenii – Russian diplomat, journalist, St Petersburg correspondent for *Le Temps*, travelled widely in the Balkans

Smuts, Jan* – Rhodes' protégé in South Africa before the Boer War, changed sides to Kruger in dubious circumstances, post-Boer War he held high office in South Africa, remained firm friend of Alfred Milner, Order of Merit, privy counsellor, Companion of Honour

Tankosić, Major Vojislav – Major in Serbian army, trained Young Bosnian assassins in run up to Sarajevo

von Bethmann-Hollweg, Theobald – German chancellor 1909–17

von Benckendorff, Count – Russian ambassador at London 1903–17, close to Sir Edward Grey, popular in London society

von Jagow, Gottlieb – German foreign minister 1913–16

Warburg, Paul* – German-born US banker, linked to Rothschilds, instrumental in setting up Federal Reserve System

Wilson, Woodrow* – President of United States of America 1912–20, funded and controlled by Secret Elite associates

Young Bosnians – Revolutionary student group who imagined that the assassination of Franz Ferdinand would lead to socialism in the Balkan States, included Danilo Ilić, Gavrilo Princip

Notes

Introduction

1 Niall Ferguson, *Empire*, p. 313.
2 Hew Strachan, *The First World War*, p. 43.
3 Norman Stone, *World War One: A Short History*, p. 9.
4 David Stevenson, *1914–1918: The History of the First World War*, p. 16.
5 Christopher Clark, *The Sleepwalkers: How Europe Went to War in 1914.*
6 The German defensive strategy was created by Count Alfred von Schlieffen and circulated in 1905.
7 Interview can be heard at www.youtube.com/watch?v=JeuF8rYgJPk
8 Carroll Quigley, *The Anglo-American Establishment*, p. x.
9 Ibid.
10 Ibid., p. xi.
11 www.youtube.com/watch?v=JeuF8rYgJPk
12 Quigley, *Anglo-American Establishment*, p. x.

Chapter 1 – The Secret Society

1 W.T. Stead, *The Last Will and Testament of Cecil John Rhodes*, p. 62.
2 Virginia Cowles, *The Rothschilds: A Family of Fortune*, p. 161.
3 The serial killer known as Jack the Ripper murdered between five and eleven prostitutes in the Whitehall district of London in 1888–91. A combination of legend, serious research and folklore still surrounds the killings, but our point is simply to highlight the social chasm that divided Victorian Britain at the same time as the secret society took root.
4 Carroll Quigley, *Anglo-American Establishment*, p. 3.
5 Edward Griffin, *The Creature From Jekyll Island*, p. 272.
6 Quigley, *Anglo-American Establishment*, pp. 4–5.
7 James Lees-Milne, *The Enigmatic Edwardian*, p. 84.
8 Stead, *Last Will and Testament*, p. 59.
9 Quigley, *Anglo-American Establishment*, p. ix.

10 Neil Parsons, *A New History of Southern Africa*, pp. 179–81.
11 Niall Ferguson, *The House of Rothschild: The World's Banker, 1849–1999*, p. 363.
12 Joan Veon, *The United Nations Global Straitjacket*, p. 68.
13 J.A. Hobson, *John Ruskin: Social Reformer*, p. 187.
14 Stead, *Last Will and Testament*, p. 59.
15 Will Podmore, *British Foreign Policy Since 1870*, p. 21.
16 Joseph Ward Swain, *Beginning the Twentieth Century* (first edition), p. 243.
17 Sidney Low, *Nineteenth Century* (magazine), May 1902.
18 Stead, *Last Will and Testament*, p. 23.
19 Ibid., p. 55.
20 W.T. Stead, 'The Maiden Tribute of Modern Babylon', *Pall Mall Gazette*, 6–10 July 1885.
21 W.T. Stead, 'The Case of Eliza Armstrong' at http://www.attackingthedevil.co.uk/pmg/tribute/(W. T. Stead resources site).
22 J. Lee Thompson, *Forgotten Patriot: A Life of Alfred, Viscount Milner of St James's and Cape Town*, p. 34.
23 These included Edmund Garrett (*Cape Times*), E.T. Cook (editor of the *Pall Mall Gazette* and the *Westminster Gazette*) and Geoffrey Dawson (editor of *The Times*), all members of the secret society's inner circle and personal friends and colleagues of Alfred Milner.
24 See the official James Lees-Milne website at http://www.jamesleesmilne.com/books.html
25 Carroll Quigley, *Tragedy and Hope: A History of the World in Our Time*, p. 137.
26 Ferguson, *House of Rothschild*, p. 251.
27 Cowles, *The Rothschilds*, p. 153.
28 E.C. Knuth, *The Empire of the City*, p. 70.
29 Griffin, *Creature from Jekyll Island*, p. 233.
30 Derek Wilson, *Rothschild: The Wealth and Power of a Dynasty*, pp. 98–9.
31 Ferguson, *House of Rothschild*, p. xxvii.
32 Stanley Chapman, *The Rise of Merchant Banking*, p. 25.
33 Knuth, *Empire of the City*, p. 68.
34 Ferguson, *House of Rothschild*, p. xxvii.
35 Ibid., p. 65.
36 Ibid., p. 38.
37 Taken from http://projects.exeter.ac.uk/RDavies/arian/current/howmuch.html 'Measuring Worth', created by Lawrence H. Officer, professor of economics at the University of Illinois at Chicago and Samuel

H. Williamson, professor of economics, emeritus, from Miami University. In all cases, we have used their valuation from the Retail Price Index and all consequent valuations will carry, in brackets, a 2011 value equivalence.

38 Cowles, *The Rothschilds*, p. 147.
39 Ferguson, *House of Rothschild*, p. 251.
40 Ibid., p. 332.
41 Ibid., p. 319.
42 Griffin, *Creature from Jekyll Island*, p. 220.
43 Ferguson, *House of Rothschild*, p. 417.
44 Ibid., p. 319.
45 Ibid., p. 327.
46 Quigley, *Tragedy and Hope*, p. 131.
47 Thompson, *Forgotten Patriot*, p. 75.
48 Quigley, *Anglo-American Establishment*, p. 37.
49 A more balanced view on Milner's contribution to British imperial history was not published until 2007, when J. Lee Thompson's *Forgotten Patriot* was first published.
50 Quigley, *Anglo-American Establishment*, p. 317.
51 Stead, *Last Will and Testament*, p. 108.
52 Quigley, *Anglo-American Establishment*, pp. 16–17.
53 Ibid., p. 45.

CHAPTER 2 – SOUTH AFRICA – DISREGARD THE SCREAMERS

1 Swain, *Beginning the Twentieth Century*, p. 234.
2 Ferguson, *House of Rothschild*, p. 363.
3 Ibid.
4 Quigley, *Anglo-American Establishment*, p. 33, quoting Rhodes' first will of 1877.
5 Swain, *Beginning the Twentieth Century*, p. 234.
6 Quigley, *Tragedy and Hope*, p. 136.
7 Quigley, *Anglo-American Establishment*, p. 312.
8 Podmore, *British Foreign Policy Since 1870*, p. 21.
9 William Engdahl, *A Century of War*, p. 48.
10 Donald McCormick, *Mask of Merlin*, p. 48.
11 Podmore, *British Foreign Policy Since 1870*, p. 21.
12 Quigley, *Tragedy and Hope*, pp. 136–7.
13 Saul David, *Military Blunders*, p. 73.
14 Quigley, *Anglo-American Establishment*, p. 313.
15 Polly Guerin, 'Flora Shaw: A Visionary Journalist' at http://amazingartdecodivas.blogspot.co.uk/2011/02/shaw-flora-visionary-journalist-c-by.html

16 Quigley, *Anglo-American Establishment*, pp. 106–7.
17 Ibid., p. 313.
18 Quigley, *Tragedy and Hope*, pp. 135–7.
19 Thomas Pakenham, *The Boer War*, p. 29.
20 Quigley, *Anglo-American Establishment*, p. 110.
21 Pakenham, *Boer War*, p. 29.
22 Ibid.
23 Quigley, *Anglo-American Establishment*, pp. 110–11.
24 Quigley, *Tragedy and Hope*, p. 137.
25 Pakenham, *Boer War*, p. 22.
26 Jean van der Poel, *The Jameson Raid*, p. 135.
27 John C.G. Rohl, *Wilhelm II: The Kaiser's Personal Monarchy*, p. 792.
28 Swain, *Beginning the Twentieth Century*, p. 38.
29 Quigley, *Anglo-American Establishment*, p. 47.
30 Letters: Esher to Stead, 19 February 1897, cited in Thompson, *Forgotten Patriot*, p. 105.
31 Milner Papers, Milner's Diary, 30 November 1898, dep. 68, Bodleian Library.
32 Thompson, *Forgotten Patriot*, p. 105.
33 Ibid. , p. 108.
34 Quigley, *Anglo-American Establishment*, p. 312.
35 Milner to Chamberlain, dispatch 23 February 1898, cited in Thompson, *Forgotten Patriot*, p. 119.
36 Milner Papers, Selborne to Milner, 21 January 1898, Bodleian Library, Ms.Eng.Hist. c.686.
37 Thompson, *Forgotten Patriot*, p. 124.
38 All are named by Quigley in *Anglo-American Establishment*.
39 Pakenham, *Boer War*, p. 571.
40 Thompson, *Forgotten Patriot*, p. 126.
41 Engdahl, *A Century of War*, p. 49.
42 Pakenham, *Boer War*, p. 21.
43 www.gutenberg.org/ebooks/16494 – *The Transvaal Within*, J. Percy Fitzpatrick, chapter XI.
44 Pakenham, *Boer War*, pp. 54–5.
45 Ibid., p. 88.
46 Milner Papers, Milner to Selborne, 14 June 1899, Bodleian Library, Ms.Eng.Hist. c.686.
47 Quigley, *Tragedy and Hope*, p. 137.
48 Pakenham, *Boer War*, p. 43.
49 Quigley, *Tragedy and Hope*, p. 137.
50 Walter Nimocks, *Milner's Young Men*, p. 4.

51 Pakenham, *Boer War*, p. 54.
52 Ibid., p. 100.
53 Ibid., p. 63.
54 Ibid., p. 109.
55 Ibid., p. 115.
56 Milner Papers, Milner to Selborne, 5 May 1898, Bodleian Library, Ms.Eng.Hist. c.686.
57 Winston Churchill, *My Early Life*, pp. 311–13.
58 Milner Papers, Churchill to Milner, 24 November 1899, Bodleian Library, Ms.Eng.Hist. c.686.
59 Roy Jenkins, *Churchill*, p. 54.
60 Ibid., p. 54; originally *Churchill War Papers*, I, pt. 2, p. 1085.
61 Ibid., p. 60.
62 Earl of Birkenhead, *Churchill: 1874–1922*, p. 96.
63 Virginia Cowles, *Winston Churchill: The Era and the Man*, p. 65.
64 Jenkins, *Churchill*, p. 61.
65 Pakenham, *Boer War*, p. 318.
66 Ibid., p. 319.
67 Milner to Violet Cecil, 27 December 1900, cited in Pakenham, *Boer War*, p. 485.
68 Pakenham, *Boer War*, pp. 487–8.
69 Ibid., p. 464.
70 Kitchener to St John Brodrick, 22 March 1901, cited in Pakenham, *Boer War*, p. 500.
71 Ibid., p. 493. Chapter 39 in Pakenham, *Boer War*, 'When is a War not a War?', gives a very full account of the concentration camps.
72 Emily Hobhouse, 'The Brunt of War, and Where it Fell' at http://archive.org/details/bruntwarandwher01hobhgoog
73 Ibid., p. 174.
74 W.T. Stead, cited in Hennie Barnard, *The Concentration Camps 1899–1902* at http://www.boer.co.za/boerwar/hellkamp.htm
75 Pakenham, *Boer War*, pp. 503–04.
76 http://www-sul.stanford.edu/depts/ssrg/africa/hansxcv2.html#573
77 War Office Official Statistics, Cd. 694.
78 Milner Papers, Haldane to Milner, 26 January 1902, Bodleian Library, Ms.Eng.Hist. c.688.
79 Pakenham, *Boer War*, p. 517.
80 St John Brodrick to Kitchener, as cited in Pakenham, *Boer War*, p. 495.
81 *Journal of the South African Institute of Mining and Metallurgy*, April 1989, p. 118.

82 Thompson, *Forgotten Patriot*, p. 193.
83 Podmore, *British Foreign Policy Since 1870*, pp. 29–30.
84 Bouda Etemad, 'Possessing the World', *European Expansion and Global Interaction*, vol. 6, p. 73.
85 Quigley, *Anglo-American Establishment*, p. 312.
86 Quigley, *Tragedy and Hope*, p. 138.
87 Nimocks, *Milner's Young Men*, p. 21.
88 Ibid.
89 Leo Amery, *Times History of the War in South Africa*, vol. 1, p. 147.
90 The relationship between members of the Secret Elite and All Souls, Oxford, has long been very close indeed. Carroll Quigley pointed out that the select membership opened the door to top jobs in politics, the Foreign Office and diplomatic services. See *Anglo-American Establishment*, pp. 52–3.
91 Quigley, *Anglo-American Establishment*, p. 65.
92 Ibid., chapter 4, pp. 50–83.
93 John Hamill, *The Strange Career of Mr. Hoover Under Two Flags*, pp. 151–2.
94 Ibid., pp. 162–3.
95 The ruthless organisers in China, Herbert Hoover and Emile Francqui, will re-emerge in our narrative in a different guise as directors of crucial Secret Elite activities during the First World War. Hoover's firm shipped over 50,000 of these unfortunate Chinamen with a profit of around $25 a head.
96 Podmore, *British Foreign Policy Since 1870*, p. 30.
97 Hamill, *Strange Career of Mr. Hoover*, p. 165.
98 Thompson, *Forgotten Patriot*, p. 483.
99 Nimocks, *Milner's Young Men*, p. 54.
100 Milner to Balfour, 27 March 1905, cited in Thompson, *Forgotten Patriot*, p. 234.
101 Thompson, *Forgotten Patriot*, p. 240.
102 Quigley, *Anglo-American Establishment*, p. 77.
103 Ibid., pp. 77–8.
104 Ibid., p. 149.
105 Hansard, House of Commons, Debate, 21 March 1906, vol. 154, cc464–511.
106 Hobson, *John Ruskin*, p. 193.
107 Pakenham, *Boer War*, p. 551.
108 Lord Milner's 'Credo', published in *The Times*, 27 July 1925.

Chapter 3 – The Edward Conspiracy – First steps and New Beginnings

1 David S. Landes, *The Unbound Prometheus*, p. 327.
2 Ibid., p. 326.
3 Niall Ferguson, *The Pity of War*, pp. 34–5.
4 John S. Ewart, *The Roots and Causes of the Wars*, vol. II, p. 680.
5 Ibid., p. 681.
6 Landes, *Unbound Prometheus*, p. 327.
7 Keith Hitchins, *Romania 1866–1947*, p. 192.
8 Podmore, *British Foreign Policy Since 1870*, pp. 11–20.
9 Ferguson, *Pity of War*, p. 41.
10 Ibid., p. 42.
11 Hansard, House of Commons, Debate, 13 February 1902, vol. 102, cc1272–313.
12 Hansard, House of Commons, Debate, 26 February 1900, vol. 79, cc1111–79.
13 Ferguson, *Pity of War*, p. 42.
14 Ewart, *Roots and Causes of the Wars*, vol. II, p. 677.
15 Harry Elmer Barnes, *The Genesis of the World War*, p. 456.
16 Grey of Fallodon, *Twenty-Five Years: 1892–1916*, vol. 1, p. 102.
17 Landes, *Unbound Prometheus*, p. 327.
18 Sidney B. Fay, *The Origins of the World War*, vol. I, p. 139.
19 E.D. Morel, *Diplomacy Revealed*, pp. 5–6.
20 Hence the phrase, 'Bob's your uncle'.
21 Kaiser Wilhelm II, *My Memoirs*, p. 99.
22 Virginia Cowles, *The Kaiser*, p. 124.
23 Keith Middlemas, *The Life and Times of Edward VII*, p. 31.
24 Sidney Lee, *Dictionary of National Biography*, Second Supplement, vol. 1, pp. 583–5.
25 Ian Dunlop, *Edward VII and the Entente Cordiale*, p. 169.
26 *The Times*, 23 January 1901.
27 Dunlop, *Edward VII*, p. 170.
28 A.J. Grant and Harold Temperley, *Europe in the Nineteenth and Twentieth Centuries (1789–1932)*, p. 423.
29 Fay, *Origins of the World War*, vol. I, p. 51.
30 Ibid.
31 The term Revanchard was given to French politicians whose main policy was revenge against Germany for the loss of Alsace-Lorraine. Delcassé was deeply involved with the Revanchard movement.
32 Lee, *Dictionary of National Biography*, Second Supplement, vol. 1, p. 593.

33 Ibid., p. 572.
34 Stanley Weintraub, *Edward the Caresser*, p. 126.
35 Article in *The Times*, 17 January 2004, and, *Paris Brothel*, BBC Four documentary, 2003.
36 Andrew Marr, *The Making of Modern Britain*, p. 44.
37 *New York Times*, 28 March 1903.
38 *The London Gazette*, 2 June 1903.
39 Grant and Temperley, *Europe*, p. 423.
40 Fay, *Origins of the World War*, vol. I, p. 153.
41 Grey, *Twenty-Five Years*, vol. 1, p. 107.
42 Morel, *Diplomacy Revealed*, p. 45.
43 Ibid., p. 73.
44 Quigley, *Anglo-American Establishment*, p. 42.
45 Lord Esher had a proclivity for promiscuity with adolescent boys, which, according to his biographer, James Lees-Milne, extended to an unusual relationship with his younger son, Maurice. Like many other upper-class Victorian hypocrites, Esher practised that for which Oscar Wilde was jailed.
46 Lees-Milne, *Enigmatic Edwardian*, p. 142.
47 Nicholas D'Ombrain, *War Machinery and High Policy Defence Administration in Peacetime Britain, 1902–1914*, p. 125.

Chapter 4 – Testing Warmer Waters

1 Ewart, *Roots and Causes of the Wars*, vol. II, p. 762.
2 Quigley, *Anglo-American Establishment*, pp. 101–16.
3 *The Times*, 9 April 1904.
4 Dunlop, *Edward VII*, p. 220.
5 Thompson, *Forgotten Patriot*, p. 68.
6 Grant and Temperley, *Europe*, p. 452.
7 Richard F. Hamilton and Holger H. Herwig, *Decisions for War, 1914–1917*, p. 188.
8 Ewart, *Roots and Causes of the Wars*, vol. I, p. 242.
9 Morel, *Diplomacy Revealed*, p. xvi.
10 E.D. Morel, *Ten Years of Secret Diplomacy*, p. 71.
11 Ibid., p. 58.
12 Ibid., pp. 58–9.
13 Grant and Temperley, *Europe*, p. 425 footnote.
14 Ibid., p. 426.
15 Ewart, *Roots and Causes of the Wars*, vol. II, pp. 768–9.
16 Kaiser William II, *My Memoirs*, p. 104.
17 *New York Times*, 1 April 1905.

18 Morel, *Ten Years of Secret Diplomacy*, p. 61.
19 Ewart, *Roots and Causes of the Wars*, vol. II, pp. 773–4.
20 Ibid., p. 775.
21 Morel, *Diplomacy Revealed*, p. 3.
22 Francis Neilson, *How Diplomats Make War*, p. 101.
23 Morel, *Ten Years of Secret Diplomacy*, p. 63.
24 *Cambridge History of British Foreign Policy*, vol. III, p. 343.
25 Ewart, *Roots and Causes of the Wars*, vol. II, p. 801.
26 *Cambridge History of British Foreign Policy*, vol. III, pp. 483–4.
27 Ewart, *Roots and Causes of the Wars*, vol. II, p. 778.
28 Morel, *Ten Years of Secret Diplomacy*, p. 78.
29 Dunlop, *Edward VII*, p. 237.
30 Fay, *Origins of the World War*, vol. I, p. 188.
31 Morel, *Ten Years of Secret Diplomacy*, pp. 84–5.
32 Ibid., pp. 42–3.
33 Fay, *Origins of the World War*, vol. I, p. 188.
34 Sidney Lee, *King Edward VII: A Biography*, p. 344.
35 Ibid., p. 360.
36 The idea of a British invasion of Schleswig-Holstein was first mooted by Admiral Sir John Fisher, who argued that in the event of a war in Europe against Germany this action would have the immediate effect of drawing a million German soldiers from the front in France. While it was rejected by the Committee of Imperial Defence, the plan was known in diplomatic circles and reached the kaiser's ear in 1905.
37 Lee, *King Edward VII*, p. 360.
38 Ewart, *Roots and Causes of the Wars*, vol. II, p. 786.
39 Lee, *King Edward VII*, p. 361.
40 Ibid.

CHAPTER 5 – TAMING THE BEAR

1 Ewart, *Roots and Causes of the Wars*, vol. II, p. 725.
2 Hansard, House of Commons, Debate, 22 January 1902, vol. 101, cc574–628.
3 Grant and Temperley, *Europe*, p. 415.
4 A.L. Kennedy, *Old Diplomacy and New: From Salisbury to Lloyd George, 1866–1922*, p. 98.
5 George Kennan, *The Fateful Alliance: France, Russia and the Coming of the First World War*, p. 76.
6 Ferguson, *House of Rothschild*. p. 382.
7 Quigley, *Tragedy and Hope*, p. 93.
8 Sir Claude MacDonald presided over the Tokyo Legation in years of

harmony between Britain and Japan (1900–12). MacDonald was in Tokyo when the alliance was renewed in 1905 and 1911. He became Britain's first ambassador to Japan and was made a privy councillor in 1906.

9 Ferguson, *Pity of War*, p. 495.

10 For detailed information see http://www.clydesite.co.uk/viewship.asp?id=5173

11 The *Mikasa* was the flagship of Admiral Togo at the Battle of Tsushima. Built in Barrow, England, she was the last of four battleships ordered under the 1896 Japanese Naval plan.

12 Ewart, *Roots and Causes of the Wars*, vol. II, p. 726.

13 Kennedy, *Old Diplomacy and New*, p. 97.

14 Grant and Temperley, *Europe*, p. 419.

15 Ewart, *Roots and Causes of the Wars*, vol. II, p. 762.

16 Hansard, House of Commons, Debate, 13 February 1902, vol. 102, cc1272–313.

17 Ian Nish, *The Anglo-Japanese: The Diplomacy of Two Island Empires 1894–1907*, pp. 23–50.

18 Kurt Kulhman, 'The Renewal of the Anglo-Japanese Alliance, 1905', academic paper, Department of History, Duke University, 9 January 1992, p. 3.

19 Hansard, House of Commons, Debate, 13 February 1902, vol. 102, cc1272–313.

20 Ibid.

21 Hansard, House of Commons, Debate, 3 July 1902, vol. 110, cc702–59.

22 *Scarborough Evening News*, 24 October 1904.

23 B.H. Liddell Hart, *History of the World War*, p. 9.

24 Recorded in a special cable from Paris to *New York Times*, 27 October 1904.

25 *New York Times*, 25 October 1904.

26 Ibid.

27 *New York Times*, 26 October 1904.

28 *The Times*, 28 October 1904.

29 *New York Times*, 31 October 1904.

30 In 1908, an international committee of enquiry concluded that the fishing fleet was entirely blameless, and the majority of the commissioners (not the Russian representative) agreed that there were no torpedo boats among the trawlers nor anywhere near them. The Dogger Bank Case (Great Britain v Russia), 1908 2 Am. J. Int'L. 931–936 (I.C.I. Report of 26 February 1905).

31 The Imperial Russian Fleet sailed from the Baltic and thus left it at the

mercy of the Imperial German Fleet. Without the generous support of Kaiser Wilhelm in providing coaling facilities and supplies, the Russian Baltic Fleet could never have reached the Far East, as the kaiser was later to remind the czar. (Herman Bernstein, *Willy–Nicky Correspondence*, pp. 68–75.)

32 Ibid., pp. 68–9.

33 *New York Times*, 19 April 1905.

34 *The Times*, 8 May 1905.

35 Article IV of the Anglo-Japanese Treaty of 1905, as detailed in the *New York Times*, 27 September 1905.

36 Hansard, House of Commons, Debate, 22 January 1902, vol. 101, cc574–628.

37 Vladimir Semenoff, *The Battle of Tsushima*, translated by Captain A.B. Lindsay at http://archive.org/stream/battleoftsushima01seme/battleoftsushima01seme_djvu.txt

38 Takahashi Korekiyo, *The Rothschilds and the Russo-Japanese War, 1904–06*, pp. 20–1.

39 Ibid.

40 Fay, *Origins of the World War*, vol. I, p. 197 and footnote.

41 Bernstein, *Willy–Nicky Correspondence*, telegram no. 13, p. 69.

42 Willy–Nicky letters, 22 August 1905, and Kaiser–Bulow letter quoted in Fay, *Origins of the World War*, vol. I, p. 175 and footnote.

43 Bernstein, *Willy–Nicky Correspondence*, telegram 49, p. 139.

44 Willy–Nicky letters, 22 August 1905, in Fay, *Origins of the World War*, vol. I, p. 175 and footnote.

45 Ferguson, *House of Rothschild*, p. 398.

46 Bernstein, *Willy–Nicky Correspondence*, telegram 46, p. 131.

47 Ferguson, *House of Rothschild*, p. 398.

48 Bernstein, *Willy–Nicky Correspondence*, telegram 46, pp. 130–2.

49 Morel, *Diplomacy Revealed*, p. 68.

50 Ferguson, *Pity of War*, pp. 60–1.

51 Ewart, *Roots and Causes of the Wars*, vol. I, p. 41.

52 Sir Arthur Nicolson's career blossomed under the patronage of Secret Elite approval. He was ambassador at St Petersburg from 1906 to 1910, where he dealt regularly with Isvolsky. Nicolson was promoted to the top diplomatic post in the Foreign Office in 1910 and advised Sir Edward Grey on all his crucial decisions up to 1916, when both 'retired'. Some believed that he was the 'man who made the war'. Lord Carnock, as Nicolson became, was a member of The Club, along with Asquith, Grey and Haldane.

53 Barnes, *In Quest of Truth and Justice*. p. 17.

54 Friedrich Stieve, *Isvolsky and the World War*. p. 13.
55 Hansard, House of Lords, Debate, 6 February 1908, vol. 183, cc999–1047.
56 Ibid.

CHAPTER 6 – THE CHANGING OF THE GUARD

1 Representation of the People Act 1884 (48 and 49 Vict. c. 3); The Third Reform Act.
2 Neilson, *How Diplomats Make War*, p. 99.
3 Jeffrey G. Williamson, 'The Structure of Pay in Britain, 1710–1911', *Research in Economic History*, vol. 7, 1982, p. 22.
4 Quigley, *Anglo-American Establishment*, p. 15.
5 Quigley, *Tragedy and Hope*, p. 471–2.
6 Terence H. O'Brien, *Milner*, p. 187.
7 Milner Papers, Haldane to Milner, Bodleian Library, Ms.Eng.Hist. c.687.
8 Milner Papers, Haldane to Milner, 13 May 1902, Bodleian Library, Ms.Eng.Hist. c.688.
9 Quigley, *Tragedy and Hope*, p. 482.
10 Thompson, *Forgotten Patriot*, p. 30.
11 Quigley, *Tragedy and Hope*, p. 475.
12 Quigley, *Anglo-American Establishment*, p. 31.
13 Ibid., p. 30.
14 Ibid., p. 140.
15 Sir Frederick Maurice, *Haldane 1856–1915*, pp. 49–50.
16 Ibid., p. 69.
17 Richard Burdon Haldane, *An Autobiography*, p. 162.
18 Maurice, *Haldane*, p. 94.
19 John Wilson, *C.B.: A Life of Sir Henry Campbell-Bannerman*, p. 318.
20 Maurice, *Haldane*, p. 111.
21 Haldane, *An Autobiography*, p, 142. This was undoubtedly a personal gift from King Edward VII, who, between 1901 and 1902, made Alfred Milner, Nathaniel Rothschild, Edward Grey, Richard Haldane, George Wyndham and Sir Edward Cassel members of his Privy Council.
22 Maurice, *Haldane*, p. 116.
23 Lees-Milne, *Enigmatic Edwardian*, p. 158.
24 Ibid.
25 Haldane, *An Autobiography*, p. 159.
26 K.M. Wilson, 'The Making and Putative Implementation of a British Foreign Policy of Gesture, December 1905–August 1914: The Anglo-French Entente Revisited', *Canadian Journal of History*, no. XXXI, August 1996, pp. 227–55.

27 Asquith MSS, Haldane to Asquith, 6 October 1905, Bodleian Library, vol. 10.
28 Lees-Milne, *Enigmatic Edwardian*, p. 155.
29 Minutes of the Committee of Imperial Defence, CAB 38/9/1905, no. 65.
30 Fay, *Origins of the World War*, vol. I, p. 203.
31 Ibid.
32 Quigley, *Anglo-American Establishment*, pp. 8–9.
33 Ibid., pp. 101–15.
34 In fact, the War Office presented a paper on this action to the Committee of Imperial Defence in September 1905. CAB 38/10/ 1905, no. 73.
35 CAB 38/9/ 1905, no. 65.
36 CAB 38/10/ 1905, no. 67, p. 6.
37 Maurice, *Haldane*, p. 175.
38 Confidential report of General Ducarne to the Belgian minister of war, 10 April 1906, as quoted by Dr Bernhard Demburg in *The International Monthly,* New York, at http://libcudl.colorado.edu/wwi/pdf/i73726928.pdf
39 Ibid.
40 Maurice, *Haldane*, p. 176.
41 Alexander Fuehr, *The Neutrality of Belgium*, p. 72.
42 Sir George Clarke was governor of Victoria but returned to Britain in 1903 to be part of the three-man Esher Committee with Admiral Jacky Fisher. He was appointed first secretary of the Committee of Imperial Defence. Later elevated to peerage as Lord Sydenham.
43 Sir George Clarke to Lord Esher, 9 January 1906, Esher papers, ESHR 10/38.
44 Grey to Haldane, quoted in Maurice, *Haldane*, pp. 172–3.
45 Fay, *Origins of the World War*, vol. I, p. 202.
46 Neilson, *How Diplomats Make War*, p. 87.
47 *The Times*, 22 December 1905, p. 7.
48 John W. Coogan and Peter F. Coogan, 'The British Cabinet and the Anglo-French Staff Talks, 1905–1914: Who Knew What and When Did He Know It?', *Journal of British Studies*, no. 24, January 1985, p. 112.
49 Wilson, *C.B.*, pp. 527–8.
50 Ibid.
51 Charles Repington, *The First World War*, p. 13.
52 Wilson, *C.B.*, p. 528.
53 Haldane Papers, NLS, M.S. 200058, Memorandum of Events between 1906–15, p. 34.

54 Wilson, *C.B.*, p. 524.
55 J.A. Spender, *The Life of the Right Honourable Sir Henry Campbell-Bannerman*, p. 251.
56 Roy Hattersley, *Campbell-Bannerman*, p. 100.
57 Wilson, *C.B.*, p. 531.
58 Grey, *Twenty-Five Years*, vol. I, p. 153.
59 Haldane, *An Autobiography*, p. 191.

CHAPTER 7 – 1906 – LANDSLIDE TO CONTINUITY

1 David Lloyd George, *War Memoirs*, p. 27.
2 T.P. O'Connor, *Sir Henry Campbell-Bannerman*, pp. 125–6.
3 Lloyd George, *War Memoirs*, p. 28.
4 Kennedy, *Old Diplomacy and New*, p. 141.
5 E. & D. Grey, *Cottage Book, Ichen Abbas, 1894–1905.*
6 Alfred F. Havinghurst, *Britain in Transition: The Twentieth Century*, p. 84.
7 Spender, *Life of the Right Hon. Sir Henry Campbell-Bannerman*, vol. II, p. 194.
8 Quigley, *Anglo-American Establishment*, p. 25.
9 Lloyd George, *War Memoirs*, pp. 56–7.
10 Ferguson, *Pity of War*, pp. 85–9.
11 Susan Hansen, 'The Identification of Radicals in the British Parliament, 1906–1914: Some Attitudes to Foreign Policy', *The Meijo Review*, vol. 6, no. 4, p. 6.
12 Lloyd George, *War Memoirs*, p. 59.
13 Lees-Milne, *Enigmatic Edwardian*, pp. 157–8.
14 Hansard, House of Commons, Debate, 12 July 1906, vol. 160, cc1074–171.
15 Maurice, *Haldane*, p. 204.
16 Ibid., p. 176.
17 Ibid., p. 228.
18 Ibid., p. 243.
19 Ibid., pp. 174–5.
20 Ewart, *Roots and Causes of the Wars*, vol. II, p. 682.
21 Robert K. Massie, *Dreadnought: Britain, Germany and the Coming of the Great War*, p. 423.
22 Ibid., p. 403.
23 Baron John Arbuthnot Fisher, *Memories and Records*, vol. II, pp. 134–5.
24 Ibid. pp. 184–96 gives Fisher's arguments and calculations in favour of oil.
25 Keith Middlemas, *Pursuit of Pleasure: High Society in the 1900s*, p. 107.

26 Minutes of the Committee of Imperial Defence, CAB/ 38/9/1905, no. 32.
27 Swain, *Beginning the Twentieth Century*, p. 271.
28 Ewart, *Roots and Causes of the Wars*, vol. II, p. 778.
29 Wilson, *C.B.*, p. 621.
30 Richard Toye, *Lloyd George and Churchill: Rivals for Greatness*, p. 46.
31 Esher Diaries, 20 March 1908, as quoted in Toye above.
32 Quoted in Toye, *Lloyd George and Churchill.*, p. 46.
33 Milner Papers, Churchill to Milner, 31 December 1900, Bodleian Library, Ms.Eng.Hist. c.687.
34 Toye, *Lloyd George and Churchill*, p. 13.
35 Ibid., p. 17.
36 Ibid., p. 20.
37 Edward David, *Inside Asquith's Cabinet: From the Diaries of Charles Hobhouse*, p. 73.
38 Norman and Jeanne MacKenzie (eds), *Diary of Beatrice Webb, Vol. III: The Power to Alter Things, 1905–1924*, p. 94.

CHAPTER 8 – ALEXANDER ISVOLSKY – HERO AND VILLAIN

1 Hansard, House of Commons, Debate, 26 May 1908, vol. 189, cc963–5.
2 Herman Bernstein, 'The Czar of Russia, From a Study at Close Range' *New York Times*, 13 Sept 1908.
3 Hansard, House of Commons, Debate, 28 May 1908, vol. 189, cc1261–2.
4 J.A. Farrer, *England Under Edward VII*, p. 217.
5 Edward Legge, *King Edward in his True Colours*, p. 173.
6 Hansard, House of Commons, Debate, 1 June 1908, vol. 89, cc1570–2.
7 Hansard, House of Commons, Debate, 28 May 1908, vol. 89, cc1290–1.
8 Lee, *King Edward VII*, part II, p. 594.
9 Ibid.
10 Committee of Imperial Defence, CAB 38/13/1907.
11 Farrer, *England Under Edward VII*, p. 218.
12 Fisher, *Memories*, p. 230–3.
13 Farrer, *England Under Edward VII*, p. 218.
14 Ibid.
15 Morel, *Diplomacy Revealed*, p. 138.
16 Farrer, *England Under Edward VII*, p. 218.
17 Morel, *Diplomacy Revealed*, pp. 127–8.
18 Hansard, House of Commons, Debate, 27 July 1908, vol. 193, cc939–88.
19 Alexander Spiridovich, *Les Dernières Années de la Cour de Tzarskoie Selo*, vol. 1, chapter 16.
20 *New York Times*, 3 August 1908.

21 Stieve, *Isvolsky and the World War*, p. 12.
22 Ibid., p. 113.
23 Stevenson, *1914–18*, p. 11.
24 Ewart, *Roots and Causes of the Wars*, vol. II, p. 928.
25 Barnes, *Genesis of the World War*, p. 83.
26 Ewart, *Roots and Causes of the Wars*, vol. II, p. 927.
27 Hansard, House of Commons, Debate, 12 October 1908, vol. 194, cc38–9.
28 Luigi Albertini, *Origins of the War of 1914*, vol. 1, pp. 222–3.
29 James Joll and Gordon Martel, *The Origins of the First World War*, p. 69.
30 Ewart, *The Roots and Causes of the Wars*, vol. II, p. 913.
31 Ibid., p. 930.
32 Ibid., p. 936.
33 Eugenii Nikolaevich Shelking, and L.W. Mavoski, *Recollections of a Russian Diplomat: The Suicide of Monarchies*, p. 183.
34 Middlemas, *Life and Times of Edward VII*, p. 170.
35 Stieve, *Isvolsky and the World War*, p. 16.
36 Ibid., p. 17.
37 Ibid., p. 13.

Chapter 9 – Scams and Scandals

1 MacDonald, J. Ramsay, 'Why We Are at War,' *The Open Court*, vol. 1915, issue 4, article 4, p. 246. Available at: http://opensiuc.lib.siu.edu/ocj/vol1915/iss4/4. It is a reproduction in America of MacDonald's article in the *Continental Times* of 4 December 1914.
2 Francis Neilson, *The Makers of War*, p. 21.
3 Strachan, *The First World War*, p. 45.
4 Ferguson, *Pity of War*, p. 86.
5 Anver Offer, *First World War: An Agrarian Interpretation*, p. 232.
6 Fay, *Origins of the World War*, vol. I, pp. 202–3.
7 Hansard, House of Commons, Debate, 5 March 1912, vol. 35, cc205–76.
8 Ferguson, *Pity of War*, pp. 63.
9 Fay, *Origins of the World War*, vol. I, p. 213.
10 Winston Churchill, *The World Crisis*, pp. 36–7.
11 Fay, *Origins of the World War*, vol. I, p. 211.
12 Quigley, *Tragedy and Hope*, p. 145.
13 Quigley, *Anglo-American Establishment*, pp. 153–4.
14 Cabinet Papers, CAB/ 38/113/1907, p. 12.
15 Ewart, *Roots and Causes of the Wars*, vol. I, p. 512.
16 Morel, *Truth and the War*, p. 157.

17 Ewart, *Roots and Causes of the Wars*, vol. I, pp. 510–13.
18 H.A.L. Fisher, *A History of Europe*, p. 1083.
19 Barnes, *In Quest of Truth and Justice*, pp. 18–19.
20 Ewart, *Roots and Causes of the Wars*, vol. I, pp. 561–3.
21 Ibid.
22 George Herbert Perris, *The War Traders: An Exposure*, p. 25.
23 Fisher, *Memories*, vol. 1, pp. 30–4.
24 Neilson, *How Diplomats Make War*, p. 133.
25 Perris, *War Traders*, p. 29.
26 Hansard, House of Commons, Debate, 29 March 1909, vol. 3, cc39–149.
27 Ibid.
28 Ewart, *Roots and Causes of the Wars*, vol. II, p. 689.
29 *New York Times*, 1 April 1909.
30 Neilson, *How Diplomats Make War*, p. 121.
31 Neilson, *Makers of War*, p. 20.
32 Churchill, *World Crisis*, pp. 23–4.
33 Hansard, House of Commons, Debate, 8 November 1934, vol. 293, cc1293–416.
34 The man sent in to replace Mulliner at the Coventry works, Rear-Admiral Bacon, was a close friend of Jacky Fisher. From that point in time, Coventry Ordnance received big orders from the government and increased its capital by 40 per cent.
35 Neilson, *How Diplomats Make War*, p. 328.
36 Perris, *War Traders*, p. 9.
37 H. Robertson Murray, *Krupps and the International Armaments Ring*, p. 3.
38 J.T. Walton Newbold, *How Asquith Helped the Armaments Ring*, p. 8.
39 *The Secret International: Armament Firms at Work*, p. 10 (published by Union of Democratic Control, author and date not listed, published in 1930s).
40 David, *Inside Asquith's Cabinet*, p. 86.
41 J.T. Walton Newbold, *The War Trust Exposed*, pp. 4–16.
42 Hansard, House of Commons, Debate, 13 June 1911, vol. 26, cc1459–97.
43 Perris, *War Traders*, pp. 4–6.
44 Newbold, *War Trust Exposed*, p. 17.
45 H.C. Engelbrecht and F.C. Hanighen, *Merchants of Death*, chapter IX, p. 3.
46 Ferguson, *House of Rothschild*, p. 413.
47 Ibid.

48 Newbold, *War Trust Exposed*, p. 7.
49 Hansard, House of Commons, Debate, 7 July 1913, vol. 55, cc10–11.
50 J.T. Walton Newbold, *How Europe Armed for War*, pp. 76–7.
51 Perris, *War Traders*, p. 10.
52 Murray, *Krupps*, p. 9.
53 Sir Charles Ottley was utterly brazen in his contempt for propriety. He went from the exalted position of advisor to the government as secretary of the Committee of Imperial Defence to director of a firm making exorbitant profits from the same source. Questions were asked in Parliament on 22 July 1912 and again on 30 July 1914 when Ottley's involvement with the Imperial Ottoman Docks company caused serious concern.
54 Murray, *Krupps*, p. 3.
55 Newbold, *War Trust Exposed*, pp. 14–15.
56 Ibid.
57 The First Sub-Committee of the Temporary Mixed Commission of the League of Nations, Report A.81, 1921, p. 5.

Chapter 10 – Creating the Fear

1 Quigley, *Anglo-American Establishment*, pp. 311–12.
2 E. Moberly Bell, *Flora Shaw*, p. 224.
3 Ibid., p. 226.
4 Quigley, *Anglo-American Establishment*, p. 112.
5 Lees-Milne, *Enigmatic Edwardian*, p. 185.
6 Quigley, *Anglo-American Establishment*, p. 102.
7 J. Lee Thompson, A *Wider Patriotism: Alfred Milner and the British Empire*, p. 89.
8 Thompson, *Forgotten Patriot*, p. 234.
9 Quigley, *Anglo-American Establishment*, p. 115.
10 Thompson, *Forgotten Patriot*, pp. 155–6.
11 'Remarkable Career of Northcliffe', *New York Times*, 15 August 1922.
12 Ibid.
13 Quigley, *Anglo-American Establishment*, p. 42.
14 Linda B. Fritzinger, *Diplomat without Portfolio: Valentine Chirol – His Life and The Times*, p. 329.
15 *New York Times*, 15 August 1922.
16 Quigley, *Anglo-American Establishment*, p. 42.
17 Ibid., p. 313.
18 Paul Ferris, *The House of Northcliffe: A Biography of an Empire*, p. 64.
19 Christopher Andrew, *Secret Service: The Making of the British Intelligence Community*, p. 39.

20 Erskine Childers is a most amazing character. Here in 1905 he played the role of patriot to the British national cause. In 1914, Childers was gun-running for the Irish Volunteers.
21 Erskine Childers, *The Riddle of the Sands*, p. 284.
22 Andrew Boyle, *The Riddle of Erskine Childers*, p. 111.
23 *The Riddle of the Sands* remains a popular Penguin Classic, and in 2003 was voted number 37 in the *Observer*'s best 100 books over the last 300 years.
24 The full title is *The Invasion of 1910: With a full account of the Siege of London*, by William Le Queux; naval chapters by H.W. Wilson.
25 Ignatius Frederick Clarke, *The Great War with Germany 1890–1914*, p. 250.
26 Ibid., p. 252.
27 Ignatius Frederick Clarke, *Voices Prophesying War*, p. 145.
28 Andrew, *Secret Service*, p. 40.
29 *Die Invasion von 1910: Einfall der Deutschen in England*, translated by Traugott Tamm.
30 Farrer, *England Under Edward VII*, p. 143.
31 Belgian Diplomatic Documents 30; quoted in Morel, *Diplomacy Revealed*, p. 77.
32 E. Philips Oppenheim, *A Maker of History*.
33 Andrew, *Secret Service*, p. 43.
34 Randolph S. Churchill, *Winston S. Churchill*, vol. II, p. 513.
35 R. F. Mackay, *Fisher of Kilverstone*, p. 385.
36 Cabinet Papers, CAB 38/13/07.
37 Report and Proceedings of the sub-committee of the Committee of Imperial Defence, 30 March 1909, PRO 16/8.
38 Rosamund M. Thomas, *Espionage and Secrecy: The Official Secrets Act 1911–1989*, pp. 2–4.
39 Hansard, House of Lords, Debate, 25 July 1911, series 5, vol. 9, cc641–7.
40 Thomas, *Espionage and Secrecy*, p. 5.
41 Andrew, *Secret Service*, pp. 58–9.
42 The 1905 Aliens Act described some groups of immigrants as 'undesirable', thereby making entry to Britain discretionary rather than automatic.
43 Section 6, Official Secrets Act, 1911.

Chapter 11 – Preparing the Empire – Alfred Milner and The Round Table

1 Quigley, *Anglo-American Establishment*, p. 312.
2 Milner to Violet Markham, June 1906, quoted in J. Lee Thompson, *Forgotten Patriot*, p. 248.

3 Ferguson, *Pity of War*, p. 93.

4 Alfred Milner, 'Some Reflections on the Coming Conference', *National Review*, April 1907.

5 Ibid.

6 Thompson, *Forgotten Patriot*, p. 256.

7 A.M. Gollin, *Proconsul in Politics: A Study of Lord Milner*, pp. 136–7.

8 Quigley, *Anglo-American Establishment*, p. 153.

9 Thompson, *Forgotten Patriot*, p. 257.

10 Gollin, *Proconsul in Politics*, pp. 138–9.

11 O.D. Skelton, *Life and Letters of Sir Wilfrid Laurier*, p. 300.

12 Gollin, *Proconsul in Politics*, p. 145.

13 Quigley, *Anglo-American Establishment*, p. 312.

14 Viscount Milner, *Speeches delivered in Canada in the Autumn of 1908*, pp. 1–12 at http://archive.org/stream/speechesdelivere00milnuoft#page/n3/mode/2up

15 Ibid., pp. 85–93.

16 *Daily Mail*, 19 January 1909.

17 Thompson, *Forgotten Patriot*, p. 276.

18 J. Lee Thompson, *Northcliffe: Press Baron in Politics 1865–1922*, p. 168.

19 Ibid., p. 169.

20 Thompson, *Forgotten Patriot*, p. 270.

21 *The Argus* (Melbourne), 29 July, 1909.

22 As quoted in Thompson, *Northcliffe*, p. 170.

23 Reginald Pound and Geoffrey Harmsworth, *Northcliffe*, p. 369.

24 Thompson, *Forgotten Patriot*, p. 270.

25 Gollin, *Proconsul in Politics*, p. 163.

26 Nimocks, *Milner's Young Men*, p. 147.

27 Quigley, *Tragedy and Hope*, p. 144.

28 Gollin, *Proconsul in Politics*, p. 164.

29 Thompson, *A Wider Patriotism*, p. 138.

30 Quigley, *Anglo-American Establishment*, p. 121.

31 Quigley, *Tragedy and Hope*, pp. 131 and 951.

32 These men played a major role in influencing politics and the British-race dream. Leopold Amery was the only one to put his head above the political parapet. A fellow of All Souls, Amery turned down the chance to be editor of *The Observer* in 1908 and *The Times* in 1912 in order to concentrate on politics. In May 1911, he was elected unopposed as a Conservative (Liberal Unionist) MP. Philip Kerr was chosen by Viscount Milner to be Lloyd George's private secretary in 1916 when the final war government was put in place. He became marquess of Lothian. Robert Brand mainly wrote about financial matters for the

Round Table and was both a director of Lazards, the merchant bankers, and *The Times*. Geoffrey Dawson was appointed editor of *The Times* when he eventually returned from South Africa in 1912. Lionel Curtis, the most ardent of the Round Tablers, became Beit lecturer in Colonial history at Oxford University and a fellow of All Souls. F.S. Oliver was involved in a plot in 1916 to remove Asquith from 10 Downing Street. And here in a nutshell are all the component parts of the Secret Elite's multi-pronged attack by their men in government, influencing government, in the press influencing public opinion, in finance and business to provide the backing, and in the universities to teach official history.

33 Nimocks, *Milner's Young Men*, p. 157.
34 Quigley, *Anglo-American Establishment*, p. 326.
35 Quigley, *Tragedy and Hope*, p. 146.
36 Nimocks, *Milner's Young Men*, p. 166.
37 Ibid.
38 Quigley, *Anglo-American Establishment*, p. 125.
39 Ferguson, *Pity of War*, p. 199.
40 Stevenson, *1914–1918*, p. 233.
41 Ibid., p. 201.
42 Ibid.

Chapter 12 – Catch a Rising Star and Put it in Your Pocket

1 Quigley, *Anglo-American Establishment*, p. x.
2 Lloyd George took enormous risks in defying the jingoistic mob by speaking out against the war in South Africa. His presence in Birmingham town hall on 18 January 1901 ended in a riot. The *Birmingham Daily Mail* had ranted against him for a fortnight, prophesying that 'the most anti-British Member of Parliament' would never be allowed to 'peddle his sedition' in Birmingham. Despite a plea from the chief constable, the meeting went ahead, but a mob rushed the doors and attacked the platform party. Lloyd George had to be smuggled out by a back door dressed as a policeman. (Hattersley, *The Great Outsider*, p. 141.)
3 Toye, *Lloyd George and Churchill*, p. 17.
4 D. R. Daniel, unpublished memoir (translated by Dr Prys Morgan, National Library of Wales, Aberystwyth), quoted him as admitting that 'I could not write down what my convictions are.' (Hattersley, *The Great Outsider*, p. 13.)
5 Hattersley, *The Great Outsider*, p. 245.
6 McCormick, *Mask of Merlin*, pp. 57–8.

7 Ibid., p. 59.
8 *The Times*, 8 November 1907.
9 Ffion Hague, *The Pain and the Privilege*, p. 174.
10 John Grigg, *Lloyd George: The People's Champion*, pp. 99–100.
11 Hattersley, *The Great Outsider*, p. 92–3.
12 W.R.P. George, *Backbencher*, p. 390.
13 Many very rich Liberal MPs and unnamed 'friends' offered him access to a lifestyle he could not afford and his friend, Lord George Riddell, gifted him a new house at Walton Heath in 1913. Suffragettes duly attempted to blow it up.
14 Hague, *The Pain and the Privilege*, p. 105.
15 Hattersley, *The Great Outsider*, pp. 104–5.
16 His private secretary, A.J. Sylvester, on seeing Lloyd George rising from the bath, wrote in his 1931 diary that he had 'the biggest organ I have ever seen. It resembles a donkey's more than anything else.' (Hague, *The Pain and the Privilege*, p. 469.)
17 Hague, *The Pain and the Privilege*, pp. 128–34.
18 Grigg, *Lloyd George*, p. 181.
19 Ibid.
20 Richard Lloyd George, *My Father*, p. 112.
21 Although he was shunned by society, Oscar Wilde was secretly visited in prison by Richard Haldane on at least two occasions. In Holloway Prison, Haldane met with Wilde alone in his cell, and he arranged for him to receive books, pen and paper. Haldane visited Wilde again in Wandsworth Prison, and he later persuaded the Home Secretary to transfer Wilde to Reading Gaol. (Haldane, *An Autobiography*, pp. 166–7.)
22 Hansard, House of Commons, Debate, 29 April 1909, vol. 4, c548.
23 Ferguson, *House of Rothschild*, p. 427.
24 Parliamentary Archives, LG/C/33/2/11.
25 Budget League Pamphlet 22, 'The Budget and the People', p. 2.
26 Speech of 9 October 1901 quoted in Richard Toye, *Lloyd George and Churchill*, p. 62.
27 Ibid.
28 Hansard, House of Lords, Debate, 22 November 1909, vol. 4, cc730–820.
29 Hansard, House of Commons, Debate, 6 July 1908, vol. 191, cc1343–415.
30 Viscount Milner, *Constructive Imperialism, Unionists and Social Reform*, p. 37.
31 Thompson, *Forgotten Patriot*, pp. 274.
32 Ferguson, *Pity of War*, p. 424.
33 The general election of January 1910 produced a hung parliament.

The Liberals lost 123 seats but had 274 MPs returned to the House of Commons. The Conservatives gained 116 seats but had 272 MPs when the final count was announced, and so had lost the election by 2 seats. This meant that the Liberals relied on the 82 Irish MPs and the 40 Labour to push through their planned legislation. That strong wedge of Labour Party seats was a threat to a Liberal recovery, and the Irish support was predicated entirely on the success of an Irish Home Rule Bill.

34 Toye, *Lloyd George and Churchill*, p. 66.
35 Thompson, *Forgotten Patriot*, p. 278.
36 Hattersley, *The Great Outsider*, p. 276.
37 *The Observer*, 8 May 1910.
38 Hattersley, *The Great Outsider*, p. 277.
39 McCormick, *Mask of Merlin*, p. 72.
40 Grigg, *Lloyd George*, pp. 362–8.
41 'Mr Lloyd George's Memorandum on the Formation of a Coalition', 17 August 1910, see Appendix to Grigg, *Lloyd George*, p. 362.
42 Lucy Masterman, *C.F.G. Masterman*, p. 169.
43 David, *Inside Asquith's Cabinet*, p. 98.
44 Austen Chamberlain, *Politics from the Inside: An Epistolary Chronicle, 1906–1914*, p. 288.
45 The general election of December 1910 again resulted in virtual stalemate. Liberals held 272 seats and Conservatives 271. Although they had the fractional advantage of one seat, the Liberals remained in hock to the Irish and Labour MPs. In effect, nothing had changed.
46 Masterman, *C.F.G. Masterman*, p. 200.
47 O'Brien, *Milner*, p. 245.
48 Attributed to Lloyd George in Hattersley, *The Great Outsider*, p. 287.
49 Hattersley, *The Great Outsider*, p. 288.

Chapter 13 – Moroccan Myths – Fez and Agadir

1 Morel, *Ten Years of Secret Diplomacy*, p. 104.
2 Ewart, *Roots and Causes of the Wars*, vol. II, p. 810.
3 Ibid.
4 Frederick Bausman, *Let France Explain*, p. 149.
5 *The Sydney Morning Herald*, 2 August 1907, p. 7.
6 *Daily Mail*, 1 August 1907.
7 Francis Charmes, *Revue de Deux Mondes*, 17 August 1907.
8 *New York Times*, 18 August 1907.
9 Morel, *Ten Years of Secret Diplomacy*, p. 102.
10 Morel, *Diplomacy Revealed*, p. 170.

11 Stieve, *Isvolsky and the World War*, p. 17, (letter of 17 January 1924, in *L' Humanité*, from Ernest Judet).
12 Ewart, *Roots and Causes of the Wars*, vol. II, p. 836.
13 Stieve, *Isvolsky and the World War*, p. 31.
14 Fay, *Origins of the World War*, vol. I, p. 278.
15 Morel, *Ten Years of Secret Diplomacy*, p. 107.
16 Fay, *Origins of the World War*, vol. I, p. 279.
17 Kennedy, *Old Diplomacy and New*, p. 170.
18 Morel, *Diplomacy Revealed*, p. 215.
19 Hansard, House of Commons, Debate, 4 May 1911, vol. 25, cc574–5.
20 Ibid.
21 Hansard, House of Commons, Debate, 25 April 1911, vol. 24, cc1601–2.
22 This French company was in fact a cartel of some of the major European capitalists, including Schneider; Krupp; and Guest, Keen and Nettle-folds, set up after Algeciras to take advantage of Moroccan natural resources.
23 Grey, *Twenty-Five Years*, vol. 2, p. 32.
24 Morel, *Diplomacy Revealed*, p. 185.
25 Morel, *Truth and the War*, p. 78.
26 Christopher Clark, *Kaiser Wilhelm II: Profiles in Power*, p. 145.
27 Morel, *Ten Years of Secret Diplomacy*, pp. 108–109.
28 Max Montgelas, *British Foreign Policy under Sir Edward Grey*, p. 29.
29 Max Montgelas, *The Case for the Central Powers*, pp. 42–4.
30 Churchill, *World Crisis*, p. 29.
31 Morel, *Diplomacy Revealed* p. 217.
32 Grey, *Twenty-Five Years*, vol. II, pp. 60–2.
33 Neilson, *Makers of War*, p. 15.
34 Barnes, *In Quest of Truth and Justice*, p. 18.
35 Montgelas, *Case for the Central Powers*, p. 43.
36 Hermann Lutz, *Lord Grey and the World War*, p. 127.
37 Grey, *Twenty-Five Years*, vol. II, p. 33.
38 Strachan, *The First World War*, p. 41.
39 *Evening Post*, Spithead Review, Volume LXXXI, 26 June 1911, p. 7.
40 Bausman, *Let France Explain*, p. 150.
41 The 74th French prime minister, Ernest Monis, took office on 2 March 1911. He was the man responsible for returning Delcassé to the Cabinet Office. He and his son were seriously injured at the Paris to Madrid Air Race in July 1911 and he had to resign from government. He was replaced by the more radical socialist, Joseph Caillaux.
42 Morel, *Truth and the War*, p. 79.
43 Lloyd George, *War Memoirs*, p. 26.

44 Ibid.
45 Grey, *Twenty-Five Years*, vol. II, pp. 39–40.
46 Montgelas, *British Foreign Policy under Sir Edward Grey*, p. 32.
47 Morel, *Diplomacy Revealed*, pp. 201–2.
48 *The Times*, 22 July 1907.
49 Morel, *Ten Years of Secret Diplomacy*, pp. 144–6.
50 David, *Inside Asquith's Cabinet*, p. 104.
51 Churchill, *World Crisis*, pp. 38–9.
52 Ibid., p. 42.
53 Ibid., p. 46.
54 Ibid., p. 47.
55 Spencer Tucker, *World War I*, p. 248.
56 Neilson, *How Diplomats Make War*, p. 198.

CHAPTER 14 – CHURCHILL AND HALDANE – BUYING TIME AND TELLING LIES

1 Haldane to Asquith, as recorded in Maurice, *Haldane*, p. 283.
2 Haldane, *An Autobiography*, p. 230.
3 Ibid., p. 227.
4 Jenkins, *Churchill*, p. 206.
5 Churchill, *World Crisis*, p. 49.
6 E.D. Morel, *The Secret History of a Great Betrayal*, p. 15.
7 Cowles, *Winston Churchill*, p. 157.
8 Churchill, *World Crisis*, p. 53.
9 Ibid., p. 52.
10 Hansard, House of Commons, Debate, 18 February 1914, series 5, vol. 58, cc920–1.
11 David, *Inside Asquith's Cabinet*, p. 107.
12 Grey, *Twenty-Five Years*, vol. II, p. 166.
13 David, *Inside Asquith's Cabinet*, p. 108.
14 Asquith Papers, Bodleian Library, vol. 6, ff.79–80.
15 Morel, *Secret History of a Great Betrayal*, p. 16.
16 Hansard, House of Commons, Debate, 27 November 1911, vol. 32, cc43–165.
17 In Morel, *Secret History of a Great Betrayal*, p. 16.
18 Albert Ballin was the owner of the Hamburg-America shipping line and had many contacts with both British and American businessmen. He had access to politicians like Churchill, was on personal terms with the kaiser, and met regularly with Max Warburg.
19 Wilhelm II, *My Memoirs*, pp. 142–5.
20 Ibid., p. 144.

21 David, *Inside Asquith's Cabinet*, p. 111.
22 Grey, *Twenty-Five Years*, vol. II, pp. 74–5.
23 Churchill, *World Crisis*, pp. 71–2.
24 Maurice, *Haldane*, p. 292.
25 Sir Ernest Cassel to Herr Ballin, 3 February 1912, in Churchill, *World Crisis*, p. 75.
26 Maurice, *Haldane*, p. 292.
27 Ibid., p. 297.
28 Ibid., p. 309.
29 Ibid.
30 Kennedy, *Old Diplomacy and New*, p. 198.
31 Annika Mombauer, *The Origins of the First World War*, p. 6.
32 Montgelas, *British Foreign Policy under Sir Edward Grey*, p. 35.
33 Fay, *Origins of the World War*, vol. I, p. 304.
34 Haldane, *An Autobiography*, p. 241.
35 Ferguson, *Pity of War*, p. 71.
36 Haldane, *An Autobiography*, p. 242.
37 Swain, *Beginning the Twentieth Century*, pp. 307–8.
38 Ibid., p. 308.
39 Ibid.
40 Maurice, *Haldane*, p. 298.
41 Ibid., p. 299.
42 Wilhelm II, *My Memoirs*, p. 152.
43 Morel, *Secret History of a Great Betrayal*, p. 16.
44 Hansard, House of Commons, Debate, 18 March 1912, vol. 35, cc1549–618.
45 Ibid.
46 David, *Inside Asquith's Cabinet*, p. 118.
47 Grey, *Twenty-Five Years*, vol. 1, p. 168.

Chapter 15 – The Roberts Academy

1 As listed in *London Gazettes* from 1887 to 1914.
2 Anne Pimlott Baker, *The Pilgrims of Great Britain: A Centennial History*, p. 7.
3 See *Oxford Dictionary of National Biography*.
4 Ferguson, *Pity of War*, p. 15.
5 Hansard, House of Lords, Debate, 12 July 1909, vol. 2, cc255–352.
6 Andrew, *Secret Service*, p. 42.
7 Lord Roberts, *Lord Roberts' Message to the Nation*, pp. vii–viii.
8 Quigley, *Anglo-American Establishment*, pp. 52–83.
9 D'Ombrain, *War Machinery and High Policy*, p. 143.

10 Ibid., p. 141.
11 Ibid., p. 146.
12 Keith Jeffery, *Field Marshal Sir Henry Wilson: A Political Soldier*, p. 39.
13 D'Ombrain, *War Machinery and High Policy*, pp. 142–3.
14 Ibid.
15 A.P. Ryan, *Mutiny at the Curragh*, p. 100.
16 Walter Reid, *Architect of Victory: Douglas Haig*, p. 53.
17 Denis Winter, *Haig's Command: A Reassessment*, p. 31.
18 Barbara Tuchman, *The Guns of August*, p. 199.
19 Ibid., pp. 198–9.
20 Ibid.
21 Major-General Sir Frederick Maurice and Tasker H. Bliss, *Soldier, Artist, Sportsman: The Life of General Lord Rawlinson of Trent*, pp. xi–xii.
22 Anthony Heathcote, *The British Field Marshals, 1736–1997*, p. 304.
23 Ryan, *Mutiny at the Curragh*, p. 101.
24 Jeffery, *Field Marshal Sir Henry Wilson*, p. 67.
25 Ibid., pp. 65–6.
26 Major-General Sir C.E. Callwell, *Field Marshal Henry Wilson Bart: His Life and His Diaries*, p. 74.
27 Ibid., p. 86.
28 Ibid., p. 89.
29 Ibid., p. 92.
30 Ibid., pp. 92–3.
31 Tuchman, *Guns of August*, pp. 49–52.
32 Ibid., p. 54.
33 Ibid.
34 Major Huguet was appointed an honorary member of the Royal Victorian Order by King Edward VII in 1907 in recognition of his services.
35 William Robertson, *From Private to Field Marshal*, p. 169.
36 Winter, *Haig's Command*, pp. 18–19.
37 Ibid., p. 20.
38 Hart, *History of the First World War*, p. 62.
39 Ibid., p. 61.
40 Ibid., p. 58.
41 Jeffery, *Field Marshal Sir Henry Wilson*, p. 66.

Chapter 16 – Poincaré – The Man Who Would be Bought

1 Swain, *Beginning the Twentieth Century*, p. 95.

2 Barnes, *Genesis of the World War*, pp. 387–8.
3 Stieve, *Isvolsky and the World War*, p. 117.
4 Swain, *Beginning the Twentieth Century*, p. 95.
5 Stieve, *Isvolsky and the World War*, p. 54.
6 Fay, *Origins of the World War*, vol. I, p. 329.
7 Stieve, *Isvolsky and the World War*, p. 57.
8 Ibid., p. 60.
9 Fay, *Origins of the World War*, vol. I, pp. 330–1.
10 W.L. Langer, *New Republic*, 15 April 1925, Part II, pp. 13–14.
11 Fay, *Origins of the World War*, vol. I, p. 315.
12 Barnes, *Genesis of the World War*, p. 124.
13 Stieve, *Isvolsky and the World War*, p. 78.
14 Ibid., pp. 75–6.
15 Rene Marchand, *Un Livre Noir*, vol. I, p. 269.
16 Fay, *Origins of the World War*, vol. I, p. 329.
17 Morel, *Diplomacy Revealed*, p. 269.
18 Barnes, *Genesis of the World War*, p. 113.
19 Fay, *Origins of the World War*, vol. I, pp. 323–30.
20 Stieve, *Isvolsky and the World War*, p. 88.
21 F. McHarg, *Pistoleros*, p. 186.
22 Herbert Feis, *Europe: The World's Banker, 1870–1914*, p. 211.
23 Bausman, *Let France Explain*, p. 161, quoting Herman Frobenius, *Germany's Hour of Destiny*, p. 43.
24 Quigley, *Tragedy and Hope*, p. 520.
25 Ibid., p. 525.
26 Stieve, *Isvolsky and the World War*, p. 56.
27 Barnes, *Genesis of the World War*, p. 117.
28 Stieve, *Isvolsky and the World War*, p. 133.
29 Barnes, *Genesis of the World War*, p. 121.
30 Ibid., p. 117.
31 Langer, *New Republic*, 15 April 1925, Part II, pp. 13–14.
32 Swain, *Beginning the Twentieth Century*, p. 97.
33 Stieve, *Isvolsky and the World War*, pp. 170–4.
34 Ibid., pp. 137–40.
35 Morel, *Pre-War Diplomacy*, p. 29.
36 Morel, *Diplomacy Revealed*, p. 226.
37 Ibid., p. 258.

Chapter 17 – America – A Very Special Relationship

1 Stead, *Last Will and Testament* at http://publicintelligence.net/the-last-will-and-testament-of-cecil-john-rhodes-1902/

2 Ibid., p. 59.
3 Ibid., p. 34.
4 Ibid., p. 55.
5 Quigley, *Tragedy and Hope*, pp. 60–1.
6 Chapman, *Rise of Merchant Banking*, pp. 158–61.
7 Dawkins to Milner, 26 July 1900, 16 August 1900, 21 March 1902, as quoted in Chapman, *Rise of Merchant Banking*, p. 161.
8 Quigley, *Anglo-American Establishment*, p. 49.
9 Ibid.
10 Baker, *Pilgrims of Great Britain*, p. 12.
11 *New York Times*, 3 March 1903.
12 Baker, *Pilgrims of Great Britain*, p. 13.
13 Knuth, *Empire of 'The City'*, p. 64.
14 Baker, *Pilgrims of the United States*, p. 3.
15 Baker, *Pilgrims of Great Britain*, p. 16.
16 While it is possible to list all of those in whose honour these dinners were organised, the individual members who attended remains a secret.
17 Baker, *Pilgrims of the United States*, p. 9.
18 Quigley, *Anglo-American Establishment*, p. 15.
19 Ferguson, *House of Rothschild*, p. 82.
20 Griffin, *Creature From Jekyll Island*, p. 415.
21 Cecil Roth, *The Magnificent Rothschilds*, p. 106.
22 Webster G. Tarpley and Anton Chaitkin, *George Bush: The Unauthorized Biography*, p. 136.
23 W.G. Carr, *Pawns in the Game*, p. 60.
24 G. Edward Griffin, interview at http://educate-yourself.org/cn/gedwardgriffininterview02apr04.shtml
25 Quigley, *Tragedy and Hope*, p. 951.
26 Ron Chernow, *The Warburgs*, pp. 46–8.
27 Stephen Birmingham, *Our Crowd*, p. 175.
28 Chernow, *The Warburgs*, p. 51.
29 Carr, *Pawns in the Game*, p. 61.
30 Chernow, *The Warburgs*, p. 12.
31 Ibid., p. 38.
32 Ibid., p. 86.
33 Proctor W. Hansl, *Years of Plunder*, pp. 37–8.
34 Ron Chernow, *Titan: The Life of John D. Rockefeller, Sr.*, pp. 575–7.
35 Initially an outspoken critic of Standard Oil, Archbold was recruited by Rockefeller to a directorship of the company, where he later served as vice president and then president until its 'demise' in 1911.
36 Chernow, *The Warburgs*, p. 248.

37 Ferguson, *House of Rothschild*, p. 117.
38 Chernow, *The Warburgs*, p. 390.
39 George R. Conroy, *Truth* magazine, Boston, 16 December 1912.
40 Griffin, *Creature From Jekyll Island*, p. 436.
41 Irving Katz, *August Belmont: A Political Biography*, p. 82.
42 Murray N. Rothbard, *Wall Street, Banks, and American Foreign Policy*, Centre for Libertarian Studies, 1995.
43 Chernow, *The Warburgs*, p. 548.
44 *The Crisis of 1907*, pamphlet taken from the *Boston Post*, 17 October 1907, p. 3.
45 House of Representatives Report No. 1593, Committee Appointed to investigate the Concentration of Control of Money and Credit, pp. 59–60.
46 Jon Moen, 'The Bank Panic of 1907', *Journal of Economic History*, no. 52, pp. 611–30.
47 *The Crisis of 1907*, p. 5.
48 Ibid., p. 6.
49 Ibid., p. 9.
50 Ibid., p. 11.
51 Ibid.
52 Antony C. Sutton, *The Federal Reserve Conspiracy*, p. 65.
53 House of Representatives Report No. 1593, pp. 24–5.
54 Ibid., p. 46.
55 Ibid., the cited case of the Mechanics and Traders Bank, p. 27.
56 Ibid., pp. 40–1. Morgan was accused in the Pujo Committee Report of disenfranchising shareholders in the Southern Railway Company.
57 Ibid., p. 56.
58 House of Representatives Report No. 1593.
59 Griffin, *Creature From Jekyll Island*, p. 444.
60 Ibid.
61 Quigley, *Tragedy and Hope*, p. 324.
62 Nicholas Stoskopf, Manuscrit auteur, publie dans; *Journee d'etudes sur l'historie de la haute banque France* (2000) at http://hal.archives-ouvertes.fr/docs/00/44/11/64/PDF/STOSKOPF_PARISIAN_HAUTE_BANQUE.pdf
63 Quigley, *Tragedy and Hope*, p. 520.
64 John Thom Holdsworth, *Money and Banking*, pp. 325–30.
65 Chernow, *The Warburgs*, p. 131.
66 Ibid.
67 Paul M. Warburg, 'A Plan for a Modified Central Bank', in *The Federal Reserve System: Its Origin and Growth*, Vol. 2, p. 29.

68 Gary Allen, *None Dare Call it Conspiracy*, chapter 3, p. 8.
69 Chernow, *Titan*, p. 352.
70 Organisation for the Study of Globalisation and Covert Politics, https://wikispooks.com/ISGP/organisations/Pilgrims_Society02.htm
71 Griffin, *Creature From Jekyll Island*, pp. 3–13.
72 Frank A. Vanderlip and Boyden Sparkes, *From Farm Boy to Financier*, p. 214.
73 Griffin, *Creature From Jekyll Island*, p. 23.
74 Joseph Patrick Tumulty, *Woodrow Wilson as I Know Him*, p. 10.
75 Sutton, *Federal Reserve Conspiracy*, pp. 82–3.
76 Quigley, *Tragedy and Hope*, p. 76.
77 The name 'Bull Moose' Party stemmed from Roosevelt's reaction to a question about his physical fitness to stand for the presidency. He replied that he was as fit as a bull moose.
78 Griffin, *Creature From Jekyll Island*, p. 453.
79 Tarpley and Chaitkin, *George Bush*, p. 330.
80 Edward Mandell House and Charles Seymour, *The Intimate Papers of Colonel House*, p. 5.
81 Library of Congress Resource Guide, *Presidential Election of 1912.*
82 Griffin, *Creature From Jekyll Island*, p. 240.
83 Ibid., p. 458.
84 George Sylvester Viereck, *The Strangest Friendship in History: Woodrow Wilson and Colonel House*, p. 4.
85 Ibid., pp. 35–7.
86 Congressional Record, House of Representatives, 23 December 1913, p. 1468.
87 Senator Bristow, Kansas, Congressional Record, House of Representatives, 23 December 1913, p. 1472.
88 Congressional Record, House of Representatives, 23 December 1913, p. 1488.
89 Representative Finlay H. Gray, Congressional Record, House of Representatives, 23 December 1913, p. 1491.

Chapter 18 – The Balkan Pressure Cooker – 1912–13

1 Even excellent sources like Fay, Ewart, Barnes and Stieve make this assumption. However, much of the funding for Serbia came from France. Note that Poincaré threatened to pull funding when Apis contemplated a civil war in 1914.
2 In 1912, Trotsky was sent to cover the Balkan War by the radical Russian newspaper *Kievskaya Mysil* and often wrote articles for them

under a pseudonym. His presence there and contemporary accounts raise the suspicion that he might have been more than a mere observer of the Balkan troubles.

3 Leon Trotsky, *The Balkan Wars 1912–13*, p. 112.
4 Kennedy, *Old Diplomacy and New*, p. 151.
5 Swain, *Beginning the Twentieth Century*, p. 169.
6 Trotsky, *Balkan Wars*, p. 112.
7 Albert Jay Nock, *The Myth of a Guilty Nation*, p. 60.
8 Ibid., p. 110.
9 Ibid., p. 114.
10 H.W. Wilson and J.A. Hammerton, *The Great War: An Illustrated History of the First World War*, vol. 1, p. 12.
11 Vladimir Dedijer, *The Road to Sarajevo*, p. 431.
12 Fay, *Origins of the World War*, vol. I, p. 439.
13 Eugenii Nicolaevich Shelking, *The Game of Diplomacy*, p. 192.
14 Dedijer, *Road to Sarajevo*, p. 432.
15 King Alexander of Serbia caused a sensation when he married his mistress rather than a member of the German royal family. They were unloved, especially by the military, who removed them in a bloody coup that shocked European courts. The two were brutally murdered at the old Turkish palace in Konak.
16 Wilson and Hammerton, *The Great War*, vol. I, ch.1, p. 21.
17 Dedijer, *Road to Sarajevo*, p. 85.
18 David MacKenzie, *Apis: The Congenial Conspirator*, p. 275.
19 Fay, *Origins of the World War*, vol. I, p. 27.
20 Barnes, *Genesis of the First World War*, p. 156.
21 Fay, *Origins of the World War*, vol. I, p. 442.
22 Kennedy, *Old Diplomacy and New*, p. 178.
23 Stieve, *Isvolsky and the First World War*, p. 116, and Engdahl, *A Century of War*, p. 34.
24 Edith Durham, *Twenty Years of Balkan Tangle*, chapter 19, pp. 2–3.
25 Fay, *Origins of the World War*, vol. I, p. 399.

CHAPTER 19 – FROM BALMORAL TO THE BALKANS

1 Sergei Sazonov, *Fateful Years, 1909–1916*, p. 57.
2 Grey, *Twenty-Five Years*, vol. II, pp. 139–40.
3 Stieve, *Isvolsky and the World War*, pp. 89–90.
4 Grey, *Twenty-Five Years*, vol. II, p. 139.
5 Gooch and Temperley, *British Documents on the Origin of the War, 1898–1914*, p. 765, no. 809.
6 Sazonov arrived in London on 20 September and spent three days there

before travelling to Balmoral. He left Balmoral on 27 September and went to visit Lord Crewe. (Gooch and Temperley, *British Documents on the Origin of the War*, p. 719.)

7 Grey, *Twenty-Five Years*, vol. II, p. 88.
8 Sazonov, *Fateful Years*, p. 58.
9 Gooch and Temperley, *British Documents on the Origin of the War*, p. 771.
10 Ibid., p. 769, no. 810.
11 Ibid., p. 764, no. 808, Sir G. Buchanan to Sir Edward Grey.
12 Ibid., p. 763, no. 807, Sir A. Nicolson to Lord Stamfordham.
13 Stieve, *Isvolsky and the World War*, p. 93.
14 Montgelas, *The Case for the Central Powers*, p. 55.
15 Bausman, *Let France Explain*, p. 169.
16 Ibid., p. 171.
17 Durham, *Twenty Years of Balkan Tangle*, chapter 19, pp. 18–19.
18 Stieve, *Isvolsky and the World War*, p. 96.
19 Engdahl, *A Century of War*, p. 34.
20 Montgelas, *The Case for the Central Powers*, p. 53.
21 Clark, *Kaiser Wilhelm II*, p. 192.
22 Grey, *Twenty-Five Years*, vol. II, p. 90.
23 Fay, *Origins of the World War*, vol. I, p. 439.
24 Ewart, *Roots and Causes of the Wars*, vol. I, p. 178.
25 Stieve, *Isvolsky and the World War*, p. 116.
26 Ibid.
27 Ewart, *Roots and Causes of the Wars*, vol. I, p. 178.
28 Stieve, *Isvolsky and the World War*, p. 126.
29 Barnes, *Genesis of the World War*, p. 148.
30 Neilson, *How Diplomats Make War*, p. 179.
31 *New York Times*, 16 September 1914.
32 Demburg in *The International Monthly*, New York at http://libcudl.colorado.edu/wwi/pdf/i73726928.pdf
33 Mombauer, *Origins of the First World War*, p. 12.
34 Trotsky, *Balkan Wars*, p. 20.
35 Durham, *Twenty Years of Balkan Tangle*, chapter 20, p. 1.
36 Grey, *Twenty-Five Years*, vol. II, p. 88.
37 Fay, *Origins of the World War*, vol. I, p. 473.
38 Stieve, *Isvolsky and the World War*, p. 94.
39 Clark, *Kaiser Wilhelm II*, p. 200.
40 Many Liberal and Radical MPs were extremely critical of the czarist regime in Russia. One example amongst many is Mr Joseph King (Hansard, House of Commons, Debate, 1 May 1913, vol. 52, c1343).

Chapter 20 – Sarajevo – The Web of Culpability

1 Editorial, *New York Times Current History of the European War*, vol. 28 (1928), issue 4, p. 619.
2 Harry Elmer Barnes, 'Germany Not Responsible for Austria's Actions', *New York Times Current History of the European War*, vol. 28 (1928), issue 4, p. 621.
3 Editorial, *New York Times Current History of the European War*, vol. 28 (1928), issue 4, p. 619.
4 Fay, *Origins of the World War*, vol. I, p. 439.
5 Ibid., p. 27.
6 Edith Durham, *Sarajevo Crime*, pp. 197–201.
7 MacKenzie, *Apis*, p. 275.
8 Barnes, *In Quest of Truth and Justice*, p. 43.
9 Dedijer, *Road to Sarajevo*, pp. 236–70.
10 Friedrich von Wiesner, 'Austria's Life and Death Struggle Against Irredentism', *New York Times Current History of the European War*, vol. 28 (1928), issue 4, p. 63.
11 Dedijer, *Road to Sarajevo*, p. 175.
12 Luigi Albertini, *Origins of the War of 1914*, vol. II, pp. 27–28, and 79.
13 Dedijer, *Road to Sarajevo*, pp. 388–9.
14 Albertini, *Origins of the War of 1914*, vol. II, pp. 282–3.
15 Dedijer, *Road to Sarajevo*, p. 388.
16 MacKenzie, *Apis*, p. 120.
17 Ibid., p. 121.
18 Dedijer, *Road to Sarajevo*, p. 385.
19 Barnes, 'Germany Not Responsible for Austria's Actions', p. 620.
20 David James Smith, *One Morning in Sarajevo: 28 June 1914*, p. 166.
21 Dedijer, *Road to Sarajevo*, pp. 317–19.
22 Smith, *One Morning in Sarajevo*, p. 193.
23 Alexander, Count Hoyos, 'Russia Chief Culprit in Precipitation of World War', *New York Times Current History of the European War*, vol. 28 (1928), p. 628 and seven other articles therein.
24 von Wiesner, 'Austria's Life and Death Struggle Against Irredentism', pp. 630–3.
25 Ibid., p. 632.
26 Ibid.
27 Barnes, 'Germany Not Responsible for Austria's Actions', p. 622.
28 W.A. Dolph Owings, *The Sarajevo Trial, Part 1*, pp. 527–30.
29 Ibid.
30 Princip endured a painful death. Following tuberculosis, he had an arm

amputated, and in prison conditions that became markedly harsher during the war, he died from malnutrition, blood loss and disease, weighing around 40 kilograms. He survived Ferdinand's assassination by three years and ten months.

31 Barnes, 'Germany Not Responsible for Austria's Actions', p. 620.
32 *The Times*, 16 July 1914.
33 MacKenzie, *Apis*, pp. 329 and 344–7.
34 Ibid., pp. 129–30.
35 Dedijer, *Road to Sarajevo*, pp. 398–400.
36 Barnes, *Genesis of the World War*, p. 731.
37 Victor Serge, 'La Verité sur l'Attentat de Sarajevo', in *Clarte*, no. 74, 1 May 1924.
38 Dedijer, *Road to Sarajevo*, p. 513.

Chapter 21 – July 1914 – Deception, Manipulation and Misrepresentation

1 King George I of Greece was assassinated in 1913; Mahmud Sevket Pasha, prime minister of Turkey in 1913; José Canalejas, prime minister of Spain in 1912; Prime Minister Stolypin in Russia in 1911; Grand Duke Alexandrovitch Romanov in 1911. Many survived attempted assassination, including Prince Albert Edward in 1900, Kaiser Wilhelm II in 1900 and Theodore Roosevelt in 1912.
2 Prime Minister Herbert Asquith in Hansard, House of Commons, Debate, 30 June 1914, vol. 64, cc214–6.
3 Imanuel Geiss, *July 1914: The Outbreak of the First World War: Selected Documents*, p. 55.
4 Ferdinand's marriage caused controversy because he chose to wed Countess Sophie Maria rather than royalty. Both parties had to accept that the marriage would be morganatic, meaning that none of the archduke's titles, property or privileges would be inherited by his wife or children.
5 Geiss, *July 1914*, p. 63.
6 *New York Times*, 3 July 1914.
7 Fay, *Origins of the World War*, vol. II, p. 205.
8 Ibid., p. 206.
9 Stieve, *Isvolsky and the World War*, p. 209.
10 Ibid. He asks the rhetorical question: 'Is this the result of a prudent holocaust?'
11 Gooch, Temperley and Headlam-Morley, *British Documents on the Origins of the War*, vol. XI, p. 22.
12 Fay, *Origins of the World War*, vol. II, p. 186.

13 Morel, *Diplomacy Revealed*, pp. 299–300.
14 Ibid.
15 *Novoe Vremya* was a daily newspaper in St Petersburg. In its earlier years it was liberal and published articles and extracts from Karl Marx. By 1914 it had become an anti-Semitic, reactionary government rag. The day after the Bolsheviks came to power, Lenin shut it down.
16 Quigley, *Anglo-American Establishment*, p. 12.
17 Fay, *Origins of the World War*, vol. II, p. 332.
18 Irene Cooper Willis, *England's Holy War*, p. 59.
19 Ibid., p. 25.
20 Jonathan Bardon, *A History of Ireland in 250 Episodes*, p. 435.
21 Count Leopold Berchtold, 'Austria's Challenge Justified by Serbian Menace', *New York Times Current History of the European War*, vol. 28 (1928), p. 626.
22 Geiss, *July 1914*, p. 71.
23 Ibid., p. 72.
24 Barnes, *In Quest of Truth and Justice*, p. 52.
25 Fay, *Origins of the World War*, vol. II, p. 175.
26 Barnes, *Genesis of the World War*, p. 241.
27 Gooch and Temperley, *British Documents on the Origins of the War*, vol. XI; Bunsen to Grey, 5 July, BD 40.
28 'Origin of the World War: Minutes of a Historic Council', *New York Times Current History of the European War*, vol. 11, (1919), pp. 455–60.
29 Geiss, *July 1914*, pp. 80–7.
30 Hansard, House of Commons, Debate, 7 July 1914, vol. 64, cc1032–55, Anglo-Persian Oil Company (Acquisition of Capital).
31 Geiss, *July 1914*, p. 105.
32 Hansard, Foreign Office, Class II, House of Commons, Debate, 10 July 1914, vol. 64, cc1383–463.
33 Arthur Ponsonby, Hansard, House of Commons, Debate, 10 July 1914, vol. 64, cc1397–398.
34 Joseph King pointed out in that debate that Mr Cassel, a distinguished financier, Sir P. Magnus, a world renowned medical scientist, Mr Montagu, the secretary to the Treasury, Mr Herbert Samuel, president of the Local Government Board, and the lord chief justice himself, Isaac Rufus, were all barred by their Jewish faith from entering Russia.
35 Joseph King, Hansard, House of Commons, Debate, 10 July 1914, vol. 64, cc1438–50.
36 Fay, *Origins of the World War*, vol. II, p. 236.
37 Berchtold, 'Austria's Challenge Justified by Serbian Menace', pp. 626–8.

38 Barnes, *In Quest of Truth and Justice*, p. 46.
39 Bunsen to Grey, 16 July, BD 50, but suppressed from the British Blue Book (BBB). Thus the official documents published in this 'book', *Great Britain and the European Crisis, Correspondence and Statements*, together with an *Introductory Narrative of Events*, published in 1914, deliberately sifted out incriminating evidence; also in Fay, *Origins of the World War*, vol. II, p. 247, footnote.
40 Ibid.
41 Barnes, 'Germany Not Responsible for Austria's Actions', p. 624.
42 Grey to Rumbold telegram 197, BD 116, in Geiss, *July 1914*, p. 212.
43 'Did Germany Incite Austria in 1914? Evidence in the War Guilt Controversy', *New York Times Current History of the European War*, vol. 28 (1928), pp. 619–25.

Chapter 22 – July 1914 – Leading Europe Towards the Brink

1 Fay, *Origins of the World War*, vol. II, p. 363.
2 Pasic to Serbian legations, 19 July 1914, Serbian Blue Book (SBB 30). As quoted in Fay, *Origins of the World War*, vol. II, p. 335.
3 It was very important for Poincaré to camouflage his real intentions in visiting the czar and Sazonov. The official visit had been agreed at the start of 1914, but a fixed date was only agreed after the assassination of Franz Ferdinand.
4 Fay, *Origins of the World War*, vol. II, p. 278.
5 Barnes, *Genesis of the World War*, p. 320.
6 Stieve, *Isvolsky and the World War*, p. 210.
7 *The Times*, 22 July 1914.
8 *The Times*, 21 July 1914.
9 Fay, *Origins of the World War*, vol. II, p. 280.
10 A detailed analysis of the French official telegrams was printed in 1927 showing the omissions and alterations to original documents that had been approved at the Quai d'Orsay. In particular, details of Poincaré's visit to St Petersburg and subsequent Russian military manoeuvres were removed. G. Demartial, *L'Evangile du Quai d'Orsay*, p. 11.
11 Fay, *Origins of the World War*, vol. II, p. 280.
12 Ibid., p. 283.
13 Barnes, *Genesis of the World War*, p. 331.
14 Buchanan to Grey, 24 July, BD 101, in Geiss, *July 1914*, p. 196.
15 Stieve, *Isvolsky and the World War*, p. 215.
16 Buchanan to Grey 24 July, BD 101. The notes appended to this telegram are particularly valuable. Sir Eyre Crowe at the Foreign Office, a rabid

anti-German, advocated immediate preparations to back up France and Russia. The telegram was then passed to the permanent under-secretary, Sir Arthur Nicolson, who added his support to Crowe. Sir Edward Grey responded that he had discussed the matter with Churchill. Layers of support and influence surrounded Grey.

17 Geiss, *July 1914*, p. 198.
18 Ibid., p. 199.
19 Hansard, House of Commons, Debate, 10 July 1914, vol. 64, cc1397–398.
20 Lloyd George, Hansard, House of Commons, Debate, 23 July 1914, vol. 65, cc666–781.
21 Geiss, *July 1914*, p. 133, and Rumbold to Grey, BD 77, 22 July 1914, p. 158.
22 Ewart, *Roots and Causes of the Wars*, vol. II, footnote p. 1071.
23 Bethmann Hollweg to the ambassadors at St Petersburg, Paris and London, DD100; Berlin, 21 July 1914, in Geiss, *July 1914*, p. 149.
24 Geiss, *July 1914*, p. 150.
25 Montgelas, *British Foreign Policy under Sir Edward Grey*, p. 65.
26 Ewart, *Roots and Causes of the Wars*, vol. II, pp. 1062–3.
27 Montgelas, *British Foreign Policy under Sir Edward Grey*, p. 66.
28 Barnes, *Genesis of the World War*, p. 200.
29 Extract from the Austrian Red Book, OD 10616, 24 July 1914, in Geiss, *July 1914*, p. 174.
30 Geiss, *July 1914*, p. 178.
31 Geiss, *July 1914*, p. 175. Mensdorff to Berchtold, 24 July 1914.
32 Willis, *England's Holy War*, p. 32.
33 *Manchester Guardian*, 25 July 1914.
34 *The Times*, 22 July 1914.
35 Fay, *Origins of the World War*, vol. II, p. 369.
36 H.H. Asquith, *Letters to Venetia Stanley*, edited by Michael and Eleanor Brock, 26 July 1914, p. 125.
37 Asquith, Grey, Haldane, Lloyd George and Churchill were exclusively 'in the know' in Cabinet.
38 Churchill, *World Crisis*, p. 155.
39 David, *Inside Asquith's Cabinet*, pp. 176–7.
40 Fay, *Origins of the World War*, vol. II, p. 369.
41 Berchtold, 'Austria's Challenge Justified by Serbian Menace', p. 226.
42 Barnes, *In Quest of Truth and Justice*, p. 44.
43 Pierre Renouvin, *The Immediate Origins of the War*, p. 99.
44 Fay, *Origins of the World War*, vol. II, p. 340.
45 Ibid., p. 337.

46 Ibid., p. 339.
47 Barnes, *Genesis of the World War*, p. 201.
48 Fay, *Origins of the World War*, vol. II, p. 338.
49 *The Times*, 22 July 1914.
50 Fay, *Origins of the World War*, vol. II, p. 338.
51 Barnes, *Genesis of the World War*, pp. 200–1.
52 Ferguson, *Pity of War*, p. 156.
53 Fay, *Origins of the World War*, vol. II, p. 348.
54 Ferguson, *Pity of War*, p. 156.
55 Renouvin, *Immediate Origins of the War*, p. 98.
56 Swain, *Beginning the Twentieth Century*. p. 353.
57 Ewart, *Roots and Causes of the Wars*, vol. II, p. 1040.
58 Stone, *World War One*, p. 21.
59 Barnes, *In Quest of Truth and Justice*, p. 47
60 Buchanan to Grey, 25 July 1914, BD 125, in Geiss, *July 1914*, p. 213.

CHAPTER 23 – JULY 1914 – THE FIRST MOBILISATIONS

1 Jack Levy, 'Organisational Routines and the Causes of War', *International Studies Quarterly*, vol. 30, no. 2, June 1986, p. 196.
2 Ibid., p. 195.
3 Barnes, *Genesis of the World War*, p. 354.
4 Kennan, *Fateful Alliance*, p. 161.
5 Barnes, *Genesis of the World War*, p. 374.
6 Kennan, *Fateful Alliance*, pp. 250–1.
7 Marc Trachtenberg, 'The Meaning of Mobilization in 1914', *International Security*, vol, 15, issue 3, Winter 1990–91, pp. 120–50.
8 Fay, *Origins of the World War*, vol. II, pp. 307–8.
9 Sergei Dobrorolsky, *The Mobilisation of the Russian Army, 1914* at http://www.vlib.us/wwi/resources/archives/texts/t040831b.html
10 Memorandum of the day of the Russian Ministry for Foreign Affairs, St Petersburg, 24 July 1914, in Geiss, *July 1914*, p. 190.
11 *Special Journal of the Russian Council of Ministers*, St Petersburg, 24 July 1914, in Geiss, *July 1914*, pp. 186–7.
12 Alexander Solzhenitsyn, *August 1914*, pp. 92–3.
13 Geiss, *July 1914*, p. 214.
14 Barnes, *Genesis of the World War*, p. 324.
15 Buchanan to Grey, St Petersburg, 25 July 1914, BD 125, in Geiss, *July 1914*, p. 214.
16 Ibid.
17 *Special Journal of the Russian Council of Ministers*, St Petersburg, 25 July 1914, in Geiss, *July 1914*, p. 207.

18 Fay, *Origins of the World War*, vol. II, p. 309.
19 Stephen J. Cimbala, *Military Persuasion: Deterrence and Provocation in Crisis and War*, p. 58.
20 George Buchanan, *My Mission to Russia and Other Diplomatic Memories*, vol. 1, p. 93.
21 Ibid., p. 94.
22 Montgelas, *Case for the Central Powers*, p. 129.
23 Lutz, *Lord Grey and the World War*, p. 244.
24 Grey to Buchanan, London, 25 July 1914, BD 112, in Geiss, *July 1914*, p. 211.
25 Grey to Rumbold, London, 25 July 1914, BD 116, in Geiss, *July 1914*, p. 212.
26 Lutz, *Lord Grey and the World War*, pp. 241–2.
27 Barnes, *Genesis of the World War*, p. 336.
28 Trachtenberg, 'The Meaning of Mobilization in 1914', p. 126.
29 Fay, *Origins of the World War*, vol. II, pp. 302–3.
30 Trachtenberg, 'The Meaning of Mobilization in 1914', pp. 120–50.
31 Fay, *Origins of the World War*, vol. II, pp. 306–7.
32 Barnes, *Genesis of the World War*, p. 337.

Chapter 24 – July 1914 – Buying Time – The Charade of Mediation

1 *Illustrated History of the Great War*, vol. 1, p. 17. Created by Northcliffe's Amalgamated Press in 1914 to provide instant propaganda and glorify the war effort.
2 Geiss, *July 1914*, pp. 214–15.
3 George Malcolm Thomson, *The Twelve Days*, p. 80.
4 Fay, *Origins of the World War*, vol. II, p. 377.
5 Barnes, *Genesis of the World War*, p. 26.
6 Pierre Renouvin, *La Crise Européene et la Grande Guerre*, p. 112.
7 Thomson, *Twelve Days*, p. 86.
8 Fay, *Origins of the World War*, vol. II, p. 383.
9 Renouvin, *La Crise Européene*, p. 117.
10 Ibid., p. 113.
11 Thomson, *Twelve Days*, p. 114.
12 Barnes, *Genesis of the World War*, p. 337.
13 Ibid., p. 340.
14 Grey, *Twenty-Five Years*, vol. II, p. 162.
15 Lutz, *Lord Grey and the World War*, p. 244.
16 Ibid.
17 Fay, *Origins of the World War*, vol. II, p. 321.

18 Geiss, *July 1914*, p. 240.
19 Fay, *Origins of the World War*, vol. II, p. 405.
20 Lutz, *Lord Grey and the World War*, p. 251.
21 Telegram 328, Berlin, 30 July 1914, OD.110130, in Geiss, *July 1914*, p. 302.
22 Fay, *Origins of the World War*, vol. II, p. 409.
23 In fact, the Austrian army did not cross the Serbian frontier until 13 August, by which time the world war had already erupted: a testimony to how urgently the Secret Elite precipitated the conflagration.
24 Handwritten by Wilhelm II, 28 July 1914, DD293, in Geiss, *July 1914*, p. 256.
25 Ibid.
26 Buchanan to Grey, St Petersburg, 28 July 1914, BD 247, in Geiss, *July 1914*, p. 264.
27 Asquith, *Letters to Venetia Stanley*, p. 131 and footnote 5. Rothschild was particularly hostile to associations with Russia because of the notorious pogroms.
28 Ibid. It was ominous. He received news that Austria had declared war on Serbia, but since it was a quiet evening in Parliament, he set up dinner and a game of bridge.
29 The Schlieffen Plan, Germany's defensive plan, was widely known across Europe.
30 Fay, *Origins of the World War*, vol. II, p. 431.
31 Moltke to Bethmann, Berlin, 29 July 1914, DD349, in Geiss, *July 1914*, p. 284.
32 Fay, *Origins of the World War*, vol. II, p. 435.
33 Lichnowsky to Jagow, London, 29 July 1914, DD357, in Geiss, *July 1914*, p. 286.
34 Ibid.
35 Lichnowsky to Jagow, London, 29 July 1914, DD368, in Geiss, *July 1914*, pp. 288–90.
36 This was a booklet of diplomatic correspondence, selected, altered and added to, which purported to prove to Parliament and the country that war had been forced on Britain by Austria-Hungry and Germany.
37 Prince Henry to Kaiser, Kiel, 28 July 1914, KD 374, in Fay, *Origins of the World War*, vol. II, p. 500.
38 Lloyd George, *War Memoirs*, p. 34.
39 Nicholas II to Wilhelm II, St Petersburg, 29 July 1914, DD332, in Geiss, *July 1914*, p. 260.
40 Kaiser Wilhelm made a number of observations on the above telegram. He clung to his belief that there was still time for negotiations and that Russia had 'no reason at all' for mobilisation.

41 Ewart, *Roots and Causes of the Wars*, vol. I, p. 158.
42 Ibid., p. 159.
43 Wilhelm II to Nicholas II, Berlin, 29 July 1914, DD359, in Geiss, *July 1914*, p. 290.
44 Sergei Dobrorolsky, *The Mobilisation of the Russian Army, 1914* at http://www.vlib.us/wwi/resources/archives/txtarchive.html
45 Moltke to Bethmann, Berlin, 29 July 1914, DD349, in Geiss, *July 1914*, p. 282.
46 Asquith, *Letters to Venetia Stanley*, p. 132.
47 *Illustrated History of the Great War*, vol. 1, p. 29.
48 Neilson, *How Diplomats Make War*, p. 258.
49 Goschen to Grey, Berlin, 29 July 1914, BD 293, in Geiss, *July 1914*, p. 300.
50 Ibid., p. 301.
51 Grey, *Twenty-Five Years*, vol. II, p. 216.
52 Neilson, *How Diplomats Make War*, p. 268.
53 International Situation, Hansard, House of Commons, Debate, 30 July 1914, vol. 65, c1574.
54 Asquith, *Letters to Venetia Stanley*, pp. 136–7.
55 Goschen to Grey, Berlin, 29 July 1914, BD 293, in Geiss, *July 1914*, pp. 300–1.
56 Whether or not the relationship was ever consummated, Asquith wrote to Venetia as a lover. His indiscretions in sending her absolutely confidential texts, telegrams, reports and detailed opinion raised serious concerns in official circles about national security.
57 Barnes, *Genesis of the World War*, p. 267.
58 Bethmann to Tschirschky (his ambassador in Austria), 30 July 1914, DD441, in Geiss, *July 1914*, pp. 305–6.
59 Barnes, *Genesis of the World War*, p. 355.
60 Wilhelm II to Nicholas II, Berlin, 30 July 1914, DD420, in Geiss, *July 1914*, p. 304.
61 Nicholas II to Wilhelm II, St Petersburg, 30 July 1914, KD390, in Fay, *Origins of the World War*, vol. II, p. 430.
62 Barnes, *Genesis of the World War*, p. 350; and Fay, *Origins of the World War*, vol. II, p. 301, footnote 54.
63 Dobrorolsky, *The Mobilisation of the Russian Army in 1914*, p. 28.
64 Thomson, *Twelve Days*, p. 126.
65 Dobrorolsky, *The Mobilisation of the Russian Army in 1914*, p. 29.
66 Ewart, *Roots and Causes of the Wars*, vol. II, p. 1165.
67 Nielson, *How Diplomats Make War*, p. 293.
68 Wilhelm II to Nicholas II, Berlin, 31 July 1914, DD 480, in Geiss, *July 1914*, p. 324.

69 Ibid.
70 Barnes, *Genesis of the World War*, pp. 268–9.
71 Fay, *Origins of the World War*, vol. II, p. 523.

Chapter 25 – Ireland – Plan B

1 Quigley, *Anglo-American Establishment*, p. 312.
2 Milner Papers, Gell to Milner, 12 July 1899, Bodleian Library, MS.Eng. Hist. c.686.
3 Ibid.
4 Pakenham, *Boer War*, p. 41.
5 Churchill, *World Crisis*, p. 148.
6 *Dundee Courier*, 31 July 1914, p. 5.
7 Francis Hackett, *The Story of the Irish Nation*, p. 338.
8 Hansard, House of Commons, Debates from 24 to 31 March and beyond.
9 Asquith, *Letters to Venetia Stanley*, pp. 135–6. The letters show that he met privately with Carson and Bonar Law, then Redmond and Dillon on 30 July alone.
10 Ryan, *Mutiny at the Curragh*, p. 76.
11 Quigley, *Anglo-American Establishment*, p. 176.
12 Patrick Buckland, *James Craig*, p. 8.
13 The Carson Papers, The Public Record Office of Northern Ireland (PRONI) (D1507), p. 4.
14 Ibid.
15 The Carson Papers, The Third Home Rule Bill, The Public Record Office of Northern Ireland (PRONI) (D1507), p. 5.
16 The Public Record Office of Northern Ireland (PRONI) (INF/7A/2/8).
17 Quigley, *Anglo-American Establishment*, p. 31 and p. 86.
18 Rudyard Kipling's poem 'Ulster 1912' was unadulterated Secret Elite propaganda. Its emotional appeal to endangered Unionism was whipped into a frenzy of imagined consequence: 'Rebellion, rapine, hate, Oppression, wrong and greed, Are loosed to rule on fate, By England's act and deed . . .'
19 The Protestant Dutchman, King William of Orange, defeated the army of the Catholic King James II in 1690 at the Battle of the Boyne. It ensured the Protestant ascendancy in Ireland and is celebrated annually on 12 July by the Orange order. The Boyne Standard has an orange background with the cross of St George in the top left-hand corner and a purple star in the lower right.

20 The Public Record Office of Northern Ireland (PRONI) (INF/7/A/2/47).
21 Bardon, *A History of Ireland*, pp. 431–2.
22 The Carson Papers, The Public Record Office of Northern Ireland (PRONI) (D1507), p. 4.
23 Ronald McNeill, *Ulster's Stand for Union*, chapter XV, letter of 4 June 1914.
24 Ibid.
25 Gollin, *Proconsul in Politics*, p. 180.
26 Ian Colvin, *The Life of Lord Carson*, vol. II, p. 241.
27 Gollin, *Proconsul in Politics*, p. 188.
28 Ibid., footnote.
29 Quigley, *Anglo-American Establishment*, p. 312.
30 Gollin, *Proconsul in Politics*, p. 188.
31 Alfred Milner considered that one way to 'paralyse the arm' was to block the annual Army Act and bring about a constitutional crisis. The act, which had been passed routinely since 1688, was a reminder to the army that Parliament held the purse strings and the army was subordinate to parliamentary authority.
32 Brevet Colonel Hacket Pain served throughout the Boer War and was among the select group of officers specifically selected by Roberts for duty with the UVF.
33 Geoffrey Lewis, *Carson: The Man Who Divided Ireland*, p. 136.
34 McNeill, *Ulster's Stand for Union*, chap. XVI.
35 *The Times*, 18 March 1914.
36 Wilson Diaries, 14 November 1913, cited in C.E. Callwell and Marshal Foch, *Field Marshal Sir Henry Wilson, Vol. 1: His Life and Diaries*, p. 132.
37 Milner Papers, Carson to Milner, 18 March 1914, in Gollin, *Proconsul in Politics*, p. 200.
38 K.W.W. Aikin, *The Last Years of Liberal England, 1900–1914*, pp. 112–13.
39 Ryan, *Mutiny at the Curragh*, p. 120.
40 Jeffery, *Field Marshal Sir Henry Wilson*, p. 39.
41 Robert Kee, *Ireland: A History*, p. 149.
42 Gollin, *Proconsul in Politics*, p. 202.
43 Hansard, House of Commons, Debate, 7 April 1914, vol. 60, cc1787–9.
44 Hansard, House of Commons, Debate, 2 April 1914, vol. 60, cc1359–64.
45 Ibid.
46 Jeffery, *Field Marshal Sir Henry Wilson*, p. 39.

47 Kee, *Ireland*, p. 149.
48 Haldane, *An Autobiography*, pp. 267–8; Hansard, House of Lords, Debate, 23 March 1914, vol. 15, cc619–53, gives verbatim report.
49 David, *Inside Asquith's Cabinet*, p. 168, citing Hansard, House of Commons, 16 April 1914, vol. 61, cc322–5.
50 Iain McLean and Tom Lubbock, *The Curious Incident of the Guns in the Night Time*, p. 11.
51 Churchill, *World Crisis*, p. 148.
52 *The Times*, 23 March 1914.
53 Toye, *Lloyd George and Churchill*, p. 116.
54 Major Fred Crawford, who played a leading role in the Ulster arms smuggling, was a Boer War veteran who served in South Africa as an artillery captain.
55 The precise number of weapons imported varies with the persons recording this incident. The weapons were not all of uniform type.
56 McLean and Lubbock, *The Curious Incident*, p. 13, citing PRONI D/1700/5/17/2/4 Fred Crawford, 'Diary of the gunrunning'.
57 Alvin Jackson, *Home Rule: An Irish History, 1800–2000*, p. 133.
58 McLean and Lubbock, *The Curious Incident*, p. 13, citing PRONI D/1700/5/17/2/4.
59 Bardon, *A History of Ireland*, p. 444.
60 Wilfred Spender was a promising British soldier who served on the Committee of Imperial Defence in London. He was allowed to retire from his army commission and went to help the UVF. His cousin, A.J. Spender, was editor of the *Westminster Gazette* and close to many in the Secret Elite.
61 Ryan, *Mutiny at the Curragh*, p. 182.
62 Warre B. Wells, *John Redmond: A Biography*, p 122.
63 Diarmid Ferriter, *The Transformation of Ireland, 1900–2000*, p. 125.
64 Jackson, *Ireland, 1798–1998*, p 167.
65 Ibid.
66 Childers, *The Riddle of the Sands*, p. 281.
67 Frederick Bridgham, *The First World War as a Clash of Cultures*, pp. 55–6.
68 K.O. Morgan, 'The Boer War and the Media, 1899–1902', Twentieth Centruy British History, vol. 13, no. 1, march 2002, p. 6.
69 Erskine Childers, *War and the Arme Blanche*, pp. v–xvi.
70 Quigley, *Anglo-American Establishment*, p. 313.
71 Boyle, *The Riddle of Erskine Childers*, p. 118.
72 Ibid., p. 71.
73 Ibid., p. 144.

74 Angus Mitchell, *Casement*, p. 85.
75 Leonard Piper, *The Tragedy of Erskine Childers*, p. 124.
76 Quigley, *Anglo-American Establishment*, p. 314.
77 Rodger Casement was knighted in 1911 for his humanitarian campaigns.
78 John M. Bourne, *Who's Who in World War I*, p. 264.
79 Erskine Childers' log book at http://www.rmg.co.uk/explore/sea-and-ships/in-depth/erskine-childers/
80 Asquith, *Letters to Venetia Stanley*, p. 84.
81 Ibid., pp. 129–30, letter to Venetia Stanley, Monday, 27 July 1914.
82 Bardon, *A History of Ireland*, p. 438.
83 Ibid., p. 82.
84 Boyle, *Riddle of Erskine Childers*, p. 196.
85 Ibid., p. 200.

Chapter 26 – August 1914 – Of Neutrality and Just Causes

1 Isvolsky to Sazonov, 31 July 1914, in Fay, *Origins of the World War*, vol. II, p. 531.
2 Fay, *Origins of the World War*, vol. II, p. 532.
3 Lawrence Lafore, *The Long Fuse: An Interpretation of the Origins of World War*, p. 261.
4 Thomson, *The Twelve Days*, p. 152.
5 Hamilton and Herwig, *Decisions for War*, p. 140.
6 Fay, *Origins of the World War*, vol. II, p. 532.
7 Barnes, *In Quest of Truth and Justice*, p. 87.
8 Lichnowsky to von Jagow, London, 1 August 1914, DD596, in Geiss, *July 1914*, p. 346.
9 Ibid.
10 Ibid., p. 347.
11 Ewart, *Roots and Causes of the Wars*, vol. I, p. 136.
12 Hamilton and Herwig, *Decisions for War*, p. 141.
13 David, *Inside Asquith's Cabinet*, p. 179.
14 Morel, *Truth and the War*, pp. 47–9.
15 Morel, *The Makers of War*, p. 47.
16 David, *Inside Asquith's Cabinet*, p. 179.
17 Hamilton and Herwig, *Decisions for War*, pp. 138–9.
18 Grey, *Twenty-Five Years*, vol. II, p. 175.
19 Strachan, *The First World War*, p. 50.
20 Arthur Ponsonby, *Falsehood in Wartime*, p. 53.
21 Ewart, *Roots and Causes of the Wars*, vol. I, pp. 541–2.
22 Ibid., pp. 542–6.

23 Minutes of the conference between General Jungbluth and Colonel Bridges, 23 April 1912, as cited in 'The Case of Belgium, etc.', Document 2, in *The International Monthly Inc.*, New York, 1914.
24 Barnes, *Genesis of the World War*, p. 559.
25 Goschen to Grey, Berlin, 29 July 1914, BD 293, in Geiss, *July 1914*, p. 300.
26 Ewart, *Roots and Causes of the Wars*, vol. I, p. 137.
27 Swain, *Beginning the Twentieth Century*, p. 368.
28 Neilson, *How Diplomats Make War*, pp. 265–6.
29 Ewart, *Roots and Causes of the Wars*, vol. I, p. 432.
30 Crowe to Grey, BD 369, memo by Sir Eyre Crowe, 31 July 1914, in Geiss, *July 1914*, pp. 330–1.
31 Ibid.
32 Thomson, *The Twelve Days*, p. 171.
33 Barnes, *Genesis of the World War*, p. 515.
34 John Burns was a truly remarkable individual and the first working-class man to hold a government ministry. He resigned from Asquith's Cabinet in 1914, declaring the war to be a 'universal crime'.
35 David, *Inside Asquith's Cabinet*, p. 180.
36 Asquith, *Letters to Venetia Stanley*, Sunday, 2 August 1914, p. 146.
37 Ibid.
38 Ibid., p. 140.
39 Thomson, *The Twelve Days*, p. 173.
40 Toye, *Lloyd George and Churchill*, p. 125.
41 Hamilton and Herwig, *Decisions for War*, p. 143.
42 Ferguson, *Pity of War*, p. 161.
43 Geiss, *July 1914*, p. 231.
44 Fay, *Origins of the World War*, vol. II, p. 541.
45 Barnes, *Genesis of the World War*, pp. 558–9.
46 Ibid., p. 464.
47 Churchill, *World Crisis*, p. 174.
48 *The Times*, 3 August 1914, p. 7.

Chapter 27 – The Speech That Cost a Million Dead

1 'The lamps are going out all over Europe. We shall not see them lit again in our time' was attributed to Sir Edward Grey, as claimed in his autobiography, *Twenty-Five Years*, vol. 2, chapter XVIII, p. 223. Isvolsky to Sazonov, 31 July 1914, in Fay, *Origins of the World War*, vol. II, p. 531.
2 Stephen Lucius Gwynn, *John Redmond's Last Years*, p. 128.

3 Haldane, *An Autobiography*, pp. 275–6.
4 Statement by Sir Edward Grey, Hansard, House of Commons, Debate, 3 August 1914, vol. 65, cc1809–32.
5 Morel, *Secret History of a Great Betrayal*, p. 11.
6 Leo Amery, *The Leo Amery Diaries, 1896–1929*, vol. I, p. 106.
7 Statement by Sir Edward Grey, Hansard, House of Commons, 3 August 1914, vol. 65, cc1809–32.
8 Ibid. His fraudulence was to become the official British government position.
9 Crowe to Grey, 31 July 1914, BD 369, in Geiss, *July 1914*, p. 330.
10 Statement by Sir Edward Grey, Hansard, House of Commons, 3 August 1914, vol. 65, cc1810. According to *The Guardian* of 4 July 1914, this promise was greeted by ministerial cheers.
11 Fay, *Origins of the World War*, vol. I, pp. 14–15.
12 Morel, *Secret History of a Great Betrayal*, pp. 11–12.
13 Asquith in Hansard, House of Commons, Debate, 27 November 1911, vol. 32, cc106–107, and in Morel, *Secret History of a Great Betrayal*, p. 16.
14 Grey, *Twenty-Five Years*, vol. II, pp. 218–19.
15 Nicolson to Grey, London, 1 August 1914, BD 424, in Geiss, *July 1914*, p. 349.
16 The Committee of Imperial Defence concluded in September 1905 that 'Recent history shows . . . that the value of a collective guarantee of the neutrality and independence of a State must be largely discounted. Whatever may be the legal interpretation of the obligations involved in such a guarantee, nations usually act mainly in accordance with their real or supposed interests at the moment, and independently of their Treaty engagements.' CAB 38/10/67, p. 7.
17 Morel, *Secret History of a Great Betrayal*, p. 16.
18 Statement by Sir Edward Grey, Hansard, House of Commons, 3 August 1914, vol. 65, cc1822–23.
19 Arthur Conan Doyle, *The Crime of the Congo, 1908*, is a noted work on this subject.
20 'A Fateful Sitting of the House of Commons', *The Guardian*, 4 July 1914.
21 Ibid., p. 6.
22 Statement by Sir Edward Grey, Hansard, House of Commons, 3 August 1914, vol. 65, cc1823–24.
23 Amery, *Leo Amery Diaries*, p. 106.
24 Ibid.
25 Joseph King in Hansard, House of Commons, War in Europe Debate, 3 August 1914, vol. 65, cc1864.

26 Mr Bonar Law in Hansard, House of Commons, Foreign Office Debate, 10 July 1914, vol. 64, cc1438–9.

27 Churchill, *World Crisis*, p. 174.

28 Asquith, *Letters to Venetia Stanley*, Monday, 3 August 1914, p. 148.

29 Ibid., p. 149, footnote 6.

30 Gwynn, *John Redmond's Last Years*, p. 129.

31 *The Times*, 1 August 1914, p. 6.

32 Asquith, *Letters to Venetia Stanley*, p. 149, footnote 4.

33 Ramsay MacDonald in Hansard, House of Commons, Debate, 3 August 1914, vol. 65, cc1830.

34 Grey, *Twenty-Five Years*, vol. II, p. 211.

35 Churchill, *World Crisis*, p. 178.

36 Haldane, *An Autobiography*, p. 278.

37 This was the second of three parts to the sitting of the House of Commons that day. Hansard, House of Commons, Debate, 3 August 1914, vol. 65, cc1833–48.

38 Paul Cambon to Vivani, 3 August 1914, FYB 143, in Geiss, *July 1914*, p. 356.

39 Philip Morrell was Liberal MP for Burnley. Strongly opposed to the war, he was part of the Union of Democratic Control organised to oppose the secrecy of foreign policy and military influences on government. The UDC included Ramsay MacDonald, E.D. Morel and Charles Trevelyan.

40 Edmund Harvey, Liberal MP for Leeds West, was a Quaker and pacifist who worked to have conscientious objectors permitted to take on non-combatant duties in the army.

41 Germany and Belgium, Hansard, House of Commons, Adjournment Debate, 3 August 1914, vol. 65, cc1839.

42 Keir Hardie was MP for Merthyr Tydfil. Hansard, House of Commons, Germany and Belgium Adjournment Debate, 3 August 1914, vol. 65, cc1840.

43 Hansard, House of Commons, War in Europe Debate, 3 August 1914, vol. 65, cc1848–84.

44 Percy Molteno, Liberal MP for Dumfriesshire, in Hansard, House of Commons, War in Europe Debate, 3 August 1914, vol. 65, cc1848–51.

45 Ibid.

46 Llewellyn Williams, Liberal MP for Carmarthen Boroughs, in Hansard, House of Commons, War in Europe Debate, 3 August 1914, vol. 65, cc1856–58.

47 Joseph King, Liberal MP for North Somerset, Hansard, in House of Commons, War in Europe Debate, 3 August 1914, vol. 65, cc1865–66.

48 Ibid., cc1868.
49 Arthur Balfour in Hansard, House of Commons, War in Europe Debate, 3 August 1914, vol. 65, cc1881–82.
50 Ibid.
51 *The Guardian*, 4 August 1914, p. 6.
52 Amery, *The Leo Amery Diaries*, p. 106.
53 After hours of debate, all that *The Times* reported was: 'The sitting was suspended for a time, and later on the adjournment motion, several Radicals criticised the government after Sir Edward Grey had acquainted the House with the terms of the German ultimatum to Belgium.' *The Times*, 4 August 1914.
54 A.J.P. Taylor, *English History 1914–1945*, p. 27, footnote 2.
55 Chancellor Bethmann, speech to the Reichstag on 4 August, at http://www.firstworldwar.com/source/bethmannspeech1914.htm.
56 Quigley, *Anglo-American Establishment*, p. 177.
57 Ibid.
58 Taylor, *English History 1914–1945*, p. 28.
59 William Lygon, 7th Earl Beauchamp, First Commissioner of Works, a man who is more remembered for his public exile following revelations of his sexual preferences than his involvement in witnessing the declaration of war. His reward was to be appointed lord president of the Council to replace Lord Morley, who had resigned from Asquith's Cabinet in protest over the war.

Conclusion – Lies, Myths and Stolen History

1 Anthony Arnoux, *The European War*, vol. 1, p. 270.
2 J.A. White, *Transition to Global Rivalry*, p. 181.
3 Alexander Fuehr, *The Neutrality of Belgium*, pp. 73–5.
4 Albert J. Knock, *The Myth of a Guilty Nation*, p. 37, ebook at http://library.mises.org/books/Albert%20Jay%20Nock/The%20Myth%20of%20a%20Guilty%20Nation.pdf
5 Fay, *Origins of the World War*, vol. I, p. 5.
6 George Buchanan, *My Mission to Russia*, vol. 1, p. 100.
7 Fay, *Origins of the World War*, vol. I, p. 29.
8 Ibid., p. 5.
9 Barnes, *Genesis of the World War*, p. 40.
10 Fay, *Origins of the World War*, p. 6.
11 The German White Book was titled *Preliminary Memoir and Documents Concerning the Outbreak of the War.*
12 Fay, *Origins of the World War*, vol. I, p. 4.

13 Ibid., vol. I, pp. 8–10.
14 Alfred von Wegerer, 'A Refutation of the Versailles War Guilt Thesis', p. 146.
15 Ibid., p. 354.
16 Peace Treaty of Versailles, Part VIII, Reparation, Section 1, Article 231.
17 Barnes, *Genesis of the World War*, p. 35.
18 Quigley, *Anglo-American Establishment*, p. 197.
19 Gollin, *Proconsul in Politics*, p. 551, noted in a footnote.
20 Milner Papers, Milner to Selborne, 5 April 1899, Bodleian Library, Ms.Eng.Hist. c.688.
21 Fisher, *Memories and Records*, vol. 1, p. 21.
22 Ferguson, *House of Rothschild*, vol. II, p. 319.
23 Cabinet Papers, CAB 37/120/ 69, 81, 90.
24 List of Cabinet Papers, 1880–1914. PRO booklet.
25 D'Ombrain, *War Machinery and High Policy*, preface, p. xiii.
26 Ibid.
27 Lloyd George, *War Memoirs*, p. 70.
28 Meriel Buchanan, *The Dissolution of an Empire*, pp. 192–207.
29 Quigley, *Anglo-American Establishment*, p. 98.
30 Ibid., p. 99.
31 Barnes, *In Quest of Truth and Justice*, p. x.
32 *New York Times Current History Magazine*, July 1928, pp. 619–40.
33 Quigley, *Anglo-American Establishment*, p. 314.
34 M.H. Cochran, *Germany Not Guilty in 1914*, p. xix.
35 *Times Literary Supplement*, 4 May 1962.
36 Marc Trachtenberg, 'The Craft of International History: A Guide to Method' at http://mises.org/misesreview_detail.aspx?control=303
37 Stone, *World War One*, p. 19.
38 Strachan, *First World War*, p. 16.
39 Ibid., p. 36.
40 See Chapter 13.
41 A.J.P. Taylor, *The First World War: An Illustrated History*, p. 20.
42 Michael Howard, *The First World War: A Very Short Introduction*, p. 24.
43 Walter W. Ligget, *The Rise of Herbert Hoover*, p. 51.
44 Ibid., p. 55.
45 Ibid., p. 120.
46 Hamill, *Strange Career of Mr. Hoover*, p. 150.
47 See Chapter 2.
48 Hamill, *Strange Career of Mr. Hoover*, pp. 156–7.
49 Cissie Dore Hill, *Collecting the Twentieth Century*, p. 1 at http://www.

hoover.org/publications/hoover-digest/article/8041
50 Charles G. Palm and Dale Reed, *Guide to the Hoover Institution Archives*, p. 5.
51 Whittaker Chambers, Hoover Library http://whittakerchambers.org/articles/time-a/hoover-library/
52 *New York Times*, 5 February 1921.
53 Hill, *Collecting the Twentieth Century*, p. 1 at http://www.hoover.org/publications/hoover-digest/article/8041
54 Whittaker Chambers, Hoover Library at http://whittakerchambers.org/articles/time-a/hoover-library/
55 Ibid.
56 *New York Times*, 5 February 1921.
57 Whittaker Chambers, Hoover Library, as above.
58 *New York Times*, 5 February 1921.
59 Hoover Institution, Stanford University at http://www.hoover.org/about/herbert-hoover
60 Ibid.
61 Ian Bell, *Sunday Herald*, 16 December 2012.

List of References

Original Papers and Sources

Asquith Papers, Oxford, Bodleian Library, Special Collections, Asquith MSS 1–150

Carson Papers (D1507) Public Record Office of Northern Ireland (PRONI)

Milner Collection, Oxford, Bodleian Library, Special Collections, MSS. Eng. hist. 686–688

Haldane Papers, National Library of Scotland, Special collections, MS. 20058

League of Nations Report, 1921

National Archives, Kew, Minutes of the Committee of Imperial Defence (CAB)

National Archives, Kew, Cabinet Minutes (CAB)

Public Records Office Northern Ireland (PRONI)

Carson Papers (PRONI) D1 507

United States House of Representatives No. 1593 Report of the Pujo Committee, Library of congress, Washington DC

United States Congressional Record December 1913, Library of Congress, Washington DC

Hansard House of Commons Debates

Hansard House of Lords Debates

Newspapers and Magazines

Boston Post

Daily Chronicle

Daily Express

Daily Mirror

Daily News

Daily Telegraph

Dundee Courier

Evening News

Fortnightly Review
International Monthly Inc.
Irish Times
Johannesburg Star
John Bull
Kievskaya Mysil
Le Matin
Le Temps
Manchester Guardian
Melbourne Argus
Morning Post
Nation
National Review
New Republic
New York Times
Nineteenth Century
North German Gazette
Novoe Vremya
The Observer
Pall Mall Gazette
Pijemont
Quarterly Review
The Radical
Rand Star
Review of Reviews
Round Table Quarterly Review
Scarborough Evening News
Standard
Sunday Herald
Sunday People
Sunday Times
Sydney Morning Herald
The Times
Times Literary Supplement
Weekly Dispatch
Westminster Gazette

Published Articles and Pamphlets

Barnes, Harry Elmer, 'Germany Not Responsible for Austria's Action', *Current History Magazine*, published by the *New York Times*, July 1928, pp. 620–6

Berchtold, Count Leopold, 'Austria's Challenge Justified by Serbian Menace', *Current History Magazine*, published by the *New York Times*, July 1928, pp. 626–7

Budget League Pamphlet 22, 'The Budget and the People'

Coakley, John, 'Ethnic Conflict and the Two-State Solution: The Irish Experience of Partition', Institute for British–Irish Studies & Centre for International Borders Research, MFPP Ancillary Papers, no. 3

Coogan, John W. and Coogan, Peter F., 'The British Cabinet and the Anglo-French Staff Talks, 1905–1914: Who Knew What and When Did He Know It?' *Journal of British Studies*, no. 24 (January 1985)

Eckstein, Michael, 'Some Notes on Sir Edward Grey's Policy in July 1914', *The Historical Journal* XV, 2 (1972), pp. 321–4

Fay, Sidney B., 'The Kaiser's Secret Negotiations with the Tsar, 1904–1905', *The American Historical Review*, vol. 24, no. 1 (October 1918), pp. 48–72

Hoyos, Count Alexander, 'Russia Chief Culprit in Precipitation of World War', *Current History Magazine*, published by the *New York Times*, July 1928, pp. 628–30

Jagow, Gottlieb von, 'Germany's Reasons for Supporting Her Ally's Anti-Serb Policy', *Current History Magazine*, published by the *New York Times*, July 1928, pp. 633–5

Kulhman, Kurt, 'The Renewal of the Anglo-Japanese Alliance', 1905, Duke University 9 January, 1992

Langer, W.L., *New Republic*, 15 April 1925

Levy, Jack, 'Organisational Routines and the Causes of War', *International Studies Quarterly*, vol. 30, no. 2, June 1986

MacDonald, J. Ramsay, 'Why We Are At War', *The Open Court*, vol. 1, 1915, issue 4 article 4

McLean, Iain and Lubbock, Tom, 'The Curious Incident of the Guns in the Night-time: Curragh, Larne and the UK Constitution' at http://www.scribd.com/doc/94418905/Curious-Incident-of-the-Guns-in-the-Night-Time

Milner Alfred, 'Lord Milner's Credo', reprinted from *The Times*, 27 July 1925

Moen, Jon, and Tollman, Ellis, 'The Bank Panic of 1907: The Role of Trust Companies', *The Journal of Economic History*, no. 52

Morgan, K.O., 'The Boer War and the Media, 1899–1902', *Twentieth Century British History*, vol. 13, no. 1, March 2002

Serge, Victor, 'La Verité sur l'Attentat de Sarajevo', *Clarte*, no. 74, 1 May 1924

Smethurst, K.M. Richard, and Korekiyo, Takahashi, 'The Rothschilds and the Russo-Japanese War 1904–1907', essay in the *Occasional Papers* series of the Suntory Centre at the London School of Economics

Stoskopf, Nicholas, *Journee d'etudes sur l'historie de la haute banque France* (2000)

Trachtenberg, Marc, 'The Meaning of Mobilization in 1914', *International Security*, vol. 15, issue 3, Winter 1990–91

von Wegerer, Alfred, 'A Refutation of the Versailles War Guilt Thesis', *The Nation*, April 1927, pp. 485–6

von Wiesner, Dr Friedrich, 'Austria's Life and Death Struggle Against Irredentism', *Current History Magazine*, published by the *New York Times*, July 1928, pp. 630–3

Warburg, Paul M., 'A Plan for a Modified Central Bank', in *The Federal Reserve System: Its Origin and Growth*, vol. 2, 1914

Williamson, J.G., 'The Structure of Pay in Britain, 1710–1911', *Research in Economic History*, vol., 7, 1982

Wilson, K.W., 'The Making and Putative Implementation of a British Foreign Policy of Gesture, December 1905–August 1914: The Anglo-French Entente Revisited', *Canadian Journal of History*, no. XXXI, August

Select Bibliography

Abrahams, Ray H., *Preachers Present Arms*, Pennsylvania, Herald Press, 1933

Aikin, K.W.W, *The Last Years of Liberal England, 1900–1914*, London, Collins, 1972

Albertini, Luigi, *Origins of the War of 1914*, Oxford University Press, 1952

Allen, Gary, with Abraham, Larry, *None Dare Call it Conspiracy*, New York, Amereon Ltd, 1972

Amery, Leo, *Times History of the War in South Africa*, London, Low Marston and Co. Ltd, 1900

Amery, Leo, *The Leo Amery Diaries, 1896–1929*, London, Hutchinson, 1980, vol. 1

Andrew, Christopher, S*ecret Service: The Making of the British Intelligence Community*, London, Heinemann, 1985

Andrew, Christopher, *The Defence of the Realm: The Authorised History of MI5*, London, Penguin Books, 2009

Arrighi, Giovanni, *The Long Twentieth Century*, London,Verso, 1994

Arthur, Max, *Last Post*, London, Cassel, 2005

Arthur, Max, *Forgotten Voices of the Great War*, London, Ebury Press, 2002

Arthur, Max, *Lest We Forget*, London, Ebury Press, 2007

Baker, Anne Pimlott, *The Pilgrims of Great Britain: A Centennial History*, London, Profile Books, 2002

Baker, Anne Pimlott, *The Pilgrims of The United States: A Centennial History*, London, Profile Books, 2003

Ballard, Robert, *Lusitania*, New Jersey, Madison Press Books, 1995

Bardon, Jonathan, *A History of Ireland in 250 Episodes*, Dublin, Gill & Macmillan Ltd, 2008

Barnes, Harry Elmer, *In Quest of Truth and Justice: De-Bunking the War-Guilt Myth*, Colorado Springs, Ralph Myles Publisher, 1972

Barnes, Harry Elmer, *Who Started the First World War?*, California, Institute for Historical Review, 1984

Barnes, Harry Elmer, *The Genesis of the World War*, New York, Alfred A. Knopf, 1927

Bausman, Frederick, *Let France Explain*, London, George Allen & Unwin Ltd, 1922

Bell, E. Moberly, *Flora Shaw*, London, Constable, 1947

Bernstein, Herman, *The Willy-Nicky Correspondence*, Toronto, Gundy, 1918

Bird, G.E. and Merwin, F.E., *The Press and Society*, New York, Prentice-Hall, 1951

Birinyi, Louis K., *Why the Treaty of Trianon is Void*, Michigan, Simmons Inc., 1928

Birkenhead, Earl of, *Churchill: 1874–1922*, London, Harrap, 1989

Birmingham, Stephen, *Our Crowd*, London, Macdonald & Co., 1967

Bourne, John M., *Who's Who in World War I*, London, Routledge, 2001

Brett, Maurice V., *The Journals and Letters of Lord Esher*, London, Nicholson and Watson, 1934

Bridgham, Frederick, *The First World War as a Clash of Cultures*, Boydell and Brewer, 2006

Boyle, Andrew, *The Riddle of Erskine Childers*, Hutchison of London, 1977

Brock, Michael and Eleanor (eds), H.H. Asquith: *Letters to Venetia Stanley*, Oxford University Press, 1982

Buchan, John, *Memory Hold the Door*, London, Hodder and Stoughton Ltd, 1940

Buchan, John, *A History of the First World War*, Moffat, Lochar Publishing, 1991

Buchan, John, *Mr Standfast*, Ware, Wordsworth Editions Ltd, 1994

Buchan, John, *Greenmantle*, Ware, Wordsworth Editions Ltd, 1994

Buchanan, George, *My Mission to Russia and Other Diplomatic Memories*, vols 1 and 2, London, Cassell, 1923

Buchanan, Meriel, *The Dissolution of an Empire*, London, John Murray, 1932

Buckland, Patrick, *James Craig*, Dublin, Gill & MacMillan, 1980

Burton, J. Endrick, *The Life and Letters of Walter H. Page*, 3 vols, London, William Heinemann, 1923

Callwell, Major-General Sir C. E., *Field Marshal Henry Wilson Bart: His Life and His Diaries*, London, Cassell, 1927

Carlyon, L.A., *Gallipoli*, London, Bantam Books, 2002
Carnegie, Andrew, *Problems of Today*, London, George Allen & Sons, 1908
Carr, E.H., *What is History?*, London, Macmillan, 1961
Carr, W.G., *Pawns in the Game*, Ontario, Federation of Christian Laymen, 1958
Chamberlain, Austen, *Politics From the Inside: An Epistolary Chronicle, 1906–1914*, Yale University Press, 1937
Chapman, Stanley, *The Rise of Merchant Banking*, London, George Allen and Unwin, 1984
Chatterton, Kebble, *The Big Blockade*, London, Hutchinson and Co, 1932
Chernow, Ron, *The Warburgs*, New York, Random House, 1993
Chernow, Ron, *Titan: The Life of John D. Rockefeller, Sr.*, New York, Vintage Books, 2004
Chevalier, Gabriel, *Fear*, English translation of *La Peur* (1930), London, Profile Books, 2008
Childers, Erskine, *The Riddle of the Sands*, London, Penguin Books, 1903
Childers, Erskine, and Lord Roberts, *War and the Arme Blanche*, London, E. Arnold, 1910
Chomsky, Noam, *Understanding Power*, London, Vintage, 2003
Churchill, Randolph S., *Winston S. Churchill, Vol. II*, Boston, Houghton Mifflin, 1967
Churchill, Winston, *The World Crisis 1911–1918*, London, Odhams Press, 1938
Churchill, Winston, *My Early Life*, London, Butterworth, 1930
Cimbala, Stephen, J., *Military Persuasion: Deterrence and Provocation in Crisis and War*, Pennsylvania University Press, 1994
Clark, Christopher, *Kaiser Wilhelm II: Profiles in Power*, London, Longman, 2000
Clarke, Ignatius Frederick, *The Great War with Germany, 1890–1914*, Liverpool University Press
Clarke, Ignatius Frederick, *Voices Prophesying War*, Oxford University Press, 1966
Cochran, M.H., *Germany Not Guilty in 1914*, Colorado Springs, Ralph Myles Publisher, 1972
Cole, Margaret, *Beatrice Webb*, London, Longmans Green and Co., 1945
Colingwood, W.G., *The Life and Work of John Ruskin*, London, Methven & Co., 1893
Colvin, Ian, *The Life of Lord Carson*, London, Victor Gollancz, 1934
Consett, M.W.W.P., *The Triumph of Unarmed Forces (1914–1918)*, London, Williams and Norgate, 1923
Cowles, Virginia, *The Kaiser*, New York, Harper and Row, 1963

Cowles, Virginia, *The Rothschilds:A Family of Fortune*, London, Futura Publications Ltd, 1973

Cowles, Virginia, *Winston Churchill: The Era and the Man*, London, Hamish Hamilton Ltd, 1953

Croy, Marie de, Princess of, *War Memories*, London, Macmillan, 1932

Davenport, Guiles, *Zaharoff, High Priest of War*, Massachusetts, Lothrop, Lee and Shepard Company, 1934

David, Edward, *Inside Asquith's Cabinet*, London, John Murray, 1977

David, Saul, *Military Blunders: The How and Why of Military Failure*, London, Robinson Publishing, 1997

Dedijer, Vladimir, *The Road to Sarajevo*, London, Macgibbon & Kee, 1967

Demartial, G., *L'Evangile du Quai d'Orsay*, Paris, (publisher unknown), 1926

Dobrorolsky, Sergei, *The Mobilisation of the Russian Army, 1914*, Berlin, Deutsche Verlagsgesellschaft für Politik und Geschichte m.b.h, 1922

D'Ombrain, Nicholas, *War Machinery and High Policy Defence Administration in Peacetime Britain, 1902–1914*, Oxford University Press, 1974 Dunlop, Ian, *Edward VII and the Entente Cordiale*, London, Constable, 2004

Dunlop, Ian, *Edward VII and the Entente Cordiale*, London, Constable, 2004

Durham, Edith, *The Sarajevo Crime*, Allen and Unwin, London, 1925

Durham, Edith, *Twenty Years of Balkan Tangle*, London, Allen & Unwin, 1920

Emden, Richard van, *Boy Soldiers of the Great War*, London, Hodder Headline, 2005

Engdahl, William, *A Century of War*, London, Pluto Press, 1992

Engelbrecht, H.C. and Hanighen, F.C., *Merchants of Death*, New York, Dodd, Mead & Co, 1934

Etemad, Bouda, *Possessing the World: European Expansion and Global Interaction*, New York, Berghahn Books, 2007

Ewart, J.S., *The Roots and Causes of the Wars*, vols I and II, New York, George H. Doran Company, 1925

Farrer, J.A., *England Under Edward VII*, London, Allen & Unwin, 1922

Fay, Sidney B., *The Origins of the World War*, New York, The Macmillan Company, 1936

Feis, Herbert, *Europe: The World's Banker, 1870–1914*, New York, Norton & Co., 1965

Ferguson, Niall, *The House of Rothschild: The World's Banker, 1849–1999*, London, Penguin Books, 1998

F*erguson, Niall, 1914: Why the World went to War*, London, Penguin Books, 2003

Ferguson, Niall, *The Pity of War*, London, Penguin Books, 1998

Ferris, Paul, *The House of Northcliffe: A Biography of an Empire*, New York, World Publishing, 1972

Ferriter, Diarmid, *The Transformation of Ireland, 1900–2000*, London, Profile Books, 2004

Fischer, Fritz, *Germany's Aims in the First World War*, London, Chatto and Windus, 1967

Fisher, H.A.L., *A History of Europe*, London, Edward Arnold and Co., 1936

Fisher, Baron John Arbuthnot, *Memories and Records*, vols 1 & 2, New York, George H. Doran Co., 1920

Fitzpatrick, J. Percy, *The Transvaal Within*, Charlestown, Bibliobazaar, 2009

Fleming, Thomas, *The Illusion of Victory: America in World War I*, New York, Perseus Book Group, 2003

Foy, Michael T., *Michael Collins's Intelligence War*, Stroud, The History Press, 2008

Fremont-Barnes, Gregory, *The Boer War (1899–1902)* Oxford, Osprey Publishing, 2003

Fritzinger, Linda B., *Diplomat Without Portfolio: Valentine Chirol – His Life and The Times*, London and New York, I.B. Tauris, 2006

Fromm, Erich, *The Anatomy of Human Destructiveness*, London, Pimlico, 1973

Fuehr, Alexander, *The Neutrality of Belgium*, New York and London, Funk and Wagnall, 1915

Gallacher, William, *Revolt on the Clyde*, London, Lawrence & Wishart, 1936

Gallagher, Charles F., *The United States and North Africa, Morocco, Algeria and Tunisia*, Harvard University Press, 1963

Gardiner, A., *The War Lords*, Toronto, J.M. Dent & Co., 1915

Gates, Robert, *The Conspiracy That Will Not Die*, Oregon, Red Anvil Press, 2011

Geiss, Imanuel, *July 1914: The Outbreak of the First World War: Selected Documents*, London, B.T. Batsford Ltd, 1965

George, W.R.P., *Backbencher*, Ceredigion, Gomer Press, 1983

Gerard, James W., *My Four Years in Germany*, London, Hodder and Stoughton, 1917

Gerard, James W., *Face to Face with Kaiserism*, London, Hodder and Stoughton, 1928

Gerretson, Dr F.C., *History of the Royal Dutch*, 4 vols, The Netherlands, Leiden, 1957

Gollin, A.M., *Proconsul in Politics: A Study of Lord Milner*, London, Anthony Blond Ltd, 1964

Gooch & Temperley, *British Documents on the Origin of the War, 1898–1914*, London, H.M.S.O., 1927

Gottlieb, W.W., *Studies in Secret Diplomacy*, London, Allen & Unwin, 1957
Grant and Temperley, *Europe in the Nineteenth and Twentieth Centuries*, London, Longmans Green and Co, 1934
Greider, William, *The Secrets of the Temple*, New York, Simon & Schuster, 1987
Grenfell, Captain Russell, *Unconditional Hatred*, New York, The Devin-Adair Company, 1953
Grey, Edward and Dorothy, *Cottage Book, Ichen Abbas, 1894–1905*, London, Gollancz, 1999
Grey of Fallodon, *Twenty-five Years: 1892–1916*, London, Hodder and Stoughton, 1928
Griffin, G. Edward, *The Creature From Jekyll Island: A Second Look at the Federal Reserve*, California, American Media, 1994
Grigg, John, *Lloyd George: The People's Champion (1902–1911)* Berkeley, University of California Press, 1978
Gunther, John, *Inside Europe*, London, Hamish Hamilton, 1936
Gwynn, Stephen Lucius, *John Redmond's Last Years*, New York, Longmans, Green and Company, 1919
Hackett, Francis, *The Story of the Irish Nation*, The Library of the University of California, 1923
Hague, Ffion, *The Pain and the Privilege*, London, Harper Press, 2008
Haldane, Richard Burdon, *An Autobiography*, London, Hodder and Stoughton, 1924
Halperin, Vladimir, *Lord Milner and the Empire*, London, Odhams Press Ltd, 1952
Hamilton, Richard F., and Herwig, Holger H., *Decisions for War, 1914-1917*, Cambridge, Cambridge University Press, 2004
Hamill, John, *The Strange Career of Mr. Hoover Under Two Flags*, New York, William Faro, Inc., 1931
Hansl, Proctor W., *Years of Plunder*, New York, H. Smith and R. Haas, 1935
Hardach, Gerd, *The First World War, 1914–1918*, London, Pelican Books, 1977
Hart, B.H. Liddell, *History of the First World War*, London, Pan Books, 1930
Harvey, A.D., *Collision of Empires: Britain in Three World Wars*, London, Hambledon Press, 1992
Hattersley, Roy, *Campbell-Bannerman*, London, Haus Publishing, 2006
Hattersley, Roy, *David Lloyd George: The Great Outsider*, London, Abacus, 2010
Havinghurst, Alfred F., *Britain in Transition, The Twentieth Century*, London, University of Chicago Press, 1979

Heathcote, Anthony, *The British Field Marshals, 1736–1997*, Barnsley, Penn and Sword Books Ltd, 1999

Henig, Ruth, *The Origins of the First World War*, London, Routledge, 1989

Hill, Cissie Dore, *Collecting the Twentieth Century*, Hoover Digest, Hoover Institute on War, Revolution and Peace, 2000

Hill, William Thomson, *The Martyrdom of Nurse Edith Cavell*, London, Hutchinson and Co., 1915

Hitchins, Keith, *Romania 1866–1947*, Oxford University Press, 1994

Hobsbawm, E.J., *Industry and Empire*, London, Penguin Books, 1968

Hobson, J.A., *John Ruskin: Social Reformer*, London, James Nisbet & Co. Ltd, 1898

Holdsworth, John Thom, *Money and Banking*, New York, D. Appleton and Co., 1917

Holmes, Richard, *Tommy: The British Soldiers on the Western Front 1914–1918*, London, Harper Perennial, 2005

Hough, Richard, *Winston and Clementine: The Triumphs and Tragedies of the Churchills*, London, Bantam Books, 1989

House, Edward Mandell, *Philip Dru: Administrator*, New York, B.W. Huebsch, 1912

House, Edward Mandell and Seymour, Charles, *The Intimate Papers of Colonel House*, Boston, Houghton Mifflin, 1926

Howard, Michael, *The First World War: A Very Short Introduction*, Oxford University Press, 2002

Jackson, Alvin, *Home Rule: An Irish History, 1800–2000*, Oxford University Press, 2003

Jackson, Alvin, *Ireland, 1798–1998: War, Peace and Beyond*, Chichester, Wiley-Blackwell, 2010

Jeffery, Keith, *Field Marshal Sir Henry Wilson: A Political Soldier*, Oxford University Press, 2008

Jenkins, Roy, *Churchill*, London, Pan Books, 2001

Joll, James and Martel, Gordon, *The Origins of the First World War*, London, Pearson, 1984

Katz, Irving, *August Belmont: A Political Biography*, Columbia University Press, 1968

Kee, Robert, *Ireland: A History*, London, Abacus Books, 1982

Keegan, John, *The Penguin Book of War*, London, Penguin Books, 2000

Keegan, John, *The First World War*, London, Hutchinson, 2011

Kelen, Emery, *Peace in Their Time*, London, Victor Gollancz, 1964

Kennan, George F., *The Fateful Alliance: France, Russia, and the Coming of the First World War*, New York, Pantheon Books, 1984

Kennedy, A.L., *Old Diplomacy and New: From Salisbury to Lloyd George, 1866–1922*, London, John Murray, 1922

Kipling, Rudyard, *Ulster 1912*, Classic Poetry Series, 2004

Knock, Albert J., *The Myth of a Guilty Nation*, Alabama, Ludwig von Mises Institute, 2011

Knuth, E.C., *The Empire of 'the City'*, California, The Book Tree, 1944

Kulhman,Kurt, 'The Renewal of the Anglo-Japanese Alliance 1905', Duke University, 9 January 1992 (paper submitted)

Lafore, Laurence, *The Long Fuse: An Interpretation of the Origins of World War*, Illinois, Wavelength Press, 1997

Landes, Davis S., *The Unbound Prometheus*, Cambridge University Press, 1969

Langewiesche, Dieter, *Liberalism in Germany*, New Jersey, Princeton University Press, 1988

Lapping, Brian, *End of Empire*, London, Paladin Grafton Books, 1989

Lee, Dwight E., *The Outbreak of the First World War*, Boston, D.C. Heath and Co., 1958

Lee, Sidney, *King Edward VII: A Biography*, London, Macmillan and Co., 1925

Lee, Sidney, *Dictionary of National Biography*, Second Supplement, London, Smith Elder, 1912

Lees-Milne, James, *The Enigmatic Edwardian: The Life of Reginald, Second Viscount Esher*, London, Sidgwick and Jackson, 1986

Legge, Edward, *King Edward in his True Colours*, Charleston, Nabu Press, 2011

Legge, Edward, *More about King Edward*, London, Eveleigh Nash, 1913

Lewinsohn, Richard, *Sir Basil Zaharoff*, London, Victor Gollancz, 1929

Lewis, Geoffrey, *Carson: The Man Who Divided Ireland*, London, Hambledon Continuum, 2005

Ligget, Walter W., *The Rise of Herbert Hoover*, New York, The H.K. Fly Company, 1932

Lincoln, Ignatius T., *Revelations of an International Spy*, New York, Robert M. McBride and Co., 1916

Lindqvist, Sven, *Exterminate All The Brutes*, London, Granta Books, 1997

Lloyd George, David, *War Memoirs*, vols 1 & 2, London, Odhams Press, 1938

Lloyd George, Richard, *My Father*, New York, Crown Publishers, 1961

Lockhart, R.H. Bruce, *Memoirs of a British Agent*, London, Putnam, 1932

Lutz, Hermann, *Lord Grey and the World War*, New York, Alfred A. Knopf, 1928

Lynch, E.P.F., *Somme Mud*, London, Bantam Books, 2008

McArthur, Brian, *For King and Country*, London, Abacus, 2008

McCormick, Donald, *The Mask of Merlin: A Critical Biography of David Lloyd George*, New York, Holt, Rinehart and Wilson, 1963

McDonald, Donna, *Lord Strathconna*, Toronto, Dundurn Press, 1996

McHarg, F., *Pistoleros!: The Chronicles of Farquhar McHarg*, Vol. I, Oakland, PM Press, 2011

Mackay, R.F., *Fisher of Kilverstone*, Oxford University Press, 1973

MacKenzie, David, *Apis: The Congenial Conspirator: The Life of Colonel Dragutin T. Dimitrijevic*, New York, Boulder Press, 1989

MacKenzie, Norman and Jeanne (eds), *Diary of Beatrice Webb – Vol. III: The Power to Alter Things, 1905–1924*, Harvard University Press, 1985

McMahon, Paul, *British Spies & Irish Rebels*, Woodbridge, Suffolk, The Boydell Press, 2008

MacMillan, Margaret, *Peacemakers: Six Months that Changed the World*, London, John Murray, 2001

McNeill, Ronald, *Ulster's Stand for Union*, New York, Dutton, 1922

Malatesta, Errico, *Anarchy*, London, Freedom Press, 1974

Manchester, William, *The Arms of Krupp (1587–1968)*, London, Michael Joseph Ltd, 1964

Marchand, Rene, *Un Livre Noir*, University of Toronto Libraries, 2012

Martel, Gordon, *The Origins of the First World War*, London, Pearson Longman, 1987

Marr, Andrew, *A History of Modern Britain*, London, Macmillan, 2007

Marr, Andrew, *The Making of Modern Britain*, London, Macmillan, 2009

Marwick, Arthur, *The Deluge, British Society and the First World War*, Middlesex, Pelican Books, 1965

Massie, Robert K., *Dreadnought: Britain, Germany and the Coming of the Great War*, New York, Random House, 1991

Masterman, Lucy, *C.F.G. Masterman: A Biography*, London, Nicholson and Watson, 1939

Maurice, Major-General Sir Frederick and Bliss, Tasker H., *Soldier, Artist, Sportsman: The Life of General Lord Rawlinson of Trent*, Montana, Kessinger Publications, 2004

Maurice, Major-General Sir Frederick, *Haldane 1856–1915*, London, Faber and Faber, 1937

Middlemas, Keith, *The Life and Times of Edward VII*, London, Weidenfeld & Nicolson, 1972

Middlemas, Keith, *Pursuit of Pleasure: High Society in the 1900s*, London, Book Club Associates, 1977

Millis, Walter, *Road to War: America, 1914–1917*, Massachusetts, The Riverside Press, 1935

Milner, Viscount, *Constructive Imperialism: Unionists and Social Reform*, Slough, Dodo Press, 2009

Mitchell, Angus, *Casement*, London, Haus Publishing, 2003

Mock, James R., and Larson, Cedric, *Words That Won the War*, Connecticut, Cobden Press, 1984.

Morgan, Kenneth O., *The Boer War and the Media (1899–1902), Twentieth Century British History*, vol. 13, no. 1, Oxford University Press, 2002

Mombauer, Annika, *The Origins of the First World War*, London, Longman, 2002

Montefiore, Simon, *Young Stalin*, London, Phoenix, 2007

Montgelas, Max, *British Foreign Policy under Sir Edward Grey*, New York, Alfred. A. Knopf, 1928

Montgelas, Max, *The Case for the Central Powers*, London, Allen & Unwin Ltd, 1925

Morel, E.D. *Diplomacy Revealed*, London, National Labour Press, 1921

Morel, E.D., *Pre-war Diplomacy: Fresh Revelations*, London, Independent Labour Party, 1919

Morel, E.D., *The Secret History of a Great Betrayal*, London, Caledonian Press, 1923

Morel, E.D., *Ten Years of Secret Diplomacy*, London, National Labour Press Ltd, 1915

Morel, E.D., *Truth and the War*, London, National Labour Press, 1918

Morgan, Janet, *The Secrets of Rue St Roch*, London, Penguin Books, 2005

Moore, R.K., *Escaping the Matrix*, Ireland, Cyberjournal, 2005

Mr Punch's History of the Great War, London, Cassell and Co. Ltd, 1919

Murphy, Brian P., *Patrick Pearse and the Lost Republican Ideal*, Dublin, James Duffy and Company, 1991

Murray, H. Robertson, *Krupps and the International Armaments Ring*, London, Holden & Hardingham, 1915

Nash, George H., *The Life of Herbert Hoover, The Humanitarian 1914–1917*, New York, W.W. Norton and Co., 1988

Neilson, Francis, *How Diplomats Make War*, New York, Bibliolife, 1923

Neilson, Francis, *The Makers of War*, Wisconsin, C.C. Nelson Publishing Company, 1950

Neumann, Robert, *Zaharoff, the Armaments King*, London, Allen & Unwin Ltd, 1936

Newbold, J.T. Walton, *How Asquith Helped the Armaments Ring*, Manchester and London, National Labour Press [undated pamphlet]

Newbold, J.T. Walton, *How Europe Armed for War, 1871–1914*, London, Blackfriars Press Ltd, 1916

Newbold, J.T. Walton, *The War Trust Exposed*, Manchester, The National Labour Press, 1913

Nimocks, Walter, *Milner's Young Men*, London, Hodder and Stoughton, 1968

Nish, Ian, *The Anglo-Japanese: The Diplomacy of Two Island Empires 1894–1907*, London, Routledge, 1966

Nock, Albert Jay, *The Myth of a Guilty Nation*, New York, B.W. Huebsch Inc., 1922

O'Brien, Terence H., *Milner*, London, Constable and Co., 1979

O'Connor, Thomas Power MP, *Sir Henry Campbell-Bannerman*, London, Hodder and Stoughton, 1908

Offer, Anver, *First World War: An Agrarian Interpretation*, Oxford University Press, 1990

Oppenheim, E. Philips, *A Maker of History*, Boston, IndyPublish.com, 2007

Owings, W.A. Dolph, and Pribic, Elizabeth and Nikola, *The Sarajevo Trial, Part 1*, Chapel Hill, Documentary Publications, 1984

Pakenham, Thomas, *The Boer War*, London, Abacus, 1979

Palm, Charles G. and Reed, Dale, *Guide to the Hoover Institution Archives*, Stanford, California, Hoover Institution Press, 1980

Parsons, Neil, *A New History of Southern Africa*, Teaneck, Holmes and Meier, 1983

Pelling, Henry, *Modern Britain 1885–1955*, London, Sphere Books, 1960

Perris, George Herbert, *The War Traders: An Exposure*, London, National Peace London Council, 1913

Peterson, H.C. and Fite, Gilbert C., *Opponents of War, 1917–1918*, Connecticut, Greenwood Press, 1957

Piper, Leonard, *The Tragedy of Erskine Childers*, London, Hambledon, 2003

Pitt, Barrie, *Zeebrugge*, London, Cassell, 1958

Podmore, Will, *British Foreign Policy Since 1870*, London (self-published) 2008

Poel, Jean van der, *The Jameson Raid*, Oxford University Press, 1951

Ponsonby, Arthur, *Falsehood in Wartime*, London, Allen and Unwin, 1928

Pound, Reginald and Harmsworth, Geoffrey, *Northcliffe*, Westport, Praeger, 1960

Preston, Diana, *Wilful Murder: The Sinking of the Lusitania*, London, Corgi Books, 2002

Quigley, Carroll, *Tragedy & Hope, A History of the World in Our Time*, California, GSC & Associates (first printing: New York, The Macmillan Company, 1966)

Quigley, Carroll, *The Anglo-American Establishment*, California, GSC & Associates, 1981

Rankin, Raymond, *The Inner History of the Balkan War*, London, Constable & Co., 1914

Reeves, John, *The Rothschilds: The Financial Rulers of Nations*, London, Sampson Low, 1887

Reid, Walter, *Architect of Victory: Douglas Haig*, Edinburgh, Birlinn, 2006

Remak, Joachim, *Sarajevo: The Story of a Political Murder*, New York, Criterion Books Inc., 1959

Renouvin, Pierre, *The Immediate Origins of the War (28th June–4th August 1914)*, USA, Yale University Press, 1928

Renouvin, Pierre, *La Crise Europeene et la Grande Guerre*, Paris (publisher unknown), 1939

Repington, Charles, *The First World War*, Boston and New York, Houghton Mifflin, 1920

Roberts, Lord, *Lord Roberts' Message to the Nation*, London, John Murray, 1912

Robertson, William, *From Private to Field Marshal*, New York, Houghton Mifflin, 1921

Rohl, John C.G., *Wilhelm II: The Kaiser's Personal Monarchy*, Cambridge University Press, 2004

Roth, Cecil, *The Magnificent Rothschilds*, London, R. Hale, 1939

Rothbard, Murray N., *Wall Street, Banks and American Foreign Policy*, New York, Center for Libertarian Studies, 1995

Royle, Trevor, *The Flowers of the Forest*, Edinburgh, Birlinn, 2007

Royle, Trevor, *The Kitchener Enigma*, London, Michael Joseph, 1985.

Royle, Trevor, *War Report*, Edinburgh, Mainstream Publishing, 1987.

Ryan, A.P., *Mutiny at the Curragh*, London, Macmillan and Company, 1956

Sampson, Anthony, *The Seven Sisters: The Great Oil Companies and the World They Shaped*, London, PFD, 2009

Sazonov, Sergei, *Fateful Years, 1909–1916*, New York, Ishi Press, first printing 1928

The Secret International: Armaments Firms at Work, Union of Democratic Control, London

Semenoff, Vladimir, *The Battle of Tsushima*, New York, E.P. Dutton and Co., 1912

Seymour, Charles, *The Intimate Papers of Colonel House*, Boston, Houghton Mifflin Company, 1926

Sheehan, James, *The Monopoly of Violence*, London, Faber and Faber, 2007

Shelking, Eugenii Nikolaevich, *The Game of Diplomacy*, London, Hutchinson and Co., 1918

Shelking, Eugenii Nikolaevich and Makvoski, L.W., *Recollections of a Russian Diplomat: The Suicide of Monarchies*, New York, Macmillan 1918

Simpson, Colin, *Lusitania*, Wirral, UK, Avid publications, 1972

Skelton, Oscar Douglas, *Life and Letters of Sir Wilfrid Laurier*, Toronto, Oxford University Press, 1921

Sladen, Douglas, *The Real Truth about Germany*, New York, Knickerbocker Press, 1914

Smith, Janet Adam, *John Buchan and his World*, London, Thames and Hudson, 1979

Smith, David James, *One Morning in Sarajevo: 28 June 1914*, London, Phoenix, 2008

Solzhenitsyn, Alexander, *August 1914*, London, Penguin Books, 1992

Spender, J.A., *The Life of the Right Honourable Sir Henry Campbell-Bannerman*, London, Hodder and Stoughton, 1923

Spiridovich, Alexander, *Les Dernières Années de la Cour de Tzarskoie Selo*, vol. 1, Paris, Payot, 1928

Stevenson, David, *1914–1918: The History of the First World War*, London, Penguin Books, 2004

Stone, Norman, *World War One: A Short History*, London, Allen Lane, 2007

Strachan, Hew, *The First World War*, London, Simon & Schuster, 2006

Stead, William T., *The Last Will and Testament of Cecil John Rhodes*, London, 1902

Stieve, Friedrich, *Isvolsky and the World War*, New York, Alfred A. Knopf, 1926

Sutton, Antony C., *The Federal Reserve Conspiracy*, Oregon, CPA Book Publishers, 1995

Sutton, Antony C., *The Best Enemy Money Can Buy*, Montana, Liberty House Press, 1986

Swain, Joseph Ward, *Beginning the Twentieth Century*, New York, W.W. Norton & Company Inc., 1933

Tarpley, Webster G. and Chaitkin, Anton, *George Bush: The Unauthorized Biography*, Washington, DC, Executive Intelligence Review, 1992

Taylor, A.J.P., *The First World War: An Illustrated History*, London, Penguin, 1966

Taylor, A.J.P., *English History 1914–1945*, Middlesex, Penguin Books, 1965

Taylor, Edmond, *The Fall of the Dynasties: The Collapse of the Old Order, 1905–1922*, New York, Doubleday Inc., 1922

Thomas, Rosamund M., *Espionage and Secrecy: The Official Secrets Act 1911–1989*, London, Taylor and Francis, 1991

Thompson, J. Lee, *Forgotten Patriot*, New Jersey, Rosemount Publishing, 2007

Thompson, J. Lee, *A Wider Patriotism: Alfred Milner and the British Empire*, London, Pickering & Chatto, 2007

Thompson, J. Lee, *Northcliffe: Press Baron in Politics 1865–1922*, London, John Murray, 2000

Thomson, David, *England in the Nineteenth Century*, Middlesex, Penguin Books, 1950

Thomson, George Malcolm, *The Twelve Days*, London, The History Book Club, 1966

Toye, Richard, *Lloyd George and Churchill: Rivals for Greatness*, London, Pan Books, 2007

Trachtenberg, Marc, '*The Craft of International History: A Guide to Method*' at http://mises.org/misesreview_detail.aspx?control=303

Trevelyan, G.M., *Grey of Fallodon*, London, Longmans Green and Company, 1937

Trotsky, Leon, *The Balkan Wars 1912–13*, New York, Pathfinder Press, 1921

Tuchman, Barbara W., *The Guns of August*, New York, Ballantine Books, 1962

Tucker, Spencer, *World War I*, ABC-Clio ebook, 2006

Tumulty, Joseph Patrick, *Woodrow Wilson as I Know Him*, Garden City, Doubleday Publishing Company, 1927

Turner, John, *Lloyd George's Secretariat*, Cambridge University Press, 1980

Union of Democratic Control, *The Secret International: Armaments Firms at Work*, London, 1932

Vanderlip, Frank A. and Sparkes, Boyden, *From Farm Boy to Financier*, New York, D. Appleton-Century Company, 1935

Veon, Joan M., *The United Nations Global Straitjacket*, New Jersey, Hearthstone Publications, 2000

Viereck, George Sylvester, *The Strangest Friendship in History: Woodrow Wilson and Colonel House*, West Point, Connecticut, Greenwood Press, 1976

Waller, W., *War in the Twentieth Century*, New York, Revisionist Press, 1974

Walter, George, *Rupert Brooke & Wilfred Owen*, London, Everyman, 1997

Ward, A.W. and Gooch, G.P., *Cambridge History of British Foreign Policy*, vol. 3, Cambridge University Press, 1924

Weintraub, Stanley, *Edward the Caresser: The Playboy Prince who became Edward VII*, New York, The Free Press, 2001

Wells, Warre B., *John Redmond: A Biography*, London, Nisbet and Co., 1919

Wells, H.G., *A Short History of the World*, Leipzig, Bernhard Tauchnitz, 1935

Westwell, Ian, *World War I*, London, Hermes House, 2008

Wheeler, George, *Pierpont Morgan and Friends: The Anatomy of a Myth*, New Jersey, Prentice-Hall, Inc., 1973

White, J.A., *Transition to Global Rivalry: Alliance Diplomacy and the Quadruple Entente, 1895–1907*, Cambridge University Press, 2002

Wile, Frederic William, *Men Around the Kaiser*, Danvers USA, General Books, 2009

Wilhelm II, Kaiser, *My Memoirs (1878–1918)*, London, Cassell and Co., 1922

Willis, Irene Cooper, *England's Holy War*, New York, Alfred A. Knopf, 1928

Wilson, Derek A., *Rothschild: The Wealth and Power of a Dynasty*, London, Simon & Schuster, 1988

Wilson, H.W., and Hammerton, J.A., *The Great War: An Illustrated History of the First World War*, vol. 1, London, The Amalgamated Press Limited, 1914

Wilson, John, *C.B.: A Life of Sir Henry Campbell-Bannerman*, London, Constable, 1973

Winter, Denis, *Haig's Command: A Reassessment*, London, Viking Books, 1991

Wrangell, Baron C., *Before the Storm: A True Picture of Life in Russia Prior to 1917*, Italy, Tipo-Litografia, 1923

Yergin, Daniel, *The Prize: The Epic Quest for Oil, Money and Power*, New York, Simon & Schuster Ltd, 1991

Index